POCKET VISUAL
dictionary

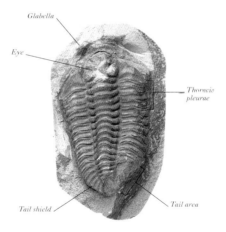

Glabella

Eye

Thoracic
pleurae

Tail shield

Tail area

PREHISTORIC TRILOBITE

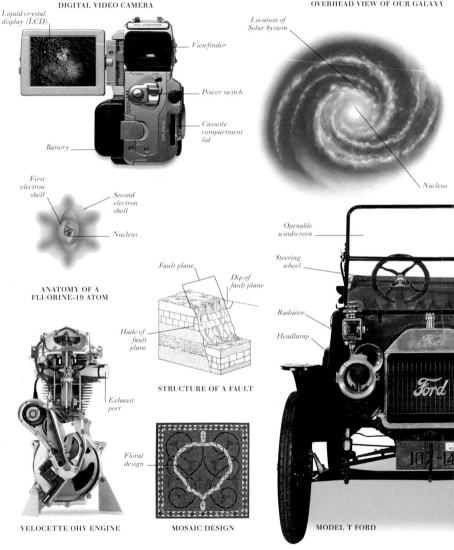

DIGITAL VIDEO CAMERA

Liquid crystal display (LCD)

Viewfinder

Power switch

Cassette compartment lid

Battery

OVERHEAD VIEW OF OUR GALAXY

Location of Solar System

Nucleus

First electron shell

Second electron shell

Nucleus

ANATOMY OF A FLUORINE-19 ATOM

Fault plane

Dip of fault plane

Hade of fault plane

STRUCTURE OF A FAULT

Openable windscreen

Steering wheel

Radiator

Headlamp

Exhaust port

Floral design

VELOCETTE OHV ENGINE

MOSAIC DESIGN

MODEL T FORD

POCKET VISUAL
dictionary

Pedicel
(flower stalk)

Sepal

Achene
(one-seeded
dry fruit)

Remains
of stigma
and style

STRAWBERRY

THIS EDITION

DK LONDON

Editorial Consultants Ian Graham, Darren Naish, Carole Stott
Picture Researcher Karen VanRoss
Jacket Designer Silke Spingies
Digital Conversion Coordinator Linda Zacharia
Production Editor Joanna Byrne
Production Controller Linda Dare
Managing Editor Julie Ferris
Managing Art Editor Owen Peyton Jones
Art Director Philip Ormerod
Associate Publishing Director Liz Wheeler
Publishing Director Jonathan Metcalf

DK DELHI

Managing Art Editor Arunesh Talapatra
Managing Editor Saloni Talwar
Deputy Managing Art Editor Priyabrata Roy Chowdhury
Senior Art Editor Rajnish Kashyap
Senior Editor Neha Gupta
Art Editors Arijit Ganguly, Pooja Pipil
Assistant Art Editor Pooja Pawwar
DTP Manager Balwant Singh
DTP Designer Jaypal Singh Chauhan
Managing Director Aparna Sharma

Anatomical And Botanical Models Supplied By Somso Modelle, Coburg, Germany

ORIGINAL EDITION (*Ultimate Visual Dictionary*)
Project Art Editors Heather McCarry, Johnny Pau, Chris Walker, Kevin Williams
Designer Simon Murrell
Project Editors Luisa Caruso, Peter Jones, Jane Mason, Geoffrey Stalker
Editor Jo Evans
DTP Designer Zirrinia Austin
Picture Researcher Charlotte Bush
Managing Art Editor Toni Kay
Senior Editor Roger Tritton
Managing Editor Sean Moore
Production Manager Hilary Stephens

THIS EDITION PUBLISHED IN 2017
FIRST PUBLISHED IN GREAT BRITAIN IN 1994
UNDER THE TITLE *ULTIMATE VISUAL DICTIONARY* BY
DORLING KINDERSLEY LIMITED
80 STRAND, LONDON WC2R 0RL
A PENGUIN RANDOM HOUSE COMPANY

17 18 19 20 21 10 9 8 7 6 5 4 3 2
002–299759–Jan/17
REVISED EDITIONS IN 1996, 1997, 1998, 1999, 2000, 2002, 2006, 2011, 2016, 2017

COPYRIGHT © 1994, 1996, 1997, 1998, 1999, 2000, 2002, 2006, 2011, 2016, 2017 DORLING KINDERSLEY LIMITED

A CIP CATALOGUE RECORD FOR THIS BOOK IS AVAILABLE FROM THE BRITISH LIBRARY

ISBN 978-0-2412-8729-5

Printed and bound in China

A WORLD OF IDEAS:
SEE ALL THERE IS TO KNOW
www.dk.com

Prosoma (cephalothorax) — *Spinneret*

Leg

EXTERNAL FEATURES OF A SPIDER

Canopy — *Fin*

G-BNHB

Main landing gear

SIDE VIEW OF ARV SUPER 2 AEROPLANE

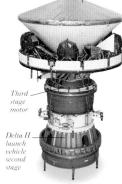

Heat shield

Third stage motor

Delta II launch vehicle second stage

MARS PATHFINDER

Barrel

Permanent black ink

FOUNTAIN PEN AND INK

CONTENTS

Face light emitting diodes (LEDs)

Movable tail

SONY AIBO ROBOT DOG

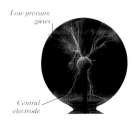

Low pressure gases

Central electrode

BALL CONTAINING HIGH TEMPERATURE GAS (PLASMA)

Parallel bands

ONYX

Non-breakable plastic

Shock absorber

AMERICAN FOOTBALL HELMET

Introduction

THE VISUAL DICTIONARY is a completely new kind of reference book. It provides a link between pictures and words in a way that no ordinary dictionary ever has. Most dictionaries simply tell you what a word means, but the *Visual Dictionary* shows you – through a combination of detailed annotations, explicit photographs, and illustrations. In the *Visual Dictionary*, pictures define the annotations around them. You do not read definitions of the annotated words, you see them. The highly accessible format of the *Visual Dictionary*, the thoroughness of its annotations, and the range of its subject matter make it a unique and helpful reference tool.

How to use the VISUAL DICTIONARY

You will find the *Visual Dictionary* simple to use. Instead of being organized alphabetically, it is divided by subject into 14 sections – The Universe, Prehistoric Earth, Plants, Animals, The Human Body, etc. Each section begins with a table of contents listing the major entries within that section. For example, The Visual Arts section has entries on *Drawing, Tempera, Fresco, Oils, Watercolour, Pastels, Acrylics, Calligraphy, Printmaking, Mosaic,* and *Sculpture*. Every entry has a short introduction explaining the purpose of the photographs and illustrations, and the significance of the annotations.

If you know what something looks like, but don't know its name, find the term you need by turning to the annotations surrounding the pictures; if you know a word, but don't know what it refers to, use the comprehensive index to direct you to the appropriate page.

Suppose that you want to know what the bone at the end of your little finger is called. With a standard dictionary, you wouldn't know where to begin. But with the *Visual Dictionary* you simply turn to the entry called *Hands* – within The Human Body section – where you will find four fully

annotated, colour photographs showing the skin, muscles, and bones of the human hand. In this entry you will quickly find that the bone you are searching for is called the distal phalanx, and for good measure you will discover that it is attached to the middle phalanx by the distal interphalangeal joint.

Perhaps you want to know what a catalytic converter looks like. If you look up "catalytic converter" in an ordinary dictionary, you will be told what it is and possibly what it does – but you will not be able to tell what shape it is or what it is made of. However, if you look up "catalytic converter" in the index of the *Visual Dictionary*, you will be directed to the *Modern engines* entry on page 344 – where the introduction gives you basic information about what a catalytic converter is – and to page 350 – where there is a spectacular exploded-view photograph of the mechanics of a Renault Clio. From these pages you will find out not only what a catalytic converter looks like, but also that it is attached at one end to an exhaust downpipe and at the other to a silencer.

Whatever it is that you want to find a name for, or whatever name you want to find a picture for, you will find it quickly and easily in the *Visual Dictionary*. Perhaps you need to know where the vamp on a shoe is; or how to tell obovate and lanceolate leaves apart; or what a spiral galaxy looks like; or whether birds have nostrils. With the *Visual Dictionary* at hand, the answers to each of these questions, and thousands more, are readily available.

The *Visual Dictionary* does not just tell you what the names of the different parts of an object are. The photographs, illustrations, and annotations are all specially arranged to help you understand which parts relate to one another and how objects function.

With the *Visual Dictionary* you can find in seconds the words or pictures that you are looking for; or you can simply browse through the pages of the book for your own pleasure. The *Visual Dictionary* is not intended to replace a standard dictionary or conventional encyclopedia, but is instead a stimulating and valuable companion to ordinary reference volumes. Giving you instant access to the language that is used by astronomers and architects, musicians and mechanics, scientists and sportspeople, it is the ideal reference book for specialists and generalists of all ages.

Sections of the VISUAL DICTIONARY

The 14 sections of the *VISUAL DICTIONARY* contain a total of more than 30,000 terms, encompassing a wide range of topics:

• In the first section, THE UNIVERSE, spectacular photographs and illustrations are used to show the names of the stars and planets and to explain the structure of solar systems, galaxies, nebulae, comets, and black holes.

• PREHISTORIC EARTH tells the story in annotations of how our own planet has evolved since its formation. It includes examples of prehistoric flora and fauna, and fascinating dinosaur models – some with parts of the body stripped away to show anatomical sections.

• PLANTS covers a huge range of species – from the familiar to the exotic. In addition to the colour photographs of plants included in this section, there is a series of micrographic photographs illustrating plant details – such as pollen grains, spores, and cross-sections of stems and roots – in close-up.

• In the ANIMALS section, skeletons, anatomical diagrams, and different parts of animals' bodies have been meticulously annotated. This section provides a comprehensive guide to the vocabulary of zoological classification and animal physiology.

• The structure of the human body, its parts, and its systems are presented in THE HUMAN BODY. The section includes lifelike, three-dimensional models and the latest false-colour images. Clear and authoritative annotations indicate the correct anatomical terms.

• GEOLOGY, GEOGRAPHY, AND METEOROLOGY describes the structure of the Earth – from the inner core to the exosphere – and the physical phenomena – such as volcanoes, rivers, glaciers, and climate – that shape its surface.

• PHYSICS AND CHEMISTRY is a visual journey through the fundamental principles underlying the physical universe, and provides the essential vocabulary of these sciences.

• In RAIL AND ROAD, a wide range of trains, trams and buses, cars, bicycles, and motorcycles are described. Exploded-view photographs show mechanical details with striking clarity.

• SEA AND AIR gives the names for hundreds of parts of ships and aeroplanes. The section includes civil and fighting craft, both historical and modern.

• THE VISUAL ARTS shows the equipment and materials used by painters, sculptors, printers, and other artists. Well-known compositions have been chosen to illustrate specific artistic techniques and effects.

• ARCHITECTURE includes photographs of exemplary architectural models and illustrates dozens of additional features such as columns, domes, and arches.

• MUSIC provides a visual introduction to the special language of music and musical instruments. It includes clearly annotated photographs of each of the major groups of traditional instruments – brass, woodwind, strings, and percussion – together with modern electronic instruments.

• The SPORTS section is a guide to the playing areas, formations, equipment, and techniques needed for many of today's most popular sports.

• In THE MODERN WORLD, items that are a familiar part of our daily lives are taken apart to reveal their inner workings and give access to the language used by their manufacturers. It also includes systems and concepts, such as the Internet, that increasingly influence our 21st century world.

THE UNIVERSE

Anatomy of the Universe

THE UNIVERSE CONTAINS EVERYTHING that exists, from the tiniest subatomic particles to galactic superclusters (the largest structures known). Nobody knows how big the Universe is, but astronomers estimate that it contains at least 125 billion galaxies, each comprising an average of 100 billion stars. The most widely accepted theory about the origin of the Universe is the Big Bang theory, which states that the Universe came into being in a huge explosion – the Big Bang – that took place between 10 and 20 billion years ago. The Universe initially consisted of a very hot, dense fireball of expanding, cooling gas. After about one million years, the gas began to condense into localized clumps called protogalaxies. During the next five billion years, the protogalaxies continued condensing, forming galaxies in which stars were being born. Today, billions of years later, the Universe as a whole is still expanding, although there are localized areas in which objects are held together by gravity; for example, many galaxies are found in clusters. The Big Bang theory is supported by the discovery of faint, cool background radiation coming evenly from all directions. This radiation is believed to be the remnant of the radiation produced by the Big Bang. Small "ripples" in the temperature of the cosmic background radiation are thought to be evidence of slight fluctuations in the density of the early Universe, which resulted in the formation of galaxies. Astronomers do not yet know if the Universe is "closed", which means it will eventually stop expanding and begin to contract, or if it is "open", which means it will continue expanding forever.

Fireball of rapidly expanding, extremely hot gas lasting about one million years

FALSE-COLOUR MICROWAVE MAP OF COSMIC BACKGROUND RADIATION

Pink indicates "warm ripples" in background radiation

Pale blue indicates "cool ripples" in background radiation

Deep blue indicates background radiation corresponding to -270°C (remnant of the Big Bang)

Red and pink band indicates radiation from our galaxy

Low-energy microwave radiation corresponding to about -270°C

High-energy gamma radiation corresponding to about 3,000°C

ORIGIN AND EXPANSION OF THE UNIVERSE

Quasar (probably the centre of a galaxy containing a massive black hole)

Universe about five billion years after Big Bang

Protogalaxy (condensing gas cloud)

Galaxy spinning and flattening to become spiral shaped

Dark cloud (dust and gas condensing to form a protogalaxy)

Elliptical galaxy in which stars form rapidly

Universe today (13–17 billion years after Big Bang)

Cluster of galaxies held together by gravity

Elliptical galaxy containing old stars and little gas and dust

Irregular galaxy

Spiral galaxy containing gas, dust, and young stars

OBJECTS IN THE UNIVERSE

CLUSTER OF GALAXIES IN VIRGO

FALSE-COLOUR IMAGE OF 3C273 (QUASAR)

NGC 4406 (ELLIPTICAL GALAXY)

NGC 5236 (BARRED SPIRAL GALAXY)

NGC 6822 (IRREGULAR GALAXY)

THE ROSETTE NEBULA (EMISSION NEBULA)

THE JEWEL BOX (STAR CLUSTER)

THE SUN (MAIN SEQUENCE STAR)

EARTH

THE MOON

Galaxies

**SOMBRERO,
A SPIRAL GALAXY**

A GALAXY IS A HUGE MASS OF STARS, nebulae, and interstellar material. The smallest galaxies contain about 100,000 stars, while the largest contain up to 3,000 billion stars. There are three main types of galaxy, classified according to their shape: elliptical, which are oval shaped; spiral, which have arms spiralling outwards from a central bulge (those whose arms spiral from a bar-shaped bulge are called spirals); and irregular, which have no obvious shape. Sometimes, the shape of a galaxy is distorted by a collision with another galaxy. Quasars (quasi-stellar objects) are thought to be galactic nuclei but are so far away that their exact nature is still uncertain. They are compact, highly luminous objects in the outer reaches of the known Universe: while the furthest known "ordinary" galaxies are about 12 billion light years away, the furthest known quasar is about 13 billion light years away. Active galaxies, such as Seyfert galaxies and radio galaxies, emit intense radiation. In a Seyfert galaxy, this radiation comes from the galactic nucleus; in a radio galaxy, it also comes from huge lobes on either side of the galaxy. The radiation from active galaxies and quasars is thought to be caused by material falling into central black holes (see pp. 28-29).

**OPTICAL IMAGE OF NGC 4486
(ELLIPTICAL GALAXY)**

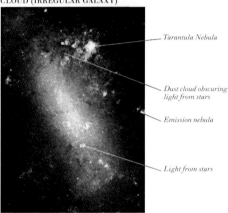

Globular cluster containing very old red giants

Central region containing old red giants

Less densely populated region

Neighbouring galaxy

**OPTICAL IMAGE OF LARGE MAGELLANIC
CLOUD (IRREGULAR GALAXY)**

Tarantula Nebula

Dust cloud obscuring light from stars

Emission nebula

Light from stars

OPTICAL IMAGE OF NGC 2997 (SPIRAL GALAXY)

Glowing nebula in spiral arm

Spiral arm containing young stars

Galactic nucleus containing old stars

Dust in spiral arm reflecting blue light from hot young stars

Hot, ionized hydrogen gas emitting red light

Dust lane

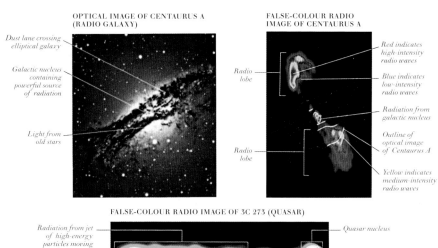

OPTICAL IMAGE OF CENTAURUS A (RADIO GALAXY)

Dust lane crossing elliptical galaxy

Galactic nucleus containing powerful source of radiation

Light from old stars

FALSE-COLOUR RADIO IMAGE OF CENTAURUS A

Red indicates high-intensity radio waves

Blue indicates low-intensity radio waves

Radiation from galactic nucleus

Outline of optical image of Centaurus A

Radio lobe

Radio lobe

Yellow indicates medium-intensity radio waves

FALSE-COLOUR RADIO IMAGE OF 3C 273 (QUASAR)

Radiation from jet of high-energy particles moving away from quasar

Quasar nucleus

Blue indicates low-intensity radio waves

White indicates high-intensity radio waves

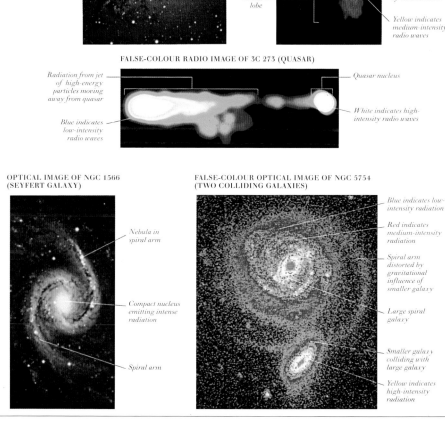

OPTICAL IMAGE OF NGC 1566 (SEYFERT GALAXY)

Nebula in spiral arm

Compact nucleus emitting intense radiation

Spiral arm

FALSE-COLOUR OPTICAL IMAGE OF NGC 5754 (TWO COLLIDING GALAXIES)

Blue indicates low-intensity radiation

Red indicates medium-intensity radiation

Spiral arm distorted by gravitational influence of smaller galaxy

Large spiral galaxy

Smaller galaxy colliding with large galaxy

Yellow indicates high-intensity radiation

The Milky Way

**VIEW TOWARDS
GALACTIC CENTRE**

THE MILKY WAY IS THE NAME GIVEN TO THE FAINT BAND OF LIGHT that stretches across the night sky. This light comes from stars and nebulae in our galaxy, known as the Milky Way Galaxy or simply as "the Galaxy". The Galaxy is believed to be a barred spiral, with a dense central bar of stars encircled by four arms spiralling outwards and surrounded by a less dense halo. We cannot see the spiral shape because the Solar System is in one of the spiral arms, the Orion Arm (also called the Local Arm). From our position, the centre of the Galaxy is completely obscured by dust clouds; as a result, optical maps give only a limited view of the Galaxy. However, a more complete picture can be obtained by studying radio, infra-red, and other radiation. The central part of the Galaxy is relatively small and dense and contains mainly older red and yellow stars. The halo is a less dense region in which the oldest stars are situated; some of these stars are as old as the Galaxy itself (possibly 13 billion years). The spiral arms contain main sequence stars and hot, young, blue stars, as well as nebulae (clouds of dust and gas inside which stars are born). The Galaxy is vast, about 100,000 light years across (a light year is about 9,460 billion kilometres); in comparison, the Solar System seems small, at about 12 light hours across (about 13 billion kilometres). The entire Galaxy is rotating in space, although the inner stars travel faster than those further out. The Sun, which is about two-thirds out from the centre, completes one lap of the Galaxy about every 220 million years.

SIDE VIEW OF OUR GALAXY

Disc of spiral arms containing mainly young stars

Central bulge containing mainly older stars

Halo containing oldest stars

Nucleus

100,000 light years

OVERHEAD VIEW OF OUR GALAXY

Central bulge

Nucleus

Perseus Arm

Crux-Centaurus Arm

Emission nebula

Sagittarius Arm

Dust in spiral arm reflecting blue light from hot young stars

Location of Solar System

Patch of dust clouds

Orion Arm (Local Arm)

PANORAMIC OPTICAL MAP OF OUR GALAXY AND NEARBY GALAXIES

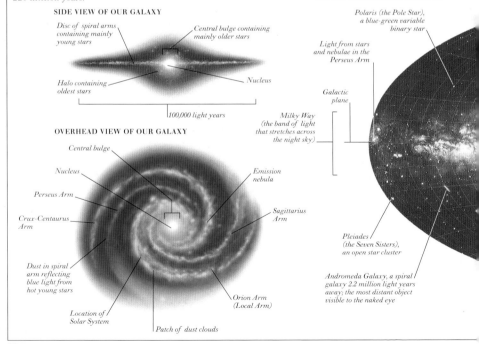

Polaris (the Pole Star), a blue-green variable binary star

Light from stars and nebulae in the Perseus Arm

Galactic plane

Milky Way (the band of light that stretches across the night sky)

Pleiades (the Seven Sisters), an open star cluster

Andromeda Galaxy, a spiral galaxy 2.2 million light years away; the most distant object visible to the naked eye

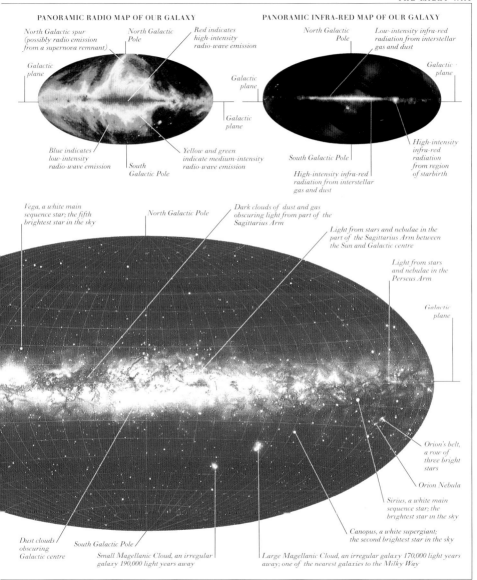

PANORAMIC RADIO MAP OF OUR GALAXY

*North Galactic spur
(possibly radio emission
from a supernova remnant)*

*North Galactic
Pole*

*Red indicates
high-intensity
radio-wave emission*

*Galactic
plane*

*Galactic
plane*

*Galactic
plane*

*Blue indicates
low-intensity
radio-wave emission*

*South
Galactic Pole*

*Yellow and green
indicate medium-intensity
radio-wave emission*

PANORAMIC INFRA-RED MAP OF OUR GALAXY

*North Galactic
Pole*

*Low-intensity infra-red
radiation from interstellar
gas and dust*

*Galactic
plane*

South Galactic Pole

*High-intensity infra-red
radiation from interstellar
gas and dust*

*High-intensity
infra-red
radiation
from region
of starbirth*

*Vega, a white main
sequence star; the fifth
brightest star in the sky*

North Galactic Pole

*Dark clouds of dust and gas
obscuring light from part of the
Sagittarius Arm*

*Light from stars and nebulae in the
part of the Sagittarius Arm between
the Sun and Galactic centre*

*Light from stars
and nebulae in the
Perseus Arm*

*Galactic
plane*

*Orion's belt,
a row of
three bright
stars*

Orion Nebula

*Sirius, a white main
sequence star; the
brightest star in the sky*

*Canopus, a white supergiant;
the second brightest star in the sky*

*Dust clouds
obscuring
Galactic centre*

South Galactic Pole

*Small Magellanic Cloud, an irregular
galaxy 190,000 light years away*

*Large Magellanic Cloud, an irregular galaxy 170,000 light years
away; one of the nearest galaxies to the Milky Way*

Nebulae and star clusters

HODGE 11, A GLOBULAR CLUSTER

A NEBULA IS A CLOUD OF DUST AND GAS inside a galaxy. Nebulae become visible if the gas glows, or if the cloud reflects starlight or obscures light from more distant objects. Emission nebulae shine because their gas emits light when it is stimulated by radiation from hot young stars. Reflection nebulae shine because their dust reflects light from stars in or around the nebula. Dark nebulae appear as silhouettes because they block out light from shining nebulae or stars behind them. Two types of nebula are associated with dying stars: planetary nebulae and supernova remnants. Both consist of expanding shells of gas that were once the outer layers of a star. A planetary nebula is a gas shell drifting away from a dying stellar core. A supernova remnant is a gas shell moving away from a stellar core at great speed following a violent explosion called a supernova (see pp. 26-27). Stars are often found in groups known as clusters. Open clusters are loose groups of a few thousand young stars that were born from the same cloud and are drifting apart. Globular clusters are densely packed, roughly spherical groups of hundreds of thousands of older stars.

TRIFID NEBULA (EMISSION NEBULA)

Reflection nebula

Emission nebula

Dust lane

Starbirth region (area in which dust and gas clump together to form stars)

PLEIADES (OPEN STAR CLUSTER) WITH A REFLECTION NEBULA

Wisps of dust and hydrogen gas. The cluster is passing through a region of inter-stellar material

Young star in an open cluster of more than 1,000 stars

Reflection nebula

HORSEHEAD NEBULA (DARK NEBULA)

Glowing filament of hot, ionized hydrogen gas

Alnitak (star in Orion's belt)

Dust lane

Emission nebula

Star near southern end of Orion's belt

Emission nebula

Horsehead Nebula

Reflection nebula

Dark nebula obscuring light from distant stars

ORION NEBULA (DIFFUSE EMISSION NEBULA)

Glowing cloud of dust and hydrogen gas forming part of Orion Nebula

Gas cloud emitting light due to ultraviolet radiation from the four young Trapezium stars

Dust cloud

Trapezium (group of four young stars)

Green light from hot, ionized oxygen gas

Red light from hot, ionized hydrogen gas

Glowing filament of hot, ionized hydrogen gas

HELIX NEBULA (PLANETARY NEBULA)

Planetary nebula (gas shell expanding outwards from dying stellar core)

Remnant of core with a surface temperature of about 100,000°C

Red light from hot, ionized hydrogen gas

Blue-green light from hot, ionized oxygen and nitrogen gases

VELA SUPERNOVA REMNANT

Supernova remnant (gas shell consisting of outer layers of star thrown off in supernova explosion)

Hydrogen gas emitting red light due to being heated by supernova explosion

Glowing filament of hot, ionized hydrogen gas

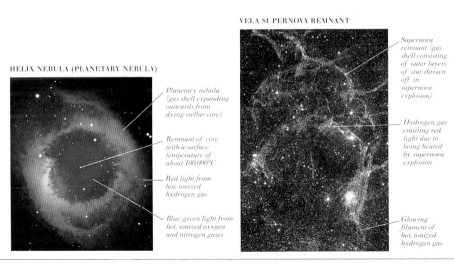

Stars of northern skies

When you look at the northern sky, you look away from the densely populated Galactic centre, so the northern sky generally appears less bright than the southern sky (see pp. 20-21). Among the best-known sights in the northern sky are the constellations Ursa Major (the Great Bear) and Orion. Some ancient civilizations believed that the stars were fixed to a celestial sphere surrounding the Earth, and modern maps of the sky are based on a similar idea. The North and South Poles of this imaginary celestial sphere are directly above the North and South Poles of the Earth, at the points where the Earth's axis of rotation intersects the sphere. The celestial North Pole is at the centre of the map shown here, and Polaris (the Pole Star) lies very close to it. The celestial equator marks a projection of the Earth's equator on the sphere. The ecliptic marks the path of the Sun across the sky as the Earth orbits the Sun. The Moon and planets move against the background of the stars because the stars are much more distant; the nearest star outside the Solar System (Proxima Centauri) is more than 50,000 times further away than the planet Jupiter.

ORION

Chi₂ Orionis, Chi₁ Orionis, Nu Orionis, Xi Orionis, Heka, Mu Orionis, Bellatrix, Betelgeuse, Orion's belt, Omicron Orionis, Alnitak, Pi₂ Orionis, Pi₃ Orionis, Pi₄ Orionis, Pi₅ Orionis, Saiph, Pi₆ Orionis, Mintaka, Eta Orionis, Orion Nebula, Tau Orionis, Rigel, Alnilam

VISIBLE STARS IN THE NORTHERN SKY

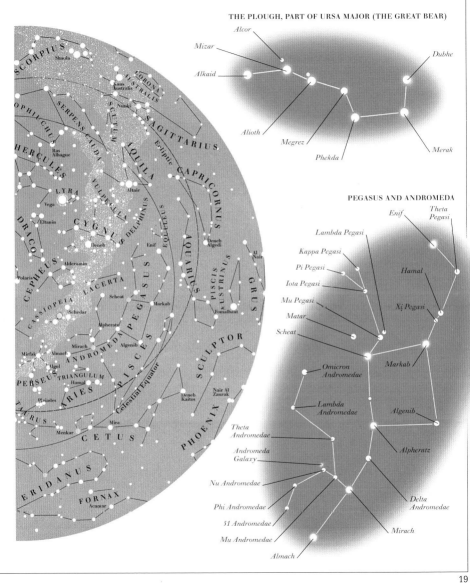

THE PLOUGH, PART OF URSA MAJOR (THE GREAT BEAR)

Alcor
Mizar
Alkaid
Alioth
Megrez
Phekda
Dubhe
Merak

PEGASUS AND ANDROMEDA

Enif
Theta Pegasi
Lambda Pegasi
Kappa Pegasi
Pi Pegasi
Iota Pegasi
Mu Pegasi
Matar
Scheat
Hamal
Xi Pegasi
Markab
Algenib
Alpheratz
Omicron Andromedae
Lambda Andromedae
Theta Andromedae
Andromeda Galaxy
Nu Andromedae
Phi Andromedae
51 Andromedae
Mu Andromedae
Almach
Delta Andromedae
Mirach

SCORPIUS
Shaula
CORONA AUSTRALIS
Kaus Australis
OPHIUCHUS
SERPENS CAUDA
SCUTUM
Nunki
SAGITTARIUS
Ras Alhague
HERCULES
AQUILA
Ecliptic
CAPRICORNUS
LYRA
Vega
VULPECULA
Altair
Eltanin
CYGNUS
DELPHINUS
EQUULEUS
Enif
Deneb Algedi
DRACO
Deneb
AQUARIUS
Al Nair
CEPHEUS
Alderamin
LACERTA
Scheat
PEGASUS
PISCIS AUSTRINUS
GRUS
Polaris
CASSIOPEIA
Schedar
Markab
Fomalhaut
Mirach
Alpheratz
Algenib
ANDROMEDA
PISCES
SCULPTOR
Mirfak
Almach
Algol
TRIANGULUM
Celestial Equator
Nair Al Zaurak
PERSEUS
ARIES
Hamal
Deneb Kaitos
Pleiades
TAURUS
Mira
PHOENIX
Menkar
CETUS
ERIDANUS
FORNAX
Acamar

Stars of southern skies

WHEN YOU LOOK AT THE SOUTHERN SKY, you look towards the Galactic centre, which has a huge population of stars. As a result, the Milky Way appears brighter in the southern sky than in the northern sky (see pp. 18-19). The southern sky is rich in nebulae and star clusters. It contains the Large and Small Magellanic Clouds, which are two of the nearest galaxies to our own. Stars make fixed patterns in the sky called constellations. However, the constellations are only apparent groupings of stars, since the distances to the stars in a constellation may vary enormously. The shapes of constellations may change over many thousands of years due to the relative motions of the stars. The movement of the constellations across the sky is due to the Earth's motion in space. The daily rotation of the Earth causes the constellations to move across the sky from east to west, and the orbit of the Earth around the Sun causes different areas of sky to be visible in different seasons. The visibility of areas of sky also depends on the location of the observer. For instance, stars near the celestial equator may be seen from either hemisphere at some time during the year, whereas stars close to the celestial poles (the celestial South Pole is at the centre of the map shown here) can never be seen from the opposite hemisphere.

HYDRUS (THE WATER SNAKE) AND MENSA (THE TABLE)

VISIBLE STARS IN THE SOUTHERN SKY

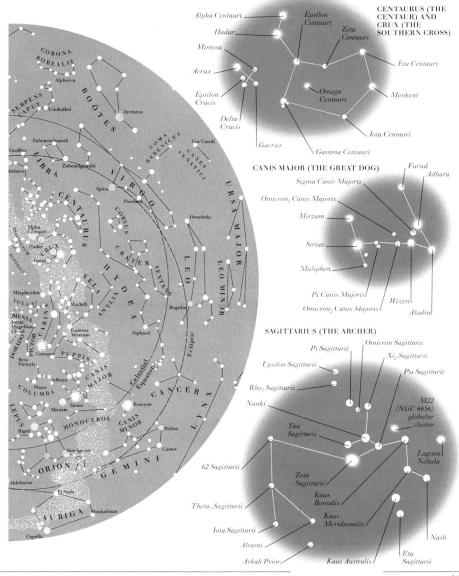

CENTAURUS (THE CENTAUR) AND CRUX (THE SOUTHERN CROSS)

Alpha Centauri
Epsilon Centauri
Hadar
Zeta Centauri
Mimosa
Eta Centauri
Acrux
Epsilon Crucis
Omega Centauri
Menkent
Delta Crucis
Iota Centauri
Gacrux
Gamma Centauri

CANIS MAJOR (THE GREAT DOG)

Furud
Adhara
Sigma Canis Majoris
Omicron₁ Canis Majoris
Mirzam
Sirius
Muliphen
Pi Canis Majoris
Wezen
Omicron₂ Canis Majoris
Aludra

SAGITTARIUS (THE ARCHER)

Pi Sagittarii
Omicron Sagittarii
Upsilon Sagittarii
Xi₂ Sagittarii
Psi Sagittarii
Rho₁ Sagittarii
Nunki
M22 (NGC 6656) globular cluster
Tau Sagittarii
Lagoon Nebula
62 Sagittarii
Zeta Sagittarii
Kaus Borealis
Theta₁ Sagittarii
Kaus Meridionalis
Iota Sagittarii
Nash
Alrami
Eta Sagittarii
Arkab Prior
Kaus Australis

CORONA BOREALIS
Alphecca
SERPENS CAPUT
Unukalhai
BOÖTES
Arcturus
COMA BERENICES
CANES VENATICI
Cor Caroli
Zubeneschamali
Graffias
LIBRA
Zubenelgenubi
VIRGO
URSA MAJOR
Antares
CENTAURUS
Spica
Porrima
CORVUS
LEO MINOR
Alpha Centauri
CRUX
CRATER
Denebola
LEO
Hadar
HYDRA
SEXTANS
Acrux
TRIANGULUM AUSTRALE
VELA
ANTLIA
Markeb
Miaplacidus
VOLANS
CARINA
Regulus
Ecliptic
MENSA
Gamma Velorum
Alphard
Large Magellanic Cloud
DORADO
PICTOR
PUPPIS
CANIS MINOR
Canopus
Beta Pictoris
Phact
COLUMBA
Adhara
CANIS MAJOR
Procyon
Celestial Equator
CANCER
LEPUS
Mirzam
Sirius
MONOCEROS
Pollux
LYNX
Rigel
Castor
Betelgeuse
ORION
GEMINI
Aldebaran
El Nath
AURIGA
Menkalinan
Capella

Stars

OPEN STAR CLUSTER AND DUST CLOUD

STARS ARE BODIES of hot, glowing gas that are born in nebulae (see pp. 24-27). They vary enormously in size, mass, and temperature: diameters range from about 450 times smaller to over 1,000 times bigger than that of the Sun; masses range from about a twentieth to over 50 solar masses; and surface temperatures range from about 3,000°C to over 50,000°C. The colour of a star is determined by its temperature: the hottest stars are blue and the coolest are red. The Sun, with a surface temperature of 5,500°C, is between these extremes and appears yellow. The energy emitted by a shining star is usually produced by nuclear fusion in the star's core. The brightness of a star is measured in magnitudes – the brighter the star, the lower its magnitude. There are two types of magnitude: apparent magnitude, which is the brightness seen from Earth, and absolute magnitude, which is the brightness that would be seen from a standard distance of 10 parsecs (32.6 light years). The light emitted by a star may be split to form a spectrum containing a series of dark lines (absorption lines). The patterns of lines indicate the presence of particular chemical elements, enabling astronomers to deduce the composition of the star's atmosphere. The magnitude and spectral type (colour) of stars may be plotted on a graph called a Hertzsprung-Russell diagram, which shows that stars tend to fall into several well-defined groups. The principal groups are main sequence stars (those which are fusing hydrogen to form helium), giants, supergiants, and white dwarfs.

STAR SIZES

Red giant (diameters between about 15 million and 150 million km)

The Sun (main sequence star with diameter about 1.4 million km)

White dwarf (diameters between about 3,000 and 50,000 km)

ENERGY EMISSION FROM THE SUN

Nuclear fusion in core produces gamma rays and neutrinos

Neutrinos travel to Earth directly from Sun's core in about 8 minutes

Lower-energy radiation travels to Earth in about 8 minutes

Earth

Lower-energy radiation (mainly ultraviolet, infra-red, and light rays) leaves surface

Sun

High-energy radiation (gamma rays) loses energy while travelling to surface over 2 million years

STAR MAGNITUDES

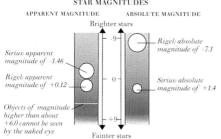

APPARENT MAGNITUDE — ABSOLUTE MAGNITUDE

Brighter stars

Sirius: apparent magnitude of -1.46

Rigel: apparent magnitude of +0.12

Objects of magnitude higher than about +6.0 cannot be seen by the naked eye

Rigel: absolute magnitude of -7.1

Sirius: absolute magnitude of +1.4

Fainter stars

NUCLEAR FUSION IN MAIN SEQUENCE STARS LIKE THE SUN

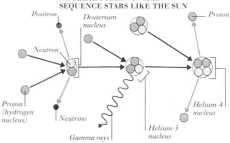

Positron

Deuterium nucleus

Proton

Neutron

Proton (hydrogen nucleus)

Neutrino

Helium-4 nucleus

Gamma rays

Helium-3 nucleus

HERTZSPRUNG-RUSSELL DIAGRAM

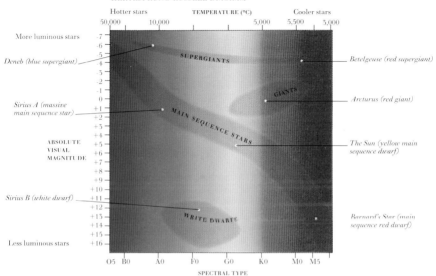

Hotter stars   TEMPERATURE (°C)   Cooler stars

More luminous stars

Deneb (blue supergiant)

Betelgeuse (red supergiant)

SUPERGIANTS

Sirius A (massive main sequence star)

GIANTS

Arcturus (red giant)

MAIN SEQUENCE STARS

ABSOLUTE
VISUAL
MAGNITUDE

The Sun (yellow main sequence dwarf)

Sirius B (white dwarf)

WHITE DWARFS

Barnard's Star (main sequence red dwarf)

Less luminous stars

SPECTRAL TYPE

STELLAR SPECTRAL ABSORPTION LINES

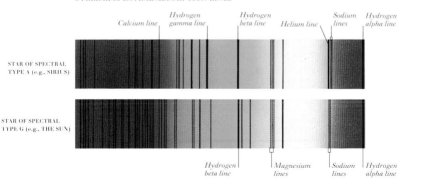

Calcium line Hydrogen gamma line Hydrogen beta line Helium line Sodium lines Hydrogen alpha line

STAR OF SPECTRAL
TYPE A (e.g., SIRIUS)

STAR OF SPECTRAL
TYPE G (e.g., THE SUN)

Hydrogen beta line Magnesium lines Sodium lines Hydrogen alpha line

Small stars

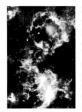

**REGION OF
STAR FORMATION
IN ORION**

SMALL STARS HAVE A MASS of up to about one and a half times that of the Sun. They begin to form when a region of higher density in a nebula condenses into a huge globule of gas and dust that contracts under its own gravity. Within a globule, regions of condensing matter heat up and begin to glow, forming protostars. If a protostar contains enough matter, the central temperature reaches about 8 million °C. At this temperature, nuclear reactions in which hydrogen fuses to form helium can start. This process releases energy, which prevents the star from contracting further and also causes it to shine; it is now a main sequence star. A star of about one solar mass remains on the main sequence for about 10 billion years, until much of the hydrogen in the star's core has been converted into helium. The helium core then contracts, and nuclear reactions continue in a shell around the core. The core becomes hot enough for helium to fuse to form carbon, while the outer layers of the star expand and cool. The expanding star is known as a red giant. When the helium in the core runs out, the outer layers of the star may be blown away as an expanding gas shell called a planetary nebula. The remaining core (about 80 per cent of the original star) is now in its final stages. It becomes a white dwarf star that gradually cools and dims. When it finally stops shining altogether, the dead star will become a black dwarf.

STRUCTURE OF A MAIN SEQUENCE STAR

Core containing hydrogen fusing to form helium

Radiative zone

Convective zone

Surface temperature about 5,500°C

Core temperature about 15 million °C

STRUCTURE OF A NEBULA

Young main sequence star

Dense region of dust and gas (mainly hydrogen) condensing under gravity to form globules

Hot, ionized hydrogen gas emitting red light due to being stimulated by radiation from hot young stars

Dark globule of dust and gas (mainly hydrogen) contracting to form protostars

LIFE OF A SMALL STAR OF ABOUT ONE SOLAR MASS

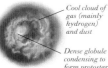

Cool cloud of gas (mainly hydrogen) and dust

Dense globule condensing to form protostars

NEBULA

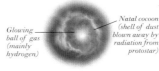

Glowing ball of gas (mainly hydrogen)

Natal cocoon (shell of dust blown away by radiation from protostar)

PROTOSTAR
Duration: 50 million years

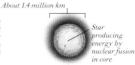

About 1.4 million km

Star producing energy by nuclear fusion in core

MAIN SEQUENCE STAR
Duration: 10 billion years

STRUCTURE OF A RED GIANT

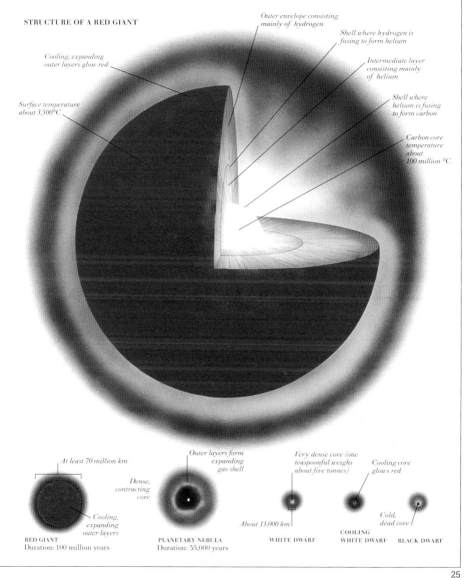

Cooling, expanding outer layers glow red

Surface temperature about 3,500°C

Outer envelope consisting mainly of hydrogen

Shell where hydrogen is fusing to form helium

Intermediate layer consisting mainly of helium

Shell where helium is fusing to form carbon

Carbon core temperature about 100 million °C

At least 70 million km

Cooling, expanding outer layers

Dense, contracting core

Outer layers form expanding gas shell

Very dense core (one teaspoonful weighs about five tonnes)

Cooling core glows red

About 13,000 km

Cold, dead core

RED GIANT
Duration: 100 million years

PLANETARY NEBULA
Duration: 35,000 years

WHITE DWARF

COOLING WHITE DWARF

BLACK DWARF

Massive stars

MASSIVE STARS HAVE A MASS AT LEAST THREE TIMES that of the Sun, and some stars are as massive as about 50 Suns. A massive star evolves in a similar way to a small star until it reaches the main sequence stage (see pp. 24-25). During its life as a main sequence star, it shines steadily until the hydrogen in its core has fused to form helium. This process takes billions of years in a small star, but only millions of years in a massive star. A massive star then becomes a red supergiant, which initially consists of a helium core surrounded by outer layers of cooling, expanding gas. Over the next few million years, a series of nuclear reactions form different elements in shells around an iron core. The core eventually collapses in less than a second, causing a massive explosion called a supernova, in which a shock wave blows away the outer layers of the star. Supernovae shine brighter than an entire galaxy for a short time. Sometimes, the core survives the supernova explosion. If the surviving core is between about one and a half and three solar masses, it contracts to become a tiny, dense neutron star. If the core is greater than three solar masses, it contracts to become a black hole (see pp. 28-29).

SUPERNOVA

TARANTULA NEBULA BEFORE SUPERNOVA

STRUCTURE OF A RED SUPERGIANT

Outer envelope consisting mainly of hydrogen

Layer consisting mainly of helium

Layer consisting mainly of carbon

Layer consisting mainly of oxygen

Layer consisting mainly of silicon

Shell of hydrogen fusing to form helium

Shell of helium fusing to form carbon

Shell of carbon fusing to form oxygen

Shell of oxygen fusing to form silicon

Shell of silicon fusing to form iron core

Surface temperature about 3,000°C

Cooling, expanding outer layers glow red

Core of mainly iron at a temperature of 3-5 billion °C

LIFE OF A MASSIVE STAR OF ABOUT 10 SOLAR MASSES

Dense globule condensing to form protostars

Cool cloud of gas (mainly hydrogen) and dust

NEBULA

Glowing ball of gas (mainly hydrogen)

Natal cocoon (shell of dust blown away by radiation from protostar)

PROTOSTAR
Duration: a few hundred thousand years

About 3 million km

Star producing energy by nuclear fusion in core

MAIN SEQUENCE STAR
Duration: 10 million years

FEATURES OF A SUPERNOVA

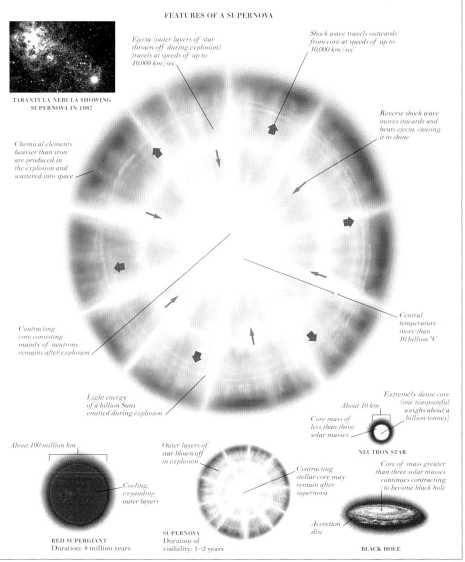

TARANTULA NEBULA SHOWING
SUPERNOVA IN 1987

Ejecta (outer layers of star thrown off during explosion) travels at speeds of up to 10,000 km/sec

Shock wave travels outwards from core at speeds of up to 30,000 km/sec

Reverse shock wave moves inwards and heats ejecta, causing it to shine

Chemical elements heavier than iron are produced in the explosion and scattered into space

Contracting core consisting mainly of neutrons remains after explosion

Light energy of a billion Suns emitted during explosion

Central temperature more than 10 billion °C

About 100 million km

Cooling, expanding outer layers

RED SUPERGIANT
Duration: 4 million years

Outer layers of star blown off in explosion

Contracting stellar core may remain after supernova

SUPERNOVA
Duration of visibility: 1–2 years

About 10 km

Core mass of less than three solar masses

Extremely dense core (one teaspoonful weighs about a billion tonnes)

NEUTRON STAR

Core of mass greater than three solar masses continues contracting to become black hole

Accretion disc

BLACK HOLE

Neutron stars and black holes

Neutron stars and black holes form from the stellar cores that remain after stars have exploded as supernovae (see pp. 26-27). If the remaining core is between about one and a half and three solar masses, it contracts to form a neutron star. If the remaining core is greater than about three solar masses, it contracts to form a black hole. Neutron stars are typically only about 10 kilometres in diameter and consist almost entirely of subatomic particles called neutrons. Such stars are so dense that a teaspoonful would weigh about a billion tonnes. Neutron stars are observed as pulsars, so-called because they rotate rapidly and emit two beams of radio waves, which sweep across the sky and are detected as short pulses. Black holes are characterized by their extremely strong gravity, which is so powerful that not even light can escape; as a result, black holes are invisible. However, they can be detected if they have a close companion star. The gravity of the black hole pulls gas from the other star, forming an accretion disc that spirals around the black hole at high speed, heating up and emitting radiation. Eventually, the matter spirals in to cross the event horizon (the boundary of the black hole), thereby disappearing from the visible Universe.

Nebula of gas and dust surrounds pulsar

Rapidly rotating pulsar

Beam of radiation from pulsar

X-RAY IMAGE OF PULSAR AND CENTRAL REGION OF CRAB NEBULA (SUPERNOVA REMNANT)

PULSAR (ROTATING NEUTRON STAR)

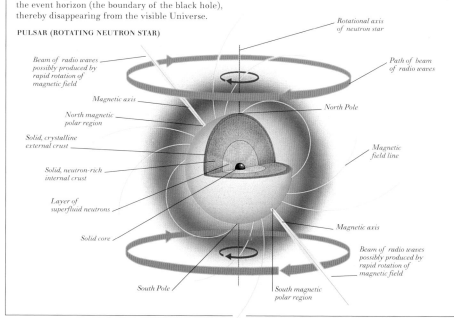

Rotational axis of neutron star

Beam of radio waves possibly produced by rapid rotation of magnetic field

Path of beam of radio waves

Magnetic axis

North magnetic polar region

North Pole

Solid, crystalline external crust

Magnetic field line

Solid, neutron-rich internal crust

Layer of superfluid neutrons

Solid core

Magnetic axis

Beam of radio waves possibly produced by rapid rotation of magnetic field

South Pole

South magnetic polar region

STELLAR BLACK HOLE

Blue supergiant star

Gas current (outer layers of nearby blue supergiant pulled towards black hole by gravity)

Singularity (theoretical region in which the physics of the material is unknown)

Hot spot (region of intense friction where gas current joins accretion disc)

Gas in outer part of accretion disc emitting low-energy radiation

Event horizon (boundary of black hole)

Hot gas in inner part of accretion disc emitting high-energy X-rays

Accretion disc (matter spiralling around black hole)

Black hole

Gas at temperatures of millions °C spiralling at close to the speed of light

FORMATION OF A BLACK HOLE

Stellar core remains after supernova explosion

Light rays increasingly bent by gravity as core collapses

Core shrinks beyond its event horizon to become a black hole

Light rays cannot escape because gravity is so strong

Outer layers of massive star thrown off in explosion

Core greater than three solar masses collapses under its own gravity

Density, pressure, and temperature of core increase as core collapses

Event horizon

Singularity (theoretical region in which the physics of the material is unknown)

SUPERNOVA

COLLAPSING STELLAR CORE

BLACK HOLE

The Solar System

THE SUN

THE SOLAR SYSTEM consists of a central star (the Sun) and the bodies that orbit it. These bodies include eight planets and their more than 160 known moons; dwarf planets; Kuiper Belt objects; asteroids; comets; and meteoroids. The Solar System also contains interplanetary gas and dust. The planets fall into two groups: four small rocky planets near the Sun (Mercury, Venus, Earth, and Mars); and four planets further out, the giants (Jupiter, Saturn, Uranus, and Neptune). Between the rocky planets and giants is the asteroid belt, which contains thousands of chunks of rock orbiting the Sun. Beyond Neptune is the Kuiper Belt and, more distant, the Oort Cloud. Most of the bodies in the planetary part of the Solar System move around the Sun in elliptical orbits located in a thin disc around the Sun's equator. All the planets orbit the Sun in the same direction (anticlockwise when viewed from above) and all but Venus and Uranus also spin about their axes in this direction. Moons also spin as they, in turn, orbit their planets. The entire Solar System orbits the centre of our galaxy, the Milky Way (see pp. 14-15).

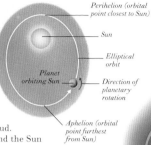

Perihelion (orbital point closest to Sun)

Sun

Elliptical orbit

Planet orbiting Sun

Direction of planetary rotation

Aphelion (orbital point furthest from Sun)

Aphelion of Neptune: 4,545 million km

ORBITS OF INNER PLANETS

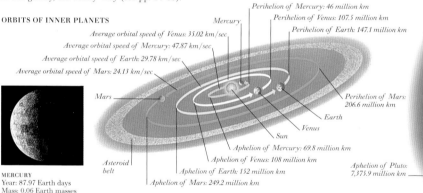

Perihelion of Mercury: 46 million km

Perihelion of Venus: 107.5 million km

Mercury

Perihelion of Earth: 147.1 million km

Average orbital speed of Venus: 35.02 km/sec

Average orbital speed of Mercury: 47.87 km/sec

Average orbital speed of Earth: 29.78 km/sec

Average orbital speed of Mars: 24.13 km/sec

Mars

Perihelion of Mars: 206.6 million km

Earth

Venus

Sun

Aphelion of Mercury: 69.8 million km

Asteroid belt

Aphelion of Venus: 108 million km

Aphelion of Earth: 152 million km

Aphelion of Mars: 249.2 million km

Aphelion of Pluto: 7,375.9 million km

MERCURY
Year: 87.97 Earth days
Mass: 0.06 Earth masses
Diameter: 4,878 km

VENUS
Year: 224.7 Earth days
Mass: 0.81 Earth masses
Diameter: 12,103 km

EARTH
Year: 365.26 days
Mass: 1 Earth mass
Diameter: 12,756 km

MARS
Year: 1.88 Earth years
Mass: 0.11 Earth masses
Diameter: 6,786 km

JUPITER
Year: 11.87 Earth years
Mass: 317.83 Earth masses
Diameter: 142,984 km

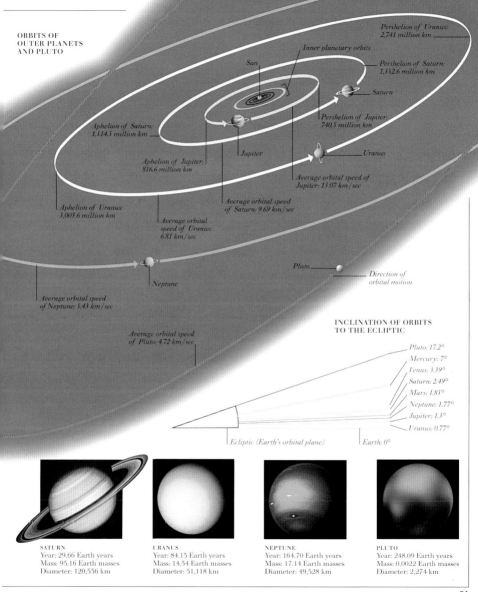

**ORBITS OF
OUTER PLANETS
AND PLUTO**

Perihelion of Uranus:
2,741 million km

Inner planetary orbits

Sun

Perihelion of Saturn:
1,352.6 million km

Saturn

Perihelion of Jupiter:
740.3 million km

Aphelion of Saturn:
1,514.5 million km

Jupiter

Aphelion of Jupiter:
816.6 million km

Uranus

Average orbital speed of
Jupiter: 13.07 km/sec

Aphelion of Uranus:
3,003.6 million km

Average orbital
speed of Uranus:
6.81 km/sec

Average orbital speed
of Saturn: 9.69 km/sec

Neptune

Pluto

Direction of
orbital motion

Average orbital speed
of Neptune: 5.43 km/sec

Average orbital speed
of Pluto: 4.72 km/sec

**INCLINATION OF ORBITS
TO THE ECLIPTIC**

Pluto: 17.2°

Mercury: 7°

Venus: 3.39°

Saturn: 2.49°

Mars: 1.85°

Neptune: 1.77°

Jupiter: 1.3°

Uranus: 0.77°

Ecliptic (Earth's orbital plane)

Earth: 0°

SATURN
Year: 29.66 Earth years
Mass: 95.16 Earth masses
Diameter: 120,536 km

URANUS
Year: 84.13 Earth years
Mass: 14.54 Earth masses
Diameter: 51,118 km

NEPTUNE
Year: 164.70 Earth years
Mass: 17.14 Earth masses
Diameter: 49,528 km

PLUTO
Year: 248.09 Earth years
Mass: 0.0022 Earth masses
Diameter: 2,274 km

The Sun

SOLAR
PHOTOSPHERE

THE SUN IS THE STAR AT THE CENTRE of the Solar System.
It is about five billion years old and will continue to shine
as it does now for about another five billion years. The
Sun is a yellow main sequence star (see pp. 22-23) about
1.4 million kilometres in diameter. It consists almost
entirely of hydrogen and helium. In the Sun's core,
hydrogen is converted to helium by nuclear fusion,
releasing energy in the process. The energy travels
from the core, through the radiative and convective zones, to the
photosphere (visible surface), where it leaves the Sun in the form of
heat and light. On the photosphere there are often dark, relatively cool
areas called sunspots, which usually appear in pairs or groups and are
caused by the cooling effect of the magnetic field. Other types of solar
activity are flares, which are usually associated with sunspots, and
prominences. Flares are sudden discharges of high-energy radiation
and atomic particles. Prominences are huge loops or filaments of gas
extending into the solar atmosphere; some last for hours, others for
months. Beyond the photosphere is the chromosphere (inner
atmosphere) and the extremely rarified corona (outer atmosphere),
which extends millions of kilometres into space. Tiny particles that
escape from the corona give rise to the solar wind, which streams
through space at hundreds of kilometres per second. The
chromosphere and corona can be seen from Earth when the Sun
is totally eclipsed by the Moon.

Sun

*Moon passes
between Sun
and Earth*

*Region of
Earth from
which total
eclipse is visible*

*Region of Earth
from which partial
eclipse is visible*

*Umbra (inner, total
shadow) of Earth*

*Penumbra (outer,
partial shadow)
of Earth*

*Umbra
(inner, total
shadow) of
Moon*

*Penumbra
(outer,
partial
shadow)
of Moon*

Earth

SURFACE FEATURES

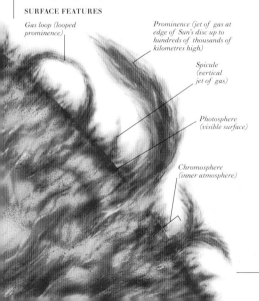

*Gas loop (looped
prominence)*

*Prominence (jet of gas at
edge of Sun's disc up to
hundreds of thousands of
kilometres high)*

*Spicule
(vertical
jet of gas)*

*Photosphere
(visible surface)*

*Chromosphere
(inner atmosphere)*

TOTAL SOLAR ECLIPSE

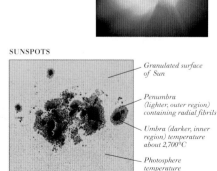

*Corona (outer
atmosphere
of extremely
hot, diffuse gas)*

*Moon covers
Sun's disc*

SUNSPOTS

*Granulated surface
of Sun*

*Penumbra
(lighter, outer region)
containing radial fibrils*

*Umbra (darker, inner
region) temperature
about 2,700°C*

*Photosphere
temperature
about 5,500°C*

EXTERNAL FEATURES AND
INTERNAL STRUCTURE OF THE SUN

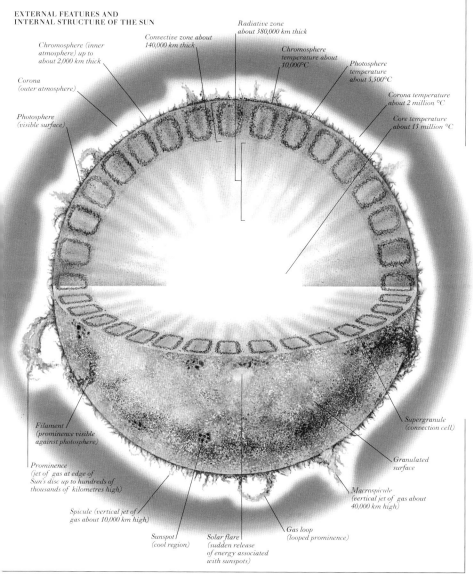

Radiative zone
about 380,000 km thick

Convective zone about
140,000 km thick

Chromosphere (inner
atmosphere) up to
about 2,000 km thick

Chromosphere
temperature about
10,000°C

Photosphere
temperature
about 5,500°C

Corona
(outer atmosphere)

Corona temperature
about 2 million °C

Core temperature
about 15 million °C

Photosphere
(visible surface)

Filament
(prominence visible
against photosphere)

Prominence
(jet of gas at edge of
Sun's disc up to hundreds of
thousands of kilometres high)

Spicule (vertical jet of
gas about 10,000 km high)

Sunspot
(cool region)

Solar flare
(sudden release
of energy associated
with sunspots)

Gas loop
(looped prominence)

Macrospicule
(vertical jet of gas about
40,000 km high)

Granulated
surface

Supergranule
(convection cell)

Mercury

MERCURY

MERCURY IS THE NEAREST PLANET to the Sun, orbiting at an average distance of about 58 million kilometres. Because Mercury is the closest planet to the Sun, it moves faster than any other planet, travelling at an average speed of nearly 48 kilometres per second and completing an orbit in just under 88 days. Mercury is very small (only 40 per cent bigger than the Moon) and rocky. Most of the surface has been heavily cratered by the impact of meteorites, although there are also smooth, sparsely cratered lava-covered plains. The Caloris Basin is the largest crater, measuring about 1,300 kilometres across. It is thought to have been formed when a 60-kilometre-diameter asteroid hit the planet, and is surrounded by concentric rings of mountains thrown up by the impact. The surface also has many cliff-like ridges (called rupes) that are thought to have been formed when the hot core of the young planet cooled and shrank about four billion years ago, buckling the planet's surface in the process. The planet rotates about its axis very slowly, taking nearly 59 Earth days to complete one rotation. As a result, a solar day (sunrise to sunrise) on Mercury is about 176 Earth days – twice as long as the 88-day Mercurian year. Mercury has extreme surface temperatures, ranging from a maximum of 430°C on the sunlit side to -170°C on the dark side. At nightfall, the temperature drops very quickly because the planet's atmosphere is almost non-existent. It consists only of minute amounts of helium and hydrogen captured from the solar wind, plus traces of other gases.

TILT AND ROTATION OF MERCURY

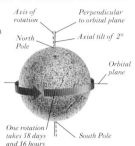

Axis of rotation

Perpendicular to orbital plane

North Pole

Axial tilt of 2°

Orbital plane

One rotation takes 58 days and 16 hours

South Pole

DEGAS AND BRONTË (RAY CRATERS)

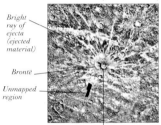

Bright ray of ejecta (ejected material)

Brontë

Unmapped region

Degas with central peak

FORMATION OF A RAY CRATER

Debris thrown out by impact

Path of meteorite colliding with planet

Wall of rock thrown up around crater

Impact forms saucer-shaped crater

Fractured rock

METEORITE IMPACT

Path of rocky ejecta (ejected material)

Ejecta forms secondary craters

Loose debris on crater floor

SECONDARY CRATERING

Wall of rock forms ring of mountains

Ray of ejecta (ejected material)

Small secondary crater

Loose ejected rock

Central mountain rings form if floor of large crater recoils from meteorite impact

Falling debris forms ridges on side of wall

RAY CRATER

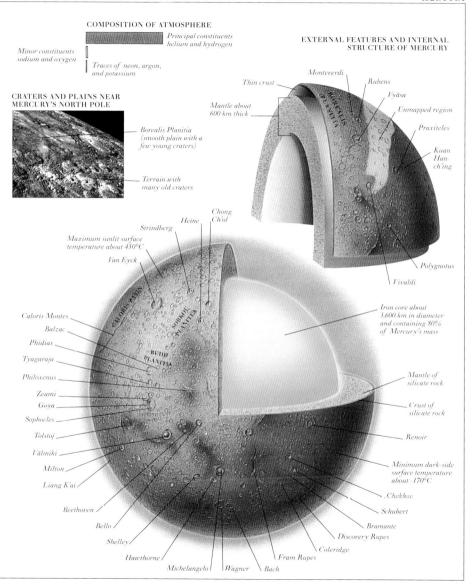

COMPOSITION OF ATMOSPHERE

Principal constituents
helium and hydrogen

Minor constituents
sodium and oxygen

Traces of neon, argon,
and potassium

EXTERNAL FEATURES AND INTERNAL
STRUCTURE OF MERCURY

Thin crust

Monteverdi

Rubens

Vyāsa

Mantle about
600 km thick

Unmapped region

Praxiteles

Kuan
Han-
ch'ing

BOREALIS PLANITIA

CRATERS AND PLAINS NEAR
MERCURY'S NORTH POLE

Borealis Planitia
(smooth plain with a
few young craters)

Terrain with
many old craters

Polygnotus

Vivaldi

Chong
Ch'ol

Heine

Strindberg

Maximum sunlit surface
temperature about 430°C

Van Eyck

Caloris Montes

Balzac

Phidias

Tyagaraja

Philoxenus

Zeami

Goya

Sophocles

Tolstoj

Vālmiki

Milton

Liang K'ai

Beethoven

Bello

Shelley

Hawthorne

Michelangelo

Wagner

Bach

CALORIS PLANITIA

SOBKOU PLANITIA

BUDH
PLANITIA

Iron core about
3,600 km in diameter
and containing 80%
of Mercury's mass

Mantle of
silicate rock

Crust of
silicate rock

Renoir

Minimum dark-side
surface temperature
about -170°C

Chekhov

Schubert

Bramante

Discovery Rupes

Coleridge

Fram Rupes

Venus

RADAR IMAGE OF VENUS

VENUS IS A ROCKY PLANET and the second planet from the Sun. Venus spins slowly backwards as it orbits the Sun, causing its rotational period to be the longest in the Solar System, at about 243 Earth days. It is slightly smaller than Earth and probably has a similar internal structure, consisting of a semi-solid metal core, surrounded by a rocky mantle and crust. Venus is the brightest object in the sky after the Sun and Moon because its clouds reflect sunlight strongly. The main component of the atmosphere is carbon dioxide, which traps heat in a greenhouse effect far stronger than that on Earth. As a result, Venus is the hottest planet, with a maximum surface temperature of about 480°C. The thick cloud layers contain droplets of sulphuric acid and are driven around the planet by winds at speeds of up to 360 kilometres per hour. Although the planet takes 243 Earth days to rotate once, the high-speed winds cause the clouds to circle the planet in only four Earth days. The high temperature, acidic clouds, and enormous atmospheric pressure (about 90 times greater at the surface than that on Earth) make the environment extremely hostile. However, space probes have managed to land on Venus and photograph its dry, dusty surface. The Venusian surface has also been mapped by probes with radar equipment that can "see" through the cloud layers. Such radar maps reveal a terrain with craters, mountains, volcanoes, and areas where craters have been covered by plains of solidified volcanic lava. There are two large highland regions called Aphrodite Terra and Ishtar Terra.

TILT AND ROTATION OF VENUS

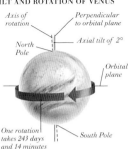

Axis of rotation

Perpendicular to orbital plane

North Pole

Axial tilt of 2°

Orbital plane

One rotation takes 243 days and 14 minutes

South Pole

CLOUD FEATURES

Polar hood

Dark, mid latitude band

Cloud features swept around planet by winds of up to 360 km/h

Dirty yellow hue due to sulphuric acid in atmosphere

Bright polar band

VENUSIAN CRATERS

Danilova

Ejecta (ejected material)

Central peak

Howe

FALSE-COLOUR RADAR MAP OF THE SURFACE OF VENUS

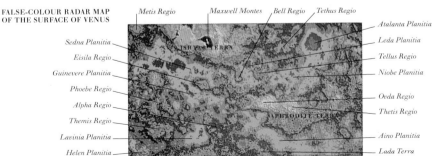

Metis Regio

Maxwell Montes

Bell Regio

Tethus Regio

Atalanta Planitia

Sedna Planitia

Leda Planitia

Eisila Regio

ISHTAR TERRA

Tellus Regio

Guinevere Planitia

Niobe Planitia

Phoebe Regio

Alpha Regio

Ovda Regio

Themis Regio

APHRODITE TERRA

Thetis Regio

Lavinia Planitia

Aino Planitia

Helen Planitia

Lada Terra

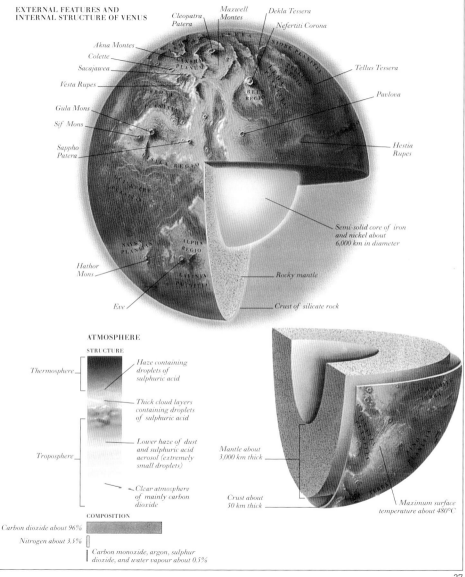

EXTERNAL FEATURES AND
INTERNAL STRUCTURE OF VENUS

Cleopatra Patera
Maxwell Montes
Dekla Tessera
Nefertiti Corona
Akna Montes
Colette
Sacajawea
Vesta Rupes
Gula Mons
Sif Mons
Sappho Patera
Tellus Tessera
Pavlova
Hestia Rupes
Hathor Mons
Eve

Semi-solid core of iron and nickel about 6,000 km in diameter
Rocky mantle
Crust of silicate rock

ATMOSPHERE

STRUCTURE

Thermosphere

Haze containing droplets of sulphuric acid

Thick cloud layers containing droplets of sulphuric acid

Lower haze of dust and sulphuric acid aerosol (extremely small droplets)

Troposphere

Clear atmosphere of mainly carbon dioxide

Mantle about 3,000 km thick

Crust about 50 km thick

Maximum surface temperature about 480°C

COMPOSITION

Carbon dioxide about 96%

Nitrogen about 3.5%

Carbon monoxide, argon, sulphur dioxide, and water vapour about 0.5%

The Earth

THE EARTH

THE EARTH IS THE THIRD of the eight planets that orbit the Sun. It is the largest and densest rocky planet, and the only one known to support life. About 70 per cent of the Earth's surface is covered by water, which is not found in liquid form on the surface of any other planet. There are four main layers: the inner core, the outer core, the mantle, and the crust. At the heart of the planet the solid inner core has a temperature of about 6,600°C. The heat from this inner core causes material in the molten outer core and mantle to circulate in convection currents. It is thought that these convection currents generate the Earth's magnetic field, which extends into space as the magnetosphere. The Earth's atmosphere helps screen out some of the harmful radiation from the Sun, stops most meteoroids from reaching the planet's surface, and traps enough heat to prevent extremes of cold. The Earth has one natural satellite, the Moon, which is thought to have formed when a huge asteroid impacted Earth in the distant past.

TILT AND ROTATION OF THE EARTH

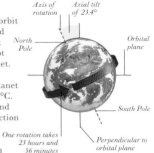

Axis of rotation

Axial tilt of 23.4°

North Pole

Orbital plane

South Pole

One rotation takes 23 hours and 56 minutes

Perpendicular to orbital plane

THE FORMATION OF THE EARTH

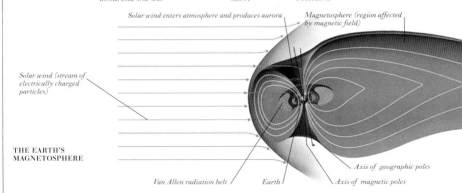

The heat of the collisions caused the planet to glow red

The cloud formed a disc of material around the young Sun's equator. The disc material stuck together to form planets

Micro-organisms began to photosynthesize, creating a build up of oxygen

4,600 MILLION YEARS AGO, THE SOLAR SYSTEM FORMED FROM A CLOUD OF ROCK, ICE, AND GAS

THE EARTH WAS FORMED FROM COLLIDING ROCKS

4,500 MILLION YEARS AGO THE SURFACE COOLED TO FORM THE CRUST

THE CONTINENTS BROKE UP AND REFORMED, GRADUALLY MOVING TO THEIR PRESENT POSITIONS

Solar wind enters atmosphere and produces aurora

Magnetosphere (region affected by magnetic field)

Solar wind (stream of electrically charged particles)

THE EARTH'S MAGNETOSPHERE

Axis of geographic poles

Axis of magnetic poles

Van Allen radiation belt

Earth

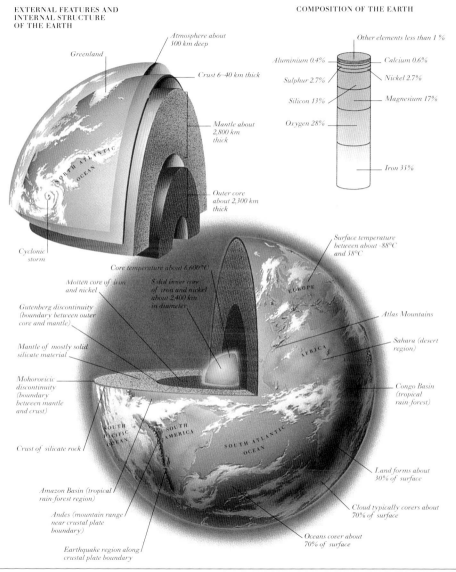

EXTERNAL FEATURES AND INTERNAL STRUCTURE OF THE EARTH

Greenland

Atmosphere about 500 km deep

Crust 6–40 km thick

Mantle about 2,800 km thick

Outer core about 2,300 km thick

Cyclonic storm

NORTH ATLANTIC OCEAN

COMPOSITION OF THE EARTH

Other elements less than 1 %

Aluminium 0.4%

Calcium 0.6%

Sulphur 2.7%

Nickel 2.7%

Silicon 13%

Magnesium 17%

Oxygen 28%

Iron 35%

Core temperature about 6,600°C

Surface temperature between about -88°C and 58°C

Molten core of iron and nickel

Solid inner core of iron and nickel about 2,400 km in diameter

Gutenberg discontinuity (boundary between outer core and mantle)

Mantle of mostly solid silicate material

Mohorovicic discontinuity (boundary between mantle and crust)

Crust of silicate rock

Amazon Basin (tropical rain-forest region)

Andes (mountain range near crustal plate boundary)

Earthquake region along crustal plate boundary

EUROPE

AFRICA

Atlas Mountains

Sahara (desert region)

Congo Basin (tropical rain forest)

Land forms about 30% of surface

Cloud typically covers about 70% of surface

Oceans cover about 70% of surface

SOUTH PACIFIC OCEAN

SOUTH AMERICA

SOUTH ATLANTIC OCEAN

The Moon

THE MOON FROM EARTH

THE MOON IS THE EARTH'S only natural satellite. It is relatively large for a moon, with a diameter of about 3,470 kilometres − just over a quarter that of the Earth. The Moon takes the same time to rotate on its axis as it takes to orbit the Earth (27.3 days), and so the same side (the near side) always faces us. However, the amount of the surface we can see − the phase of the Moon − depends on how much of the near side is in sunlight. The Moon is dry and barren, with negligible atmosphere and water. It consists mainly of solid rock, although its core may contain molten rock or iron. The surface is dusty, with highlands covered in craters caused by meteorite impacts, and lowlands in which large craters have been filled by solidified lava to form dark areas called maria or "seas". Maria occur mainly on the near side, which has a thinner crust than the far side. Many of the craters are rimmed by mountain ranges that form the crater walls and can be thousands of metres high.

TILT AND ROTATION OF THE MOON

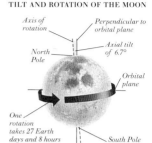

Axis of rotation
Perpendicular to orbital plane
North Pole
Axial tilt of 6.7°
Orbital plane
One rotation takes 27 Earth days and 8 hours
South Pole

CRATERS ON OCEANUS PROCELLARUM

Aristarchus
Cobra Head (head of Schröter's Valley)
Herodotus

NEAR SIDE OF THE MOON

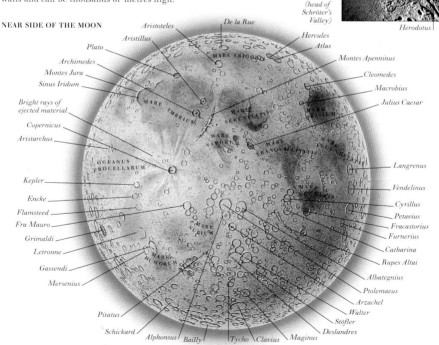

Aristoteles
De la Rue
Aristillus
Hercules
Plato
Atlas
Archimedes
Montes Apenninus
Montes Jura
Cleomedes
Sinus Iridum
Macrobius
Bright rays of ejected material
Julius Caesar
Copernicus
Aristarchus
Langrenus
Kepler
Vendelinus
Encke
Cyrillus
Flamsteed
Petavius
Fra Mauro
Fracastorius
Grimaldi
Furnerius
Letronne
Catharina
Gassendi
Rupes Altai
Mersenius
Albategnius
Ptolemaeus
Arzachel
Walter
Pitatus
Stöfler
Deslandres
Schickard
Alphonsus
Bailly
Tycho
Clavius
Maginus

MARE FRIGORIS
MARE IMBRIUM
MARE SERENITATIS
MARE VAPORUM
MARE TRANQUILLITATIS
OCEANUS PROCELLARUM
MARE NUBIUM
MARE HUMORUM

40

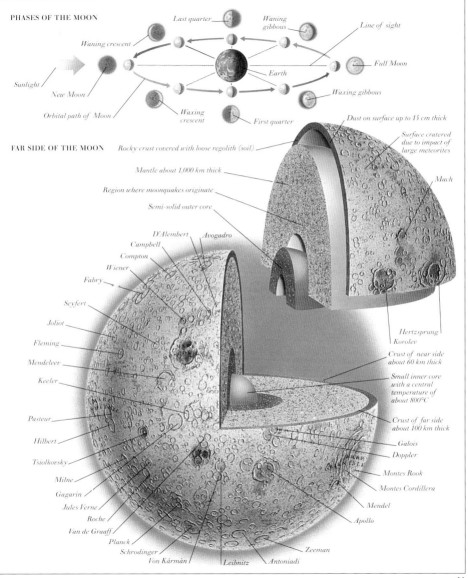

PHASES OF THE MOON

Last quarter

Waning gibbous

Line of sight

Waning crescent

Earth

Full Moon

Sunlight

New Moon

Waxing gibbous

Orbital path of Moon

Waxing crescent

First quarter

FAR SIDE OF THE MOON

Rocky crust covered with loose regolith (soil)

Dust on surface up to 15 cm thick

Surface cratered due to impact of large meteorites

Mantle about 1,000 km thick

Mach

Region where moonquakes originate

Semi-solid outer core

D'Alembert

Avogadro

Campbell

Compton

Wiener

Fabry

Seyfert

Joliot

Fleming

Mendeleev

Keeler

Pasteur

Hilbert

Tsiolkovsky

Milne

Gagarin

Jules Verne

Roche

Van de Graaff

Planck

Schrodinger

Von Kármàn

Leibnitz

Antoniadi

Zeeman

Apollo

Mendel

Montes Cordillera

Montes Rook

Doppler

Galois

Crust of far side about 100 km thick

Small inner core with a central temperature of about 800°C

Crust of near side about 60 km thick

Hertzsprung Korolev

Mars

MARS

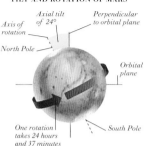

Axial tilt of 24°

Perpendicular to orbital plane

Axis of rotation

North Pole

Orbital plane

One rotation takes 24 hours and 37 minutes

South Pole

MARS, KNOWN AS THE RED PLANET, is the fourth planet from the Sun and the outermost rocky planet. In the 19th century, astronomers first observed what were thought to be signs of life on Mars. These signs included apparent canal-like lines on the surface, and dark patches that were thought to be vegetation. It is now known that the "canals" are an optical illusion, and the dark patches are areas where the red dust that covers most of the planet has been blown away. The fine dust particles are often whipped up by winds into dust storms that occasionally obscure almost all the surface. Residual fine dust in the atmosphere gives the Martian sky a pinkish hue. The northern hemisphere of Mars has many large plains formed of solidified volcanic lava, whereas the southern hemisphere has many craters and large impact basins. There are also several huge, extinct volcanoes, including Olympus Mons, which, at 600 kilometres across and 25 kilometres high, is the largest known volcano in the Solar System. The surface also has many canyons and branching channels. The canyons were formed by movements of the surface crust, but the channels are thought to have been formed by flowing water that has now dried up. The Martian atmosphere is much thinner than Earth's, with only a few clouds and morning mists. Mars has two tiny, irregularly shaped moons called Phobos and Deimos. Their small size indicates that they may be asteroids that have been captured by the gravity of Mars.

SURFACE FEATURES OF MARS

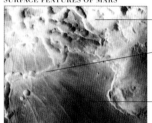

Bright water-ice fog

Fog in canyon about 20 km wide at end of Valles Marineris

Syria Planum

NOCTIS LABYRINTHUS (CANYON SYSTEM)

Summit caldera consisting of overlapping collapsed volcanic craters

Gentle slope produced by lava flow

Cloud formation

OLYMPUS MONS (EXTINCT SHIELD VOLCANO)

THE SURFACE OF MARS

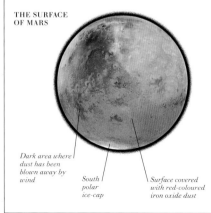

Dark area where dust has been blown away by wind

South polar ice-cap

Surface covered with red-coloured iron oxide dust

MOONS OF MARS

PHOBOS
Average diameter: 22 km
Average distance from planet: 9,400 km

DEIMOS
Average diameter: 13 km
Average distance from planet: 23,500 km

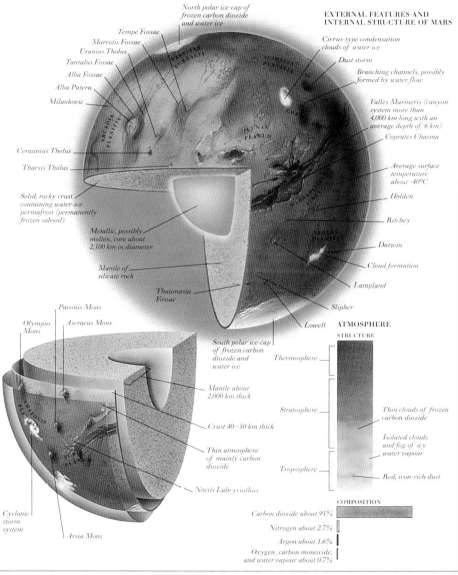

EXTERNAL FEATURES AND
INTERNAL STRUCTURE OF MARS

North polar ice-cap of
frozen carbon dioxide
and water ice

Tempe Fossae
Mareotis Fossae
Uranius Tholus
Tantalus Fossae
Alba Fossae
Alba Patera
Milankovic

Ceraunius Tholus
Tharsis Tholus

Solid, rocky crust
containing water-ice
permafrost (permanently
frozen subsoil)

Metallic, possibly
molten, core about
2,500 km in diameter

Mantle of
silicate rock

Thaumasia
Fossae

Cirrus-type condensation
clouds of water ice

Dust storm

Branching channels, possibly
formed by water flow

Valles Marineris (canyon
system more than
4,000 km long with an
average depth of 6 km)

Coprates Chasma

Average surface
temperature
about −40°C

Holden

Ritchey

Darwin

Cloud formation

Lampland

Slipher

Lowell

Olympus
Mons
Pavonis Mons
Ascraeus Mons

South polar ice-cap
of frozen carbon
dioxide and water ice

Mantle about
2,000 km thick

Crust 40−50 km thick

Thin atmosphere
of mainly carbon
dioxide

Noctis Labyrinthus

Cyclonic
storm
system

Arsia Mons

ATMOSPHERE

STRUCTURE

Thermosphere

Stratosphere

Troposphere

Thin clouds of frozen
carbon dioxide

Isolated clouds
and fog of icy
water vapour

Red, iron-rich dust

COMPOSITION

Carbon dioxide about 95%
Nitrogen about 2.7%
Argon about 1.6%
Oxygen, carbon monoxide,
and water vapour about 0.7%

43

Jupiter

JUPITER

JUPITER IS THE FIFTH PLANET from the Sun and the innermost of the four giant planets. It is the largest and the most massive planet, with a diameter about 11 times that of the Earth and a mass about 2.5 times the combined mass of the seven other planets. Jupiter is thought to have a small rocky core surrounded by an inner mantle of metallic hydrogen (liquid hydrogen that acts like a metal). Outside the inner mantle is an outer mantle of liquid hydrogen and helium that merges into the gaseous atmosphere. Jupiter's rapid rate of rotation causes the clouds in its atmosphere to form belts and zones that encircle the planet parallel to the equator. Belts are dark, low-lying, relatively warm cloud layers, and zones are bright, high-altitude, cooler cloud layers. Within the belts and zones, turbulence causes the formation of cloud features such as white ovals and red spots, both of which are huge storm systems. The most prominent cloud feature is a storm called the Great Red Spot, which consists of a spiralling column of clouds three times wider than the Earth that rises about eight kilometres above the upper cloud layer. Jupiter has a thin, faint, main ring, inside which is a tenuous halo ring of tiny particles. Beyond the main ring's outer edge is a broad and faint two-part gossamer ring. There are 63 known Jovian moons. The four largest moons (called the Galileans) are Ganymede, Callisto, Io, and Europa. Ganymede and Callisto are cratered and icy. Europa is smooth and icy and is thought to have a subsurface water ocean. Io is covered in bright red, orange, and yellow splotches. This colouring is caused by sulphurous material from active volcanoes that shoot plumes of lava hundreds of kilometres above the surface.

TILT AND ROTATION OF JUPITER

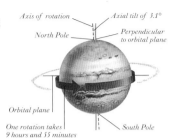

Axis of rotation

Axial tilt of 3.1°

North Pole

Perpendicular to orbital plane

Orbital plane

One rotation takes 9 hours and 55 minutes

South Pole

GREAT RED SPOT AND WHITE OVAL

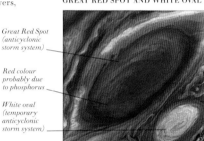

Great Red Spot (anticyclonic storm system)

Red colour probably due to phosphorus

White oval (temporary anticyclonic storm system)

INNER RINGS OF JUPITER

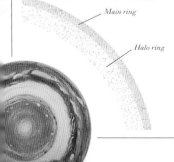

Main ring

Halo ring

GALILEAN MOONS OF JUPITER

EUROPA
Diameter: 3,130 km
Average distance from planet: 670,900 km

CALLISTO
Diameter: 4,806 km
Average distance from planet: 1,883,000 km

GANYMEDE
Diameter: 5,268 km
Average distance from planet: 1,070,000 km

IO
Diameter: 3,642 km
Average distance from planet: 421,800 km

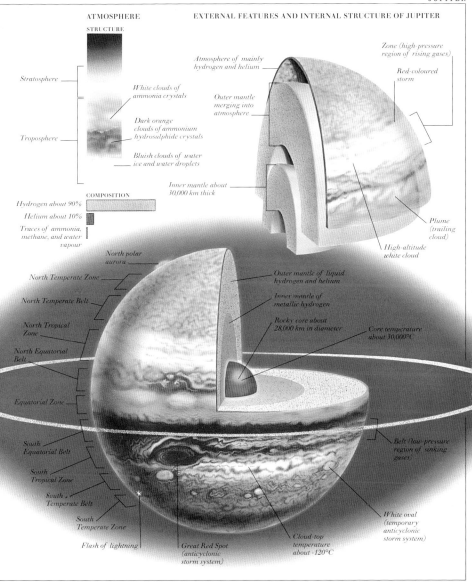

ATMOSPHERE

EXTERNAL FEATURES AND INTERNAL STRUCTURE OF JUPITER

STRUCTURE

Stratosphere

Troposphere

White clouds of
ammonia crystals

Dark orange
clouds of ammonium
hydrosulphide crystals

Bluish clouds of water
ice and water droplets

Atmosphere of mainly
hydrogen and helium

Outer mantle
merging into
atmosphere

Zone (high-pressure
region of rising gases)

Red-coloured
storm

Inner mantle about
30,000 km thick

Plume
(trailing
cloud)

High-altitude
white cloud

COMPOSITION

Hydrogen about 90%

Helium about 10%

Traces of ammonia,
methane, and water
vapour

North polar
aurora

North Temperate Zone

North Temperate Belt

North Tropical
Zone

North Equatorial
Belt

Equatorial Zone

South
Equatorial Belt

South
Tropical Zone

South
Temperate Belt

South
Temperate Zone

Flash of lightning

Great Red Spot
(anticyclonic
storm system)

Cloud-top
temperature
about -120°C

Outer mantle of liquid
hydrogen and helium

Inner mantle of
metallic hydrogen

Rocky core about
28,000 km in diameter

Core temperature
about 30,000°C

Belt (low-pressure
region of sinking
gases)

White oval
(temporary
anticyclonic
storm system)

45

Saturn

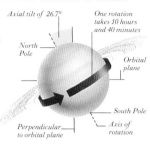

FALSE-COLOUR
IMAGE OF SATURN

SATURN IS THE SIXTH PLANET from the Sun. It is a gas giant almost as big as Jupiter, with an equatorial diameter of about 120,500 kilometres. Saturn is thought to consist of a small core of rock and ice surrounded by an inner mantle of metallic hydrogen (liquid hydrogen that acts like a metal). Outside the inner mantle is an outer mantle of liquid hydrogen that merges into a gaseous atmosphere. Saturn's clouds form belts and zones similar to those on Jupiter, but obscured by overlying haze. Storms and eddies, seen as red or white ovals, occur in the clouds. Saturn has an extremely thin but wide system of rings that is less than one kilometre thick but extends outwards to about 420,000 kilometres from the planet's surface. The main rings comprise thousands of narrow ringlets, each made of icy rock lumps that range in size from tiny particles to chunks several metres across. The D, E, and G rings are very faint, the F ring is brighter, and the A, B, and C rings are bright enough to be seen from Earth with binoculars. In 2009, a huge dust ring was discovered 6 kilometres (4 million miles) beyond the main system. Saturn has more than 60 known moons, some of which orbit inside the rings and are thought to exert a gravitational influence on the shapes of the rings. Unusually, seven of the moons are co-orbital – they share an orbit with another moon. Astronomers believe that such co-orbital moons may have originated from a single satellite that broke up.

TILT AND ROTATION OF SATURN

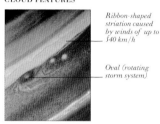

Axial tilt of 26.7°

One rotation takes 10 hours and 40 minutes

North Pole

Orbital plane

South Pole

Perpendicular to orbital plane

Axis of rotation

FALSE-COLOUR IMAGE OF SATURN'S CLOUD FEATURES

Ribbon-shaped striation caused by winds of up to 540 km/h

Oval (rotating storm system)

INNER RINGS OF SATURN

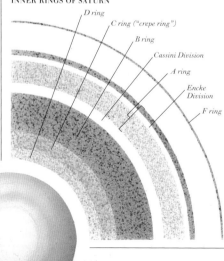

D ring

C ring ("crepe ring")

B ring

Cassini Division

A ring

Encke Division

F ring

MOONS OF SATURN

ENCELADUS
Diameter: 498 km
Average distance from planet: 258,000 km

TETHYS
Diameter: 1,066 km
Average distance from planet: 295,000 km

DIONE
Diameter: 1,123 km
Average distance from planet: 577,000 km

MIMAS
Diameter: 397 km
Average distance from planet: 186,000 km

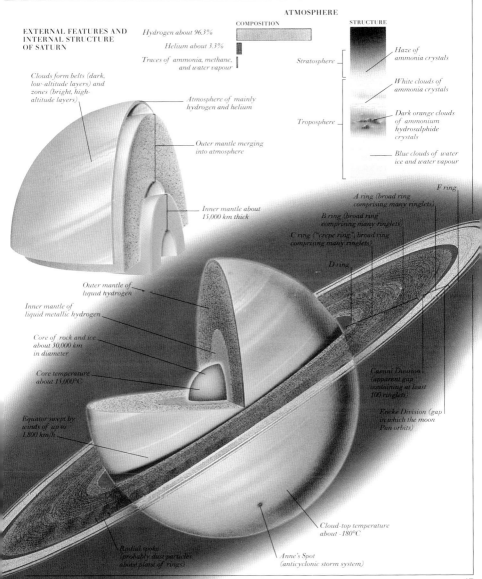

EXTERNAL FEATURES AND
INTERNAL STRUCTURE
OF SATURN

ATMOSPHERE

COMPOSITION

Hydrogen about 96.3%

Helium about 3.3%

Traces of ammonia, methane,
and water vapour

STRUCTURE

Stratosphere

Troposphere

Haze of ammonia crystals

White clouds of
ammonia crystals

Dark orange clouds
of ammonium
hydrosulphide
crystals

Blue clouds of water
ice and water vapour

Clouds form belts (dark,
low-altitude layers) and
zones (bright, high-
altitude layers)

Atmosphere of mainly
hydrogen and helium

Outer mantle merging
into atmosphere

Inner mantle about
15,000 km thick

F ring

A ring (broad ring
comprising many ringlets)

B ring (broad ring
comprising many ringlets)

C ring ("crepe ring", broad ring
comprising many ringlets)

D ring

Outer mantle of
liquid hydrogen

Inner mantle of
liquid metallic hydrogen

Core of rock and ice
about 30,000 km
in diameter

Core temperature
about 15,000°C

Equator swept by
winds of up to
1,800 km/h

Cassini Division
(apparent gap
containing at least
100 ringlets)

Encke Division (gap
in which the moon
Pan orbits)

Cloud-top temperature
about -180°C

Radial spokes
(probably dust particles
about plane of rings)

Anne's Spot
(anticyclonic storm system)

47

Uranus

FALSE-COLOUR
IMAGE OF URANUS

URANUS IS THE SEVENTH PLANET from the Sun
and the third largest, with a diameter of about
51,000 kilometres. It is thought to consist of
a dense mixture of different types of ice and
gas around a solid core. Its atmosphere contains
traces of methane, giving the planet a blue-green
hue, and the temperature at the cloud tops is
about -210°C. Uranus is the most featureless
planet to have been closely observed: only a
few icy clouds of methane have been seen so far. Uranus is unique
among the planets in that its axis of rotation lies close to its orbital
plane. As a result of its strongly tilted rotational axis, Uranus rolls on
its side along its orbital path around the Sun, whereas other planets spin
more or less upright. Uranus is encircled by main rings that consist of rocks
interspersed with dust lanes and too distant outer rings made of dust. The rings
contain some of the darkest matter in the Solar System and are extremely
narrow, making them difficult to detect: most of them are less than 10
kilometres wide, whereas most of Saturn's rings are thousands of kilometres in
width. There are 27 known Uranian moons, all of which are icy and most of
which are further out than the rings. The 13 inner moons are small and dark,
with diameters of less than 160 kilometres, and the five major moons are
between about 470 and 1,600 kilometres in diameter. The major moons have a
wide variety of surface features. Miranda has the most varied surface, with
cratered areas broken up by huge ridges and cliffs 20 kilometres high. Beyond
these are nine much more distant moons with diameters less than 150 km.

TILT AND ROTATION OF URANUS

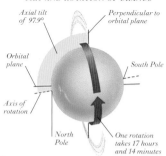

Axial tilt
of 97.9°

Perpendicular to
orbital plane

Orbital
plane

South Pole

Axis of
rotation

North
Pole

One rotation
takes 17 hours
and 14 minutes

MAJOR MOONS

MIRANDA
Diameter: 470 km
Average distance from
planet: 129,800 km

RINGS OF URANUS

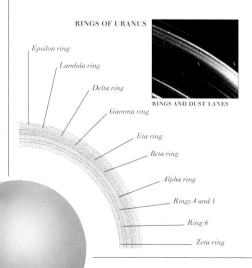

Epsilon ring

Lambda ring

Delta ring

Gamma ring

Eta ring

Beta ring

Alpha ring

Rings 4 and 5

Ring 6

Zeta ring

RINGS AND DUST LANES

ARIEL
Diameter: 1,158 km
Average distance from
planet: 191,200 km

UMBRIEL
Diameter: 1,170 km
Average distance from
planet: 266,000 km

TITANIA
Diameter: 1,578 km
Average distance from
planet: 435,800 km

OBERON
Diameter: 1,523 km
Average distance from
planet: 583,600 km

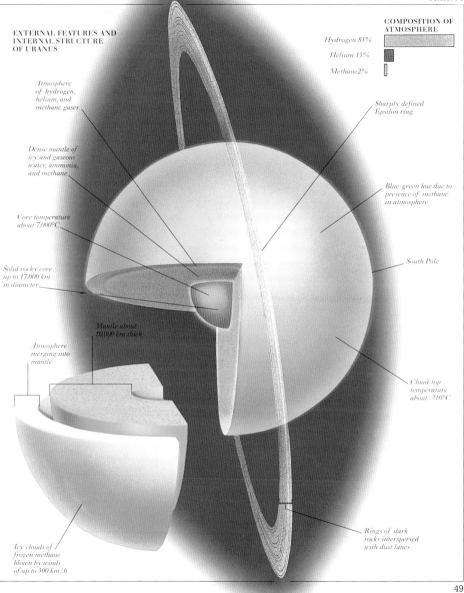

EXTERNAL FEATURES AND
INTERNAL STRUCTURE
OF URANUS

COMPOSITION OF
ATMOSPHERE

Hydrogen 83%

Helium 15%

Methane 2%

Atmosphere
of hydrogen,
helium, and
methane gases

Dense mantle of
icy and gaseous
water, ammonia,
and methane

Core temperature
about 7,000°C

Solid rocky core
up to 17,000 km
in diameter

Mantle about
10,000 km thick

Atmosphere
merging into
mantle

Icy clouds of
frozen methane
blown by winds
of up to 300 km/h

Sharply defined
Epsilon ring

Blue-green hue due to
presence of methane
in atmosphere

South Pole

Cloud-top
temperature
about -210°C

Rings of dark
rocks interspersed
with dust lanes

Neptune and Pluto

**FALSE-COLOUR
IMAGE OF NEPTUNE**

NEPTUNE IS the furthest planet from the Sun, at an average distance of about 4,500 million kilometres. Neptune is the smallest of the giant planets and is thought to consist of a small rocky core surrounded by a mixture of liquids and gases. Several transient cloud features have been observed in its atmosphere. The largest of these were the Great Dark Spot, which was as wide as the Earth, the Small Dark Spot, and the Scooter. The Great and Small Dark Spots were huge storms that were swept around the planet by winds of about 2,000 kilometres per hour. The Scooter was a large area of cirrus cloud. Neptune has six tenuous rings and 13 known moons. Triton is the largest Neptunian moon and the coldest object in the Solar System, with a temperature of -240°C. Unlike most moons in the Solar System, Triton orbits its mother planet in the opposite direction to the planet's rotation. The region extending out from Neptune's orbit is populated by Kuiper Belt objects and dwarf planets. They make a dough-nut shaped belt called the Kuiper Belt. The Kuiper Belt objects are a mix of rock and ice, irregular in shape, and less than 1,000 kilometres across. The larger dwarf planets, which include Pluto, are almost round bodies. Pluto was the first object discovered beyond Neptune and was considered a planet until the dwarf planet category was introduced in 2006. It is made of rock and ice and is 2,274 kilometres across. It has three known moons. The largest, Charon, is about half Pluto's size and the two probably had a common origin.

TILT AND ROTATION OF NEPTUNE

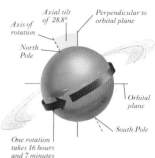

Axis of rotation

Axial tilt of 28.8°

Perpendicular to orbital plane

North Pole

Orbital plane

South Pole

One rotation takes 16 hours and 7 minutes

CLOUD FEATURES OF NEPTUNE

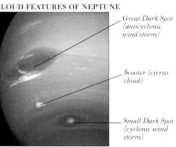

Great Dark Spot (anticyclonic wind storm)

Scooter (cirrus cloud)

Small Dark Spot (cyclonic wind storm)

RINGS OF NEPTUNE

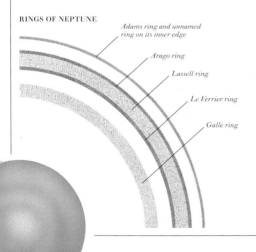

Adams ring and unnamed ring on its inner edge

Arago ring

Lassell ring

Le Verrier ring

Galle ring

HIGH-ALTITUDE CLOUDS

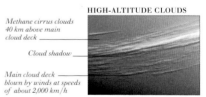

Methane cirrus clouds 40 km above main cloud deck

Cloud shadow

Main cloud deck blown by winds at speeds of about 2,000 km/h

MOONS OF NEPTUNE

TRITON
Diameter: 2,705 km
Average distance from planet: 354,800 km

PROTEUS
Diameter: 416 km
Average distance from planet: 117,600 km

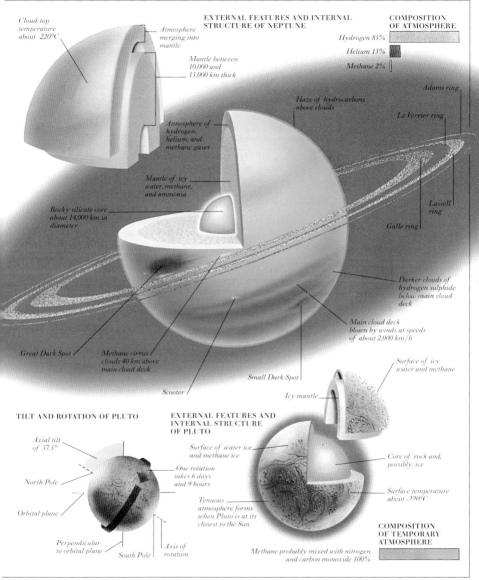

EXTERNAL FEATURES AND INTERNAL
STRUCTURE OF NEPTUNE

COMPOSITION
OF ATMOSPHERE

Hydrogen 85%

Helium 13%

Methane 2%

Cloud-top
temperature
about -220°C

Atmosphere
merging into
mantle

Mantle between
10,000 and
15,000 km thick

Haze of hydrocarbons
above clouds

Adams ring

Le Verrier ring

Atmosphere of
hydrogen,
helium, and
methane gases

Mantle of icy
water, methane,
and ammonia

Rocky silicate core
about 14,000 km in
diameter

Lassell
ring

Galle ring

Darker clouds of
hydrogen sulphide
below main cloud
deck

Main cloud deck
blown by winds at speeds
of about 2,000 km/h

Great Dark Spot

Methane cirrus
clouds 40 km above
main cloud deck

Small Dark Spot

Scooter

Surface of icy
water and methane

Icy mantle

TILT AND ROTATION OF PLUTO

EXTERNAL FEATURES AND
INTERNAL STRUCTURE
OF PLUTO

Axial tilt
of 57.5°

Surface of water ice
and methane ice

Core of rock and,
possibly, ice

North Pole

One rotation
takes 6 days
and 9 hours

Orbital plane

Tenuous
atmosphere forms
when Pluto is at its
closest to the Sun

Surface temperature
about -220°C

Perpendicular
to orbital plane

South Pole

Axis of
rotation

COMPOSITION
OF TEMPORARY
ATMOSPHERE

Methane probably mixed with nitrogen
and carbon monoxide 100%

51

Asteroids, comets, and meteoroids

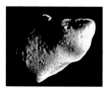

ASTEROID 951 GASPRA

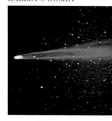

ASTEROIDS, COMETS, AND METEOROIDS are all debris remaining from the nebula from which the Solar System formed 4.6 billion years ago. Asteroids are rocky bodies up to about 1,000 kilometres in diameter, although most are much smaller. Most of them orbit the Sun in the asteroid belt, which lies between the orbits of Mars and Jupiter. Cometary nuclei exist in a huge cloud (called the Oort Cloud) that surrounds the planetary part of the Solar System. They are made of frozen water and dust, and are a few kilometres in diameter. Occasionally, a comet is deflected from the Oort Cloud on to a long, elliptical path that brings it much closer to the Sun. As the comet approaches the Sun, the cometary nucleus starts to vaporize in the heat, producing both a brightly shining coma (a huge sphere of gas and dust around the nucleus), and a gas tail, and a dust tail. Meteoroids are small chunks of stone or stone and iron, which are fragments of asteroids or comets. Meteoroids range in size from tiny dust particles to objects tens of metres across. If a meteoroid enters the Earth's atmosphere, it is heated by friction and appears as a glowing streak of light called a meteor (also known as a shooting star). Meteor showers occur when the Earth passes through the trail of dust particles left by a comet. Most meteoroids burn up in the atmosphere. The remnants of the few that are large enough to reach the Earth's surface are termed meteorites.

FALSE-COLOUR IMAGE
OF HALLEY'S COMET

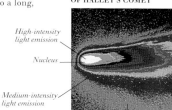

High-intensity light emission

Nucleus

Medium-intensity light emission

Low-intensity light emission

FALSE-COLOUR IMAGE OF A
LEONID METEOR SHOWER

METEORITES

DEVELOPMENT OF COMET TAILS

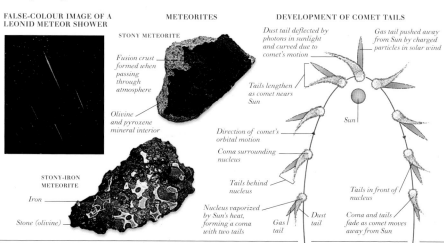

STONY METEORITE

Fusion crust formed when passing through atmosphere

Olivine and pyroxene mineral interior

STONY-IRON METEORITE

Iron

Stone (olivine)

Dust tail deflected by photons in sunlight and curved due to comet's motion

Gas tail pushed away from Sun by charged particles in solar wind

Tails lengthen as comet nears Sun

Sun

Direction of comet's orbital motion

Coma surrounding nucleus

Tails behind nucleus

Tails in front of nucleus

Nucleus vaporized by Sun's heat, forming a coma with two tails

Gas tail

Dust tail

Coma and tails fade as comet moves away from Sun

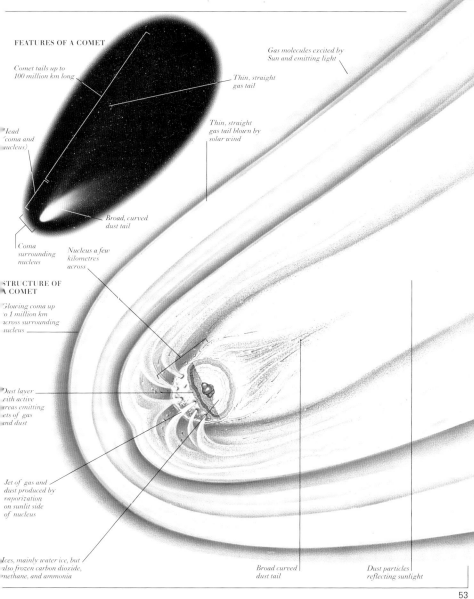

FEATURES OF A COMET

Comet tails up to
100 million km long

Thin, straight
gas tail

Gas molecules excited by
Sun and emitting light

Head
(coma and
nucleus)

Thin, straight
gas tail blown by
solar wind

Coma
surrounding
nucleus

Broad, curved
dust tail

Nucleus a few
kilometres
across

STRUCTURE OF A COMET

Glowing coma up
to 1 million km
across surrounding
nucleus

Dust layer
with active
areas emitting
jets of gas
and dust

Jet of gas and
dust produced by
vaporization
on sunlit side
of nucleus

Ices, mainly water ice, but
also frozen carbon dioxide,
methane, and ammonia

Broad curved
dust tail

Dust particles
reflecting sunlight

PREHISTORIC EARTH

The changing Earth

THE EARTH FORMED FROM A CLOUD OF DUST and gas drifting through space about 4,600 million years ago. Dense minerals sank to the centre while lighter ones formed a thin rocky crust. However, the first known life-forms – bacteria and blue-green algae – did not appear until about 3,400 million years ago, and it was only about 700 million years ago that more complex plants and animals began to develop. Since then, thousands of animal and plant species have evolved; some, such as the dinosaurs, survived for many millions of years, while others died out quickly. The Earth itself is continually changing. Although continents neared their present locations about 50 million years ago, they are still drifting slowly over the planet's surface, and mountain ranges such as the Himalayas – which began to form 40 million years ago – are continually being built up and worn away. Climate is also subject to change: the Earth has undergone a series of ice ages interspersed with warmer periods (the most recent glacial period was at its height about 20,000 years ago).

Small mammals appeared (e.g., Crusafontia)

Dinosaurs became extinct

Global mountain building occurred

Multicellular soft-bodied animals appeared (e.g., worms and jellyfish)

Shelled invertebrates appeared (e.g., trilobites)

Marine plants flourished

Land plants appeared (e.g., Cooksonia)

Unicellular organisms appeared (e.g., blue-green algae)

Earth formed

Coral reefs appeared

Vertebrates appeared (e.g., Hemicyclaspis)

More complex types of algae appeared

Amphibians appeared (e.g., Ichthyostega)

CRETACEOUS

PRECAMBRIAN TIME

CAMBRIAN

ORDOVICIAN

SILURIAN

DEVONIAN

GEOLOGICAL TIMESCALE

MILLIONS OF
YEARS AGO (MYA)

4,600	570	510	439	409	363	323	290

					MISSISSIPPIAN (NORTH AMERICA)	PENNSYLVANIAN (NORTH AMERICA)	
	CAMBRIAN	ORDOVICIAN	SILURIAN	DEVONIAN	CARBONIFEROUS		
PRECAMBRIAN TIME	PALAEOZOIC						

EVOLUTION OF THE EARTH

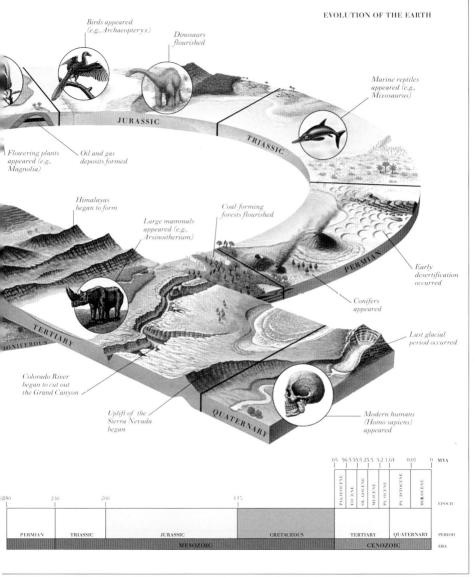

Birds appeared
(e.g., Archaeopteryx)

Dinosaurs
flourished

Marine reptiles
appeared (e.g.,
Mixosaurus)

JURASSIC

TRIASSIC

Flowering plants
appeared (e.g.,
Magnolia)

Oil and gas
deposits formed

Himalayas
began to form

Coal-forming
forests flourished

Large mammals
appeared (e.g.,
Arsinoitherium)

PERMIAN

Early
desertification
occurred

Conifers
appeared

Last glacial
period occurred

TERTIARY

CONIFEROUS

Colorado River
began to cut out
the Grand Canyon

Uplift of the
Sierra Nevada
began

QUATERNARY

Modern humans
(Homo sapiens)
appeared

			65	56.5	35.5	23.5	5.2	1.64	0.01	0	MYA
				PALAEOCENE	EOCENE	OLIGOCENE	MIOCENE	PLIOCENE	PLEISTOCENE	HOLOCENE	EPOCH

	290	240	200	115				
PERMIAN	TRIASSIC	JURASSIC		CRETACEOUS	TERTIARY	QUATERNARY		PERIOD
		MESOZOIC			CENOZOIC			ERA

57

The Earth's crust

THE EARTH'S CRUST IS THE SOLID outer shell of the Earth. It includes continental crust (about 40 kilometres thick) and oceanic crust (about six kilometres thick). The crust and the topmost layer of the mantle form the lithosphere. The lithosphere consists of semi-rigid plates that move relative to each other on the underlying asthenosphere (a partly molten layer of the mantle). This process is known as plate tectonics and helps explain continental drift. Where two plates move apart, there are rifts in the crust. In mid-ocean, this movement results in sea-floor spreading and the formation of ocean ridges; on continents, crustal spreading can form rift valleys. When plates move towards each other, one may be subducted beneath (forced under) the other. In mid-ocean, this causes ocean trenches, seismic activity, and arcs of volcanic islands. Where oceanic crust is subducted beneath continental crust or where continents collide, land may be uplifted and mountains formed (see pp. 62–65). Plates may also slide past each other – along the San Andreas fault, for example. Crustal movement on continents may result in earthquakes, while movement under the seabed can lead to tidal waves.

ELEMENTS IN THE EARTH'S CRUST

Other elements 2%

Potassium 2.6%

Calcium 3.6%

Aluminium 8%

Magnesium 2%

Sodium 2.8%

Iron 5%

Silicon 28%

Oxygen 46%

FEATURES OF PLATE MOVEMENTS

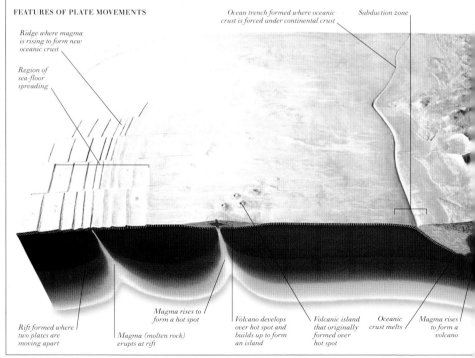

Ridge where magma is rising to form new oceanic crust

Region of sea-floor spreading

Ocean trench formed where oceanic crust is forced under continental crust

Subduction zone

Rift formed where two plates are moving apart

Magma rises to form a hot spot

Magma (molten rock) erupts at rift

Volcano develops over hot spot and builds up to form an island

Volcanic island that originally formed over hot spot

Oceanic crust melts

Magma rises to form a volcano

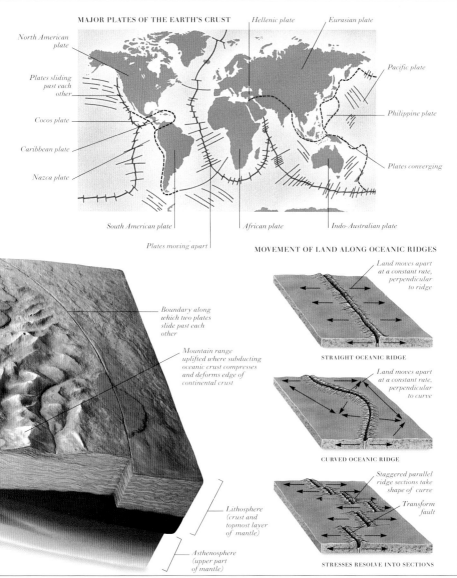

MAJOR PLATES OF THE EARTH'S CRUST

Hellenic plate

Eurasian plate

North American plate

Pacific plate

Plates sliding past each other

Philippine plate

Cocos plate

Caribbean plate

Plates converging

Nazca plate

South American plate

African plate

Indo-Australian plate

Plates moving apart

Boundary along which two plates slide past each other

Mountain range uplifted where subducting oceanic crust compresses and deforms edge of continental crust

Lithosphere (crust and topmost layer of mantle)

Asthenosphere (upper part of mantle)

MOVEMENT OF LAND ALONG OCEANIC RIDGES

Land moves apart at a constant rate, perpendicular to ridge

STRAIGHT OCEANIC RIDGE

Land moves apart at a constant rate, perpendicular to curve

CURVED OCEANIC RIDGE

Staggered parallel ridge sections take shape of curve

Transform fault

STRESSES RESOLVE INTO SECTIONS

Faults and folds

THE CONTINUOUS MOVEMENT of the Earth's crustal plates (see pp. 58–59) can squeeze, stretch, or break rock strata, deforming them and producing faults and folds. A fault is a fracture in a rock along which there is movement of one side relative to the other. The movement can be vertical, horizontal, or oblique (vertical and horizontal). Faults develop when rocks are subjected to compression or tension. They tend to occur in hard, rigid rocks, which are more likely to break than bend. The smallest faults occur in single mineral crystals and are microscopically small, whereas the largest – the Great Rift Valley in Africa, which formed between 5 million and 100,000 years ago – is more than 9,000 kilometres long. A fold is a bend in a rock layer caused by compression. Folds occur in elastic rocks, which tend to bend rather than break. The two main types of fold are anticlines (upfolds) and synclines (downfolds). Folds vary in size from a few millimetres long to folded mountain ranges hundreds of kilometres long, such as the Himalayas (see pp. 62–63) and the Alps, which are repeatedly folding. In addition to faults and folds, other features associated with rock deformations include boudins, mullions, and *en échelon* fractures.

STRUCTURE OF A FOLD

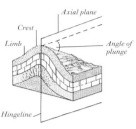

Axial plane
Crest
Limb
Angle of plunge
Hingeline

STRUCTURE OF A FAULT

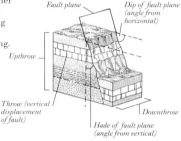

Fault plane
Dip of fault plane (angle from horizontal)
Upthrow
Throw (vertical displacement of fault)
Downthrow
Hade of fault plane (angle from vertical)

STRUCTURE OF A SLOPE

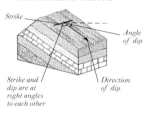

Strike
Angle of dip
Strike and dip are at right angles to each other
Direction of dip

FOLDED ROCK

Steeply dipping limbs
Crest of anticline
Plunge

SECTION THROUGH FOLDED ROCK STRATA THAT HAVE BEEN ERODED

Dipping bed
Anticlinal fold
Monoclinal fold
Mineral-filled fault

Upper Carboniferous Millstone Grit
Lower Carboniferous Limestone

EXAMPLES OF FOLDS

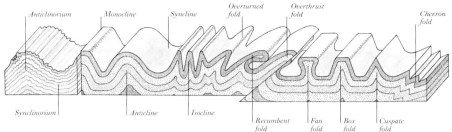

Anticlinorium   *Monocline*   *Syncline*   *Overturned fold*   *Overthrust fold*   *Chevron fold*

Synclinorium   *Anticline*   *Isocline*   *Recumbent fold*   *Fan fold*   *Box fold*   *Cuspate fold*

EXAMPLES OF FAULTS

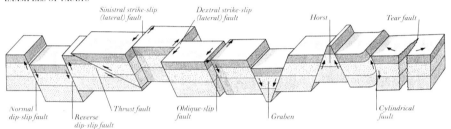

Sinistral strike-slip (lateral) fault   *Dextral strike-slip (lateral) fault*   *Horst*   *Tear fault*

Normal dip-slip fault   *Reverse dip-slip fault*   *Thrust fault*   *Oblique-slip fault*   *Graben*   *Cylindrical fault*

SMALL-SCALE ROCK DEFORMATIONS

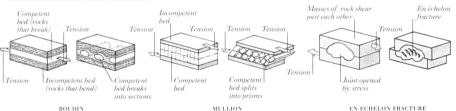

Competent bed (rocks that break)   *Tension*   *Incompetent bed*   *Tension*   *Tension*   *Masses of rock shear past each other*   *En échelon fracture*

Tension   *Tension*   *Tension*

Tension   *Incompetent bed (rocks that bend)*   *Competent bed breaks into sections*   *Competent bed*   *Competent bed splits into prisms*   *Joint opened by stress*

BOUDIN   MULLION   EN ECHELON FRACTURE

Horizontal bed

Dipping bed   *Gently folded bed*   *Mineral-filled fault*

Mineral-filled fault   *Dipping bed*

Upper Carboniferous Millstone Grit   *Upper Carboniferous Coal Measures*

Mountain building

THE PROCESSES INVOLVED in mountain building – termed orogenesis – occur
as a result of the movement of the Earth's crustal plates (see pp. 58–59).
There are three main types of mountains: volcanic mountains, fold
mountains, and block mountains. Most volcanic mountains have been
formed along plate boundaries where plates have come together or
moved apart and lava and other debris have been ejected onto the
Earth's surface. The lava and debris may have built up to form a
dome around the vent of a volcano. Fold mountains are formed
where plates push together and
cause the rock to buckle upwards.
Where oceanic crust meets less dense
continental crust, the oceanic crust
is forced under the continental crust. The
continental crust is buckled by the impact.
This is how folded mountain ranges, such as the
Appalachian Mountains in North America, were
formed. Fold mountains are also formed where
two areas of continental crust meet. The
Himalayas, for example, began to form when
India collided with Asia, buckling the sediments
and parts of the oceanic crust between them. Block mountains are formed when a block
of land is uplifted between two faults as a result of compression or tension in the Earth's
crust (see pp. 60–61). Often, the movement along faults has taken place gradually over
millions of years. However, two plates may cause an earthquake by suddenly sliding past
each other along a faultline.

BHAGIRATHI PARBAT,
HIMALAYAS

Asia

*Himalayas
formed by
buckling of
sediment and
part of the
oceanic crust
between two
colliding
continents*

*India moves
north*

*India collides
with Asia about 40
million years ago*

EXAMPLES OF MOUNTAINS

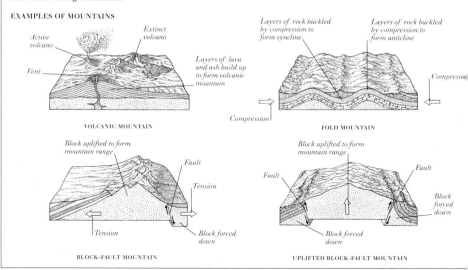

*Active
volcano*

*Extinct
volcano*

Vent

*Layers of lava
and ash build up
to form volcanic
mountain*

VOLCANIC MOUNTAIN

*Layers of rock buckled
by compression to
form syncline*

*Layers of rock buckled
by compression to
form anticline*

Compression

Compression

FOLD MOUNTAIN

*Block uplifted to form
mountain range*

Fault

Tension

Tension

*Block forced
down*

BLOCK-FAULT MOUNTAIN

*Block uplifted to form
mountain range*

Fault

Fault

*Block
forced
down*

*Block forced
down*

UPLIFTED BLOCK-FAULT MOUNTAIN

STAGES IN THE FORMATION OF THE HIMALAYAS

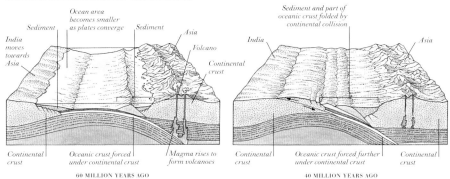

Sediment
India moves towards Asia
Ocean area becomes smaller as plates converge
Sediment
Asia
Volcano
Continental crust
Continental crust
Oceanic crust forced under continental crust
Magma rises to form volcanoes

60 MILLION YEARS AGO

Sediment and part of oceanic crust folded by continental collision
India
Asia
Continental crust
Oceanic crust forced further under continental crust
Continental crust

40 MILLION YEARS AGO

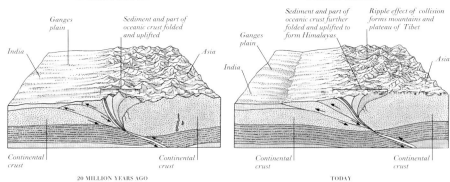

Ganges plain
India
Sediment and part of oceanic crust folded and uplifted
Asia
Continental crust
Continental crust

20 MILLION YEARS AGO

Sediment and part of oceanic crust further folded and uplifted to form Himalayas
Ripple effect of collision forms mountains and plateau of Tibet
Ganges plain
India
Asia
Continental crust
Continental crust

TODAY

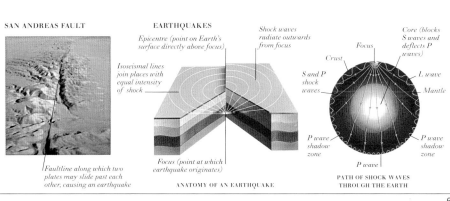

SAN ANDREAS FAULT

Faultline along which two plates may slide past each other, causing an earthquake

EARTHQUAKES

Epicentre (point on Earth's surface directly above focus)
Shock waves radiate outwards from focus
Isoseismal lines join places with equal intensity of shock
Focus (point at which earthquake originates)

ANATOMY OF AN EARTHQUAKE

Core (blocks S waves and deflects P waves)
Focus
Crust
S and P shock waves
L wave
Mantle
P wave shadow zone
P wave shadow zone
P wave

PATH OF SHOCK WAVES THROUGH THE EARTH

Precambrian to Devonian periods

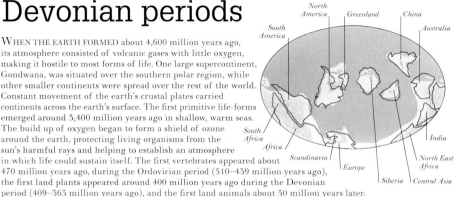

WHEN THE EARTH FORMED about 4,600 million years ago, its atmosphere consisted of volcanic gases with little oxygen, making it hostile to most forms of life. One large supercontinent, Gondwana, was situated over the southern polar region, while other smaller continents were spread over the rest of the world. Constant movement of the earth's crustal plates carried continents across the earth's surface. The first primitive life-forms emerged around 3,400 million years ago in shallow, warm seas. The build up of oxygen began to form a shield of ozone around the earth, protecting living organisms from the sun's harmful rays and helping to establish an atmosphere in which life could sustain itself. The first vertebrates appeared about 470 million years ago, during the Ordovician period (510–439 million years ago), the first land plants appeared around 400 million years ago during the Devonian period (409–363 million years ago), and the first land animals about 30 million years later.

EXAMPLES OF PRECAMBRIAN TO DEVONIAN PLANT GROUPS

A PRESENT-DAY CLUBMOSS
(*Lycopodium sp.*)

**A PRESENT-DAY
LAND PLANT**
(*Asparagus setaceous*)

FOSSIL OF AN EXTINCT LAND PLANT
(*Cooksonia hemisphaerica*)

FOSSIL OF AN EXTINCT SWAMP PLANT
(*Zosterophyllum llanoveranum*)

EXAMPLES OF PRECAMBRIAN TO DEVONIAN TRILOBITES

ACADAGNOSTUS
Group: Agnostidae
Length: 8 mm (⅓ in)

PHACOPS
Group: Phacopidae
Length: 4.5 cm (1¾ in)

OLENELLUS
Group: Olenellidae
Length: 6 cm (2½ in)

ELRATHIA
Group: Ptychopariidae
Length: 2 cm (¾in)

THE EARTH DURING THE MIDDLE ORDOVICIAN PERIOD

Siberia

Laurentia

China

Kazakstania

Gondwana

Baltica

FOSSIL NAUTILOID
(*Estonioceras
perforatum*)

FOSSIL BRACHIOPOD
(*Dicoelosia bilobata*)

TRACE FOSSIL
(*Maursonites spriggi*)

FOSSIL GRAPTOLITE
(*Monograptus
convolutus*)

EXAMPLES OF DEVONIAN FISH

RHAMPHODOPSIS
Group: Ptyctodontidae
Length: 15 cm (6 in)

PTERASPIS
Group: Pteraspidae
Length: 25 cm (10 in)

COCCOSTEUS
Group: Coccosteidae
Length: 35 cm (14 in)

BOTHRIOLEPIS
Group: Bothriolepididae
Length: 40 cm (16 in)

CHEIRACANTHUS
Group: Acanthodidae
Length: 30 cm (12 in)

PTERICHTHYODES
Group: Asterolepididae
Length: 15 cm (6 in)

CHEIROLEPIS
Group: Cheirolepidae
Length: 17 cm (6¾ in)

CEPHALASPIS
Group: Cephalaspidae
Length: 22 cm (8¾ in)

Carboniferous to Permian periods

LATE CARBONIFEROUS POSITIONS
OF PRESENT-DAY LAND-MASSES

THE CARBONIFEROUS PERIOD (363–290 million years ago) takes its name from the thick, carbon-rich layers – now coal – that were produced during this period as swampy tropical forests were repeatedly drowned by shallow seas. The humid climate across northern and equatorial continents throughout Carboniferous times produced the first dense plant cover on Earth. During the early part of this period, the first reptiles appeared. Their development of a waterproof egg with a protective internal structure ended animal life's dependence on an aquatic environment. Towards the end of Carboniferous times, the earth's continents Laurasia and Gondwana collided, resulting in the huge land-mass of Pangaea. Glaciers smothered much of the southern hemisphere during the Permian period (290–245 million years ago), covering Antarctica, parts of Australia, and much of South America, Africa, and India. Ice locked up much of the world's water and large areas of the northern hemisphere experienced a drop in sea-level. Away from the poles, deserts and a hot dry climate predominated. As a result of these conditions, the Permian period ended with the greatest mass extinction of life on earth ever.

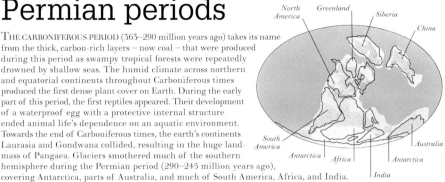

LATE CARBONIFEROUS POSITIONS
OF PRESENT-DAY LAND-MASSES

North America · Greenland · Siberia · China · South America · Antarctica · Africa · Antarctica · India · Australia

EXAMPLES OF CARBONIFEROUS AND PERMIAN PLANT GROUPS

A PRESENT-DAY FIR
(Abies concolor)

FOSSIL OF AN EXTINCT FERN
(Zeilleria frenzlii)

**FOSSIL OF AN
EXTINCT HORSETAIL**
(Equisetites sp.)

**FOSSIL OF AN
EXTINCT CLUBMOSS**
(Lepidodendron sp.)

EXAMPLES OF CARBONIFEROUS AND PERMIAN TREES

PECOPTERIS
Group: Marattiaceae
Height: 4 m (13 ft)

PARIPTERIS
Group: Medullosaceae
Height: 5 m (16 ft 6 in)

MARIOPTERIS
Group: Lyginopteridales
Height: 5 m (16 ft 6 in)

MEDULLOSA
Group: Medullosaceae
Height: 5 m (16 ft 6 in)

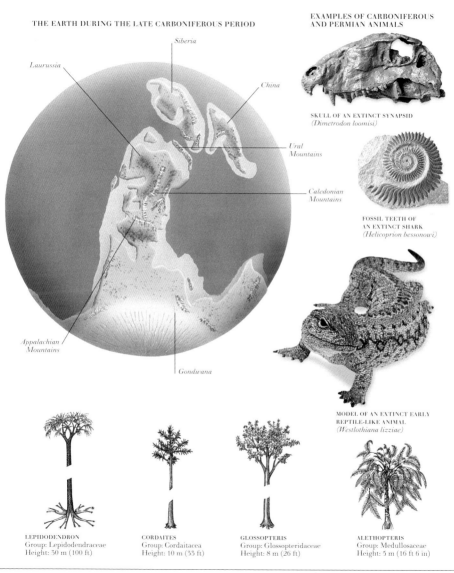

THE EARTH DURING THE LATE CARBONIFEROUS PERIOD

Siberia

Laurussia

China

Ural
Mountains

Caledonian
Mountains

Appalachian
Mountains

Gondwana

EXAMPLES OF CARBONIFEROUS
AND PERMIAN ANIMALS

SKULL OF AN EXTINCT SYNAPSID
(*Dimetrodon loomisi*)

FOSSIL TEETH OF
AN EXTINCT SHARK
(*Helicoprion bessonowi*)

MODEL OF AN EXTINCT EARLY
REPTILE-LIKE ANIMAL
(*Westlothiana lizziae*)

LEPIDODENDRON
Group: Lepidodendraceae
Height: 30 m (100 ft)

CORDAITES
Group: Cordaitacea
Height: 10 m (33 ft)

GLOSSOPTERIS
Group: Glossopteridaceae
Height: 8 m (26 ft)

ALETHOPTERIS
Group: Medullosaceae
Height: 5 m (16 ft 6 in)

Triassic period

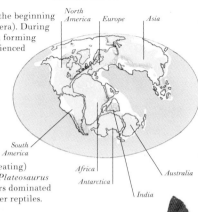

THE TRIASSIC PERIOD (250–200 million years ago) marked the beginning of what is known as the Age of the Dinosaurs (the Mesozoic era). During this period, the present-day continents were massed together, forming one huge continent known as Pangaea. This land-mass experienced extremes of climate, with lush green areas around the coast or by lakes and rivers, and arid deserts in the interior. The only forms of plant life were non-flowering plants, such as conifers, ferns, cycads, and ginkgos; flowering plants had not yet evolved. The principal forms of animal life included diverse, often gigantic, amphibians, rhynchosaurs ("beaked lizards"), and primitive crocodilians. Dinosaurs first appeared about 230 million years ago, at the beginning of the Late Triassic period. Among the earliest dinosaurs were the carnivorous (flesh-eating) herrerasaurids, such as *Herrerasaurus* and *Staurikosaurus*. Early herbivorous (plant-eating) dinosaurs first appeared in Late Triassic times and included *Plateosaurus* and *Technosaurus*. By the end of the Triassic period, dinosaurs dominated Pangaea, possibly contributing to the extinction of many other reptiles.

EXAMPLES OF TRIASSIC
PLANT GROUPS

A PRESENT-DAY
CYCAD
(*Cycas revoluta*)

A PRESENT-DAY GINKGO
(*Ginkgo biloba*)

A PRESENT-DAY CONIFER
(*Araucaria araucana*)

FOSSIL OF AN
EXTINCT FERN
(*Pachypteris sp.*)

FOSSIL LEAF OF AN
EXTINCT CYCAD
(*Cycas sp.*)

EXAMPLES OF TRIASSIC DINOSAURS

MELANOROSAURUS
Group: Melanorosauridae
Length: 12.2 m (40 ft)

MUSSAURUS
Group: Sauropodomorpha
Length: 2–3 m (6 ft 6 in–10 ft)

HERRERASAURUS
Group: Herrerasauridae
Length: 3 m (10 ft)

PISANOSAURUS
Group: Ornithischia
Length: 90 cm (3 ft)

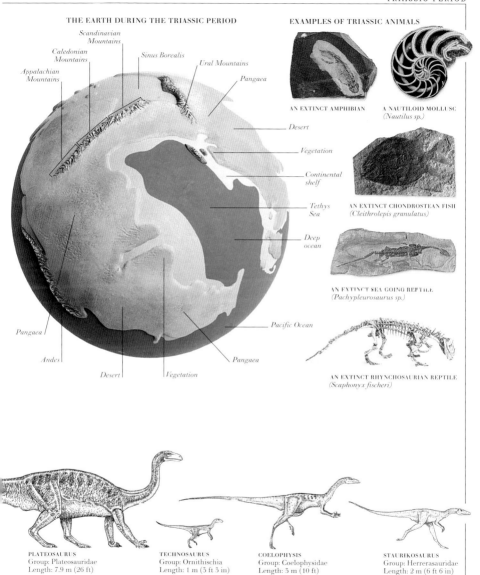

THE EARTH DURING THE TRIASSIC PERIOD

Scandinavian Mountains

Caledonian Mountains

Sinus Borealis

Ural Mountains

Appalachian Mountains

Pangaea

Desert

Vegetation

Continental shelf

Tethys Sea

Deep ocean

Pangaea

Andes

Pacific Ocean

Desert

Vegetation

Pangaea

EXAMPLES OF TRIASSIC ANIMALS

AN EXTINCT AMPHIBIAN

A NAUTILOID MOLLUSC
(*Nautilus sp.*)

AN EXTINCT CHONDROSTEAN FISH
(*Cleithrolepis granulatus*)

AN EXTINCT SEA GOING REPTILE
(*Pachypleurosaurus sp.*)

AN EXTINCT RHYNCHOSAURIAN REPTILE
(*Scaphonyx fischeri*)

PLATEOSAURUS
Group: Plateosauridae
Length: 7.9 m (26 ft)

TECHNOSAURUS
Group: Ornithischia
Length: 1 m (3 ft 3 in)

COELOPHYSIS
Group: Coelophysidae
Length: 3 m (10 ft)

STAURIKOSAURUS
Group: Herrerasauridae
Length: 2 m (6 ft 6 in)

Jurassic period

THE JURASSIC PERIOD, the middle part of the Mesozoic era, lasted from 199 to 145 million years ago. During Jurassic times, the land-mass of Pangaea broke up into the continents of Gondwana and Laurasia, and sea-levels rose, flooding areas of lower land. The Jurassic climate was warm and moist. Plants such as ginkgos, horsetails, and conifers thrived, and giant redwood trees appeared, as did the first flowering plants. The abundance of plant food coincided with the proliferation of herbivorous (plant-eating) dinosaurs, such as the large sauropods (e.g., *Diplodocus*) and stegosaurs (e.g., *Stegosaurus*). Carnivorous (flesheating) dinosaurs, such as *Compsognathus* and *Allosaurus*, also flourished by hunting the many animals that existed – among them other dinosaurs. Further Jurassic animals included shrew-like mammals, and pterosaurs (flying reptiles), as well as plesiosaurs and ichthyosaurs (both marine reptiles).

JURASSIC POSITIONS OF PRESENT-DAY LAND-MASSES

North America *Europe* *Arabia* *Asia* *South America* *Africa* *Antarctica* *India* *Australia*

EXAMPLES OF JURASSIC PLANT GROUPS

A PRESENT-DAY FERN
(Dicksonia antarctica)

A PRESENT-DAY HORSETAIL
(Equisetum arvense)

A PRESENT-DAY CONIFER
(Taxus baccata)

FOSSIL LEAF OF AN EXTINCT CONIFER
(Taxus sp.)

FOSSIL LEAF OF AN EXTINCT REDWOOD
(Sequoiadendron affinis)

EXAMPLES OF JURASSIC DINOSAURS

DIPLODOCUS
Group: Diplodocidae
Length: 26.8 m (88 ft)

CAMPTOSAURUS
Group: Iguanodontia
Length: 4.9–7 m (16–23 ft)

DRYOSAURUS
Group: Dryosauridae
Length: 3–4 m (10–13 ft)

THE EARTH DURING THE JURASSIC PERIOD

EXAMPLES OF JURASSIC ANIMALS

Laurasia

Laurasia

Ural Mountains

North Atlantic Ocean

Turgai Strait

North American Cordillera

Vegetation

Laurasia

Desert

Tethys Sea

Deep ocean

Continental shelf

Desert

Vegetation

Andes

Gondwana

Gondwana

Pacific Ocean

AN EXTINCT PTEROSAUR
(*Rhamphorhynchus sp.*)

AN EXTINCT BELEMNITE MOLLUSC
(*Belemnoteuthis sp.*)

AN EXTINCT RHYNCHOSAURIAN REPTILE
(*Homeosaurus pulchellus*)

AN EXTINCT PLESIOSAUR
(*Peloneustes philarcus*)

AN EXTINCT ICHTHYOSAUR
(*Stenopterygius megacephalus*)

ALLOSAURUS
Group: Allosauroidea
Length: 11 m (36 ft)

SCELIDOSAURUS
Group: Thyreophora
Length: 4 m (13 ft)

STEGOSAURUS
Group: Stegosauridae
Length: 9.1 m (30 ft)

71

Cretaceous period

THE MESOZOIC ERA ENDED WITH the Cretaceous period, which lasted from 146 to 65 million years ago. During this period, Gondwana and Laurasia were breaking up into smaller land-masses that more closely resembled the modern continents. The climate remained mild and moist but the seasons became more marked. Flowering plants, including deciduous trees, replaced many cycads, seed ferns, and conifers. Animal species became more varied, with the evolution of new mammals, insects, fish, crustaceans, and turtles. Dinosaurs evolved into a wide variety of species during Cretaceous times; more than half of all known dinosaurs – including *Iguanodon, Deinonychus, Tyrannosaurus,* and *Hypsilophodon* – lived during this period. At the end of the Cretaceous period, however, most dinosaurs became extinct. The reason for this mass extinction is unknown but it is thought to have been caused by climatic changes due to either a catastrophic meteor impact with the Earth or extensive volcanic eruptions.

CRETACEOUS POSITIONS OF PRESENT-DAY LAND-MASSES

North America
Europe
Arabia
Asia
South America
Africa
India
Antarctica
Australia

EXAMPLES OF CRETACEOUS PLANT GROUPS

A PRESENT-DAY CONIFER
(*Pinus muricata*)

A PRESENT-DAY DECIDUOUS TREE
(*Magnolia sp.*)

FOSSIL OF AN EXTINCT FERN
(*Sphenopteris latiloba*)

FOSSIL OF AN EXTINCT GINKGO
(*Ginkgo pluripartita*)

FOSSIL LEAVES OF AN EXTINCT DECIDUOUS TREE
(*Cercidyphyllum sp.*)

EXAMPLES OF CRETACEOUS DINOSAURS

SALTASAURUS
Group: Saltasauridae
Length: 12.2 m (40 ft)

TOROSAURUS
Group: Ceratopsidae
Length: 7.6 m (25 ft)

HYPSILOPHODON
Group: Ornithopoda
Length: 1.4–2.3 m (4 ft 6 in–7 ft 6 in)

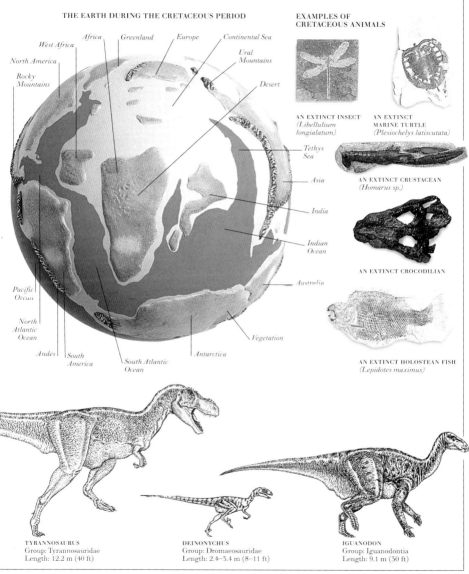

THE EARTH DURING THE CRETACEOUS PERIOD

West Africa
North America
Rocky Mountains
Africa
Greenland
Europe
Continental Sea
Ural Mountains
Desert
Tethys Sea
Asia
India
Indian Ocean
Australia
Vegetation
Antarctica
South Atlantic Ocean
South America
Andes
North Atlantic Ocean
Pacific Ocean

EXAMPLES OF CRETACEOUS ANIMALS

AN EXTINCT INSECT
(*Libellulium longialatum*)

AN EXTINCT MARINE TURTLE
(*Plesiochelys latiscutata*)

AN EXTINCT CRUSTACEAN
(*Homarus sp.*)

AN EXTINCT CROCODILIAN

AN EXTINCT HOLOSTEAN FISH
(*Lepidotes maximus*)

TYRANNOSAURUS
Group: Tyrannosauridae
Length: 12.2 m (40 ft)

DEINONYCHUS
Group: Dromaeosauridae
Length: 2.4–3.4 m (8–11 ft)

IGUANODON
Group: Iguanodontia
Length: 9.1 m (30 ft)

Tertiary period

FOLLOWING THE DEMISE OF THE DINOSAURS at the end of the Cretaceous period, the Tertiary period (65–1.6 million years ago), which formed the first part of the Cenozoic era (65 million years ago–present), was characterized by a huge expansion of mammal life. Placental mammals nourish and maintain the young in the mother's uterus; only a few groups of placental mammals existed during Cretaceous times, compared with several tens of groups during the Tertiary period. One of these tens included the early human (see pp.108–109), *Ardipithecus*, which appeared in Africa. By the beginning of the Tertiary period, the continents had almost reached their present position. The Tethys Sea, which had separated the northern continents from Africa and India, began to close up, forming the Mediterranean Sea and allowing the migration of terrestrial animals between Africa and western Europe. India's collision with Asia led to the formation of the Himalayas. During the middle part of the Tertiary period, the forest-dwelling and browsing mammals were replaced by mammals such as the horses, better suited to grazing the open savannahs that began to dominate. Repeated cool periods throughout the Tertiary period established the Antarctic as an icy island continent.

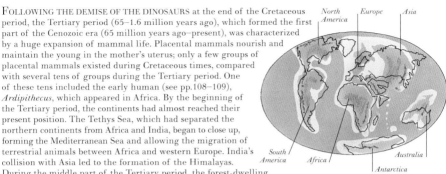

North America
Europe
Asia
South America
Africa
Australia
Antarctica

EXAMPLES OF TERTIARY PLANT GROUPS

A PRESENT-DAY OAK
(Quercus palustris)

A PRESENT-DAY BIRCH
(Betula grossa)

FOSSIL LEAF OF AN EXTINCT BIRCH
(Betulites sp.)

FOSSILIZED STEM OF AN EXTINCT PALM
(Palmoxylon sp.)

EXAMPLES OF TERTIARY ANIMAL GROUPS

HYAENODON
Group: Hyaenodontidae
Length: 2 m (6 ft 6 in)

TITANOHYRAX
Group: Pliohyracidae
Length: 2 m (6 ft 6 in)

PHORUSRHACOS
Group: Phorusrhacidae
Length: 1.5 m (5 ft)

SAMOTHERIUM
Group: Giraffidae
Length: 3 m (10 ft)

THE EARTH DURING THE TERTIARY PERIOD

EXAMPLES OF TERTIARY ANIMALS

North America
Rocky Mountains
Sierra Nevada
Appalachian Mountains
Pyrenees
Europe
Alps
Asia
Continental sea
Zagros Mountains
Himalayas
Tethys Sea
Australia
India
Andes
South America
Atlantic Ocean
Atlas Mountains
Africa
Antarctica
Vegetation
Indian Ocean

AN EXTINCT MAMMAL
(Arsinoitherium)

AN EXTINCT MAMMAL
(Merycoidodon culbertsonii)

AN EXTINCT PRIMATE
(Aegyptopithecus sp.)

AN EXTINCT
GASTROPOD MOLLUSC
(Ecphora quadricostata)

MAMMUT
Group: Mammutidae
Length: 2.5 m (8 ft)

TETRALOPHODON
Group: Gomphotheriidae
Length: 2.5 m (8 ft)

Quaternary period

THE QUATERNARY PERIOD (1.6 million years ago–present) forms the second part of the Cenozoic era (65 million years ago–present): it has been characterized by alternating cold (glacial) and warm (interglacial) periods. During cold periods, ice sheets and glaciers have formed repeatedly on northern and southern continents. The cold environments in North America and Eurasia, and to a lesser extent in southern South America and parts of Australia, have caused the migration of many life forms towards the Equator. Only the specialized ice age mammals such as *Mammuthus* and *Coelodonta*, with their thick wool and fat insulation, were suited to life in very cold climates. Humans developed throughout the Pleistocene period (1.6 million–10,000 years ago) in Africa and migrated northward into Europe and Asia. Modern humans, *Homo sapiens*, lived on the cold European continent 30,000 years ago and hunted other mammals. The end of the last ice age and the climatic changes that occurred about 10,000 years ago brought extinction to many Pleistocene mammals, but enabled humans to flourish.

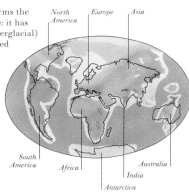

North America   Europe   Asia

South America   Africa   India   Australia

Antarctica

EXAMPLES OF QUATERNARY PLANT GROUPS

A PRESENT-DAY BIRCH
(Betula lenta)

A PRESENT-DAY SWEETGUM
(Liquidambar styraciflua)

FOSSIL LEAF OF A SWEETGUM
(Liquidambar europeanum)

FOSSIL LEAF OF A BIRCH
(Betula sp.)

EXAMPLES OF QUATERNARY ANIMAL GROUPS

PROCOPTODON
Group: Macropodidae
Length: 3 m (10 ft)

DIPROTODON
Group: Diprotodontidae
Length: 3 m (10 ft)

TOXODON
Group: Toxodontidae
Length: 3 m (10 ft)

MAMMUTHUS
Group: Elephantidae
Length: 3 m (10 ft)

THE EARTH DURING THE QUATERNARY PERIOD

Appalachian Mountains
Pyrenees
Alps
Ice sheet
Rocky Mountains
Asia
Vegetation
North America
Carpathian Mountains
Taurus Mountains
Himalayas
India
Australia
Desert
Andes
South America
Indian Ocean
Atlantic Ocean
Ice cap
Atlas Mountains
Africa
Antarctica

EXAMPLES OF QUATERNARY ANIMALS

A MAMMAL SKELETON
(*Hippopotamus amphibius*)

SKULL OF AN EXTINCT CAVE BEAR
(*Ursus spelaeus*)

SKULL OF AN EXTINCT TORTOISE
(*Meiolania platyceps*)

A MAMMOTH TOOTH
(*Mammuthus primigenius*)

DEINOTHERIUM
Group: Deinotheriidae
Length: 4 m (13 ft)

COELODONTA
Group: Rhinocerotidae
Length: 4 m (13 ft)

AUSTRALOPITHECUS
Group: Hominidae
Length: 1.2 m (4 ft)

77

Early signs of life

FOR ALMOST A THOUSAND MILLION YEARS after its formation, there was no known life on Earth. The first simple, sea-dwelling organic structures appeared about 3,500 million years ago; they may have formed when certain chemical molecules joined together. Prokaryotes, single-celled micro-organisms such as blue-green algae, were able to photosynthesize (see pp. 138–139), and thus produce oxygen. A thousand million years later, sufficient oxygen had built up in the earth's atmosphere to allow multicellular organisms to proliferate in the Precambrian seas (before 570 million years ago). Soft-bodied jellyfish, corals, and seaworms flourished about 700 million years ago. Trilobites, the first animals with hard body frames, developed during the Cambrian period (570–510 million years ago). However, it was not until the beginning of the Devonian period (409–363 million years ago) that early land plants, such as *Asteroxylon*, formed a water-retaining cuticle, which ended their dependence on an aquatic environment. About 360 million years ago, the first amphibians (see pp. 80–81) crawled onto the land, although they probably still returned to the water to lay their soft eggs. By the time the first reptiles and synapsids appeared late in the Carboniferous, animals with backbones had become fully independent of water.

STROMATOLITIC LIMESTONE

Alternate layers of mud and sand

Layers bound by algae

Layered structure

Limestone

Long, beak-like snout

Growth line

Dorsal plate

Dorsal spine base

Fixed lateral plate

Bony dorsal shield

FOSSILIZED JAWLESS FISH

Glabella

Eye

Thoracic pleurae

Tail shield

Tail area

FOSSILIZED TRILOBITE

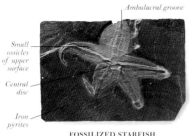

Ambulacral groove

Small ossicles of upper surface

Central disc

Iron pyrites

FOSSILIZED STARFISH

Row of ossicles

Row of ossicles

Broad disc

Short arm

UPPER SURFACE OF FOSSILIZED STARFISH

LOWER SURFACE OF FOSSILIZED STARFISH

Jointed leg

Chelicera (jointed pincer)

Jointed leg with oar-shaped paddle

Segmented abdomen

UNDERSIDE OF FOSSILIZED EURYPTERID

Telson (tail spine)

Abdominal segments

Shell contains eight somites (thoracic segments)

Hingeless, bivalved shell

FOSSIL OF AN EXTINCT SHRIMP

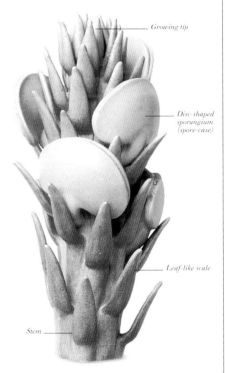

Growing tip

Disc-shaped sporangium (spore-case)

Leaf-like scale

Stem

RECONSTRUCTION OF ASTEROXYLON

Amphibians and reptiles

THE EARLIEST KNOWN AMPHIBIANS, such as *Acanthostega* and *Ichthyostega*, lived about 363 million years ago at the end of the Devonian period (409–363 million years ago). Their limbs may have evolved from the muscular fins of lungfish-like creatures. These fish can use their fins to push themselves along the bottom of lakes and some can breathe at the water's surface. While amphibians (see pp. 182–183) can exist on land, they are dependent on a wet environment because their skin does not retain moisture and most species must return to the water to lay their eggs. Evolving from amphibians, reptiles (see pp. 184–187) first appeared during the Carboniferous period (363–290 million years ago): *Westlothiana*, a possible early reptile, lived on land 338 million years ago. The development of the amniotic egg, with an embryo enclosed in its own wet environment (the amnion) and protected by a waterproof shell, freed reptiles from the amphibian's dependence on a wet habitat. A scaly skin protected the reptile from desiccation on land and enabled it to exploit ways of life closed to its amphibian ancestors. Reptiles include the dinosaurs, which came to dominate life on land during the Mesozoic era (245–65 million years ago).

Orbit

Pocket enclosing nostril

Sculpted or pitted bone surface

Spiracle to draw in water

Mandible

Small tooth

FOSSIL SKULL OF ACANTHOSTEGA

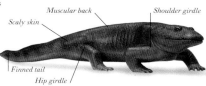

Muscular back

Shoulder girdle

Scaly skin

Finned tail

Hip girdle

MODEL OF ICHTHYOSTEGA

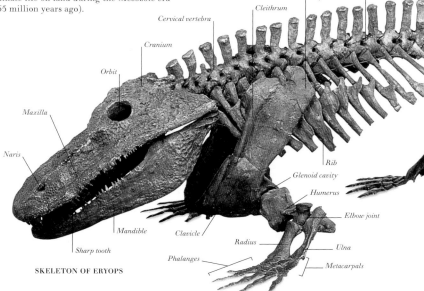

Dorsal vertebra

Scapula

Cleithrum

Cervical vertebra

Cranium

Orbit

Maxilla

Naris

Rib

Glenoid cavity

Humerus

Elbow joint

Mandible

Clavicle

Radius

Ulna

Sharp tooth

Phalanges

Metacarpals

SKELETON OF ERYOPS

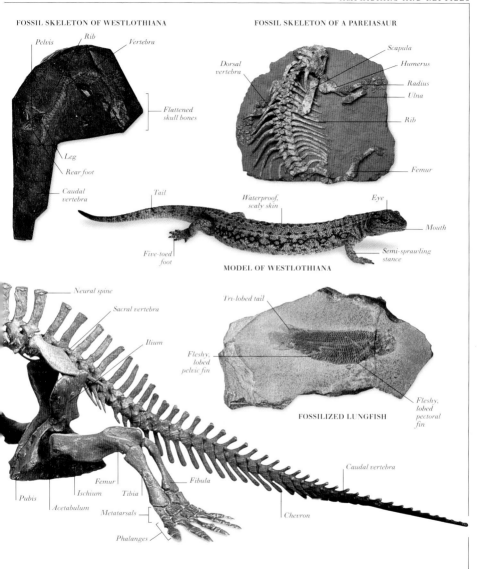

FOSSIL SKELETON OF WESTLOTHIANA

Pelvis

Rib

Vertebra

Flattened
skull bones

Leg

Rear foot

Caudal
vertebra

FOSSIL SKELETON OF A PAREIASAUR

Dorsal
vertebra

Scapula

Humerus

Radius

Ulna

Rib

Femur

Tail

Waterproof,
scaly skin

Eye

Mouth

Five-toed
foot

Semi-sprawling
stance

MODEL OF WESTLOTHIANA

Neural spine

Sacral vertebra

Ilium

Tri-lobed tail

Fleshy,
lobed
pelvic fin

Fleshy,
lobed
pectoral
fin

FOSSILIZED LUNGFISH

Pubis

Ischium

Acetabulum

Femur

Tibia

Fibula

Metatarsals

Phalanges

Chevron

Caudal vertebra

The dinosaurs

THE DINOSAURS WERE A LARGE GROUP of reptiles that were the dominant land vertebrates (animals with backbones) for most of the Mesozoic era (245–65 million years ago). They appeared some 230 million years ago and were distinguished from other scaly, egg-laying reptiles by an important feature: dinosaurs had an erect limb stance. This enabled them to keep their bodies well above the ground, unlike the sprawling and semi-sprawling stance of other reptiles. The head of the dinosaur's femur (thigh-bone) fitted into a socket in its pelvis (hip-bone), producing efficient and mobile locomotion. Dinosaurs are categorized into two groups according to the structure of their pelvis: saurischian (lizard-hipped) and ornithischian (bird-hipped) dinosaurs. In the case of most saurischians, the pubis (part of the pelvis) jutted forward, while in ornithischians it slanted back, parallel to the ischium (another part of the pelvis). Dinosaurs ranged in size from smaller than a domestic cat to the biggest land animals ever known. The Dinosauria were the most successful land vertebrates ever, and survived for 165 million years, until most became extinct 65 million years ago.

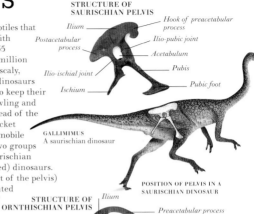

STRUCTURE OF SAURISCHIAN PELVIS

Ilium
Hook of preacetabular process
Postacetabular process
Ilio-pubic joint
Acetabulum
Ilio-ischial joint
Pubis
Ischium
Pubic foot

GALLIMIMUS
A saurischian dinosaur

POSITION OF PELVIS IN A SAURISCHIAN DINOSAUR

STRUCTURE OF ORNITHISCHIAN PELVIS

Ilium
Preacetabular process
Postacetabular process
Ilio-pubic joint
Prepubis
Ilio-ischial joint
Acetabulum
Pubis
Ischium

HYPSILOPHODON
An ornithischian dinosaur

POSITION OF PELVIS IN AN ORNITHISCHIAN DINOSAUR

BAROSAURUS
A saurischian dinosaur

COMPARISON OF ANIMAL STANCES

SPRAWLING STANCE
The thighs and upper arms project straight out from the body so that the knees and elbows are bent at right angles.

COMMON IGUANA
(*Iguana iguana*)
A present-day reptile

ERECT STANCE
The thighs and upper arms project straight down from the body so that the knees and elbows are straight.

SEMI-SPRAWLING STANCE
The thighs and upper arms project downwards and outwards so that the knees and elbows are slightly bent.

DWARF CROCODILE
(*Osteolaemus tetraspis*)
A present-day reptile

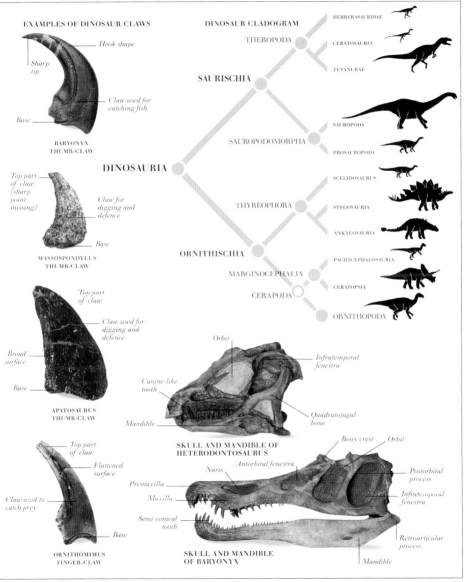

EXAMPLES OF DINOSAUR CLAWS

Hook shape

Sharp tip

Claw used for catching fish

Base

BARYONYX THUMB-CLAW

Top part of claw (sharp point missing)

Claw for digging and defence

Base

MASSOSPONDYLUS THUMB-CLAW

Top part of claw

Claw used for digging and defence

Broad surface

Base

APATOSAURUS THUMB-CLAW

Top part of claw

Flattened surface

Claw used to catch prey

Base

ORNITHOMIMUS FINGER-CLAW

DINOSAUR CLADOGRAM

HERRERASAURIDAE

THEROPODA

CERATOSAURIA

TETANURAE

SAURISCHIA

SAUROPODA

SAUROPODOMORPHA

PROSAUROPODA

DINOSAURIA

SCELIDOSAURUS

THYREOPHORA

STEGOSAURIA

ANKYLOSAURIA

ORNITHISCHIA

PACHYCEPHALOSAURIA

MARGINOCEPHALIA

CERATOPSIA

CERAPODA

ORNITHOPODA

Orbit

Infratemporal fenestra

Canine-like tooth

Quadratojugal bone

Mandible

SKULL AND MANDIBLE OF HETERODONTOSAURUS

Bony crest

Orbit

Antorbital fenestra

Naris

Postorbital process

Premaxilla

Maxilla

Infratemporal fenestra

Semi-conical tooth

Retroarticular process

Mandible

SKULL AND MANDIBLE OF BARYONYX

Theropods 1

AN ENORMOUSLY SUCCESSFUL SUBGROUP of the Saurischia, the bipedal (two-footed) theropods ("beast feet") emerged 230 million years ago in Late Triassic times; the oldest known example comes from South America. Theropods spanned the age of most dinosaurs (230–65 million years ago) and beyond, and included most of the known predatory dinosaurs. The typical theropod had smallish arms with sharp, clawed fingers; powerful jaws lined with sharp teeth; an S-shaped neck; long, muscular hind limbs; and clawed, usually four-toed feet. Many theropods may have been warm-blooded; most were exclusively carnivorous. Theropods ranged from animals no larger than a chicken to huge creatures, such as *Tyrannosaurus* and *Baryonyx*. The group also included ostrich-like omnivores and herbivores with toothless beaks, such as *Struthiomimus* and *Gallimimus*. Birds are dinosaurs and evolved from within a group of tetanuran theropods called maniraptorans. *Archaeopteryx*, small and feathered, was the first known bird and lived alongside other dinosaurs.

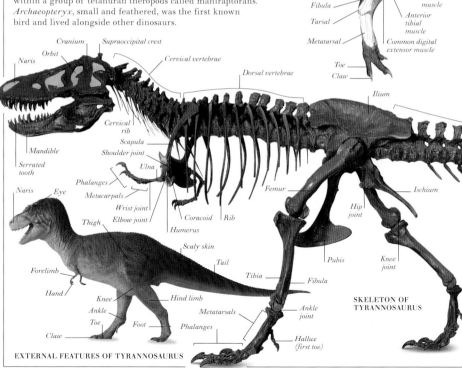

INTERNAL ANATOMY OF ALBERTOSAURUS LEG

Ilio-tibial muscle
Ilio-femoral muscle
Femoro-tibial muscle
Internal tibial flexor muscle
Femur
Ilio-fibular muscle
Gastrocnemius muscle
Digital flexor muscle
Fibula
Tarsal
Metatarsal
Toe
Claw
Ambiens muscle
Femoro-tibial muscle
Anterior tibial muscle
Common digital extensor muscle

SKELETON OF TYRANNOSAURUS

Cranium
Orbit
Naris
Supraoccipital crest
Cervical vertebrae
Dorsal vertebrae
Cervical rib
Scapula
Shoulder joint
Mandible
Serrated tooth
Phalanges
Metacarpals
Ulna
Wrist joint
Elbow joint
Coracoid
Rib
Humerus
Ilium
Femur
Ischium
Hip joint
Pubis
Knee joint
Ankle joint
Hallux (first toe)
Tibia
Fibula
Phalanges
Metatarsals

EXTERNAL FEATURES OF TYRANNOSAURUS

Naris
Eye
Forelimb
Hand
Thigh
Scaly skin
Tail
Knee
Ankle
Toe
Foot
Claw
Hind limb
Phalanges

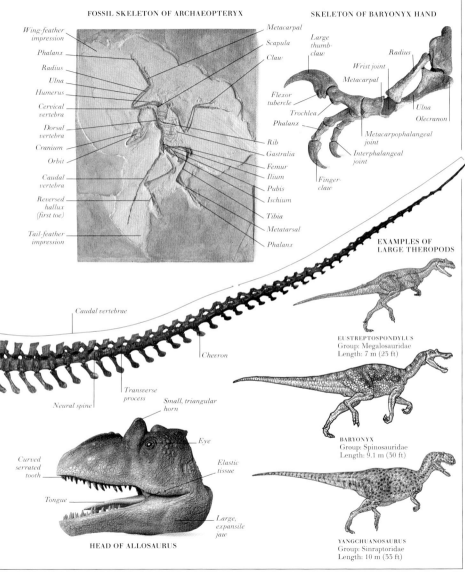

FOSSIL SKELETON OF ARCHAEOPTERYX

Wing-feather impression
Phalanx
Radius
Ulna
Humerus
Cervical vertebra
Dorsal vertebra
Cranium
Orbit
Caudal vertebra
Reversed hallux (first toe)
Tail-feather impression

Metacarpal
Scapula
Claw

Rib
Gastralia
Femur
Ilium
Pubis
Ischium
Tibia
Metatarsal
Phalanx

SKELETON OF BARYONYX HAND

Large thumb-claw
Wrist joint
Metacarpal
Radius
Flexor tubercle
Trochlea
Phalanx
Ulna
Olecranon
Metacarpophalangeal joint
Interphalangeal joint
Finger-claw

EXAMPLES OF LARGE THEROPODS

EUSTREPTOSPONDYLUS
Group: Megalosauridae
Length: 7 m (23 ft)

BARYONYX
Group: Spinosauridae
Length: 9.1 m (30 ft)

YANGCHUANOSAURUS
Group: Sinraptoridae
Length: 10 m (33 ft)

Caudal vertebrae
Chevron
Transverse process
Neural spine
Small, triangular horn
Eye
Curved serrated tooth
Elastic tissue
Tongue
Large, expansile jaw

HEAD OF ALLOSAURUS

Theropods 2

Eye

Toothless
beak

**EXAMPLES OF
ORNITHOMIMOSAURS**

DROMICEIOMIMUS
Length: 3.5 m (11 ft 6 in)

GARUDIMIMUS
Length: 3.5 m (11 ft 6 in)

Cervical
musculature

Scapula

Trachea

Lung

Rib

Gizzard

Dorsal
vertebra

Ovary

Kidney

Ilium

Hip joint

Femur

Shoulder joint

Coracoid

Heart

Posterior brachial
muscle

Anterior brachial
muscle

Humerus

Liver

Claw

Anterior
antebrachial
muscle

Ulna

Posterior
antebrachial
muscle

Metacarpal

Intestine

Pubis

Femoral
musculature

Tibia

Anterior
crural muscle

Eye

Snout

Short
forelimb

Grasping
claw

Long
shin

Hallux
(first toe)

Ankle

Foot

Tail

**EXTERNAL FEATURES OF AN EARLY
THEROPOD (HERRERASAURUS)**

**INTERNAL ANATOMY OF
FEMALE GALLIMIMUS**

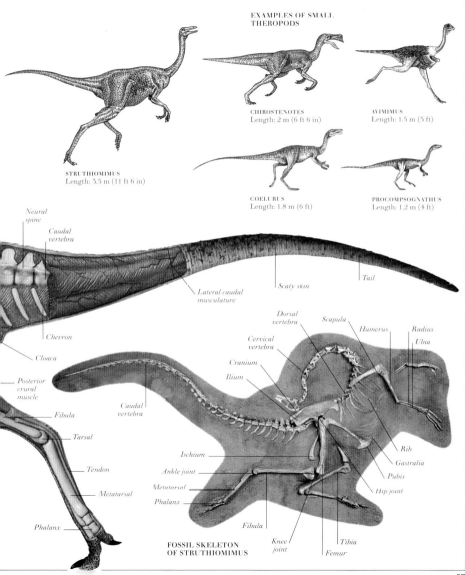

EXAMPLES OF SMALL THEROPODS

CHIROSTENOTES
Length: 2 m (6 ft 6 in)

AVIMIMUS
Length: 1.5 m (5 ft)

STRUTHIOMIMUS
Length: 3.5 m (11 ft 6 in)

COELURUS
Length: 1.8 m (6 ft)

PROCOMPSOGNATHUS
Length: 1.2 m (4 ft)

Neural spine

Caudal vertebra

Scaly skin

Tail

Lateral caudal musculature

Chevron

Cloaca

Posterior crural muscle

Dorsal vertebra

Scapula

Humerus

Radius

Ulna

Cervical vertebra

Cranium

Ilium

Fibula

Caudal vertebra

Tarsal

Tendon

Metatarsal

Ischium

Rib

Gastralia

Pubis

Hip joint

Ankle joint

Metatarsal

Phalanx

Phalanx

Fibula

Knee joint

Tibia

Femur

FOSSIL SKELETON OF STRUTHIOMIMUS

Sauropodomorphs 1

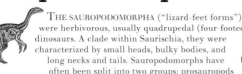

THECODONTOSAURUS

THE SAUROPODOMORPHA ("lizard-feet forms") were herbivorous, usually quadrupedal (four-footed) dinosaurs. A clade within Saurischia, they were characterized by small heads, bulky bodies, and long necks and tails. Sauropodomorphs have often been split into two groups: prosauropods and sauropods. Prosauropods lived from Late Triassic to Early Jurassic times (225–180 million years ago) and included beasts such as the small *Anchisaurus* and one of the first very large dinosaurs, *Plateosaurus*. By Middle Jurassic times (about 165 million years ago), sauropods had replaced prosauropods and spread worldwide. They included the heaviest and longest land animals ever, such as *Diplodocus* and *Brachiosaurus*. Sauropods persisted to the end of the Cretaceous period (65 million years ago). Many of these dinosaurs moved in herds, protected from predatory theropods by their huge bulk and powerful tails, which they could use to lash out at attackers. Sauropodomorphs were the most common large herbivores until Late Jurassic times (about 145 million years ago), and appear to have survived in both southern and northern continents until the end of the Cretaceous period.

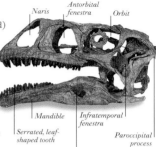

SKULL AND MANDIBLE OF PLATEOSAURUS

- *Naris*
- *Antorbital fenestra*
- *Orbit*
- *Mandible*
- *Infratemporal fenestra*
- *Serrated, leaf-shaped tooth*
- *Paroccipital process*
- *Mandibular fenestra*

SKELETON OF PLATEOSAURUS

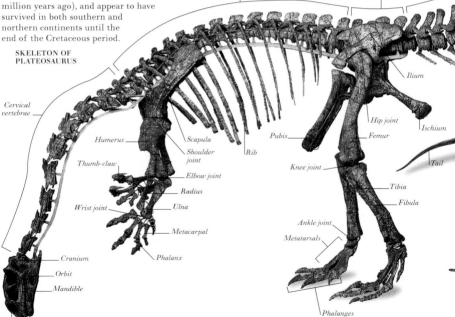

- *Dorsal vertebrae*
- *Sacral vertebrae*
- *Cervical vertebrae*
- *Ilium*
- *Humerus*
- *Scapula*
- *Shoulder joint*
- *Pubis*
- *Hip joint*
- *Femur*
- *Ischium*
- *Rib*
- *Thumb-claw*
- *Elbow joint*
- *Knee joint*
- *Tail*
- *Radius*
- *Wrist joint*
- *Ulna*
- *Tibia*
- *Fibula*
- *Metacarpal*
- *Ankle joint*
- *Cranium*
- *Metatarsals*
- *Orbit*
- *Phalanx*
- *Mandible*
- *Phalanges*
- *Naris*

THUMB-CLAW OF MASSOSPONDYLUS

Top part of claw (sharp point missing)

Curved body of claw

Base of claw

Caudal vertebrae

Neural spine

Chevron

Transverse process

EXAMPLES OF PROSAUROPODS

MASSOSPONDYLUS
Group: Massospondylidae
Length: 5 m (16 ft)

LUFENGOSAURUS
Group: Massospondylidae
Length: 6.1 m (20 ft)

RIOJASAURUS
Group: Riojasauridae
Length: 11 m (36 ft)

MELANOROSAURUS
Group: Melanorosauridae
Length: 7 m (23 ft)

EXTERNAL FEATURES OF ANCHISAURUS

Thigh
Toe
Claw
Forelimb
Hind limb
TOP VIEW OF ANCHISAURUS

Naris
Eye
Leaf-shaped tooth
Slender snout
Long, flexible neck
Long body
Hip
Scaly skin
Thigh
Shoulder
Tail
Forelimb
Elbow
Hand
Knee
Large, curved thumb-claw
Ankle
Hind limb
Hallux (first toe)
Toe
Finger
Foot
Claw
SIDE VIEW OF ANCHISAURUS

Sauropodomorphs 2

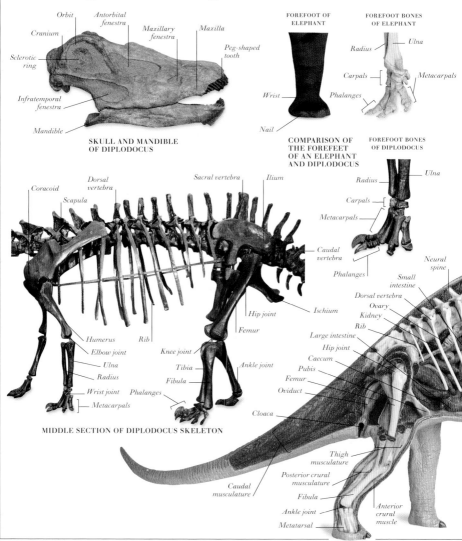

SKULL AND MANDIBLE OF DIPLODOCUS

Orbit
Antorbital fenestra
Cranium
Maxillary fenestra
Maxilla
Sclerotic ring
Peg-shaped tooth
Infratemporal fenestra
Mandible

FOREFOOT OF ELEPHANT

Wrist
Nail

FOREFOOT BONES OF ELEPHANT

Radius
Ulna
Carpals
Metacarpals
Phalanges

COMPARISON OF THE FOREFEET OF AN ELEPHANT AND DIPLODOCUS

FOREFOOT BONES OF DIPLODOCUS

Radius
Ulna
Carpals
Metacarpals
Phalanges

MIDDLE SECTION OF DIPLODOCUS SKELETON

Coracoid
Dorsal vertebra
Scapula
Sacral vertebra
Ilium
Caudal vertebra
Neural spine
Small intestine
Dorsal vertebra
Ovary
Kidney
Rib
Large intestine
Hip joint
Hip joint
Ischium
Caecum
Femur
Pubis
Femur
Oviduct
Humerus
Rib
Elbow joint
Knee joint
Ulna
Radius
Tibia
Ankle joint
Cloaca
Fibula
Wrist joint
Phalanges
Metacarpals
Thigh musculature
Posterior crural musculature
Caudal musculature
Fibula
Ankle joint
Anterior crural muscle
Metatarsal

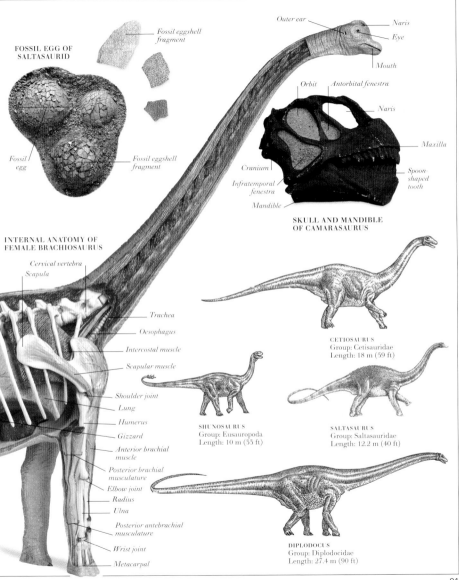

FOSSIL EGG OF SALTASAURID

Fossil eggshell fragment

Fossil egg

Fossil eggshell fragment

Outer ear

Naris

Eye

Mouth

Orbit

Antorbital fenestra

Naris

Maxilla

Cranium

Spoon-shaped tooth

Infratemporal fenestra

Mandible

SKULL AND MANDIBLE OF CAMARASAURUS

INTERNAL ANATOMY OF FEMALE BRACHIOSAURUS

Cervical vertebra

Scapula

Trachea

Oesophagus

Intercostal muscle

Scapular muscle

Shoulder joint

Lung

Humerus

Gizzard

Anterior brachial muscle

Posterior brachial musculature

Elbow joint

Radius

Ulna

Posterior antebrachial musculature

Wrist joint

Metacarpal

CETIOSAURUS
Group: Cetisauridae
Length: 18 m (59 ft)

SHUNOSAURUS
Group: Eusauropoda
Length: 10 m (33 ft)

SALTASAURUS
Group: Saltasauridae
Length: 12.2 m (40 ft)

DIPLODOCUS
Group: Diplodocidae
Length: 27.4 m (90 ft)

Thyreophorans 1

THYREOPHORANS ("SHIELD BEARERS") were a group of
quadrupedal armoured dinosaurs. They were one clade
among several within the Ornithischia (bird-hipped
dinosaurs), they were characterized by rows of bony studs, plates, or spikes along
the back, which protected some from predators and may have helped others
regulate body temperature. Up to 9 m (30 ft) long, with a small head and
small cheek teeth, thyreophorans had shorter forelimbs than hind limbs and
probably browsed on low-level vegetation. The earliest thyreophorans
were small and lived in Early Jurassic times
(about 200 million years ago) in Europe,
North America, and China. Stegosaurs,
such as *Stegosaurus* and *Kentrosaurus*,
replaced these older forms. The earliest
stegosaur remains come mainly from
China. Several genera of stegosaurs
survived into the Early Cretaceous
period (145–100 million years ago).
Ankylosaurs, with a combination of
beak and teeth in close proximity,
and cheek teeth adapted for
cropping vegetation, appeared
at the same time as stegosaurs.
They originated in the
Late Jurassic period
(155 million years ago)
and in North America
survived until 65 million
years ago.

TUOJIANGOSAURUS
Group: Stegosauridae
Length: 7 m (23 ft)

_Dorsal plate

_Hip

_Thigh

Cervical plate

Eye

Naris

Beak |*Cheek*   *Neck*|

Outer ear|

Knee
Shoulder

*Long
hind limb*

Short forelimb __

Nail   *Elbow*

Wrist   *Ankle*   *Hind foot*

**EXTERNAL FEATURES OF
STEGOSAURUS**

Nail   *Forefoot*

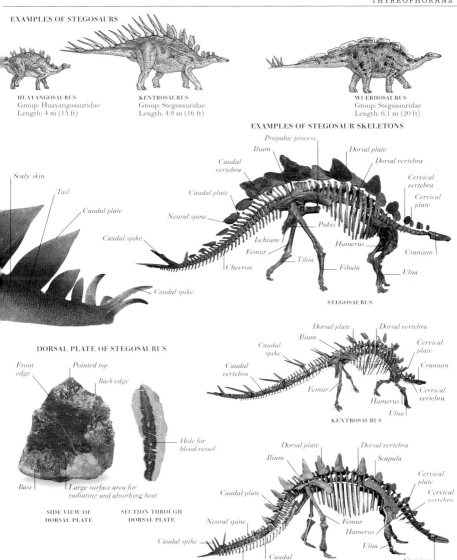

EXAMPLES OF STEGOSAURS

HUAYANGOSAURUS
Group: Huayangosauridae
Length: 4 m (13 ft)

KENTROSAURUS
Group: Stegosauridae
Length: 4.9 m (16 ft)

WUERHOSAURUS
Group: Stegosauridae
Length: 6.1 m (20 ft)

Scaly skin

Tail

Caudal plate

Caudal spike

Caudal spike

EXAMPLES OF STEGOSAUR SKELETONS

Prepubic process

Ilium

Dorsal plate

Dorsal vertebra

Caudal vertebra

Dorsal plate

Caudal plate

Cervical vertebra

Neural spine

Cervical plate

Caudal spike

Pubis

Ischium

Humerus

Femur

Cranium

Chevron

Tibia

Fibula

Ulna

STEGOSAURUS

Dorsal plate

Dorsal vertebra

Caudal spike

Ilium

Cervical plate

Caudal vertebra

Cranium

Femur

Humerus

Cervical vertebra

Ulna

KENTROSAURUS

DORSAL PLATE OF STEGOSAURUS

Front edge

Pointed top

Back edge

Hole for blood vessel

Base

Large surface area for radiating and absorbing heat

SIDE VIEW OF DORSAL PLATE

SECTION THROUGH DORSAL PLATE

Dorsal plate

Dorsal vertebra

Ilium

Scapula

Cervical plate

Caudal plate

Cervical vertebra

Neural spine

Femur

Humerus

Caudal spike

Ulna

Chevron

Caudal vertebra

Cranium

TUOJIANGOSAURUS

Thyreophorans 2

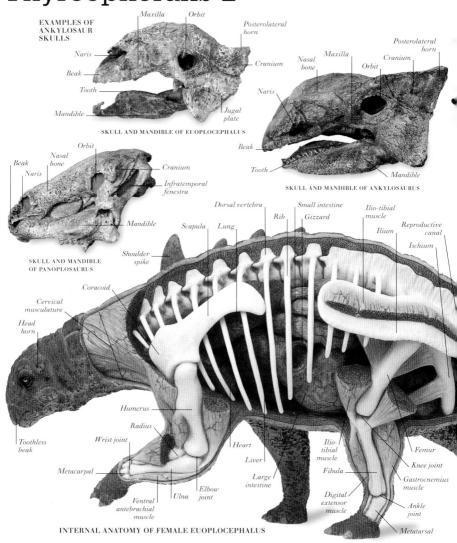

EXAMPLES OF ANKYLOSAUR SKULLS

Maxilla

Orbit

Posterolateral horn

Naris

Cranium

Beak

Tooth

Mandible

Jugal plate

SKULL AND MANDIBLE OF EUOPLOCEPHALUS

Nasal bone

Maxilla

Orbit

Posterolateral horn

Naris

Cranium

Beak

Tooth

Mandible

SKULL AND MANDIBLE OF ANKYLOSAURUS

Orbit

Nasal bone

Beak

Naris

Cranium

Infratemporal fenestra

Mandible

SKULL AND MANDIBLE OF PANOPLOSAURUS

Dorsal vertebra

Small intestine

Ilio-tibial muscle

Rib

Gizzard

Ilium

Reproductive canal

Scapula

Lung

Ischium

Shoulder spike

Coracoid

Cervical musculature

Head horn

Humerus

Radius

Wrist joint

Toothless beak

Metacarpal

Ventral antebrachial muscle

Ulna

Elbow joint

Heart

Liver

Large intestine

Ilio-tibial muscle

Fibula

Digital extensor muscle

Femur

Knee joint

Gastrocnemius muscle

Ankle joint

Metatarsal

INTERNAL ANATOMY OF FEMALE EUOPLOCEPHALUS

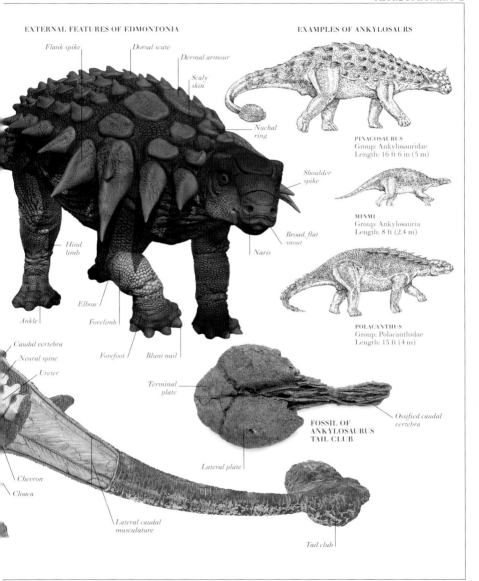

EXTERNAL FEATURES OF EDMONTONIA

Flank spike
Dorsal scute
Dermal armour
Scaly skin
Nuchal ring
Shoulder spike
Broad, flat snout
Naris
Hind limb
Elbow
Forelimb
Ankle
Forefoot
Blunt nail
Caudal vertebra
Neural spine
Ureter
Terminal plate
Chevron
Cloaca
Lateral caudal musculature
Lateral plate
Ossified caudal vertebra
Tail club

EXAMPLES OF ANKYLOSAURS

PINACOSAURUS
Group: Ankylosauridae
Length: 16 ft 6 in (5 m)

MINMI
Group: Ankylosauria
Length: 8 ft (2.4 m)

POLACANTHUS
Group: Polacanthidae
Length: 13 ft (4 m)

FOSSIL OF ANKYLOSAURUS TAIL CLUB

Ornithopods 1

ORNITHOPODS ("BIRD FEET") were a group of ornithischian ("bird-hipped") dinosaurs. These bipedal and quadrupedal herbivores had a horny beak, plant-cutting or grinding cheek teeth, and a pelvic and tail region stiffened by bony tendons. They evolved teeth and jaws adapted to pulping vegetation and flourished from the Middle Jurassic to the Late Cretaceous period (165–65 million years ago) in North America, Europe, Africa, China, Australia, and Antarctica. Some ornithopods were no larger than a dog, while others were immense creatures up to 15 m (49 ft) long. Iguanodonts, an ornithopod group, had a broad, toothless beak at the end of a long snout, large jaws with long rows of ridged, closely packed teeth for grinding vegetation, a bulky body, and a heavy tail. *Iguanodon* and some other iguanodonts had large thumb-spikes that were strong enough to stab attackers. Another group, the hadrosaurs, such as *Gryposaurus* and *Hadrosaurus*, lived in Late Cretaceous times (97–65 million years ago) and with their broad beaks are sometimes known as "duckbills". They were characterized by their deep skulls and closely packed rows of teeth, while some, such as *Corythosaurus* and *Lambeosaurus*, had tall, hollow, bony head crests.

IGUANODON TOOTH

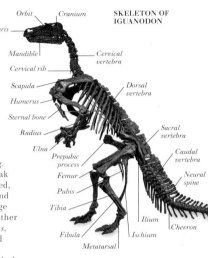

SKELETON OF IGUANODON

Orbit
Cranium
Naris
Mandible
Cervical vertebra
Cervical rib
Scapula
Humerus
Dorsal vertebra
Sternal bone
Radius
Sacral vertebra
Ulna
Caudal vertebra
Prepubic process
Neural spine
Femur
Pubis
Tibia
Ilium
Chevron
Fibula
Ischium
Metatarsal

EXTERNAL FEATURES OF MANTELLISAURUS

Thigh

Heavy, stiff tail

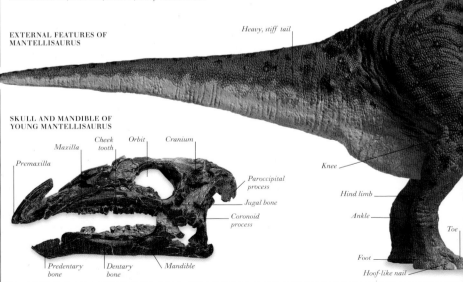

SKULL AND MANDIBLE OF YOUNG MANTELLISAURUS

Cheek tooth
Maxilla
Orbit
Cranium
Premaxilla
Paroccipital process
Jugal bone
Coronoid process
Predentary bone
Dentary bone
Mandible

Knee
Hind limb
Ankle
Toe
Foot
Hoof-like nail

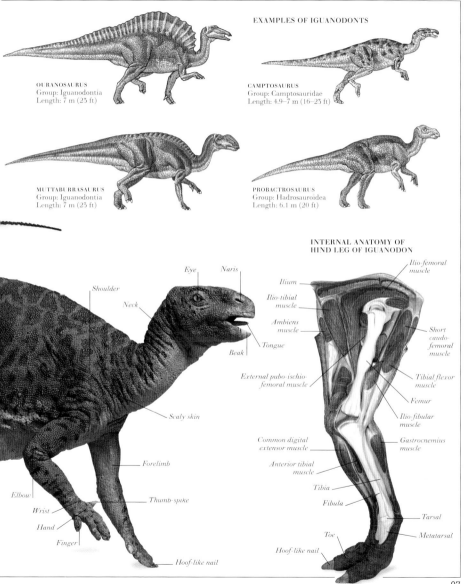

EXAMPLES OF IGUANODONTS

OURANOSAURUS
Group: Iguanodontia
Length: 7 m (23 ft)

CAMPTOSAURUS
Group: Camptosauridae
Length: 4.9–7 m (16–23 ft)

MUTTABURRASAURUS
Group: Iguanodontia
Length: 7 m (23 ft)

PROBACTROSAURUS
Group: Hadrosauroidea
Length: 6.1 m (20 ft)

**INTERNAL ANATOMY OF
HIND LEG OF IGUANODON**

Eye

Naris

Shoulder

Neck

Ilio-femoral
muscle

Ilium

Ilio-tibial
muscle

Ambiens
muscle

Tongue

Beak

Short
caudo-
femoral
muscle

External pubo-ischio-
femoral muscle

Tibial flexor
muscle

Femur

Ilio-fibular
muscle

Scaly skin

Common digital
extensor muscle

Gastrocnemius
muscle

Anterior tibial
muscle

Forelimb

Tibia

Fibula

Elbow

Thumb-spike

Wrist

Tarsal

Hand

Metatarsal

Finger

Toe

Hoof-like nail

Hoof-like nail

Ornithopods 2

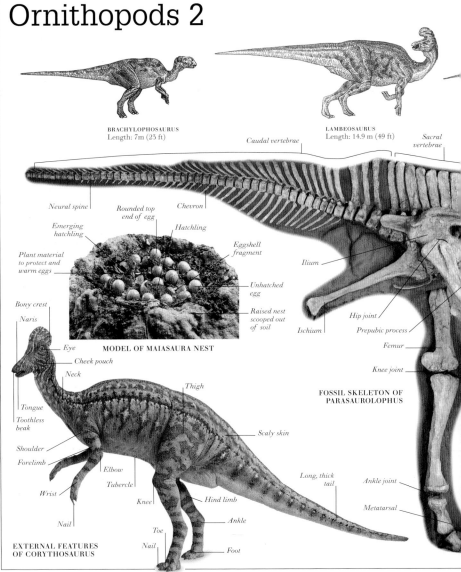

BRACHYLOPHOSAURUS
Length: 7m (23 ft)

LAMBEOSAURUS
Length: 14.9 m (49 ft)

Caudal vertebrae

Sacral vertebrae

Neural spine

Rounded top end of egg

Chevron

Emerging hatchling

Hatchling

Eggshell fragment

Plant material to protect and warm eggs

Ilium

Unhatched egg

Bony crest

Raised nest scooped out of soil

Naris

MODEL OF MAIASAURA NEST

Ischium

Hip joint

Prepubic process

Eye

Cheek pouch

Neck

Thigh

Femur

Knee joint

Tongue

Toothless beak

Scaly skin

**FOSSIL SKELETON OF
PARASAUROLOPHUS**

Shoulder

Forelimb

Elbow

Tubercle

Wrist

Knee

Hind limb

Long, thick tail

Ankle joint

Metatarsal

Nail

Ankle

Toe

Nail

Foot

**EXTERNAL FEATURES
OF CORYTHOSAURUS**

EXAMPLES OF HADROSAURS

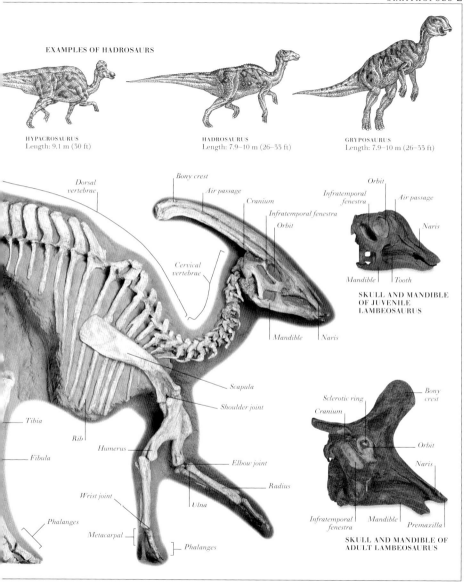

HYPACROSAURUS
Length: 9.1 m (30 ft)

HADROSAURUS
Length: 7.9–10 m (26–33 ft)

GRYPOSAURUS
Length: 7.9–10 m (26–33 ft)

Dorsal vertebrae

Bony crest

Air passage

Cranium

Infratemporal fenestra

Orbit

Cervical vertebrae

Orbit

Infratemporal fenestra

Air passage

Naris

Mandible

Tooth

SKULL AND MANDIBLE OF JUVENILE LAMBEOSAURUS

Mandible

Naris

Scapula

Shoulder joint

Tibia

Rib

Fibula

Humerus

Elbow joint

Radius

Wrist joint

Ulna

Phalanges

Metacarpal

Phalanges

Sclerotic ring

Cranium

Bony crest

Orbit

Naris

Infratemporal fenestra

Mandible

Premaxilla

SKULL AND MANDIBLE OF ADULT LAMBEOSAURUS

Marginocephalians 1

HEAD-BUTTING PRENOCEPHALES

MARGINOCEPHALIA ("margined heads") were a group of bipedal and quadrupedal ornithischian dinosaurs with a narrow shelf or deep, bony frill at the back of the skull. Marginocephalians were probably descended from the same ancestor as the ornithopods and lived in what are now North America, Africa, Asia, and Europe during the Cretaceous period (145–65 million years ago). They were divided into two groups: Pachycephalosauria ("thickheaded lizards"), such as *Pachycephalosaurus* and *Stegoceras*, and Ceratopsia ("horned faces"), such as *Triceratops* and *Psittacosaurus*. The thick skulls of Pachycephalosauria may have protected their brains during possible head-butting contests fought to win territory and mates; their hips and spines may also have been strengthened to withstand the shock. The bony frill of Ceratopsia would have added to their frightening appearance when charging; the neck was strengthened for impact and to support the huge head, with its snipping beak and powerful slicing toothed jaws. A charging ceratopsian would have been a formidable opponent for even the largest predators. Ceratopsians were among the most abundant herbivorous dinosaurs of the Late Cretaceous period (97–65 million years ago).

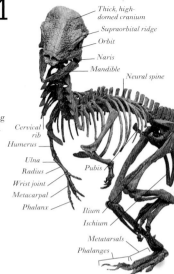

Thick, high-domed cranium
Supraorbital ridge
Orbit
Naris
Mandible
Neural spine
Cervical rib
Humerus
Ulna
Radius
Wrist joint
Metacarpal
Phalanx
Pubis
Ilium
Ischium
Metatarsals
Phalanges

EXAMPLES OF SKULLS OF PACHYCEPHALOSAURS

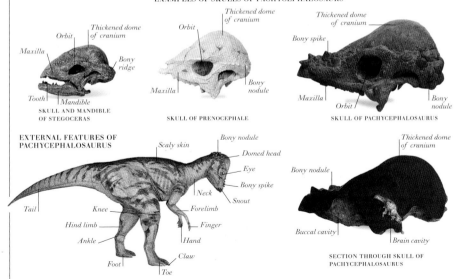

Orbit
Maxilla
Thickened dome of cranium
Bony ridge
Tooth
Mandible
SKULL AND MANDIBLE OF STEGOCERAS

Thickened dome of cranium
Orbit
Maxilla
Bony nodule
SKULL OF PRENOCEPHALE

Thickened dome of cranium
Bony spike
Maxilla
Orbit
Bony nodule
SKULL OF PACHYCEPHALOSAURUS

EXTERNAL FEATURES OF PACHYCEPHALOSAURUS

Scaly skin
Bony nodule
Domed head
Eye
Bony spike
Neck
Snout
Tail
Knee
Hind limb
Ankle
Foot
Toe
Forelimb
Finger
Hand
Claw

Bony nodule
Thickened dome of cranium
Buccal cavity
Brain cavity
SECTION THROUGH SKULL OF PACHYCEPHALOSAURUS

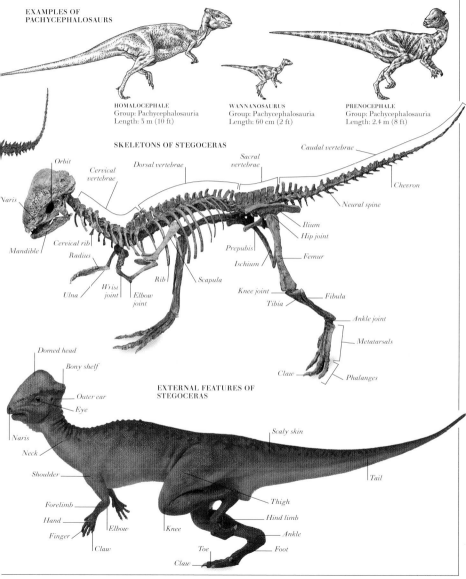

EXAMPLES OF
PACHYCEPHALOSAURS

HOMALOCEPHALE
Group: Pachycephalosauria
Length: 3 m (10 ft)

WANNANOSAURUS
Group: Pachycephalosauria
Length: 60 cm (2 ft)

PRENOCEPHALE
Group: Pachycephalosauria
Length: 2.4 m (8 ft)

SKELETONS OF STEGOCERAS

Orbit

Cervical
vertebrae

Dorsal vertebrae

Sacral
vertebrae

Caudal vertebrae

Chevron

Naris

Neural spine

Mandible

Ilium

Hip joint

Cervical rib

Prepubis

Femur

Radius

Ischium

Ulna

Wrist
joint

Rib

Scapula

Knee joint

Fibula

Elbow
joint

Tibia

Ankle joint

Metatarsals

Claw

Phalanges

Domed head

Bony shelf

Outer ear

EXTERNAL FEATURES OF
STEGOCERAS

Eye

Scaly skin

Naris

Neck

Tail

Shoulder

Forelimb

Thigh

Hand

Hind limb

Finger

Elbow

Knee

Ankle

Claw

Toe

Foot

Claw

Marginocephalians 2

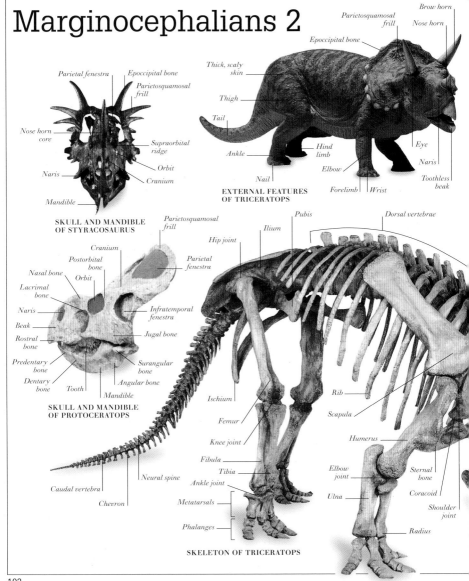

SKULL AND MANDIBLE OF STYRACOSAURUS

Parietal fenestra
Epoccipital bone
Parietosquamosal frill
Nose horn core
Naris
Supraorbital ridge
Orbit
Cranium
Mandible

EXTERNAL FEATURES OF TRICERATOPS

Parietosquamosal frill
Brow horn
Nose horn
Epoccipital bone
Thick, scaly skin
Thigh
Tail
Ankle
Nail
Hind limb
Elbow
Forelimb
Wrist
Eye
Naris
Toothless beak

SKULL AND MANDIBLE OF PROTOCERATOPS

Cranium
Postorbital bone
Nasal bone
Lacrimal bone
Orbit
Naris
Beak
Rostral bone
Predentary bone
Dentary bone
Tooth
Mandible
Parietosquamosal frill
Parietal fenestra
Infratemporal fenestra
Jugal bone
Surangular bone
Angular bone

SKELETON OF TRICERATOPS

Pubis
Ilium
Hip joint
Parietosquamosal frill
Dorsal vertebrae
Rib
Scapula
Humerus
Ischium
Femur
Knee joint
Fibula
Tibia
Ankle joint
Metatarsals
Phalanges
Caudal vertebra
Chevron
Neural spine
Elbow joint
Sternal bone
Ulna
Coracoid
Shoulder joint
Radius

**EXTERNAL FEATURES
OF PSITTACOSAURUS**

Eye

Cheek horn

Beak

Claw

Finger

Scaly skin

Thigh

Elbow

Forelimb

Knee

Claw

Toe

Ankle

Hind limb

Parietosquamosal
frill

Tail

EXAMPLES OF CERATOPSIA

PROTOCERATOPS
Group: Protoceratopsidae
Length: 2.7 m (9 ft)

STYRACOSAURUS
Group: Centrosaurinae
Length: 5.5 m (18 ft)

TRICERATOPS
Group: Chasmosaurinae
Length: 9.1 m (30 ft)

PACHYRHINOSAURUS
Group: Centrosaurinae
Length: 5.5 m (18 ft)

LEPTOCERATOPS
Group: Leptoceratopsidae
Length: 2.1 m (7 ft)

Cranium

Orbit

Brow horn
core

Nose horn
core

Naris

Cervical
rib

Infratemporal
fenestra

Jugal bone

Tooth

Metacarpals

Mandible

Phalanges

Predentary
bone

Rostral bone

Mammals 1

**TETRALOPHODON
CHEEK TEETH**

SINCE THE EXTINCTION of most of the dinosaurs 65 million years ago, mammals (along with birds) have been the dominant vertebrates on land. This class includes terrestrial, aerial, and aquatic forms. Having developed from the therapsids, the first true mammals – small, nocturnal, shrew-like creatures, such as *Megazostrodon* – appeared over 200 million years ago during the Triassic period (250–200 million years ago). Mammals had several features that differed from those of their ancestors: an efficient four-chambered heart allowed these warm-blooded animals to sustain high levels of activity; a covering of hair helped them maintain a constant body temperature; an improved limb structure gave them more efficient locomotion; and the birth of live young and the immediate supply of food from the mother's milk aided their rapid growth. Since the end of the Mesozoic era (65 million years ago), the number of major mammal groups and the abundance of species in each have varied dramatically. For example, the Perissodactyla (the group that includes *Coelodonta* and modern horses) was a common group during the Early Tertiary period (about 54 million years ago). Today, the mammalian groups with the most species include the Rodentia (rats and mice), the Chiroptera (bats), the Primates (monkeys and apes), the Carnivora (bears, cats, and dogs), and the Artiodactyla (cattle, deer, and pigs), while the Proboscidea group, which formerly included many genera, such as *Phiomia*, *Moeritherium*, *Tetralophodon*, and *Mammuthus*, now has only three species of elephant. In Australia and South America, millions of years of continental isolation led to increased diversity of the marsupials, a group of mammals distinct from the placentals (see p. 74) that existed elsewhere.

Long tail aids balance

Insulating hair

Neural spine

Scapula

Cervical vertebra

Humerus

Nasal horn

Naris

Orbit

Mandible

Premaxilla bone

Radius

Ulna

Chisel-edged molar

Metacarpal

Phalanx

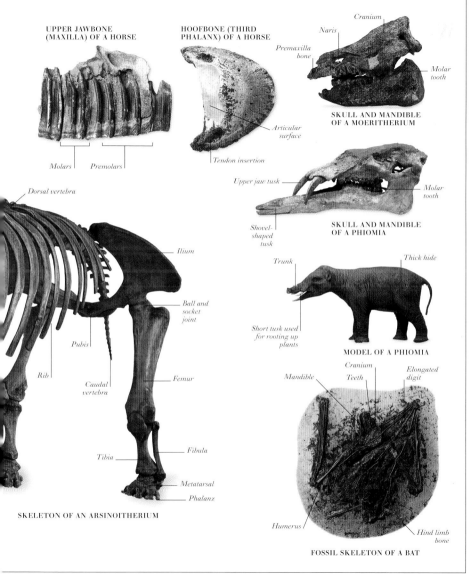

UPPER JAWBONE (MAXILLA) OF A HORSE

Molars
Premolars

HOOFBONE (THIRD PHALANX) OF A HORSE

Articular surface

Tendon insertion

SKULL AND MANDIBLE OF A MOERITHERIUM

Cranium

Naris

Premaxilla bone

Molar tooth

SKULL AND MANDIBLE OF A PHIOMIA

Upper jaw tusk

Molar tooth

Shovel-shaped tusk

MODEL OF A PHIOMIA

Trunk

Thick hide

Short tusk used for rooting up plants

SKELETON OF AN ARSINOITHERIUM

Dorsal vertebra

Ilium

Ball and socket joint

Pubis

Rib

Caudal vertebra

Femur

Tibia

Fibula

Metatarsal

Phalanx

FOSSIL SKELETON OF A BAT

Mandible

Cranium

Teeth

Elongated digit

Humerus

Hind limb bone

Mammals 2

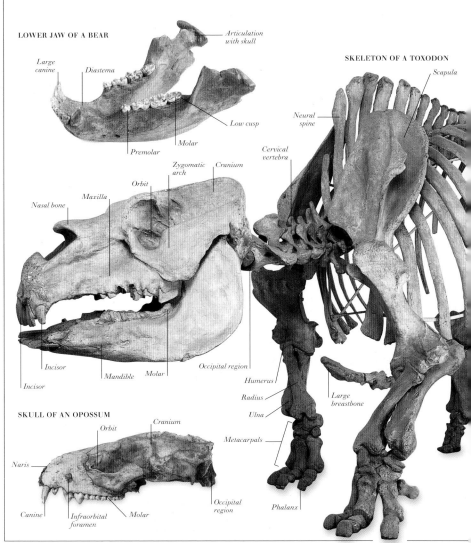

LOWER JAW OF A BEAR

Articulation with skull

Large canine

Diastema

Low cusp

Premolar

Molar

SKELETON OF A TOXODON

Scapula

Neural spine

Cervical vertebra

Zygomatic arch

Cranium

Orbit

Maxilla

Nasal bone

Incisor

Incisor

Mandible

Molar

Occipital region

Humerus

Radius

Ulna

Large breastbone

Metacarpals

Phalanx

SKULL OF AN OPOSSUM

Orbit

Cranium

Naris

Occipital region

Canine

Infraorbital foramen

Molar

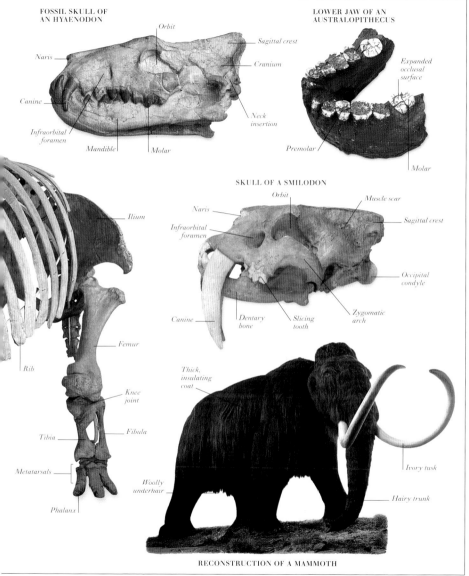

**FOSSIL SKULL OF
AN HYAENODON**

Orbit

Naris

Sagittal crest

Cranium

Canine

*Neck
insertion*

*Infraorbital
foramen*

Mandible

Molar

**LOWER JAW OF AN
AUSTRALOPITHECUS**

*Expanded
occlusal
surface*

Premolar

Molar

SKULL OF A SMILODON

Orbit

Muscle scar

Naris

Sagittal crest

*Infraorbital
foramen*

*Occipital
condyle*

Canine

*Dentary
bone*

*Slicing
tooth*

*Zygomatic
arch*

Ilium

Femur

*Knee
joint*

Rib

Tibia

Fibula

Metatarsals

Phalanx

*Thick,
insulating
coat*

Ivory tusk

*Woolly
underhair*

Hairy trunk

RECONSTRUCTION OF A MAMMOTH

The first humans

MODERN HUMANS BELONG TO THE MAMMALIAN order of primates (see pp. 202–203), which originated about 55 million years ago; primates included the only extant hominid species. The earliest members of the human clade include *Ardipithecus* ("ground ape") and *Australopithecus* ("southern ape"), both small-brained intermediates between apes and humans that were capable of standing and walking upright. *Homo habilis*, the earliest member of the genus *Homo*, appeared at least 2 million years ago. This larger-brained "handy man" began making tools for hunting. *Homo ergaster* first appeared in Africa about 1.8 million years ago and spread into Asia about 800,000 years later. Smaller-toothed than *Homo habilis*, H. ergaster – followed by Homo erectus – developed fire as a tool, which enabled it to cook food. Neanderthals, a near relative of modern humans, originated about 200,000 years ago, and *Homo sapiens* (modern humans) appeared in Africa about 100,000 years later. The two co-existed for thousands of years, but by 30,000 years ago, *Homo sapiens* had become dominant and the Neanderthals had died out. Classification of *Homo sapiens* in relation to its ancestors is enormously problematic: modern humans must be classified not only by bone structure, but also by specific behaviour – the ability to plan future action; to follow traditions; and to use symbolic communication, including complex language and the ability to use and recognize symbols.

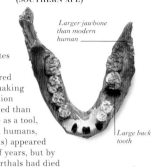

JAWBONE OF AUSTRALOPITHECUS
(SOUTHERN APE)

Larger jawbone than modern human

Large back tooth

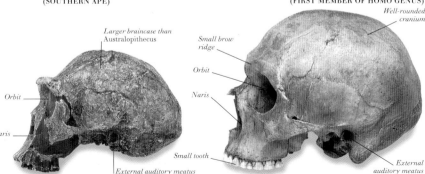

SKULL OF AUSTRALOPITHECUS
(SOUTHERN APE)

Jutting brow ridge

Cranium

Orbit

Naris

Jutting jawbone

SKULL OF HOMO HABILIS
(FIRST MEMBER OF HOMO GENUS)

Orbit

Naris

Well-rounded cranium

SKULL OF HOMO ERECTUS (UPRIGHT MAN)

Larger braincase than Australopithecus

Orbit

Naris

External auditory meatus

SKULL OF HOMO SAPIENS (MODERN HUMAN)

Small brow ridge

Orbit

Naris

Small tooth

External auditory meatus

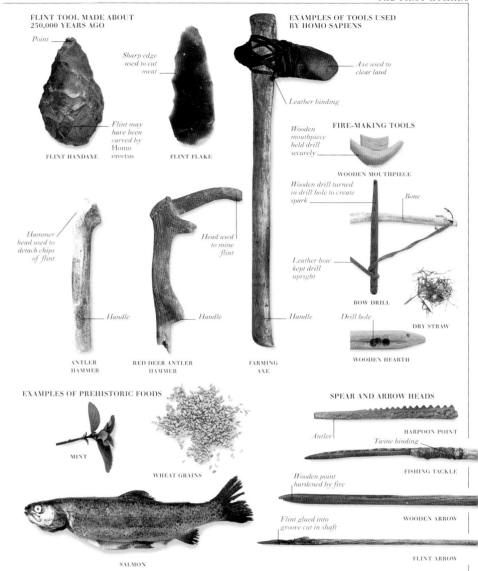

FLINT TOOL MADE ABOUT 250,000 YEARS AGO

Point

Sharp edge used to cut meat

Flint may have been carved by Homo erectus

FLINT HANDAXE

FLINT FLAKE

EXAMPLES OF TOOLS USED BY HOMO SAPIENS

Axe used to clear land

Leather binding

FIRE-MAKING TOOLS

Wooden mouthpiece held drill securely

WOODEN MOUTHPIECE

Wooden drill turned in drill hole to create spark

Bone

Leather bow kept drill upright

BOW DRILL

DRY STRAW

Hammer head used to detach chips of flint

Head used to mine flint

Drill hole

Handle

Handle

Handle

WOODEN HEARTH

ANTLER HAMMER

RED DEER ANTLER HAMMER

FARMING AXE

EXAMPLES OF PREHISTORIC FOODS

MINT

WHEAT GRAINS

SALMON

SPEAR AND ARROW HEADS

Antler

HARPOON POINT

Twine binding

FISHING TACKLE

Wooden point hardened by fire

WOODEN ARROW

Flint glued into groove cut in shaft

FLINT ARROW

PLANTS

Plant variety

THERE ARE MORE THAN 300,000 SPECIES of plants.
They show a wide diversity of forms and life-styles, ranging, for example,
from delicate liverworts, adapted for life in a damp habitat, to cacti, capable of surviving
in the desert, and from herbaceous plants, such as corn, which completes its life-cycle in one year,
to the giant redwood tree, which can live for thousands of years. This diversity reflects the adaptations
of plants to survive in a wide range of habitats. This is seen most clearly in the flowering plants (phylum
Angiospermophyta), which are the most numerous, with over 250,000 species, and the most widespread,
being found from the tropics to the poles. Despite their diversity, plants share certain characteristics: typically,
plants are green, and make their food by photosynthesis; and most plants live in or on a substrate, such as
soil, and do not actively move. Algae (kingdom Protista) and fungi (kingdom Fungi) have
some plant-like characteristics and are often studied alongside plants, although they
are not true plants.

FLOWERING PLANT
Bromeliad
(*Acanthostachys strobilacea*)

Leaf

GREEN ALGA
Micrograph of desmid
(*Micrasterias sp.*)

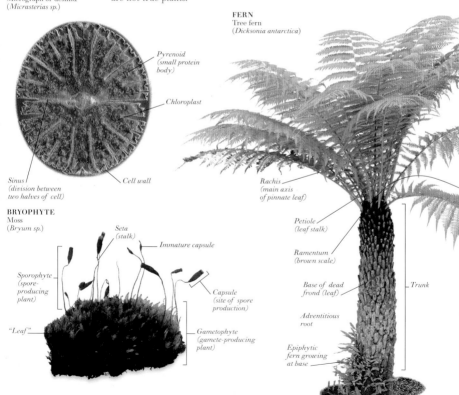

*Pyrenoid
(small protein
body)*

Chloroplast

*Sinus
(division between
two halves of cell)*

Cell wall

FERN
Tree fern
(*Dicksonia antarctica*)

*Rachis
(main axis
of pinnate leaf)*

BRYOPHYTE
Moss
(*Bryum sp.*)

*Seta
(stalk)*

Immature capsule

*Sporophyte
(spore-
producing
plant)*

*Capsule
(site of spore
production)*

"Leaf"

*Gametophyte
(gamete-producing
plant)*

*Petiole
(leaf stalk)*

*Ramentum
(brown scale)*

*Base of dead
frond (leaf)*

Trunk

*Adventitious
root*

*Epiphytic
fern growing
at base*

FLOWERING PLANT
Succulent
(*Kedrostis africana*)

Petiole
(leaf stalk)

Leaf

Stem

FLOWERING PLANT
Micrograph of cross section
through leaf of marram grass
(*Ammophila arenaria*)

Spine   *Flower*

Bract
(leaf-like structure)

Inflorescence

Stem

Cuticle
(waterproof
covering)

Sclerenchyma
(strengthening
tissue)

Stiff trichome
(hair)

Xylem

Phloem

Vascular
tissue

Interlocked
trichomes (hairs)

Epidermis
(outer layer
of cells)

Hinge cells
(cause curling of leaf to
reduce water loss)

Mesophyll
(photosynthetic
tissue)

Caudex
(swollen
stem
base)

Root

Pinna
(leaflet)

FLOWERING PLANT
Couch grass
(*Agropyron repens*)

FLOWERING PLANT
Pitcher plant
(*Sarracenia purpurea*)

Caryopsis
(type of
dry fruit)

Rachis
(main axis of
grass inflorescence)

Fruit
surrounded
by floral parts

Sepal

Umbrella
of style

Pitcher (leaf
modified to trap
insects)

Pedicel
(flower
stalk)

Frond (leaf)

Hood

Downward-pointing
hair (encourages
insect prey into
pitcher)

Node

Midrib of
pinna (leaflet)

Wing

Lamina
(blade)

Round, hollow
stem

Sheathing
leaf base

Immature
pitcher

Adventitious
root

Fungi and lichens

FUNGI WERE ONCE THOUGHT OF AS PLANTS but are now classified as a separate kingdom. This kingdom includes not only the familiar mushrooms, puffballs, stinkhorns, and moulds, but also yeasts, smuts, rusts, and lichens. Most fungi are multicellular, consisting of a mass of thread-like hyphae that together form a mycelium. However, the simpler fungi (e.g., yeasts) are microscopic, single-celled organisms. Typically, fungi reproduce by means of spores. Most fungi feed on dead or decaying matter, or on living organisms. A few fungi obtain their food from plants or algae, with which they have a symbiotic (mutually advantageous) relationship. Lichens are a symbiotic partnership between algae and fungi. Of the six types of lichens the three most common are crustose (flat and crusty), foliose (leafy), and fruticose (shrub-like). Some lichens (e.g., *Cladonia floerkeana*) are a combination of types. Lichens reproduce by means of spores or soredia (powdery vegetative fragments).

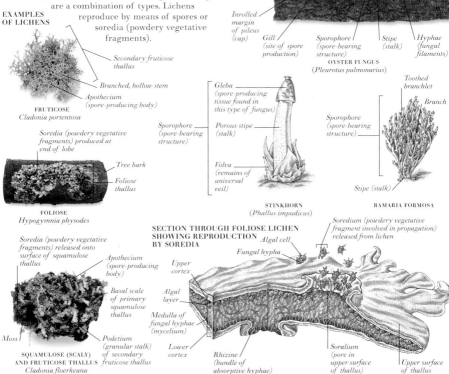

EXAMPLES OF LICHENS

Secondary fruticose thallus

Branched, hollow stem

Apothecium (spore-producing body)

FRUTICOSE
Cladonia portentosa

Soredia (powdery vegetative fragments) produced at end of lobe

Tree bark

Foliose thallus

FOLIOSE
Hypogymnia physodes

Soredia (powdery vegetative fragments) released onto surface of squamulose thallus

Apothecium (spore-producing body)

Basal scale of primary squamulose thallus

Moss

Podetium (granular stalk) of secondary fruticose thallus

SQUAMULOSE (SCALY) AND FRUTICOSE THALLUS
Cladonia floerkeana

Emerging sporophore (spore-bearing structure)

Pileus (cap) continuous with stipe (stalk)

Bark of dead beech tree

Inrolled margin of pileus (cap)

Gill (site of spore production)

Sporophore (spore-bearing structure)

Stipe (stalk)

Hyphae (fungal filaments)

OYSTER FUNGUS
(Pleurotus pulmonarius)

Gleba (spore-producing tissue found in this type of fungus)

Sporophore (spore-bearing structure)

Porous stipe (stalk)

Volva (remains of universal veil)

STINKHORN
(Phallus impudicus)

Toothed branchlet

Branch

Sporophore (spore-bearing structure)

Stipe (stalk)

RAMARIA FORMOSA

SECTION THROUGH FOLIOSE LICHEN SHOWING REPRODUCTION BY SOREDIA

Algal cell

Fungal hypha

Soredium (powdery vegetative fragment involved in propagation) released from lichen

Upper cortex

Algal layer

Medulla of fungal hyphae (mycelium)

Lower cortex

Rhizine (bundle of absorptive hyphae)

Soralium (pore in upper surface of thallus)

Upper surface of thallus

LIFE-CYCLE OF A MUSHROOM

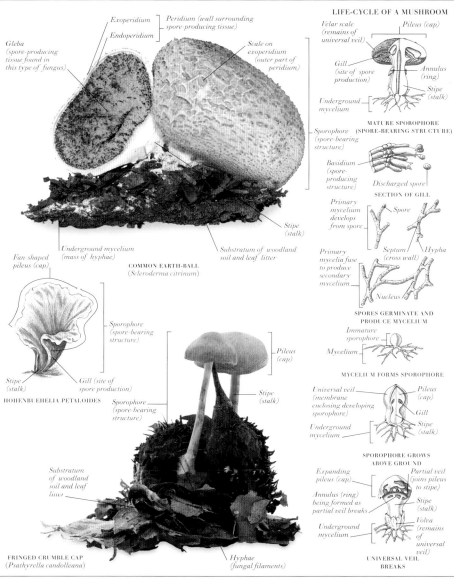

Gleba
(spore-producing
tissue found in
this type of fungus)

Exoperidium

Endoperidium

Peridium (wall surrounding
spore-producing tissue)

Scale on
exoperidium
(outer part of
peridium)

Underground mycelium
(mass of hyphae)

COMMON EARTH-BALL
(Scleroderma citrinum)

Substratum of woodland
soil and leaf litter

Stipe
(stalk)

Velar scale
(remains of
universal veil)

Pileus (cap)

Gill
(site of spore
production)

Annulus
(ring)

Stipe
(stalk)

Underground
mycelium

MATURE SPOROPHORE
(SPORE-BEARING STRUCTURE)

Sporophore
(spore-bearing
structure)

Basidium
(spore-
producing
structure)

Discharged spore

SECTION OF GILL

Primary
mycelium
develops
from spore

Spore

Primary
mycelia fuse
to produce
secondary
mycelium

Septum
(cross wall)

Hypha

Nucleus

SPORES GERMINATE AND
PRODUCE MYCELIUM

Immature
sporophore

Mycelium

MYCELIUM FORMS SPOROPHORE

Universal veil
(membrane
enclosing developing
sporophore)

Pileus
(cap)

Gill

Underground
mycelium

Stipe
(stalk)

SPOROPHORE GROWS
ABOVE GROUND

Expanding
pileus (cap)

Partial veil
(joins pileus
to stipe)

Annulus (ring)
being formed as
partial veil breaks

Stipe
(stalk)

Underground
mycelium

Volva
(remains
of
universal
veil)

UNIVERSAL VEIL
BREAKS

Fan-shaped
pileus (cap)

Sporophore
(spore-bearing
structure)

Stipe
(stalk)

Gill (site of
spore production)

HOHENBUEHELIA PETALOIDES

Sporophore
(spore-bearing
structure)

Pileus
(cap)

Stipe
(stalk)

Substratum
of woodland
soil and leaf
litter

FRINGED CRUMBLE CAP
(Psathyrella candolleana)

Hyphae
(fungal filaments)

Algae and seaweeds

ALGAE ARE NOT TRUE PLANTS. They form a diverse group
of plant-like organisms that belong to the kingdom Protista.
Like plants, algae possess the green pigment chlorophyll
and make their own food by photosynthesis (see pp. 138-139).
Many algae also possess other pigments by which they can be
classified; for example, the brown pigment fucoxanthin is
found in the brown algae. Some of the ten phyla of algae are
exclusively unicellular (single-celled); others also contain
aggregates of cells in filaments or colonies. Three phyla –
the Chlorophyta (green algae), Rhodophyta (red algae),
and Phaeophyta (brown algae) – contain larger, multicellular,
thalloid (flat), marine organisms commonly known as seaweeds.

Most algae can reproduce sexually. For
example, in the brown seaweed
Fucus vesiculosus, gametes
(sex cells) are produced in
conceptacles (chambers) in
the receptacles (fertile tips
of fronds); after their release
into the sea, antherozoids
(male gametes) and oospheres
(female gametes) fuse; the
resulting zygote settles on a rock
and develops into a new seaweed.

BROWN SEAWEED
Channelled wrack
(*Pelvetia canaliculata*)

*Receptacle
(fertile tip
of frond)*

*Thallus
(plant
body)*

*Apical
notch*

*Margin of
lamina (blade)
rolled inwards
to form channel*

Hapteron (holdfast)

BROWN SEAWEED
Spiral wrack
(*Fucus spiralis*)

Apical notch

*Conceptacle
(chamber)*

*Receptacle
(fertile tip
of frond)*

*Thallus
(plant
body)*

*Lamina
(blade)*

Smooth margin

Midrib

Hapteron (holdfast)

Apical notch

*Receptacle
(fertile tip
of frond)*

*Conceptacle
(chamber)
containing
reproductive
structures*

*Lamina
(blade)*

Midrib

RECEPTACLE
Spiral wrack
(*Fucus spiralis*)

EXAMPLES OF ALGAE

*Reproductive
chamber*

Cap

Sterile whorl

Cell wall

Stalk

Rhizoid

GREEN ALGA
Acetabularia sp.

Flagellum

Eyespot

*Contractile
vacuole*

Cytoplasm

*Cell
wall*

Nucleus

Chloroplast

*Pyrenoid
(small protein
body)*

*Starch
grain*

GREEN ALGA
Chlamydomonas sp.

*Coenobium
(colony of cells)*

*Daughter
coenobium*

Girdle

*Gelatinous
sheath*

Nucleus

Biflagellate cell

GREEN ALGA
Volvox sp.

Spine

Cytoplasm

Vacuole

*Plastid
(photosynthetic
organelle)*

DIATOM
Thalassiosira sp.

BROWN SEAWEED
Oarweed
(*Laminaria digitata*)

Thallus (plant body)

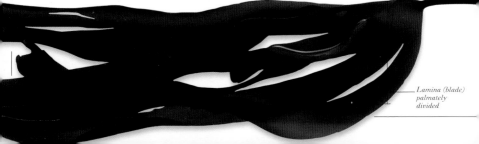

*Lamina (blade)
palmately
divided*

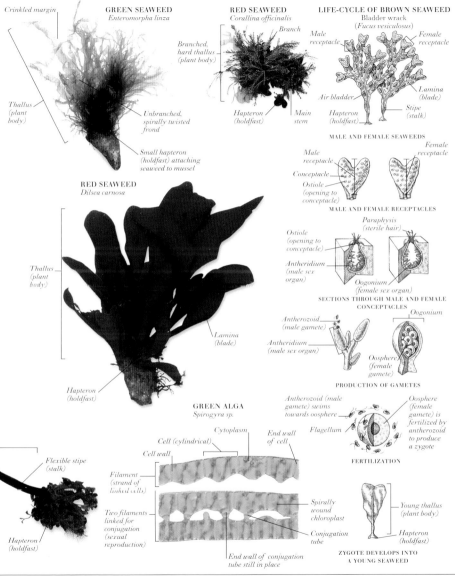

GREEN SEAWEED
Enteromorpha linza

Crinkled margin

Thallus (plant body)

Unbranched, spirally twisted frond

Small hapteron (holdfast) attaching seaweed to mussel

RED SEAWEED
Corallina officinalis

Branch

Branched, hard thallus (plant body)

Hapteron (holdfast)

Main stem

LIFE-CYCLE OF BROWN SEAWEED
Bladder wrack
(*Fucus vesiculosus*)

Male receptacle

Female receptacle

Air bladder

Lamina (blade)

Hapteron (holdfast)

Stipe (stalk)

MALE AND FEMALE SEAWEEDS

Male receptacle

Female receptacle

Conceptacle

Ostiole (opening to conceptacle)

MALE AND FEMALE RECEPTACLES

RED SEAWEED
Dilsea carnosa

Thallus (plant body)

Lamina (blade)

Hapteron (holdfast)

Paraphysis (sterile hair)

Ostiole (opening to conceptacle)

Antheridium (male sex organ)

Oogonium (female sex organ)

SECTIONS THROUGH MALE AND FEMALE CONCEPTACLES

Antherozoid (male gamete)

Oogonium

Antheridium (male sex organ)

Oosphere (female gamete)

PRODUCTION OF GAMETES

GREEN ALGA
Spirogyra sp.

Antherozoid (male gamete) swims towards oosphere

Flagellum

Oosphere (female gamete) is fertilized by antherozoid to produce a zygote

Flexible stipe (stalk)

Hapteron (holdfast)

Cytoplasm

Cell (cylindrical)

Cell wall

End wall of cell

Filament (strand of linked cells)

Two filaments linked for conjugation (sexual reproduction)

Spirally wound chloroplast

Conjugation tube

End wall of conjugation tube still in place

FERTILIZATION

Young thallus (plant body)

Hapteron (holdfast)

ZYGOTE DEVELOPS INTO A YOUNG SEAWEED

Liverworts and mosses

LIVERWORTS AND MOSSES ARE SMALL, LOW-GROWING PLANTS that belong to the phylum Bryophyta. Bryophytes do not have true stems, leaves, or roots (they are anchored to the ground by rhizoids), nor do they have the vascular tissues (xylem and phloem) that transport water and nutrients in higher plants. With no outer, waterproof cuticle, bryophytes are susceptible to drying out, and most grow in moist habitats. The bryophyte life-cycle has two stages. In stage one, the green plant (gametophyte) produces male and female gametes (sex cells), which fuse to form a zygote. In stage two, the zygote develops into a sporophyte that remains attached to the gametophyte. The sporophyte produces spores, which are released and germinate into new green plants. Liverworts (class Hepaticae) grow horizontally and may be thalloid (flat and ribbon-like) or "leafy". Mosses (class Musci) typically have an upright "stem" with spirally arranged "leaves".

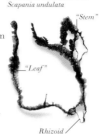

"Stem"

"Leaf"

Rhizoid

A THALLOID LIVERWORT
Marchantia polymorpha

Gemma cup

Gemma (detachable tissue that produces new plants)

Thallus (plant body)

Toothed margin of cup

DETAIL OF GEMMA CUP

Archegoniophore (stalked structure carrying archegonia)

Disc

Lobe

Stalk

Thallus (plant body)

Apical notch

Rhizoid

Stalk

Disc

Lobe

SIDE VIEW OF ARCHEGONIOPHORE

Lobe

Disc

Ray (radial groove)

Stalk

ARCHEGONIOPHORE FROM BELOW

Pore

Ray (radial groove)

MICROGRAPH OF LOBE

Gemma cup

Thallus (plant body)

Midrib

Archegoniophore (stalked structure carrying archegonia)

FEMALE GAMETOPHYTE

MICROGRAPH OF THALLUS
Conocephalum conicum

Position of air chamber

Pore for exchange of gases

Upper surface

Rhizoid

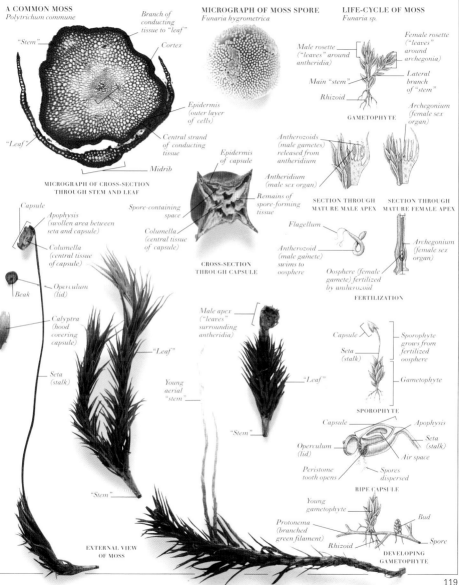

A COMMON MOSS
Polytrichum commune

Branch of conducting tissue to "leaf"

"Stem"

Cortex

Epidermis (outer layer of cells)

"Leaf"

Central strand of conducting tissue

Midrib

MICROGRAPH OF CROSS-SECTION THROUGH STEM AND LEAF

MICROGRAPH OF MOSS SPORE
Funaria hygrometrica

LIFE-CYCLE OF MOSS
Funaria sp.

Female rosette ("leaves" around archegonia)

Male rosette ("leaves" around antheridia)

Main "stem"

Lateral branch of "stem"

Rhizoid

GAMETOPHYTE

Antherozoids (male gametes) released from antheridium

Antheridium (male sex organ)

Archegonium (female sex organ)

SECTION THROUGH MATURE MALE APEX

SECTION THROUGH MATURE FEMALE APEX

Epidermis of capsule

Spore-containing space

Columella (central tissue of capsule)

Remains of spore-forming tissue

CROSS-SECTION THROUGH CAPSULE

Flagellum

Antherozoid (male gamete) swims to oosphere

Archegonium (female sex organ)

Oosphere (female gamete) fertilized by antherozoid

FERTILIZATION

Capsule

Apophysis (swollen area between seta and capsule)

Columella (central tissue of capsule)

Operculum (lid)

Beak

Calyptra (hood covering capsule)

Seta (stalk)

"Leaf"

Young aerial "stem"

"Stem"

Male apex ("leaves" surrounding antheridia)

"Leaf"

"Stem"

Capsule

Seta (stalk)

Sporophyte grows from fertilized oosphere

Gametophyte

SPOROPHYTE

Capsule

Operculum (lid)

Peristome tooth opens

Apophysis

Seta (stalk)

Air space

Spores dispersed

RIPE CAPSULE

"Stem"

EXTERNAL VIEW OF MOSS

Young gametophyte

Protonema (branched green filament)

Rhizoid

Bud

Spore

DEVELOPING GAMETOPHYTE

Horsetails, clubmosses, and ferns

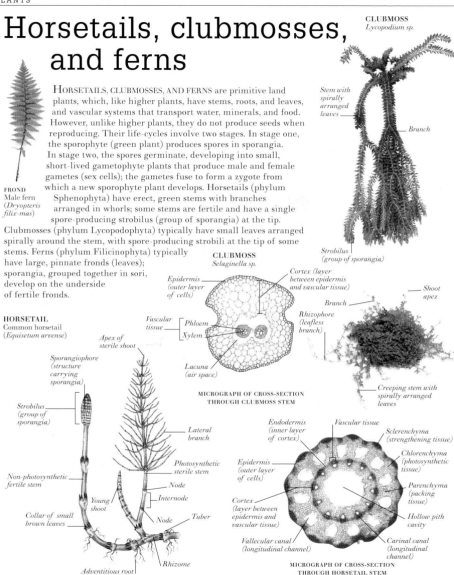

HORSETAILS, CLUBMOSSES, AND FERNS are primitive land plants, which, like higher plants, have stems, roots, and leaves, and vascular systems that transport water, minerals, and food. However, unlike higher plants, they do not produce seeds when reproducing. Their life-cycles involve two stages. In stage one, the sporophyte (green plant) produces spores in sporangia. In stage two, the spores germinate, developing into small, short-lived gametophyte plants that produce male and female gametes (sex cells); the gametes fuse to form a zygote from which a new sporophyte plant develops. Horsetails (phylum Sphenophyta) have erect, green stems with branches arranged in whorls; some stems are fertile and have a single spore-producing strobilus (group of sporangia) at the tip. Clubmosses (phylum Lycopodophyta) typically have small leaves arranged spirally around the stem, with spore-producing strobili at the tip of some stems. Ferns (phylum Filicinophyta) typically have large, pinnate fronds (leaves); sporangia, grouped together in sori, develop on the underside of fertile fronds.

FROND
Male fern
(*Dryopteris filix-mas*)

CLUBMOSS
Lycopodium sp.

Stem with spirally arranged leaves

Branch

Strobilus (group of sporangia)

CLUBMOSS
Selaginella sp.

Epidermis (outer layer of cells)

Cortex (layer between epidermis and vascular tissue)

Vascular tissue — Phloem / Xylem

Lacuna (air space)

MICROGRAPH OF CROSS-SECTION THROUGH CLUBMOSS STEM

Rhizophore (leafless branch)

Branch

Shoot apex

Creeping stem with spirally arranged leaves

HORSETAIL
Common horsetail
(*Equisetum arvense*)

Apex of sterile shoot

Sporangiophore (structure carrying sporangia)

Strobilus (group of sporangia)

Non-photosynthetic fertile stem

Young shoot

Collar of small brown leaves

Lateral branch

Photosynthetic sterile stem

Node

Internode

Node

Tuber

Rhizome

Adventitious root

Endodermis (inner layer of cortex)

Vascular tissue

Sclerenchyma (strengthening tissue)

Epidermis (outer layer of cells)

Chlorenchyma (photosynthetic tissue)

Cortex (layer between epidermis and vascular tissue)

Parenchyma (packing tissue)

Hollow pith cavity

Vallecular canal (longitudinal channel)

Carinal canal (longitudinal channel)

MICROGRAPH OF CROSS-SECTION THROUGH HORSETAIL STEM

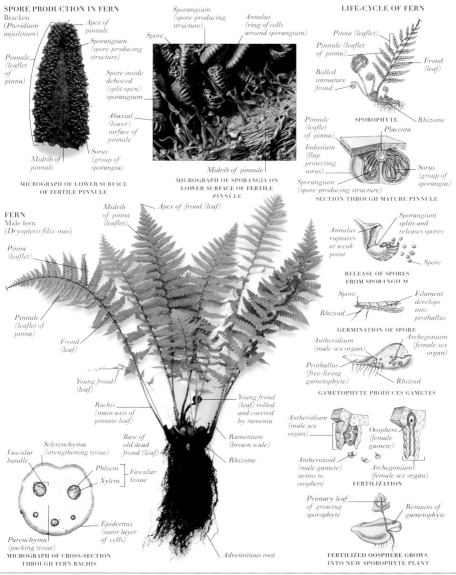

SPORE PRODUCTION IN FERN
Bracken
(*Pteridium
aquilinum*)

Apex of
pinnule

Sporangium
(spore-producing
structure)

Pinnule
(leaflet
of pinna)

Spore inside
dehisced
(split open)
sporangium

Abaxial
(lower)
surface of
pinnule

Midrib of
pinnule

Sorus
(group of
sporangia)

MICROGRAPH OF LOWER SURFACE
OF FERTILE PINNULE

Sporangium
(spore-producing
structure)

Spore

Annulus
(ring of cells
around sporangium)

Midrib of pinnule

MICROGRAPH OF SPORANGIA ON
LOWER SURFACE OF FERTILE
PINNULE

LIFE-CYCLE OF FERN

Pinna (leaflet)

Pinnule (leaflet
of pinna)

Rolled
immature
frond

Frond
(leaf)

Rhizome

SPOROPHYTE

Pinnule
(leaflet
of pinna)

Placenta

Indusium
(flap
protecting
sorus)

Sporangium
(spore-producing structure)

Sorus
(group of
sporangia)

SECTION THROUGH MATURE PINNULE

Sporangium
splits and
releases spores

Annulus
ruptures
at weak
point

Spore

RELEASE OF SPORES
FROM SPORANGIUM

Spore

Rhizoid

Filament
develops
into
prothallus

GERMINATION OF SPORE

Antheridium
(male sex organ)

Archegonium
(female sex
organ)

Prothallus
(free-living
gametophyte)

Rhizoid

GAMETOPHYTE PRODUCES GAMETES

Antheridium
(male sex
organ)

Oosphere
(female
gamete)

Antherozoid
(male gamete)
swims to
oosphere

Archegonium
(female sex organ)

FERTILIZATION

Primary leaf
of growing
sporophyte

Remains of
gametophyte

FERTILIZED OOSPHERE GROWS
INTO NEW SPOROPHYTE PLANT

FERN
Male fern
(*Dryopteris filix-mas*)

Midrib
of pinna
(leaflet)

Apex of frond (leaf)

Pinna
(leaflet)

Pinnule
(leaflet of
pinna)

Frond
(leaf)

Young frond
(leaf)

Rachis
(main axis of
pinnate leaf)

Young frond
(leaf) rolled
and covered
by ramenta

Ramentum
(brown scale)

Rhizome

Base of
old dead
frond (leaf)

Vascular
bundle

Sclerenchyma
(strengthening tissue)

Phloem

Xylem

Vascular
tissue

Epidermis
(outer layer
of cells)

Parenchyma
(packing tissue)

MICROGRAPH OF CROSS-SECTION
THROUGH FERN RACHIS

Adventitious root

121

Gymnosperms 1

THE GYMNOSPERMS ARE FOUR RELATED PHYLA of seed-producing plants; their seeds, however, lack the protective, outer covering which surrounds the seeds of flowering plants. Typically, gymnosperms are woody, perennial shrubs or trees, with stems, leaves, and roots, and a well-developed vascular (transport) system. The reproductive structures in most gymnosperms are cones: male cones produce microspores in which male gametes (sex cells) develop; female cones produce megaspores in which female gametes develop. Microspores are blown by the wind to female cones, male and female gametes fuse during fertilization, and a seed develops. The four gymnosperm phyla are the conifers (phylum Coniferophyta), mostly tall trees; cycads (phylum Cycadophyta), small palm-like trees; the ginkgo or maidenhair tree (phylum Ginkgophyta), a tall tree with bilobed leaves; and gnetophytes (phylum Gnetophyta), a diverse group of plants, mainly shrubs, but also including the horizontally growing welwitschia.

LIFE-CYCLE OF SCOTS PINE
(*Pinus sylvestris*)

Needle (foliage leaf)
Cone
Ovuliferous scale (ovule- then seed-bearing structure)

MALE CONES
YOUNG FEMALE CONE

Pollen grain in micropyle (entrance to ovule)
Ovuliferous scale
Pollen grain
Ovule (contains female gamete)
Nucleus
Air sac
POLLINATION

Integument (outer part of ovule)
Archegonium (containing female gamete)
Pollen tube (carries male gamete from pollen grain to ovum)
FERTILIZATION

SCALE AND SEEDS
Pine (*Pinus sp.*)

Ovuliferous scale (ovule- then seed-bearing structure)
Wing scar
Wing of seed derived from ovuliferous scale
Seed
Seed
Point of attachment to axis of cone
Seed scar
OVULIFEROUS SCALE FROM THIRD-YEAR FEMALE CONE

Ovuliferous scale (ovule- then seed-bearing structure)
Seed
Seed
Wing
MATURE FEMALE CONE AND WINGED SEED

Microsporangium (structure in which pollen grains are formed)

Microsporophyll (modified leaf carrying microsporangia)

Axis of cone
Scale leaf
Ovuliferous scale (ovule- then seed-bearing structure)
Ovule (contains female gametes)
Bract scale
Axis of cone

MICROGRAPH OF LONGITUDINAL SECTION THROUGH YOUNG MALE CONE

MICROGRAPH OF LONGITUDINAL SECTION THROUGH SECOND-YEAR FEMALE CONE

Plumule (embryonic shoot)
Cotyledon (seed leaf)
Root
GERMINATION OF PINE SEEDLING

WELWITSCHIA
(*Welwitschia mirabilis*)

Frayed end of leaf

SMOOTH CYPRESS
(*Cupressus glabra*)

Immature female cone

Ovuliferous scale (ovule- then seed-bearing structure)

Ovuliferous scale

Ovule (contains female gamete)

CROSS-SECTION THROUGH IMMATURE CONE

Scale-like leaf

Seed

Ovuliferous scale (ovule- then seed-bearing structure)

CROSS-SECTION THROUGH MATURE CONE

Mature female cone

Immature male cone

Woody scale

Opening between woody scales through which seeds are released

DISCARDED CONE

Stem

YEW
(*Taxus baccata*)

Single ovule (contains female gamete)

Scale

Female "cone"

Scale

Developing seed

Scale

FEMALE "CONES" AT VARIOUS STAGES OF DEVELOPMENT

Seed

Aril (fleshy outgrowth from seed)

Stem

Needle (foliage leaf)

CYCAD
Sago palm
(*Cycas revoluta*)

Pinna (leaflet)

Pinnate leaf

Scale leaf

Old leaf base

Stem covered by scale leaves

MAIDENHAIR TREE
(*Ginkgo biloba*)

Girdle scar

Stem

Petiole (leaf stalk)

Bilobed leaf

Continuously growing leaf

Site of cone growth

Adaxial (upper) surface of leaf

Frayed end of leaf

Abaxial (lower) surface of leaf

Immature cone

Stalk scar

Woody stem

123

Gymnosperms 2

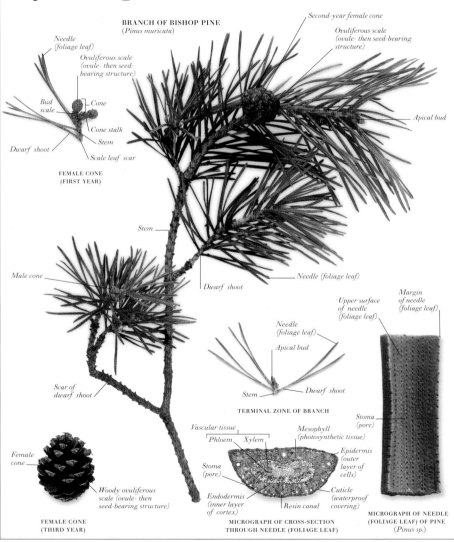

BRANCH OF BISHOP PINE
(*Pinus muricata*)

Second-year female cone

Ovuliferous scale
(ovule- then seed-bearing
structure)

Needle
(foliage leaf)

Ovuliferous scale
(ovule- then seed-
bearing structure)

Apical bud

Bud
scale

Cone

Cone stalk

Stem

Scale leaf scar

Dwarf shoot

**FEMALE CONE
(FIRST YEAR)**

Stem

Male cone

Needle (foliage leaf)

Dwarf shoot

Upper surface
of needle
(foliage leaf)

Margin
of needle
(foliage leaf)

Needle
(foliage leaf)

Apical bud

Scar of
dwarf shoot

Stem

Dwarf shoot

TERMINAL ZONE OF BRANCH

Stoma
(pore)

Female
cone

Vascular tissue

Phloem   Xylem

Mesophyll
(photosynthetic tissue)

Epidermis
(outer
layer of
cells)

Stoma
(pore)

Woody ovuliferous
scale (ovule- then
seed-bearing structure)

Endodermis
(inner layer
of cortex)

Cuticle
(waterproof
covering)

Resin canal

**FEMALE CONE
(THIRD YEAR)**

**MICROGRAPH OF CROSS-SECTION
THROUGH NEEDLE (FOLIAGE LEAF)**

**MICROGRAPH OF NEEDLE
(FOLIAGE LEAF) OF PINE**
(*Pinus sp.*)

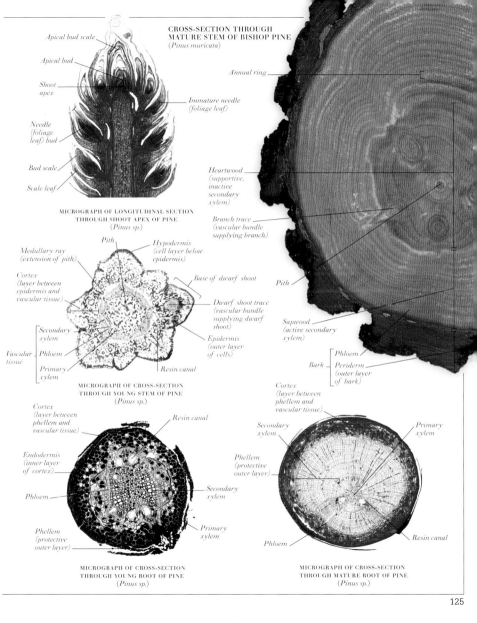

CROSS-SECTION THROUGH MATURE STEM OF BISHOP PINE
(*Pinus muricata*)

Apical bud scale

Apical bud

Shoot apex

Immature needle (foliage leaf)

Needle (foliage leaf) bud

Bud scale

Scale leaf

Annual ring

Heartwood (supportive, inactive secondary xylem)

Branch trace (vascular bundle supplying branch)

Pith

Sapwood (active secondary xylem)

Phloem

Bark — Periderm (outer layer of bark)

MICROGRAPH OF LONGITUDINAL SECTION THROUGH SHOOT APEX OF PINE
(*Pinus sp.*)

Medullary ray (extension of pith)

Pith

Hypodermis (cell layer below epidermis)

Cortex (layer between epidermis and vascular tissue)

Base of dwarf shoot

Dwarf shoot trace (vascular bundle supplying dwarf shoot)

Secondary xylem

Phloem

Vascular tissue

Primary xylem

Epidermis (outer layer of cells)

Resin canal

MICROGRAPH OF CROSS-SECTION THROUGH YOUNG STEM OF PINE
(*Pinus sp.*)

Cortex (layer between phellem and vascular tissue)

Resin canal

Endodermis (inner layer of cortex)

Secondary xylem

Phloem

Primary xylem

Phellem (protective outer layer)

MICROGRAPH OF CROSS-SECTION THROUGH YOUNG ROOT OF PINE
(*Pinus sp.*)

Cortex (layer between phellem and vascular tissue)

Secondary xylem

Phloem

Phellem (protective outer layer)

Primary xylem

Resin canal

MICROGRAPH OF CROSS-SECTION THROUGH MATURE ROOT OF PINE
(*Pinus sp.*)

125

Monocotyledons and dicotyledons

FLOWERING PLANTS (PHYLUM ANGIOSPERMOPHYTA) are divided into two classes: monocotyledons (class Monocotyledoneae) and dicotyledons (class Dicotyledoneae). Typically, monocotyledons have seeds with one cotyledon (seed leaf); their foliage leaves are narrow with parallel veins; the flower components occur in multiples of three; sepals and petals are indistinguishable and are known as tepals; vascular (transport) tissues are scattered in random bundles throughout the stem; and, since they lack stem cambium (actively dividing cells that produce wood), most monocotyledons are herbaceous (see pp. 128-129). Dicotyledons have seeds with two cotyledons; leaves are broad with a central midrib and branched veins; flower parts occur in multiples of four or five; sepals are generally small and green; petals are large and colourful; vascular bundles are arranged in a ring around the edge of the stem; and, because many dicotyledons possess wood-producing stem cambium, there are woody forms (see pp. 130-131) as well as herbaceous ones.

CROSS-SECTION
THROUGH
MONOCOTYLEDONOUS
LEAF BASES

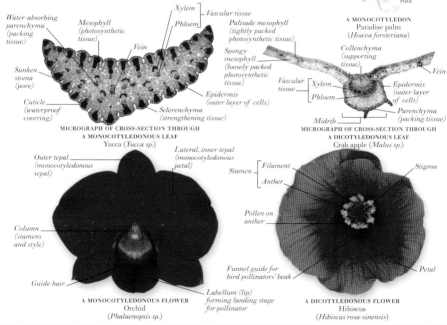

Vein (parallel venation)

Leaflet

Petiole (leaf stalk)

Emerging leaf

Leaf base

Adventitious root

A MONOCOTYLEDON
Paradise palm
(Howea forsteriana)

Water-absorbing parenchyma (packing tissue)

Mesophyll (photosynthetic tissue)

Vein

Sunken stoma (pore)

Cuticle (waterproof covering)

Xylem
Phloem
Vascular tissue

Palisade mesophyll (tightly packed photosynthetic tissue)

Spongy mesophyll (loosely packed photosynthetic tissue)

Vascular tissue

Epidermis (outer layer of cells)

Sclerenchyma (strengthening tissue)

MICROGRAPH OF CROSS-SECTION THROUGH
A MONOCOTYLEDONOUS LEAF
Yucca (Yucca sp.)

Collenchyma (supporting tissue)

Xylem
Phloem

Vein

Epidermis (outer layer of cells)

Parenchyma (packing tissue)

Midrib

MICROGRAPH OF CROSS-SECTION THROUGH
A DICOTYLEDONOUS LEAF
Crab apple (Malus sp.)

Outer tepal (monocotyledonous sepal)

Lateral, inner tepal (monocotyledonous petal)

Stamen
Filament
Anther

Pollen on anther

Stigma

Column (stamens and style)

Guide hair

Labellum (lip) forming landing stage for pollinator

Funnel guide for bird pollinators' beak

Petal

A MONOCOTYLEDONOUS FLOWER
Orchid
(Phalaenopsis sp.)

A DICOTYLEDONOUS FLOWER
Hibiscus
(Hibiscus rosa-sinensis)

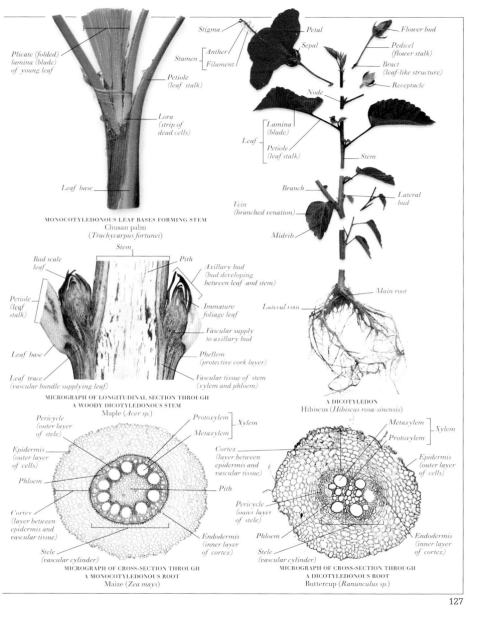

Plicate (folded) lamina (blade) of young leaf

Petiole (leaf stalk)

Lora (strip of dead cells)

Leaf base

MONOCOTYLEDONOUS LEAF BASES FORMING STEM
Chusan palm (*Trachycarpus fortunei*)

Stigma

Petal

Sepal

Stamen { Anther / Filament

Node

Leaf { Lamina (blade) / Petiole (leaf stalk)

Stem

Branch

Vein (branched venation)

Midrib

Flower bud

Pedicel (flower stalk)

Bract (leaf-like structure)

Receptacle

Lateral bud

Stem

Bud scale leaf

Pith

Petiole (leaf stalk)

Axillary bud (bud developing between leaf and stem)

Immature foliage leaf

Vascular supply to axillary bud

Leaf base

Leaf trace (vascular bundle supplying leaf)

Phellem (protective cork layer)

Vascular tissue of stem (xylem and phloem)

MICROGRAPH OF LONGITUDINAL SECTION THROUGH A WOODY DICOTYLEDONOUS STEM
Maple (*Acer sp.*)

Main root

Lateral root

A DICOTYLEDON
Hibiscus (*Hibiscus rosa-sinensis*)

Pericycle (outer layer of stele)

Protoxylem } Xylem

Metaxylem

Epidermis (outer layer of cells)

Phloem

Cortex (layer between epidermis and vascular tissue)

Pith

Cortex (layer between epidermis and vascular tissue)

Stele (vascular cylinder)

Endodermis (inner layer of cortex)

MICROGRAPH OF CROSS-SECTION THROUGH A MONOCOTYLEDONOUS ROOT
Maize (*Zea mays*)

Metaxylem } Xylem

Protoxylem

Cortex (layer between epidermis and vascular tissue)

Epidermis (outer layer of cells)

Pericycle (outer layer of stele)

Phloem

Stele (vascular cylinder)

Endodermis (inner layer of cortex)

MICROGRAPH OF CROSS-SECTION THROUGH A DICOTYLEDONOUS ROOT
Buttercup (*Ranunculus sp.*)

Herbaceous flowering plants

HERBACEOUS FLOWERING PLANTS TYPICALLY HAVE GREEN, NON-WOODY STEMS, and tend to be relatively short-lived. Many herbaceous plants live for only one or two years. Annuals (e.g., sweet peas) grow from seed, produce flowers and then seeds, and die within a single year. Biennials (e.g., carrots) have a two-year life cycle. In the first year, seeds grow into plants, which produce leaves and store food in underground storage organs; the stems and foliage then die back in winter. In the second year, new stems grow from the storage organs, produce leaves, flowers, and seeds, and then die. Some herbaceous plants (e.g., potatoes) are perennial. They grow back year after year, producing shoots and flowers in spring, storing food in underground tubers or rhizomes during summer, dying back in autumn, and surviving underground during winter.

Young plant forming

Petiole (stalk) of young leaf

Lateral root

Stipule (structure at base of leaf)

Trifoliate leaf

Node

Simple ovate leaflet

Root nodule

Main root

SWEET PEA
(*Lathyrus odoratus*)

STRAWBERRY
(*Fragaria* x *ananassa*)

Runner (creeping stem)

Lateral root scar

Remains of leaves

Stem

Leaf scar

Rib

Lateral root

Tap root

Leaf base

CARROT
(*Daucus carota*)

Leaf scar

Petiole (leaf stalk)

Spine (modified leaf)

Slender rhizome

Stem tuber

Adventitious root

Stem

Narrow, succulent leaf

Simple deltoid leaf

POTATO
(*Solanum tuberosum*)

ROCK STONECROP
(*Sedum rupestre*)

Adventitious root

PARTS OF HERBACEOUS FLOWERING PLANTS

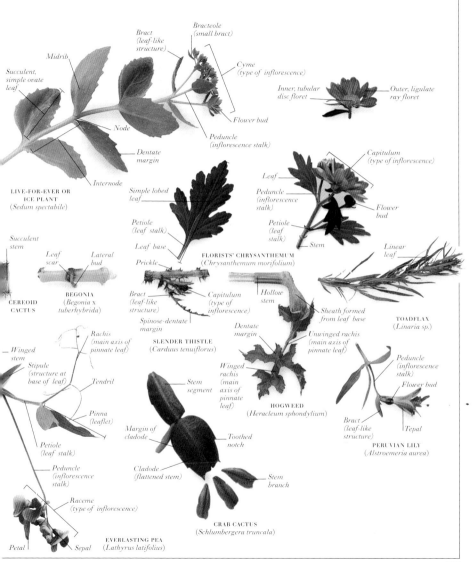

Succulent, simple ovate leaf

Midrib

Bract (leaf-like structure)

Bracteole (small bract)

Cyme (type of inflorescence)

Inner, tubular disc floret

Outer, ligulate ray floret

Flower bud

Node

Peduncle (inflorescence stalk)

Dentate margin

Internode

LIVE-FOR-EVER OR ICE PLANT
(Sedum spectabile)

Simple lobed leaf

Capitulum (type of inflorescence)

Leaf

Peduncle (inflorescence stalk)

Flower bud

Petiole (leaf stalk)

Leaf base

Prickle

Petiole (leaf stalk)

Stem

Linear leaf

Succulent stem

Leaf scar

Lateral bud

CEREOID CACTUS

BEGONIA
(Begonia x tuberhybrida)

FLORISTS' CHRYSANTHEMUM
(Chrysanthemum morifolium)

Bract (leaf-like structure)

Capitulum (type of inflorescence)

Hollow stem

Sheath formed from leaf base

TOADFLAX
(Linaria sp.)

Spinose-dentate margin

SLENDER THISTLE
(Carduus tenuiflorus)

Dentate margin

Unwinged rachis (main axis of pinnate leaf)

Winged stem

Rachis (main axis of pinnate leaf)

Stipule (structure at base of leaf)

Tendril

Pinna (leaflet)

Petiole (leaf stalk)

Peduncle (inflorescence stalk)

Raceme (type of inflorescence)

Stem segment

Winged rachis (main axis of pinnate leaf)

HOGWEED
(Heracleum sphondylium)

Peduncle (inflorescence stalk)

Flower bud

Bract (leaf-like structure)

Tepal

PERUVIAN LILY
(Alstroemeria aurea)

Margin of cladode

Toothed notch

Cladode (flattened stem)

Stem branch

CRAB CACTUS
(Schlumbergera truncata)

Petal

Sepal

EVERLASTING PEA
(Lathyrus latifolius)

Woody flowering plants

Woody flowering plants are perennial, that is, they continue to grow and reproduce for many years. They have one or more permanent stems above ground, and numerous smaller branches. The stems and branches have a strong woody core that supports the plant and contains vascular tissue for transporting water and nutrients. Outside the woody core is a layer of tough, protective bark, which has lenticels (tiny pores) in it to enable gases to pass through. Woody flowering plants may be shrubs, which have several stems arising from the soil; bushes, which are shrubs with dense branching and foliage; or trees, which typically have a single upright stem (the trunk) that bears branches. Deciduous woody plants (e.g., roses) shed all their leaves once a year and remain leafless during winter. Evergreen woody plants (e.g., ivy) shed their leaves gradually, so retaining full leaf cover throughout the year.

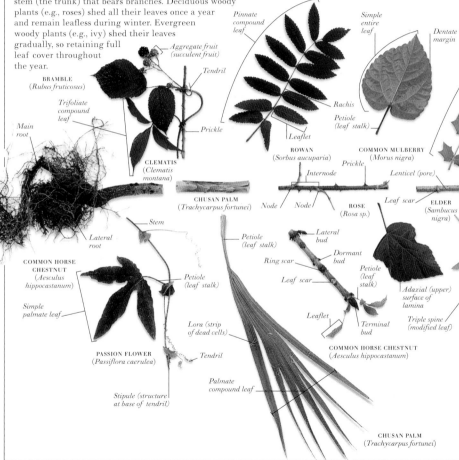

Pinnate compound leaf

Simple entire leaf

Dentate margin

BRAMBLE
(*Rubus fruticosus*)

Aggregate fruit (succulent fruit)

Tendril

Trifoliate compound leaf

Main root

CLEMATIS
(*Clematis montana*)

Prickle

Rachis

Petiole (leaf stalk)

Leaflet

ROWAN
(*Sorbus aucuparia*)

COMMON MULBERRY
(*Morus nigra*)

Prickle

Internode

Node

Node

ROSE
(*Rosa sp.*)

Lenticel (pore)

Leaf scar

ELDER
(*Sambucus nigra*)

CHUSAN PALM
(*Trachycarpus fortunei*)

Lateral root

Stem

COMMON HORSE CHESTNUT
(*Aesculus hippocastanum*)

Petiole (leaf stalk)

Simple palmate leaf

Petiole (leaf stalk)

Lateral bud

Dormant bud

Ring scar

Leaf scar

Petiole (leaf stalk)

Adaxial (upper) surface of lamina

Leaflet

Terminal bud

Triple spine (modified leaf)

COMMON HORSE CHESTNUT
(*Aesculus hippocastanum*)

Lora (strip of dead cells)

PASSION FLOWER
(*Passiflora caerulea*)

Tendril

Stipule (structure at base of tendril)

Palmate compound leaf

CHUSAN PALM
(*Trachycarpus fortunei*)

PARTS OF WOODY FLOWERING PLANTS

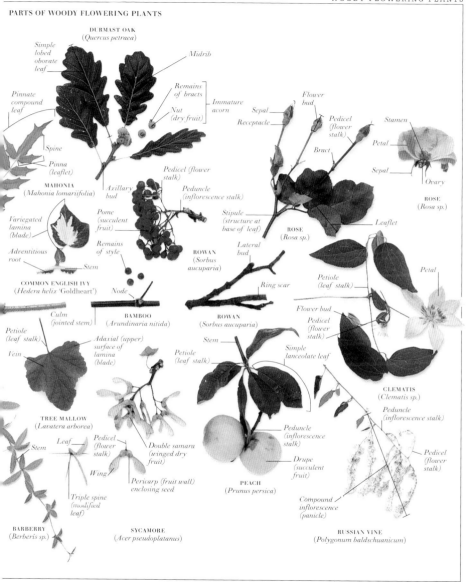

DURMAST OAK
(*Quercus petraea*)

Simple lobed obovate leaf

Midrib

Pinnate compound leaf

Remains of bracts

Nut (dry fruit)

Immature acorn

Spine

Pinna (leaflet)

MAHONIA
(*Mahonia lomariifolia*)

Axillary bud

Pedicel (flower stalk)

Peduncle (inflorescence stalk)

Pome (succulent fruit)

Variegated lamina (blade)

Adventitious root

Remains of style

Stem

COMMON ENGLISH IVY
(*Hedera helix* 'Goldheart')

Node

Culm (jointed stem)

BAMBOO
(*Arundinaria nitida*)

ROWAN
(*Sorbus aucuparia*)

Flower bud

Sepal

Receptacle

Pedicel (flower stalk)

Bract

Stamen

Petal

Sepal

Ovary

ROSE
(*Rosa sp.*)

Stipule (structure at base of leaf)

ROSE
(*Rosa sp.*)

Leaflet

Lateral bud

Ring scar

ROWAN
(*Sorbus aucuparia*)

Petiole (leaf stalk)

Petal

Flower bud

Pedicel (flower stalk)

Simple lanceolate leaf

CLEMATIS
(*Clematis sp.*)

Peduncle (inflorescence stalk)

Petiole (leaf stalk)

Vein

Adaxial (upper) surface of lamina (blade)

TREE MALLOW
(*Lavatera arborea*)

Petiole (leaf stalk)

Stem

Pedicel (flower stalk)

Double samara (winged dry fruit)

Wing

Pericarp (fruit wall) enclosing seed

Peduncle (inflorescence stalk)

Drupe (succulent fruit)

PEACH
(*Prunus persica*)

Pedicel (flower stalk)

Leaf

Stem

Triple spine (modified leaf)

BARBERRY
(*Berberis sp.*)

SYCAMORE
(*Acer pseudoplatanus*)

Compound inflorescence (panicle)

RUSSIAN VINE
(*Polygonum baldschuanicum*)

Roots

ROOTS ARE THE UNDERGROUND PARTS OF PLANTS. They have three main functions. First, they anchor the plant in the soil. Second, they absorb water and minerals from the spaces between soil particles; the roots' absorptive properties are increased by root hairs, which grow behind the root tip, allowing maximum uptake of vital substances. Third, the root is part of the plant's transport system: xylem carries water and minerals from the roots to the stem and leaves, and phloem carries nutrients from the leaves to all parts of the root system. In addition, some roots (e.g., carrots) are food stores. Roots have an outer epidermis covering a cortex of parenchyma (packing tissue), and a central cylinder of vascular tissue. This arrangement helps the roots resist the forces of compression as they grow through the soil.

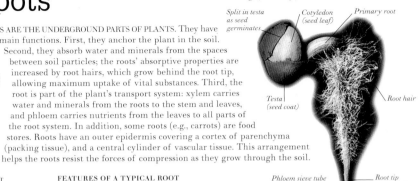

Split in testa as seed germinates

Cotyledon (seed leaf)

Primary root

Testa (seed coat)

Root hair

CARROT (*Daucus carota*)

Root tip (region of cell division)

FEATURES OF A TYPICAL ROOT
Buttercup (*Ranunculus sp.*)

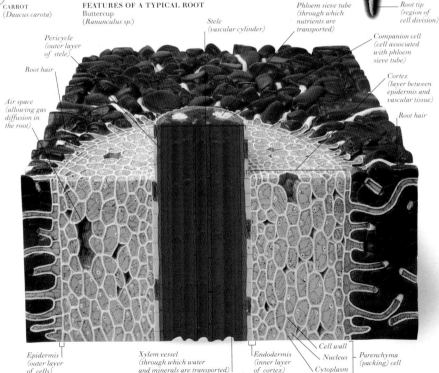

Pericycle (outer layer of stele)

Root hair

Air space (allowing gas diffusion in the root)

Stele (vascular cylinder)

Phloem sieve tube (through which nutrients are transported)

Companion cell (cell associated with phloem sieve tube)

Cortex (layer between epidermis and vascular tissue)

Root hair

Epidermis (outer layer of cells)

Xylem vessel (through which water and minerals are transported)

Endodermis (inner layer of cortex)

Cell wall

Nucleus

Cytoplasm

Parenchyma (packing) cell

PRIMARY ROOT AND MICROGRAPHS OF SECTIONS THROUGH ROOTS

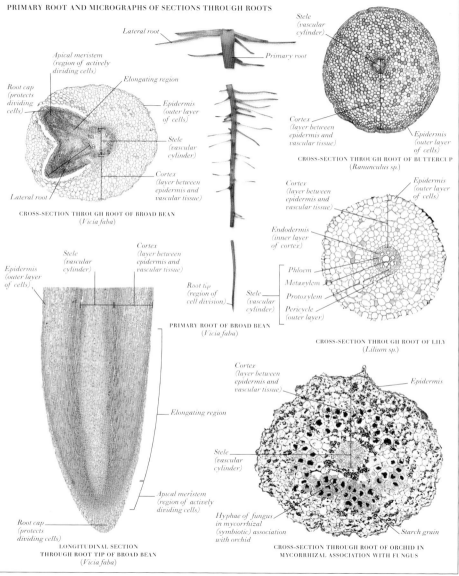

Lateral root

Primary root

Apical meristem
(region of actively
dividing cells)

Elongating region

Root cap
(protects
dividing
cells)

Epidermis
(outer layer
of cells)

Stele
(vascular
cylinder)

Cortex
(layer between
epidermis and
vascular tissue)

Lateral root

CROSS-SECTION THROUGH ROOT OF BROAD BEAN
(*Vicia faba*)

Stele
(vascular
cylinder)

Cortex
(layer between
epidermis and
vascular tissue)

Epidermis
(outer layer
of cells)

CROSS-SECTION THROUGH ROOT OF BUTTERCUP
(*Ranunculus sp.*)

Cortex
(layer between
epidermis and
vascular tissue)

Epidermis
(outer layer
of cells)

Endodermis
(inner layer
of cortex)

Phloem

Metaxylem

Protoxylem

Pericycle
(outer layer)

Stele
(vascular
cylinder)

CROSS-SECTION THROUGH ROOT OF LILY
(*Lilium sp.*)

Epidermis
(outer layer
of cells)

Stele
(vascular
cylinder)

Cortex
(layer between
epidermis and
vascular tissue)

Root tip
(region of
cell division)

Stele
(vascular
cylinder)

PRIMARY ROOT OF BROAD BEAN
(*Vicia faba*)

Elongating region

Apical meristem
(region of actively
dividing cells)

Root cap
(protects
dividing cells)

**LONGITUDINAL SECTION
THROUGH ROOT TIP OF BROAD BEAN**
(*Vicia faba*)

Cortex
(layer between
epidermis and
vascular tissue)

Epidermis

Stele
(vascular
cylinder)

Hyphae of fungus
in mycorrhizal
(symbiotic) association
with orchid

Starch grain

**CROSS-SECTION THROUGH ROOT OF ORCHID IN
MYCORRHIZAL ASSOCIATION WITH FUNGUS**

Stems

THE STEM IS THE MAIN SUPPORTIVE PART OF A PLANT that grows
above ground. Stems bear leaves (organs of photosynthesis), which
grow at nodes; buds (shoots covered by protective scales), which
grow at the stem tip (apical or terminal buds) and in the angle between a
leaf and the stem (axillary or lateral buds); and flowers (reproductive
structures). The stem forms part of the plant's transport system: xylem
tissue in the stem transports water and minerals from the roots to the
aerial parts of the plant, and phloem tissue transports nutrients
manufactured in the leaves to other parts of the plant. Stem tissues
are also used for storing water and food. Herbaceous (non-woody)
stems have an outer protective epidermis covering a cortex that
consists mainly of parenchyma (packing tissue) but also has some
collenchyma (supporting tissue). The vascular tissue of such stems
is arranged in bundles, each of which consists of xylem, phloem,
and sclerenchyma (strengthening tissue). Woody stems have an outer
protective layer of tough bark, which is perforated with lenticels (pores)
to allow gas exchange. Inside the bark is a ring of secondary phloem,
which surrounds an inner core of secondary xylem.

**MICROGRAPH OF LONGITUDINAL
SECTION THROUGH APEX OF STEM**
Coleus sp.

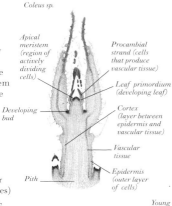

Apical
meristem
(region of
actively
dividing
cells)

Procambial
strand (cells
that produce
vascular tissue)

Leaf primordium
(developing leaf)

Developing
bud

Cortex
(layer between
epidermis and
vascular tissue)

Vascular
tissue

Epidermis
(outer layer
of cells)

Pith

YOUNG WOODY STEM
Lime
(Tilia sp.)

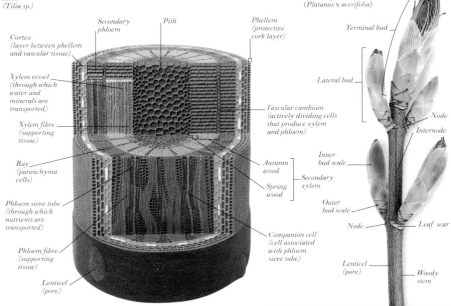

Cortex
(layer between phellem
and vascular tissue)

Xylem vessel
(through which
water and
minerals are
transported)

Xylem fibre
(supporting
tissue)

Ray
(parenchyma
cells)

Phloem sieve tube
(through which
nutrients are
transported)

Phloem fibre
(supporting
tissue)

Lenticel
(pore)

Secondary
phloem

Pith

Phellem
(protective
cork layer)

Vascular cambium
(actively dividing cells
that produce xylem
and phloem)

Autumn
wood

Spring
wood

Companion cell
(cell associated
with phloem
sieve tube)

EMERGENT BUDS
London plane
(Platanus x acerifolia)

Young
leaves
emergi

Terminal bud

Lateral bud

Node

Internode

Inner
bud scale

Secondary
xylem

Outer
bud scale

Node

Leaf scar

Lenticel
(pore)

Woody
stem

MICROGRAPHS OF CROSS-SECTIONS THROUGH VARIOUS STEMS

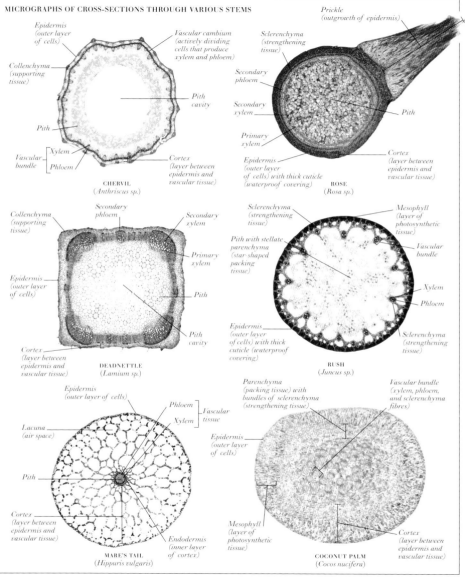

Epidermis (outer layer of cells)

Collenchyma (supporting tissue)

Pith

Vascular bundle
Xylem
Phloem

Vascular cambium (actively dividing cells that produce xylem and phloem)

Pith cavity

Cortex (layer between epidermis and vascular tissue)

CHERVIL
(*Anthriscus sp.*)

Prickle (outgrowth of epidermis)

Sclerenchyma (strengthening tissue)

Secondary phloem

Secondary xylem

Primary xylem

Epidermis (outer layer of cells) with thick cuticle (waterproof covering)

Pith

Cortex (layer between epidermis and vascular tissue)

ROSE
(*Rosa sp.*)

Collenchyma (supporting tissue)

Epidermis (outer layer of cells)

Cortex (layer between epidermis and vascular tissue)

Secondary phloem

Secondary xylem

Primary xylem

Pith

Pith cavity

DEADNETTLE
(*Lamium sp.*)

Sclerenchyma (strengthening tissue)

Pith with stellate parenchyma (star-shaped packing tissue)

Epidermis (outer layer of cells) with thick cuticle (waterproof covering)

Mesophyll (layer of photosynthetic tissue)

Vascular bundle

Xylem

Phloem

Sclerenchyma (strengthening tissue)

RUSH
(*Juncus sp.*)

Epidermis (outer layer of cells)

Lacuna (air space)

Pith

Cortex (layer between epidermis and vascular tissue)

Phloem
Xylem
Vascular tissue

Endodermis (inner layer of cortex)

MARE'S TAIL
(*Hippuris vulgaris*)

Parenchyma (packing tissue) with bundles of sclerenchyma (strengthening tissue)

Epidermis (outer layer of cells)

Mesophyll (layer of photosynthetic tissue)

Vascular bundle (xylem, phloem, and sclerenchyma fibres)

Cortex (layer between epidermis and vascular tissue)

COCONUT PALM
(*Cocos nucifera*)

Leaves

CHECKERBLOOM
(Sidalcea malviflora)

LEAVES ARE THE MAIN SITES OF PHOTOSYNTHESIS (see pp. 138-139) and transpiration (water loss by evaporation) in plants. A typical leaf consists of a thin, flat lamina (blade) supported by a network of veins; a petiole (leaf stalk); and a leaf base, where the petiole joins the stem. Leaves can be classified as simple, in which the lamina is a single unit, or compound, in which the lamina is divided into separate leaflets. Compound leaves may be pinnate, with pinnae (leaflets) on both sides of a rachis (main axis), or palmate, with leaflets arising from a single point at the tip of the petiole. Leaves can be classified further by the overall shape of the lamina, and by the shape of the lamina's apex, margin, and base.

SIMPLE LEAF SHAPES

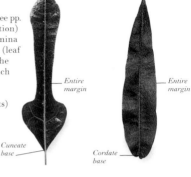

Subacute apex
Acuminate apex
Entire margin
Entire margin
Cuneate base
Cordate base

PANDURIFORM
Croton
(Codiaeum variegatum)

LANCEOLATE
Sea buckthorn
(Hippophae rhamnoides)

GENERAL LEAF FEATURES

Apex
Lamina (blade)
Midrib
Margin
Lateral vein
Lamina base
Petiole (leaf stalk)
Leaf base

Sweet chestnut
(Castanea sativa)

COMPOUND LEAF SHAPES

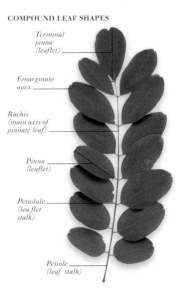

Terminal pinna (leaflet)
Emarginate apex
Rachis (main axis of pinnate leaf)
Pinna (leaflet)
Petiolule (leaflet stalk)
Petiole (leaf stalk)

ODD PINNATE
False acacia
(Robinia pseudoacacia)

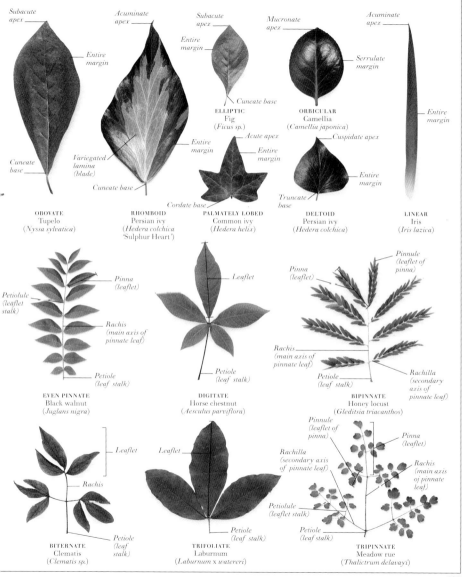

Subacute apex

Entire margin

Cuneate base

OBOVATE
Tupelo
(*Nyssa sylvatica*)

Acuminate apex

Variegated lamina (blade)

Entire margin

Cuneate base

RHOMBOID
Persian ivy
(*Hedera colchica* 'Sulphur Heart')

Subacute apex

Entire margin

Cuneate base

ELLIPTIC
Fig
(*Ficus sp.*)

Acute apex

Entire margin

Cordate base

PALMATELY LOBED
Common ivy
(*Hedera helix*)

Mucronate apex

Serrulate margin

ORBICULAR
Camellia
(*Camellia japonica*)

Cuspidate apex

Entire margin

Truncate base

DELTOID
Persian ivy
(*Hedera colchica*)

Acuminate apex

Entire margin

LINEAR
Iris
(*Iris lazica*)

Pinna (leaflet)

Petiolule (leaflet stalk)

Rachis (main axis of pinnate leaf)

Petiole (leaf stalk)

EVEN PINNATE
Black walnut
(*Juglans nigra*)

Leaflet

Petiole (leaf stalk)

DIGITATE
Horse chestnut
(*Aesculus parviflora*)

Pinnule (leaflet of pinna)

Pinna (leaflet)

Rachis (main axis of pinnate leaf)

Petiole (leaf stalk)

Rachilla (secondary axis of pinnate leaf)

BIPINNATE
Honey locust
(*Gleditsia triacanthos*)

Leaflet

Rachis

Petiole (leaf stalk)

BITERNATE
Clematis
(*Clematis sp.*)

Leaflet

Petiole (leaf stalk)

TRIFOLIATE
Laburnum
(*Laburnum x watereri*)

Pinnule (leaflet of pinna)

Pinna (leaflet)

Rachilla (secondary axis of pinnate leaf)

Rachis (main axis of pinnate leaf)

Petiolule (leaflet stalk)

Petiole (leaf stalk)

TRIPINNATE
Meadow rue
(*Thalictrum delavayi*)

Photosynthesis

PHOTOSYNTHESIS IS THE PROCESS by which plants make their food using sunlight, water, and carbon dioxide. It takes place inside special structures in leaf cells called chloroplasts. The chloroplasts contain chlorophyll, a green pigment that absorbs energy from sunlight. During photosynthesis, the absorbed energy is used to join together carbon dioxide and water to form the sugar glucose, which is the energy source for the whole plant; oxygen, a waste product, is released into the air. Leaves are the main sites of photosynthesis, and have various adaptations for that purpose: flat laminae (blades) provide a large surface for absorbing sunlight; stomata (pores) in the lower surface of the laminae allow gases (carbon dioxide and oxygen) to pass into and out of the leaves; and an extensive network of veins brings water into the leaves and transports the glucose produced by photosynthesis to the rest of the plant.

MICROGRAPH OF LEAF
Lily (*Lilium sp.*)

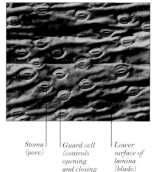

Stoma (pore)

Guard cell (controls opening and closing of stoma)

Lower surface of lamina (blade)

THE PROCESS OF PHOTOSYNTHESIS

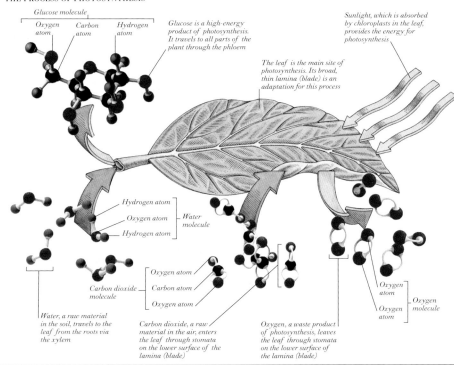

Glucose molecule

Oxygen atom

Carbon atom

Hydrogen atom

Glucose is a high-energy product of photosynthesis. It travels to all parts of the plant through the phloem

Sunlight, which is absorbed by chloroplasts in the leaf, provides the energy for photosynthesis

The leaf is the main site of photosynthesis. Its broad, thin lamina (blade) is an adaptation for this process

Hydrogen atom

Oxygen atom

Hydrogen atom

Water molecule

Carbon dioxide molecule

Oxygen atom

Carbon atom

Oxygen atom

Oxygen atom

Oxygen atom

Oxygen molecule

Water, a raw material in the soil, travels to the leaf from the roots via the xylem

Carbon dioxide, a raw material in the air, enters the leaf through stomata on the lower surface of the lamina (blade)

Oxygen, a waste product of photosynthesis, leaves the leaf through stomata on the lower surface of the lamina (blade)

CROSS-SECTION THROUGH LEAF
Christmas rose
(*Helleborus niger*)

Cuticle (waterproof covering)

Upper (adaxial) epidermis (outer layer of cells)

Cell wall

Cytoplasm

Vacuole

Chloroplast (photosynthetic organelle)

Palisade mesophyll (tightly packed layer of photosynthetic tissue)

Nucleus

Intercellular space

Sclerenchyma (strengthening tissue)

Xylem (tissue that transports water and mineral salts)

Phloem (tissue that transports sugars and other nutrients)

Spongy mesophyll (loosely packed layer of photosynthetic tissue)

Vein

Lower (abaxial) epidermis (outer layer of cells)

Parenchyma (packing tissue)

Guard cell (controls opening and closing of stoma)

Stoma (pore)

Substomatal chamber

INTERNAL VIEW OF CHLOROPLAST

Granum (stack of thylakoids that hold chlorophyll molecules in position)

Lamella (membrane of thylakoid)

Thylakoid (flat sac of granum)

Stroma (watery matrix)

Deoxyribonucleic acid (DNA) strand

Chloroplast envelope
Outer membrane
Inner membrane

Starch grain

Ribosome (site of protein synthesis)

Stroma thylakoid (link between grana)

Flowers 1

FLOWERS ARE THE SITES OF SEXUAL REPRODUCTION in flowering plants. Their component parts are arranged in whorls around the receptacle (tip of the flower stalk). The sepals (collectively called the calyx) are outermost; typically small and green, they protect the developing flower. The petals (collectively called the corolla) are typically large and brightly coloured; they are found inside the sepals. In monocotyledonous flowers (see pp. 126-127), sepals and petals are indistinguishable; individually they are called tepals (collectively called the perianth). The petals surround the male and female reproductive structures (androecium and gynoecium). The androecium consists of stamens (male organs); each stamen is made up of a filament (stalk) and anther. The gynoecium has one or more carpels (female organs); each carpel consists of an ovary, style, and stigma. Some flowers (e.g., lily) occur singly on a pedicel (flower stalk); others (e.g., elder, sunflower) are arranged in a group (inflorescence) on a peduncle (inflorescence stalk).

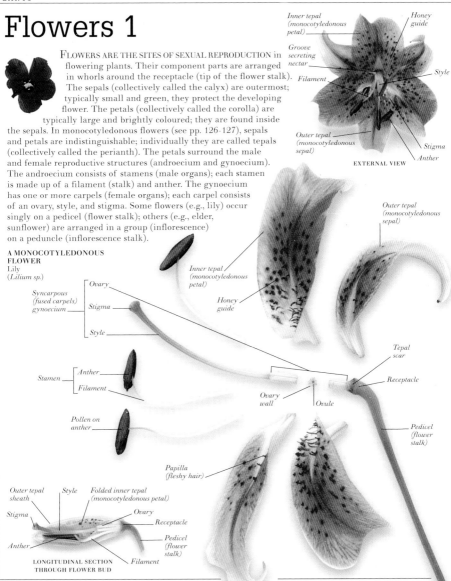

Inner tepal (monocotyledonous petal)

Honey guide

Groove secreting nectar

Filament

Style

Outer tepal (monocotyledonous sepal)

Stigma

Anther

EXTERNAL VIEW

Outer tepal (monocotyledonous sepal)

A MONOCOTYLEDONOUS FLOWER
Lily
(*Lilium sp.*)

Inner tepal (monocotyledonous petal)

Honey guide

Syncarpous (fused carpels) gynoecium

Ovary

Stigma

Style

Tepal scar

Receptacle

Stamen

Anther

Filament

Ovary wall

Ovule

Pollen on anther

Pedicel (flower stalk)

Papilla (fleshy hair)

Outer tepal sheath

Style

Folded inner tepal (monocotyledonous petal)

Stigma

Ovary

Receptacle

Anther

Pedicel (flower stalk)

LONGITUDINAL SECTION THROUGH FLOWER BUD

Filament

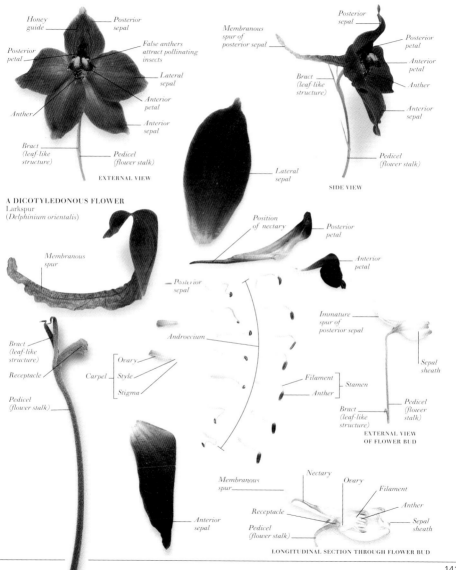

A DICOTYLEDONOUS FLOWER
Larkspur
(*Delphinium orientalis*)

Honey guide

Posterior sepal

Posterior petal

False anthers attract pollinating insects

Lateral sepal

Anterior petal

Anterior sepal

Anther

Bract (leaf-like structure)

Pedicel (flower stalk)

EXTERNAL VIEW

Membranous spur of posterior sepal

Posterior sepal

Posterior petal

Anterior petal

Anther

Bract (leaf-like structure)

Anterior sepal

Pedicel (flower stalk)

SIDE VIEW

Lateral sepal

Membranous spur

Position of nectary

Posterior petal

Anterior petal

Bract (leaf-like structure)

Receptacle

Pedicel (flower stalk)

Posterior sepal

Androecium

Carpel

Ovary

Style

Stigma

Filament

Anther

Stamen

Bract (leaf-like structure)

Immature spur of posterior sepal

Sepal sheath

Pedicel (flower stalk)

EXTERNAL VIEW OF FLOWER BUD

Membranous spur

Anterior sepal

Nectary

Ovary

Filament

Anther

Receptacle

Sepal sheath

Pedicel (flower stalk)

LONGITUDINAL SECTION THROUGH FLOWER BUD

Flowers 2

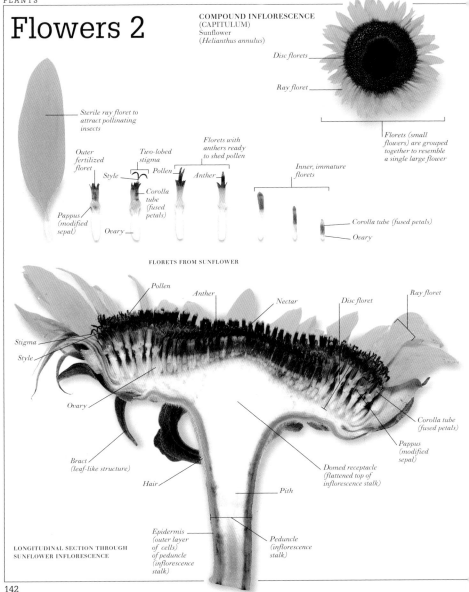

COMPOUND INFLORESCENCE
(CAPITULUM)
Sunflower
(*Helianthus annulus*)

Disc florets

Ray floret

Florets (small flowers) are grouped together to resemble a single large flower

Sterile ray floret to attract pollinating insects

Outer fertilized floret

Two-lobed stigma

Florets with anthers ready to shed pollen

Style

Pollen

Anther

Inner, immature florets

Corolla tube (fused petals)

Pappus (modified sepal)

Ovary

Corolla tube (fused petals)

Ovary

FLORETS FROM SUNFLOWER

Pollen

Anther

Nectar

Disc floret

Ray floret

Stigma

Style

Ovary

Bract (leaf-like structure)

Hair

Corolla tube (fused petals)

Pappus (modified sepal)

Domed receptacle (flattened top of inflorescence stalk)

Pith

Epidermis (outer layer of cells) of peduncle (inflorescence stalk)

Peduncle (inflorescence stalk)

LONGITUDINAL SECTION THROUGH SUNFLOWER INFLORESCENCE

ARRANGEMENT OF FLOWERS ON STEM

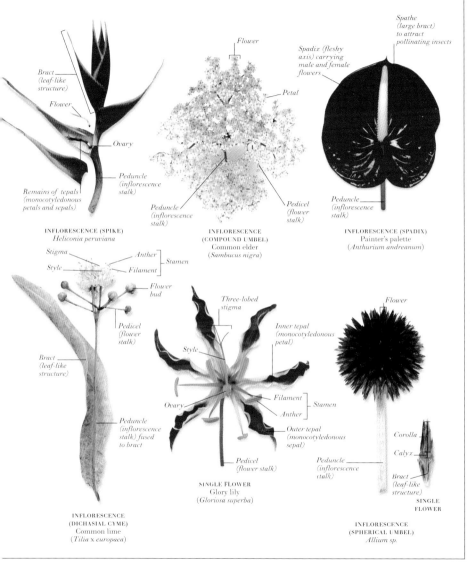

Bract (leaf-like structure)

Flower

Ovary

Peduncle (inflorescence stalk)

Remains of tepals (monocotyledonous petals and sepals)

INFLORESCENCE (SPIKE)
Heliconia peruviana

Flower

Petal

Peduncle (inflorescence stalk)

Pedicel (flower stalk)

INFLORESCENCE (COMPOUND UMBEL)
Common elder
(*Sambucus nigra*)

Spadix (fleshy axis) carrying male and female flowers

Spathe (large bract) to attract pollinating insects

Peduncle (inflorescence stalk)

INFLORESCENCE (SPADIX)
Painter's palette
(*Anthurium andreanum*)

Stigma

Style

Anther

Filament

Stamen

Flower bud

Pedicel (flower stalk)

Bract (leaf-like structure)

Peduncle (inflorescence stalk) fused to bract

INFLORESCENCE (DICHASIAL CYME)
Common lime
(*Tilia x europaea*)

Three-lobed stigma

Style

Inner tepal (monocotyledonous petal)

Ovary

Filament

Anther

Stamen

Outer tepal (monocotyledonous sepal)

Pedicel (flower stalk)

SINGLE FLOWER
Glory lily
(*Gloriosa superba*)

Flower

Peduncle (inflorescence stalk)

INFLORESCENCE (SPHERICAL UMBEL)
Allium sp.

Corolla

Calyx

Bract (leaf-like structure)

SINGLE FLOWER

143

Pollination

POLLINATION IS THE TRANSFER OF POLLEN (which contains the male sex cells) from an anther (part of the male reproductive organ) to a stigma (part of the female reproductive organ). This process precedes fertilization (see pp. 146-147). Pollination may occur within the same flower (self-pollination), or between flowers on separate plants of the same species (cross-pollination). In most plants, pollination is carried out either by insects (entomophilous pollination) or by the wind (anemophilous pollination). Less commonly, birds, bats, or water are the agents of pollination. Insect-pollinated flowers are typically brightly coloured, scented, and produce nectar, on which insects feed. Such flowers also tend to have patterns that are visible only in ultraviolet light, which many insects can see but which humans cannot. These features attract insects, which become covered with the sticky or hooked pollen grains when they visit one flower, and then transfer the pollen to the next flower they visit. Wind-pollinated flowers are generally small, relatively inconspicuous, and unscented. They produce large quantities of light pollen grains that are easily blown by the wind to other flowers.

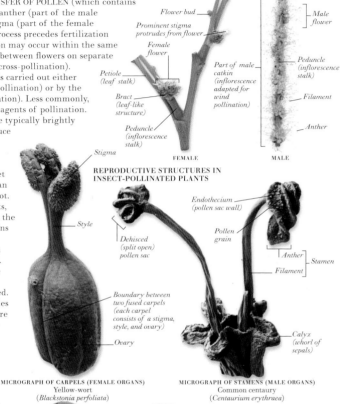

REPRODUCTIVE STRUCTURES IN WIND-POLLINATED PLANT
Sweet chestnut
(*Castanea saliva*)

Flower bud

Prominent stigma protrudes from flower

Female flower

Petiole (*leaf stalk*)

Bract (*leaf-like structure*)

Peduncle (*inflorescence stalk*)

Part of male catkin (*inflorescence adapted for wind pollination*)

FEMALE

Male flower

Peduncle (*inflorescence stalk*)

Filament

Anther

MALE

REPRODUCTIVE STRUCTURES IN INSECT-POLLINATED PLANTS

Stigma

Style

Endothecium (*pollen sac wall*)

Pollen grain

Dehisced (*split open*) pollen sac

Boundary between two fused carpels (*each carpel consists of a stigma, style, and ovary*)

Ovary

Anther

Filament

Stamen

Calyx (*whorl of sepals*)

MICROGRAPHS OF POLLEN GRAINS

Exine (*outer coat of pollen grain*)

Pore

EUROPEAN FIELD ELM
(*Ulmus minor*)

MICROGRAPH OF CARPELS (FEMALE ORGANS)
Yellow-wort
(*Blackstonia perfoliata*)

Colpus (*furrow-shaped aperture*)

Exine (*outer coat of pollen grain*)

JUSTICIA AUREA

Exine (*outer coat of pollen grain*)

Pore

MEADOW CRANESBILL
(*Geranium pratense*)

Baculum (*rod-shaped structure*)

MICROGRAPH OF STAMENS (MALE ORGANS)
Common centaury
(*Centaurium erythraea*)

Colpus (*furrow-shaped aperture*)

Exine (*outer coat of pollen grain*)

Equatorial furrow

BOX-LEAVED MILKWORT
(*Polygala chamaebuxus*)

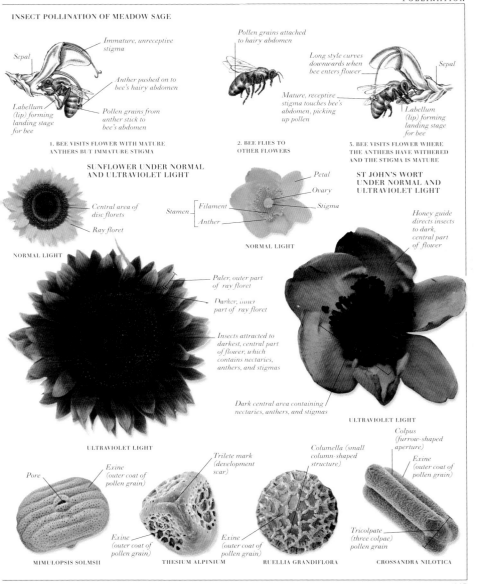

INSECT POLLINATION OF MEADOW SAGE

Sepal

Immature, unreceptive stigma

Anther pushed on to bee's hairy abdomen

Labellum (lip) forming landing stage for bee

Pollen grains from anther stick to bee's abdomen

1. BEE VISITS FLOWER WITH MATURE ANTHERS BUT IMMATURE STIGMA

Pollen grains attached to hairy abdomen

2. BEE FLIES TO OTHER FLOWERS

Long style curves downwards when bee enters flower

Sepal

Mature, receptive stigma touches bee's abdomen, picking up pollen

Labellum (lip) forming landing stage for bee

3. BEE VISITS FLOWER WHERE THE ANTHERS HAVE WITHERED AND THE STIGMA IS MATURE

SUNFLOWER UNDER NORMAL AND ULTRAVIOLET LIGHT

Central area of disc florets

Ray floret

NORMAL LIGHT

Petal

Ovary

Stamen { Filament / Anther }

Stigma

NORMAL LIGHT

ST JOHN'S WORT UNDER NORMAL AND ULTRAVIOLET LIGHT

Honey guide directs insects to dark, central part of flower

Paler, outer part of ray floret

Darker, inner part of ray floret

Insects attracted to darkest, central part of flower, which contains nectaries, anthers, and stigmas

ULTRAVIOLET LIGHT

Dark central area containing nectaries, anthers, and stigmas

ULTRAVIOLET LIGHT

Colpus (furrow-shaped aperture)

Exine (outer coat of pollen grain)

Columella (small column-shaped structure)

Trilete mark (development scar)

Pore

Exine (outer coat of pollen grain)

Exine (outer coat of pollen grain)

Tricolpate (three colpae) pollen grain

MIMULOPSIS SOLMSII

THESIUM ALPINIUM

RUELLIA GRANDIFLORA

CROSSANDRA NILOTICA

Fertilization

FERTILIZATION IS THE FUSION of male and female gametes (sex cells) to produce a zygote (embryo). Following pollination (see pp. 144-145), the pollen grains that contain the male gametes are on the stigma, some distance from the female gamete (ovum) inside the ovule. To enable the gametes to meet, the pollen grain germinates and produces a pollen tube, which grows down and enters the embryo sac (the inner part of the ovule that contains the ovum). Two male gametes, travelling at the tip of the pollen tube, enter the embryo sac. One gamete fuses with the ovum to produce a zygote that will develop into an embryo plant. The other male gamete fuses with two polar nuclei to produce the endosperm, which acts as a food store for the developing embryo. Fertilization also initiates other changes: the integument (outer part of ovule) forms a testa (seed coat) around the embryo and endosperm; the petals fall off; the stigma and style wither; and the ovary wall forms a layer (called the pericarp) around the seed. Together, the pericarp and seed form the fruit, which may be succulent (see pp. 148-149) or dry (see pp. 150-151). In some species (e.g., blackberry), apomixis can occur: the seed develops without fertilization of the ovum by a male gamete but endosperm formation and fruit development take place as in other species.

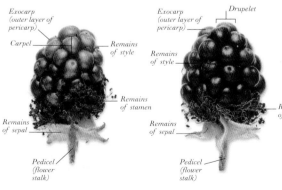

BANANA
(*Musa 'lacatan'*)

DEVELOPMENT OF A SUCCULENT FRUIT
Blackberry
(*Rubus fruticosus*)

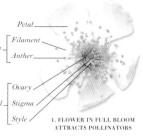

Petal

Stamen
- Filament
- Anther

Carpel
- Ovary
- Stigma
- Style

1. FLOWER IN FULL BLOOM ATTRACTS POLLINATORS

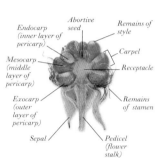

Endocarp (inner layer of pericarp)

Abortive seed

Remains of style

Carpel

Mesocarp (middle layer of pericarp)

Receptacle

Exocarp (outer layer of pericarp)

Remains of stamen

Sepal

Pedicel (flower stalk)

4. PERICARP FORMS FLESH, SKIN, AND A HARD INNER LAYER (SHOWN IN CROSS-SECTION)

Exocarp (outer layer of pericarp)

Carpel

Remains of style

Remains of stamen

Remains of sepal

Pedicel (flower stalk)

7. MESOCARP (FLESHY PART OF PERICARP) OF EACH CARPEL STARTS TO CHANGE COLOUR

Exocarp (outer layer of pericarp)

Drupelet

Remains of style

Remains of stamen

Remains of sepal

Pedicel (flower stalk)

8. CARPELS MATURE INTO DRUPELETS (SMALL FLESHY FRUITS WITH SINGLE SEEDS SURROUNDED BY HARD ENDOCARP)

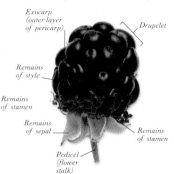

Exocarp (outer layer of pericarp)

Drupelet

Remains of style

Remains of stamen

Pedicel (flower stalk)

9. MESOCARP OF DRUPELET BECOMES DARKER AND SWEETER

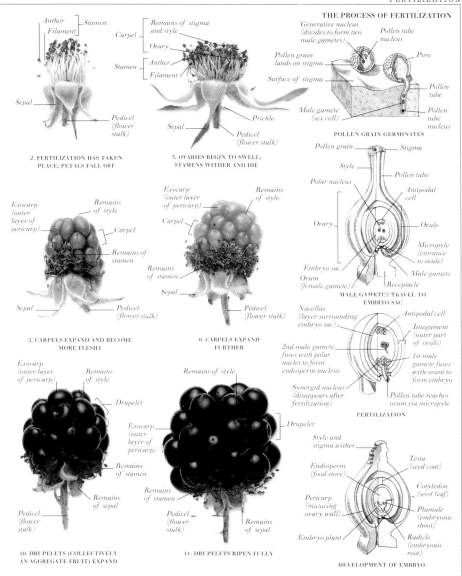

2. FERTILIZATION HAS TAKEN PLACE; PETALS FALL OFF

Anther — Stamen
Filament
Sepal
Pedicel (flower stalk)

3. OVARIES BEGIN TO SWELL; STAMENS WITHER AND DIE

Remains of stigma and style
Carpel
Ovary
Anther — Stamen
Filament
Sepal
Prickle
Pedicel (flower stalk)

THE PROCESS OF FERTILIZATION

Generative nucleus (divides to form two male gametes)
Pollen tube nucleus
Pollen grain lands on stigma
Pore
Surface of stigma
Pollen tube
Male gamete (sex cell)
Pollen tube nucleus

POLLEN GRAIN GERMINATES

5. CARPELS EXPAND AND BECOME MORE FLESHY

Exocarp (outer layer of pericarp)
Remains of style
Carpel
Remains of stamen
Sepal
Pedicel (flower stalk)

6. CARPELS EXPAND FURTHER

Exocarp (outer layer of pericarp)
Remains of style
Carpel
Remains of stamen
Sepal
Pedicel (flower stalk)

Pollen grain
Stigma
Style
Pollen tube
Polar nucleus
Antipodal cell
Ovary
Ovule
Micropyle (entrance to ovule)
Embryo sac
Male gamete
Ovum (female gamete)
Receptacle

MALE GAMETES TRAVEL TO EMBRYO SAC

Nucellus (layer surrounding embryo sac)
Antipodal cell
Integument (outer part of ovule)
2nd male gamete fuses with polar nuclei to form endosperm nucleus
1st male gamete fuses with ovum to form embryo
Synergid nucleus (disappears after fertilization)
Pollen tube reaches ovum via micropyle

FERTILIZATION

10. DRUPELETS (COLLECTIVELY AN AGGREGATE FRUIT) EXPAND

Exocarp (outer layer of pericarp)
Remains of style
Drupelet
Remains of stamen
Remains of sepal
Pedicel (flower stalk)

11. DRUPELETS RIPEN FULLY

Remains of style
Exocarp (outer layer of pericarp)
Drupelet
Remains of stamen
Pedicel (flower stalk)
Remains of sepal

Style and stigma wither
Endosperm (food store)
Testa (seed coat)
Cotyledon (seed leaf)
Pericarp (maturing ovary wall)
Plumule (embryonic shoot)
Embryo plant
Radicle (embryonic root)

DEVELOPMENT OF EMBRYO

Succulent fruits

A FRUIT IS A FULLY DEVELOPED and ripened ovary (seed-producing part of a plant's female reproductive organs). Fruits may be succulent or dry (see pp. 150-151). Succulent fruits are fleshy and brightly coloured, making them attractive to animals, which eat them and so disperse the seeds away from the parent plant. The wall (pericarp) of a succulent fruit has three layers: an outer exocarp, a middle mesocarp, and an inner endocarp. These three layers vary in thickness and texture in different types of fruits and may blend into each other. Succulent fruits can be classed as simple (derived from one ovary) or compound (derived from several ovaries). Simple succulent fruits include berries, which typically have many seeds, and drupes, which typically have a single stone or pip (e.g., cherry and peach). Compound succulent fruits include aggregate fruits, which are formed from many ovaries in one flower, and multiple fruits, which develop from the ovaries of many flowers. Some fruits, known as false fruits or pseudocarps, develop from parts of the flower in addition to the ovaries. For example, the flesh of the apple is formed from the receptacle (the upper end of the flower stalk).

BERRY
Cocoa
(*Theobroma cacao*)

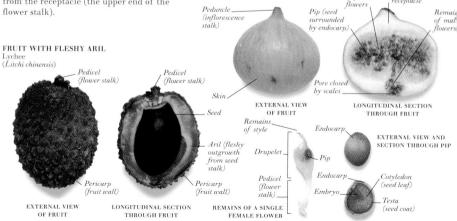

HESPERIDIUM (A TYPE OF BERRY)
Lemon
(*Citrus limon*)

Pedicel (flower stalk)
Endocarp
Mesocarp
Pedicel (flower stalk)
Exocarp
Leathery exocarp
Seed
Vesicle (juice sac)
Oil gland
Placenta
Remains of style
Remains of style

EXTERNAL VIEW OF FRUIT

LONGITUDINAL SECTION THROUGH FRUIT

Hilum (point of attachment to ovary)
Embryo
Seed
Carpel wall
Carpel
Testa (seed coat)
Cotyledon (seed leaf)
Placenta

EXTERNAL VIEW AND SECTION THROUGH SEED

CROSS-SECTION THROUGH FRUIT

SYCONIUM (A TYPE OF FALSE FRUIT)
Fig
(*Ficus carica*)

Peduncle (inflorescence stalk)
Remains of female flowers
Fleshy infolded receptacle
Pip (seed surrounded by endocarp)
Remains of male flowers
Skin
Pore closed by scales

EXTERNAL VIEW OF FRUIT

LONGITUDINAL SECTION THROUGH FRUIT

FRUIT WITH FLESHY ARIL
Lychee
(*Litchi chinensis*)

Pedicel (flower stalk)
Pedicel (flower stalk)
Seed
Skin
Aril (fleshy outgrowth from seed stalk)
Pericarp (fruit wall)
Pericarp (fruit wall)

EXTERNAL VIEW OF FRUIT

LONGITUDINAL SECTION THROUGH FRUIT

Remains of style
Drupelet
Pedicel (flower stalk)
Endocarp
Pip
Endocarp
Embryo

EXTERNAL VIEW AND SECTION THROUGH PIP

Cotyledon (seed leaf)
Testa (seed coat)

REMAINS OF A SINGLE FEMALE FLOWER

BERRY
Cape gooseberry
(*Physalis peruviana*)

Calyx (whorl of sepals)

Calyx (whorl of sepals) surrounding berry

Exocarp of berry

Pedicel (flower stalk)

Pedicel (flower stalk)

EXTERNAL VIEW OF FRUIT

INTERNAL VIEW OF FRUIT

Seed

Placenta

Pericarp

Testa (seed coat)

CROSS-SECTION THROUGH FRUIT

EXTERNAL VIEW OF SEED

AGGREGATE FRUIT
Raspberry
(*Rubus idaeus*)

Remains of stamen

Drupelet

Remains of style

Pedicel (flower stalk)

Mesocarp and exocarp

Pip (seed surrounded by endocarp)

Receptacle

Drupelet

EXTERNAL VIEW OF FRUIT

LONGITUDINAL SECTION THROUGH FRUIT

Hard endocarp

Pip

Hard endocarp

Cotyledon (seed leaf)

Seed

Testa (seed coat)

EXTERNAL VIEW AND SECTION THROUGH PIP

POME (A TYPE OF FALSE FRUIT)
Apple
(*Malus sylvestris*)

Pedicel (flower stalk)

seed

Mesocarp and exocarp

Swollen receptacle

Waxy skin

Endocarp

Vascular strand

EXTERNAL VIEW OF FRUIT

CROSS-SECTION THROUGH FRUIT

Hilum (point of attachment to ovary)

Testa (seed coat)

Embryo

Cotyledon (seed leaf)

Testa (seed coat)

EXTERNAL VIEW AND SECTION THROUGH SEED

PEPO (A TYPE OF BERRY)
Charentais melon
(*Cucumis melo*)

Pedicel (flower stalk)

Rind (fused receptacle and exocarp)

Seed

Rind (fused receptacle and exocarp)

Mesocarp and endocarp

EXTERNAL VIEW OF FRUIT

CROSS-SECTION THROUGH FRUIT

Testa (seed coat)

Embryo

Testa (seed coat)

Cotyledon (seed leaf)

EXTERNAL VIEW AND SECTION THROUGH SEED

Dry fruits

DRY FRUITS HAVE A HARD, DRY PERICARP (fruit wall) around their seeds unlike succulent fruits, which have fleshy pericarps (see pp. 148-149). Dry fruits are divided into three types: dehiscent, in which the pericarp splits open to release the seeds; indehiscent, which do not split open; and schizocarpic, in which the fruit splits but the seeds are not exposed. Dehiscent dry fruits include capsules (e.g., love-in-a-mist), follicles (e.g., delphinium), legumes (e.g., pea), and siliquas (e.g., honesty). Typically, the seeds of dehiscent fruits are dispersed by the wind. Indehiscent dry fruits include nuts (e.g., sweet chestnut), nutlets (e.g., goosegrass), achenes (e.g., strawberry), caryopses (e.g., wheat), samaras (e.g., elm), and cypselas (e.g., dandelion). Some indehiscent dry fruits are dispersed by the wind, assisted by "wings" (e.g., elm) or "parachutes" (e.g., dandelion); others (e.g., goosegrass) have hooked pericarps to aid dispersal on animals' fur. Schizocarpic dry fruits include cremocarps (e.g., hogweed), and double samaras (e.g., sycamore); these are dispersed by the wind.

NUTLET
Goosegrass
(*Galium aparine*)

LEGUME
Pea
(*Pisum sativum*)

Pedicel (flower stalk)

Receptacle

Remains of sepal

Remains of stamen

Placenta

Pericarp (fruit wall)

Remains of style and stigma

EXTERNAL VIEW OF FRUIT

Pedicel (flower stalk)

Receptacle

Remains of sepal

Funicle (stalk attaching seed to placenta)

Pericarp (fruit wall)

Seed

Remains of style and stigma

INTERNAL VIEW OF FRUIT

Funicle (stalk attaching seed to placenta)

Micropyle (pore for water absorption)

Testa (seed coat)

Cotyledon (seed leaf)

Radicle (embryonic root)

Testa (seed coat)

Plumule (embryonic shoot)

EXTERIOR VIEW AND SECTION THROUGH SEED

NUT
Sweet chestnut
(*Castanea sativa*)

Line of splitting between valves of cupule

Peduncle (inflorescence stalk)

Remains of male inflorescence

Nut (indehiscent fruit)

Spiky cupule (husk around fruit formed from bracts)

EXTERNAL VIEW OF FRUIT WITH SURROUNDING CUPULE

Remains of stigma

Remains of style

Nut (indehiscent fruit)

Remains of stigma

Remains of style

Remains of stigma

Remains of style

Embryo

Cotyledon (seed leaf)

Testa (seed coat)

Woody pericarp (fruit wall)

Woody pericarp (fruit wall)

EXTERNAL VIEW AND SECTION THROUGH FRUIT

ACHENE
Strawberry
(*Fragaria* x *ananassa*)

Sepal

Swollen receptacle

Remains of stigma and style

Achene (one-seeded dry fruit)

Pedicel (flower stalk)

Sepal

Pedicel (flower stalk)

Swollen fleshy tissues of receptacle

EXTERNAL VIEW OF FRUIT

LONGITUDINAL SECTION THROUGH FRUIT

Pericarp (fruit wall)

Pericarp (fruit wall)

Cotyledon (seed leaf)

Testa (seed coat)

EXTERNAL VIEW AND SECTION THROUGH SEED

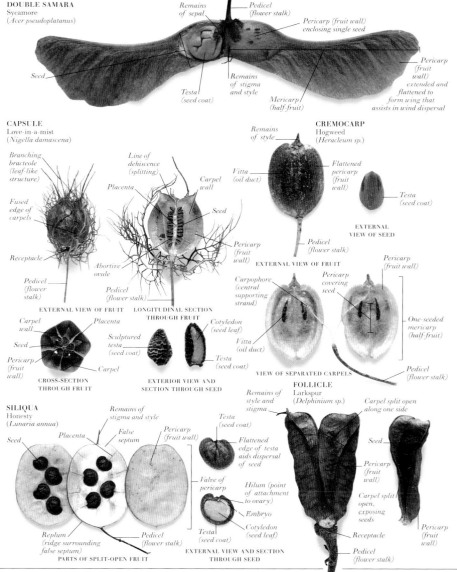

DOUBLE SAMARA
Sycamore
(*Acer pseudoplatanus*)

Remains of sepal

Pedicel (flower stalk)

Pericarp (fruit wall) enclosing single seed

Pericarp (fruit wall) extended and flattened to form wing that assists in wind dispersal

Seed

Testa (seed coat)

Remains of stigma and style

Mericarp (half-fruit)

CAPSULE
Love-in-a-mist
(*Nigella damascena*)

Branching bracteole (leaf-like structure)

Fused edge of carpels

Receptacle

Pedicel (flower stalk)

Line of dehiscence (splitting)

Placenta

Carpel wall

Seed

Pericarp (fruit wall)

Abortive ovule

Pedicel (flower stalk)

EXTERNAL VIEW OF FRUIT

LONGITUDINAL SECTION THROUGH FRUIT

Carpel wall

Placenta

Seed

Pericarp (fruit wall)

Carpel

CROSS-SECTION THROUGH FRUIT

Sculptured testa (seed coat)

Cotyledon (seed leaf)

Testa (seed coat)

EXTERIOR VIEW AND SECTION THROUGH SEED

CREMOCARP
Hogweed
(*Heracleum sp.*)

Remains of style

Vitta (oil duct)

Flattened pericarp (fruit wall)

Testa (seed coat)

EXTERNAL VIEW OF SEED

Pedicel (flower stalk)

EXTERNAL VIEW OF FRUIT

Carpophore (central supporting strand)

Pericarp (fruit wall)

Pericarp covering seed

One-seeded mericarp (half-fruit)

Vitta (oil duct)

Pedicel (flower stalk)

VIEW OF SEPARATED CARPELS

SILIQUA
Honesty
(*Lunaria annua*)

Remains of stigma and style

Placenta

Seed

False septum

Pericarp (fruit wall)

FOLLICLE
Larkspur
(*Delphinium sp.*)

Remains of style and stigma

Testa (seed coat)

Flattened edge of testa aids dispersal of seed

Valve of pericarp

Hilum (point of attachment to ovary)

Embryo

Cotyledon (seed leaf)

Testa (seed coat)

Carpel split open along one side

Seed

Pericarp (fruit wall)

Carpel split open, exposing seeds

Receptacle

Pericarp (fruit wall)

Pedicel (flower stalk)

Replum (ridge surrounding false septum)

Pedicel (flower stalk)

PARTS OF SPLIT-OPEN FRUIT

EXTERNAL VIEW AND SECTION THROUGH SEED

Germination

GERMINATION IS THE GROWTH OF SEEDS INTO SEEDLINGS. It starts when seeds become active below ground, and ends when the first foliage leaves appear above ground. A seed consists of an embryo and its food store, surrounded by a testa (seed coat). The embryo is made up of one or two cotyledons (seed leaves) attached to a central axis. The upper part of the axis consists of an epicotyl, which has a plumule (embryonic shoot) at its tip. The lower part of the axis consists of a hypocotyl and a radicle (embryonic root). After dispersal from the parent plant, the seeds dehydrate and enter a period of dormancy. Following this dormant period, germination begins, provided that the seeds have enough water, oxygen, warmth, and, in some cases, light. In the first stages of germination, the seed takes in water; the embryo starts to use its food store; and the radicle swells, breaks through the testa, and grows downwards. Germination then proceeds in one of two ways, depending on the type of seed. In epigeal germination, the hypocotyl lengthens, pulling the plumule and its protective cotyledons out of the soil. In hypogeal germination, the cotyledons remain below ground and the epicotyl lengthens, pushing the plumule upwards.

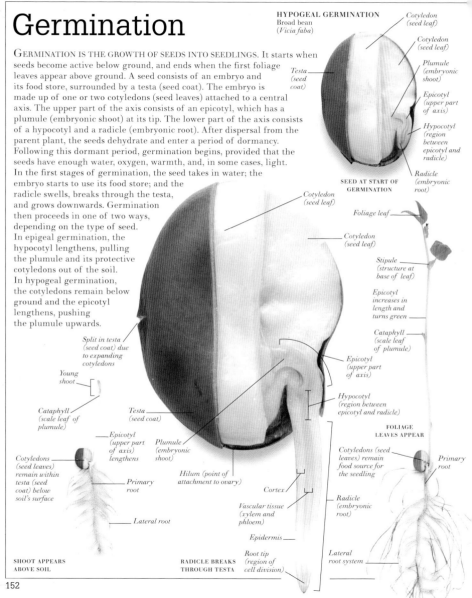

HYPOGEAL GERMINATION
Broad bean
(*Vicia faba*)

Cotyledon (seed leaf)

Cotyledon (seed leaf)

Plumule (embryonic shoot)

Epicotyl (upper part of axis)

Hypocotyl (region between epicotyl and radicle)

Testa (seed coat)

Radicle (embryonic root)

SEED AT START OF GERMINATION

Cotyledon (seed leaf)

Foliage leaf

Cotyledon (seed leaf)

Stipule (structure at base of leaf)

Epicotyl increases in length and turns green

Cataphyll (scale leaf of plumule)

Epicotyl (upper part of axis)

Hypocotyl (region between epicotyl and radicle)

FOLIAGE LEAVES APPEAR

Cotyledons (seed leaves) remain food source for the seedling

Primary root

Radicle (embryonic root)

Lateral root system

Split in testa (seed coat) due to expanding cotyledons

Young shoot

Cataphyll (scale leaf of plumule)

Testa (seed coat)

Epicotyl (upper part of axis) lengthens

Plumule (embryonic shoot)

Hilum (point of attachment to ovary)

Cortex

Vascular tissue (xylem and phloem)

Epidermis

Root tip (region of cell division)

Cotyledons (seed leaves) remain within testa (seed coat) below soil's surface

Primary root

Lateral root

SHOOT APPEARS ABOVE SOIL

RADICLE BREAKS THROUGH TESTA

Cotyledons (seed leaves) remain food source for the seedling

Primary root

Radicle (embryonic root)

Lateral root system

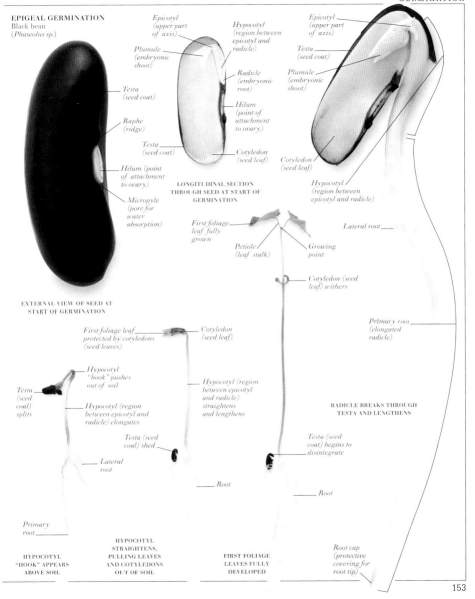

EPIGEAL GERMINATION
Black bean
(*Phaseolus sp.*)

Testa (seed coat)

Raphe (ridge)

Hilum (point of attachment to ovary)

Micropyle (pore for water absorption)

EXTERNAL VIEW OF SEED AT START OF GERMINATION

Epicotyl (upper part of axis)

Plumule (embryonic shoot)

Hypocotyl (region between epicotyl and radicle)

Radicle (embryonic root)

Hilum (point of attachment to ovary)

Testa (seed coat)

Cotyledon (seed leaf)

LONGITUDINAL SECTION THROUGH SEED AT START OF GERMINATION

Epicotyl (upper part of axis)

Testa (seed coat)

Plumule (embryonic shoot)

Cotyledon (seed leaf)

Hypocotyl (region between epicotyl and radicle)

Lateral root

Primary root (elongated radicle)

RADICLE BREAKS THROUGH TESTA AND LENGTHENS

First foliage leaf fully grown

Petiole (leaf stalk)

Growing point

Cotyledon (seed leaf) withers

First foliage leaf protected by cotyledons (seed leaves)

Cotyledon (seed leaf)

Hypocotyl "hook" pushes out of soil

Hypocotyl (region between epicotyl and radicle) straightens and lengthens

Testa (seed coat) begins to disintegrate

Testa (seed coat) splits

Hypocotyl (region between epicotyl and radicle) elongates

Testa (seed coat) shed

Lateral root

Root

Root

Primary root

Root cap (protective covering for root tip)

HYPOCOTYL "HOOK" APPEARS ABOVE SOIL

HYPOCOTYL STRAIGHTENS, PULLING LEAVES AND COTYLEDONS OUT OF SOIL

FIRST FOLIAGE LEAVES FULLY DEVELOPED

153

Vegetative reproduction

ADVENTITIOUS BUD
Mexican hat plant
(*Kalanchoe daigremontiana*)

MANY PLANTS CAN PROPAGATE THEMSELVES by vegetative reproduction. In this process, part of a plant separates off, takes root, and grows into a new plant. Vegetative reproduction is a type of asexual reproduction; that is, it involves only one parent, and there is no fusion of gametes (sex cells). Plants use various structures to reproduce vegetatively. Some plants use underground storage organs. Such organs include rhizomes (horizontal, underground stems), the branches of which produce new plants;

CORM
Gladiolus
(*Gladiolus sp.*)

bulbs (swollen leaf bases) and corms (swollen stems), which produce daughter bulbs or corms that separate off from the parent; and stem tubers (thickened underground stems) and root tubers (swollen adventitious roots), which also separate off from the parent. Other propagative structures include runners and stolons, creeping horizontal stems that take root and produce new plants; bulbils, small bulbs that develop on the stem or in the place of flowers, and then drop off and grow into new plants; and adventitious buds, miniature plants that form on leaf margins before dropping to the ground and growing into mature plants.

Apex of leaf

Lamina (blade) of leaf

Leaf margin

Notch in leaf margin containing meristematic (actively dividing) cells

Adventitious bud (detachable bud with adventitious roots) drops from leaf

Petiole (leaf stalk)

BULBIL IN PLACE OF FLOWER
Orange lily
(*Lilium bulbiferum*)

Scar left by flower

Leaf

Pedicel (flower stalk)

Detachable bulbil formed in place of flower

Peduncle (inflorescence stalk)

STOLON
Ground ivy
(*Glechoma hederacea*)

Terminal bud

Internode

Node

Node

Parent plant

Stolon (creeping stem)

Adventitious root of daughter plant

Daughter plant developed from lateral bud

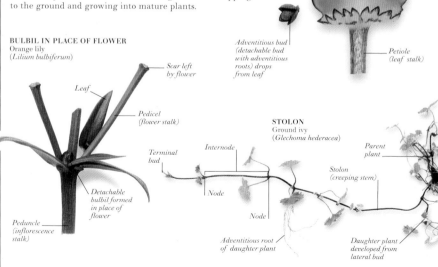

154

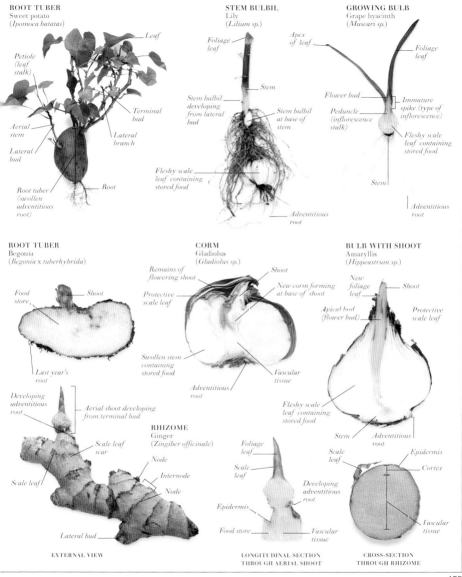

ROOT TUBER
Sweet potato
(*Ipomoea batatas*)

Leaf

Petiole
(leaf
stalk)

Terminal
bud

Aerial
stem

Lateral
branch

Lateral
bud

Root tuber
(swollen
adventitious
root)

Root

STEM BULBIL
Lily
(*Lilium sp.*)

Foliage
leaf

Stem

Stem bulbil
developing
from lateral
bud

Stem bulbil
at base of
stem

Fleshy scale
leaf containing
stored food

Adventitious
root

GROWING BULB
Grape hyacinth
(*Muscari sp.*)

Apex
of leaf

Foliage
leaf

Flower bud

Immature
spike (type of
inflorescence)

Peduncle
(inflorescence
stalk)

Fleshy scale
leaf containing
stored food

Stem

Adventitious
root

ROOT TUBER
Begonia
(*Begonia* x *tuberhybrida*)

Food
store

Shoot

Last year's
root

Developing
adventitious
root

Aerial shoot developing
from terminal bud

Scale leaf
scar

Scale leaf

Lateral bud

EXTERNAL VIEW

CORM
Gladiolus
(*Gladiolus sp.*)

Remains of
flowering shoot

Protective
scale leaf

Shoot

New corm forming
at base of shoot

Swollen stem
containing
stored food

Adventitious
root

Vascular
tissue

RHIZOME
Ginger
(*Zingiber officinale*)

Foliage
leaf

Scale
leaf

Developing
adventitious
root

Epidermis

Food store

Vascular
tissue

LONGITUDINAL SECTION
THROUGH AERIAL SHOOT

Node

Internode

Node

BULB WITH SHOOT
Amaryllis
(*Hippeastrum sp.*)

New
foliage
leaf

Shoot

Apical bud
(flower bud)

Protective
scale leaf

Fleshy scale
leaf containing
stored food

Stem

Adventitious
root

Scale
leaf

Epidermis

Cortex

Vascular
tissue

CROSS-SECTION
THROUGH RHIZOME

Dryland plants

LEAF SUCCULENT
Lithops sp.

DRYLAND PLANTS (XEROPHYTES) are able to survive in unfavourable habitats. All are found in places where little water is available; some live in high temperatures that cause excessive loss of water from the leaves. Xerophytes show a number of adaptations to dry conditions; these include reduced leaf area, rolled leaves, sunken stomata, hairs, spines, and thick cuticles. One group, succulent plants, stores water in specially enlarged spongy tissues found in leaves, roots, or stems. Leaf succulents have enlarged, fleshy, water-storing leaves. Root succulents have a large, underground water-storage organ with short-lived stems and leaves above ground. Stem succulents are represented by the cacti (family Cactaceae). Cacti stems are fleshy, green, and photosynthetic; they are typically ribbed or covered by tubercles in rows, with leaves being reduced to spines or entirely absent.

STEM SUCCULENT
Golden barrel cactus
(*Echinocactus grusonii*)

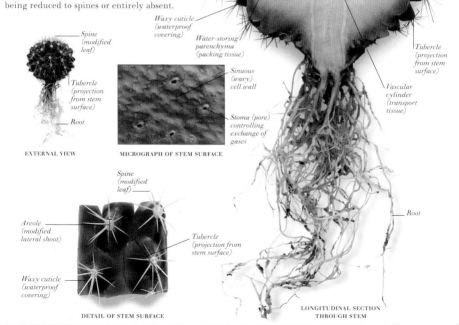

Areole (modified lateral shoot)

Trichome (hair)

Spine (modified leaf)

Waxy cuticle (waterproof covering)

Water-storing parenchyma (packing tissue)

Tubercle (projection from stem surface)

Vascular cylinder (transport tissue)

Spine (modified leaf)

Tubercle (projection from stem surface)

Root

Sinuous (wavy) cell wall

Stoma (pore) controlling exchange of gases

EXTERNAL VIEW

MICROGRAPH OF STEM SURFACE

Spine (modified leaf)

Areole (modified lateral shoot)

Tubercle (projection from stem surface)

Waxy cuticle (waterproof covering)

DETAIL OF STEM SURFACE

Root

LONGITUDINAL SECTION THROUGH STEM

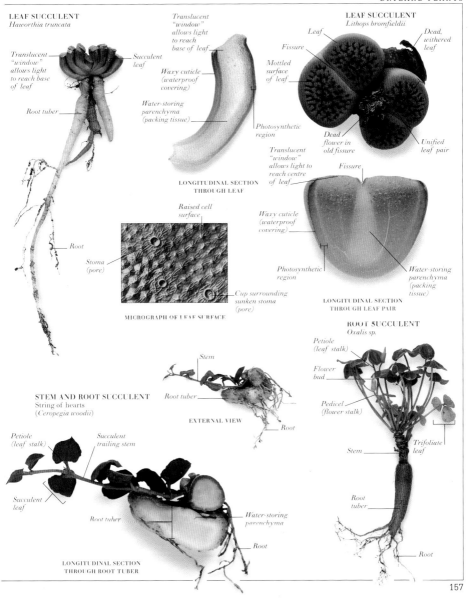

LEAF SUCCULENT
Haworthia truncata

Translucent "window" allows light to reach base of leaf

Succulent leaf

Root tuber

Root

Translucent "window" allows light to reach base of leaf

Waxy cuticle (waterproof covering)

Water-storing parenchyma (packing tissue)

Photosynthetic region

LONGITUDINAL SECTION THROUGH LEAF

LEAF SUCCULENT
Lithops bromfieldii

Leaf

Fissure

Dead, withered leaf

Mottled surface of leaf

Dead flower in old fissure

Unified leaf pair

Fissure

Translucent "window" allows light to reach centre of leaf

Waxy cuticle (waterproof covering)

Photosynthetic region

Water-storing parenchyma (packing tissue)

LONGITUDINAL SECTION THROUGH LEAF PAIR

Raised cell surface

Stoma (pore)

Cup surrounding sunken stoma (pore)

MICROGRAPH OF LEAF SURFACE

ROOT SUCCULENT
Oxalis sp.

Petiole (leaf stalk)

Flower bud

Pedicel (flower stalk)

Trifoliate leaf

Stem

Root tuber

Root

Stem

Root tuber

Root

EXTERNAL VIEW

STEM AND ROOT SUCCULENT
String of hearts
(*Ceropegia woodii*)

Petiole (leaf stalk)

Succulent trailing stem

Succulent leaf

Root tuber

Water-storing parenchyma

Root

LONGITUDINAL SECTION THROUGH ROOT TUBER

Wetland plants

WETLAND PLANTS GROW SUBMERGED IN WATER, either partially (e.g., water hyacinth) or completely (e.g., pond weeds), and show various adaptations to this habitat. Typically, there are numerous air spaces inside the stems, leaves, and roots; these aid gas exchange and buoyancy. Submerged parts generally have no cuticle (waterproof covering), enabling the plants to absorb minerals and gases directly from the water; in addition, being supported by the water, they need little of the supportive tissue found in land plants. Stomata, the gas exchange pores, are absent from plants that are completely submerged; in partially submerged plants with floating leaves (e.g., water lilies), stomata are found on the upper leaf surfaces, where they cannot be flooded.

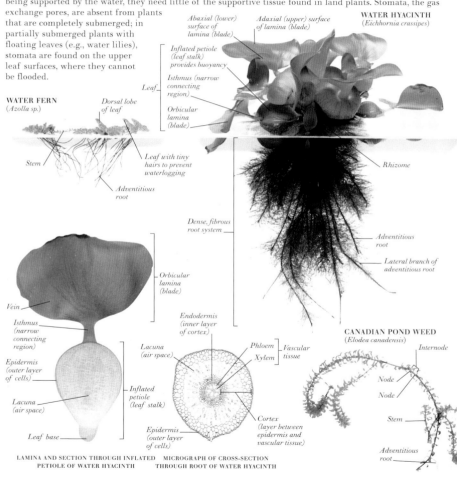

WATER FERN
(*Azolla sp.*)

Dorsal lobe of leaf

Stem

Leaf with tiny hairs to prevent waterlogging

Adventitious root

Abaxial (lower) surface of lamina (blade)

Adaxial (upper) surface of lamina (blade)

WATER HYACINTH
(*Eichhornia crassipes*)

Inflated petiole (leaf stalk) provides buoyancy

Isthmus (narrow connecting region)

Leaf

Orbicular lamina (blade)

Rhizome

Dense, fibrous root system

Adventitious root

Lateral branch of adventitious root

Orbicular lamina (blade)

Vein

Isthmus (narrow connecting region)

Epidermis (outer layer of cells)

Lacuna (air space)

Inflated petiole (leaf stalk)

Leaf base

Endodermis (inner layer of cortex)

Lacuna (air space)

Epidermis (outer layer of cells)

Phloem
Xylem

Vascular tissue

Cortex (layer between epidermis and vascular tissue)

CANADIAN POND WEED
(*Elodea canadensis*)

Internode

Node

Node

Stem

Adventitious root

LAMINA AND SECTION THROUGH INFLATED
PETIOLE OF WATER HYACINTH

MICROGRAPH OF CROSS-SECTION
THROUGH ROOT OF WATER HYACINTH

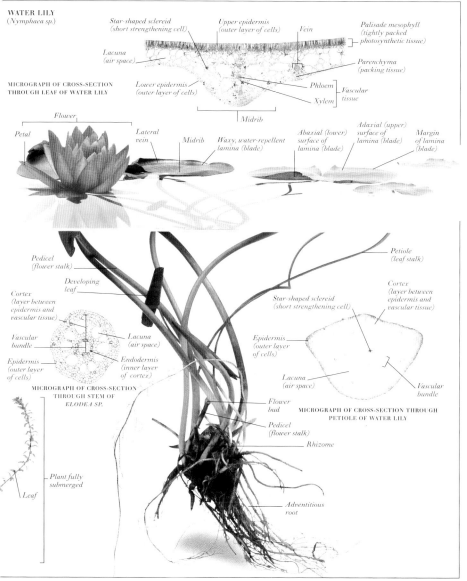

WATER LILY
(*Nymphaca sp.*)

Star-shaped sclereid
(short strengthening cell)

Upper epidermis
(outer layer of cells)

Vein

Palisade mesophyll
(tightly packed
photosynthetic tissue)

Lacuna
(air space)

Parenchyma
(packing tissue)

MICROGRAPH OF CROSS-SECTION
THROUGH LEAF OF WATER LILY

Lower epidermis
(outer layer of cells)

Phloem
Xylem

Vascular
tissue

Midrib

Flower

Petal

Lateral
vein

Midrib

Waxy, water-repellent
lamina (blade)

Abaxial (lower)
surface of
lamina (blade)

Adaxial (upper)
surface of
lamina (blade)

Margin
of lamina
(blade)

Pedicel
(flower stalk)

Developing
leaf

Petiole
(leaf stalk)

Cortex
(layer between
epidermis and
vascular tissue)

Vascular
bundle

Lacuna
(air space)

Star-shaped sclereid
(short strengthening cell)

Cortex
(layer between
epidermis and
vascular tissue)

Epidermis
(outer layer
of cells)

Epidermis
(outer layer
of cells)

Endodermis
(inner layer
of cortex)

Lacuna
(air space)

Vascular
bundle

MICROGRAPH OF CROSS-SECTION
THROUGH STEM OF
ELODEA SP.

MICROGRAPH OF CROSS-SECTION THROUGH
PETIOLE OF WATER LILY

Flower
bud

Pedicel
(flower stalk)

Rhizome

Plant fully
submerged

Leaf

Adventitious
root

159

Carnivorous plants

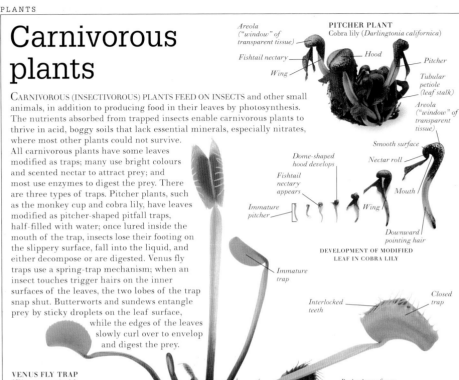

Areola ("window" of transparent tissue)

Fishtail nectary

Wing

Hood

Pitcher

Tubular petiole (leaf stalk)

Areola ("window" of transparent tissue)

CARNIVOROUS (INSECTIVOROUS) PLANTS FEED ON INSECTS and other small animals, in addition to producing food in their leaves by photosynthesis. The nutrients absorbed from trapped insects enable carnivorous plants to thrive in acid, boggy soils that lack essential minerals, especially nitrates, where most other plants could not survive. All carnivorous plants have some leaves modified as traps; many use bright colours and scented nectar to attract prey; and most use enzymes to digest the prey. There are three types of traps. Pitcher plants, such as the monkey cup and cobra lily, have leaves modified as pitcher-shaped pitfall traps, half-filled with water; once lured inside the mouth of the trap, insects lose their footing on the slippery surface, fall into the liquid, and either decompose or are digested. Venus fly traps use a spring-trap mechanism; when an insect touches trigger hairs on the inner surfaces of the leaves, the two lobes of the trap snap shut. Butterworts and sundews entangle prey by sticky droplets on the leaf surface, while the edges of the leaves slowly curl over to envelop and digest the prey.

Dome-shaped hood develops

Fishtail nectary appears

Immature pitcher

Smooth surface

Nectar roll

Wing

Mouth

Downward pointing hair

DEVELOPMENT OF MODIFIED LEAF IN COBRA LILY

Immature trap

Interlocked teeth

Closed trap

VENUS FLY TRAP
(*Dionaea muscipula*)

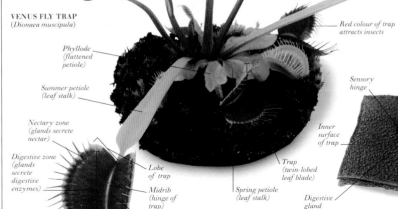

Phyllode (flattened petiole)

Summer petiole (leaf stalk)

Nectary zone (glands secrete nectar)

Digestive zone (glands secrete digestive enzymes)

Tooth

Lobe of trap

Midrib (hinge of trap)

Trigger hair

Red colour of trap attracts insects

Sensory hinge

Trigger hair

Inner surface of trap

Trap (twin-lobed leaf blade)

Spring petiole (leaf stalk)

Digestive gland

MICROGRAPH OF LOBE OF VENUS FLY TRAP

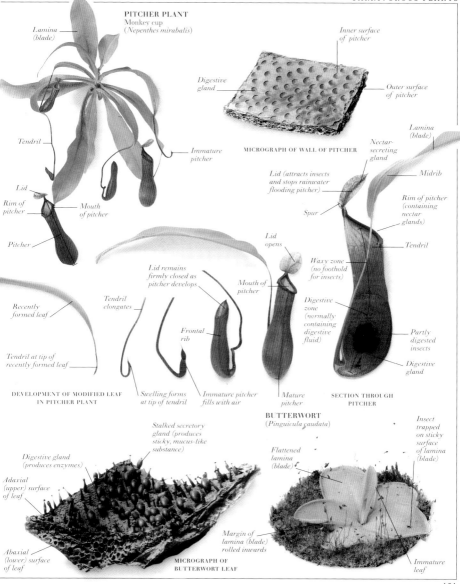

PITCHER PLANT
Monkey cup
(*Nepenthes mirabalis*)

Lamina
(blade)

Tendril

Lid

Rim of
pitcher

Mouth
of pitcher

Pitcher

Immature
pitcher

Inner surface
of pitcher

Digestive
gland

Outer surface
of pitcher

MICROGRAPH OF WALL OF PITCHER

Lamina
(blade)

Nectar-
secreting
gland

Midrib

Lid (attracts insects
and stops rainwater
flooding pitcher)

Rim of pitcher
(containing
nectar
glands)

Spur

Tendril

Waxy zone
(no foothold
for insects)

Lid
opens

Mouth of
pitcher

Digestive
zone
(normally
containing
digestive
fluid)

Partly
digested
insects

Digestive
gland

Recently
formed leaf

Lid remains
firmly closed as
pitcher develops

Tendril
elongates

Frontal
rib

Tendril at tip of
recently formed leaf

Swelling forms
at tip of tendril

Immature pitcher
fills with air

Mature
pitcher

DEVELOPMENT OF MODIFIED LEAF
IN PITCHER PLANT

SECTION THROUGH
PITCHER

BUTTERWORT
(*Pinguicula caudata*)

Stalked secretory
gland (produces
sticky, mucus-like
substance)

Insect
trapped
on sticky
surface
of lamina
(blade)

Digestive gland
(produces enzymes)

Flattened
lamina
(blade)

Adaxial
(upper) surface
of leaf

Abaxial
(lower) surface
of leaf

MICROGRAPH OF
BUTTERWORT LEAF

Margin of
lamina (blade)
rolled inwards

Immature
leaf

Epiphytic and parasitic plants

EPIPHYTIC AND PARASITIC PLANTS GROW ON OTHER LIVING PLANTS. Typically, epiphytic plants are not rooted in the soil; instead, they live above ground level on the stems and branches of other plants. Epiphytes obtain water from trapped rainwater and from moisture in the air, and minerals from organic matter that has accumulated on the surface of the plant on which they are growing. Like other green plants, epiphytes produce their food by photosynthesis. Epiphytes include tropical orchids and bromeliads (air plants), and some mosses that live in temperate regions. Parasitic plants obtain all their nutrient requirements from the host plants on which they grow. The parasites produce haustoria, root-like organs that penetrate the stem or roots of the host and grow inwards to merge with the host's vascular tissue, from which the parasite extracts water, minerals, and manufactured nutrients. As they have no need to produce their own food, parasitic plants lack chlorophyll, the green photosynthetic pigment, and they have no foliage leaves. Partial parasitic plants (e.g., mistletoe) obtain water and minerals from the host plant but have green leaves and stems and are therefore able to produce their own food by photosynthesis.

EPIPHYTIC ORCHID
Brassavola nodosa

Peduncle
(inflorescence
stalk)

Pedicel
(flower
stalk)

Flower

Scale
leaf

Leaf

Aerial
root

Node

Stem

Bark of tree to
which epiphyte
is attached

Inflorescence
(spike)

Peduncle
(inflorescence
stalk)

Flower
bud

Strap shaped
arching leaf
(part of rosette
of leaves)

Leaf margin
with spines

Overlapping leaf
bases in which
rainwater is trapped

EPIPHYTIC BROMELIAD
Aechmea miniata

Mass of
adventitious roots

Stem

Bark of tree to
which epiphyte
is attached

Velamen
(multi-layered epidermis
capable of absorbing
water from rain or
condensation)

Cortex
(layer between
epidermis and
vascular tissue)

Cortex cell
containing
chloroplasts

Vascular
tissue

Xylem

Phloem

Exodermis
(outer layer
of cortex)

Pith

Endodermis
(inner layer
of cortex)

MICROGRAPH OF CROSS-SECTION THROUGH
AERIAL ROOT OF EPIPHYTIC ORCHID

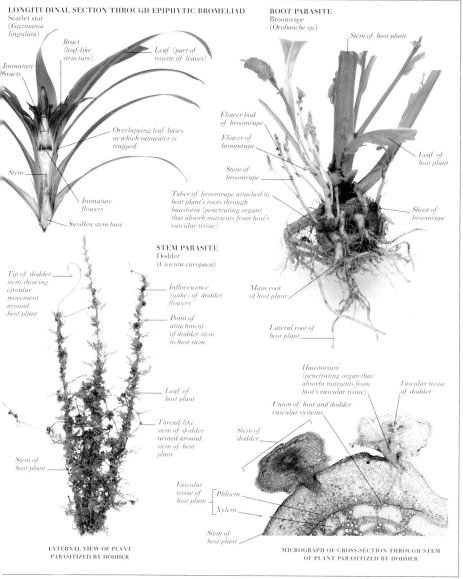

LONGITUDINAL SECTION THROUGH EPIPHYTIC BROMELIAD
Scarlet star
(*Guzmania lingulata*)

Bract (*leaf-like structure*)

Leaf (*part of rosette of leaves*)

Immature bracts

Overlapping leaf bases in which rainwater is trapped

Stem

Immature flowers

Swollen stem base

ROOT PARASITE
Broomrape
(*Orobanche sp.*)

Stem of host plant

Flower bud of broomrape

Flower of broomrape

Stem of broomrape

Tuber of broomrape attached to host plant's roots through haustoria (*penetrating organs that absorb nutrients from host's vascular tissue*)

Leaf of host plant

Shoot of broomrape

Main root of host plant

Lateral root of host plant

STEM PARASITE
Dodder
(*Cuscuta europaea*)

Tip of dodder stem showing circular movement around host plant

Inflorescence (spike) of dodder flowers

Point of attachment of dodder stem to host stem

Leaf of host plant

Thread-like stem of dodder twined around stem of host plant

Stem of host plant

Haustorium (*penetrating organ that absorbs nutrients from host's vascular tissue*)

Vascular tissue of dodder

Union of host and dodder vascular systems

Stem of dodder

Vascular tissue of host plant [Phloem / Xylem]

Stem of host plant

EXTERNAL VIEW OF PLANT PARASITIZED BY DODDER

MICROGRAPH OF CROSS-SECTION THROUGH STEM OF PLANT PARASITIZED BY DODDER

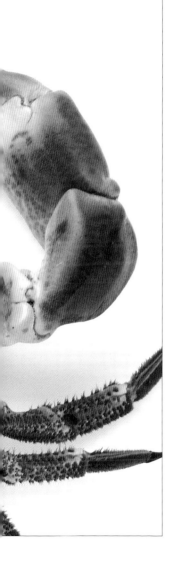

ANIMALS

Sponges, jellyfish, and sea anemones

SPONGES ARE MAINLY MARINE animals that make up the phylum Porifera. They are among the simplest of all animals, having no tissues or organs. Their bodies consist of two layers of cells separated by a jelly-like layer (mesohyal) that is strengthened by mineral spicules or protein fibres. The body is perforated by a system of pores and water channels called the aquiferous system. Special cells (choanocytes) with whip-like structures (flagella) draw water through the aquiferous system, thereby bringing tiny food particles to the sponge's cells. Jellyfish (class Scyphozoa), sea anemones (class Anthozoa), and corals (also class Anthozoa) belong to the phylum Cnidaria, also known as Coelenterata. More complex than sponges, coelenterates have simple tissues, such as nervous tissue; a radially symmetrical body; and a mouth surrounded by tentacles with unique stinging cells (cnidocytes).

INTERNAL ANATOMY OF A SPONGE

Amoebocyte
Osculum (excurrent pore)
Choanocyte (collar cell)
Ostium (incurrent pore)
Porocyte (pore cell)
Mesohyal
Spongocoel (atrium; paragaster)
Spicule
Pinacocyte (epidermal cell)
Ostium (incurrent pore)

SKELETON OF A SPONGE

Protein matrix
Pore

EXTERNAL FEATURES OF A SEA ANEMONE

Tentacle

EXAMPLES OF SEA ANEMONES

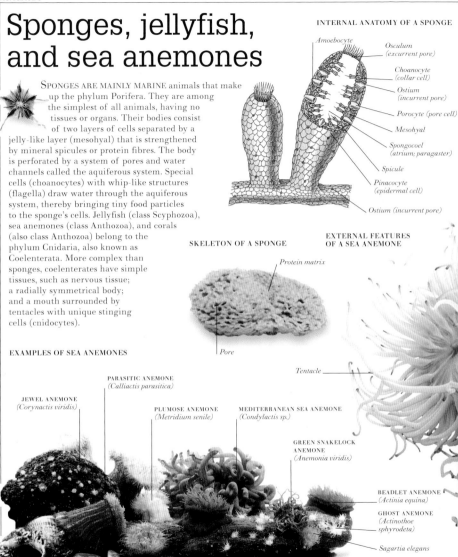

PARASITIC ANEMONE (*Calliactis parasitica*)

JEWEL ANEMONE (*Corynactis viridis*)

PLUMOSE ANEMONE (*Metridium senile*)

MEDITERRANEAN SEA ANEMONE (*Condylactis sp.*)

GREEN SNAKELOCK ANEMONE (*Anemonia viridis*)

BEADLET ANEMONE (*Actinia equina*)

GHOST ANEMONE (*Actinothoe sphyrodeta*)

Sagartia elegans

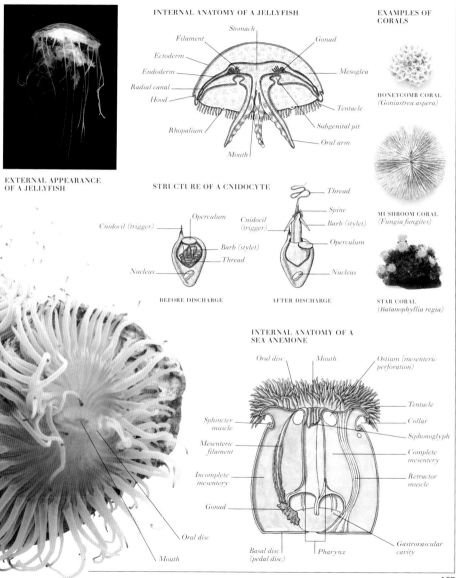

INTERNAL ANATOMY OF A JELLYFISH

- Stomach
- Filament
- Ectoderm
- Endoderm
- Radial canal
- Hood
- Rhopalium
- Gonad
- Mesoglea
- Tentacle
- Subgenital pit
- Oral arm
- Mouth

EXTERNAL APPEARANCE OF A JELLYFISH

EXAMPLES OF CORALS

HONEYCOMB CORAL
(*Goniastrea aspera*)

MUSHROOM CORAL
(*Fungia fungites*)

STAR CORAL
(*Balanophyllia regia*)

STRUCTURE OF A CNIDOCYTE

- Operculum
- Cnidocil (trigger)
- Barb (stylet)
- Thread
- Nucleus

BEFORE DISCHARGE

- Thread
- Spine
- Cnidocil (trigger)
- Barb (stylet)
- Operculum
- Nucleus

AFTER DISCHARGE

INTERNAL ANATOMY OF A SEA ANEMONE

- Oral disc
- Mouth
- Ostium (mesenteric perforation)
- Sphincter muscle
- Mesenteric filament
- Incomplete mesentery
- Gonad
- Tentacle
- Collar
- Siphonoglyph
- Complete mesentery
- Retractor muscle
- Oral disc
- Mouth
- Basal disc (pedal disc)
- Pharynx
- Gastrovascular cavity

Insects

PUPA
(CHRYSALIS)

THE WORD INSECT REFERS to small invertebrate creatures, especially those with bodies divided into sections. Insects, including beetles, ants, bees, butterflies, and moths, belong to various orders in the class Insecta, which is a division of the phylum Arthropoda. Features common to all insects are an exoskeleton (external skeleton); three pairs of jointed legs; three body sections (head, thorax, and abdomen); and one pair of sensory antennae. Beetles (order Coleoptera) are the biggest group of insects, with about 300,000 species (about 30 per cent of all known insects). They have a pair of hard elytra (wing cases), which are modified front wings. The principal function of the elytra is to protect the hind wings, which are used for flying. Ants, together with bees and wasps, form the order Hymenoptera, which contains about 200,000 species. This group is characterized by a marked narrowing between the thorax and abdomen. Butterflies and moths form the order Lepidoptera, which has about 150,000 species. They have wings covered with tiny scales, hence the name of their order (Lepidoptera means "scale wings"). The separation of lepidopterans into butterflies and moths is largely artificial as there are no features that categorically distinguish one group from the other. In general, however, most butterflies fly by day, whereas most moths are night-flyers. Some insects, including butterflies and moths, undergo complete metamorphosis (transformation) during their life-cycle. A butterfly metamorphoses from an egg to a larva (caterpillar), then to a pupa (chrysalis), and finally to an imago (adult).

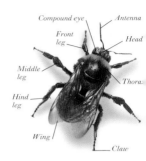

Compound eye

Antenna

Front leg

Head

Middle leg

Thorax

Hind leg

Wing

Claw

BUMBLEBEE

Compound eye

Stigma (spot)

Abdomen

Vein

DAMSELFLY

EXTERNAL FEATURES OF A BEETLE

Elytron

Tarsus

Claw

Tibia

Costal margin

Pedicel

Femur

Apex

Flagellum

Trochanter

Vein

Mandible

Scape

Coxa

Wing

Labrum

Labial palp

Compound eye

Abdomen

Head

Prothorax

Front leg

Mesothorax

Scutellum

Metathorax

Middle leg

Hind leg

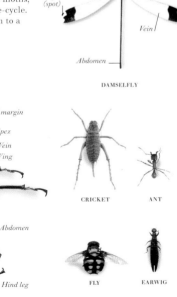

CRICKET

ANT

FLY

EARWIG

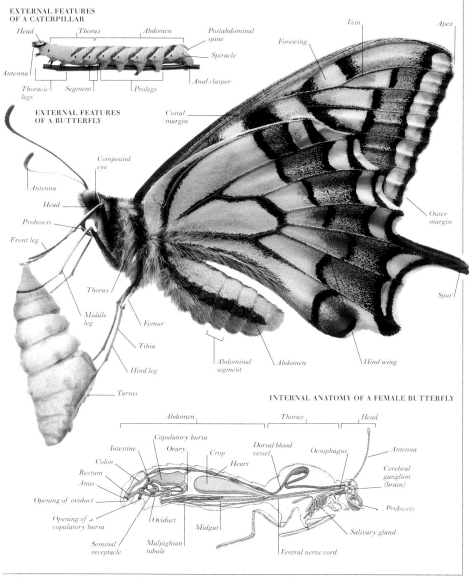

EXTERNAL FEATURES OF A CATERPILLAR

Head
Thorax
Abdomen
Postabdominal spine
Spiracle
Antenna
Thoracic legs
Segment
Prolegs
Anal clasper

Vein
Apex
Forewing

Costal margin

EXTERNAL FEATURES OF A BUTTERFLY

Antenna
Compound eye
Head
Proboscis
Front leg
Thorax
Middle leg
Femur
Tibia
Hind leg
Tarsus

Outer margin

Spur

Abdominal segment
Abdomen
Hind wing

INTERNAL ANATOMY OF A FEMALE BUTTERFLY

Abdomen
Thorax
Head

Intestine
Copulatory bursa
Ovary
Crop
Dorsal blood vessel
Heart
Oesophagus
Antenna
Colon
Rectum
Cerebral ganglion (brain)
Anus
Opening of oviduct
Proboscis
Opening of copulatory bursa
Oviduct
Midgut
Salivary gland
Seminal receptacle
Malpighian tubule
Ventral nerve cord

Arachnids

THE CLASS ARACHNIDA INCLUDES SPIDERS (order Araneae) and scorpions (order Scorpiones). The class is part of the phylum Arthropoda, which also includes insects and crustaceans.

Spiders and scorpions are characterized by having four pairs of walking legs; a pair of pincer-like mouthparts called chelicerae; another pair of frontal appendages called pedipalps, which are sensory in spiders but used for grasping in scorpions; and a body divided into two sections (a combined head and thorax called a cephalothorax or prosoma, and an abdomen or opisthosoma). Unlike other arthropods, spiders and scorpions lack antennae. Spiders and scorpions are carnivorous. Spiders poison prey by biting with the fanged chelicerae, scorpions by stinging with the end of the metasoma (tail).

MEXICAN TRUE RED-LEGGED TARANTULA
(*Euathlus emilia*)

INTERNAL ANATOMY OF A FEMALE SPIDER

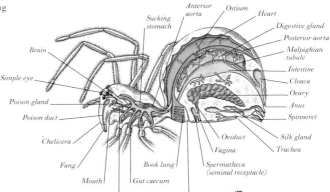

Anterior aorta
Ostium
Heart
Sucking stomach
Digestive gland
Posterior aorta
Malpighian tubule
Brain
Intestine
Simple eye
Cloaca
Ovary
Poison gland
Anus
Poison duct
Spinneret
Chelicera
Silk gland
Oviduct
Trachea
Fang
Vagina
Mouth
Book lung
Spermatheca (seminal receptacle)
Oesophagus
Gut caecum
Spiracle

EXTERNAL FEATURES OF A SCORPION

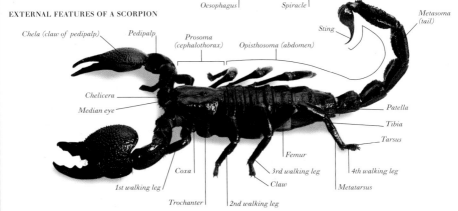

Chela (claw of pedipalp)
Pedipalp
Prosoma (cephalothorax)
Opisthosoma (abdomen)
Sting
Metasoma (tail)
Chelicera
Median eye
Patella
Tibia
Tarsus
Femur
1st walking leg
Coxa
3rd walking leg
4th walking leg
Trochanter
Claw
Metatarsus
2nd walking leg

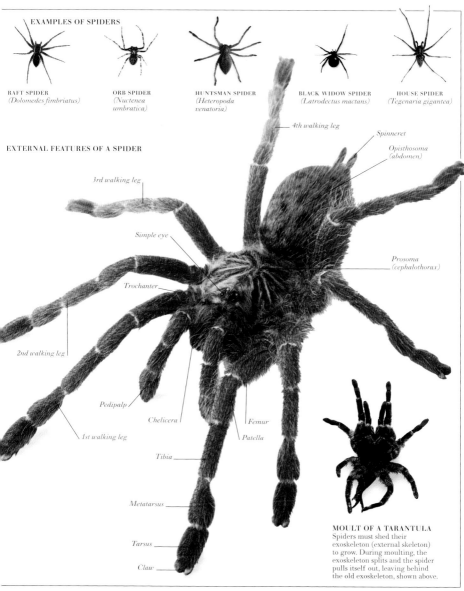

EXAMPLES OF SPIDERS

RAFT SPIDER
(Dolomedes fimbriatus)

ORB SPIDER
(Nuctenea umbratica)

HUNTSMAN SPIDER
(Heteropoda venatoria)

BLACK WIDOW SPIDER
(Latrodectus mactans)

HOUSE SPIDER
(Tegenaria gigantea)

EXTERNAL FEATURES OF A SPIDER

4th walking leg

Spinneret

Opisthosoma
(abdomen)

3rd walking leg

Simple eye

Prosoma
(cephalothorax)

Trochanter

2nd walking leg

Pedipalp

Chelicera

Femur

Patella

1st walking leg

Tibia

Metatarsus

Tarsus

Claw

MOULT OF A TARANTULA

Spiders must shed their exoskeleton (external skeleton) to grow. During moulting, the exoskeleton splits and the spider pulls itself out, leaving behind the old exoskeleton, shown above.

171

Crustaceans

THE SUBPHYLUM CRUSTACEA is one of the largest groups in the phylum Arthropoda. The subphylum is divided into several classes, the most important of which are Malacostraca and Cirripedia. The class Malacostraca includes crayfish, crabs, lobsters, and shrimps. Typical features of malacostracans include a body divided into two sections (a combined head and thorax called a cephalothorax, and an abdomen); an exoskeleton (external skeleton) with a large plate (carapace) covering the cephalothorax; stalked, compound eyes; and two pairs of antennae. The class Cirripedia includes barnacles, which, unlike other crustaceans, spend their adult lives attached to a surface, such as a rock. Other characteristics of cirripedes include an exoskeleton of overlapping calcareous plates; a body consisting almost entirely of thorax (the abdomen and head are minute); and six pairs of thoracic appendages (cirri) used for filter feeding.

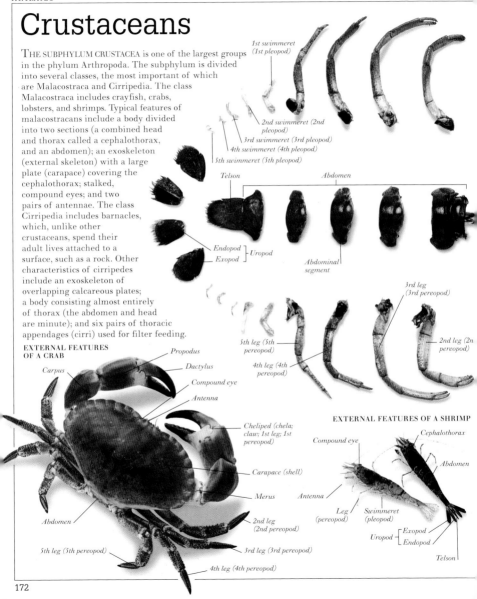

1st swimmeret (1st pleopod)

2nd swimmeret (2nd pleopod)

3rd swimmeret (3rd pleopod)

4th swimmeret (4th pleopod)

5th swimmeret (5th pleopod)

Telson

Abdomen

Endopod
Exopod ⎤ Uropod

Abdominal segment

3rd leg (3rd pereopod)

2nd leg (2nd pereopod)

5th leg (5th pereopod)

4th leg (4th pereopod)

EXTERNAL FEATURES OF A CRAB

Carpus

Propodus

Dactylus

Compound eye

Antenna

Cheliped (chela; claw; 1st leg; 1st pereopod)

Carapace (shell)

Merus

Abdomen

2nd leg (2nd pereopod)

5th leg (5th pereopod)

3rd leg (3rd pereopod)

4th leg (4th pereopod)

EXTERNAL FEATURES OF A SHRIMP

Cephalothorax

Compound eye

Abdomen

Antenna

Leg (pereopod)

Swimmeret (pleopod)

Uropod ⎤ Exopod
Endopod

Telson

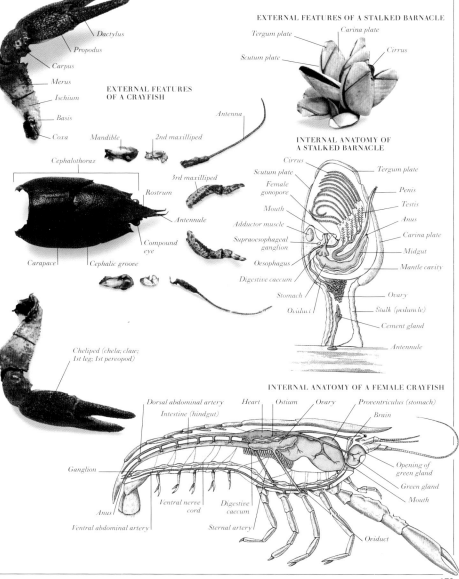

EXTERNAL FEATURES OF A STALKED BARNACLE

Tergum plate
Carina plate
Scutum plate
Cirrus

Dactylus
Propodus
Carpus
Merus
Ischium
Basis
Coxa

EXTERNAL FEATURES OF A CRAYFISH

Antenna
Mandible
2nd maxilliped
Cephalothorax
3rd maxilliped
Rostrum
Antennule
Compound eye
Carapace
Cephalic groove

INTERNAL ANATOMY OF A STALKED BARNACLE

Cirrus
Scutum plate
Female gonopore
Mouth
Adductor muscle
Supraoesophageal ganglion
Oesophagus
Digestive caecum
Stomach
Oviduct
Tergum plate
Penis
Testis
Anus
Carina plate
Midgut
Mantle cavity
Ovary
Stalk (peduncle)
Cement gland
Antennule

Cheliped (chela; claw; 1st leg; 1st pereopod)

INTERNAL ANATOMY OF A FEMALE CRAYFISH

Dorsal abdominal artery
Intestine (hindgut)
Heart
Ostium
Ovary
Proventriculus (stomach)
Brain
Ganglion
Opening of green gland
Green gland
Mouth
Anus
Ventral nerve cord
Digestive caecum
Ventral abdominal artery
Sternal artery
Oviduct

Starfish and sea urchins

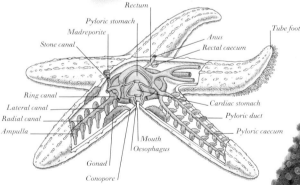

STARFISH, SEA URCHINS, AND THEIR relatives (including feather stars, brittle stars, basket stars, sea daisies, sea lilies, and sea cucumbers) make up the phylum Echinodermata. A unique feature of echinoderms is the water vascular system, which consists of a series of water-filled canals from which protrude thousands of tiny tube feet. The tube feet may be used for movement, feeding, or respiration. Other features include pentaradiate symmetry (that is, the body can be divided into five parts radiating from the centre); no head; a diffuse, decentralized nervous system that lacks a brain; and no excretory organs. Typically, echinoderms also have an endoskeleton (internal skeleton) consisting of hard calcite ossicles embedded in the body wall and often bearing protruding spines or tubercles. The ossicles may fit together to form a test (as in sea urchins) or remain separate (as in sea cucumbers).

EXTERNAL FEATURES OF A STARFISH (UPPER, OR ABORAL, SURFACE)

Disc

Madreporite

Spine

Arm

INTERNAL ANATOMY OF A STARFISH

Rectum

Pyloric stomach

Madreporite

Stone canal

Anus

Rectal caecum

Tube foot

Ring canal

Lateral canal

Radial canal

Ampulla

Cardiac stomach

Pyloric duct

Pyloric caecum

Mouth

Oesophagus

Gonad

Conopore

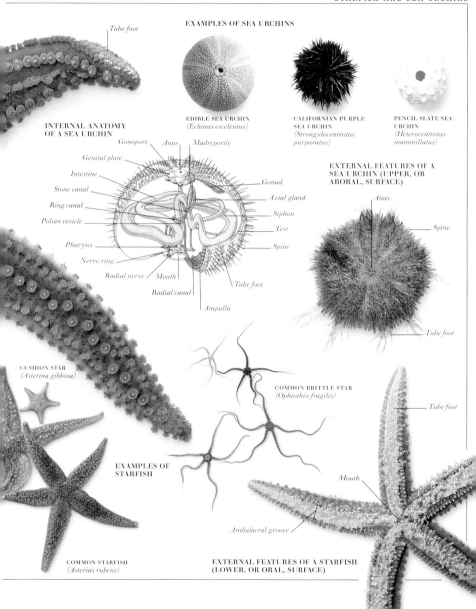

Tube foot

EXAMPLES OF SEA URCHINS

EDIBLE SEA URCHIN
(*Echinus escelentus*)

CALIFORNIAN PURPLE
SEA URCHIN
(*Strongylocentrotus
purpuratus*)

PENCIL SLATE SEA
URCHIN
(*Heterocentrotus
mammillatus*)

**INTERNAL ANATOMY
OF A SEA URCHIN**

Gonopore
Anus
Madreporite
Genital plate
Intestine
Gonad
Stone canal
Axial gland
Ring canal
Siphon
Polian vesicle
Test
Pharynx
Spine
Nerve ring
Radial nerve
Mouth
Radial canal
Tube foot
Ampulla

**EXTERNAL FEATURES OF A
SEA URCHIN (UPPER, OR
ABORAL, SURFACE)**

Anus
Spine
Tube foot

CUSHION STAR
(*Asterina gibbosa*)

COMMON BRITTLE STAR
(*Ophiothix fragilis*)

Tube foot

**EXAMPLES OF
STARFISH**

Mouth

Ambulacral groove

COMMON STARFISH
(*Asterias rubens*)

**EXTERNAL FEATURES OF A STARFISH
(LOWER, OR ORAL, SURFACE)**

Molluscs

THE PHYLUM MOLLUSCA (MOLLUSCS) is a large group of animals that includes octopuses, snails, and scallops. Octopuses and their relatives – including squid and cuttlefish – form the class Cephalopoda. Cephalopods typically have a head with a radula (a file-like feeding organ) and beak; a well-developed nervous system; sucker-bearing tentacles; a muscular mantle (part of the body wall) that can expel water through the siphon, enabling movement by jet propulsion; and a small shell or no shell. Snails and their relatives – including slugs, limpets, and abalones – make up the class Gastropoda. Gastropods typically have a coiled external shell, although some, such as slugs, have a small internal shell or no shell; a flat foot; and a head with tentacles and a radula. Scallops and their relatives – including clams, mussels, and oysters – make up the class Bivalvia (also called Pelecypoda). Features of bivalves include a shell with two halves (valves); large gills that are used for breathing and filter feeding; and no radula.

EXTERNAL FEATURES OF A SCALLOP

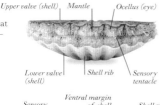

Upper valve (shell)　Mantle　Ocellus (eye)

Lower valve (shell)　Shell rib　Sensory tentacle

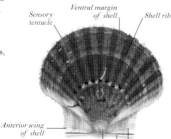

Sensory tentacle　Ventral margin of shell　Shell rib

Anterior wing of shell

Umbo　Posterior wing of shell

Dorsal margin of shell

INTERNAL ANATOMY OF AN OCTOPUS

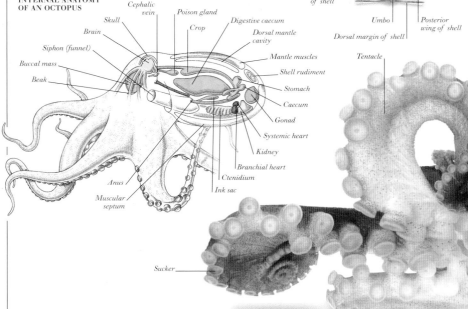

Cephalic vein
Poison gland
Skull
Crop
Digestive caecum
Brain
Dorsal mantle cavity
Siphon (funnel)
Mantle muscles
Buccal mass
Shell rudiment
Beak
Stomach
Caecum
Gonad
Systemic heart
Kidney
Branchial heart
Anus
Ctenidium
Muscular septum
Ink sac
Tentacle

Sucker

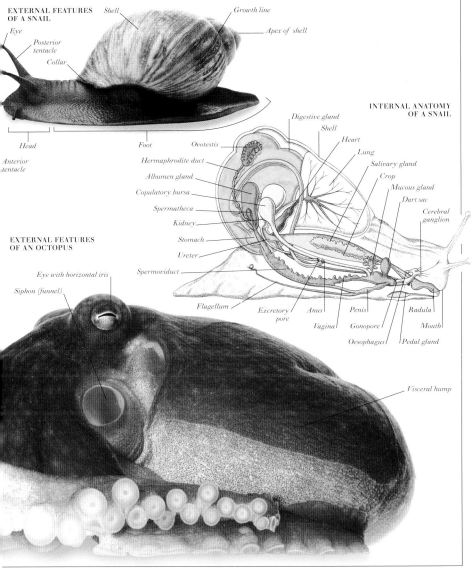

EXTERNAL FEATURES OF A SNAIL

Eye
Posterior tentacle
Collar
Shell
Growth line
Apex of shell
Head
Foot
Anterior tentacle

INTERNAL ANATOMY OF A SNAIL

Digestive gland
Shell
Heart
Lung
Salivary gland
Crop
Mucous gland
Dart sac
Cerebral ganglion
Ovotestis
Hermaphrodite duct
Albumen gland
Copulatory bursa
Spermatheca
Kidney
Stomach
Ureter
Spermoviduct
Flagellum
Excretory pore
Anus
Penis
Radula
Vagina
Gonopore
Mouth
Oesophagus
Pedal gland

EXTERNAL FEATURES OF AN OCTOPUS

Eye with horizontal iris
Siphon (funnel)
Visceral hump

Sharks and jawless fish

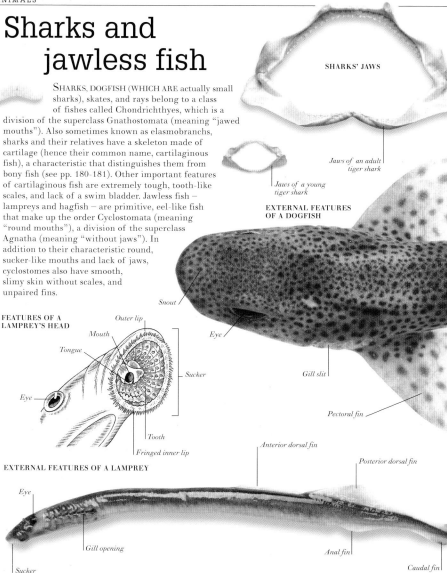

SHARKS, DOGFISH (WHICH ARE actually small sharks), skates, and rays belong to a class of fishes called Chondrichthyes, which is a division of the superclass Gnathostomata (meaning "jawed mouths"). Also sometimes known as elasmobranchs, sharks and their relatives have a skeleton made of cartilage (hence their common name, cartilaginous fish), a characteristic that distinguishes them from bony fish (see pp. 180-181). Other important features of cartilaginous fish are extremely tough, tooth-like scales, and lack of a swim bladder. Jawless fish – lampreys and hagfish – are primitive, eel-like fish that make up the order Cyclostomata (meaning "round mouths"), a division of the superclass Agnatha (meaning "without jaws"). In addition to their characteristic round, sucker-like mouths and lack of jaws, cyclostomes also have smooth, slimy skin without scales, and unpaired fins.

SHARKS' JAWS

Jaws of an adult tiger shark

Jaws of a young tiger shark

EXTERNAL FEATURES OF A DOGFISH

Snout

Eye

Gill slit

Pectoral fin

FEATURES OF A LAMPREY'S HEAD

Outer lip

Mouth

Tongue

Eye

Sucker

Tooth

Fringed inner lip

EXTERNAL FEATURES OF A LAMPREY

Eye

Anterior dorsal fin

Posterior dorsal fin

Gill opening

Anal fin

Sucker

Caudal fin

EXAMPLES OF CARTILAGINOUS FISH

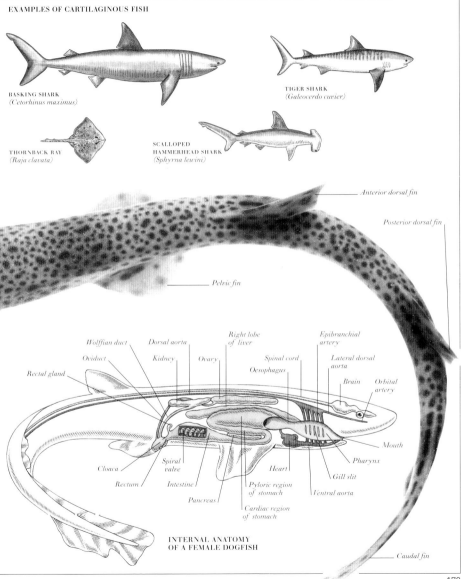

BASKING SHARK
(*Cetorhinus maximus*)

TIGER SHARK
(*Galeocerdo cuvier*)

THORNBACK RAY
(*Raja clavata*)

**SCALLOPED
HAMMERHEAD SHARK**
(*Sphyrna lewini*)

Anterior dorsal fin

Posterior dorsal fin

Pelvic fin

Wolffian duct

Dorsal aorta

*Right lobe
of liver*

*Epibranchial
artery*

Oviduct

Kidney

Ovary

Spinal cord

*Lateral dorsal
aorta*

Rectal gland

Oesophagus

Brain

*Orbital
artery*

Mouth

Cloaca

*Spiral
valve*

Heart

Pharynx

Rectum

Intestine

Gill slit

Pancreas

*Pyloric region
of stomach*

Ventral aorta

*Cardiac region
of stomach*

**INTERNAL ANATOMY
OF A FEMALE DOGFISH**

Caudal fin

Bony fish

BONY FISH, SUCH AS CARP, TROUT, SALMON, perch, and cod, are by far the best known and largest group of fish, with more than 20,000 species (over 95 per cent of all known fish). As their name suggests, bony fish have skeletons made of bone, in contrast to the cartilaginous skeletons of sharks, jawless fish, and their relatives (see pp. 178-179). Other typical features of bony fish include a swim bladder, which functions as a variable-buoyancy organ, enabling a fish to remain effortlessly at whatever depth it is swimming; relatively thin, bone-like scales; a flap (called an operculum) covering the gills; and paired pelvic and pectoral fins. Scientifically, bony fish belong to the class Osteichthyes, which is a division of the superclass Gnathostomata (meaning "jawed mouths").

HOW FISH BREATHE
Fish "breathe" by extracting oxygen from water through their gills. Water is sucked in through the mouth; simultaneously, the opercula close to prevent the water from escaping. The mouth is then closed, and muscles in the walls of the mouth, pharynx, and opercular cavity contract to pump the water inside over the gills and out through the opercula. Some fish rely on swimming with their mouths open to keep water flowing over the gills.

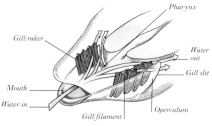

Pharynx

Gill raker

Water out

Gill slit

Mouth

Water in

Gill filament

Operculum

EXAMPLES OF BONY FISH

MANDARINFISH
(Synchiropus splendidus)

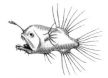

ANGLERFISH
(Caulophryne jordani)

LIONFISH
(Pterois volitans)

STURGEON
(Acipenser sturio)

OCEANIC SEAHORSE
(Hippocampus kuda)

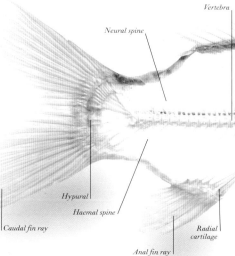

Vertebra

Neural spine

Hypural

Haemal spine

Caudal fin ray

Anal fin ray

Radial cartilage

SNOWFLAKE MORAY EEL
(Echidna nebulosa)

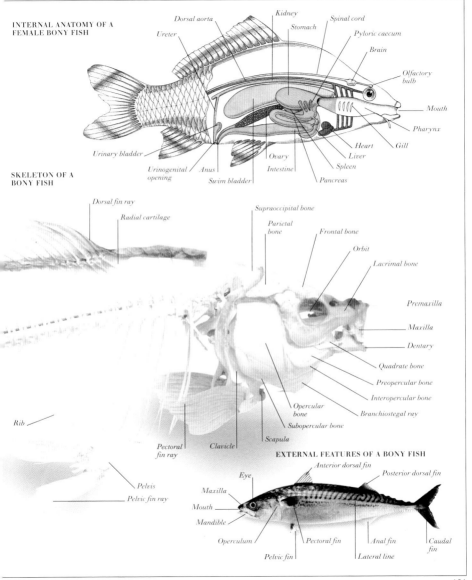

INTERNAL ANATOMY OF A FEMALE BONY FISH

Dorsal aorta
Ureter
Kidney
Stomach
Spinal cord
Pyloric caecum
Brain
Olfactory bulb
Mouth
Pharynx
Gill
Heart
Liver
Spleen
Pancreas
Intestine
Ovary
Swim bladder
Anus
Urinogenital opening
Urinary bladder

SKELETON OF A BONY FISH

Dorsal fin ray
Radial cartilage
Supraoccipital bone
Parietal bone
Frontal bone
Orbit
Lacrimal bone
Premaxilla
Maxilla
Dentary
Quadrate bone
Preopercular bone
Interopercular bone
Branchiostegal ray
Opercular bone
Subopercular bone
Scapula
Clavicle
Pectoral fin ray
Rib
Pelvis
Pelvic fin ray

EXTERNAL FEATURES OF A BONY FISH

Eye
Maxilla
Mouth
Mandible
Operculum
Pelvic fin
Pectoral fin
Anterior dorsal fin
Posterior dorsal fin
Anal fin
Lateral line
Caudal fin

Amphibians

THE CLASS AMPHIBIA INCLUDES FROGS and toads (which make up the order Anura), and newts and salamanders (which make up the order Urodela). Amphibians typically have moist, scaleless, hairless skin; lungs; and are cold-blooded. They also undergo complete metamorphosis, from eggs laid in water through various water-living larval stages (such as tadpoles) to land-living adults. Typical features of adult frogs and toads include a squat body with no tail; long, powerful hind legs; and large, often bulging, eyes. Adult newts and salamanders typically have a long body with a well-developed tail; and relatively short, equal-sized legs. However, newts and salamanders show considerable variation; for example, in some species the adults have minute legs, external gills rather than lungs, and spend their entire lives in water.

INTERNAL ANATOMY OF A FEMALE FROG

Larynx
Right bronchus
Stomach
Right lung
Heart
Liver
Posterior vena cava
Right kidney
Dorsal aorta
Cloaca
Rectum
Forelimb
External nostril
Mouth
Eye
Pulmonary artery
Left lung
Pancreas
Duodenum
Spleen
Left kidney
Mesentery
Small intestine (ileum)
Left ureter

EXTERNAL FEATURES OF A FROG

Hind limb
Trunk
Head
5 digits
Tympanum (eardrum)
4 digits
Web

EXTERNAL FEATURES OF A SALAMANDER

Eye
Tail
Forelimb
Hind limb
Digit

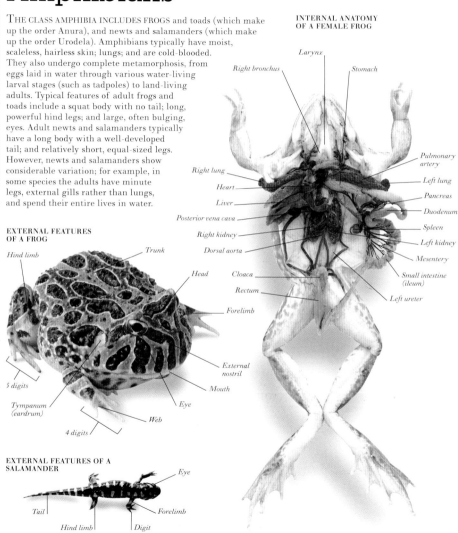

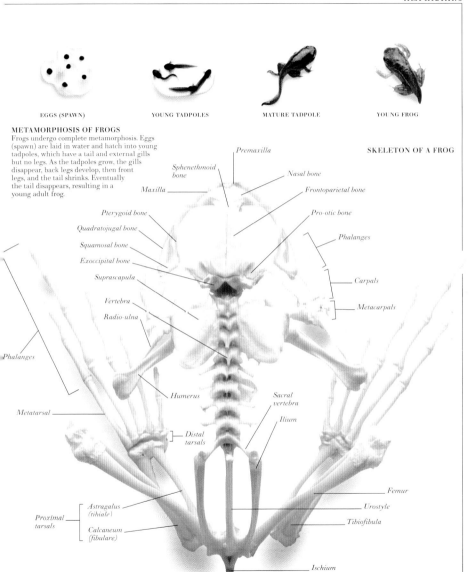

EGGS (SPAWN)

YOUNG TADPOLES

MATURE TADPOLE

YOUNG FROG

METAMORPHOSIS OF FROGS

Frogs undergo complete metamorphosis. Eggs (spawn) are laid in water and hatch into young tadpoles, which have a tail and external gills but no legs. As the tadpoles grow, the gills disappear, back legs develop, then front legs, and the tail shrinks. Eventually the tail disappears, resulting in a young adult frog.

SKELETON OF A FROG

Premaxilla

Sphenethmoid bone

Nasal bone

Maxilla

Frontoparietal bone

Pterygoid bone

Pro-otic bone

Quadratojugal bone

Phalanges

Squamosal bone

Exoccipital bone

Suprascapula

Carpals

Vertebra

Metacarpals

Radio-ulna

Phalanges

Humerus

Sacral vertebra

Metatarsal

Ilium

Distal tarsals

Astragalus (tibiale)

Femur

Proximal tarsals

Urostyle

Calcaneum (fibulare)

Tibiofibula

Ischium

Lizards and snakes

LIZARDS AND SNAKES BELONG to the order Squamata, a division of the class Reptilia. Characteristic reptilian features include scaly skin, lungs, and cold-bloodedness. Most reptiles lay leathery-shelled eggs, although some hatch the eggs inside their bodies and give birth to live young. Lizards belong to the suborder Lacertilia. Typically, they have long tails, and shed their skin in several pieces. Many lizards can regenerate a tail if it is lost; some can change colour; and some are limbless. Snakes make up the suborder Ophidia (also called Serpentes). All snakes have long, limbless bodies; can dislocate their lower jaw to swallow large prey; and have eyelids that are joined together to form a single transparent covering over the front of the eye. Most snakes shed their skin in a single piece. Constrictor snakes kill their prey by squeezing; venomous snakes poison their prey.

EXAMPLES OF SNAKES

MEXICAN MOUNTAIN KING SNAKE
(Lampropeltis triangulum annulata)

BANDED M
SNA
(Lamprope
ruthve

EXTERNAL FEATURES OF A LIZARD

Eye

Mouth

External nostril

Crest

Eardrum

Masseteric scale

Dorsal scale

SKELETON OF A LIZARD

Skull

Orbit

Scapula

Cervical vertebrae

Phalanges

Carpals

Metacarpal

Ulna

Humerus

Radius

Rib

Thoracolumbar vertebrae

Femur

Pelvis

Sacrum

Tibia

Fibula

Tarsals

Metatarsal

Caudal vertebrae

Phalanges

Dewlap

Foreleg

Belly

Ventral scale

Toe

Claw

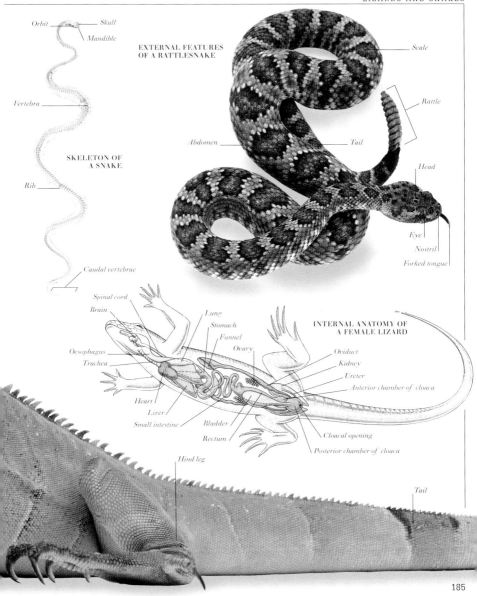

SKELETON OF A SNAKE

Orbit
Skull
Mandible
Vertebra
Rib
Caudal vertebrae

EXTERNAL FEATURES OF A RATTLESNAKE

Scale
Rattle
Abdomen
Tail
Head
Eye
Nostril
Forked tongue

INTERNAL ANATOMY OF A FEMALE LIZARD

Spinal cord
Brain
Lung
Stomach
Funnel
Ovary
Oesophagus
Trachea
Oviduct
Kidney
Ureter
Anterior chamber of cloaca
Heart
Liver
Small intestine
Bladder
Rectum
Cloacal opening
Posterior chamber of cloaca
Hind leg
Tail

Crocodilians and turtles

GHARIAL
(Gavialis gangeticus)

CROCODILIANS AND TURTLES BELONG to different orders in the class Reptilia.
The order Crocodilia includes crocodiles, alligators, caimans, and gharials.
Typically, crocodilians are carnivores (flesh-eaters), and have a long
snout, sharp teeth for gripping prey, and hard, square scales. All
crocodilians are adapted to living on land and in water: they have four
strong legs for moving on land; a powerful tail for swimming; and their
eyes and nostrils are high on the head so that they stay above water while
the rest of the body is submerged. The order Chelonia includes marine
turtles, terrapins (freshwater turtles), and tortoises (land turtles).
Characteristically, chelonians have a short, broad body encased in a
bony shell with an outer horny covering, into which the head and limbs
can be withdrawn; and a horny beak instead of teeth.

NILE CROCODILE
(Crocodylus niloticus)

AMERICAN ALLIGATOR
(Alligator mississippiensis)

SKELETON OF A CROCODILE

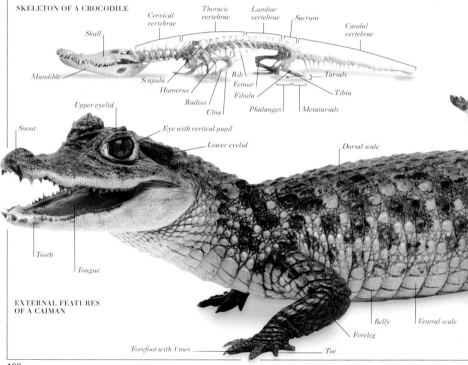

Cervical
vertebrae

Thoracic
vertebrae

Lumbar
vertebrae

Sacrum

Caudal
vertebrae

Skull

Mandible

Scapula

Humerus

Radius

Ulna

Rib

Femur

Fibula

Phalanges

Metatarsals

Tarsals

Tibia

Upper eyelid

Snout

Eye with vertical pupil

Lower eyelid

Dorsal scale

Tooth

Tongue

**EXTERNAL FEATURES
OF A CAIMAN**

Belly

Ventral scale

Foreleg

Forefoot with 5 toes

Toe

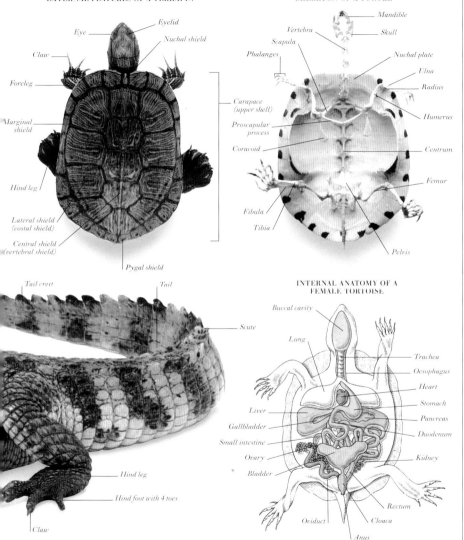

EXTERNAL FEATURES OF A TERRAPIN

Eye
Eyelid
Nuchal shield
Claw
Foreleg
Marginal shield
Hind leg
Lateral shield (costal shield)
Central shield (vertebral shield)
Pygal shield

SKELETON OF A TURTLE

Mandible
Vertebra
Skull
Scapula
Phalanges
Nuchal plate
Ulna
Radius
Carapace (upper shell)
Proscapular process
Coracoid
Humerus
Centrum
Femur
Fibula
Tibia
Pelvis

Tail crest
Tail
Scute
Hind leg
Hind foot with 4 toes
Claw

INTERNAL ANATOMY OF A FEMALE TORTOISE

Buccal cavity
Lung
Trachea
Oesophagus
Heart
Liver
Stomach
Gallbladder
Pancreas
Small intestine
Duodenum
Ovary
Bladder
Kidney
Oviduct
Rectum
Cloaca
Anus

Birds 1

BIRDS MAKE UP THE CLASS AVES. There are more than 9,000 species, almost all of which can fly (the only flightless birds are penguins, ostriches, rheas, cassowaries, and kiwis). The ability to fly is reflected in the typical bird features: forelimbs modified as wings; a streamlined body; and hollow bones to reduce weight. All birds lay hard-shelled eggs, which the parents incubate. Birds' beaks and feet vary according to diet and way of life. Beaks range from general-purpose types suitable for a mixed diet (those of thrushes, for example), to types specialized for particular foods (such as the large, curved, sieving beaks of flamingos). Feet range from the webbed "paddles" of ducks, to the talons of birds of prey. Plumage also varies widely, and in many species the male is brightly coloured for courtship display whereas the female is drab.

EXTERNAL FEATURES OF A BIRD

Forehead
Eye
Crown
Nostril
Nape
Upper mandible
Beak
Lower mandible
Chin
Throat

EXAMPLES OF BIRDS

MALE TUFTED DUCK
(*Aythya fuligula*)

Minor coverts
Lesser wing coverts
Median wing coverts

Greater wing coverts (major coverts)

Secondary flight feathers (secondary remiges)

Primary flight feathers (primary remiges)

WHITE STORK
(*Ciconia ciconia*)

Breast
Belly
Flank
Thigh

Under tail coverts

Claw

Tarsus

Toe

Tail feathers (retrices)

MALE OSTRICH
(*Struthio camelus*)

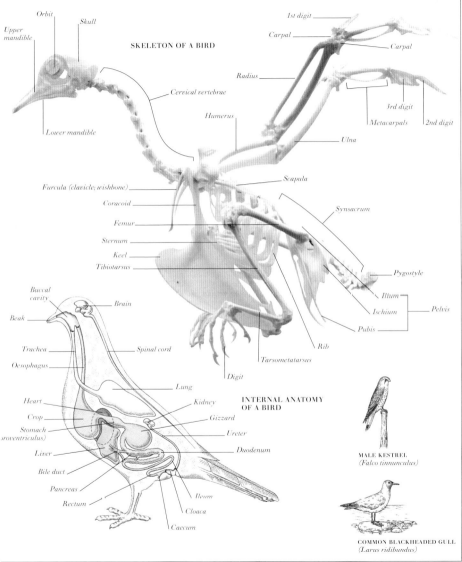

Upper mandible

Orbit

Skull

SKELETON OF A BIRD

1st digit

Carpal

Carpal

Radius

Cervical vertebrae

3rd digit

Metacarpals

2nd digit

Humerus

Lower mandible

Ulna

Scapula

Furcula (clavicle; wishbone)

Coracoid

Synsacrum

Femur

Sternum

Keel

Tibiotarsus

Pygostyle

Illum

Buccal cavity

Brain

Ischium

Pelvis

Beak

Pubis

Trachea

Spinal cord

Rib

Oesophagus

Tarsometatarsus

Digit

Lung

Heart

Kidney

INTERNAL ANATOMY OF A BIRD

Crop

Gizzard

Stomach (proventriculus)

Ureter

Liver

Duodenum

Bile duct

Pancreas

Ileum

Rectum

Cloaca

MALE KESTREL
(*Falco tinnunculus*)

Caecum

COMMON BLACKHEADED GULL
(*Larus ridibundus*)

Birds 2

EXAMPLES OF BIRDS' FEET

KITTIWAKE
(Rissa tridactyla)
The webbed feet are
adapted for paddling
through water.

LITTLE GREBE
(Tachybaptus ruficollis)
The lobed, flattened feet
are adapted for swimming
underwater.

TAWNY OWL
(Strix aluco)
The clawed feet are adapted
for gripping prey.

EXAMPLES OF BIRDS' BEAKS

KING VULTURE
(Sarcorhamphus papa)
The hooked beak is adapted
for pulling apart flesh.

GREATER FLAMINGO
(Phoenicopterus ruber)
In the living bird, the large,
curved beak contains a
cartilaginous "sieve" for
filtering food particles
from water.

MISTLE THRUSH
(Turdus viscivorus)
The general-purpose beak is
suitable for a wide range of
animal and plant foods.

BLUE-AND-YELLOW MACAW
(Ara ararauna)
The broad, powerful, hooked beak
is adapted for crushing seeds and
eating fruit.

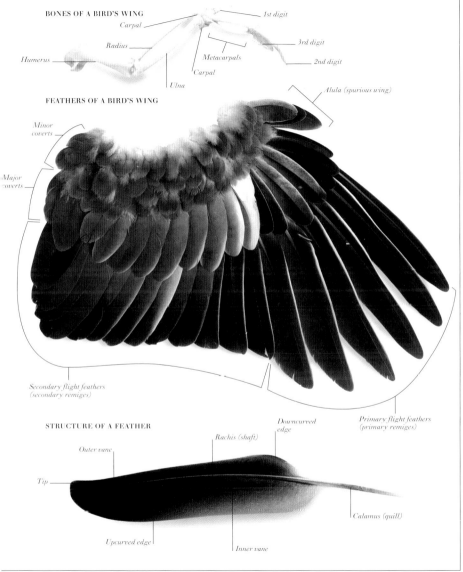

BONES OF A BIRD'S WING

1st digit
Carpal
Radius
3rd digit
Metacarpals
2nd digit
Humerus
Carpal
Ulna

FEATHERS OF A BIRD'S WING

Alula (spurious wing)

Minor coverts

Major coverts

Secondary flight feathers (secondary remiges)

Primary flight feathers (primary remiges)

STRUCTURE OF A FEATHER

Downcurved edge
Rachis (shaft)
Outer vane
Tip
Calamus (quill)
Upcurved edge
Inner vane

Eggs

AN EGG IS A SINGLE CELL, produced by the female, with the capacity to develop into a new individual. Development may take place inside the mother's body (as in most mammals) or outside, in which case the egg has a protective covering such as a shell. Egg yolk nourishes the growing young. Eggs developing inside the mother generally have little yolk, because the young are nourished from her body. Eggs developing outside may also have little yolk if they are produced by animals whose young go through a larval stage (such as a caterpillar) that feeds itself while developing into the adult form. The shelled eggs of birds and reptiles contain enough yolk to sustain the young until it hatches into a juvenile version of the adult.

SECTION THROUGH A CHICKEN'S EGG

Yolk
Yolk sac
Shell
Allantoic fluid
Allantois
Chorioallantoic membrane
Air sac
Albumen (egg white)
Amnion
Amniotic fluid
Developing chick
Developing wing
Shell membrane

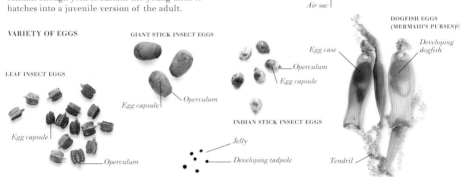

VARIETY OF EGGS

LEAF INSECT EGGS

Egg capsule
Operculum

GIANT STICK INSECT EGGS

Egg capsule
Operculum

INDIAN STICK INSECT EGGS

Operculum
Egg capsule

FROG EGGS (FROG SPAWN)

Jelly
Developing tadpole

DOGFISH EGGS (MERMAID'S PURSES)

Egg case
Developing dogfish
Tendril

HATCHING OF A QUAIL'S EGG

EGG AT THE POINT OF HATCHING

Rounded end of egg
Shell
Pointed end of egg
Shell membrane
Camouflage coloration
Crack caused by chick pecking through the shell

CUTTING THROUGH THE EGG

Chick
Shell
Crack extended by further pecking by the chick

BREAKING OUT OF THE EGG

Chick pushes off the top of the shell
Shell membrane
Shell
Eye
Beak
Egg-tooth
Crack runs completely around the shell

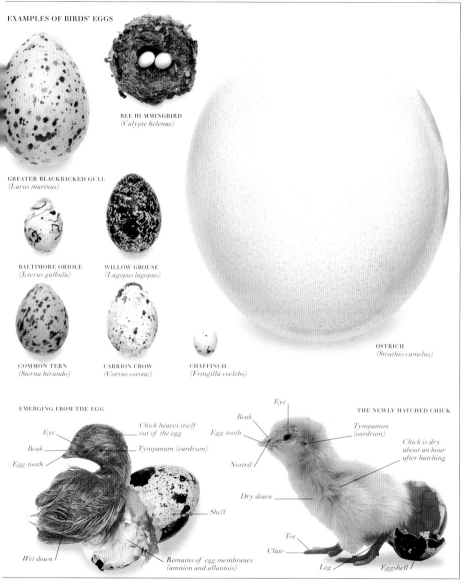

EXAMPLES OF BIRDS' EGGS

BEE HUMMINGBIRD
(*Calypte helenae*)

GREATER BLACKBACKED GULL
(*Larus marinus*)

BALTIMORE ORIOLE
(*Icterus galbula*)

WILLOW GROUSE
(*Lagopus lagopus*)

COMMON TERN
(*Sterna hirundo*)

CARRION CROW
(*Corvus corone*)

CHAFFINCH
(*Fringilla coelebs*)

OSTRICH
(*Struthio camelus*)

EMERGING FROM THE EGG

Chick heaves itself
out of the egg

Eye

Beak

Egg-tooth

Tympanum (eardrum)

Shell

Wet down

Remains of egg membranes
(amnion and allantois)

THE NEWLY HATCHED CHICK

Eye

Beak

Egg-tooth

Nostril

Tympanum
(eardrum)

Chick is dry
about an hour
after hatching

Dry down

Toe

Claw

Leg

Eggshell

Carnivores

THE MAMMALIAN ORDER CARNIVORA includes cats, dogs, bears, raccoons, pandas, weasels, badgers, skunks, otters, civets, mongooses, and hyenas. The order's name is derived from the fact that most of its members are carnivores (flesheaters). Typical carnivore features therefore reflect a hunting life-style: speed and agility; sharp claws and well-developed canine teeth for holding and killing prey; carnassial teeth (cheek teeth) for cutting flesh; and forward-facing eyes for good distance judgment. However, some members of the order – bears, badgers, and foxes, for example – have a more mixed diet, and a few are entirely herbivorous (plant-eating), notably pandas. Such animals have no carnassial teeth and tend to be slower-moving than pure flesh-eaters.

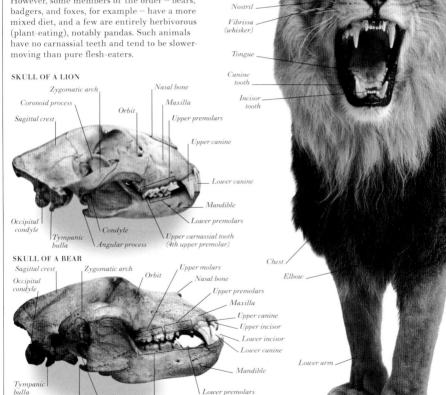

EXTERNAL FEATURES OF A MALE LION

- Nose
- Eye
- Mane
- Nostril
- Vibrissa (whisker)
- Tongue
- Canine tooth
- Incisor tooth
- Chest
- Elbow
- Lower arm
- Toe

SKULL OF A LION

- Zygomatic arch
- Coronoid process
- Sagittal crest
- Orbit
- Nasal bone
- Maxilla
- Upper premolars
- Upper canine
- Lower canine
- Mandible
- Lower premolars
- Occipital condyle
- Tympanic bulla
- Condyle
- Angular process
- Upper carnassial tooth (4th upper premolar)

SKULL OF A BEAR

- Sagittal crest
- Occipital condyle
- Zygomatic arch
- Orbit
- Upper molars
- Nasal bone
- Upper premolars
- Maxilla
- Upper canine
- Upper incisor
- Lower incisor
- Lower canine
- Mandible
- Tympanic bulla
- Angular process
- Condyle
- Lower premolars
- Lower molars

EXAMPLES OF CARNIVORES

ALSATIAN DOG
(Canis familiaris)

MANED WOLF
(Chrysocyon brachyurus)

RACCOON
(Procyon lotor)

AMERICAN BLACK BEAR
(Ursus americanus)

SKELETON OF A DOMESTIC CAT

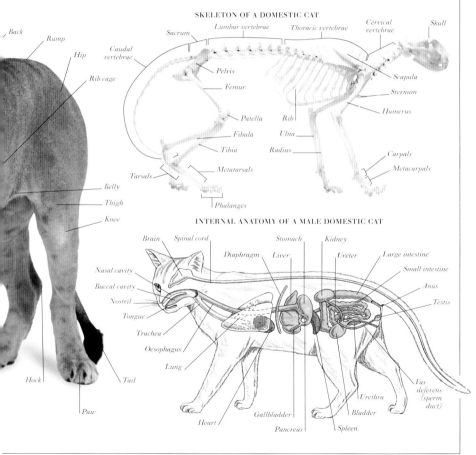

Back

Rump

Hip

Rib cage

Caudal vertebrae

Sacrum

Lumbar vertebrae

Thoracic vertebrae

Cervical vertebrae

Skull

Pelvis

Femur

Scapula

Sternum

Humerus

Patella

Rib

Fibula

Ulna

Tibia

Radius

Carpals

Metacarpals

Tarsals

Metatarsals

Belly

Thigh

Knee

Phalanges

INTERNAL ANATOMY OF A MALE DOMESTIC CAT

Brain

Spinal cord

Diaphragm

Stomach

Liver

Kidney

Ureter

Large intestine

Small intestine

Nasal cavity

Buccal cavity

Nostril

Tongue

Trachea

Oesophagus

Lung

Anus

Testis

Hock

Tail

Paw

Heart

Gallbladder

Pancreas

Spleen

Bladder

Urethra

Vas deferens (sperm duct)

Rabbits and rodents

ALTHOUGH RABBITS AND RODENTS belong
to different orders of mammals, they have some
features in common. These features include
chisel-shaped incisor teeth that grow
continually, and eating their faeces to
extract more nutrients from their plant diet. Rabbits and
hares belong to the order Lagomorpha. Characteristically,
they have four incisors in the upper jaw and two in the
lower jaw; powerful hind legs for jumping; forelimbs
adapted for burrowing; long ears; and a small tail. Rodents
make up the order Rodentia. This is the largest order of
mammals, with more than 1,700 species, including
squirrels, beavers, chipmunks, gophers, rats,
mice, lemmings, gerbils, porcupines, cavies,
and the capybara. Typical rodent features
include two incisors in each jaw;
short forelimbs for manipulating
food; and cheek pouches
for storing food.

EXTERNAL FEATURES OF A RAT

Snout
Eye
Ear
Nose
Nostril
Vibrissa (whisker)
Neck
Mouth
Tail
Forelimb
5 digits
Hind limb
5 digits

EXTERNAL FEATURES OF A RABBIT

Pinna (ear flap)
Ear
Shoulder
Eye
Nose
Nostril
Vibrissa (whisker)
Forelimb
5 digits

INTERNAL ANATOMY OF A MALE RABBIT

Brain
Gallbladder
Liver
Stomach
Kidney
Spinal cord
Colon
Ileum
Ureter
Rectum
Bladder
Anus
Urethra
Testis
Vas deferens
Appendix
Nasal cavity
Mouth
Buccal cavity
Tongue
Esophagus
Lung
Trachea
Diaphragm
Heart
Pancreas
Duodenum
Caecum

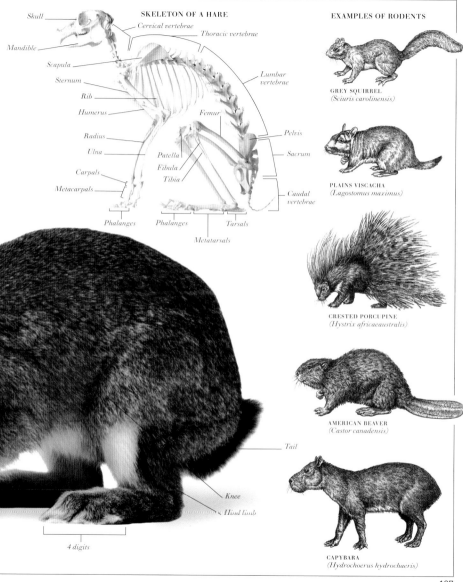

SKELETON OF A HARE

Skull

Cervical vertebrae

Mandible

Thoracic vertebrae

Scapula

Sternum

Lumbar vertebrae

Rib

Humerus

Radius

Femur

Ulna

Pelvis

Patella

Carpals

Fibula

Sacrum

Metacarpals

Tibia

Caudal vertebrae

Phalanges

Phalanges

Tarsals

Metatarsals

Tail

Knee

Hind limb

4 digits

EXAMPLES OF RODENTS

GREY SQUIRREL
(*Sciurus carolinensis*)

PLAINS VISCACHA
(*Lagostomus maximus*)

CRESTED PORCUPINE
(*Hystrix africaeaustralis*)

AMERICAN BEAVER
(*Castor canadensis*)

CAPYBARA
(*Hydrochoerus hydrochaeris*)

Ungulates

UNGULATES IS A GENERAL TERM FOR a large, varied group of mammals that includes horses, cattle, and their relatives. The ungulates are divided into two orders on the basis of the number of toes. Members of the order Perissodactyla (odd-toed ungulates) have one or three toes. Perissodactyls include horses, asses, and zebras (all of which are one-toed), and rhinoceroses and tapirs (which are three-toed). Members of the order Artiodactyla (even-toed ungulates) have two or four toes. Most artiodactyls have two toes, which are typically encased in hooves to give the so-called cloven hoof. Two-toed, cloven-hoofed artiodactyls include cows and other cattle, sheep, goats, antelopes, deer, and giraffes. The other main two-toed artiodactyls are camels and llamas. Most two-toed artiodactyls are ruminants; that is, they have a four-chambered stomach and chew the cud. The principal four-toed artiodactyls are pigs, peccaries, and hippopotamuses.

Chambers of stomach

Rumen Omasum Abomasum Reticulum

Colon

Anus

Rectum

Caecum

Small intestine

Mo...

Tongu...

Oesophagus

Duodenum

DIGESTIVE SYSTEM OF A COW

B...

Croup

Loin

Root of tail

Buttock

Tail

Thigh

COMPARISON OF THE FRONT FEET OF A HORSE AND A COW

SKELETON OF THE LEFT FRONT FOOT OF A HORSE

SKELETON OF THE RIGHT FRONT FOOT OF A COW

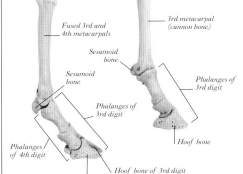

2nd metacarpal (splint bone)

Fused 3rd and 4th metacarpals

3rd metacarpal (cannon bone)

Sesamoid bone

Sesamoid bone

Phalanges of 3rd digit

Phalanges of 3rd digit

Phalanges of 4th digit

Hoof bone

Hoof bone of 3rd digit

Hoof bone of 4th digit

Pastern

Flank

Stifle

Belly

Gaskin

Hock

Chestnut

Shannon bone (cannon bone)

Coronet

Heel

Hoof

EXAMPLES OF UNGULATES

MALE RED DEER
(Cervus elephas)
An even-toed ungulate
(order Artiodactyla)

BACTRIAN CAMEL
(Camelus ferus)
An even-toed ungulate
(order Artiodactyla)

GIRAFFE
(Giraffa camelopardalis)
An even toed ungulate
(order Artiodactyla)

BLACK RHINOCEROS
(Diceros bicornis)
An odd-toed ungulate
(order Perissodactyla)

EXTERNAL FEATURES OF A HORSE

Mane
Poll
Crest
Ear
Forelock
Withers
Forehead
Eye
Muzzle
Nose
Nostril
Cheek
Mouth
Chin groove
Neck
Shoulder
Breast
Bow
Forearm
Knee
Cannon bone
Fetlock
Pastern

SKELETON OF A HORSE

Orbit
Atlas
Skull
Lumbar vertebrae
Thoracic vertebrae
Axis
Sacrum
Caudal vertebrae
Cervical vertebrae
Pelvis
Scapula
Femur
Mandible
Fibula
Sternum
Tibia
Patella
Humerus
Calcaneum
Rib
Radius
Tarsals
Ulna
2nd metatarsal
Carpals
4th metatarsal
3rd metatarsal
3rd metacarpal (cannon bone)
Phalanges of 3rd digit
Phalanges of 3rd digit

Elephants

THE TWO SPECIES OF elephants – African and Asian – are the only members of the mammalian order Proboscidea. The bigger African elephant is the largest land animal: a fully grown male may be up to 4 m (13 ft) tall and weigh as much as 7 tonnes (6.9 tons). A fully grown male Asian elephant may be 3.3 m (11 ft) tall and weigh 5.4 tonnes (5.3 tons). The trunk – an extension of the nose and upper lip – is the elephant's other most obvious feature. It is used for manipulating and lifting, feeding, drinking and spraying water, smelling, touching, and producing trumpeting sounds. Other characteristic features include a pair of tusks, used for defence and for crushing vegetation; thick, pillar-like legs and broad feet to support the massive body; and large ear flaps that act as radiators to keep the elephant cool.

DIFFERENCES BETWEEN AFRICAN AND ASIAN ELEPHANTS

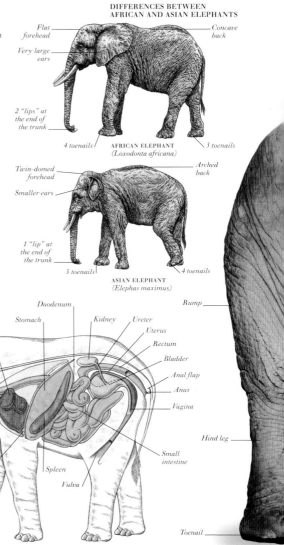

Flat forehead
Very large ears
Concave back
2 "lips" at the end of the trunk
4 toenails
3 toenails

AFRICAN ELEPHANT
(*Loxodonta africana*)

Twin-domed forehead
Smaller ears
Arched back
1 "lip" at the end of the trunk
5 toenails
4 toenails

ASIAN ELEPHANT
(*Elephas maximus*)

INTERNAL ANATOMY OF A FEMALE ELEPHANT

Spinal cord
Heart
Duodenum
Stomach
Kidney
Ureter
Uterus
Rectum
Bladder
Rump
Brain
Nasal cavity
Buccal cavity
Mouth
Tongue
Tusk
Epiglottis
Oesophagus
Trachea
Lung
Diaphragm
Nasal passage
Nostril
Spleen
Vulva
Small intestine
Anal flap
Anus
Vagina
Hind leg
Toenail

200

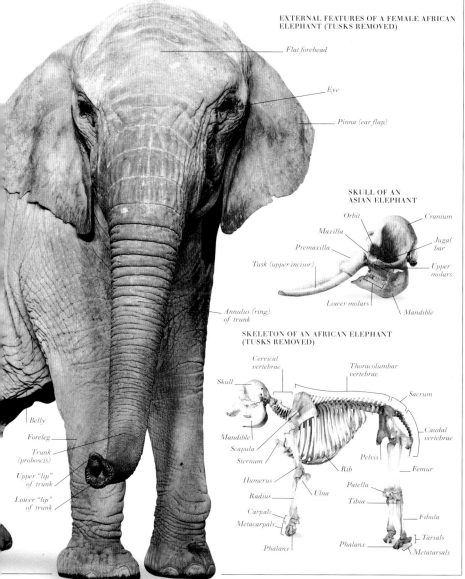

**EXTERNAL FEATURES OF A FEMALE AFRICAN
ELEPHANT (TUSKS REMOVED)**

Flat forehead

Eye

Pinna (ear flap)

Annulus (ring)
of trunk

Belly

Foreleg

Trunk
(proboscis)

Upper "lip"
of trunk

Lower "lip"
of trunk

**SKULL OF AN
ASIAN ELEPHANT**

Orbit

Cranium

Maxilla

Jugal
bar

Premaxilla

Upper
molars

Tusk (upper incisor)

Lower molars

Mandible

**SKELETON OF AN AFRICAN ELEPHANT
(TUSKS REMOVED)**

Cervical
vertebrae

Thoracolumbar
vertebrae

Skull

Sacrum

Mandible

Caudal
vertebrae

Scapula

Sternum

Pelvis

Humerus

Rib

Femur

Radius

Patella

Ulna

Tibia

Carpals

Fibula

Metacarpals

Phalanx

Phalanx

Tarsals

Metatarsals

201

Primates

THE MAMMALIAN ORDER PRIMATES consists of monkeys, apes, and their relatives (including humans). There are two suborders of primates: Prosimii, the primitive primates, which include lemurs, tarsiers, and lorises; and Anthropoidea, the advanced primates, which include monkeys, apes, and humans. The anthropoids are divided into New World monkeys, Old World monkeys, and hominids. New World monkeys typically have wide-apart nostrils that open to the side; and long tails, which are prehensile (grasping) in some species. This group of monkeys lives in South America, and includes marmosets, tamarins, and howler monkeys. Old World monkeys typically have close-set nostrils that open forwards or downwards; and non-prehensile tails. This group of monkeys lives in Africa and Asia, and includes langurs, mandrills, macaques, and baboons. Hominids typically have large brains, and no tail. This group includes the apes – chimpanzees, gibbons, gorillas, and orangutans – and humans.

INTERNAL ANATOMY OF A FEMALE CHIMPANZEE

Buccal cavity
Tongue
Trachea
Lung
Liver
Pancreas
Small intestine
Caecum
Appendix
Ovary
Uterus
Vagina
Brain
Nasal cavity
Spinal cord
Oesophagus
Heart
Diaphragm
Stomach
Spleen
Large intestine
Rectum
Bladder
Urethra

SKELETON OF A RHESUS MONKEY

Skull
Orbit
Cervical vertebrae
Mandible
Thoracic vertebrae
Clavicle
Scapula
Rib
Humerus
Lumbar vertebrae
Radius
Ulna
Femur
Sacrum
Patella
Tibia
Fibula
Carpals
Metacarpals
Pelvis
Caudal vertebrae
Tarsals
Metatarsals
Phalanges
Phalanges

SKULL OF A CHIMPANZEE

Temporal bone
Suture
Frontal bone
Parietal bone
Supraorbital ridge
Orbit
Maxilla
Premaxilla
Occipital bone
Auditory meatus
Zygomatic arch
Incisor tooth
Mandible
Molar tooth
Premolar tooth
Canine tooth

EXAMPLES OF PRIMATES

RING-TAILED LEMUR
(Lemur catta)
A prosimian

MALE RED HOWLER MONKEY
(Alouatta seniculus)
A New World monkey

MALE MANDRILL
(Mandrillus sphinx)
An Old World monkey

CHIMPANZEE
(Pan troglodytes)
An ape

EXTERNAL FEATURES OF A YOUNG GORILLA

GOLDEN LION TAMARIN
(Leontopithecus rosalia)
A New World monkey

Pinna (ear flap)

Brow ridge

Eye

Nostril

Mouth

Upper arm

Forearm

Chest

Elbow

Shoulder

Thigh

Knee

Lower leg

Hand

Foot

Toe

Finger

Toenail

Dolphins, whales, and seals

DOLPHINS, WHALES, AND SEALS belong
to two orders of mammals adapted to living
in water. Dolphins and whales make up the
order Cetacea. Typical cetacean features include
a streamlined, fish-like shape; forelimbs in the form
of flippers; no visible hind limbs; a horizontally flattened
tail; and thick blubber under the skin. There are two groups
of cetaceans: toothed whales, including sperm whales, white whales,
beaked whales, dolphins, and porpoises; and the larger whalebone (baleen)
whales, including rorquals, grey whales, and right whales. The blue whale – a
rorqual – is the largest living animal: an adult may be up to 30 m (100 ft) long
and weigh 130 tonnes (128 tons). Seals and their relatives – sea lions and
walruses – make up the order Pinnipedia. Characteristically, they have a
streamlined, torpedo-shaped body; forelimbs and hind limbs modified as
flippers; thick blubber; and no external ears.

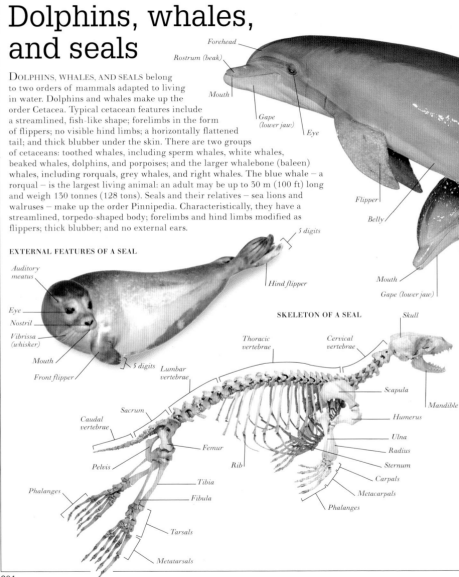

Forehead

Rostrum (beak)

Mouth

Gape (lower jaw)

Eye

Flipper

Belly

Mouth

Gape (lower jaw)

EXTERNAL FEATURES OF A SEAL

5 digits

Hind flipper

Auditory meatus

Eye

Nostril

Vibrissa (whisker)

Mouth

Front flipper

5 digits

SKELETON OF A SEAL

Skull

Thoracic vertebrae

Cervical vertebrae

Lumbar vertebrae

Scapula

Mandible

Caudal vertebrae

Sacrum

Humerus

Ulna

Radius

Sternum

Carpals

Metacarpals

Phalanges

Femur

Rib

Pelvis

Tibia

Fibula

Phalanges

Tarsals

Metatarsals

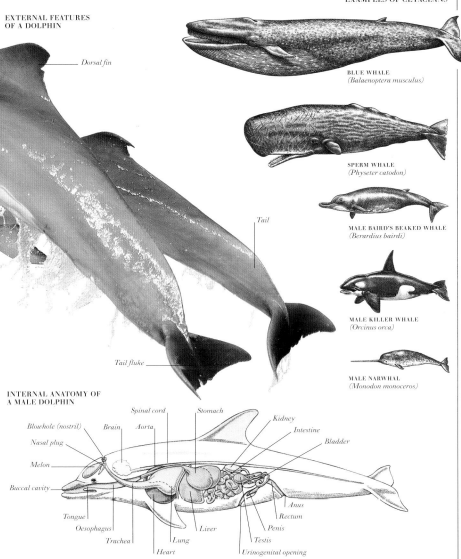

EXAMPLES OF CETACEANS

**EXTERNAL FEATURES
OF A DOLPHIN**

Dorsal fin

Tail

Tail fluke

BLUE WHALE
(Balaenoptera musculus)

SPERM WHALE
(Physeter catodon)

MALE BAIRD'S BEAKED WHALE
(Berardius bairdi)

MALE KILLER WHALE
(Orcinus orca)

MALE NARWHAL
(Monodon monoceros)

**INTERNAL ANATOMY OF
A MALE DOLPHIN**

Blowhole (nostril)
Nasal plug
Melon
Buccal cavity
Tongue
Oesophagus
Trachea
Brain
Spinal cord
Aorta
Stomach
Kidney
Intestine
Bladder
Anus
Rectum
Penis
Testis
Urinogenital opening
Liver
Lung
Heart

Marsupials and Monotremes

MARSUPIALS AND MONOTREMES are two orders of mammals that differ from other mammalian groups in the ways that their young develop. The order Marsupalia, the pouched mammals, is made up of kangaroos and their relatives. Typically, marsupials give birth to their young at a very early stage of development. The young then crawls to the mother's pouch (which is on the outside of her abdomen), where it attaches itself to a nipple and remains until fully developed. Most marsupials live in Australia, although the opossums – which are classified as marsupials despite not having a pouch – live in the Americas. The order Monotremata is made up of the platypus and its relatives (the echidnas, or spiny anteaters). The monotremes are primitive mammals that lay eggs, which the mother incubates. The monotremes are found only in Australia and New Guinea.

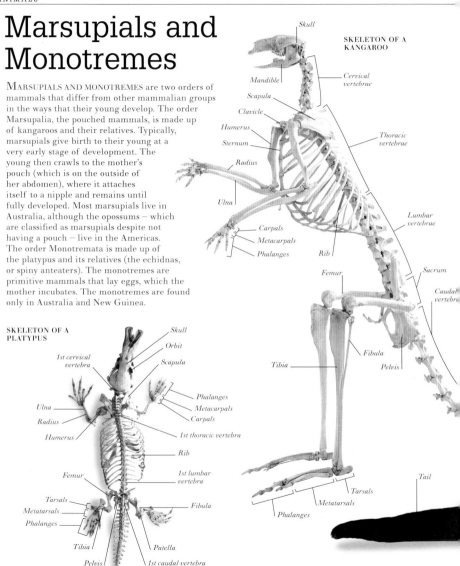

SKELETON OF A KANGAROO

Skull

Mandible

Cervical vertebrae

Scapula

Clavicle

Humerus

Sternum

Radius

Ulna

Thoracic vertebrae

Carpals

Metacarpals

Phalanges

Rib

Lumbar vertebrae

Femur

Sacrum

Caudal vertebra

Fibula

Tibia

Pelvis

Tarsals

Metatarsals

Phalanges

Tail

SKELETON OF A PLATYPUS

Skull

Orbit

Scapula

1st cervical vertebra

Ulna

Radius

Humerus

Phalanges

Metacarpals

Carpals

1st thoracic vertebra

Rib

1st lumbar vertebra

Femur

Tarsals

Metatarsals

Phalanges

Fibula

Tibia

Pelvis

Patella

1st caudal vertebra

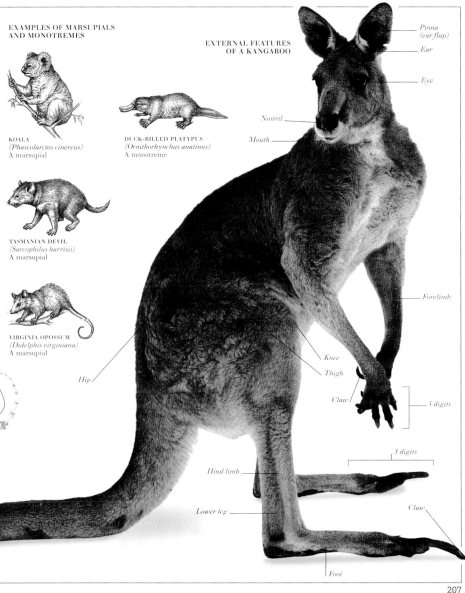

EXAMPLES OF MARSUPIALS
AND MONOTREMES

EXTERNAL FEATURES
OF A KANGAROO

Pinna
(ear flap)

Ear

Eye

Nostril

Mouth

KOALA
(Phascolarctos cinereus)
A marsupial

DUCK-BILLED PLATYPUS
(Ornithorhynchus anatinus)
A monotreme

TASMANIAN DEVIL
(Sarcophilus harrisii)
A marsupial

Forelimb

Knee

Thigh

VIRGINIA OPOSSUM
(Didelphis virginiana)
A marsupial

Hip

Claw

5 digits

3 digits

Hind limb

Claw

Lower leg

Foot

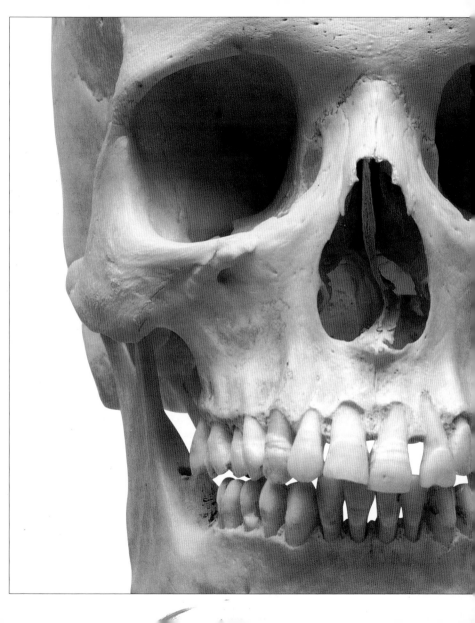

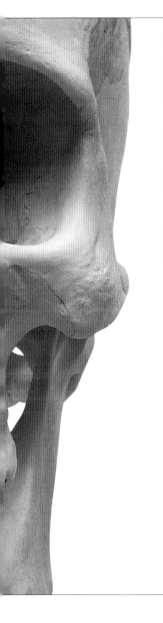

THE
HUMAN BODY

Body features

ALTHOUGH THERE IS enormous
variation between the external
appearances of humans, all bodies
contain the same basic features.
The outward form of the
human body depends on the
size of the skeleton, the shape
of the muscles, the thickness
of the fat layer beneath
the skin, the elasticity or
sagginess of the skin, and
the person's age and sex.
Males tend to be taller than
females, with broader
shoulders, more body hair,
and a different pattern of fat
deposits under the skin; the
female body tends to be
less muscular and has
a shallower and wider
pelvis to allow
for childbirth.

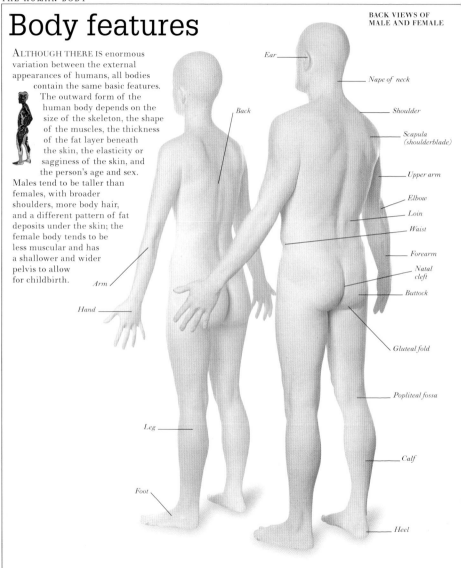

Ear

Nape of neck

Shoulder

Back

Scapula
(shoulderblade)

Upper arm

Elbow

Loin

Waist

Forearm

Natal
cleft

Arm

Buttock

Hand

Gluteal fold

Popliteal fossa

Leg

Calf

Foot

Heel

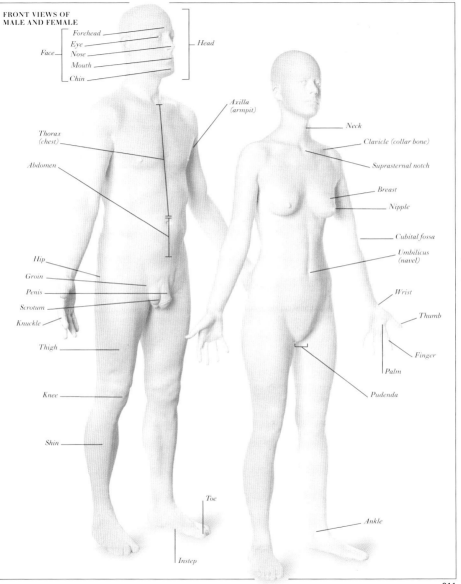

FRONT VIEWS OF MALE AND FEMALE

Forehead

Eye

Face — Nose

Mouth

Chin

Head

Axilla (armpit)

Thorax (chest)

Abdomen

Hip

Groin

Penis

Scrotum

Knuckle

Thigh

Knee

Shin

Toe

Instep

Neck

Clavicle (collar bone)

Suprasternal notch

Breast

Nipple

Cubital fossa

Umbilicus (navel)

Wrist

Thumb

Finger

Palm

Pudenda

Ankle

Head

IN A NEWBORN BABY, the head accounts for one-quarter of the total body length; by adulthood, the proportion has reduced to one-eighth. Contained in the head are the body's main sense organs: eyes, ears, olfactory nerves that detect smells, and the taste buds of the tongue. Signals from these organs pass to the body's great coordination centre: the brain, housed in the protective, bony dome of the skull. Hair on the head insulates against heat loss, and adult males also grow thick facial hair. The face has three important openings: two nostrils through which air passes, and the mouth, which takes in nourishment and helps form speech. Although all heads are basically similar, differences in the size, shape, and colour of features produce an infinite variety of appearances.

SIDE VIEW OF EXTERNAL FEATURES OF HEAD

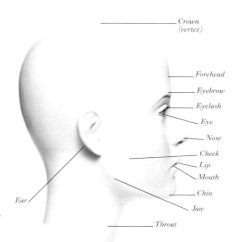

Crown (vertex)
Forehead
Eyebrow
Eyelash
Eye
Nose
Cheek
Lip
Mouth
Chin
Jaw
Throat
Ear

SECTION THROUGH HEAD

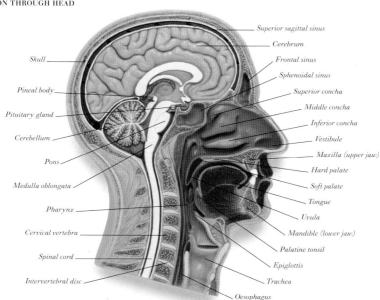

Skull
Pineal body
Pituitary gland
Cerebellum
Pons
Medulla oblongata
Pharynx
Cervical vertebra
Spinal cord
Intervertebral disc

Superior sagittal sinus
Cerebrum
Frontal sinus
Sphenoidal sinus
Superior concha
Middle concha
Inferior concha
Vestibule
Maxilla (upper jaw)
Hard palate
Soft palate
Tongue
Uvula
Mandible (lower jaw)
Palatine tonsil
Epiglottis
Trachea
Oesophagus

**FRONT VIEW OF EXTERNAL
FEATURES OF HEAD**

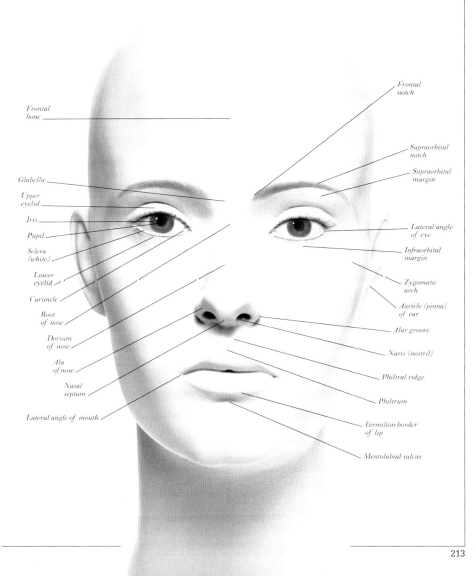

Frontal
notch

Supraorbital
notch

Supraorbital
margin

Frontal
bone

Lateral angle
of eye

Glabella

Upper
eyelid

Infraorbital
margin

Iris

Pupil

Zygomatic
arch

Sclera
(white)

Auricle (pinna)
of ear

Lower
eyelid

Alar groove

Caruncle

Naris (nostril)

Root
of nose

Philtral ridge

Dorsum
of nose

Philtrum

Ala
of nose

Nasal
septum

Lateral angle of mouth

Vermilion border
of lip

Mentolabial sulcus

Body organs

ALL THE VITAL BODY ORGANS except for the brain are enclosed within the trunk or torso (the body apart from the head and limbs). The trunk contains two large cavities separated by a muscular sheet called the diaphragm. The upper cavity, known as the thorax or chest cavity, contains the heart and lungs. The lower cavity, called the abdominal cavity, contains the stomach, intestines, liver, and pancreas, which all play a role in digesting food. Also within the trunk are the kidneys and bladder, which are part of the urinary system, and the reproductive organs, which hold the seeds of new human life. Modern imaging techniques, such as contrast X-rays and different types of scans, make it possible to see and study body organs without the need to cut through their protective coverings of skin, fat, muscle, and bone.

MAJOR INTERNAL STRUCTURES

Thyroid gland

Larynx

Heart

Right lung

Left lung

Liver

Diaphragm

Stomach

Large intestine

Small intestine

Greater omentum

IMAGING THE BODY

SCINTIGRAM OF HEART CHAMBERS

ANGIOGRAM OF RIGHT LUNG

CONTRAST X-RAY OF GALLBLADDER

SCINTIGRAM OF NERVOUS SYSTEM

DOUBLE CONTRAST X-RAY OF COLON

ULTRASOUND SCAN OF TWINS IN UTERUS

ANGIOGRAM OF KIDNEYS

ANGIOGRAM OF ARTERIES OF HEAD

CT SCAN THROUGH FEMALE CHEST

THERMOGRAM OF CHEST REGION

ANGIOGRAM OF ARTERIES OF HEART

MRI SCAN THROUGH HEAD AT EYE LEVEL

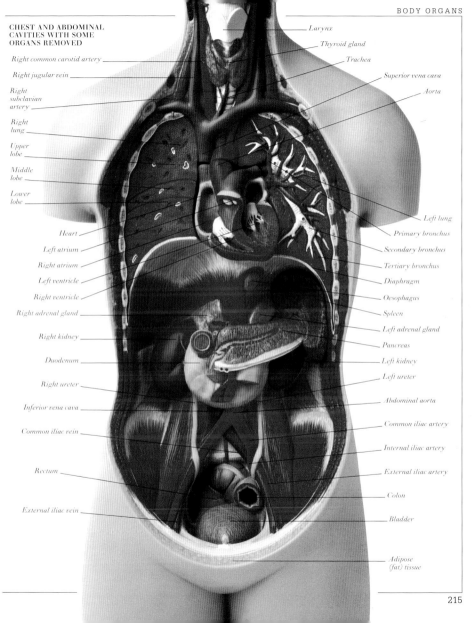

CHEST AND ABDOMINAL CAVITIES WITH SOME ORGANS REMOVED

Right common carotid artery

Right jugular vein

Right subclavian artery

Right lung

Upper lobe

Middle lobe

Lower lobe

Heart

Left atrium

Right atrium

Left ventricle

Right ventricle

Right adrenal gland

Right kidney

Duodenum

Right ureter

Inferior vena cava

Common iliac vein

Rectum

External iliac vein

Larynx

Thyroid gland

Trachea

Superior vena cava

Aorta

Left lung

Primary bronchus

Secondary bronchus

Tertiary bronchus

Diaphragm

Oesophagus

Spleen

Left adrenal gland

Pancreas

Left kidney

Left ureter

Abdominal aorta

Common iliac artery

Internal iliac artery

External iliac artery

Colon

Bladder

Adipose (fat) tissue

215

Body cells

EVERYONE IS MADE UP OF BILLIONS OF CELLS, which are the basic structural units of the body. Bones, muscles, nerves, skin, blood, and all other body tissues are formed from different types of cells. Each cell has a specific function but works with other types of cells to perform the enormous number of tasks needed to sustain life. Most body cells have a similar basic structure. Each cell has an outer layer (called the cell membrane) and contains a fluid material (cytoplasm). Within the cytoplasm are many specialized structures (organelles). The most important organelle is the nucleus, which contains vital genetic material and acts as the cell's control centre.

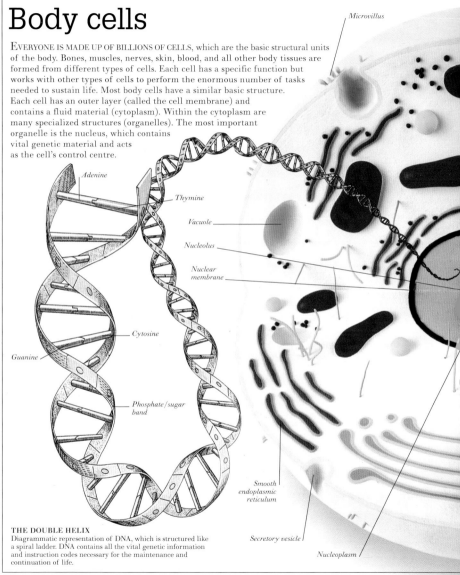

Microvillus

Adenine

Thymine

Vacuole

Nucleolus

Nuclear membrane

Cytosine

Guanine

Phosphate/sugar band

Smooth endoplasmic reticulum

Secretory vesicle

Nucleoplasm

THE DOUBLE HELIX
Diagrammatic representation of DNA, which is structured like a spiral ladder. DNA contains all the vital genetic information and instruction codes necessary for the maintenance and continuation of life.

GENERALIZED HUMAN CELL

Cytoplasm

Lysosome

Cell membrane

Mitochondrial crista

Nucleus

Rough endoplasmic reticulum

Microfilament

Pore of nuclear membrane

Ribosome

Centriole

Mitochondrion

Microtubule

Peroxisome

Pinocytotic vesicle

Golgi complex (Golgi apparatus; Golgi body)

TYPES OF CELLS

BONE-FORMING CELL

NERVE CELLS IN SPINAL CORD

SPERM CELLS IN SEMEN

SECRETORY THYROID GLAND CELLS

ACID-SECRETING STOMACH CELLS

CONNECTIVE TISSUE CELLS

MUCUS-SECRETING DUODENAL CELLS

RED AND TWO WHITE BLOOD CELLS

FAT CELLS IN ADIPOSE TISSUE

EPITHELIAL CELLS IN CHEEK

Skeleton

THE SKELETON IS A MOBILE FRAMEWORK made up of 206 bones, approximately half of which are in the hands and feet. Although individual bones are rigid, the skeleton as a whole is remarkably flexible and allows the human body a huge range of movement. The skeleton serves as an anchorage for the skeletal muscles, and as a protective cage for the body's internal organs. Female bones are usually smaller and lighter than male bones, and the female pelvis is shallower and has a wider cavity.

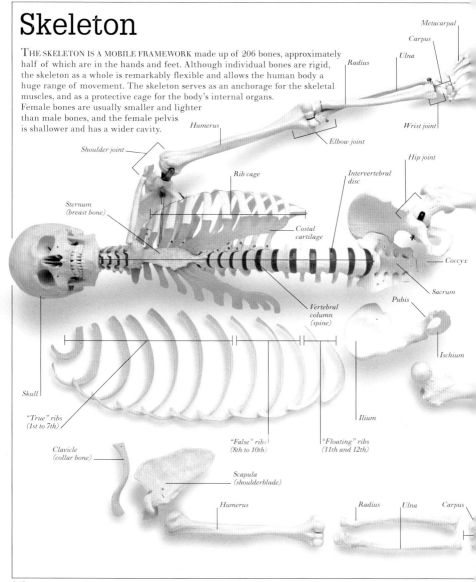

Metacarpal

Carpus

Ulna

Radius

Humerus

Shoulder joint

Wrist joint

Elbow joint

Hip joint

Rib cage

Intervertebral disc

Sternum (breast bone)

Costal cartilage

Coccyx

Sacrum

Pubis

Vertebral column (spine)

Ischium

Skull

"True" ribs (1st to 7th)

"False" ribs (8th to 10th)

"Floating" ribs (11th and 12th)

Ilium

Clavicle (collar bone)

Scapula (shoulderblade)

Humerus

Radius

Ulna

Carpus

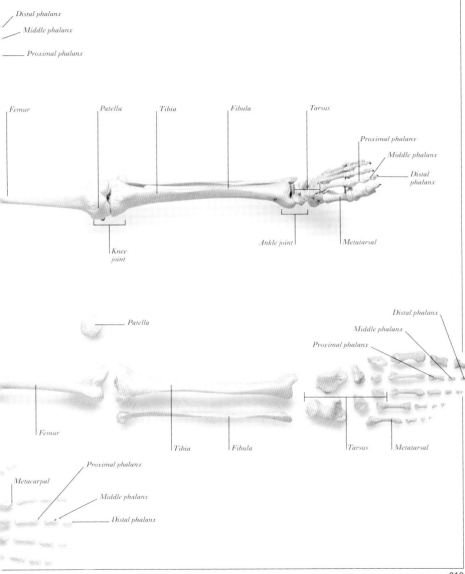

Distal phalanx

Middle phalanx

Proximal phalanx

Femur

Patella

Tibia

Fibula

Tarsus

Proximal phalanx

Middle phalanx

Distal phalanx

Knee joint

Ankle joint

Metatarsal

Patella

Distal phalanx

Middle phalanx

Proximal phalanx

Femur

Tibia

Fibula

Tarsus

Metatarsal

Metacarpal

Proximal phalanx

Middle phalanx

Distal phalanx

Skull

THE SKULL is the most complicated bony structure of the body but every feature serves a purpose. Internally, the main hollow chamber of the skull has three levels that support the brain, with every bump and hollow corresponding to the shape of the brain. Underneath and towards the back of the skull is a large round hole, the foramen magnum, through which the spinal cord passes. To the front of this are many smaller openings through which nerves, arteries, and veins pass to and from the brain. The roof of the skull is formed from four thin, curved bones that are firmly fixed together from the age of about two years. At the front of the skull are the two orbits, which contain the eyeballs, and a central hole for the airway of the nose. The jaw bone hinges on either side at ear level.

RIGHT SIDE VIEW OF A FETAL SKULL

Anterior fontanelle

Parietal bone

Coronal suture

Frontal bone

Nasal bone

Mental symphysis

Lambdoid suture

Occipital bone

Sphenoidal fontanelle

Mastoid fontanelle

External auditory meatus

RIGHT SIDE VIEW OF SKULL

Frontal bone

Coronal suture

Greater wing of sphenoid bone

Parietal bone

Squamous suture

Frontozygomatic suture

Supraorbital margin

Orbital cavity

Nasal bone

Anterior nasal spine

Maxilla (upper jaw)

Mandible (lower jaw)

Lambdoid suture

Occipital bone

Temporal bone

External auditory meatus

Condyle

Coronoid process

Zygomatic bone

Mental foramen

Mastoid process

VIEW OF SKULL FROM BELOW

External occipital crest

Foramen magnum

Occipital condyle

Carotid canal

Mastoid process

Pharyngeal tubercle

Pterygoid plate

Pterygoid hamulus

Greater palatine foramen

Posterior nasal aperture

Mandible (lower jaw)

Concha

Posterior border of vomer

Zygomatic arch

Styloid process

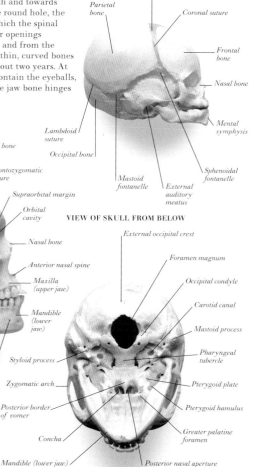

FRONT VIEW OF SKULL

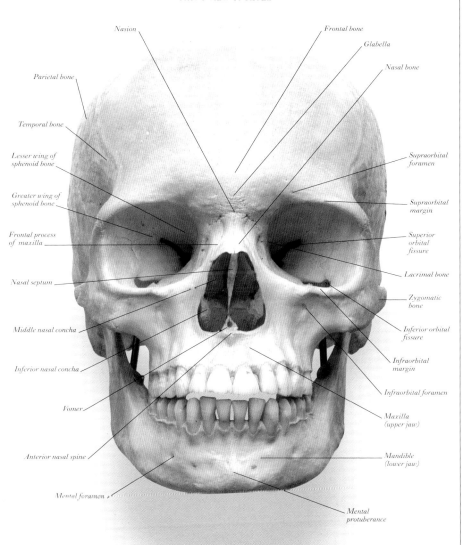

Nasion

Frontal bone

Glabella

Nasal bone

Parietal bone

Temporal bone

Lesser wing of sphenoid bone

Greater wing of sphenoid bone

Frontal process of maxilla

Nasal septum

Middle nasal concha

Inferior nasal concha

Vomer

Anterior nasal spine

Mental foramen

Supraorbital foramen

Supraorbital margin

Superior orbital fissure

Lacrimal bone

Zygomatic bone

Inferior orbital fissure

Infraorbital margin

Infraorbital foramen

Maxilla (upper jaw)

Mandible (lower jaw)

Mental protuberance

Spine

THE SPINE (OR VERTEBRAL COLUMN) has two main functions: it serves as a protective surrounding for the delicate spinal cord and forms the supporting back bone of the skeleton. The spine consists of 24 separate differently shaped bones (vertebrae) with a curved, triangular bone (the sacrum) at the bottom. The sacrum is made up of fused vertebrae; at its lower end is a small tail-like structure made up of tiny bones collectively called the coccyx. Between each pair of vertebrae is a disc of cartilage that cushions the bones during movement. The top two vertebrae differ in appearance from the others and work as a pair: the first, called the atlas, rotates around a stout vertical peg on the second, the axis. This arrangement allows the skull to move freely up and down, and from side to side.

SPINE DIVIDED INTO VERTEBRAL SECTIONS

FRONT

Cervical vertebrae —

Thoracic vertebrae —

Lumbar vertebrae —

Sacral vertebrae —

Coccygeal vertebrae —

TYPES OF VERTEBRAE (VIEWED FROM ABOVE)

ATLAS

Anterior arch

Lateral mass with superior articular facet

Posterior arch

Anterior tubercle

Posterior tubercle

Vertebral foramen

Transverse process

Transverse foramen

AXIS

Facet

Dens

Vertebral foramen

Spinous process

Lamina

Transverse process and foramen

CERVICAL VERTEBRA

Body

Superior articular process

Anterior tubercle

Spinous process

Vertebral foramen

Posterior tubercle

Transverse foramen

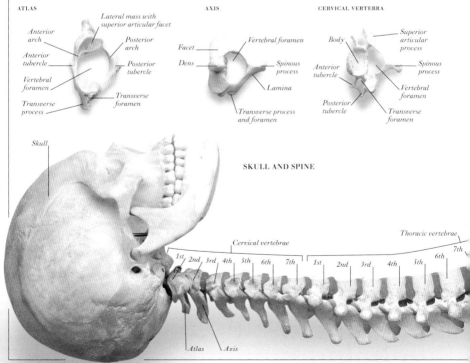

SKULL AND SPINE

Skull

Cervical vertebrae
1st 2nd 3rd 4th 5th 6th 7th

Thoracic vertebrae
1st 2nd 3rd 4th 5th 6th 7th

Atlas Axis

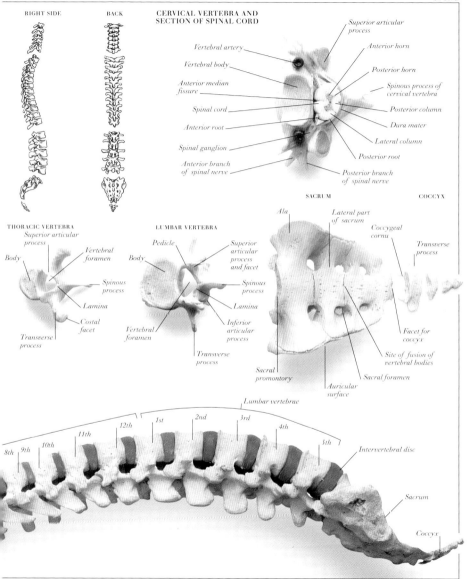

RIGHT SIDE

BACK

**CERVICAL VERTEBRA AND
SECTION OF SPINAL CORD**

Superior articular process

Anterior horn

Vertebral artery

Posterior horn

Vertebral body

Spinous process of cervical vertebra

Anterior median fissure

Posterior column

Spinal cord

Dura mater

Anterior root

Lateral column

Spinal ganglion

Posterior root

Anterior branch of spinal nerve

Posterior branch of spinal nerve

SACRUM

COCCYX

Ala

Lateral part of sacrum

Coccygeal cornu

THORACIC VERTEBRA

Transverse process

Superior articular process

Vertebral foramen

Body

Spinous process

Lamina

Costal facet

Transverse process

LUMBAR VERTEBRA

Pedicle

Body

Superior articular process and facet

Spinous process

Lamina

Inferior articular process

Vertebral foramen

Transverse process

Sacral promontory

Auricular surface

Facet for coccyx

Site of fusion of vertebral bodies

Sacral foramen

Lumbar vertebrae

1st

2nd

3rd

4th

5th

8th 9th 10th 11th 12th

Intervertebral disc

Sacrum

Coccyx

Bones and joints

BONES FORM the body's hard, strong skeletal framework. Each bone has a hard, compact exterior surrounding a spongy, lighter interior. The long bones of the arms and legs, such as the femur (thigh bone), have a central cavity containing bone marrow. Bones are composed chiefly of calcium, phosphorus, and a fibrous substance known as collagen. Bones meet at joints, which are of several different types. For example, the hip is a ball-and-socket joint that allows the femur a wide range of movement, whereas finger joints are simple hinge joints that allow only bending and straightening. Joints are held in place by bands of tissue called ligaments. Movement of joints is facilitated by the smooth hyaline cartilage that covers the bone ends and by the synovial membrane that lines and lubricates the joint.

LIGAMENTS SURROUNDING HIP JOINT

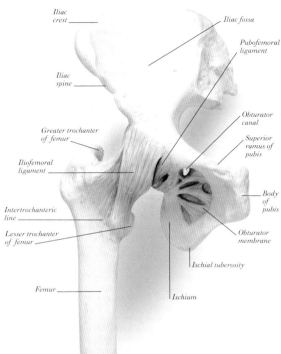

Iliac crest

Iliac fossa

Pubofemoral ligament

Iliac spine

Greater trochanter of femur

Obturator canal

Superior ramus of pubis

Iliofemoral ligament

Body of pubis

Intertrochanteric line

Lesser trochanter of femur

Obturator membrane

Ischial tuberosity

Femur

Ischium

SECTION THROUGH LEFT FEMUR

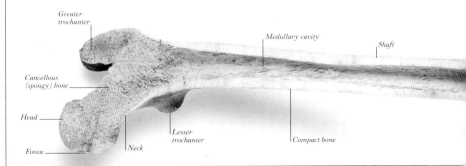

Greater trochanter

Medullary cavity

Shaft

Cancellous (spongy) bone

Head

Fovea

Neck

Lesser trochanter

Compact bone

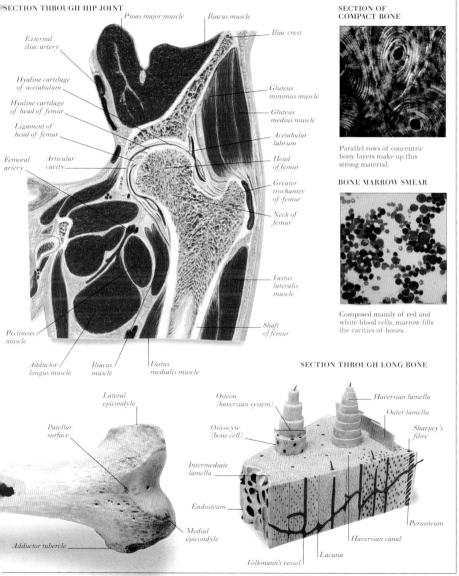

SECTION THROUGH HIP JOINT

Psoas major muscle

Iliacus muscle

External iliac artery

Iliac crest

Hyaline cartilage of acetabulum

Hyaline cartilage of head of femur

Gluteus minimus muscle

Ligament of head of femur

Gluteus medius muscle

Femoral artery

Articular cavity

Acetabular labrum

Head of femur

Greater trochanter of femur

Neck of femur

Vastus lateralis muscle

Pectineus muscle

Adductor longus muscle

Iliacus muscle

Vastus medialis muscle

Shaft of femur

SECTION OF COMPACT BONE

Parallel rows of concentric bony layers make up this strong material.

BONE MARROW SMEAR

Composed mainly of red and white blood cells, marrow fills the cavities of bones.

SECTION THROUGH LONG BONE

Lateral epicondyle

Patellar surface

Osteon (haversian system)

Haversian lamella

Outer lamella

Osteocyte (bone cell)

Sharpey's fibre

Intermediate lamella

Endosteum

Adductor tubercle

Medial epicondyle

Periosteum

Volkmann's vessel

Lacuna

Haversian canal

Muscles 1

THERE ARE THREE MAIN TYPES OF MUSCLE: skeletal muscle (also called voluntary muscle because it can be consciously controlled); smooth muscle (also called involuntary muscle because it is not under voluntary control); and the specialized muscle tissue of the heart. Humans have more than 600 skeletal muscles, which differ in size and shape according to the jobs they do. Skeletal muscles are attached either directly or indirectly (via tendons) to bones, and work in opposing pairs (one muscle in the pair contracts while the other relaxes) to produce body movements as diverse as walking, threading a needle, and an array of facial expressions. Smooth muscles occur in the walls of internal body organs and perform actions such as forcing food through the intestines, contracting the uterus (womb) in childbirth, and pumping blood through the blood vessels.

SOME OTHER MUSCLES IN THE BODY

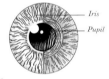

- Iris
- Pupil

IRIS
The muscle fibres contract and dilate (expand) to alter pupil size.

TONGUE
Interlacing layers of muscle allow great mobility.

ILEUM
Opposing muscle layers transport semi-digested food.

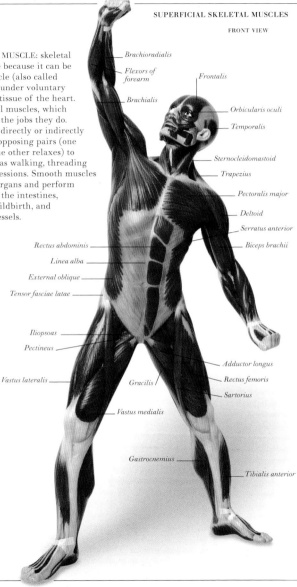

SUPERFICIAL SKELETAL MUSCLES

FRONT VIEW

- Brachioradialis
- Flexors of forearm
- Frontalis
- Brachialis
- Orbicularis oculi
- Temporalis
- Sternocleidomastoid
- Trapezius
- Pectoralis major
- Deltoid
- Serratus anterior
- Biceps brachii
- Rectus abdominis
- Linea alba
- External oblique
- Tensor fasciae latae
- Iliopsoas
- Pectineus
- Adductor longus
- Rectus femoris
- Sartorius
- Vastus lateralis
- Gracilis
- Vastus medialis
- Gastrocnemius
- Tibialis anterior

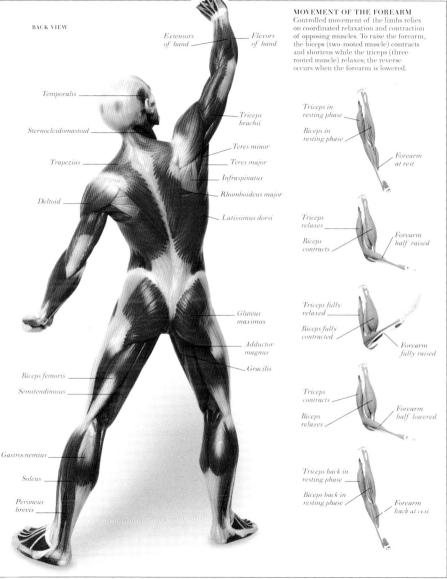

BACK VIEW

Extensors of hand

Flexors of hand

MOVEMENT OF THE FOREARM
Controlled movement of the limbs relies on coordinated relaxation and contraction of opposing muscles. To raise the forearm, the biceps (two-rooted muscle) contracts and shortens while the triceps (three-rooted muscle) relaxes; the reverse occurs when the forearm is lowered.

Temporalis

Sternocleidomastoid

Trapezius

Deltoid

Triceps brachii

Teres minor

Teres major

Infraspinatus

Rhomboideus major

Latissimus dorsi

Gluteus maximus

Adductor magnus

Gracilis

Biceps femoris

Semitendinosus

Gastrocnemius

Soleus

Peroneus brevis

Triceps in resting phase

Biceps in resting phase

Forearm at rest

Triceps relaxes

Biceps contracts

Forearm half raised

Triceps fully relaxed

Biceps fully contracted

Forearm fully raised

Triceps contracts

Biceps relaxes

Forearm half lowered

Triceps back in resting phase

Biceps back in resting phase

Forearm back at rest

Muscles 2

SKELETAL MUSCLE FIBRE

Myofibril

Sarcomere

Nucleus

Sarcoplasmic reticulum

Sarcolemma

Endomysium

Motor end plate

Synaptic knob

Schwann cell

Motor neuron

Node of Ranvier

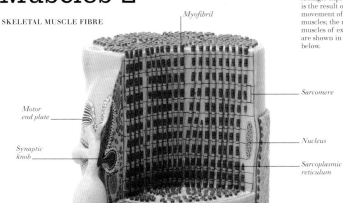

MUSCLES OF FACIAL EXPRESSION

A single expression is the result of movement of many muscles; the main muscles of expression are shown in action below.

FRONTALIS

CORRUGATOR SUPERCILII

ORBICULARIS ORIS

TYPES OF MUSCLE

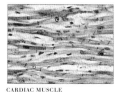

CARDIAC MUSCLE

SKELETAL MUSCLE

SMOOTH MUSCLE

ZYGOMATICUS MAJOR

CONTRACTION OF SKELETAL MUSCLE

RELAXED STATE

CONTRACTED STATE

DEPRESSOR ANGULI ORIS

MUSCLES OF HEAD AND NECK

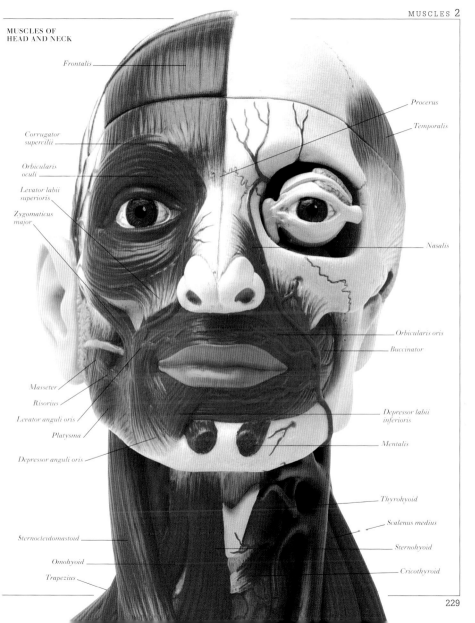

Frontalis

Procerus

Temporalis

Corrugator supercilii

Orbicularis oculi

Levator labii superioris

Zygomaticus major

Nasalis

Orbicularis oris

Buccinator

Masseter

Risorius

Levator anguli oris

Platysma

Depressor anguli oris

Depressor labii inferioris

Mentalis

Thyrohyoid

Scalenus medius

Sternocleidomastoid

Sternohyoid

Omohyoid

Cricothyroid

Trapezius

Hands

THE HUMAN HAND is an extremely versatile tool, capable of delicate manipulation as well as powerful gripping actions. The arrangement of its 27 small bones, moved by 37 skeletal muscles that are connected to the bones by tendons, allows a wide range of movements. Our ability to bring the tips of our thumbs and fingers together, combined with the extraordinary sensitivity of our fingertips due to their rich supply of nerve endings, makes our hands uniquely dextrous.

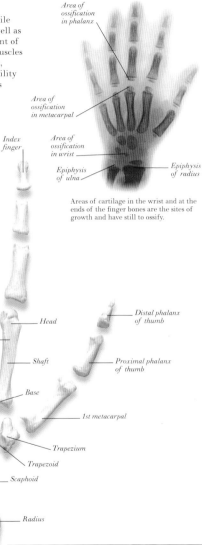

X-RAY OF LEFT HAND OF A YOUNG CHILD

Area of ossification in phalanx

Area of ossification in metacarpal

Area of ossification in wrist

Epiphysis of ulna

Epiphysis of radius

Areas of cartilage in the wrist and at the ends of the finger bones are the sites of growth and have still to ossify.

BONES OF HAND

Ring finger

Middle finger

Index finger

Little finger

Distal phalanx

Middle phalanx

Proximal phalanx

2nd metacarpal

3rd metacarpal

4th metacarpal

5th metacarpal

Hamate

Pisiform

Capitate

Triquetral

Lunate

Ulna

Head

Shaft

Base

Trapezium

Trapezoid

Scaphoid

Radius

Distal phalanx of thumb

Proximal phalanx of thumb

1st metacarpal

STRUCTURES UNDERLYING SKIN
OF PALM OF HAND

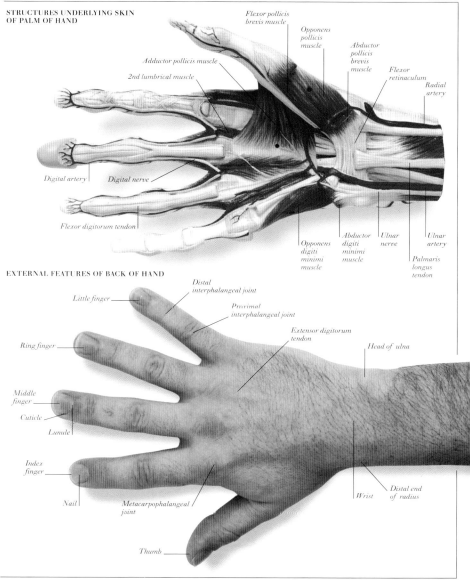

Flexor pollicis brevis muscle

Opponens pollicis muscle

Abductor pollicis brevis muscle

Flexor retinaculum

Radial artery

Adductor pollicis muscle

2nd lumbrical muscle

Digital artery

Digital nerve

Flexor digitorum tendon

Opponens digiti minimi muscle

Abductor digiti minimi muscle

Ulnar nerve

Ulnar artery

Palmaris longus tendon

EXTERNAL FEATURES OF BACK OF HAND

Little finger

Distal interphalangeal joint

Proximal interphalangeal joint

Extensor digitorum tendon

Head of ulna

Ring finger

Middle finger

Cuticle

Lunule

Index finger

Nail

Metacarpophalangeal joint

Wrist

Distal end of radius

Thumb

231

Feet

BONES OF FOOT

THE FEET AND TOES are essential elements in body movement. They bear and propel the weight of the body during walking and running, and also help to maintain balance during changes of body position. Each foot has 26 bones, more than 100 ligaments, and 33 muscles, some of which are attached to the lower leg. The heel pad and the arch of the foot act as shock absorbers, providing a cushion against the jolts that occur with every step.

LIGAMENTS OF FOOT

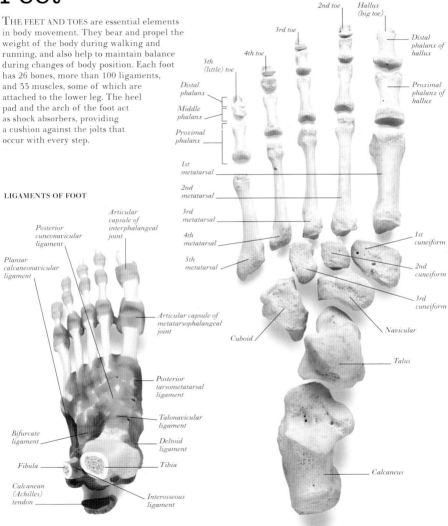

2nd toe
Hallux (big toe)
3rd toe
Distal phalanx of hallux
4th toe
Proximal phalanx of hallux
5th (little) toe
Distal phalanx
Middle phalanx
Proximal phalanx
1st metatarsal
2nd metatarsal
3rd metatarsal
4th metatarsal
5th metatarsal
1st cuneiform
2nd cuneiform
3rd cuneiform
Navicular
Cuboid
Talus
Calcaneus

Posterior cuneonavicular ligament
Articular capsule of interphalangeal joint
Plantar calcaneonavicular ligament
Articular capsule of metatarsophalangeal joint
Posterior tarsometatarsal ligament
Talonavicular ligament
Bifurcate ligament
Deltoid ligament
Fibula
Tibia
Calcanean (Achilles) tendon
Interosseous ligament

STRUCTURES UNDERLYING SKIN OF FOOT

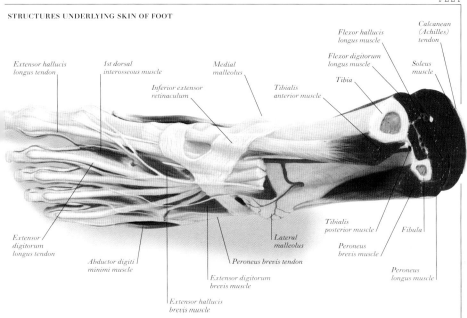

Extensor hallucis longus tendon

1st dorsal interosseous muscle

Medial malleolus

Inferior extensor retinaculum

Flexor hallucis longus muscle

Flexor digitorum longus muscle

Calcanean (Achilles) tendon

Soleus muscle

Tibialis anterior muscle

Tibia

Extensor digitorum longus tendon

Abductor digiti minimi muscle

Lateral malleolus

Peroneus brevis tendon

Extensor digitorum brevis muscle

Extensor hallucis brevis muscle

Tibialis posterior muscle

Peroneus brevis muscle

Fibula

Peroneus longus muscle

EXTERNAL FEATURES OF FOOT

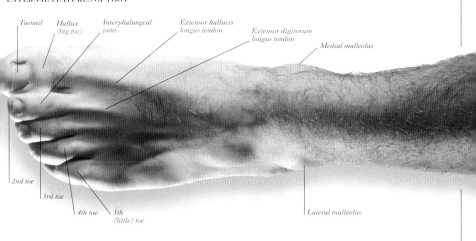

Toenail

Hallux (big toe)

Interphalangeal joint

Extensor hallucis longus tendon

Extensor digitorum longus tendon

Medial malleolus

2nd toe

3rd toe

4th toe

5th (little) toe

Lateral malleolus

Skin and hair

SKIN IS THE BODY'S LARGEST ORGAN, a waterproof barrier that protects the internal organs against infection, injury, and harmful sun rays. The skin is also an important sensory organ and helps to control body temperature. The outer layer of the skin, known as the epidermis, is coated with keratin, a tough, horny protein that is also the chief constituent of hair and nails. Dead cells are shed from the skin's surface and are replaced by new cells from the base of the epidermis, the region that also produces the skin pigment, melanin. The dermis contains most of the skin's living structures, and includes nerve endings, blood vessels, elastic fibres, sweat glands that cool the skin, and sebaceous glands that produce oil to keep the skin supple. Beneath the dermis lies the subcutaneous tissue (hypodermis), which is rich in fat and blood vessels. Hair shafts grow from hair follicles situated in the dermis and subcutaneous tissue. Hair grows on every part of the skin apart from the palms of the hands and soles of the feet.

SECTION OF HAIR

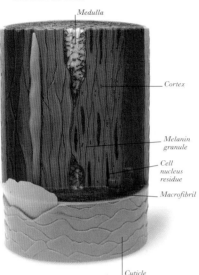

Medulla

Cortex

Melanin granule

Cell nucleus residue

Macrofibril

Cuticle

SECTIONS OF DIFFERENT TYPES OF SKIN

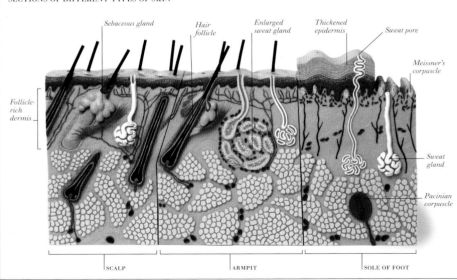

Sebaceous gland

Hair follicle

Enlarged sweat gland

Thickened epidermis

Sweat pore

Meissner's corpuscle

Follicle-rich dermis

Sweat gland

Pacinian corpuscle

SCALP

ARMPIT

SOLE OF FOOT

SECTION OF SKIN

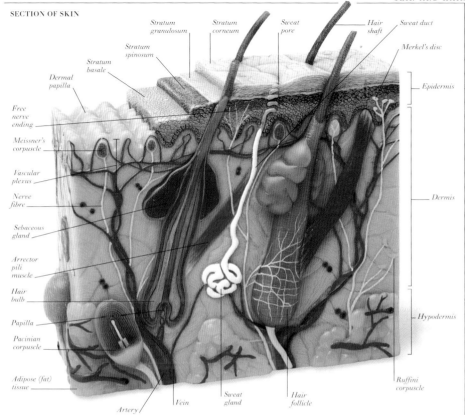

Stratum granulosum

Stratum corneum

Sweat pore

Hair shaft

Sweat duct

Stratum spinosum

Stratum basale

Merkel's disc

Dermal papilla

Epidermis

Free nerve ending

Meissner's corpuscle

Vascular plexus

Nerve fibre

Dermis

Sebaceous gland

Arrector pili muscle

Hair bulb

Papilla

Pacinian corpuscle

Hypodermis

Adipose (fat) tissue

Ruffini corpuscle

Artery

Vein

Sweat gland

Hair follicle

PHOTOMICROGRAPHS OF SKIN AND HAIR

SECTION OF SKIN
The flaky cells at the skin's surface are shed continuously.

SWEAT PORE
This allows loss of fluid as part of temperature control.

SKIN HAIR
Two hairs pushing through the outer layer of skin.

HEAD HAIR
The root and part of the shaft of a hair from the scalp.

Brain

THE BRAIN IS THE MAJOR ORGAN of the central nervous system and the control centre for all the body's voluntary and involuntary activities. It is also responsible for the complexities of thought, memory, emotion, and language. In adults, this complex organ is a mere 1.4 kg (3 lb) in weight, containing over 10 thousand million nerve cells. Three distinct regions can easily be seen – the brainstem, the cerebellum, and the large cerebrum. The brainstem controls vital body functions, such as breathing and digestion. The cerebellum's main functions are the maintenance of posture and the coordination of body movements. The cerebrum, which consists of the right and left cerebral hemispheres joined by the corpus callosum, is the site of most conscious and intelligent activities.

MRI SCAN OF TRANSVERSE SECTION THROUGH BRAIN

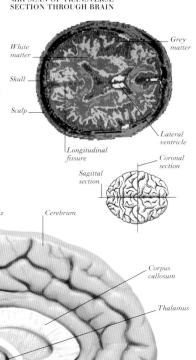

White matter
Skull
Scalp
Grey matter
Lateral ventricle
Longitudinal fissure
Sagittal section
Coronal section

SAGITTAL SECTION THROUGH BRAIN

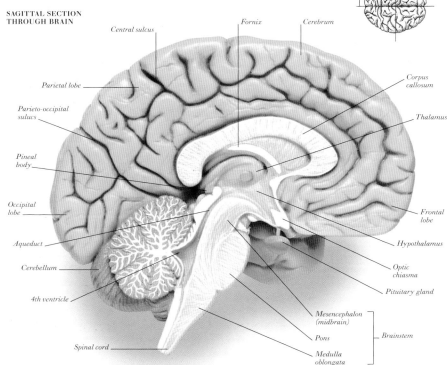

Central sulcus
Fornix
Cerebrum
Parietal lobe
Corpus callosum
Parieto-occipital sulucs
Thalamus
Pineal body
Occipital lobe
Frontal lobe
Aqueduct
Hypothalamus
Cerebellum
Optic chiasma
4th ventricle
Pituitary gland
Spinal cord
Mesencephalon (midbrain)
Pons
Medulla oblongata
Brainstem

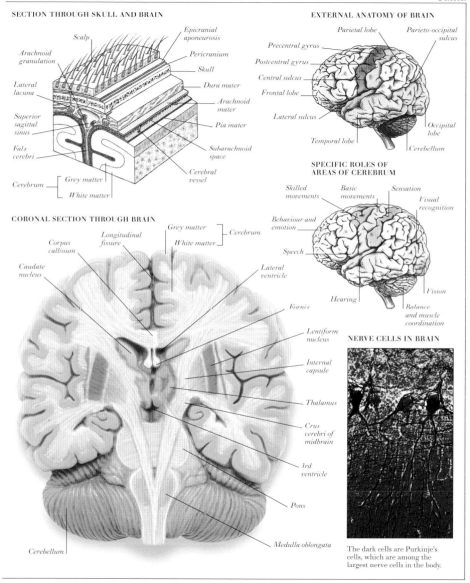

SECTION THROUGH SKULL AND BRAIN

Scalp
Epicranial aponeurosis
Pericranium
Arachnoid granulation
Skull
Dura mater
Lateral lacuna
Arachnoid mater
Superior sagittal sinus
Pia mater
Falx cerebri
Subarachnoid space
Cerebral vessel
Cerebrum — Grey matter / White matter

EXTERNAL ANATOMY OF BRAIN

Parietal lobe
Parieto-occipital sulcus
Precentral gyrus
Postcentral gyrus
Central sulcus
Frontal lobe
Lateral sulcus
Temporal lobe
Occipital lobe
Cerebellum

SPECIFIC ROLES OF AREAS OF CEREBRUM

Skilled movements
Basic movements
Sensation
Visual recognition
Behaviour and emotion
Speech
Hearing
Vision
Balance and muscle coordination

CORONAL SECTION THROUGH BRAIN

Corpus callosum
Longitudinal fissure
Grey matter / White matter — Cerebrum
Caudate nucleus
Lateral ventricle
Fornix
Lentiform nucleus
Internal capsule
Thalamus
Crus cerebri of midbrain
3rd ventricle
Pons
Medulla oblongata
Cerebellum

NERVE CELLS IN BRAIN

The dark cells are Purkinje's cells, which are among the largest nerve cells in the body.

237

Nervous system

THE NERVOUS SYSTEM IS THE BODY'S internal, electrochemical, communications network. Its main parts are the brain, spinal cord, and nerves. The brain and spinal cord form the central nervous system (CNS), the body's chief controlling and coordinating centres. Billions of long neurons, many grouped as nerves, make up the peripheral nervous system, transmitting nerve impulses between the CNS and other regions of the body. Each neuron has three parts: a cell body, branching dendrites that receive chemical signals from other neurons, and a tube-like axon that conveys these signals as electrical impulses.

CENTRAL AND PERIPHERAL NERVOUS SYSTEMS

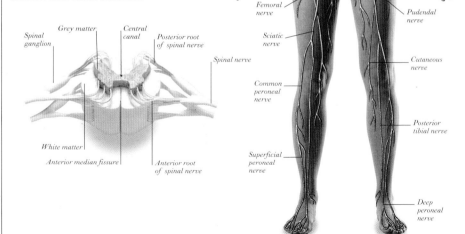

- Cranial nerves
- Cerebrum
- Cerebellum
- Cervical nerves
- Brachial plexus
- Thoracic nerves
- Spinal cord
- Radial nerve
- Median nerve
- Ulnar nerve
- Lumbar nerves
- Sacral nerves
- Sacral plexus
- Femoral nerve
- Pudendal nerve
- Sciatic nerve
- Cutaneous nerve
- Common peroneal nerve
- Posterior tibial nerve
- Superficial peroneal nerve
- Deep peroneal nerve

SECTION THROUGH SPINAL CORD

- Spinal ganglion
- Grey matter
- Central canal
- Posterior root of spinal nerve
- Spinal nerve
- White matter
- Anterior median fissure
- Anterior root of spinal nerve

STRUCTURE OF A MOTOR NEURON

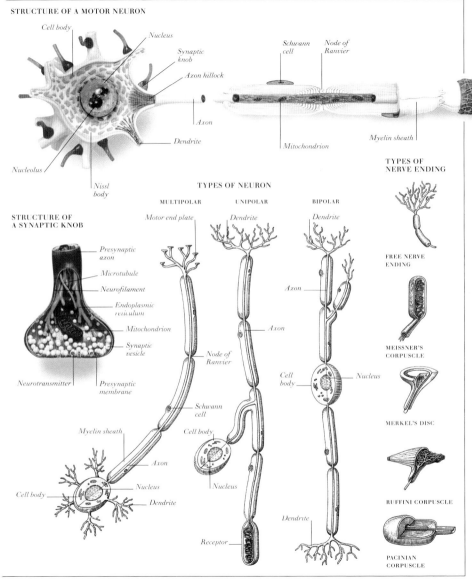

Cell body

Nucleus

Synaptic knob

Axon hillock

Axon

Dendrite

Nucleolus

Nissl body

Schwann cell

Node of Ranvier

Mitochondrion

Myelin sheath

TYPES OF NERVE ENDING

FREE NERVE ENDING

MEISSNER'S CORPUSCLE

MERKEL'S DISC

RUFFINI CORPUSCLE

PACINIAN CORPUSCLE

TYPES OF NEURON

MULTIPOLAR

UNIPOLAR

BIPOLAR

Motor end plate

Dendrite

Dendrite

Axon

Axon

Node of Ranvier

Axon

Cell body

Nucleus

Schwann cell

Cell body

Nucleus

Dendrite

Receptor

STRUCTURE OF A SYNAPTIC KNOB

Presynaptic axon

Microtubule

Neurofilament

Endoplasmic reticulum

Mitochondrion

Synaptic vesicle

Neurotransmitter

Presynaptic membrane

Myelin sheath

Axon

Cell body

Nucleus

Dendrite

Eye

Lateral
rectus muscle ___

THE EYE IS THE ORGAN OF SIGHT. The two eyeballs, protected
within bony sockets called orbits and on the outside by the
eyelids, eyebrows, and tear film, are directly connected
to the brain by the optic nerves. Each eye is moved by
six muscles, which are attached around the eyeball.
Light rays entering the eye through the pupil
are focused by the cornea and lens to form
an image on the retina. The retina contains
millions of light-sensitive cells, called
rods and cones, which convert the image
into a pattern of nerve impulses. These
impulses are transmitted along the optic
nerve to the brain. Information from
the two optic nerves is processed
in the brain to produce a
single coordinated image.

Vitreous humour ___

Macula ___

Central retinal vein ___

Central retinal artery ___

Pia mater ___

Arachnoid mater ___

Dura mater ___

Optic nerve ___

Area of
optic disc

Retina ___

Choroid ___

Sclera ___

Retinal blood vessel ___

Medial
rectus muscle ___

SECTION THROUGH LEFT EYE

LACRIMAL (TEAR-PRODUCING) APPARATUS

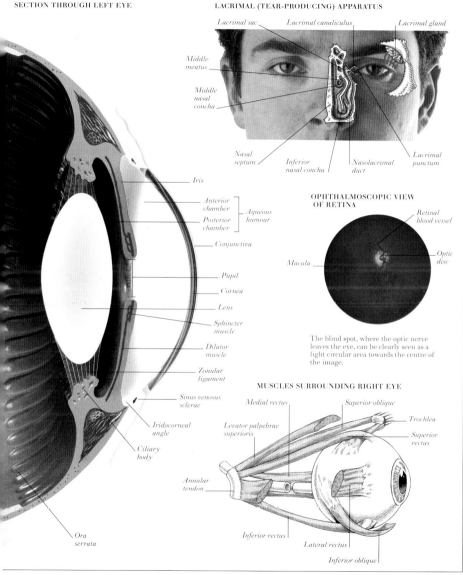

Lacrimal sac   *Lacrimal canaliculus*   *Lacrimal gland*

Middle meatus

Middle nasal concha

Nasal septum   *Inferior nasal concha*   *Nasolacrimal duct*   *Lacrimal punctum*

Iris

Anterior chamber
Posterior chamber
  } *Aqueous humour*

Conjunctiva

Pupil

Cornea

Lens

Sphincter muscle

Dilator muscle

Zonular ligament

Sinus venosus sclerae

Iridocorneal angle

Ciliary body

Ora serrata

OPHTHALMOSCOPIC VIEW OF RETINA

Retinal blood vessel

Macula   *Optic disc*

The blind spot, where the optic nerve leaves the eye, can be clearly seen as a light circular area towards the centre of the image.

MUSCLES SURROUNDING RIGHT EYE

Medial rectus   *Superior oblique*

Levator palpebrae superioris   *Trochlea*

Superior rectus

Annular tendon

Inferior rectus   *Lateral rectus*

Inferior oblique

Ear

THE EAR IS THE ORGAN OF HEARING AND BALANCE. The outer ear consists of a flap called the auricle or pinna and the auditory canal. The main functional parts – the middle and inner ears – are enclosed within the skull. The middle ear consists of three tiny bones, known as auditory ossicles, and the eustachian tube, which links the ear to the back of the nose. The inner ear consists of the spiral-shaped cochlea, and also the semicircular canals and the vestibule, which are the organs of balance. Sound waves entering the ear travel through the auditory canal to the tympanic membrane (eardrum), where they are converted to vibrations that are transmitted via the ossicles to the cochlea. Here, the vibrations are converted by millions of microscopic hairs into electrical nerve signals to be interpreted by the brain.

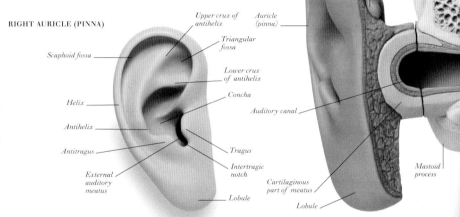

RIGHT AURICLE (PINNA)

Upper crux of antihelix

Triangular fossa

Auricle (pinna)

Scaphoid fossa

Lower crux of antihelix

Concha

Helix

Auditory canal

Antihelix

Temporal bone

Cartilage of auricle

Antitragus

Tragus

Intertragic notch

External auditory meatus

Cartilaginous part of meatus

Lobule

Mastoid process

Lobule

OSSICLES OF MIDDLE EAR

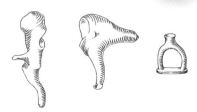

MALLEUS (HAMMER)   INCUS (ANVIL)   STAPES (STIRRUP)

These three tiny bones connect to form a bridge between the tympanic membrane and the oval window. With a system of membranes they convey sound vibrations to the inner ear.

INTERNAL STRUCTURE OF AMPULLA

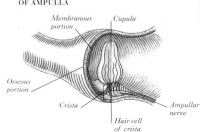

Membranous portion

Cupula

Osseous portion

Crista

Ampullar nerve

Hair cell of crista

LABYRINTH

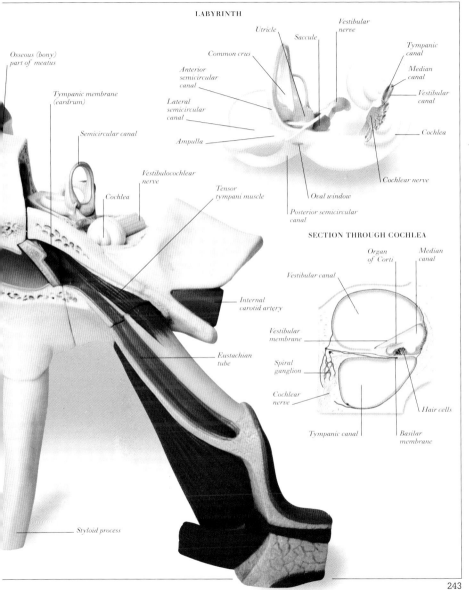

Osseous (bony) part of meatus

Tympanic membrane (eardrum)

Semicircular canal

Cochlea

Vestibulocochlear nerve

Tensor tympani muscle

Internal carotid artery

Eustachian tube

Styloid process

Common crus

Anterior semicircular canal

Lateral semicircular canal

Ampulla

Utricle

Saccule

Vestibular nerve

Tympanic canal

Median canal

Vestibular canal

Cochlea

Cochlear nerve

Oval window

Posterior semicircular canal

SECTION THROUGH COCHLEA

Organ of Corti

Median canal

Vestibular canal

Vestibular membrane

Spiral ganglion

Cochlear nerve

Hair cells

Tympanic canal

Basilar membrane

Nose, mouth, and throat

WITH EVERY BREATH, air passes through the nasal cavity down the pharynx (throat), larynx ("voice box"), and trachea (windpipe) to the lungs. The nasal cavity warms and moistens air, and the tiny layers in its lining protect the airway against damage by foreign bodies. During swallowing, the tongue moves up and back, the larynx rises, the epiglottis closes off the entrance to the trachea, and the soft palate separates the nasal cavity from the pharynx. Saliva, secreted from three pairs of salivary glands, lubricates food to make swallowing easier; it also begins the chemical breakdown of food, and helps to produce taste. The senses of taste and smell are closely linked. Both depend on the detection of dissolved molecules by sensory receptors in the olfactory nerve endings of the nose and in the taste buds of the tongue.

STRUCTURE OF TONGUE

Median glossoepiglottic fold
Epiglottis
Palatine tonsil
Sulcus terminalis
Palatoglossal arch
Foramen caecum
Vallate papilla
Median sulcus
Foliate papilla
Fungiform papilla
Filiform papilla
Apex

STRUCTURES SURROUNDING PHARYNX

Lingual nerve
Tongue
Styloglossus muscle
Hyoglossus muscle
Sublingual gland
Hypoglossal nerve
Mandible (lower jaw)
Superior laryngeal nerve
Submandibular gland
Superior thyroid artery
Hyoid bone
Laryngeal prominence (Adam's apple)
Thyrohyoid muscle
Thyrohyoid membrane
Cricothyroid ligament
Cricothyroid muscle
Thyroid gland
Trachea

TASTE AREAS ON TONGUE

Bitter
Sour
Salt
Sweet

TYPES OF PAPILLAE

FILIFORM PAPILLAE

FUNGIFORM PAPILLAE

VALLATE PAPILLAE

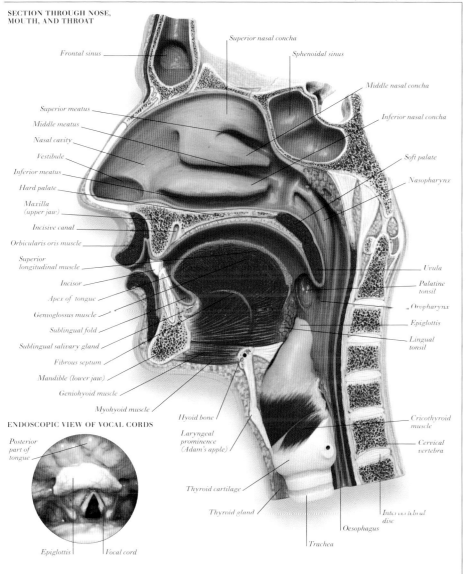

SECTION THROUGH NOSE, MOUTH, AND THROAT

Frontal sinus

Superior nasal concha

Sphenoidal sinus

Middle nasal concha

Inferior nasal concha

Superior meatus

Middle meatus

Nasal cavity

Vestibule

Soft palate

Inferior meatus

Nasopharynx

Hard palate

Maxilla (upper jaw)

Incisive canal

Orbicularis oris muscle

Superior longitudinal muscle

Uvula

Incisor

Palatine tonsil

Apex of tongue

Oropharynx

Genioglossus muscle

Sublingual fold

Epiglottis

Sublingual salivary gland

Lingual tonsil

Fibrous septum

Mandible (lower jaw)

Geniohyoid muscle

Myohyoid muscle

Hyoid bone

Cricothyroid muscle

ENDOSCOPIC VIEW OF VOCAL CORDS

Laryngeal prominence (Adam's apple)

Cervical vertebra

Posterior part of tongue

Thyroid cartilage

Intervertebral disc

Thyroid gland

Oesophagus

Epiglottis

Vocal cord

Trachea

Teeth

THE 20 PRIMARY TEETH (also called deciduous or milk teeth) usually begin to erupt when a baby is about six months old. They start to be replaced by the permanent teeth when the child is about six years old. By the age of 20, most adults have a full set of 32 teeth although the third molars (commonly called wisdom teeth) may never erupt. While teeth help people to speak clearly and give shape to the face, their main function is the chewing of food. Incisors and canines shear and tear the food into pieces; premolars and molars crush and grind it further. Although tooth enamel is the hardest substance in the body, it tends to be eroded and destroyed by acid produced in the mouth during the breakdown of food.

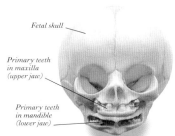

Fetal skull

Primary teeth in maxilla (upper jaw)

Primary teeth in mandible (lower jaw)

FETAL JAWS
By the sixth week of embryonic development areas of thickening occur in each jaw; these areas give rise to tooth buds. By the time the fetus is six months old, enamel has formed on the tooth buds.

DEVELOPMENT OF JAW AND TEETH

Maxilla (upper jaw)

Mandible (lower jaw)

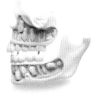

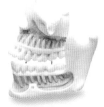

A NEWBORN BABY'S JAWS
The primary teeth can be seen developing in the jaw bones; they begin to erupt around the age of six months.

A FIVE-YEAR-OLD CHILD'S TEETH
There is a full set of 20 erupted primary teeth; the permanent teeth can be seen developing in the upper and lower jaws.

A NINE-YEAR-OLD CHILD'S TEETH
Most of the teeth are primary teeth but the permanent incisors and first molars have now emerged.

AN ADULT'S TEETH
By the age of 20, the full set of 32 permanent teeth (including the wisdom teeth) should be in position.

THE PERMANENT TEETH

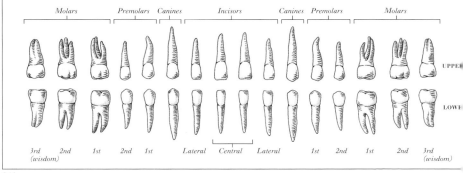

Molars | Premolars | Canines | Incisors | Canines | Premolars | Molars

UPPER

LOWER

3rd (wisdom) | 2nd | 1st | 2nd | 1st | Lateral | Central | Lateral | 1st | 2nd | 1st | 2nd | 3rd (wisdom)

STRUCTURE OF A TOOTH

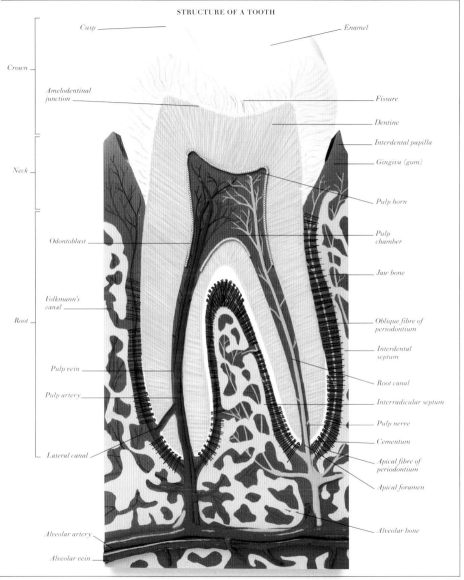

Cusp

Enamel

Crown

Amelodentinal junction

Fissure

Dentine

Interdental papilla

Neck

Gingiva (gum)

Pulp horn

Odontoblast

Pulp chamber

Jaw bone

Root

Volkmann's canal

Oblique fibre of periodontium

Interdental septum

Pulp vein

Root canal

Pulp artery

Interradicular septum

Pulp nerve

Cementum

Apical fibre of periodontium

Lateral canal

Apical foramen

Alveolar bone

Alveolar artery

Alveolar vein

Digestive system

THE DIGESTIVE SYSTEM BREAKS DOWN FOOD into particles so tiny that blood can take nourishment to all parts of the body. The system's main part is a 9 m (30 ft) tube from mouth to rectum; muscles in this alimentary canal force food along. Chewed food first travels through the oesophagus to the stomach, which churns and liquidizes food before it passes through the duodenum, jejunum, and ileum – the three parts of the long, convoluted small intestine. Here, digestive juices from the gallbladder and pancreas break down food particles; many filter out into the blood through tiny fingerlike villi that line the small intestine's inner wall. Undigested food in the colon forms faeces that leave the body through the anus.

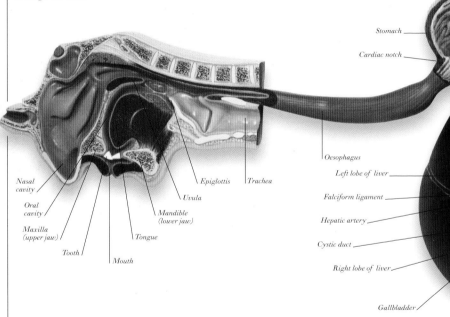

Stomach

Cardiac notch

Oesophagus

Left lobe of liver

Falciform ligament

Hepatic artery

Cystic duct

Right lobe of liver

Gallbladder

Nasal cavity

Oral cavity

Maxilla (upper jaw)

Tooth

Mouth

Tongue

Mandible (lower jaw)

Uvula

Epiglottis

Trachea

ENDOSCOPIC VIEWS INSIDE ALIMENTARY CANAL

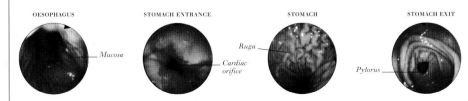

OESOPHAGUS

Mucosa

STOMACH ENTRANCE

Cardiac orifice

STOMACH

Ruga

STOMACH EXIT

Pylorus

ALIMENTARY CANAL

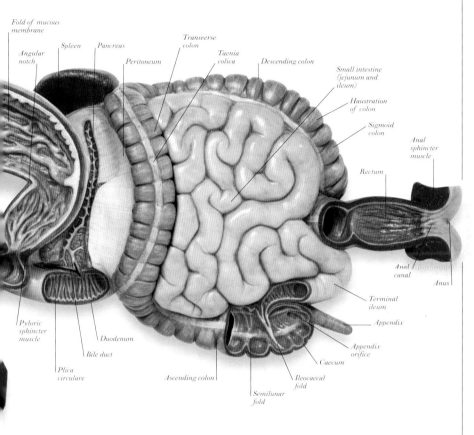

Fold of mucous membrane

Angular notch

Spleen

Pancreas

Peritoneum

Transverse colon

Taenia colica

Descending colon

Small intestine (jejunum and ileum)

Haustration of colon

Sigmoid colon

Anal sphincter muscle

Rectum

Anal canal

Anus

Terminal ileum

Appendix

Appendix orifice

Caecum

Ileocaecal fold

Semilunar fold

Ascending colon

Pyloric sphincter muscle

Bile duct

Duodenum

Plica circulare

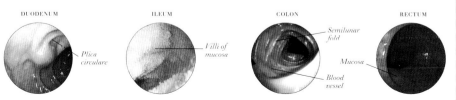

DUODENUM

Plica circulare

ILEUM

Villi of mucosa

COLON

Semilunar fold

Blood vessel

RECTUM

Mucosa

Heart

THE HEART IS A HOLLOW MUSCLE in the middle of the chest that pumps blood around the body, supplying cells with oxygen and nutrients. A muscular wall, called the septum, divides the heart lengthways into left and right sides. A valve divides each side into two chambers: an upper atrium and a lower ventricle. When the heart muscle contracts, it squeezes blood through the atria and then through the ventricles. Oxygenated blood from the lungs flows from the pulmonary veins into the left atrium, through the left ventricle, and then out via the aorta to all parts of the body. Deoxygenated blood returning from the body flows from the vena cava into the right atrium, through the right ventricle, and then out via the pulmonary artery to the lungs for reoxygenation. At rest the heart beats between 60 and 80 times a minute; during exercise or at times of stress or excitement the rate may increase to 200 beats a minute.

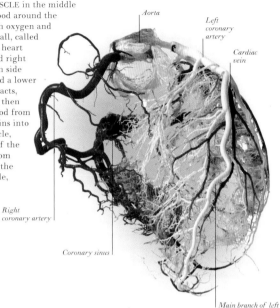

Aorta

Left coronary artery

Cardiac vein

Right coronary artery

Coronary sinus

Main branch of left coronary artery

SECTION THROUGH HEART WALL

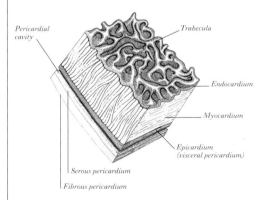

Pericardial cavity

Trabecula

Endocardium

Myocardium

Epicardium (visceral pericardium)

Serous pericardium

Fibrous pericardium

HEARTBEAT SEQUENCE

ATRIAL DIASTOLE

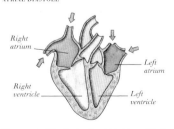

Right atrium

Left atrium

Right ventricle

Left ventricle

Deoxygenated blood enters the right atrium while the left atrium receives oxygenated blood.

STRUCTURE OF HEART

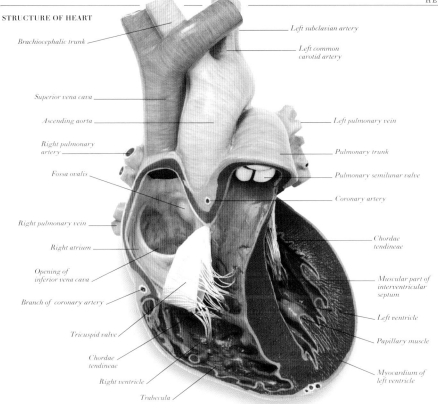

Brachiocephalic trunk

Left subclavian artery

Left common carotid artery

Superior vena cava

Ascending aorta

Right pulmonary artery

Left pulmonary vein

Pulmonary trunk

Pulmonary semilunar valve

Fossa ovalis

Coronary artery

Right pulmonary vein

Right atrium

Chordae tendineae

Opening of inferior vena cava

Muscular part of interventricular septum

Branch of coronary artery

Left ventricle

Tricuspid valve

Papillary muscle

Chordae tendineae

Right ventricle

Myocardium of left ventricle

Trabecula

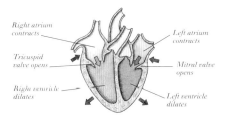

ATRIAL SYSTOLE (VENTRICULAR DIASTOLE)

Right atrium contracts

Left atrium contracts

Tricuspid valve opens

Mitral valve opens

Right ventricle dilates

Left ventricle dilates

Left and right atria contract, forcing blood into the relaxed ventricles.

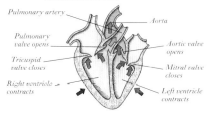

VENTRICULAR SYSTOLE

Pulmonary artery

Aorta

Pulmonary valve opens

Aortic valve opens

Tricuspid valve closes

Mitral valve closes

Right ventricle contracts

Left ventricle contracts

Ventricles contract and force blood to the lungs for oxygenation and via the aorta to the rest of the body.

Circulatory system

THE CIRCULATORY SYSTEM consists of the heart and blood vessels, which together maintain a continuous flow of blood around the body. The heart pumps oxygen-rich blood from the lungs to all parts of the body through a network of tubes called arteries, and smaller branches called arterioles. Blood returns to the heart via small vessels called venules, which lead in turn into larger tubes called veins. Arterioles and venules are linked by a network of tiny vessels called capillaries, where the exchange of oxygen and carbon dioxide between blood and body cells takes place. Blood has four main components: red blood cells, white blood cells, platelets, and liquid plasma.

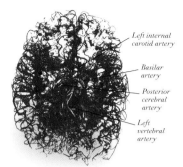

ARTERIAL SYSTEM OF BRAIN

- Left internal carotid artery
- Basilar artery
- Posterior cerebral artery
- Left vertebral artery

CIRCULATORY SYSTEM OF LIVER

- Inferior vena cava
- Portal vein
- Common bile duct
- Hepatic artery
- Gallblader

CIRCULATORY SYSTEM OF HEART AND LUNGS

- Superior vena cava
- Aorta
- Right ventricle
- Left ventricle

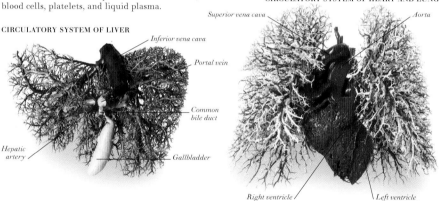

SECTION OF MAIN ARTERY

- Tunica media
- Collagen and elastic fibres
- External elastic lamina
- Tunica adventitia
- Internal elastic lamina
- Tunica intima
- Endothelium
- Arteriole

SECTION OF MAIN VEIN

- Tunica media
- Collagen and elastic fibres
- External elastic lamina
- Tunica adventitia
- Valve cusp
- Internal elastic lamina
- Tunica intima
- Endothelium

PRINCIPAL ARTERIES AND VEINS
OF CIRCULATORY SYSTEM

Common carotid artery

Subclavian artery

Arch of aorta

Axillary artery

Pulmonary artery

Coronary artery

Brachial artery

Gastric artery

Hepatic artery

Splenic artery

Superior mesenteric artery

Radial artery

Ulnar artery

Palmar arch

Digital artery

Common iliac artery

External iliac artery

Internal iliac artery

Femoral artery

Popliteal artery

Peroneal artery

Anterior tibial artery

Posterior tibial artery

Lateral plantar artery

Dorsal metatarsal artery

Internal jugular vein

Brachiocephalic vein

Subclavian vein

Axillary vein

Cephalic vein

Superior vena cava

Pulmonary vein

Basilic vein

Hepatic portal vein

Median cubital vein

Inferior vena cava

Anterior median vein

Gastroepiploic vein

Palmar vein

Digital vein

Inferior mesenteric vein

Superior mesenteric vein

Common iliac vein

External iliac vein

Internal iliac vein

Femoral vein

Great saphenous vein

Short saphenous vein

Dorsal venous arch

Digital vein

TYPES OF BLOOD CELLS

RED BLOOD CELLS
These cells are biconcave in shape to maximize their oxygen-carrying capacity.

WHITE BLOOD CELLS
Lymphocytes are the smallest white blood cells; they form antibodies against disease.

PLATELETS
Tiny cells that are activated whenever blood clotting or repair to vessels is necessary.

BLOOD CLOTTING

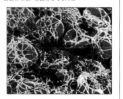

Filaments of fibrin enmesh red blood cells as part of the process of blood clotting.

Respiratory system

THE RESPIRATORY SYSTEM supplies the oxygen needed by body cells and carries off their carbon dioxide waste. Inhaled air passes via the trachea (windpipe) through two narrower tubes, the bronchi, to the lungs. Each lung comprises many fine, branching tubes called bronchioles that end in tiny clustered chambers called alveoli. Gases cross the thin alveolar walls to and from a network of tiny blood vessels. Intercostal (rib) muscles and the muscular diaphragm below the lungs operate the lungs like bellows, drawing air in and forcing it out at regular intervals.

BRONCHIOLE AND ALVEOLI

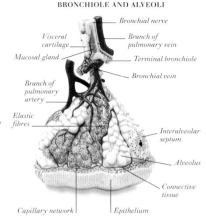

Bronchial nerve

Visceral cartilage

Branch of pulmonary vein

Mucosal gland

Terminal bronchiole

Bronchial vein

Branch of pulmonary artery

Elastic fibres

Interalveolar septum

Alveolus

Connective tissue

Capillary network

Epithelium

SEGMENTS OF BRONCHIAL TREE

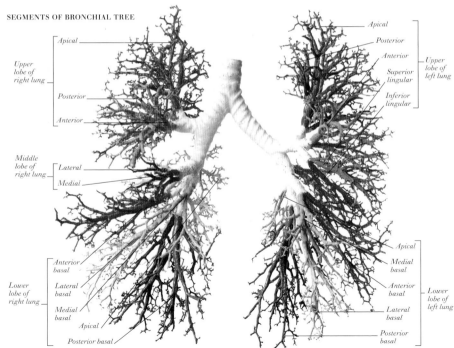

Apical

Upper lobe of right lung

Posterior

Anterior

Apical

Posterior

Anterior

Superior lingular

Inferior lingular

Upper lobe of left lung

Middle lobe of right lung

Lateral

Medial

Lower lobe of right lung

Anterior basal

Lateral basal

Medial basal

Apical

Posterior basal

Apical

Medial basal

Anterior basal

Lateral basal

Posterior basal

Lower lobe of left lung

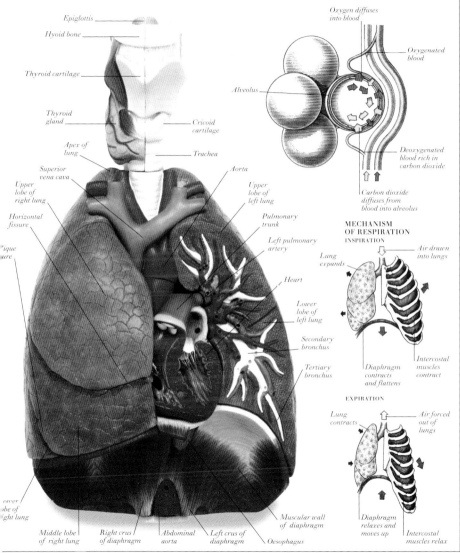

STRUCTURES OF THORACIC CAVITY

Epiglottis

Hyoid bone

Thyroid cartilage

Thyroid gland

Cricoid cartilage

Apex of lung

Trachea

Superior vena cava

Aorta

Upper lobe of right lung

Upper lobe of left lung

Horizontal fissure

Pulmonary trunk

Left pulmonary artery

Oblique fissure

Heart

Lower lobe of left lung

Secondary bronchus

Tertiary bronchus

Lower lobe of right lung

Middle lobe of right lung

Right crus of diaphragm

Abdominal aorta

Left crus of diaphragm

Oesophagus

Muscular wall of diaphragm

GASEOUS EXCHANGE IN ALVEOLUS

Oxygen diffuses into blood

Oxygenated blood

Alveolus

Deoxygenated blood rich in carbon dioxide

Carbon dioxide diffuses from blood into alveolus

MECHANISM OF RESPIRATION

INSPIRATION

Lung expands

Air drawn into lungs

Diaphragm contracts and flattens

Intercostal muscles contract

EXPIRATION

Lung contracts

Air forced out of lungs

Diaphragm relaxes and moves up

Intercostal muscles relax

Urinary system

THE URINARY SYSTEM FILTERS WASTE PRODUCTS from the blood and removes them from the body via a system of tubes. Blood is filtered in the two kidneys, which are fist-sized, bean-shaped organs. The renal arteries carry blood to the kidneys; the renal veins remove blood after filtering. Each kidney contains about one million tiny units called nephrons. Each nephron is made up of a tubule and a filtering unit called a glomerulus, which consists of a collection of tiny blood vessels surrounded by the hollow Bowman's capsule. The filtering process produces a watery fluid that leaves the kidney as urine. The urine is carried via two tubes called ureters to the bladder, where it is stored until its release from the body through another tube called the urethra.

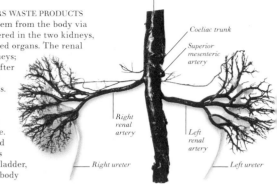

Aorta

Coeliac trunk

Superior mesenteric artery

Right renal artery

Left renal artery

Right ureter

Left ureter

SECTION THROUGH LEFT KIDNEY

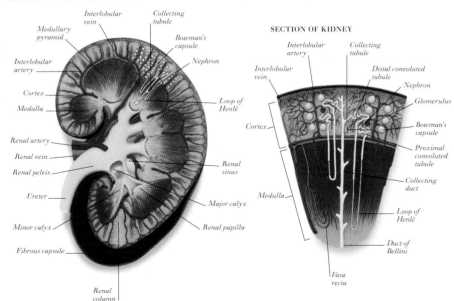

Interlobular vein

Collecting tubule

Medullary pyramid

Bowman's capsule

Nephron

Interlobular artery

Cortex

Medulla

Loop of Henlé

Renal artery

Renal vein

Renal pelvis

Renal sinus

Ureter

Major calyx

Minor calyx

Renal papilla

Fibrous capsule

Renal column

SECTION OF KIDNEY

Interlobular artery

Collecting tubule

Interlobular vein

Distal convoluted tubule

Nephron

Cortex

Glomerulus

Bowman's capsule

Proximal convoluted tubule

Medulla

Collecting duct

Loop of Henlé

Duct of Bellini

Vasa recta

MALE URINARY TRACT

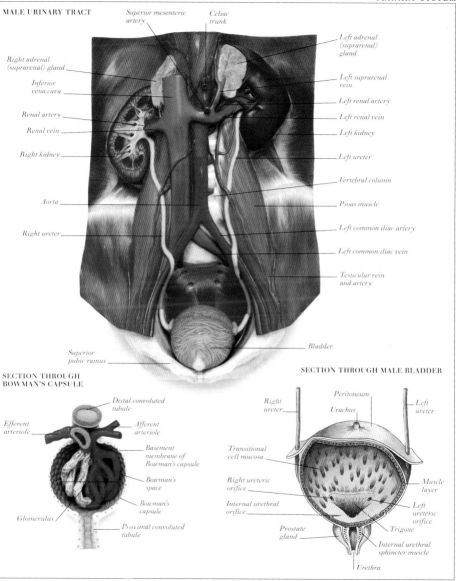

Superior mesenteric artery

Celiac trunk

Left adrenal (suprarenal) gland

Right adrenal (suprarenal) gland

Inferior vena cava

Left suprarenal vein

Left renal artery

Renal artery

Left renal vein

Renal vein

Left kidney

Right kidney

Left ureter

Vertebral column

Aorta

Psoas muscle

Right ureter

Left common iliac artery

Left common iliac vein

Testicular vein and artery

Superior pubic ramus

Bladder

SECTION THROUGH BOWMAN'S CAPSULE

Distal convoluted tubule

Efferent arteriole

Afferent arteriole

Basement membrane of Bowman's capsule

Bowman's space

Bowman's capsule

Glomerulus

Proximal convoluted tubule

SECTION THROUGH MALE BLADDER

Right ureter

Peritoneum

Urachus

Left ureter

Transitional cell mucosa

Right ureteric orifice

Muscle layer

Internal urethral orifice

Left ureteric orifice

Trigone

Prostate gland

Internal urethral sphincter muscle

Urethra

Reproductive system

SEX ORGANS LOCATED IN THE PELVIS create new human lives. Each month a ripe egg is released from one of the female's ovaries into a fallopian tube leading to the uterus (womb), a muscular pear-sized organ. A male produces minute tadpole-like sperm in two oval glands called testes. When the male is ready to release sperm into the female's vagina, many millions pass into his urethra and leave his body through the fleshy penis. The sperm travel up through the vagina into the uterus and fallopian tubes, and one sperm may enter and fertilize an egg. The fertilized egg becomes embedded in the uterus wall and starts to grow into a new human being.

SECTION THROUGH OVARY

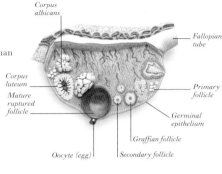

Corpus albicans

Fallopian tube

Corpus luteum

Primary follicle

Mature ruptured follicle

Germinal epithelium

Graffian follicle

Oocyte (egg)

Secondary follicle

SECTION THROUGH FEMALE PELVIC REGION

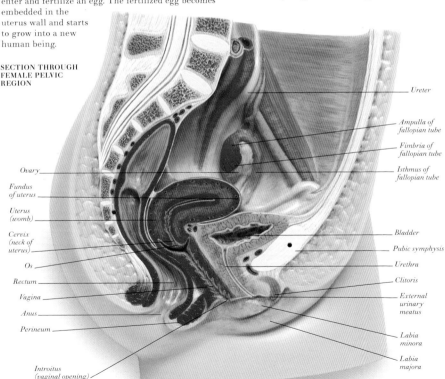

Ureter

Ampulla of fallopian tube

Fimbria of fallopian tube

Isthmus of fallopian tube

Ovary

Fundus of uterus

Uterus (womb)

Cervix (neck of uterus)

Os

Rectum

Vagina

Anus

Perineum

Bladder

Pubic symphysis

Urethra

Clitoris

External urinary meatus

Labia minora

Labia majora

Introitus (vaginal opening)

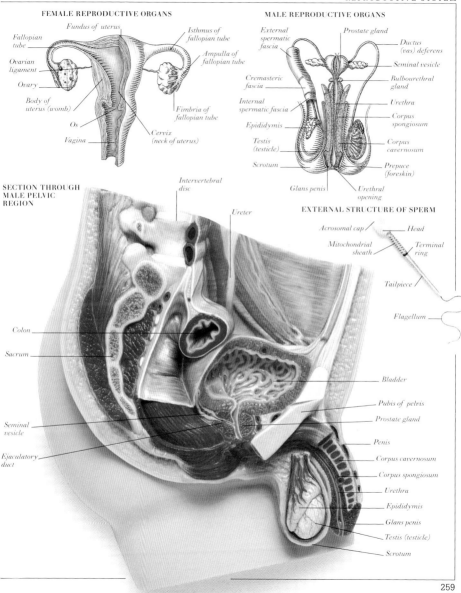

FEMALE REPRODUCTIVE ORGANS

- Fallopian tube
- Fundus of uterus
- Isthmus of fallopian tube
- Ampulla of fallopian tube
- Ovarian ligament
- Ovary
- Body of uterus (womb)
- Os
- Cervix (neck of uterus)
- Vagina
- Fimbria of fallopian tube

MALE REPRODUCTIVE ORGANS

- External spermatic fascia
- Prostate gland
- Ductus (vas) deferens
- Seminal vesicle
- Cremasteric fascia
- Bulbourethral gland
- Internal spermatic fascia
- Urethra
- Corpus spongiosum
- Epididymis
- Testis (testicle)
- Corpus cavernosum
- Scrotum
- Prepuce (foreskin)
- Glans penis
- Urethral opening

SECTION THROUGH MALE PELVIC REGION

- Intervertebral disc
- Ureter
- Colon
- Sacrum
- Seminal vesicle
- Ejaculatory duct
- Bladder
- Pubis of pelvis
- Prostate gland
- Penis
- Corpus cavernosum
- Corpus spongiosum
- Urethra
- Epididymis
- Glans penis
- Testis (testicle)
- Scrotum

EXTERNAL STRUCTURE OF SPERM

- Acrosomal cap
- Head
- Mitochondrial sheath
- Terminal ring
- Tailpiece
- Flagellum

Development of a baby

A FERTILIZED EGG IS NOURISHED AND PROTECTED as it develops into an embryo and then a fetus during the 40 weeks of pregnancy. The placenta, a mass of blood vessels implanted in the uterus lining, delivers nourishment and oxygen, and removes waste through the umbilical cord. Meanwhile, the fetus lies snugly in its amniotic sac, a bag of fluid that protects it against any sudden jolts. In the last weeks of the pregnancy, the rapidly growing fetus turns head-down: a baby ready to be born.

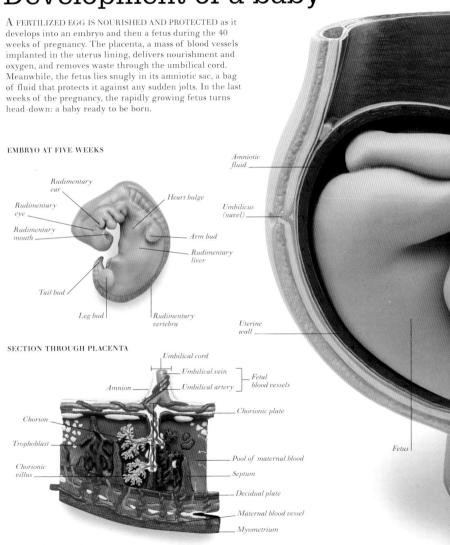

EMBRYO AT FIVE WEEKS

Rudimentary ear

Rudimentary eye

Rudimentary mouth

Heart bulge

Arm bud

Rudimentary liver

Tail bud

Leg bud

Rudimentary vertebra

Amniotic fluid

Umbilicus (navel)

Uterine wall

Fetus

SECTION THROUGH PLACENTA

Umbilical cord

Umbilical vein

Umbilical artery

Amnion

Fetal blood vessels

Chorionic plate

Chorion

Trophoblast

Chorionic villus

Pool of maternal blood

Septum

Decidual plate

Maternal blood vessel

Myometrium

SECTION THROUGH PELVIS IN NINTH MONTH OF PREGNANCY

THE DEVELOPING FETUS

Placenta

Uterine wall

Fallopian tube

SECOND MONTH
All the internal organs have developed by this stage.

Fetus

Intervertebral disc

Vertebra

Spinal cord

Umbilical cord

THIRD MONTH
The fetus is fully formed and now begins a period of rapid growth.

FIFTH MONTH
Although the fetus is here in breech (bottom down) position, it will probably turn by 180° before birth. By the fifth month the baby is moving actively and responds to sound.

Cervix

SEVENTH MONTH
The internal organs are maturing in preparation for life outside the uterus. The baby has grown to such a size that there is less room for movement within the uterus.

Bladder

Cervix

Rectum

Anus

Pubic bone

Placenta

Vagina

Urethra

GEOLOGY, GEOGRAPHY, AND METEOROLOGY

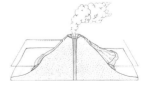

Mapping the Earth

THE EARTH'S SURFACE FEATURES can be represented in various ways, such as on maps and globes. The earliest know map of the whole world dates back to between 750-500 BCE. The first globe was constructed in the mid-2nd century BCE, about 100 years after ancient Greek astronomers established that the Earth was spherical. Advances in mathematics, science, and geography – combined with an increasing number of people exploring the world – have meant that Earth's surface features have been mapped with increasing accuracy throughout history. In modern times, advances in technology have revolutionized the mapping process. In 1972, NASA launched the first civilian remote-sensing vehicle into Earth's orbit, which allowed the Earth to be mapped by satellite for the first time. Today, the surface of the Earth is surveyed every day by thousands of satellites, which send mappable data back to Earth to be analysed and used by a range of people, from cartographers to scientists. The ability to use satellites has substantially sped up data collection – areas that would have once taken months or even years to survey can now be mapped within minutes. However, even with these advances in map-making, globes remain a more accurate way to represent the Earth's surface features. This is because only a globe can correctly represent areas, shapes, sizes, and directions, as there is always distortion when a spherical surface like the Earth's is projected on to the flat surface of a map. A map projection is therefore always a compromise: it shows some features accurately but distorts others. Even satellite mapping does not produce completely accurate maps, although they can show physical features with great clarity.

EXAMPLES OF MAP PROJECTIONS

CYLINDRICAL PROJECTION

CYLINDRICAL-PROJECTION MAP

SATELLITE MAPPING OF THE EARTH

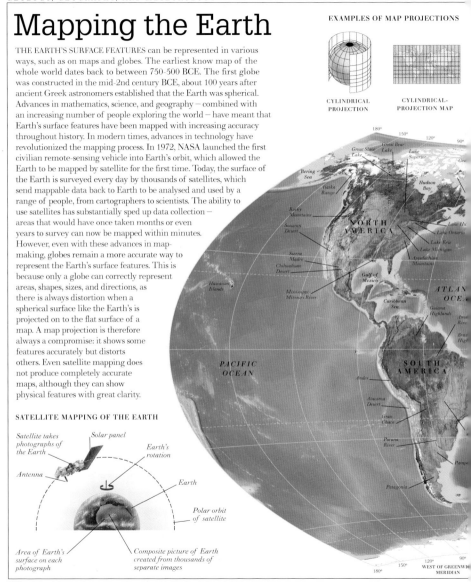

Satellite takes photographs of the Earth

Solar panel

Earth's rotation

Antenna

Earth

Polar orbit of satellite

Area of Earth's surface on each photograph

Composite picture of Earth created from thousands of separate images

Great Slave Lake

Great Bear Lake

Lake Superior

Bering Sea

Alaska Range

Hudson Bay

Rocky Mountains

Sonoran Desert

NORTH AMERICA

Lake Hu

Lake Ontario

Lake Erie

Lake Michigan

Appalachian Mountains

Sierra Madre

Chihuahuan Desert

Gulf of Mexico

ATLAN OCE

Hawaiian Islands

Mississippi-Missouri River

Caribbean Sea

Guiana Highlands

Ama Riv

Braz Rive

PACIFIC OCEAN

SOUTH AMERICA

Andes

Atacama Desert

Gran Chaco

Paraná River

Pampa

Patagonia

WEST OF GREENWI MERIDIAN

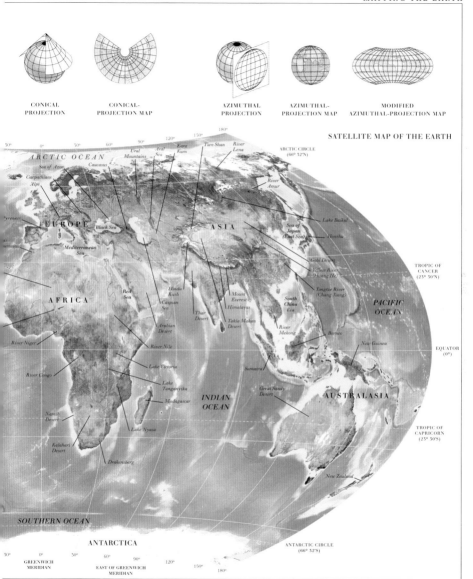

CONICAL
PROJECTION

CONICAL-
PROJECTION MAP

AZIMUTHAL
PROJECTION

AZIMUTHAL-
PROJECTION MAP

MODIFIED
AZIMUTHAL-PROJECTION MAP

SATELLITE MAP OF THE EARTH

ARCTIC OCEAN

Ural Mountains

Aral Sea

Kara Kum

Tien Shan

River Lena

ARCTIC CIRCLE
(66° 52'N)

Sea of Azov

Caucasus

Carpathians

Alps

River Amur

Pyrenees

EUROPE

Black Sea

ASIA

*Sea of Japan
(East Sea)*

Lake Baikal

Honshu

*Mediterranean
Sea*

Gobi Desert

TROPIC OF
CANCER
(23° 30'N)

Red Sea

Hindu Kush

*Yellow River
(Huang He)*

AFRICA

Caspian Sea

Mount Everest

Himalayas

*Yangtze River
(Chang Jiang)*

PACIFIC
OCEAN

Thar Desert

Takla Makan Desert

South China Sea

Arabian Desert

River Niger

River Nile

River Mekong

Borneo

New Guinea

EQUATOR
(0°)

River Congo

Lake Victoria

Sumatra

Lake Tanganyika

Madagascar

INDIAN
OCEAN

Great Sandy Desert

AUSTRALASIA

Namib Desert

Lake Nyasa

TROPIC OF
CAPRICORN
(23° 30'S)

Kalahari Desert

Drakensberg

New Zealand

SOUTHERN OCEAN

ANTARCTICA

ANTARCTIC CIRCLE
(66° 52'S)

GREENWICH
MERIDIAN

EAST OF GREENWICH
MERIDIAN

The rock cycle

THE ROCK CYCLE IS A CONTINUOUS PROCESS through which old rocks are transformed into new ones. Rocks can be divided into three main groups: igneous, sedimentary, and metamorphic. Igneous rocks are formed when magma (molten rock) from the Earth's interior cools and solidifies (see pp. 274-275). Sedimentary rocks are formed when sediment (rock particles, for example) becomes compressed and cemented together in a process known as lithification (see pp. 276-277). Metamorphic rocks are formed when igneous, sedimentary, or other metamorphic rocks are changed by heat or pressure (see pp. 274-275). Rocks are added to the Earth's surface by crustal movements and volcanic activity. Once exposed on the surface, the rocks are broken down into rock particles by weathering (see pp. 282-283). The particles are then transported by glaciers, rivers, and wind, and deposited as sediment in lakes, deltas, deserts, and on the ocean floor. Some

HEXAGONAL BASALT
COLUMNS, ICELAND

of this sediment undergoes lithification and forms sedimentary rock. This rock may be thrust back to the surface by crustal movements or forced deeper into the Earth's interior, where heat and pressure transform it into metamorphic rock. The metamorphic rock in turn may be pushed up to the surface or may be melted to form magma. Eventually, the magma cools and solidifies – below or on the surface – forming igneous rock. When the sedimentary, igneous, and metamorphic rocks are exposed once more on the Earth's surface, the cycle begins again.

THE ROCK CYCLE

Igneous rock

Cooling and solidification (crystallization)

Weathering, transport, and deposition

Sediment

Heat and pressure (metamorphism)

Weathering, transport, and deposition

Weathering, transport, and deposition

Compression and cementation (lithification)

Magma

Melting

Heat and pressure (metamorphism)

Metamorphic rock

Sedimentary rock

STAGES IN THE ROCK CYCLE

Magma extruded as lava, which solidifies to form igneous rock

Lava flow

Vent

Main conduit

Secondary conduit

Lava

Ash

Rock surrounding magma changed by heat to form metamorphic rock

Intense heat of rising magma melts some of the surrounding rock

Sedimentary rock crushed and folded to form metamorphic rock

266

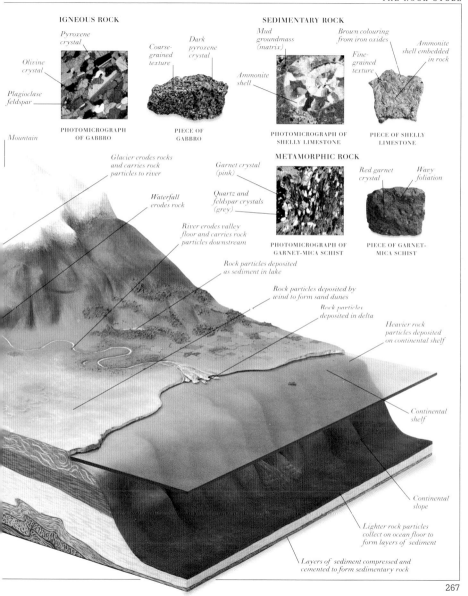

IGNEOUS ROCK

Pyroxene crystal

Olivine crystal

Plagioclase feldspar

Coarse-grained texture

Dark pyroxene crystal

PHOTOMICROGRAPH OF GABBRO

PIECE OF GABBRO

SEDIMENTARY ROCK

Mud groundmass (matrix)

Ammonite shell

Brown colouring from iron oxides

Fine-grained texture

Ammonite shell embedded in rock

PHOTOMICROGRAPH OF SHELLY LIMESTONE

PIECE OF SHELLY LIMESTONE

METAMORPHIC ROCK

Garnet crystal (pink)

Quartz and feldspar crystals (grey)

Red garnet crystal

Wavy foliation

PHOTOMICROGRAPH OF GARNET-MICA SCHIST

PIECE OF GARNET-MICA SCHIST

Mountain

Glacier erodes rocks and carries rock particles to river

Waterfall erodes rock

River erodes valley floor and carries rock particles downstream

Rock particles deposited as sediment in lake

Rock particles deposited by wind to form sand dunes

Rock particles deposited in delta

Heavier rock particles deposited on continental shelf

Continental shelf

Continental slope

Lighter rock particles collect on ocean floor to form layers of sediment

Layers of sediment compressed and cemented to form sedimentary rock

267

Minerals

A MINERAL IS A NATURALLY OCCURRING SUBSTANCE that has a characteristic chemical composition and specific physical properties, such as habit and streak (see pp. 270-271). A rock, by comparison, is an aggregate of minerals and need not have a specific chemical composition. Minerals are made up of elements (substances that cannot be broken down chemically into simpler substances), each of which can be represented by a chemical symbol. Minerals can be divided into two main groups: native elements and compounds. Native elements are made up of a pure element. Examples include gold (chemical symbol Au), silver (Ag), copper (Cu), and carbon (C); carbon occurs as a native element in two forms, diamond and graphite. Compounds are combinations of two or more elements. For example, sulphides are compounds of sulphur (S) and one or more other elements, such as lead (Pb) in the mineral galena, or antimony (Sb) in the mineral stibnite.

Dendritic (branching) copper

Limonite groundmass (matrix)

COPPER
(Cu)

SULPHIDES

Cubic galena crystal

GALENA
(PbS)

Dendritic (branching) gold

Kimberlite groundmass (matrix)

Quartz vein

GOLD
(Au)

White diamond

DIAMOND
(C)

Hexagonal graphite crystal

GRAPHITE
(C)

OXIDES/HYDROXIDES

Milky quartz groundmass (matrix)

Smoky quartz crystal

SMOKY QUARTZ
(SiO_2)

Rounded bauxite grains in groundmass (matrix)

Mass of specular haematite crystals

SPECULAR HAEMATITE
(Fe_2O_3)

BAUXITE
(FeO(OH) and $Al_2O_3.2H_2O$)

Prismatic stibnite crystal

Quartz groundmass (matrix)

STIBNITE
(Sb_2S_3)

Perfect octahedral pyrites crystal

Quartz crystal

PYRITES
(FeS_2)

Parallel bands of onyx

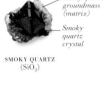

ONYX
(SiO_2)

Kidney ore haematite

Specular crystals of haematite

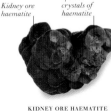

KIDNEY ORE HAEMATITE
(Fe_2O_3)

PHOSPHATES

Limonite groundmass (matrix)

Rock groundmass (matrix)

Radiating wavellite crystals

WAVELLITE
($Al_3(PO_4)_2(OH,F)_3.5H_2O$)

Prismatic pyromorphite crystals

PYROMORPHITE
($Pb_5(PO_4)_3Cl$)

CARBONATES

Striated cerussite crystal

Dog tooth calcite crystal

CERUSSITE
($PbCO_3$)

CALCITE
($CaCO_3$)

SULPHATES

Rock groundmass (matrix)

Radiating crystal mass of daisy gypsum

Radiating cyanotrichite crystals

CYANOTRICHITE
$Cu_4Al_2(SO_4)(OH)_{12}.2H_2O$

DAISY GYPSUM
($CaSO_4.2H_2O$)

MOLYBDATE

Tabular wulfenite crystal

Dark rock groundmass (matrix)

WULFENITE
($PbMoO_4$)

SILICATES

Feldspar groundmass (matrix)

Transparent bicolored tourmaline crystal

Dodecahedral sodalite crystal

SODALITE
($Na_8Al_6Si_6O_{24}Cl_2$)

Striated surface of olivine crystal

TOURMALINE
($Na(Mg,Fe,Li,Mn,Al)_3Al_6(BO_3)_3Si_6O_{18}(OH,F)_4$)

OLIVINE
($Fe_2SiO_4 - Mg_2SiO_4$)

Striated prismatic epidote crystal

EPIDOTE
($Ca_2(Al,Fe)_3(SiO_4)_3(OH)$)

Tabular muscovite crystal

Orthoclase crystal

MUSCOVITE
($KAl_2(Si_3Al)O_{10}(OH,F)_2$)

ORTHOCLASE
($KAlSi_3O_8$)

HALIDES

Cubic fluorite crystal

Cubic rock salt crystal

GREEN FLUORITE
(CaF_2)

ORANGE HALITE (ROCK SALT)
($NaCl$)

Mineral features

MINERALS CAN BE IDENTIFIED BY STUDYING features such as fracture, cleavage, crystal system, habit, hardness, colour, and streak. Minerals can break in different ways. If a mineral breaks in an irregular way, leaving rough surfaces, it possesses fracture. If a mineral breaks along well-defined planes of weakness, it possesses cleavage. Specific minerals have distinctive patterns of cleavage; for example, mica cleaves along one plane. Most minerals form crystals, which can be categorized into crystal systems according to their symmetry and number of faces. Within each system, several different but related forms of crystal are possible; for example, a cubic crystal can have six, eight, or twelve sides. A mineral's habit is the typical form taken by an aggregate of its crystals. Examples of habit include botryoidal (like a bunch of grapes) and massive (no definite form). The relative hardness of a mineral may be assessed by testing its resistance to scratching. This property is usually measured using Mohs scale, which increases in hardness from 1 (talc) to 10 (diamond). The colour of a mineral is not a dependable guide to its identity as some minerals have a range of colours. Streak (the colour the powdered mineral makes when rubbed across an unglazed tile) is a more reliable indicator.

CLEAVAGE

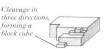

Cleavage in one direction

CLEAVAGE ALONG ONE PLANE

Cleavage in three directions, forming a block cube

CLEAVAGE ALONG THREE PLANES

Horizontal cleavage

Vertical cleavage

CLEAVAGE ALONG TWO PLANES

Cleavage in four directions, forming a double-pyramid crystal

CLEAVAGE ALONG FOUR PLANES

CRYSTAL SYSTEMS

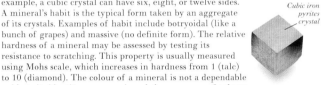

Cubic iron pyrites crystal

Tetragonal idocrase crystal

Representation of tetragonal system

TETRAGONAL SYSTEM

CUBIC SYSTEM

Representation of cubic system

Hexagonal beryl crystal

Representation of hexagonal/trigonal system

Orthorhombic barytes crystal

Representation of orthorhombic system

HEXAGONAL/TRIGONAL SYSTEM

ORTHORHOMBIC SYSTEM

FRACTURE

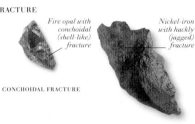

Fire opal with conchoidal (shell-like) fracture

Nickel-iron with hackly (jagged) fracture

CONCHOIDAL FRACTURE

HACKLY FRACTURE

Orpiment with uneven fracture

Garnierite with splintery fracture

UNEVEN FRACTURE

SPLINTERY FRACTURE

Monoclinic selenite crystal

Representation of monoclinic system

MONOCLINIC SYSTEM

Representation of triclinic system

Triclinic axinite crystal

TRICLINIC SYSTEM

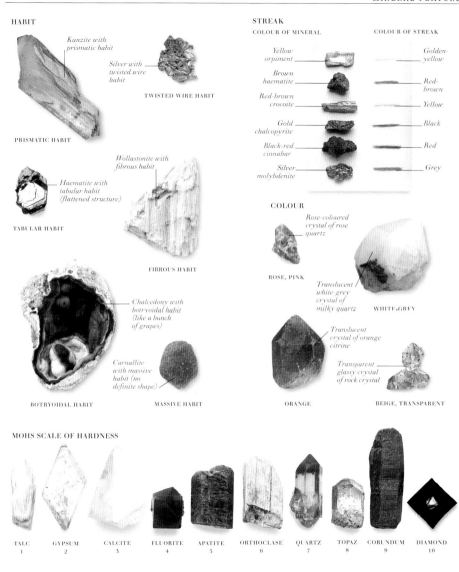

HABIT

Kunzite with prismatic habit

Silver with twisted wire habit

TWISTED WIRE HABIT

PRISMATIC HABIT

Haematite with tabular habit (flattened structure)

Wollastonite with fibrous habit

TABULAR HABIT

FIBROUS HABIT

Chalcedony with botryoidal habit (like a bunch of grapes)

Carnallite with massive habit (no definite shape)

BOTRYOIDAL HABIT

MASSIVE HABIT

STREAK

COLOUR OF MINERAL

Yellow orpiment

Brown haematite

Red-brown crocoite

Gold chalcopyrite

Black-red cinnabar

Silver molybdenite

COLOUR OF STREAK

Golden-yellow

Red-brown

Yellow

Black

Red

Grey

COLOUR

Rose-coloured crystal of rose quartz

ROSE, PINK

Translucent white-grey crystal of milky quartz

WHITE-GREY

Translucent crystal of orange citrine

Transparent glassy crystal of rock crystal

ORANGE

BEIGE, TRANSPARENT

MOHS SCALE OF HARDNESS

TALC	GYPSUM	CALCITE	FLUORITE	APATITE	ORTHOCLASE	QUARTZ	TOPAZ	CORUNDUM	DIAMOND
1	2	3	4	5	6	7	8	9	10

Volcanoes

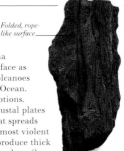

Folded, rope-like surface

VOLCANOES ARE VENTS OR FISSURES in the Earth's crust through which magma (molten rock that originates from deep beneath the crust) is forced on to the surface as lava. They occur most commonly along the boundaries of crustal plates; most volcanoes lie in a belt called the "Ring of Fire", which runs along the edge of the Pacific Ocean. Volcanoes can be classified according to the violence and frequency of their eruptions.

Non-explosive volcanic eruptions generally occur where crustal plates pull apart. These eruptions produce runny basaltic lava that spreads quickly over a wide area to form relatively flat cones. The most violent eruptions take place where plates collide. Such eruptions produce thick rhyolitic lava and may also blast out clouds of dust and pyroclasts (lava fragments). The lava does not flow far before cooling and therefore builds up steep-sided, conical volcanoes. Some volcanoes produce lava and ash eruptions, which build up composite volcanic cones. Volcanoes that erupt frequently are described as active; those that erupt rarely are termed dormant; and those that have stopped erupting altogether are termed extinct. As well as the volcanoes themselves, other features associated with volcanic regions include geysers, hot mineral springs, solfataras, fumaroles, and bubbling mud pools.

PAHOEHOE (ROPY LAVA)

HORU GEYSER, NEW ZEALAND

VOLCANO TYPES

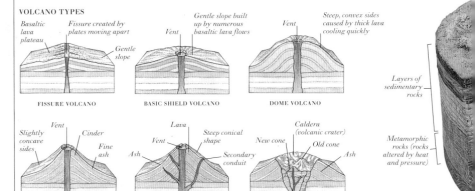

Basaltic lava plateau

Fissure created by plates moving apart

Gentle slope

FISSURE VOLCANO

Gentle slope built up by numerous basaltic lava flows

Vent

BASIC SHIELD VOLCANO

Steep, convex sides caused by thick lava cooling quickly

Vent

DOME VOLCANO

Slightly concave sides

Vent

Cinder

Fine ash

ASH-CINDER VOLCANO

Lava

Vent

Ash

Steep conical shape

Secondary conduit

COMPOSITE VOLCANO

Caldera (volcanic crater)

New cone

Old cone

Ash

CALDERA VOLCANO

Layers of sedimentary rocks

Metamorphic rocks (rocks altered by heat and pressure)

HOW VOLCANIC PLUGS BECOME EXPOSED

Extinct volcano

Solidified lava forms plug

PLUG FORMATION

Plug exposed

Volcanic cone slowly eroded away

INITIAL EROSION AROUND PLUG

Resistant lava plug remains

Volcanic cone completely eroded away

COMPLETE DENUDATION OF PLUG

LAPILLI (LAVA FRAGMENTS)

Small piece of solidified lava

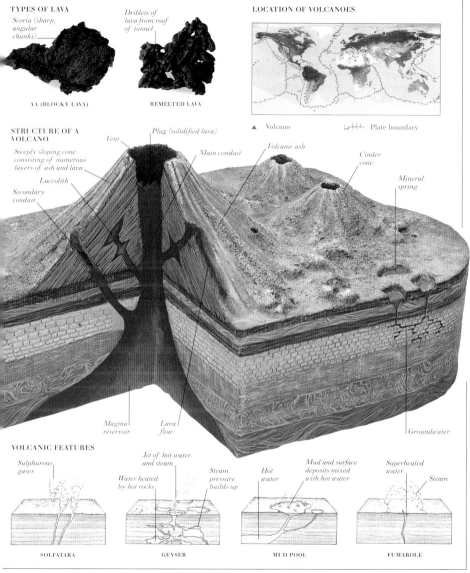

TYPES OF LAVA

Scoria (sharp, angular chunks)

Driblets of lava from roof of tunnel

AA (BLOCKY LAVA)

REMELTED LAVA

LOCATION OF VOLCANOES

▲ Volcano ⌐⊢⊹⊹ Plate boundary

STRUCTURE OF A VOLCANO

Steeply sloping cone consisting of numerous layers of ash and lava

Laccolith

Secondary conduit

Vent

Plug (solidified lava)

Main conduit

Volcanic ash

Cinder cone

Mineral spring

Magma reservoir

Lava flow

Groundwater

VOLCANIC FEATURES

Sulphurous gases

Water heated by hot rocks

Jet of hot water and steam

Steam pressure builds up

Hot water

Mud and surface deposits mixed with hot water

Superheated water

Steam

SOLFATARA

GEYSER

MUD POOL

FUMAROLE

Igneous and metamorphic rocks

IGNEOUS ROCKS ARE FORMED WHEN MAGMA (molten rock that originates from deep beneath the Earth's crust) cools and solidifies. There are two main types of igneous rock: intrusive and extrusive. Intrusive rocks are formed deep underground where magma is forced into cracks or between rock layers to form structures such as sills, dykes, and batholiths. The magma cools slowly to form coarse-grained rocks such as gabbro and pegmatite. Extrusive rocks are formed above the Earth's surface from lava (magma that has been ejected in a volcanic eruption). The molten lava cools quickly, producing fine-grained rocks such as rhyolite and basalt. Metamorphic rocks are those that have been altered by intense heat (contact metamorphism) or extreme pressure (regional metamorphism). Contact metamorphism occurs when rocks are changed by heat from, for example, an igneous intrusion or lava flow. Regional metamorphism occurs when rock is crushed in the middle of a folding mountain range. Metamorphic rocks can be formed from igneous rocks, sedimentary rocks, or even from other metamorphic rocks.

BASALT COLUMNS

IGNEOUS ROCK STRUCTURES

Cinder cone
Large eroded lava flow
Cedar-tree laccolith
Butte
Plug
Cone sheet
Ring dyke
Batholith
Dyke
Sill
Dyke swarm
Lopolith

CONTACT METAMORPHISM

Metamorphic aureole (region where contact metamorphism occurs)
Hot igneous intrusion
Limestone
Shale
Marble (metamorphosed limestone)
Slate (metamorphosed shale)

REGIONAL METAMORPHISM

Mountain range
Slate, formed under low pressure and temperature
Compression
Compression
Schist, formed under medium pressure and temperature
Crust
Gneiss, formed under high pressure and temperature
Mantle
Magma

EXAMPLES OF METAMORPHIC ROCKS

Pale feldspar
Dark mica
Dark mineral band
Pale calcite

GNEISS

FOLDED SCHIST

SKARN

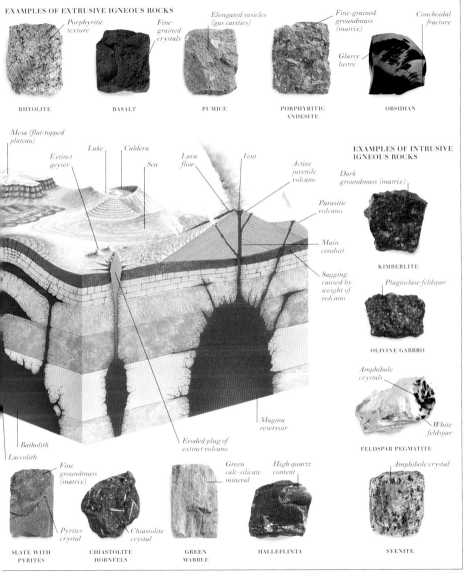

EXAMPLES OF EXTRUSIVE IGNEOUS ROCKS

Porphyritic texture

Fine-grained crystals

Elongated vesicles (gas cavities)

Fine-grained groundmass (matrix)

Conchoidal fracture

Glassy lustre

RHYOLITE

BASALT

PUMICE

PORPHYRITIC ANDESITE

OBSIDIAN

Mesa (flat-topped plateau)

Extinct geyser

Lake

Caldera

Sea

Lava flow

Vent

Active juvenile volcano

Parasitic volcano

Main conduit

Sagging caused by weight of volcano

Magma reservoir

Batholith

Laccolith

Eroded plug of extinct volcano

EXAMPLES OF INTRUSIVE IGNEOUS ROCKS

Dark groundmass (matrix)

KIMBERLITE

Plagioclase feldspar

OLIVINE GABBRO

Amphibole crystals

White feldspar

FELDSPAR PEGMATITE

Amphibole crystal

SYENITE

Fine groundmass (matrix)

Pyrites crystal

SLATE WITH PYRITES

Chiastolite crystal

CHIASTOLITE HORNFELS

Green calc-silicate mineral

GREEN MARBLE

High quartz content

HALLEFLINTA

Sedimentary rocks

SEDIMENTARY ROCKS ARE FORMED BY THE ACCUMULATION and consolidation of sediments (see pp. 266-267). There are three main types of sedimentary rock. Clastic sedimentary rocks, such as breccia or sandstone, are formed from other rocks that have been broken down into fragments by weathering (see pp. 282-283), which have then been transported and deposited elsewhere. Organic sedimentary rocks – for example, coal (see pp. 280-281) – are derived from plant and animal remains. Chemical sedimentary rocks are formed by

THE GRAND CANYON, USA

chemical processes. For example, rock salt is formed when salt dissolved in water is deposited as the water evaporates. Sedimentary rocks are laid down in layers, called beds or strata. Each new layer is laid down horizontally over older ones. There are usually some gaps in the sequence, called unconformities. These represent periods in which no new sediments were being laid down, or when earlier sedimentary layers were raised above sea level and eroded away.

EXAMPLES OF UNCONFORMITIES

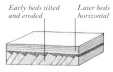

Early beds tilted and eroded   *Later beds horizontal*

ANGULAR UNCONFORMITY

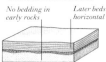

No bedding in early rocks   *Later beds horizontal*

NONCONFORMITY

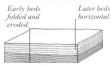

Early beds folded and eroded   *Later beds horizontal*

DISCONFORMITY

SEDIMENTARY LAYERS OF THE GRAND CANYON REGION

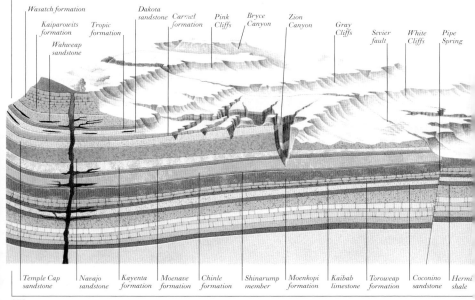

Wasatch formation
Kaiparowits formation
Tropic formation
Wahweap sandstone
Dakota sandstone
Carmel formation
Pink Cliffs
Bryce Canyon
Zion Canyon
Gray Cliffs
Sevier fault
White Cliffs
Pipe Spring

Temple Cap sandstone   *Navajo sandstone*   *Kayenta formation*   *Moenave formation*   *Chinle formation*   *Shinarump member*   *Moenkopi formation*   *Kaibab limestone*   *Toroweap formation*   *Coconino sandstone*   *Hermi shale*

EXAMPLES OF SEDIMENTARY ROCKS

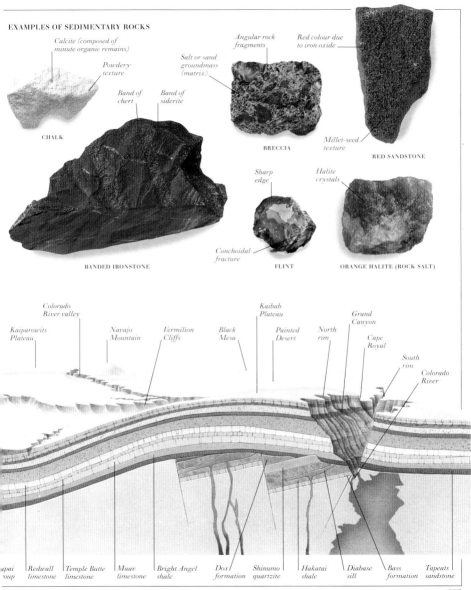

Calcite (composed of minute organic remains)

Powdery texture

CHALK

Salt or sand groundmass (matrix)

Angular rock fragments

BRECCIA

Red colour due to iron oxide

Millet-seed texture

RED SANDSTONE

Band of chert

Band of siderite

BANDED IRONSTONE

Sharp edge

Conchoidal fracture

FLINT

Halite crystals

ORANGE HALITE (ROCK SALT)

Kaiparowits Plateau

Colorado River valley

Navajo Mountain

Vermilion Cliffs

Black Mesa

Kaibab Plateau

Painted Desert

North rim

Grand Canyon

Cape Royal

South rim

Colorado River

...pai ...oup

Redwall limestone

Temple Butte limestone

Muav limestone

Bright Angel shale

Dox formation

Shinumo quartzite

Hakatai shale

Diabase sill

Bass formation

Tapeats sandstone

277

Fossils

FOSSILS ARE THE REMAINS of plants and animals that have been preserved in rock. A fossil may be the preserved remains of an organism itself, an impression of it in rock, or preserved traces (known as trace fossils) left by an organism while it was alive, such as organic carbon outlines, fossilized footprints, or droppings. Most dead organisms soon rot away or are eaten by scavengers. For fossilization to occur, rapid burial by sediment is necessary. The organism decays, but the harder parts – bones, teeth, and shells, for example – may be preserved and hardened by minerals from the surrounding sediment. Fossilization may also occur even when the hard parts of an organism are dissolved away to leave an impression called a mould. The mould is filled by minerals, thereby creating a cast of the organism. The study of fossils (palaeontology) can not only show how living things have evolved, but can also help to reveal the Earth's geological history – for example, by aiding in the dating of rock strata.

PROCESS OF FOSSILIZATION

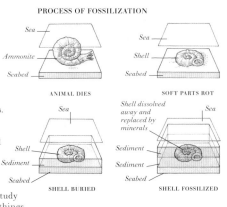

ANIMAL DIES

SOFT PARTS ROT

SHELL BURIED

SHELL FOSSILIZED

EXAMPLES OF FOSSILS

ALETHOPTERIS (SEED FERN)

FROG (AMPHIBIAN)

PAVLOVIA (AMMONITE MOLLUSC)

DICYOTHYRIS (BRACHIOPOD)

SCALLOP (BIVALVE MOLLUSC)

ACROTEUTHIS (BELEMNITE MOLLUSC)

SCORPION (ARTHROPOD)

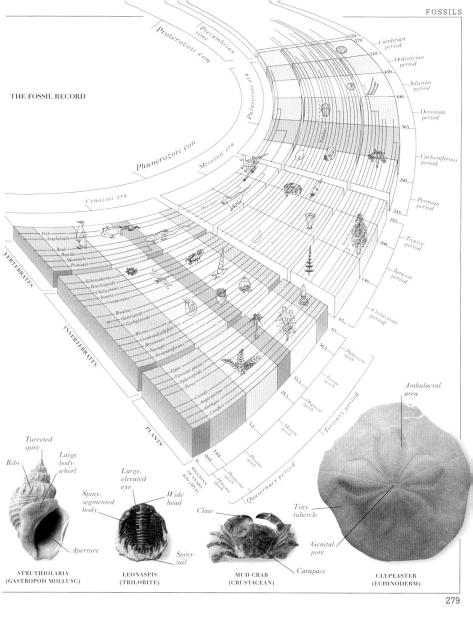

THE FOSSIL RECORD

Proterozoic eon

Precambrian time

Phanerozoic eon

Palaeozoic era

Mesozoic era

Cenozoic era

Cambrian period — 570
570

Ordovician period — 510

Silurian period — 439

Devonian period — 409

363

Carboniferous period

Permian period — 290

245
245

Triassic period — 208

Jurassic period — 146

Cretaceous period — 65

Dinosaurs

Ammonite de Belemnit

Seed plants

VERTEBRATES

Fish
Amphibians
Birds
Reptiles
Mammals
Primates

INVERTEBRATES

Echinoderms
Brachiopods
Chelicerates
Insects
Crustaceans
Bivalves
Gastropods
Cephalopods
Worms
Corals and jellyfish
Bryozoans
Sponges
Foraminiferans

PLANTS

Algae
Vascular plants
Sphenopsids
Ferns
Cycads
Angiosperms
Ginkgos
Conifers

65
65

Palaeocene epoch — 56.5

Eocene epoch — 35.5

Oligocene epoch — 23.5

Miocene epoch — 5.2

Pliocene epoch — 1.64

0.01
0.01

Pleistocene epoch

Holocene epoch

MILLIONS OF YEARS AGO (MYA)

Tertiary period

Quaternary period

Turreted spire

Ribs

Large body whorl

Aperture

STRUTHIOLARIA
(GASTROPOD MOLLUSC)

Large, elevated eye

Spiny, segmented body

Wide head

Spiny tail

LEONASPIS
(TRILOBITE)

Claw

Carapace

MUD CRAB
(CRUSTACEAN)

Ambulacral area

Tiny tubercle

Genital pore

CLYPEASTER
(ECHINODERM)

Mineral resources

Stalk   *Leaf*

PLANT MATTER

MINERAL RESOURCES CAN BE DEFINED AS naturally occurring substances that can be extracted from the Earth and are useful as fuels and raw materials. Coal, oil, and gas – collectively called fossil fuels – are commonly included in this group, but are not strictly minerals, because they are of organic origin. Coal formation begins when vegetation is buried and partly decomposed to form peat. Overlying sediments compress the peat and transform it into lignite (soft brown coal). As the overlying sediments accumulate, increasing pressure and temperature eventually transform the lignite into bituminous and hard anthracite coals. Oil and gas are usually formed from organic matter that was deposited in marine sediments. Under the effects of heat and pressure, the compressed organic matter undergoes complex chemical changes to form oil and gas. The oil and gas percolate upwards through water-saturated, permeable rocks and they may rise to the Earth's surface or accumulate below an impermeable layer of rock that has been folded or faulted to form a trap – an anticline (upfold) trap, for example. Minerals are inorganic substances that may consist of a single chemical element, such as gold, silver, or copper, or combinations of elements (see pp. 268-269). Some minerals are concentrated in mineralization zones in rock associated with crustal movements or volcanic activity. Others may be found in sediments as placer deposits – accumulations of high-density minerals that have been weathered out of rocks, transported, and deposited (on river-beds, for example).

OIL RIG, NORTH SEA

Decayed plant matter

About 60% carbon   **PEAT**   *About 70% carbon*

Crumbly texture   **LIGNITE (BROWN COAL)**   *Powdery texture*

About 80% carbon

Shiny surface   **BITUMINOUS COAL**   *About 95% carbon*

ANTHRACITE COAL

HOW COAL IS FORMED

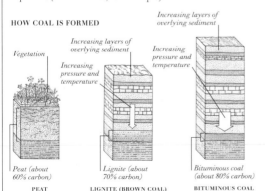

Vegetation

Increasing pressure and temperature

Increasing layers of overlying sediment

Increasing pressure and temperature

Increasing layers of overlying sediment

Increasing pressure and temperature

Peat (about 60% carbon)

PEAT

Lignite (about 70% carbon)

LIGNITE (BROWN COAL)

Bituminous coal (about 80% carbon)

BITUMINOUS COAL

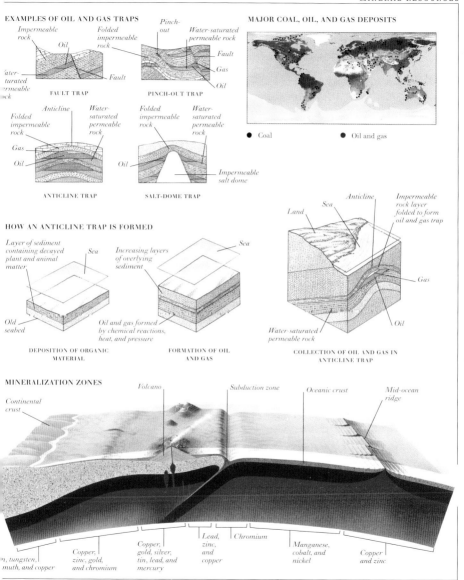

EXAMPLES OF OIL AND GAS TRAPS

Impermeable rock
Oil
Folded impermeable rock

Water-saturated permeable rock
Fault

FAULT TRAP

Pinch-out
Water-saturated permeable rock
Fault
Gas
Oil

PINCH-OUT TRAP

Anticline
Folded impermeable rock
Water-saturated permeable rock
Gas
Oil

ANTICLINE TRAP

Folded impermeable rock
Water-saturated permeable rock
Oil
Impermeable salt dome

SALT-DOME TRAP

MAJOR COAL, OIL, AND GAS DEPOSITS

● Coal   ● Oil and gas

HOW AN ANTICLINE TRAP IS FORMED

Layer of sediment containing decayed plant and animal matter
Sea
Old seabed

DEPOSITION OF ORGANIC MATERIAL

Increasing layers of overlying sediment
Sea
Oil and gas formed by chemical reactions, heat, and pressure

FORMATION OF OIL AND GAS

Land
Sea
Anticline
Impermeable rock layer folded to form oil and gas trap
Gas
Oil
Water-saturated permeable rock

COLLECTION OF OIL AND GAS IN ANTICLINE TRAP

MINERALIZATION ZONES

Continental crust
Volcano
Subduction zone
Oceanic crust
Mid-ocean ridge

..n, tungsten, ..muth, and copper
Copper, zinc, gold, and chromium
Copper, gold, silver, tin, lead, and mercury
Lead, zinc, and copper
Chromium
Manganese, cobalt, and nickel
Copper and zinc

281

Weathering and erosion

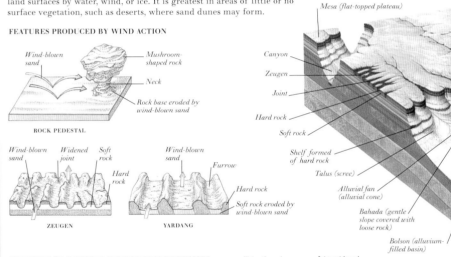

WEATHERING IS THE BREAKING DOWN of rocks on the Earth's surface. There are two main types: physical (or mechanical) and chemical. Physical weathering may be caused by temperature changes, such as freezing and thawing, or by abrasion from material carried by winds, rivers, or glaciers. Rocks may also be broken down by the actions of animals and plants, such as the burrowing of animals and the growth of roots. Chemical weathering causes rocks to decompose by changing their chemical composition – for example, rainwater may dissolve certain minerals in a rock. Erosion is the wearing away and removal of land surfaces by water, wind, or ice. It is greatest in areas of little or no surface vegetation, such as deserts, where sand dunes may form.

Wind blows away small particles

Larger particles aggregate

Hamada forms

FIRST STAGE

SECOND STAGE

FINAL STAGE

FEATURES OF WEATHERING AND EROSION

FEATURES PRODUCED BY WIND ACTION

Wind-blown sand

Mushroom-shaped rock

Neck

Rock base eroded by wind-blown sand

ROCK PEDESTAL

Wind-blown sand   *Widened joint*   *Soft rock*   *Hard rock*

ZEUGEN

Wind-blown sand   *Furrow*   *Hard rock*   *Soft rock eroded by wind-blown sand*

YARDANG

Mesa (flat-topped plateau)

Canyon

Zeugen

Joint

Hard rock

Soft rock

Shelf formed of hard rock

Talus (scree)

Alluvial fan (alluvial cone)

Bahada (gentle slope covered with loose rock)

Bolson (alluvium-filled basin)

EXAMPLES OF PHYSICAL WEATHERING PROCESSES

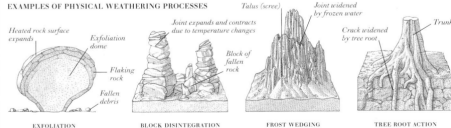

Heated rock surface expands   *Exfoliation dome*   *Flaking rock*   *Fallen debris*

EXFOLIATION (ONION-SKIN WEATHERING)

Joint expands and contracts due to temperature changes   *Block of fallen rock*

BLOCK DISINTEGRATION

Talus (scree)   *Joint widened by frozen water*

FROST WEDGING

Crack widened by tree root   *Trunk*

TREE ROOT ACTION

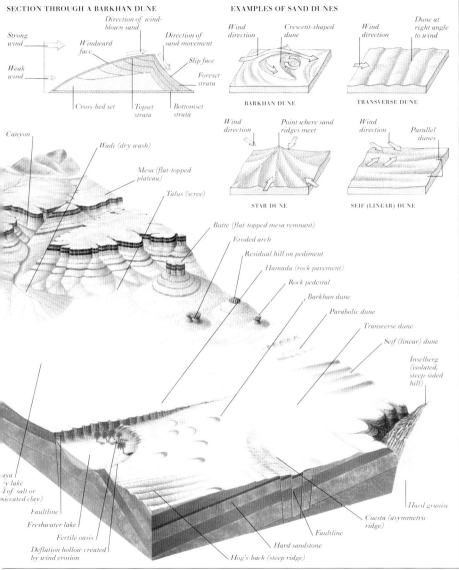

SECTION THROUGH A BARKHAN DUNE

Strong wind

Weak wind

Windward face

Direction of wind-blown sand

Direction of sand movement

Slip face

Foreset strata

Cross-bed set

Topset strata

Bottomset strata

EXAMPLES OF SAND DUNES

Wind direction

Crescent-shaped dune

BARKHAN DUNE

Wind direction

Dune at right angle to wind

TRANSVERSE DUNE

Wind direction

Point where sand ridges meet

STAR DUNE

Wind direction

Parallel dunes

SEIF (LINEAR) DUNE

Canyon

Wadi (dry wash)

Mesa (flat-topped plateau)

Talus (scree)

Butte (flat-topped mesa remnant)

Eroded arch

Residual hill on pediment

Hamada (rock pavement)

Rock pedestal

Barkhan dune

Parabolic dune

Transverse dune

Seif (linear) dune

Inselberg (isolated, steep-sided hill)

Playa (dry lake of salt or desiccated clay)

Faultline

Freshwater lake

Fertile oasis

Deflation hollow created by wind erosion

Hog's-back (steep ridge)

Hard sandstone

Faultline

Cuesta (asymmetric ridge)

Hard granite

283

Caves

CAVES COMMONLY FORM in areas of limestone, although on coastlines they also occur in other rocks. Limestone is made of calcite (calcium carbonate), which dissolves in the carbonic acid naturally present in rainwater, and in humic acids from the decay of vegetation. The acidic water trickles down through cracks and joints in the limestone and between rock layers, breaking up the surface terrain into clints (blocks of rock), separated by grikes (deep cracks), and punctuated by sink-holes (also called swallow-holes or potholes) into which surface streams may disappear. Underground, the acidic water dissolves the rock around crevices, opening up a network of passages and caves, which can become large caverns if the roofs collapse. Various features are formed when the dissolved calcite is redeposited; for example, it may be redeposited along an underground stream to form a gour (series of calcite ridges), or in caves and passages to form stalactites and stalagmites. Stalactites develop where calcite is left behind as water drips from the roof; where the drops land, stalagmites build up.

STALACTITE WITH RING MARKS

Ring mark

MERGED STALACTITES

SURFACE TOPOGRAPHY OF A CAVE SYSTEM

Doline (depression caused by collapse of cave roof)

Sink-hole

Porous limestone

Gorge where cave roof has fallen in

Resurgence

Limestone terrain with clints and grikes

Impermeable rock

STALAGMITE FORMATIONS

Calcite (calcium carbonate) crystallized under water

Thin encrustations of calcite (calcium carbonate)

Scar of bare rock

Former water table

CALCAREOUS TUFA

CRYSTALLINE STALAGMITIC FLOOR

Permeable limestone

Encrustations on dead stems of small plants

Calcite (calcium carbonate)

Resurgence

Calcite (calcium carbonate)

Encrustations with fungoid structure

STALAGMITIC FLOOR

STALAGMITIC BOSS

Layer of impermeable rock

Present water table

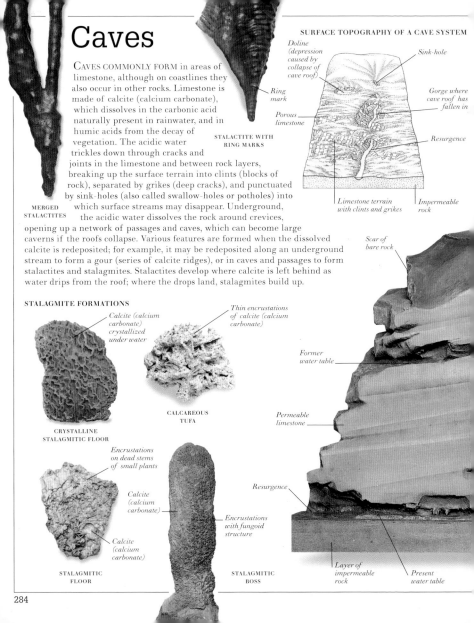

284

DEVELOPMENT OF A CAVE SYSTEM

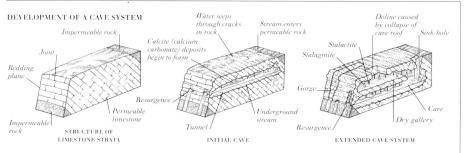

STRUCTURE OF
LIMESTONE STRATA

Impermeable rock

Joint

Bedding plane

Impermeable rock

Permeable limestone

INITIAL CAVE

Water seeps through cracks in rock

Stream enters permeable rock

Calcite (calcium carbonate) deposits begin to form

Resurgence

Tunnel

Underground stream

EXTENDED CAVE SYSTEM

Doline caused by collapse of cave roof

Sink-hole

Stalactite

Stalagmite

Gorge

Resurgence

Cave

Dry gallery

INTERCONNECTED CAVE SYSTEM

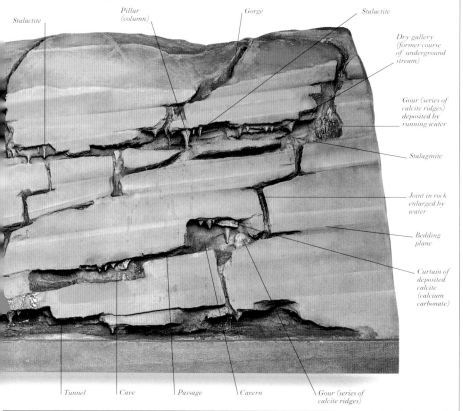

Stalactite

Pillar (column)

Gorge

Stalactite

Dry gallery (former course of underground stream)

Gour (series of calcite ridges) deposited by running water

Stalagmite

Joint in rock enlarged by water

Bedding plane

Curtain of deposited calcite (calcium carbonate)

Tunnel

Cave

Passage

Cavern

Gour (series of calcite ridges)

Glaciers

GLACIER BAY, ALASKA

A VALLEY GLACIER IS A LARGE MASS OF ICE that forms on land and moves slowly downhill under its own weight. It is formed from snow that collects in cirques (mountain hollows also known as corries) and compresses into ice as more and more snow accumulates. The cirque is deepened by frost wedging and abrasion (see pp. 282-283), and arêtes (sharp ridges) develop between adjacent cirques. Eventually, so much ice builds up that the glacier begins to move downhill. As the glacier moves it collects moraine (debris), which may range in size from particles of dust to large boulders. The rocks at the base of the glacier erode the glacial valley, giving it a U-shaped cross-section. Under the glacier, *roches moutonnées* (eroded outcrops of hard rock) and drumlins (rounded mounds of rock and clay) are left behind on the valley floor. The glacier ends at a terminus (the snout), where the ice melts as fast as it arrives. If the temperature increases, the ice melts faster than it arrives, and the glacier retreats. The retreating glacier leaves behind its moraine and also erratics (isolated single boulders). Glacial streams from the melting glacier deposit eskers and kames (ridges and mounds of sand and gravel), but carry away the finer sediment to form a stratified outwash plain. Lumps of ice carried on to this plain melt, creating holes called kettles.

VALLEY GLACIER

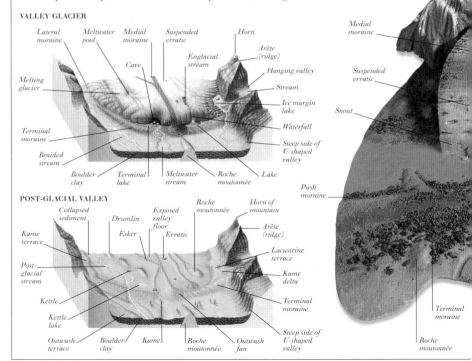

Lateral moraine
Meltwater pool
Medial moraine
Suspended erratic
Horn
Arête (ridge)
Cave
Englacial stream
Hanging valley
Melting glacier
Stream
Ice margin lake
Terminal moraine
Waterfall
Braided stream
Steep side of U-shaped valley
Boulder clay
Terminal lake
Meltwater stream
Roche moutonnée
Lake

Medial moraine
Suspended erratic
Snout
Push moraine
Terminal moraine
Roche moutonnée

POST-GLACIAL VALLEY

Collapsed sediment
Drumlin
Exposed valley floor
Roche moutonnée
Horn of mountain
Kame terrace
Esker
Erratic
Arête (ridge)
Post-glacial stream
Lacustrine terrace
Kame delta
Kettle
Terminal moraine
Kettle lake
Outwash terrace
Boulder clay
Kame
Roche moutonnée
Outwash fan
Steep side of U-shaped valley

FEATURES OF A GLACIER

Firn (compressed snow)

Tributary glacier

Moving ice

U-shaped valley

Medial moraine

Lateral moraine

Subglacial stream

Cirque (corrie)

Arête (ridge)

Tributary moraine joins medial moraine

Rock being eroded by ice

Brittle surface ice

Viscous flowing ice

Englacial moraine

Crevasse

Ribbon lake

Outwash plain

Meltwater

Stream

Sediment deposited by meltwater

ICE-FALL

Slope flattens

Rougher surface

Ice recompresses

Ice block tilts and twists

Steep slope

Gentle slope

Smooth surface

Crevasse deepens and widens

Ice breaks into blocks

CIRQUE FORMATION

Firn (compressed snow)

Material loosened by frost wedging

Fresh snowfall

EARLY STAGE

Moraine pulled from ground

Glacier

Base of cirque eroded by glacier's pivoting action

Rock lip

Steep back wall

LATER STAGE

U-SHAPED VALLEY FORMATION

Arête (ridge)

Horn

Glacier

Cirque overspills

DURING GLACIATION

Deepened cirque

Hanging valley

Tarn

Deep U-shaped valley

AFTER GLACIATION

287

Rivers

RIVERS FORM PART of the water cycle – the continuous circulation of water between the land, sea, and atmosphere. The source of a river may be a mountain spring or lake, or a melting glacier. The course that the river subsequently takes depends on the slope of the terrain and on the rock types and formations over which it flows. In its early, upland stages, a river tumbles steeply over rocks and boulders and cuts a steep-sided V-shaped valley. Farther downstream, it flows smoothly over sediments and forms winding meanders, eroding sideways to create broad valleys and plains. On reaching the coast, the river may deposit sediment to form an estuary or delta (see pp. 290-291).

RIVER CAPTURE

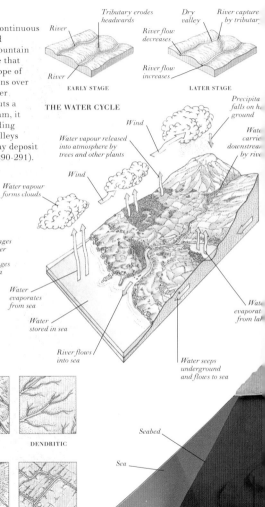

Tributary erodes headwards
River
River flow decreases
River
EARLY STAGE

Dry valley
River capture by tributary
River flow increases
LATER STAGE

THE WATER CYCLE

Precipitation falls on high ground
Wind
Water carried downstream by river
Water vapour released into atmosphere by trees and other plants
Wind
Water vapour forms clouds
Water evaporates from sea
Water stored in sea
Water evaporates from lake
River flows into sea
Water seeps underground and flows to sea

SATELLITE IMAGE OF GANGES RIVER DELTA, BANGLADESH

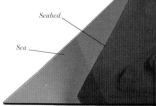

Ganges River
Ganges delta
Infertile swampland
Distributary
Large volume of sediment

Seabed
Sea
Sediment layers

RIVER DRAINAGE PATTERNS

RADIAL

CENTRIPETAL

PARALLEL

DENDRITIC

DERANGED

TRELLISED

ANNULAR

RECTANGULAR

STAGES IN A RIVER'S DEVELOPMENT

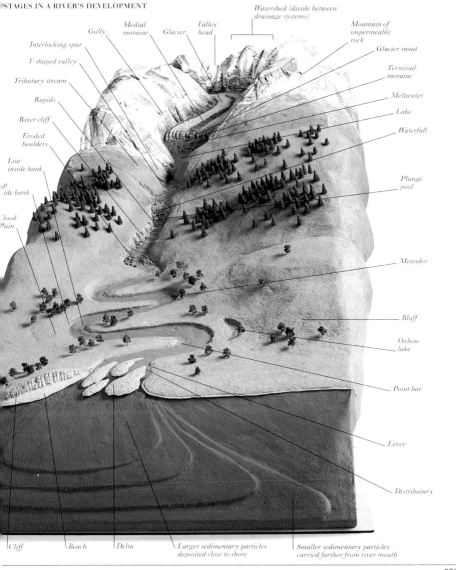

Watershed (divide between drainage systems)

Medial moraine

Gully

Glacier

Valley head

Mountain of impermeable rock

Glacier snout

Interlocking spur

V-shaped valley

Tributary stream

Rapids

River cliff

Eroded boulders

Low inside bank

p ide bank

Flood-ain

Terminal moraine

Meltwater

Lake

Waterfall

Plunge pool

Meander

Bluff

Oxbow lake

Point bar

Levee

Distributary

Cliff

Beach

Delta

Larger sedimentary particles deposited close to shore

Smaller sedimentary particles carried farther from river mouth

289

River features

RIVERS ARE ONE OF THE MAJOR FORCES that shape the landscape. Near its source, a river is steep (see pp. 288-289). It erodes downwards, carving out V-shaped valleys and deep gorges. Waterfalls and rapids are formed where the river flows from hard rock to softer, more easily eroded rock. Farther downstream, meanders may form and there is greater sideways erosion, resulting in a broad river valley. The river sometimes erodes through the neck of a meander to form an oxbow lake. Sediment deposited on the valley floor by meandering rivers and during floods helps to create a flood-plain. Floods may also deposit sediment on the banks of the river to form levees. As a river spills into the sea or a lake, it deposits large amounts of sediment, and may form a delta. A delta is an area of sand-bars, swamps, and lagoons through which the river flows in several channels called distributaries – the Mississippi delta, for example. Often, a rise in sea level may have flooded the river-mouth to form a broad estuary, a tidal section where seawater mixes with fresh water.

HOW WATERFALLS AND RAPIDS ARE FORMED

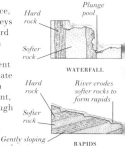

WATERFALL

RAPIDS

A RIVER VALLEY DRAINAGE SYSTEM

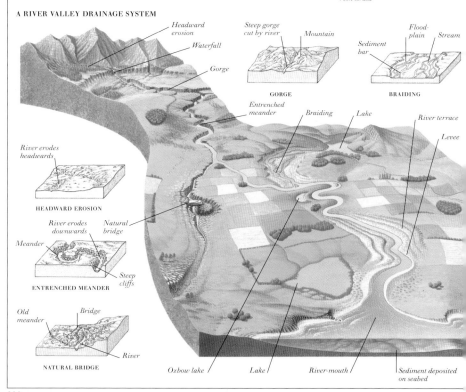

GORGE

BRAIDING

HEADWARD EROSION

ENTRENCHED MEANDER

NATURAL BRIDGE

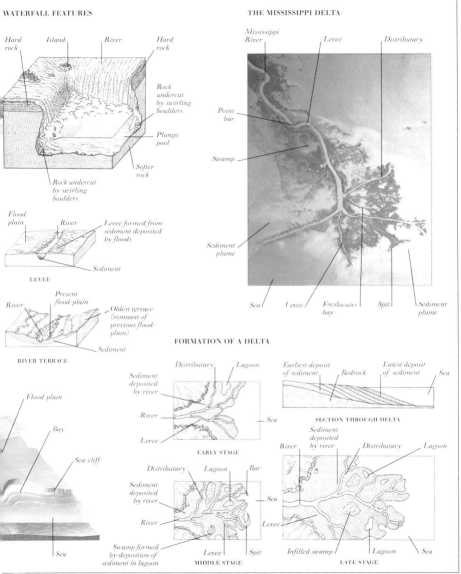

WATERFALL FEATURES

Hard rock

Island

River

Hard rock

Rock undercut by swirling boulders

Plunge pool

Softer rock

Rock undercut by swirling boulders

Flood-plain

River

Levee formed from sediment deposited by floods

Sediment

LEVEE

River

Present flood-plain

Oldest terrace (remnant of previous flood-plain)

Sediment

RIVER TERRACE

Flood-plain

Bay

Sea-cliff

Sea

THE MISSISSIPPI DELTA

Mississippi River

Levee

Distributary

Point bar

Swamp

Sediment plume

Sea

Levee

Fresh-water bay

Spit

Sediment plume

FORMATION OF A DELTA

Distributary

Lagoon

Sediment deposited by river

River

Levee

Sea

EARLY STAGE

Earliest deposit of sediment

Bedrock

Latest deposit of sediment

Sea

SECTION THROUGH DELTA

Distributary

Lagoon

Bar

Sediment deposited by river

River

Sea

Swamp formed by deposition of sediment in lagoon

Levee

Spit

MIDDLE STAGE

River

Sediment deposited by river

Distributary

Lagoon

Levee

Infilled swamp

Lagoon

Sea

LATE STAGE

291

Lakes and groundwater

NATURAL LAKE OCCUR WHERE a large quantity of water collects in a hollow in impermeable rock, or is prevented from draining away by a barrier, such as moraine (glacial deposits) or solidified lava. Lakes are often relatively short-lived landscape features, as they tend to become silted up by sediment from the streams and rivers that feed them. Some of the more long-lasting

lakes are found in deep rift valleys formed by vertical movements of the Earth's crust (see pp. 58-59) – for example, Lake Baikal in Russia, the world's largest freshwater lake, and the Dead Sea in the Middle East, one of the world's saltiest lakes. Where water is able to drain away, it sinks into the ground until it reaches a layer of impermeable rock, then accumulates in the permeable rock above it; this water-saturated permeable rock is called an aquifer. The saturated zone varies in depth according to seasonal and climatic changes. In wet conditions, the water

LAKE BAIKAL, RUSSIA

stored underground builds up, while in dry periods it becomes depleted. Where the upper edge of the saturated zone – the water table – meets the ground surface, water emerges as springs. In an artesian basin, where the aquifer is below an aquiclude (layer of impermeable rock), the water table throughout the basin is determined by its height at the rim. In the centre of such a basin, the water table is above ground level. The water in the basin is thus trapped below the water table and can rise under its own pressure along faultlines or well shafts.

EXAMPLES OF SPRINGS

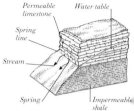

LIMESTONE SPRING

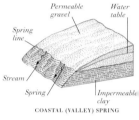

COASTAL (VALLEY) SPRING

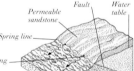

FAULT SPRING

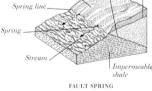

LAVA SPRING

STRUCTURE OF AN ARTESIAN BASIN

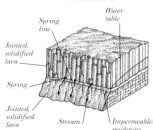

FEATURES OF A GROUNDWATER SYSTEM

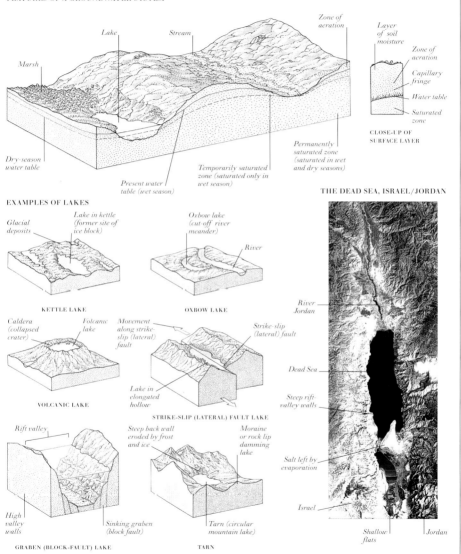

Zone of aeration

Lake

Stream

Marsh

Layer of soil moisture

Zone of aeration

Capillary fringe

Water table

Saturated zone

CLOSE-UP OF SURFACE LAYER

Dry-season water table

Permanently saturated zone (saturated in wet and dry seasons)

Temporarily saturated zone (saturated only in wet season)

Present water table (wet season)

EXAMPLES OF LAKES

Glacial deposits

Lake in kettle (former site of ice block)

KETTLE LAKE

Oxbow lake (cut-off river meander)

River

OXBOW LAKE

Caldera (collapsed crater)

Volcanic lake

VOLCANIC LAKE

Movement along strike-slip (lateral) fault

Strike-slip (lateral) fault

Lake in elongated hollow

STRIKE-SLIP (LATERAL) FAULT LAKE

Rift valley

High valley walls

Sinking graben (block fault)

GRABEN (BLOCK-FAULT) LAKE

Steep back wall eroded by frost and ice

Moraine or rock lip damming lake

Tarn (circular mountain lake)

TARN

THE DEAD SEA, ISRAEL/JORDAN

River Jordan

Dead Sea

Steep rift-valley walls

Salt left by evaporation

Israel

Shallow flats

Jordan

293

Coastlines

COASTLINES ARE AMONG THE MOST RAPIDLY changing landscape
features. Some are eroded by waves, wind, and rain, causing
cliffs to be undercut and caves to be hollowed out of solid rock.
Others are built up by waves transporting sand and small rocks in a
process known as longshore drift, and by rivers depositing sediment in
deltas. Additional influences include the activities of living organisms
such as coral, crustal movements, and sea-level variations due to
climatic changes. Rising land or a drop in sea level creates an emergent
coastline, with cliffs and beaches stranded above the new shoreline.
Sinking land or a rise in sea level produces a drowned coastline, typified
by fjords (submerged glacial valleys) or submerged river valleys.

FEATURES OF A SEA-CLIFF

Cliff-top
Cliff-face
High tide level
Low tide level
Offshore deposits
Wave-cut platform
Undercut area of cliff

FEATURES OF WAVES

Wave height
Crest
Wavelength
Trough
Shorter wavelength near beach
Circular orbit of water and suspended particles
Orbit deformed into ellipse as water gets shallower

Mature river
Headland
Bedding plane
Sea-cliff
Remnants of former headland
Estuary

LONGSHORE DRIFT

Movement of material along beach
Build-up of material against groyne
Pebble
Backwash
Beach
Groyne
Waves approaching shore at an oblique angle
Swash zone
Swash

DEPOSITIONAL FEATURES OF COASTLINES

Bay-head beach
Wave direction
Headland

Wave direction
Tombolo
Island

Wave direction
Cuspate foreland

Wave direction
Barrier beach
Lagoon

BAY HEAD BEACH   TOMBOLO   CUSPATE FORELAND   BARRIER BEACH

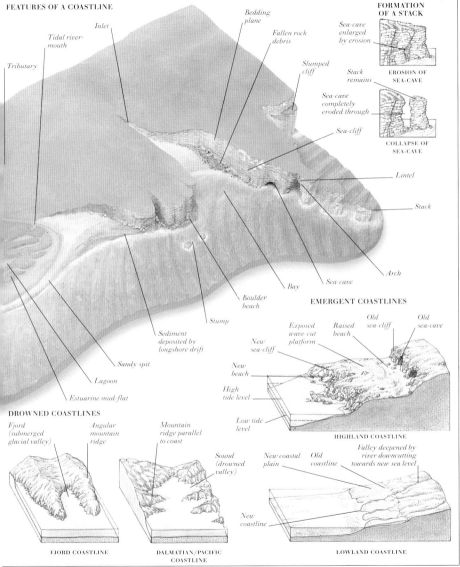

FEATURES OF A COASTLINE

Tributary

Tidal river-mouth

Inlet

Bedding plane

Fallen rock debris

Slumped cliff

Sea-cliff

Lintel

Stack

Arch

Sea-cave

Bay

Boulder beach

Stump

Sediment deposited by longshore drift

Sandy spit

Lagoon

Estuarine mud-flat

FORMATION OF A STACK

Sea-cave enlarged by erosion

EROSION OF SEA-CAVE

Sea-cave completely eroded through

Stack remains

COLLAPSE OF SEA-CAVE

EMERGENT COASTLINES

Exposed wave-cut platform

Raised beach

Old sea-cliff

Old sea-cave

New sea-cliff

New beach

High tide level

Low tide level

HIGHLAND COASTLINE

DROWNED COASTLINES

Fjord (submerged glacial valley)

Angular mountain ridge

FJORD COASTLINE

Mountain ridge parallel to coast

Sound (drowned valley)

DALMATIAN/PACIFIC COASTLINE

New coastal plain

Old coastline

Valley deepened by river downcutting towards new sea level

New coastline

LOWLAND COASTLINE

Oceans and seas

OCEANS AND SEAS COVER ABOUT 70 PER CENT of the Earth's surface and account for about 97 per cent of its total water. These oceans and seas play a crucial role in regulating temperature variations and determining climate. Their waters absorb heat from the Sun, especially in tropical regions, and the surface currents distribute it around the Earth, warming overlying air masses and neighbouring land in winter and cooling them in summer. The oceans are never still. Differences in temperature and salinity drive deep current systems, while surface currents are generated by winds blowing over the oceans. All currents are deflected – to the right in the Northern Hemisphere, to the left in the Southern Hemisphere – as a result of the Earth's rotation. This deflective factor is known as the Coriolis force. A current that begins on the surface is immediately deflected. This current in turn generates a current in the layer of water beneath, which is also deflected. As the movement is transmitted downwards, the deflections form an Ekman spiral. The waters of the oceans and seas are also moved by the constant ebb and flow of tides. These are caused by the gravitational pull of the Moon and Sun. The highest tides (Spring tides) occur at full and new Moon; the lowest tides (neap tides) occur at first and last quarter.

North Pacific Current
Alaska Current
East-Greenland Current
North Atlantic Current
Gulf Stream
Florida Current
NORTH PACIFIC GYRE
NORTH ATLANTIC GYRE
North Equatorial Current
North Equatorial Current
Equatorial Countercurrent
Equatorial Countercurrent
South Equatorial Current
South Equatorial Current
Peru Current
Brazil Current
SOUTH PACIFIC GYRE
SOUTH ATLANTIC GYRE
Humboldt Current
Falkland Current
Antarctic Circumpolar Current

SALT CONTENT OF SEAWATER

Potassium 1.1%
Magnesium 3.7%
Sodium 30.2%
Others 1.9%
Calcium 1.2%
Sulphate 7.6%
Chloride 54.3%

Surface ocean current
Wind drives water along coast
Cold-water upwelling replaces warm surface water
Continental slope

COLD-WATER UPWELLING (SOUTHERN HEMISPHERE)

Surface ocean current
Pack-ice formation increases water salinity and density
Cold, dense water sinks
Continental slope

POLAR BOTTOM WATER

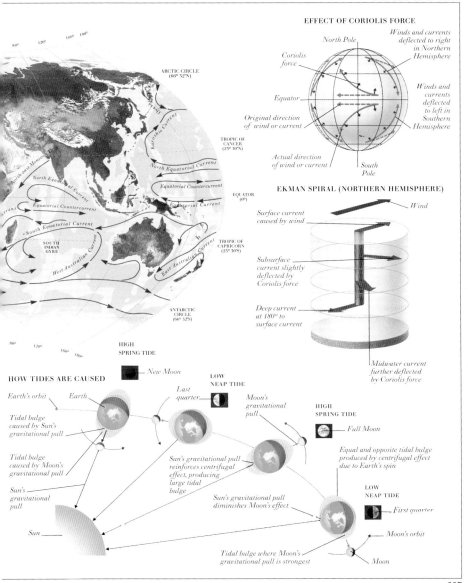

EFFECT OF CORIOLIS FORCE

Winds and currents deflected to right in Northern Hemisphere

North Pole

Coriolis force

Equator

Original direction of wind or current

Actual direction of wind or current

South Pole

Winds and currents deflected to left in Southern Hemisphere

ARCTIC CIRCLE
(66° 32'N)

Oyashio Current

Kuroshio Current

North Equatorial Current

North-east Monsoon Drift

TROPIC OF
CANCER
(23° 30'N)

North Equatorial Current

Equatorial Countercurrent

EQUATOR
(0°)

Equatorial Countercurrent

Equatorial Current

South Equatorial Current

SOUTH
INDIAN
GYRE

West Australian Current

East Australian Current

TROPIC OF
CAPRICORN
(23° 30'S)

ANTARCTIC
CIRCLE
(66° 32'S)

80°   120°   160°   180°

EKMAN SPIRAL (NORTHERN HEMISPHERE)

Surface current caused by wind

Wind

Subsurface current slightly deflected by Coriolis force

Deep current at 180° to surface current

Midwater current further deflected by Coriolis force

HOW TIDES ARE CAUSED

HIGH
SPRING TIDE

New Moon

LOW
NEAP TIDE

Last quarter

Moon's gravitational pull

HIGH
SPRING TIDE

Full Moon

Earth's orbit   *Earth*

Tidal bulge caused by Sun's gravitational pull

Tidal bulge caused by Moon's gravitational pull

Sun's gravitational pull

Sun's gravitational pull reinforces centrifugal effect, producing large tidal bulge

Equal and opposite tidal bulge produced by centrifugal effect due to Earth's spin

LOW
NEAP TIDE

First quarter

Sun's gravitational pull diminishes Moon's effect

Sun

Tidal bulge where Moon's gravitational pull is strongest

Moon's orbit

Moon

297

The ocean floor

THE OCEAN FLOOR COMPRISES TWO SECTIONS: the continental
shelf and slope, and the deep-ocean floor. The continental shelf and
slope are part of the continental crust, but may extend far into the ocean.
Sloping quite gently to a depth of about 140 metres, the continental shelf
is covered in sandy deposits shaped by waves and tidal currents. At the
edge of the continental shelf, the seabed slopes down to the abyssal plain,
which lies at an average depth of about 3,800 metres. On this deep-
ocean floor is a layer of sediment made up of clays, fine oozes formed
from the remains of tiny sea creatures, and occasional mineral-rich
deposits. Echo-sounding and remote sensing from satellites has revealed
that the abyssal plain is divided by a system of mountain ranges, far
bigger than any on land – the mid-ocean ridge. Here, magma (molten
rock) wells up from the Earth's interior and solidifies, widening the
ocean floor (see pp. 58-59). As the ocean floor spreads, volcanoes that
have formed over hot spots in the crust move away from their magma
source; they become extinct and are increasingly submerged and
eroded. Volcanoes eroded below sea level remain as seamounts
(underwater mountains). In warm waters, a volcano that projects
above the ocean surface often acquires a fringing coral reef, which
may develop into an atoll as the volcano becomes submerged.

CONTINENTAL-SHELF FLOOR

Bedrock
exposed by
tidal scour

Shoreline

Parallel strips
of coarse
material left
by strong
tidal currents

Sand
deposited
in wavy
pattern by
weaker
currents

FEATURES OF THE OCEAN FLOOR

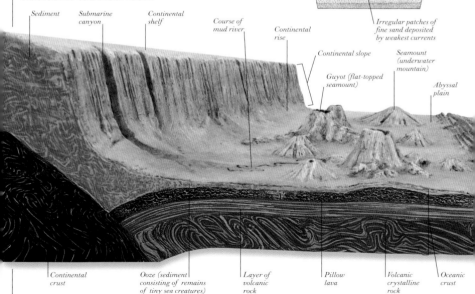

Sediment

Submarine
canyon

Continental
shelf

Course of
mud river

Continental
rise

Irregular patches of
fine sand deposited
by weakest currents

Continental slope

Seamount
(underwater
mountain)

Guyot (flat-topped
seamount)

Abyssal
plain

Continental
crust

Ooze (sediment
consisting of remains
of tiny sea creatures)

Layer of
volcanic
rock

Pillow
lava

Volcanic
crystalline
rock

Oceanic
crust

KEY

- [ ] Calcareous ooze
- [ ] Pelagic clay
- [ ] Glacial sediments
- [ ] Siliceous ooze
- [ ] Terrigenous sediments
- [ ] Continental margin sediments
- [ ] Metalliferous muds
- [ ] Major nodule fields

DEEP-OCEAN FLOOR SEDIMENTS

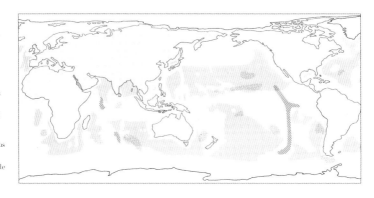

ECHO-SOUND PROFILE OF OCEAN FLOOR

Sand wave

Event mark indicates synchronization of survey equipment

Minor oscillations caused by ship's movement

Sand wave

Seabed profile

22 1493 22

Velocity of sound in water (1,493 m/sec)

Reference code

DEVELOPMENT OF AN ATOLL

Volcanic island

Sea level

Coral grows on shoreline

FRINGING REEF

Lagoon

Coral continues to grow, forming barrier reef

Eroded volcanic island subsides

BARRIER REEF

Coral continues to grow where waves bring food

Lagoon

Dead coral

Volcanic island becomes submerged

ATOLL

Coral submerged too deeply to grow

Volcanic island is submerged further

SUBMERGED ATOLL

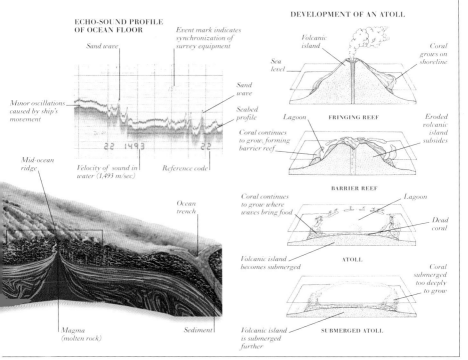

Mid-ocean ridge

Ocean trench

Magma (molten rock)

Sediment

299

The atmosphere

JET STREAM

THE EARTH IS SURROUNDED BY ITS ATMOSPHERE, a blanket of gases that enables life to exist on the planet. This layer has no definite outer edge, gradually becoming thinner until it merges into space, but over 80 per cent of atmospheric gases are held by gravity within about 20 kilometres of the Earth's surface. The atmosphere blocks out much harmful ultraviolet solar radiation, and insulates the Earth against extremes of temperature by limiting both incoming solar radiation and the escape of re-radiated heat into space. This natural balance may be distorted by the greenhouse effect, as gases such as carbon dioxide have built up in the atmosphere, trapping more heat. Close to the Earth's surface, differences in air temperature and pressure cause air to circulate between the equator and poles. This circulation, together with the Coriolis force, gives rise to the prevailing surface winds and the high-level jet streams.

Exosphere (altitude above about 500 km)

Corona

Thermosphere (altitude about 100–500 km)

Ozone layer absorbs ultraviolet radiation from Sun

Mesosphere (altitude about 50–100 km)

Stratosphere (altitude about 10–50 km)

Troposphere (altitude up to about 10 km)

ATMOSPHERIC CIRCULATION AND WINDS

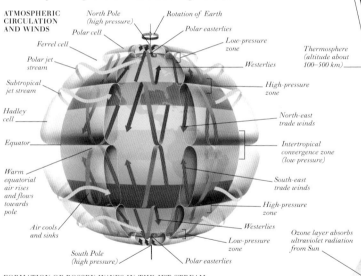

North Pole (high pressure)
Rotation of Earth
Polar cell
Polar easterlies
Ferrel cell
Low-pressure zone
Polar jet stream
Westerlies
Subtropical jet stream
High-pressure zone
Hadley cell
North-east trade winds
Equator
Intertropical convergence zone (low pressure)
Warm equatorial air rises and flows towards pole
South-east trade winds
High-pressure zone
Air cools and sinks
Westerlies
Low-pressure zone
South Pole (high pressure)
Polar easterlies

FORMATION OF ROSSBY WAVES IN THE JET STREAM

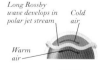

Long Rossby wave develops in polar jet stream
Cold air
Rossby wave becomes more pronounced
Fully developed Rossby wave
Warm air

INITIAL UNDULATION

DEEPENING WAVE

DEVELOPED WAVE

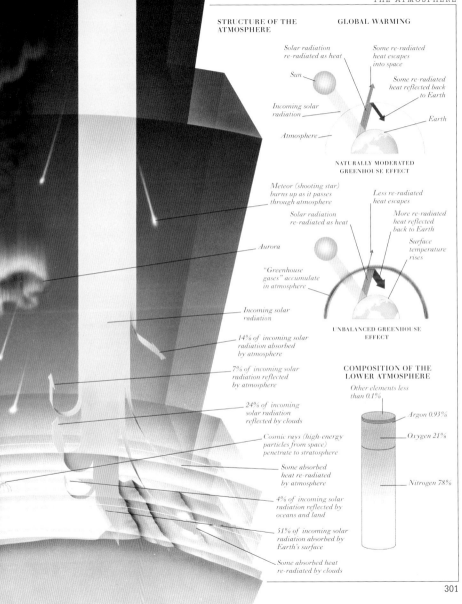

STRUCTURE OF THE ATMOSPHERE

GLOBAL WARMING

Solar radiation re-radiated as heat

Some re-radiated heat escapes into space

Sun

Some re-radiated heat reflected back to Earth

Incoming solar radiation

Earth

Atmosphere

NATURALLY MODERATED GREENHOUSE EFFECT

Meteor (shooting star) burns up as it passes through atmosphere

Less re-radiated heat escapes

Solar radiation re-radiated as heat

More re-radiated heat reflected back to Earth

Surface temperature rises

Aurora

"Greenhouse gases" accumulate in atmosphere

Incoming solar radiation

UNBALANCED GREENHOUSE EFFECT

14% of incoming solar radiation absorbed by atmosphere

7% of incoming solar radiation reflected by atmosphere

COMPOSITION OF THE LOWER ATMOSPHERE

Other elements less than 0.1%

24% of incoming solar radiation reflected by clouds

Argon 0.93%

Cosmic rays (high-energy particles from space) penetrate to stratosphere

Oxygen 21%

Some absorbed heat re-radiated by atmosphere

4% of incoming solar radiation reflected by oceans and land

Nitrogen 78%

51% of incoming solar radiation absorbed by Earth's surface

Some absorbed heat re-radiated by clouds

Weather

WEATHER IS DEFINED AS THE ATMOSPHERIC CONDITIONS at a particular time and place; climate is the average weather conditions for a given region over time. Weather is assessed in terms of temperature, wind, cloud cover, and precipitation, such as rain or snow. Fine weather is associated with high-pressure areas, where air is sinking. Cloudy, wet, changeable weather is common in low-pressure zones with rising, unstable air. Such conditions occur at temperate latitudes, where warm air meets cool air along the polar fronts. Here, spiralling low-pressure cells known as depressions (mid-latitude cyclones) often form. A depression usually contains a sector of warmer air, beginning at a warm front and ending at a cold front. If the two fronts merge, forming an occluded front, the warm air is pushed upwards. An extreme form of low-pressure cell is a hurricane (also called a typhoon or tropical cyclone), which brings torrential rain and exceptionally strong winds.

TYPES OF OCCLUDED FRONT

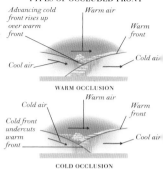

Advancing cold front rises up over warm front

Warm air

Warm front

Cool air

Cold air

WARM OCCLUSION

Cold air

Warm air

Warm front

Cold front undercuts warm front

Cool air

COLD OCCLUSION

FORMS OF PRECIPITATION

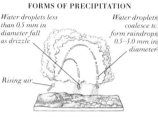

Water droplets less than 0.5 mm in diameter fall as drizzle

Water droplets coalesce to form raindrops 0.5–5.0 mm in diameter

Rising air

RAIN FROM CLOUDS NOT REACHING FREEZING LEVEL

Coalesced water droplets fall as rain

Ice crystal

Snowflakes grown from ice crystals fall as snow

Snowflakes melt to fall as rain

Rising air

RAIN AND SNOW FROM CLOUDS REACHING FREEZING LEVEL

Vertical air currents toss frozen water droplets up and down

Alternate freezing and melting builds up layers of ice

Ice falls as hailstones

Rising air

HAIL

TYPES OF CLOUD

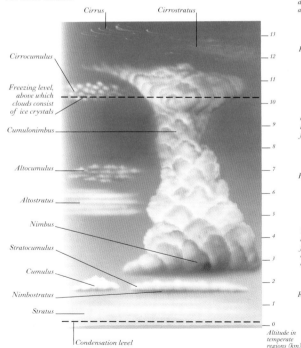

Cirrus

Cirrostratus

Cirrocumulus

Freezing level, above which clouds consist of ice crystals

Cumulonimbus

Altocumulus

Altostratus

Nimbus

Stratocumulus

Cumulus

Nimbostratus

Stratus

Condensation level

— 13
— 12
— 11
— 10
— 9
— 8
— 7
— 6
— 5
— 4
— 3
— 2
— 1
— 0

Altitude in temperate regions (km)

STRUCTURE OF A HURRICANE

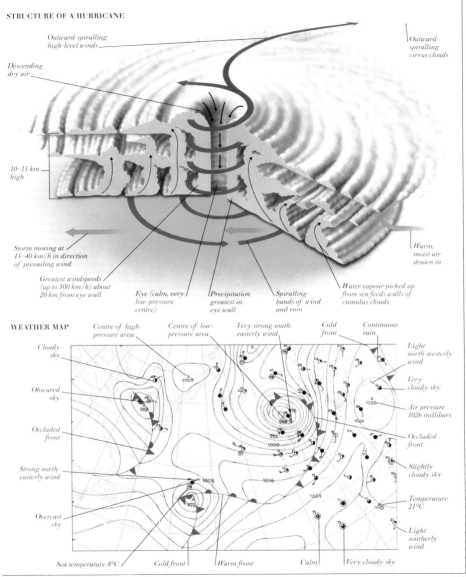

Outward-spiralling
high-level winds

Outward-
spiralling
cirrus clouds

Descending
dry air

10–15 km
high

Storm moving at
15–40 km/h in direction
of prevailing wind

Warm,
moist air
drawn in

Greatest windspeeds
(up to 300 km/h) about
20 km from eye wall

Eye (calm, very
low-pressure
centre)

Precipitation
greatest in
eye wall

Spiralling
bands of wind
and rain

Water vapour picked up
from sea feeds walls of
cumulus clouds

WEATHER MAP

Centre of high-
pressure area

Centre of low-
pressure area

Very strong south-
easterly wind

Cold
front

Continuous
rain

Cloudy
sky

Light
north-westerly
wind

Obscured
sky

Very
cloudy sky

Air pressure
1026 millibars

Occluded
front

Occluded
front

Strong north-
easterly wind

Slightly
cloudy sky

Temperature
21°C

Overcast
sky

Light
southerly
wind

Sea temperature 8°C

Cold front

Warm front

Calm

Very cloudy sky

303

Physics and Chemistry

The variety of matter

PLANT AND INSECT
(LIVING MATTER)

MATTER IS ANYTHING THAT HAS A MASS. It includes everything from natural substances, such as minerals or living organisms, to synthetic materials. Matter can exist in three distinct states – solid, liquid, and gas. A solid is rigid and retains its shape. A liquid is fluid, has a definite volume, and will take the shape of its container. A gas (also fluid) fills a space, so its volume will be the same as the volume of its container. Most substances can exist as a solid, a liquid, or a gas: the state is determined by temperature. At very high temperatures, matter becomes plasma, often considered to be a fourth state of matter. All matter is composed of microscopic particles, such as atoms and molecules (see pp. 308–309). The arrangement and interactions of these particles give a substance its physical and chemical properties, by which matter can be identified. There is a huge variety of matter because particles can arrange themselves in countless ways, in one substance or by mixing with others. Natural glass, for example, seems to be a solid but is, in fact, a supercool liquid: the atoms are not locked into a pattern and can flow. Pure substances known as elements (see p. 310) combine to form compounds or mixtures. Mixtures called colloids are made up of larger particles of matter suspended in a solid, liquid, or gas, while a solution is one substance dissolved in another.

HAIR GEL (SOLID IN LIQUID)

SHAVING FOAM
(AIR IN LIQUID)

MIST
(LIQUID IN GAS)

EXAMPLES OF MATTER

The element silicon in pure crystalline form

Polythene is made by combining natural materials in new ways

POLYTHENE
(SYNTHETIC POLYMER)

PURE SILICON
(SEMICONDUCTOR)

Low pressure gases

Central electrode

BALL CONTAINING
HIGH-TEMPERATURE GAS
(PLASMA)

Streaks of plasma (mixture of electrons and charged atoms)

Voltage tears electrons from atoms of low pressure gases inside

Obsidian is molten volcanic rock that cools quickly, so atoms cannot form a regular pattern

OBSIDIAN
(NATURAL GLASS)

Azurite is found naturally with deposits of copper ore

AZURITE
(CRYSTALLINE MINERAL)

Solid crystals dissolve in liquid water

Water

Potassium permanganate crystals

POTASSIUM PERMANGANATE AND WATER
(SOLUTION)

STATES OF MATTER

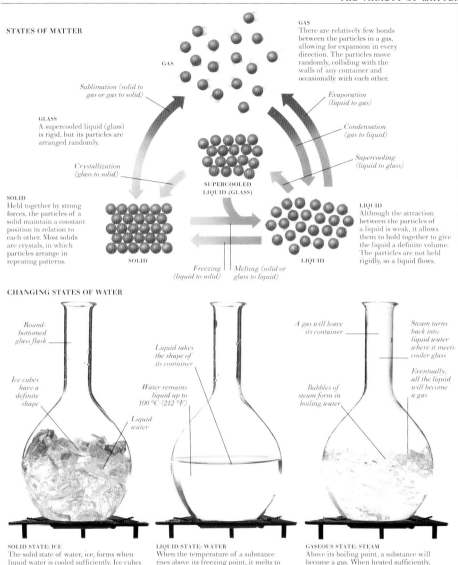

GAS
There are relatively few bonds between the particles in a gas, allowing for expansion in every direction. The particles move randomly, colliding with the walls of any container and occasionally with each other.

GAS

Sublimation (solid to gas or gas to solid)

Evaporation (liquid to gas)

GLASS
A supercooled liquid (glass) is rigid, but its particles are arranged randomly.

Condensation (gas to liquid)

Crystallization (glass to solid)

Supercooling (liquid to glass)

SUPERCOOLED LIQUID (GLASS)

SOLID
Held together by strong forces, the particles of a solid maintain a constant position in relation to each other. Most solids are crystals, in which particles arrange in repeating patterns.

LIQUID
Although the attraction between the particles of a liquid is weak, it allows them to hold together to give the liquid a definite volume. The particles are not held rigidly, so a liquid flows.

SOLID

Freezing (liquid to solid) | *Melting (solid or glass to liquid)*

LIQUID

CHANGING STATES OF WATER

Round-bottomed glass flask

Ice cubes have a definite shape

Liquid water

Liquid takes the shape of its container

Water remains liquid up to 100 °C (212 °F)

A gas will leave its container

Steam turns back into liquid water where it meets cooler glass

Bubbles of steam form in boiling water

Eventually, all the liquid will become a gas

SOLID STATE: ICE
The solid state of water, ice, forms when liquid water is cooled sufficiently. Ice cubes are rigid, with a definite shape and volume.

LIQUID STATE: WATER
When the temperature of a substance rises above its freezing point, it melts to become a liquid. Ice changes to water.

GASEOUS STATE: STEAM
Above its boiling point, a substance will become a gas. When heated sufficiently, liquid water turns to steam, a colourless gas.

Atoms and molecules

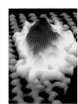

FALSE-COLOUR
IMAGE OF ACTUAL
GOLD ATOMS

ATOMS ARE THE smallest individual parts of an element (see pp. 310-311). They are tiny, with diameters in the order of one ten-thousand-millionth of a metre (10^{-10} m). Two or more atoms join together (bond) to form a molecule of a substance known as a compound. For example, when atoms of the elements hydrogen and fluorine join together, they form a molecule of the compound hydrogen fluoride. So molecules are the smallest individual parts of a compound. Atoms themselves are not indivisible – they possess an internal structure. At their centre is a dense nucleus, consisting of protons, which have a positive electric charge (see p. 316), and neutrons, which are uncharged. Around the nucleus are the negatively charged electrons. It is the electrons that give a substance most of its physical and chemical properties. They do not follow definite paths around the nucleus. Instead, electrons are said to be found within certain regions, called orbitals. These are arranged around the nucleus in "shells", each containing electrons of a particular energy. For example, the first shell (1) can hold up to two electrons, in a so-called s-orbital (1s). The second shell (2) can hold up to eight electrons, in s-orbitals (2s) and p-orbitals (2p). If an atom loses an electron, it becomes a positive ion (cation). If an electron is gained, an atom becomes a negative ion (anion). Ions of opposite charges will attract and join together, in a type of bonding known as ionic bonding. In covalent bonding, the atoms bond by sharing their electrons in what become molecular orbitals.

ATOMIC ORBITALS

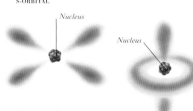

S-ORBITAL

P-ORBITAL

Nucleus

Nucleus

D-ORBITALS

MOLECULAR ORBITALS

Nucleus

Nucleus

Nucleus

Nucleus

Σ- (SIGMA) ORBITAL

π- (PI) ORBITAL

Nucleus

SP³-HYBRID ORBITAL

EXAMPLE OF IONIC BONDING

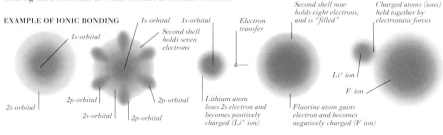

1s-orbital

1s-orbital

1s-orbital

Second shell holds seven electrons

Electron transfer

Second shell now holds eight electrons, and is "filled"

Charged atoms (ions) held together by electrostatic forces

2s-orbital

2p-orbital

2p-orbital

2s-orbital

2p-orbital

Lithium atom loses 2s electron and becomes positively charged (Li^+ ion)

Li^+ ion

F^- ion

Fluorine atom gains electron and becomes negatively charged (F^- ion)

1. NEUTRAL LITHIUM
ATOM (Li)

NEUTRAL FLUORINE
ATOM (F)

2. ELECTRON TRANSFER

3. IONIC BONDING:
LITHIUM FLUORIDE MOLECULE (LiF)

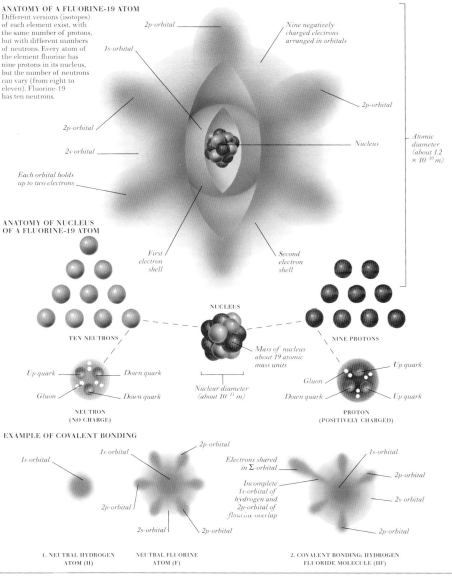

ANATOMY OF A FLUORINE-19 ATOM
Different versions (isotopes) of each element exist, with the same number of protons, but with different numbers of neutrons. Every atom of the element fluorine has nine protons in its nucleus, but the number of neutrons can vary (from eight to eleven). Fluorine-19 has ten neutrons.

2p-orbital

1s-orbital

Nine negatively charged electrons arranged in orbitals

2p-orbital

2p-orbital

2s-orbital

Nucleus

Atomic diameter (about 1.2 × 10⁻¹⁰ m)

Each orbital holds up to two electrons

First electron shell

Second electron shell

ANATOMY OF NUCLEUS OF A FLUORINE-19 ATOM

NUCLEUS

Mass of nucleus about 19 atomic mass units

TEN NEUTRONS

NINE PROTONS

Up quark

Down quark

Gluon

Down quark

Nuclear diameter (about 10⁻¹⁵ m)

Up quark

Gluon

Down quark

Up quark

NEUTRON (NO CHARGE)

PROTON (POSITIVELY CHARGED)

EXAMPLE OF COVALENT BONDING

1s-orbital

1s-orbital

2p-orbital

Electrons shared in Σ-orbital

1s-orbital

2p-orbital

Incomplete 1s-orbital of hydrogen and 2p-orbital of fluorine overlap

2s-orbital

2p-orbital

2s-orbital

2p-orbital

2p-orbital

1. **NEUTRAL HYDROGEN ATOM (H)**

NEUTRAL FLUORINE ATOM (F)

2. **COVALENT BONDING: HYDROGEN FLUORIDE MOLECULE (HF)**

The periodic table

AN ELEMENT is a substance that consists of atoms of one type only. The 92 elements that occur naturally, and the 17 elements created artificially, are often arranged into a chart called the periodic table. Each element is defined by its atomic number – the number of protons in the nucleus of each of its atoms (it is also the number of electrons present). Atomic number increases along each row (period) and down each column (group). The shape of the table is determined by the way in which electrons arrange themselves around the nucleus: the positioning of elements in order of increasing atomic number brings together atoms with a similar pattern of orbiting electrons (orbitals). These appear in blocks. Electrons occupy shells of a certain energy (see pp. 308-309). Periods are ordered according to the filling of successive shells with electrons, while groups reflect the number of electrons in the outer shell (valency electrons). These outer electrons are important – they decide the chemical properties of the atom. Elements that appear in the same group have similar properties because they have the same number of electrons in their outer shell. Elements in Group 0 have "filled shells", where the outer shell holds its maximum number of electrons, and are stable. Atoms of Group I elements have just one electron in their outer shell. This makes them unstable – and ready to react with other substances.

METALS AND NON-METALS

Elements at the left-hand side of each period are metals. Metals easily lose electrons and form positive ions. Non-metals, on the right of a period, tend to become negative ions. Semi-metals, which have properties of both metals and non-metals, are between the two.

TYPES OF ELEMENT KEY:

- Alkali metals
- Alkaline earth metals
- Transition metals
- Lanthanides
- Actinides
- Poor metals
- Semi-metals
- Non-metals
- Noble gases
- Unknown chemical properties

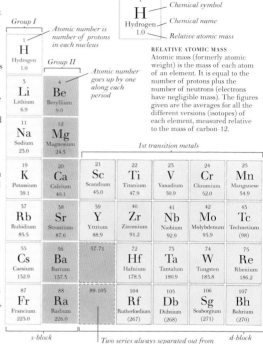

Atomic number

1
H
Hydrogen
1.0

Chemical symbol
Chemical name
Relative atomic mass

RELATIVE ATOMIC MASS
Atomic mass (formerly atomic weight) is the mass of each atom of an element. It is equal to the number of protons plus the number of neutrons (electrons have negligible mass). The figures given are the averages for all the different versions (isotopes) of each element, measured relative to the mass of carbon-12.

Group I
Atomic number is number of protons in each nucleus

1
H
Hydrogen
1.0

Group II
Atomic number goes up by one along each period

1st transition metals

Group I	Group II							
1 **H** Hydrogen 1.0								
3 **Li** Lithium 6.9	4 **Be** Beryllium 9.0							
11 **Na** Sodium 25.0	12 **Mg** Magnesium 24.3							
19 **K** Potassium 39.1	20 **Ca** Calcium 40.1	21 **Sc** Scandium 45.0	22 **Ti** Titanium 47.9	23 **V** Vanadium 50.9	24 **Cr** Chromium 52.0	25 **Mn** Manganese 54.9		
37 **Rb** Rubidium 85.5	38 **Sr** Strontium 87.6	39 **Y** Yttrium 88.9	40 **Zr** Zirconium 91.2	41 **Nb** Niobium 92.9	42 **Mo** Molybdenum 95.9	43 **Tc** Technetium (98)		
55 **Cs** Caesium 152.9	56 **Ba** Barium 157.5	57-71	72 **Hf** Hafnium 178.5	75 **Ta** Tantalum 180.9	74 **W** Tungsten 183.8	75 **Re** Rhenium 186.2		
87 **Fr** Francium 223.0	88 **Ra** Radium 226.0	89-105	104 **Rf** Rutherfordium (267)	105 **Db** Dubnium (268)	106 **Sg** Seaborgium (271)	107 **Bh** Bohrium (270)		

s-block

Two series always separated out from the table to give it a coherent shape

d-block

Soft, silvery, and highly reactive metal

Silvery, reactive metal

Hard, silvery metal

SODIUM: GROUP 1 METAL

MAGNESIUM: GROUP 2 METAL

CHROMIUM: 1ST TRANSITION METAL

Radioactive metal

PLUTONIUM: ACTINIDE SERIES METAL

57 **La** Lanthanum 158.9	58 **Ce** Cerium 140.1	59 **Pr** Praseodymium 140.9	60 **Nd** Neodymium 144.2
89 **Ac** Actinium (227)	90 **Th** Thorium 232.0	91 **Pa** Protactinium 251.0	92 **U** Uranium 258.0

DIAMOND

ALLOTROPES OF CARBON
Some elements exist in more than one form – these are known as allotropes. Carbon powder, graphite, and diamond are allotropes of carbon. They all consist of carbon atoms, but have very different physical properties.

Bright yellow crystal

SULPHUR:
GROUP 6 SOLID NON-METAL

IODINE:
GROUP 7
SOLID NON-METAL

Purple-black solid turns to gas easily

GRAPHITE

CARBON POWDER

Boron and carbon groups

Nitrogen and oxygen groups

Halogens

Group 0

Period

| | | | | | | | | | 2 **He** Helium 4.0 |

2nd transition metals   *3rd transition metals*

Group III	Group IV	Group V	Group VI	Group VII	
5 **B** Boron 10.8	6 **C** Carbon 12.0	7 **N** Nitrogen 14.0	8 **O** Oxygen 16.0	9 **F** Fluorine 19.0	10 **Ne** Neon 20.2
13 **Al** Aluminium 27.0	14 **Si** Silicon 28.1	15 **P** Phosphorus 31.0	16 **S** Sulphur 52.1	17 **Cl** Chlorine 35.5	18 **Ar** Argon 40.0

Short period

26 **Fe** Iron 55.8	27 **Co** Cobalt 58.9	28 **Ni** Nickel 58.7	29 **Cu** Copper 63.5	30 **Zn** Zinc 65.4	31 **Ga** Gallium 69.7	32 **Ge** Germanium 72.6	33 **As** Arsenic 74.9	34 **Se** Selenium 79.0	35 **Br** Bromine 79.9	36 **Kr** Krypton 83.8
44 **Ru** Ruthenium 101.1	45 **Rh** Rhodium 102.9	46 **Pd** Palladium 106.4	47 **Ag** Silver 107.9	48 **Cd** Cadmium 112.4	49 **In** Indium 114.8	50 **Sn** Tin 118.7	51 **Sb** Antimony 121.8	52 **Te** Tellurium 127.6	53 **I** Iodine 126.9	54 **Xe** Xenon 131.3
76 **Os** Osmium 190.2	77 **Ir** Iridium 192.2	78 **Pt** Platinum 195.1	79 **Au** Gold 197.0	80 **Hg** Mercury 200.6	81 **Tl** Thallium 204.4	82 **Pb** Lead 207.2	83 **Bi** Bismuth 209.0	84 **Po** Polonium (209)	85 **At** Astatine (210)	86 **Rn** Radon (222)
108 **Hs** Hassium (269)	109 **Mt** Meitnerium (278)	110 **Ds** Darmstadtium (281)	111 **Rg** Roentgenium (281)	112 **Cn** Copernicium (285)	113 **Uut** Ununtrium (286)	114 **Uuq** Ununquadium (289)	115 **Uup** Ununpentium (289)	116 **Uuh** Ununhexium (293)	117 **Uus** Ununseptium (294)	118 **Uuo** Ununoctium (294)

Long period

d-block   *p-block*

Unreactive, colourless gas glows red in discharge tube

Yellow, unreactive precious metal

GOLD:
3RD TRANSITION METAL

Soft, shiny, reactive metal

Shiny semi-metal

TIN:
GROUP 4 POOR METAL

ANTIMONY:
GROUP 5 SEMI-METAL

NOBLE GASES
Group 0 contains elements that have a filled (complete) outer shell of electrons, which means the atoms do not need to lose or gain electrons by bonding with other atoms. This makes them stable and they do not easily form ions or react with other elements. Noble gases are also called rare or inert gases.

NEON:
GROUP 0
COLOURLESS GAS

| 61 **Pm** Promethium (145) | 62 **Sm** Samarium 150.4 | 63 **Eu** Europium 152.0 | 64 **Gd** Gadolinium 157.5 | 65 **Tb** Terbium 158.9 | 66 **Dy** Dysprosium 162.5 | 67 **Ho** Holmium 164.9 | 68 **Er** Erbium 167.3 | 69 **Tm** Thulium 168.9 | 70 **Yb** Ytterbium 173.0 | 71 **Lu** Lutetium 175.0 |
| 93 **Np** Neptunium (237) | 94 **Pu** Plutonium (244) | 95 **Am** Americium (243) | 96 **Cm** Curium (247) | 97 **Bk** Berkelium (247) | 98 **Cf** Californium (251) | 99 **Es** Einsteinium (252) | 100 **Fm** Fermium (257) | 101 **Md** Mendelevium (258) | 102 **No** Nobelium (259) | 103 **Lr** Lawrencium (262) |

f-block

Chemical reactions

A CHEMICAL REACTION TAKES PLACE whenever bonds between atoms are broken or made. In each case, atoms or groups of atoms rearrange, making new substances (products) from the original ones (reactants). Reactions happen naturally, or can be made to happen; they may take years, or only an instant. Some of the main types are shown here. A reaction usually involves a change in energy (see pp. 314-315). In a burning reaction, for example, the making of new bonds between atoms releases energy as heat and light. This type of reaction, in which heat is given off, is an exothermic reaction. Many reactions, like burning, are irreversible, but some can take place in either direction, and are said to be reversible. Reactions can be used to form solids from solutions: in a double decomposition reaction, two compounds in solution break down and re-form into two new substances, often creating a precipitate (insoluble solid); in displacement, an element (eg. copper) displaces another element (eg. silver) from a solution. The rate (speed) of a reaction is determined by many different factors, such as temperature, and the size and shape of the reactants. To describe and keep track of reactions, internationally recognized chemical symbols and equations are used. Reactions are also used in the laboratory to identify matter. An experiment with candle wax, for example, demonstrates that it contains carbon and hydrogen.

SALT FORMATION (ACID ON METAL)

Glass beaker

Hydrogen gas (H_2) given off

Zinc (Zn) replaces hydrogen in acid (HCl) to form zinc chloride solution ($ZnCl_2$)

Hydrogen in acid driven off when acid meets a reactive metal

Hydrochloric acid (HCl)

Effervescence

Zinc metal chippings (Zn)

Zinc metal chippings (Zn)

THE REACTION
Hydrochloric acid added to zinc produces zinc chloride and hydrogen.
$Zn + 2HCl \rightarrow ZnCl_2 + H_2$

BURNING MATTER

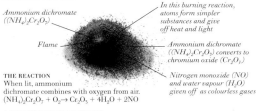

Ammonium dichromate ((NH_4)$_2Cr_2O_7$)

Flame

In this burning reaction, atoms form simpler substances and give off heat and light

Ammonium dichromate ((NH_4)$_2Cr_2O_7$) converts to chromium oxide (Cr_2O_3)

Nitrogen monoxide (NO) and water vapour (H_2O) given off as colourless gases

THE REACTION
When lit, ammonium dichromate combines with oxygen from air.
$(NH_4)_2Cr_2O_7 + O_2 \rightarrow Cr_2O_3 + 4H_2O + 2NO$

DISPLACEMENT

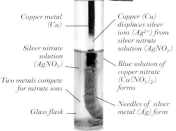

Copper metal (Cu)

Silver nitrate solution ($AgNO_3$)

Two metals compete for nitrate ions

Glass flask

Copper (Cu) displaces silver ions (Ag^{2+}) from silver nitrate solution ($AgNO_3$)

Blue solution of copper nitrate ($Cu(NO_3)_2$) forms

Needles of silver metal (Ag) form

THE REACTION
Copper metal added to silver nitrate solution produces copper nitrate and silver metal.
$Cu + 2AgNO_3 \rightarrow Cu(NO_3)_2 + 2Ag$

A REVERSIBLE REACTION

Flat-bottomed glass flask

Potassium Chromate solution (K_2CrO_4)

Bright yellow solution contains potassium and chromate ions

1. THE REACTANT
Potassium chromate dissolves in water to form potassium ions and chromate ions.
$K_2CrO_4 \rightarrow 2K^+ + CrO_4^{2-}$

Pipette

Hydrochloric acid (HCl) added in drops

Acid causes reaction to take place

Chromate ions converted to orange dichromate ions

Potassium dichromate (KCr_2O_7) forms

2. THE REACTION
Addition of hydrochloric acid changes chromate ions into dichromate ions.
$2CrO_4^{2-} \rightarrow Cr_2O_7^{2-}$

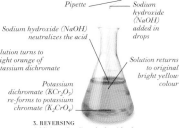

Pipette

Sodium hydroxide (NaOH) added in drops

Sodium hydroxide (NaOH) neutralizes the acid

Solution turns to bright orange of potassium dichromate

Solution returns to original bright yellow colour

Potassium dichromate (KCr_2O_7) re-forms to potassium chromate (K_2CrO_4)

3. REVERSING
Addition of sodium hydroxide changes dichromate ions back into chromate ions.
$Cr_2O_7^{2-} \rightarrow 2CrO_4^{2-}$

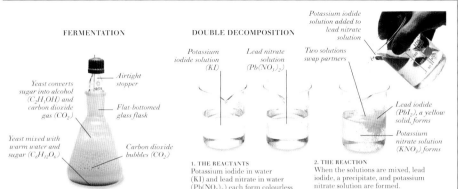

FERMENTATION

Yeast converts sugar into alcohol (C_2H_5OH) and carbon dioxide gas (CO_2)

Airtight stopper

Flat-bottomed glass flask

Yeast mixed with warm water and sugar ($C_6H_{12}O_6$)

Carbon dioxide bubbles (CO_2)

THE REACTION
Yeast converts sugar and warm water into alcohol and carbon dioxide.
$C_6H_{12}O_6 \rightarrow 2C_2H_5OH + 2CO_2$

DOUBLE DECOMPOSITION

Potassium iodide solution (KI)

Lead nitrate solution ($Pb(NO_3)_2$)

Potassium iodide solution added to lead nitrate solution

Two solutions swap partners

Lead iodide (PbI_2), a yellow solid, forms

Potassium nitrate solution (KNO_3) forms

1. THE REACTANTS
Potassium iodide in water (KI) and lead nitrate in water ($Pb(NO_3)_2$) each form colourless solutions.

2. THE REACTION
When the solutions are mixed, lead iodide, a precipitate, and potassium nitrate solution are formed.
$2KI + Pb(NO_3)_2 \rightarrow PbI_2 + 2KNO_3$

TESTING CANDLE WAX, AN ORGANIC COMPOUND

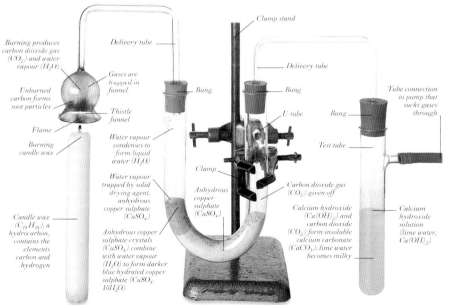

Burning produces carbon dioxide gas (CO_2) and water vapour (H_2O)

Unburned carbon forms soot particles

Flame

Burning candle wax

Candle wax ($C_{18}H_{38}$), a hydrocarbon, contains the elements carbon and hydrogen

Delivery tube

Gases are trapped in funnel

Thistle funnel

Water vapour condenses to form liquid water (H_2O)

Water vapour trapped by solid drying agent, anhydrous copper sulphate ($CuSO_4$)

Anhydrous copper sulphate crystals ($CuSO_4$) combine with water vapour (H_2O) to form darker blue hydrated copper sulphate ($CuSO_4$. $10H_2O$).

Clamp stand

Delivery tube

Bung

Bung

U-tube

Clamp

Anhydrous copper sulphate ($CuSO_4$)

Carbon dioxide gas (CO_2) given off

Calcium hydroxide ($Ca(OH)_2$) and carbon dioxide (CO_2) form insoluble calcium carbonate ($CaCO_3$): lime water becomes milky

Tube connection to pump that sucks gases through

Bung

Test tube

Calcium hydroxide solution (lime water, $Ca(OH)_2$)

1. THE BURNING REACTION
Burning wax produces carbon dioxide gas and water vapour.
$2C_{18}H_{38} + 55O_2 \rightarrow 36CO_2 + 38H_2O$

2. TESTING FOR WATER VAPOUR
A solid drying agent traps water vapour, proving the presence of hydrogen in the candle wax.
$CuSO_4 + 10H_2O \rightarrow CuSO_4 . 10H_2O$

3. TESTING FOR CARBON DIOXIDE
Calcium hydroxide in solution reacts with carbon dioxide, forming a carbonate and turning milky.
$Ca(OH)_2 + CO_2 \rightarrow CaCO_3 + H_2O$

Energy

ANYTHING THAT HAPPENS – from a pin-drop to an explosion – requires energy. Energy is the capacity for "doing work" (making something happen). Various forms of energy exist, including light, heat, sound, electrical, chemical, nuclear, kinetic, and potential energies. The Law of Conservation of Energy states that the total amount of energy in the Universe is fixed – energy cannot be created or destroyed. It means that energy can only change from one form to another (energy transfer). For example, potential energy is energy that is "stored", and can be used in the future. An object gains potential energy when it is lifted; as the object is released, potential energy changes into the energy of motion (kinetic energy). During transference, some of the energy converts into heat. A combined heat and power station can put some of the otherwise "waste" heat to useful effect in local schools and housing. Most of the Earth's energy is provided by the Sun, in the form of electromagnetic radiation (see pp. 316-317). Some of this energy transfers to plant and animal life, and ultimately to fossil fuels, where it is stored in chemical form. Our bodies obtain energy from the food we eat, while energy needed for other tasks, such as heating and transport, can be obtained by burning fossil fuels – or by harnessing natural forces like wind or moving water – to generate electricity. Another source is nuclear power, where energy is released by reactions in the nucleus of an atom. All energy is measured by the international unit, the joule (J). As a guide, one joule is about equal to the amount of energy needed to lift an apple one metre.

SANKEY DIAGRAM SHOWING ENERGY FLOW IN A COAL-FIRED COMBINED HEAT AND POWER STATION

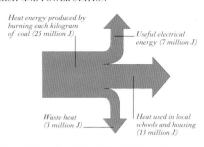

Heat energy produced by burning each kilogram of coal (25 million J)

Useful electrical energy (7 million J)

Waste heat (5 million J)

Heat used in local schools and housing (13 million J)

CROSS-SECTION OF HYDROELECTRIC POWER STATION WITH FRANCIS TURBINE

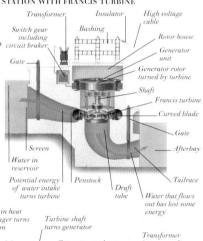

Transformer
Insulator
High voltage cable
Switch gear including circuit braker
Bushing
Rotor house
Gate
Generator unit
Generator rotor turned by turbine
Shaft
Francis turbine
Curved blade
Gate
Screen
Afterbay
Water in reservoir
Potential energy of water intake turns turbine
Penstock
Draft tube
Tailrace
Water that flows out has lost some energy

CROSS-SECTION OF NUCLEAR POWER STATION WITH PRESSURIZED WATER REACTOR

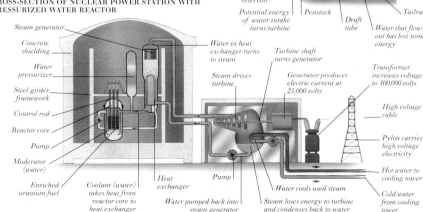

Steam generator
Concrete shielding
Water pressurizer
Steel girder framework
Control rod
Reactor core
Pump
Moderator (water)
Enriched uranium fuel
Coolant (water) takes heat from reactor core to heat exchanger
Heat exchanger
Pump
Water pumped back into steam generator
Water in heat exchanger turns to steam
Steam drives turbine
Turbine shaft turns generator
Generator produces electric current at 25,000 volts
Water cools used steam
Steam loses energy to turbine and condenses back to water
Transformer increases voltage to 300,000 volts
High voltage cable
Pylon carries high voltage electricity
Hot water to cooling tower
Cold water from cooling tower

ENERGY SYSTEMS

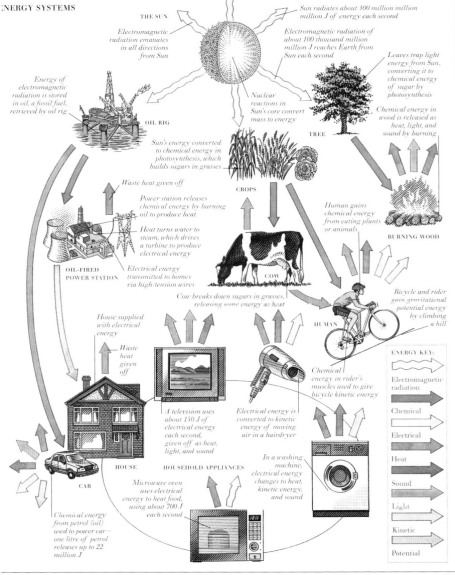

THE SUN

Electromagnetic radiation emanates in all directions from Sun

Sun radiates about 300 million million million J of energy each second

Electromagnetic radiation of about 100 thousand million million J reaches Earth from Sun each second

Leaves trap light energy from Sun, converting it to chemical energy of sugar by photosynthesis

Energy of electromagnetic radiation is stored in oil, a fossil fuel, retrieved by oil rig

OIL RIG

Nuclear reactions in Sun's core convert mass to energy

Chemical energy in wood is released as heat, light, and sound by burning

TREE

Sun's energy converted to chemical energy in photosynthesis, which builds sugars in grasses

CROPS

Waste heat given off

Power station releases chemical energy by burning oil to produce heat

Heat turns water to steam, which drives a turbine to produce electrical energy

Human gains chemical energy from eating plants or animals

BURNING WOOD

OIL-FIRED POWER STATION

Electrical energy transmitted to homes via high-tension wires

COW

Cow breaks down sugars in grasses, releasing some energy as heat

Bicycle and rider gain gravitational potential energy by climbing a hill

HUMAN

House supplied with electrical energy

Waste heat given off

Chemical energy in rider's muscles used to give bicycle kinetic energy

A television uses about 150 J of electrical energy each second, given off as heat, light, and sound

Electrical energy is converted to kinetic energy of moving air in a hairdryer

In a washing machine, electrical energy changes to heat, kinetic energy, and sound

HOUSE

HOUSEHOLD APPLIANCES

CAR

Chemical energy from petrol (oil) used to power car – one litre of petrol releases up to 22 million J

Microwave oven uses electrical energy to heat food, using about 700 J each second

ENERGY KEY:

Electromagnetic radiation

Chemical

Electrical

Heat

Sound

Light

Kinetic

Potential

Electricity and magnetism

ELECTRICAL EFFECTS result from an imbalance of electric charge. There are two types of electric charge, named positive (carried by protons) and negative (carried by electrons). If charges are opposite (unlike), they attract one another, while like charges repel. Forces of attraction and repulsion (electrostatic forces) exist between any two charged particles. Matter is normally uncharged, but if

LIGHTNING

electrons are gained, an object will gain an overall negative charge; if they are removed, it becomes positive. Objects with an overall negative or positive charge are said to have an imbalance of charge, and exert the same forces as individual negative and positive charges. On this larger scale, the forces will always act to regain the balance of charge. This causes static electricity. Lightning, for example, is produced by clouds discharging a huge excess of negative electrons. If charges are "free" – in a wire or material that allows

electrons to pass through it – the forces cause a flow of charge called an electric current. Some substances exhibit the strange phenomenon of magnetism – which also produces attractive and repulsive forces. Magnetic substances consist of small regions called domains. Normally unmagnetized, they can be magnetized by being placed in a magnetic field. Magnetism and electricity are inextricably linked, a fact put to use in motors and generators.

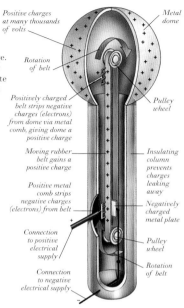

Positive charges at many thousands of volts

Metal dome

Rotation of belt

Positively charged belt strips negative charges (electrons) from dome via metal comb, giving dome a positive charge

Moving rubber belt gains a positive charge

Positive metal comb strips negative charges (electrons) from belt

Connection to positive electrical supply

Connection to negative electrical supply

Pulley wheel

Insulating column prevents charges leaking away

Negatively charged metal plate

Pulley wheel

Rotation of belt

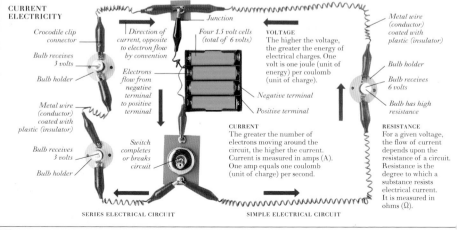

CURRENT ELECTRICITY

Junction

Crocodile clip connector

Direction of current, opposite to electron flow by convention

Four 1.5 volt cells (total of 6 volts)

Metal wire (conductor) coated with plastic (insulator)

VOLTAGE
The higher the voltage, the greater the energy of electrical charges. One volt is one joule (unit of energy) per coulomb (unit of charge).

Bulb receives 3 volts

Bulb holder

Electrons flow from negative terminal to positive terminal

Negative terminal

Positive terminal

Bulb holder

Bulb receives 6 volts

Bulb has high resistance

Metal wire (conductor) coated with plastic (insulator)

Bulb receives 3 volts

Bulb holder

Switch completes or breaks circuit

CURRENT
The greater the number of electrons moving around the circuit, the higher the current. Current is measured in amps (A). One amp equals one coulomb (unit of charge) per second.

RESISTANCE
For a given voltage, the flow of current depends upon the resistance of a circuit. Resistance is the degree to which a substance resists electrical current. It is measured in ohms (Ω).

SERIES ELECTRICAL CIRCUIT

SIMPLE ELECTRICAL CIRCUIT

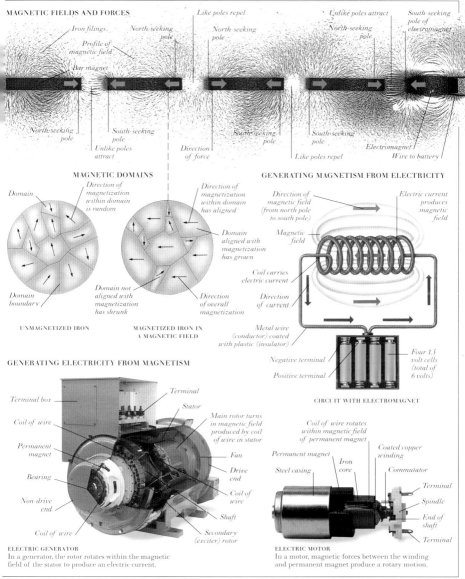

MAGNETIC FIELDS AND FORCES

Iron filings

Profile of magnetic field

Bar magnet

North-seeking pole

North-seeking pole

Like poles repel

Unlike poles attract

North-seeking pole

South-seeking pole of electromagnet

North-seeking pole

South-seeking pole

Unlike poles attract

South-seeking pole

Direction of force

South-seeking pole

Like poles repel

Electromagnet

Wire to battery

MAGNETIC DOMAINS

Domain

Direction of magnetization within domain is random

Direction of magnetization within domain has aligned

Domain aligned with magnetization has grown

Domain not aligned with magnetization has shrunk

Direction of overall magnetization

Domain boundary

UNMAGNETIZED IRON

MAGNETIZED IRON IN A MAGNETIC FIELD

GENERATING MAGNETISM FROM ELECTRICITY

Direction of magnetic field (from north pole to south pole)

Electric current produces magnetic field

Magnetic field

Coil carries electric current

Direction of current

Metal wire (conductor) coated with plastic (insulator)

Negative terminal

Positive terminal

Four 1.5 volt cells (total of 6 volts)

CIRCUIT WITH ELECTROMAGNET

GENERATING ELECTRICITY FROM MAGNETISM

Terminal box

Terminal

Stator

Main rotor turns in magnetic field produced by coil of wire in stator

Coil of wire

Permanent magnet

Bearing

Non-drive end

Coil of wire

Fan

Drive end

Coil of wire

Shaft

Secondary (exciter) rotor

ELECTRIC GENERATOR
In a generator, the rotor rotates within the magnetic field of the stator to produce an electric current.

Coil of wire rotates within magnetic field of permanent magnet

Permanent magnet

Iron core

Steel casing

Coated copper winding

Commutator

Terminal

Spindle

End of shaft

Terminal

ELECTRIC MOTOR
In a motor, magnetic forces between the winding and permanent magnet produce a rotary motion.

317

Light

LIGHT IS A FORM OF ENERGY. It is a type of electromagnetic radiation, like X-rays or radio waves. All electromagnetic radiation is produced by electric charges (see pp. 316-317): it is caused by the effects of oscillating electric and magnetic fields as they travel through space. Electromagnetic radiation is considered to have both wave and particle properties. It can be thought of as a wave of electricity and magnetism. In that case, the difference between the various forms of radiation is their wavelength. Radiation can also be said to consist of particles, or packets of energy, called photons. The difference between light and X-rays, for instance, is the amount of energy that each photon carries. The complete range of radiation is referred to as the electromagnetic spectrum, extending from low energy, long wavelength radio waves to high energy, short wavelength gamma rays. Light is the only part of the electromagnetic spectrum that is visible. White light from the Sun is made up of all the visible wavelengths of radiation, which can be seen when it is separated by using a prism. Light, like all forms of electromagnetic radiation, can be reflected (bounced back) and refracted (bent). Different parts of the electromagnetic spectrum are produced in different ways. Sometimes visible light – and infra-red radiation – is generated by the vibrating particles of warm or hot objects. The emission of light in this way is called incandescence. Light can also be produced by fluorescence, a phenomenon in which electrons gain and lose energy within atoms.

INFRA-RED IMAGE OF A HOUSE

MAXWELLIAN DIAGRAM OF ELECTROMAGNETIC RADIATION AS WAVES

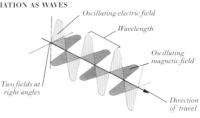

Oscillating electric field

Wavelength

Oscillating magnetic field

Two fields at right angles

Direction of travel

ELECTROMAGNETIC RADIATION AS PARTICLES

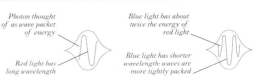

Photon thought of as wave packet of energy

Blue light has about twice the energy of red light

Red light has long wavelength

Blue light has shorter wavelength: waves are more tightly packed

PHOTON OF RED LIGHT

PHOTON OF BLUE LIGHT

SPLITTING WHITE LIGHT INTO THE SPECTRUM

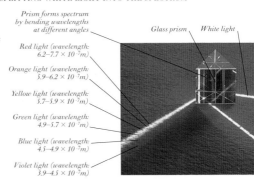

Prism forms spectrum by bending wavelengths at different angles

Glass prism *White light*

Red light (wavelength: 6.2–7.7 × 10⁻⁷m)

Orange light (wavelength: 5.9–6.2 × 10⁻⁷m)

Yellow light (wavelength: 5.7–5.9 × 10⁻⁷m)

Green light (wavelength: 4.9–5.7 × 10⁻⁷m)

Blue light (wavelength: 4.5–4.9 × 10⁻⁷m)

Violet light (wavelength: 3.9–4.5 × 10⁻⁷m)

THE ELECTROMAGNETIC SPECTRUM

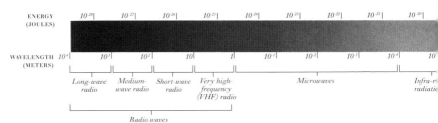

ENERGY (JOULES)	10^{-28}	10^{-27}	10^{-26}	10^{-25}	10^{-24}	10^{-23}	10^{-22}	10^{-21}	10^{-20}

WAVELENGTH (METERS) 10^4 10^3 10^2 10 1 10^{-1} 10^{-2} 10^{-3} 10^{-4} 10

Long-wave radio *Medium-wave radio* *Short-wave radio* *Very high-frequency (VHF) radio* *Microwaves* *Infra-red radiation*

Radio waves

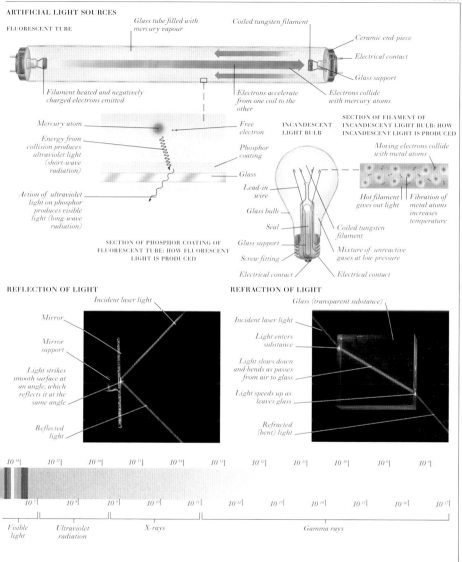

ARTIFICIAL LIGHT SOURCES

FLUORESCENT TUBE

Glass tube filled with mercury vapour

Coiled tungsten filament

Ceramic end-piece

Electrical contact

Glass support

Filament heated and negatively charged electrons emitted

Electrons accelerate from one coil to the other

Electrons collide with mercury atoms

Mercury atom

Free electron

Energy from collision produces ultraviolet light (short-wave radiation)

Phosphor coating

Glass

Action of ultraviolet light on phosphor produces visible light (long-wave radiation)

SECTION OF PHOSPHOR COATING OF FLUORESCENT TUBE: HOW FLUORESCENT LIGHT IS PRODUCED

INCANDESCENT LIGHT BULB

SECTION OF FILAMENT OF INCANDESCENT LIGHT BULB: HOW INCANDESCENT LIGHT IS PRODUCED

Moving electrons collide with metal atoms

Hot filament gives out light

Vibration of metal atoms increases temperature

Lead-in wire

Glass bulb

Seal

Glass support

Screw fitting

Electrical contact

Coiled tungsten filament

Mixture of unreactive gases at low pressure

Electrical contact

REFLECTION OF LIGHT

Incident laser light

Mirror

Mirror support

Light strikes smooth surface at an angle, which reflects it at the same angle

Reflected light

REFRACTION OF LIGHT

Glass (transparent substance)

Incident laser light

Light enters substance

Light slows down and bends as passes from air to glass

Light speeds up as leaves glass

Refracted (bent) light

10^{18} 10^{17} 10^{16} 10^{15} 10^{14} 10^{13} 10^{12} 10^{11} 10^{10} 10^{9} 10^{8}

10^{7} 10^{8} 10^{9} 10^{10} 10^{11} 10^{12} 10^{13} 10^{14} 10^{15} 10^{16} 10^{17}

Visible light

Ultraviolet radiation

X-rays

Gamma rays

Force and motion

FORCES ARE PUSHES OR PULLS that change the motion of objects. To make a stationary object move, or a moving object stop, a force is needed. A force is also required to change the speed or direction of an object. This change in speed or direction is known as acceleration. Acceleration depends on the size (magnitude) of the force, and on the mass of the object. The effects of forces were first summarized by Isaac Newton in his three laws of motion. The international unit of force, named after him, is the newton (N), which is approximately equal to the weight of one apple. Gravity – the force of attraction between any two masses – can be measured using a newton meter (spring balance). Forces are put to useful effect in machines. A simple machine, such as a wheel and axle, is a device that changes the size or direction of an applied force. It allows an applied force (the effort) to produce another force (the load). A lever uses a bar that turns on a fulcrum to exert force. In all simple machines, there is a relationship between force and distance. A small force (in a compound pulley, for instance) moves through a large distance to lift a heavy object a small distance. This is called the Law of Simple Machines.

SIMPLE MACHINES

Single-pulley system (simple pulley)

Pulley wheel

Simple pulley only changes direction of a force

Effort is the same size as the load (10 N) and is pulled the same distance

One rope attached to load

Load of 10 N

Two-pulley system (simple pulley)

Pulley wheel

Effort is half the load (5 N), but the rope must be pulled twice the distance

Two ropes share the force and distance

Pulley wheel

Load of 10 N

Four-pulley system (compound pulley)

Two pulley wheels

Effort is one quarter of the load (2.5 N), but the rope must be pulled four times the distance

Four ropes share the force and distance

SIMPLE AND COMPOUND PULLEYS

Two pulley wheels

Load of 10 N

NEWTON METERS (SPRING BALANCES)

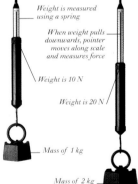

Weight is measured using a spring

When weight pulls downwards, pointer moves along scale and measures force

Weight is 10 N

Weight is 20 N

Mass of 1 kg

Mass of 2 kg

WEIGHT AND MASS
The "mass" of an object is a measure of the quantity of matter that it possesses. Mass is usually measured in grams (g) or kilograms (kg). The "weight" of an object is the force exerted on the object's mass by gravity. Since weight is a force, its unit is the newton (N).

Wheel and axle multiplies the effort

Force is transmitted to the wheels by the chain

Pedal

Crank

Effort, provided by cyclist's muscles, is smaller than the load, but moves through a greater distance

A larger force, the load, is produced at the axle

WHEEL AND AXLE

A screw, acting like a wedge wrapped around a shaft, multiplies the effort

Effort, a turning force supplied through a screwdriver

Pitch (the angle of the screw thread)

The smaller the angle of pitch, the less force is required, but more turns are needed to move it through a greater distance

A larger force, the load, pulls the screw into wood

SCREW

Effort pushes axe into wood

Axe blade has wedge shape

Wedge multiplies effort

A larger force, the load, moves through a smaller distance to push wood apart

WEDGE

NEWTON'S THREE LAWS OF MOTION

NEWTON'S FIRST LAW
When no force acts on a body, it will continue in a state of rest or uniform motion.

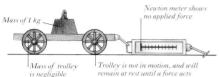

Newton meter shows no applied force

Constant speed

Mass of 1 kg

Newton meter shows no applied force

Mass of 1 kg

Mass of trolley is negligible

Trolley is not in motion, and will remain at rest until a force acts

Trolley is in motion, and will continue at a constant speed in a straight line until a force acts

NO FORCE, NO ACCELERATION: STATE OF REST

NO FORCE, NO ACCELERATION: UNIFORM MOTION

NEWTON'S SECOND LAW
When a force acts on a body, the motion of the body will change. The size of the change will depend upon the mass of the object and the magnitude of the applied force.

Acceleration is 2 ms⁻²

Trolley and mass (1 kg) gain 2 metres per second of speed each second (2 ms⁻²)

Mass of 1 kg

Newton meter registers force of 2 N

Acceleration is 1 ms⁻²

Trolley and mass (2 kg) gain 1 metre per second of speed each second (1 ms⁻²)

Mass of 2 kg

Newton meter registers force of 2 N

With the same applied force, an object with 2 kg mass accelerates at half the rate of object with 1 kg mass

FORCE AND ACCELERATION: SMALL MASS, LARGE ACCELERATION

FORCE AND ACCELERATION: LARGE MASS, SMALL ACCELERATION

NEWTON'S THIRD LAW
If one object exerts a force on another, an equal and opposite force, called the reaction force, is applied by the second object on the first.

Newton meters pull on each other with equal and opposite forces

Acceleration: the trolley and mass accelerate at 2 ms⁻²

Newton meter registers force of 2 N to the left

Newton meter registers force of 2 N to the right

Mass of 1 kg

Person experiences a reaction force

ACTION AND REACTION

THREE CLASSES OF LEVER

Fulcrum, between effort and load

Effort

Fulcrum

Load, between effort and fulcrum

Load is applied at open end

Effort forces tongs together

...d is ...ter than ..t, but moves ...gh smaller ...nce

Effort is smaller than load, but moves through greater distance

Load is smaller than effort, but moves through greater distance

Effort, between fulcrum and load

Fulcrum

CLASS 1 LEVER
Pliers consist of two class 1 levers.

CLASS 2 LEVER
Nutcrackers consist of two class 2 levers.

CLASS 3 LEVER
Tongs consist of two class 3 levers.

Rail and Road

Steam locomotives

WAGONS THAT ARE PULLED along tracks have been used to transport material since the 16th century, but these trains were drawn by men or horses until the invention of the steam locomotive. Steam locomotives enabled the basic railway system to realize its true potential. In 1804, Richard Trevithick built the world's first working steam locomotive in South Wales. It was not entirely successful, but it encouraged others to develop new designs. By 1829, the British engineer Robert Stephenson had built the "Rocket", considered to be the forerunner of the modern locomotive. The "Rocket" was a self-sufficient unit, carrying coal to heat the boiler and a water supply for generating steam. Steam passed from the boiler to force the pistons back and forth, and this movement turned the driving wheels, propelling the train forwards. Used steam was then expelled in characteristic "chuffs". Later steam locomotives, like "Ellerman Lines" and the "Mallard", worked in a similar way, but on a much larger scale. The simple design and reliability of steam locomotives ensured that they changed very little in 120 years of use, before being replaced from the 1950s by more efficient diesel and electric power (see pp. 326-329).

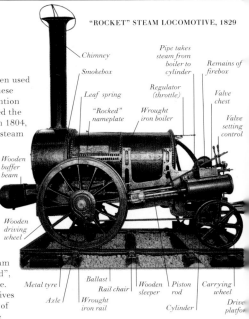

"ROCKET" STEAM LOCOMOTIVE, 1829

Chimney
Smokebox
Leaf spring
"Rocked" nameplate
Pipe takes steam from boiler to cylinder
Regulator (throttle)
Wrought iron boiler
Remains of firebox
Valve chest
Valve setting control
Wooden buffer beam
Wooden driving wheel
Metal tyre
Axle
Ballast
Rail chair
Wrought iron rail
Wooden sleeper
Piston rod
Cylinder
Carrying wheel
Drive platfor

"ELLERMAN LINES", 1949 (CUTAWAY VIEW)

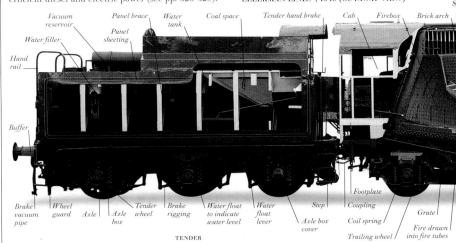

Vacuum reservoir
Panel brace
Water filler
Panel sheeting
Water tank
Coal space
Tender hand brake
Cab
Firebox
Brick arch
Hand rail
Buffer
Brake vacuum pipe
Wheel guard
Axle
Axle box
Tender wheel
Brake rigging
Water float to indicate water level
Water float lever
Step
Axle box cover
Footplate
Coupling
Coil spring
Trailing wheel
Grate
Fire drawn into fire tubes

TENDER

CAB INTERIOR OF "MALLARD" EXPRESS STEAM LOCOMOTIVE, 1938

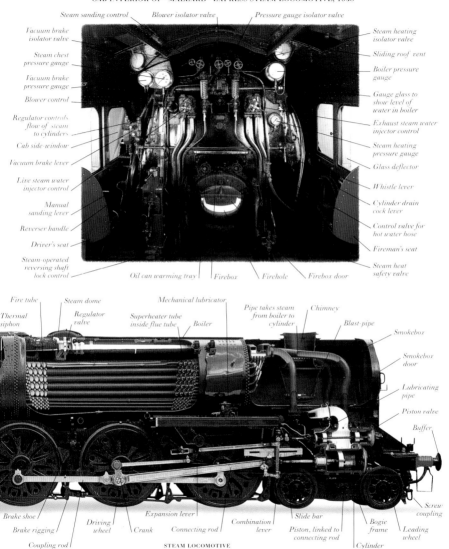

Steam sanding control

Blower isolator valve

Pressure gauge isolator valve

Vacuum brake isolator valve

Steam chest pressure gauge

Vacuum brake pressure gauge

Blower control

Regulator controls flow of steam to cylinders

Cab side-window

Vacuum brake lever

Live steam water injector control

Manual sanding lever

Reverser handle

Driver's seat

Steam-operated reversing shaft lock control

Oil can warming tray

Firebox

Firehole

Firebox door

Steam heating isolator valve

Sliding roof vent

Boiler pressure gauge

Gauge glass to show level of water in boiler

Exhaust steam water injector control

Steam heating pressure gauge

Glass deflector

Whistle lever

Cylinder drain cock lever

Control valve for hot water hose

Fireman's seat

Steam heat safety valve

Fire tube

Thermal siphon

Steam dome

Regulator valve

Mechanical lubricator

Superheater tube inside flue tube

Boiler

Pipe takes steam from boiler to cylinder

Chimney

Blast-pipe

Smokebox

Smokebox door

Lubricating pipe

Piston valve

Buffer

Brake shoe

Brake rigging

Coupling rod

Driving wheel

Crank

Expansion lever

Connecting rod

Combination lever

Slide bar

Piston, linked to connecting rod

Screw coupling

Bogie frame

Cylinder

Leading wheel

STEAM LOCOMOTIVE

Diesel trains

RUDOLF DIESEL FIRST DEMONSTRATED the diesel engine in Germany in 1898, but it was not until the 1940s that diesel locomotives were successfully established on both passenger and freight services, in the US. Early diesel locomotives like the "Union Pacific" were more expensive to build than steam locomotives, but were more efficient and cheaper to operate, especially where oil was plentiful. One feature of diesel engines is that the power output cannot be coupled directly to the wheels. To convert the mechanical energy produced by diesel engines, a transmission system is needed. Almost all diesel locomotives have electric transmissions, and are known as "diesel-electric" locomotives. The diesel engine works by drawing air into the cylinders and compressing it to increase its temperature; a small quantity of diesel fuel is then injected into it. The resulting combustion drives the generator (more recently an alternator) to produce electricity, which is fed to electric motors connected to the wheels. Diesel-electric locomotives are essentially electric locomotives that carry their own power plants, and are used worldwide today. The "Deltic" diesel-electric locomotive, similar to the one shown here, replaced classic express steam locomotives, and ran at speeds up to 160 kph (100 mph).

FRONT VIEW OF "UNION PACIFIC" DIESEL-ELECTRIC LOCOMOTIVE, 1950s

Exhaust vent · Windscreen wiper · Horn · Cab front window · Head-light · Name of operating railroad · Illuminated locomotive unit number · Railroad crest · Cab door · Cab step · Step · Motor-driven bogie axle · Air-brake coupling hose · Centre buck-eye coupler

PROTOTYPE "DELTIC" DIESEL-ELECTRIC LOCOMOTIVE, 1956

Engine room vent · Inspection hatch · Engine exhaust port · Radiator fan · Engine room window · Engine room vent

Fuel tank · Water for heating boiler · Inspection socket · Folding step · Drain for radiator coolant · Radiator coolant · Sand box · Telescopic damper · Drain for control reservoir

DELTIC

DIESEL ENGINE OF BRITISH RAIL CLASS 20 DIESEL-ELECTRIC LOCOMOTIVE

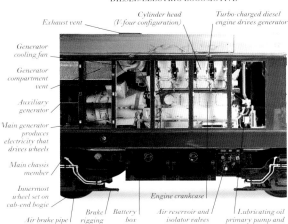

Exhaust vent

Cylinder head
(V-four configuration)

Turbo-charged diesel
engine drives generator

Generator
cooling fan

Generator
compartment
vent

Auxiliary
generator

Main generator
produces
electricity that
drives wheels

Main chassis
member

Innermost
wheel set on
cab-end bogie

Air brake pipe

Brake
rigging

Battery
box

Engine crankcase

Air reservoir and
isolator valves

Lubricating oil
primary pump and
fuel supply pump

EXAMPLES OF FREIGHT CARS

BOX CAR

HOPPER CAR

REFRIGERATOR CAR

LIVESTOCK CAR

FLAT CAR WITH BULKHEADS

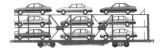

AUTOMOBILE CAR

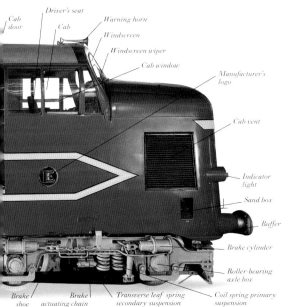

Cab
door

Driver's seat

Cab

Warning horn

Windscreen

Windscreen wiper

Cab window

Manufacturer's
logo

Cab vent

Indicator
light

Sand box

Buffer

Brake cylinder

Roller-bearing
axle box

Brake
shoe

Brake
actuating chain

Transverse leaf spring
secondary suspension

Coil spring primary
suspension

Electric and high-speed trains

THE FIRST ELECTRIC LOCOMOTIVE ran in 1879 in Berlin, Germany. In Europe, electric trains developed as a more efficient alternative to the steam locomotive and diesel-electric power. Like diesels, electric trains employ electric motors to drive the wheels but, unlike diesels, the electricity is generated externally at a power station. Electric current is picked up either from a catenary (overhead cable) via a pantograph, or from a third rail. Since it does not carry its own power-generating equipment, an electric locomotive has a better power-to-weight ratio and greater acceleration than its diesel-electric equivalent. This makes electric trains suitable for urban routes with many stops. They are also faster, quieter, and less polluting. The latest electric French TGV (Train à Grande Vitesse) reaches 300 kph (186 mph); other trains, like the London to Paris and Brussels "Eurostar", can run at several voltages and operate between different countries. Simpler electric trains perform special duties – the "People Mover" at Gatwick Airport in Britain runs between terminals.

HOW ALTERNATING CURRENT (AC) ELECTRIC TRAINS WORK

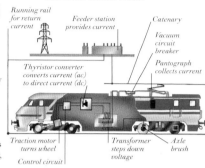

Running rail for return current

Feeder station provides current

Catenary

Vacuum circuit breaker

Pantograph collects current

Thyristor converter converts current (ac) to direct current (dc)

Traction motor turns wheel

Control circuit

Transformer steps down voltage

Axle brush

FRONT VIEW OF PARIS METRO

Route number

Windscreen wiper

Unit number

Operator's initials (Régie Autonome des Transports Parisien)

Rubber running wheel

Guard for rubber wheel

Door open/shut indicator light

Driver's seat

Handle

Front light (white)

Rear light (red)

Buffing pad

Rubber guide wheel

FRONT VIEW OF ITALIAN STATE RAILWAYS CLASS 402 ELECTRIC LOCOMOTIVE

Collector strip for electric current

Double-arm pantograph

Head-light

Windscreen wiper

Italian State Railways crest

Number of electric (E) locomotive (class 402 No. 5)

Buffer

"Jumper" cable

Conventional hook-screw coupling

Front light (white)

Rear light (red)

SIDE VIEW OF SHANGHAI MAGLEV TRAIN

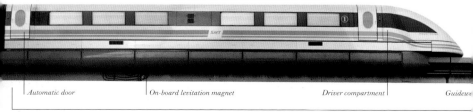

Automatic door

On-board levitation magnet

Driver compartment

Guidewe

"EUROSTAR" MULTI-VOLTAGE ELECTRIC TRAIN

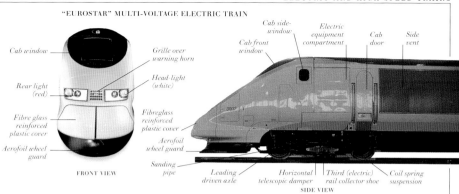

Cab window

Grille over warning horn

Rear light (red)

Head-light (white)

Fibre glass reinforced plastic cover

Fibreglass reinforced plastic cover

Aerofoil wheel guard

Aerofoil wheel guard

Sanding pipe

FRONT VIEW

Cab side-window

Cab front window

Electric equipment compartment

Cab door

Side vent

Leading driven axle

Horizontal telescopic damper

Third (electric) rail collector shoe

Coil spring suspension

SIDE VIEW

TGV ELECTRIC HIGH-SPEED TRAIN

Luggage rack

Reading light

Double-glazed and tinted side-window

Sliding curtain

Seat

Main overhead lighting

Automatic electric carriage end door

Antimacassar

Headrest

Armrest

Centre gangway

INTERIOR OF TGV

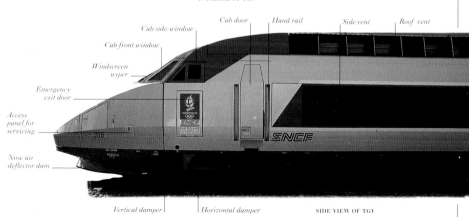

Cab door

Hand rail

Side vent

Roof vent

Cab side-window

Cab front window

Windscreen wiper

Emergency exit door

Access panel for servicing

Nose air deflector dam

Vertical damper

Horizontal damper

SIDE VIEW OF TGV

329

Train equipment

MODERN RAILWAY TRACK consists of two parallel steel rails clipped on to a support called a sleeper. Sleepers are usually made of reinforced concrete, although wood and steel are still used. The distance between the inside edges of the rails is the track gauge. It evolved in Britain, which uses a gauge of 1,435 mm (4 ft 8½ in), known as the standard gauge. As engineering grew more sophisticated, narrower gauges were adopted because they cost less to build. The loading gauge, which is equally important, determines the size of the largest loaded vehicle that may pass through tunnels and under bridges with adequate clearance. Safe train operation relies on following a signalling system. At first, signalling was based on a simple time interval between trains, but it now depends on maintaining a safe distance between successive trains travelling in the same direction. Most modern signals are colour lights, but older mechanical semaphore signals are still used. On the latest high-speed lines, train drivers receive control instructions by electronic means. Signalling depends on reliable control of the train by effective braking. For fast, modern trains, which have considerable momentum, it is essential that each vehicle in the train can be braked by the driver or by a train control system, such as Automatic Train Protection (ATP). Braking is achieved by the brake shoe acting on the wheel rim (rim brakes), by disc brakes, or, increasingly, by electrical braking.

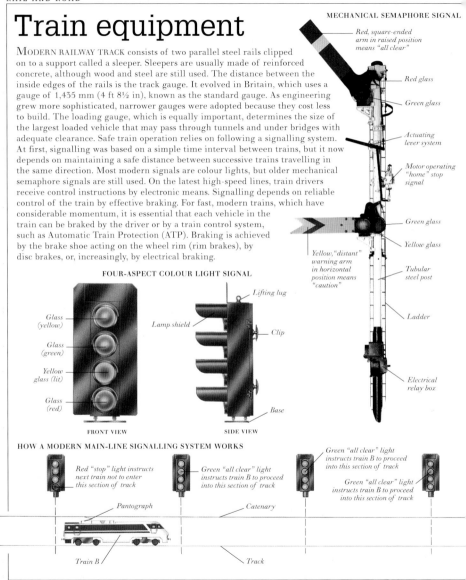

Red, square-ended arm in raised position means "all clear"

Red glass

Green glass

Actuating lever system

Motor operating "home" stop signal

Green glass

Yellow glass

Yellow, "distant" warning arm in horizontal position means "caution"

Tubular steel post

Ladder

Electrical relay box

FOUR-ASPECT COLOUR LIGHT SIGNAL

Glass (yellow)

Glass (green)

Yellow glass (lit)

Glass (red)

Lifting lug

Lamp shield

Clip

Base

FRONT VIEW

SIDE VIEW

HOW A MODERN MAIN-LINE SIGNALLING SYSTEM WORKS

Red "stop" light instructs next train not to enter this section of track

Green "all clear" light instructs train B to proceed into this section of track

Green "all clear" light instructs train B to proceed into this section of track

Green "all clear" light instructs train B to proceed into this section of track

Pantograph

Catenary

Train B

Track

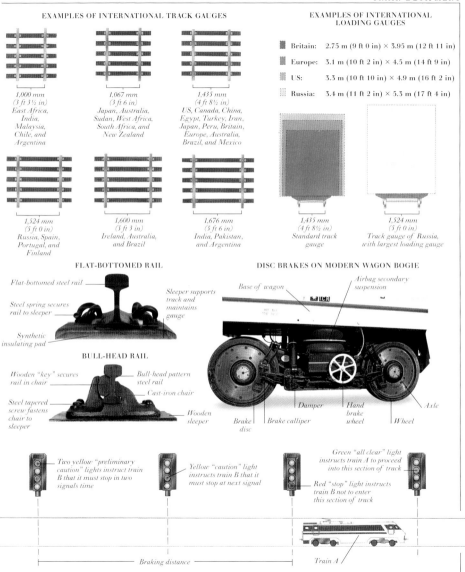

EXAMPLES OF INTERNATIONAL TRACK GAUGES

1,000 mm
(3 ft 3½ in)
East Africa,
India,
Malaysia,
Chile, and
Argentina

1,067 mm
(3 ft 6 in)
Japan, Australia,
Sudan, West Africa,
South Africa, and
New Zealand

1,435 mm
(4 ft 8½ in)
US, Canada, China,
Egypt, Turkey, Iran,
Japan, Peru, Britain,
Europe, Australia,
Brazil, and Mexico

1,524 mm
(5 ft 0 in)
Russia, Spain,
Portugal, and
Finland

1,600 mm
(5 ft 3 in)
Ireland, Australia,
and Brazil

1,676 mm
(5 ft 6 in)
India, Pakistan,
and Argentina

EXAMPLES OF INTERNATIONAL LOADING GAUGES

Britain: 2.75 m (9 ft 0 in) × 3.95 m (12 ft 11 in)

Europe: 3.1 m (10 ft 2 in) × 4.5 m (14 ft 9 in)

US: 3.3 m (10 ft 10 in) × 4.9 m (16 ft 2 in)

Russia: 3.4 m (11 ft 2 in) × 5.3 m (17 ft 4 in)

1,435 mm
(4 ft 8½ in)
Standard track
gauge

1,524 mm
(5 ft 0 in)
Track gauge of Russia,
with largest loading gauge

FLAT-BOTTOMED RAIL

Flat-bottomed steel rail

Steel spring secures rail to sleeper

Synthetic insulating pad

Sleeper supports track and maintains gauge

BULL-HEAD RAIL

Wooden "key" secures rail in chair

Steel tapered screw fastens chair to sleeper

Bull-head pattern steel rail

Cast-iron chair

Wooden sleeper

DISC BRAKES ON MODERN WAGON BOGIE

Airbag secondary suspension

Base of wagon

Damper

Brake disc

Brake calliper

Hand brake wheel

Axle

Wheel

Two yellow "preliminary caution" lights instruct train B that it must stop in two signals time

Yellow "caution" light instructs train B that it must stop at next signal

Green "all clear" light instructs train A to proceed into this section of track

Red "stop" light instructs train B not to enter this section of track

Braking distance

Train A

Trams and buses

METROLINK TRAM, MANCHESTER, BRITAIN

AS CITY POPULATIONS exploded in the 1800s, there was an urgent need for mass transportation. Trams were an early solution. The first trams, like buses, were horse-drawn, but in 1881, electric street tramways appeared in Berlin, Germany. Electric trams soon became widespread throughout Europe and North America. Trams run on rails along a fixed route, using electric motors that receive power from overhead cables. As road networks developed, motorized buses offered a flexible alternative to trams. By the 1930s, they had replaced tram systems in many cities. City buses typically have doors at both front and rear to make loading and unloading easier. Double-decker designs are popular, occupying the same amount of street space as single-decker buses but able to transport twice the number of people. Buses are also commonly used for inter-city travel and touring. Tour buses have reclining seats, large windows, luggage space, and toilets. Recently, as city traffic has become increasingly congested, many city planners have designed new tram routes to run alongside bus routes as part of an integrated transport system.

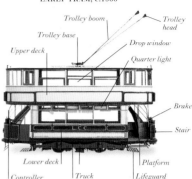

EARLY TRAM, c.1900

Trolley boom

Trolley head

Trolley base

Drop window

Upper deck

Quarter light

Brake

Stair

Lower deck

Platform

Controller

Truck

Lifeguard

MCW METROBUS, LONDON, BRITAIN

Square roof dome

Upper deck air intake

Mirror for driver to see upstairs

Window vent

Upper deck windscreen

Route number

Route information

Operator's logo

Destination screen

Destination screen

Nearside mirror

Offside mirror

Asymmetric windscreen

Nearside mirror

Windscreen wiper

Licence holder

Sidelight

Head-light

Turning indicator

Grille

Front bumper

Fog light

Number plate

Manufacturer's badge

Entrance door

Emergency door control

Turning indicator

FRONT VIEW

LONDON NORTHERN

41

ARCHWAY STN.

PAY DRIVER

mcw

KYV 739X

LONDON NORTHERN

SINGLE-DECKER BUS, NEW YORK, US

Wheelchair access
Sliding window
Sloped roof dome
Marker light
Repeater indicator
Entrance door
Side mirror
Tinted glass
Route number
Head-light
Turning indicator
Air intake
Bumper
Tyre
Axle
Exit door
Access panel
Sidelight
Entrance door
Number plate
Bumper

SIDE VIEW

FRONT VIEW

DOUBLE-DECKER TOUR BUS, PARIS, FRANCE

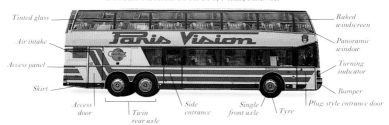

Tinted glass
Raked windscreen
Air intake
Panoramic window
Access panel
Turning indicator
Skirt
Bumper
Access door
Twin rear axle
Side entrance
Single front axle
Tyre
Plug-style entrance door

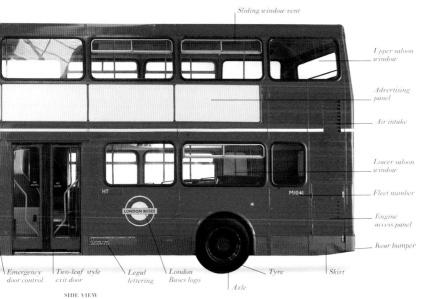

Sliding window vent

Upper saloon window

Advertising panel

Air intake

Lower saloon window

Fleet number

Engine access panel

Rear bumper

Emergency door control
Two-leaf style exit door
Legal lettering
London Buses logo
Tyre
Skirt
Axle

SIDE VIEW

The first cars

THE EARLIEST ROAD VEHICLE powered by an engine, the Cugnot steam traction engine, was built in 1770. More practical steam carriages, such as the Bordino, were available in the early 19th century, but they were heavy and cumbersome. Restrictive laws and the introduction of railways, faster and able to carry more passengers, saw the decline of "cars" powered by steam. It was not until 1860 that the first practical power unit for road vehicles was developed, with the invention of the internal combustion engine by the Belgian Etienne Lenoir. By around 1890, Karl Benz and Gottlieb Daimler in Germany, and Albert de Dion and Armand Peugeot in France were building cars for sale to the public. These early cars, despite being primitive, expensive, and produced in limited numbers, heralded the age of the motor car.

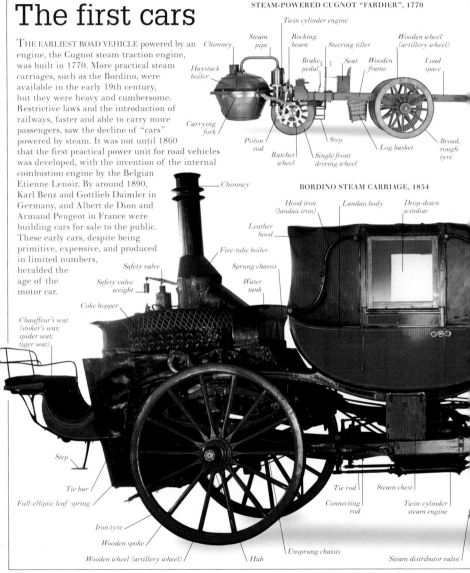

STEAM-POWERED CUGNOT "FARDIER", 1770

Twin cylinder engine
Steam pipe
Rocking beam
Chimney
Steam
Brake pedal
Steering tiller
Seat
Wooden frame
Wooden wheel (artillery wheel)
Load space
Haystack boiler
Carrying fork
Piston rod
Ratchet wheel
Single front driving wheel
Step
Log basket
Broad, rough tyre

BORDINO STEAM CARRIAGE, 1854

Chimney
Hood iron (landau iron)
Landau body
Drop-down window
Leather hood
Fire-tube boiler
Sprung chassis
Water tank
Safety valve
Safety valve weight
Coke hopper
Chauffeur's seat (stoker's seat; spider seat; tiger seat)
Step
Tie bar
Full-elliptic leaf spring
Iron tyre
Wooden spoke
Wooden wheel (artillery wheel)
Hub
Unsprung chassis
Tie rod
Connecting rod
Steam chest
Twin-cylinder steam engine
Steam distributor valve

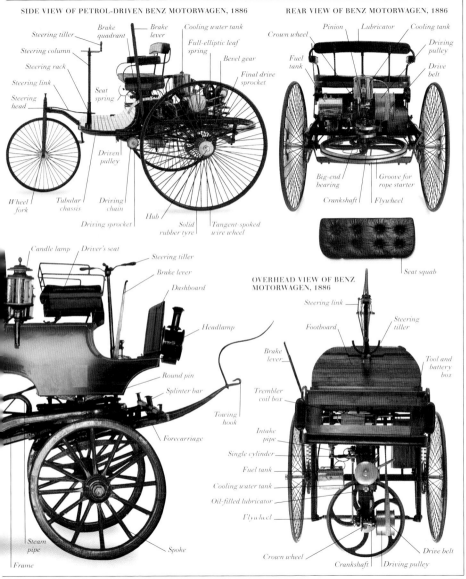

SIDE VIEW OF PETROL-DRIVEN BENZ MOTORWAGEN, 1886

Steering tiller
Brake quadrant
Brake lever
Cooling water tank
Full-elliptic leaf spring
Bevel gear
Final drive sprocket
Steering column
Steering rack
Steering link
Seat spring
Steering head
Driven pulley
Wheel fork
Tubular chassis
Driving chain
Driving sprocket
Hub
Solid rubber tyre
Tangent-spoked wire wheel

REAR VIEW OF BENZ MOTORWAGEN, 1886

Pinion
Lubricator
Cooling tank
Crown wheel
Driving pulley
Fuel tank
Drive belt
Big-end bearing
Groove for rope starter
Crankshaft
Flywheel

Seat squab

OVERHEAD VIEW OF BENZ MOTORWAGEN, 1886

Candle lamp
Driver's seat
Steering tiller
Brake lever
Dashboard
Headlamp
Round pin
Splinter bar
Towing hook
Forecarriage
Steam pipe
Spoke
Frame

Steering link
Steering tiller
Footboard
Tool and battery box
Brake lever
Trembler coil box
Intake pipe
Single cylinder
Fuel tank
Cooling water tank
Oil-filled lubricator
Flywheel
Crown wheel
Crankshaft
Driving pulley
Drive belt

Elegance and utility

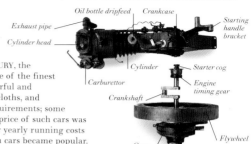

- Oil bottle dripfeed
- Crankcase
- Starting handle bracket
- Exhaust pipe
- Cylinder head
- Cylinder
- Carburettor
- Starter cog
- Engine timing gear
- Crankshaft
- Flywheel
- Gear band

DURING THE FIRST DECADE OF THE 20TH CENTURY, the motorist who could afford it had a choice of some of the finest cars ever made. These handbuilt cars were powerful and luxurious, using the finest woods, leathers, and cloths, and bodywork made to the customer's individual requirements; some had six-cylinder engines as big as 15 litres. The price of such cars was several times that of an average house, and their yearly running costs were also very high. As a result, basic, utilitarian cars became popular. Costing perhaps one-tenth of the price of a luxury car, these cars had very little trim and often had only single-cylinder engines.

FRONT VIEW OF 1906 RENAULT

SIDE VIEW OF 1906 RENAULT

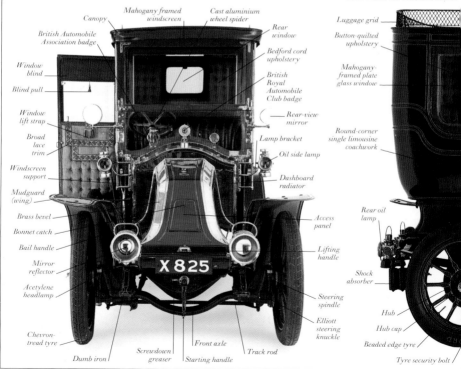

- Canopy
- Mahogany framed windscreen
- Cast aluminium wheel spider
- Rear window
- British Automobile Association badge
- Bedford cord upholstery
- Window blind
- British Royal Automobile Club badge
- Blind pull
- Window lift strap
- Rear-view mirror
- Broad lace trim
- Lamp bracket
- Windscreen support
- Oil side lamp
- Mudguard (wing)
- Dashboard radiator
- Brass bevel
- Access panel
- Bonnet catch
- Bail handle
- Lifting handle
- Mirror reflector
- Acetylene headlamp
- Steering spindle
- Chevron-tread tyre
- Elliott steering knuckle
- Dumb iron
- Screwdown greaser
- Front axle
- Starting handle
- Track rod

- Luggage grid
- Button-quilted upholstery
- Mahogany-framed plate glass window
- Round-corner single limousine coachwork
- Rear oil lamp
- Shock absorber
- Hub
- Hub cap
- Beaded edge tyre
- Tyre security bolt

X 825

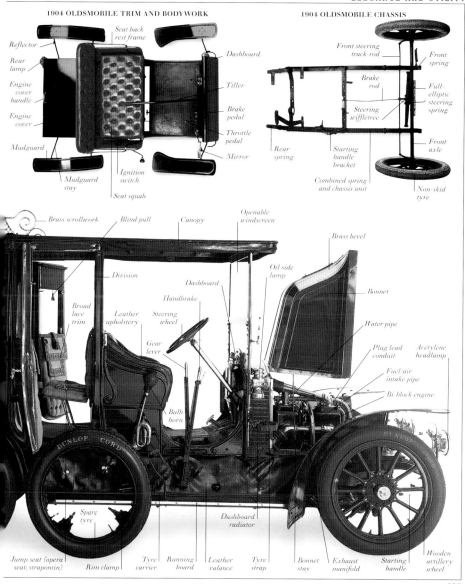

1904 OLDSMOBILE TRIM AND BODYWORK

Reflector
Rear lamp
Engine cover handle
Engine cover
Mudguard
Mudguard stay
Seat back rest frame
Ignition switch
Seat squab
Dashboard
Tiller
Brake pedal
Throttle pedal
Mirror

1904 OLDSMOBILE CHASSIS

Front steering track-rod
Brake rod
Steering wiffletree
Rear spring
Starting handle bracket
Combined spring and chassis unit
Front spring
Full-elliptic steering spring
Front axle
Non-skid tyre

Brass scrollwork
Blind pull
Canopy
Openable windscreen
Brass bevel
Division
Dashboard
Oil side lamp
Bonnet
Broad lace trim
Leather upholstery
Handbrake
Steering wheel
Water pipe
Gear lever
Plug lead conduit
Acetylene headlamp
Fuel/air intake pipe
Bi-block engine
Bulb horn
Spare tyre
Dashboard radiator
Jump seat (opera seat; strapontin)
Rim clamp
Tyre carrier
Running board
Leather valance
Tyre strap
Bonnet stay
Exhaust manifold
Starting handle
Wooden artillery wheel

Mass-production

THE FIRST CARS WERE HAND-ASSEMBLED from individually built parts, a time-consuming procedure that required skilled mechanics and made cars very expensive. This problem was solved, in America, by a Detroit car manufacturer named Henry Ford; he introduced mass-production by using standardized parts, and later combined these with a moving production line. The work was brought to the workers, each of whom performed one simple task in the construction process as the chassis moved along the line. The first mass-produced car, the Ford Model T, was launched in 1908 and was available in a limited range of body styles and colours. However, when the production line was introduced in 1914, the colour range was cut back; the Model T became available, as Henry Ford said, in "any colour you like, so long as it's black". Ford cut the production time for a car from several days to about 12 hours, and eventually to minutes, making cars much cheaper than before. As a result, by 1920 half the cars in the world were Model T Fords.

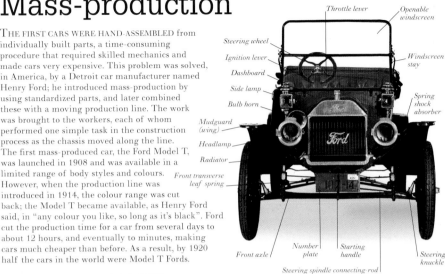

FRONT VIEW OF 1913 FORD MODEL T

Throttle lever
Openable windscreen
Steering wheel
Ignition lever
Dashboard
Side lamp
Bulb horn
Windscreen stay
Spring shock absorber
Mudguard (wing)
Headlamp
Radiator
Front transverse leaf spring
Front axle
Number plate
Starting handle
Steering knuckle
Steering spindle connecting-rod

STAGES OF FORD MODEL T PRODUCTION

Left half of differential housing
Pinion
Rear leaf spring (cross-member)
Steering arm
King pin
Demountable wheel
Hub brake shoe
Track rod
Steering wheel
Hub bolt
Pinion housing
Front transverse leaf spring
Differential housing
Chassis frame
Rear spring perch
Rear axle
Front cross-member
Battery carrier
Radius rod
Body mount
Bearing sleeve
King pin
Half-shaft
Crown wheel
Bevel pinion
Front axle
Demountable wheel
Radius rod
Right half of differential housing
Rear axle bearing
Torque tube
Running-board stay
Hub brake shoe

SIDE VIEW OF 1913 FORD MODEL T

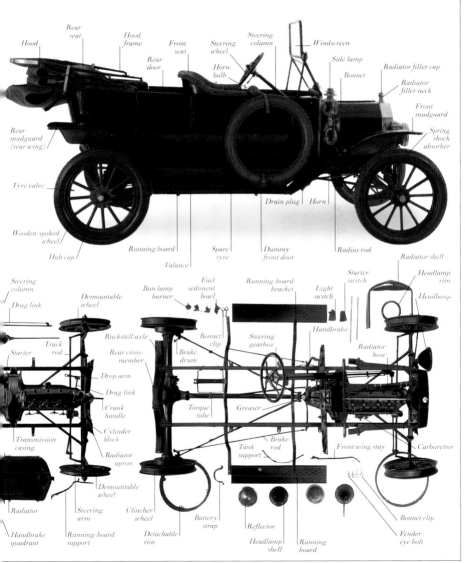

Hood

Rear seat

Hood frame

Front seat

Steering wheel

Steering column

Windscreen

Rear door

Horn bulb

Side lamp

Bonnet

Radiator filler cap

Radiator filler neck

Front mudguard

Spring shock absorber

Rear mudguard (rear wing)

Tyre valve

Drain plug

Horn

Wooden-spoked wheel

Hub cap

Running board

Spare tyre

Dummy front door

Radius rod

Radiator shell

Valance

Steering column

Bun lamp burner

Fuel sediment bowl

Running-board bracket

Light switch

Starter switch

Headlamp rim

Drag link

Demountable wheel

Bonnet clip

Steering gearbox

Handbrake

Headlamp

Starter

Track rod

Ruckstell axle

Rear cross-member

Brake drum

Radiator hose

Drop arm

Drag link

Crank handle

Cylinder block

Torque tube

Greaser

Carburettor

Transmission casing

Radiator apron

Brake rod

Front wing stay

Tank support

Radiator

Steering arm

Demountable wheel

Clincher wheel

Battery strap

Bonnet clip

Handbrake quadrant

Running-board support

Detachable rim

Reflector

Headlamp shell

Running board

Fender eye bolt

339

The "people's car"

THE MOST POPULAR CAR in the history of car manufacture is the Volkswagen Beetle, originally called the KdF Wagen. The car was developed in Germany in the 1930s by Dr. Ferdinand Porsche. At that time, Germany had only half the number of cars of Britain or France, and Adolf Hitler took a personal interest in the development of the Volkswagen ("people's car"). The intention was to provide a new industry, new jobs, and a car so cheap that anyone in work could afford it. Dr. Porsche designed a car that was cheap to build and run; its rear-mounted, air-cooled engine cut down the number of parts needed and also reduced weight. However, few civilians managed to obtain the Beetle before the outbreak of the Second World War in 1939. After the war, the Beetle proved so popular that eventually more than 20 million were sold.

CUSTOMIZED VOLKSWAGEN BEETLE

FLAT-FOUR CYLINDER ARRANGEMENT

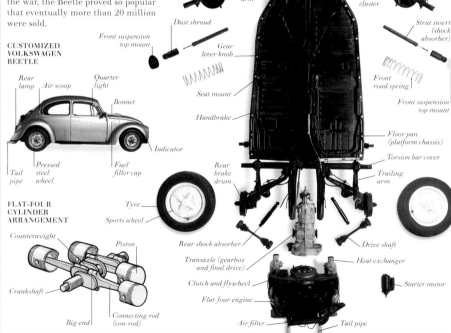

Fuel tank

Steering tie-rod

Fuel tank sender unit

Fuel filler neck

Windscreen-wiper motor assembly

Steering box assembly

Steering idler

Frame head

Suspension strut

Anti-roll bar

Brake back plate

Track control arm

Pedal cluster

Dust shroud

Strut insert (shock absorber)

Front suspension top mount

Gear lever knob

Front road spring

Rear lamp

Air scoop

Quarter light

Bonnet

Seat mount

Front suspension top mount

Handbrake

Indicator

Floor pan (platform chassis)

Torsion bar cover

Tail pipe

Pressed steel wheel

Fuel filler cap

Rear brake drum

Trailing arm

Tyre

Sports wheel

Counterweight

Piston

Rear shock absorber

Drive shaft

Transaxle (gearbox and final drive)

Heat exchanger

Crankshaft

Clutch and flywheel

Starter motor

Flat-four engine

Big end

Connecting rod (con-rod)

Air filter

Tail pipe

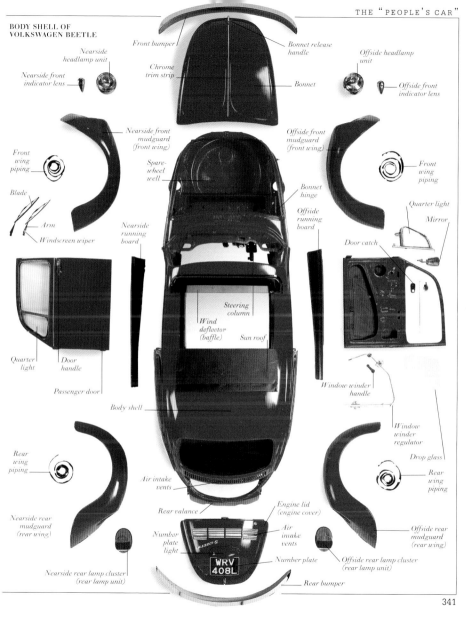

BODY SHELL OF VOLKSWAGEN BEETLE

Front bumper

Bonnet release handle

Nearside headlamp unit

Offside headlamp unit

Nearside front indicator lens

Chrome trim strip

Bonnet

Offside front indicator lens

Nearside front mudguard (front wing)

Offside front mudguard (front wing)

Front wing piping

Spare-wheel well

Front wing piping

Bonnet hinge

Quarter light

Blade

Offside running board

Mirror

Arm

Nearside running board

Door catch

Windscreen wiper

Steering column

Wind deflector (baffle)

Sun roof

Quarter light

Door handle

Passenger door

Window winder handle

Body shell

Window winder regulator

Rear wing piping

Drop glass

Air intake vents

Rear wing piping

Nearside rear mudguard (rear wing)

Rear valance

Engine lid (engine cover)

Air intake vents

Offside rear mudguard (rear wing)

Number plate light

Number plate

Offside rear lamp cluster (rear lamp unit)

Nearside rear lamp cluster (rear lamp unit)

WRV 408L

Rear bumper

341

Early engines

STEAM AND ELECTRICITY were used to power cars until early this century, but neither power source was ideal. Electric cars had to stop frequently to recharge their heavy batteries, and steam cars gave smooth power delivery but were too complicated for the average motorist to use. A rival power source, the internal combustion engine, was invented in 1860 by Etienne Lenoir (see pp. 334-335). This engine converted the force of a controlled explosion into rotary motion, to turn the wheels of a vehicle. Early variations on this basic model included sleeve valves, separately cast cylinders, and the two-stroke combustion cycle. Today, many internal combustion engines, including the Wankel rotary and diesels (see pp. 346-347), use the four-stroke cycle, first demonstrated by Nikolaus Otto in 1876. The Otto cycle, often described as "suck, squeeze, bang, blow", has proved the best method of ensuring that the engine turns over smoothly and that exhaust emissions are controllable.

BERSEY ELECTRIC CAB, 1896

Port linking combustion chambers of upper and lower cylinders

Water connection

Upper paired cylinder

Spark plug

Wide piston-ring

Transfer port

Wire gauze pad

Upper piston

Flexible, forked connecting-rod

Flywheel

Mounting for tray of 40 batteries

Housing for electric motors

Counterweight

Big end

Crankcase

SECTIONED WHITE STEAM CAR, 1903

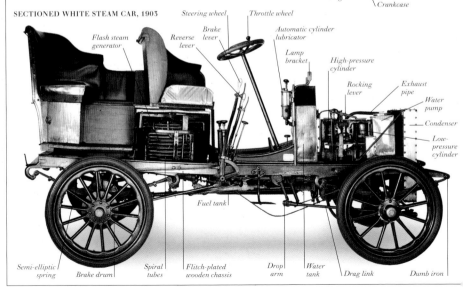

Steering wheel

Throttle wheel

Brake lever

Reverse lever

Automatic cylinder lubricator

Flash steam generator

Lamp bracket

High-pressure cylinder

Rocking lever

Exhaust pipe

Water pump

Condenser

Low-pressure cylinder

Fuel tank

Semi-elliptic spring

Brake drum

Spiral tubes

Flitch-plated wooden chassis

Drop arm

Water tank

Drag link

Dumb iron

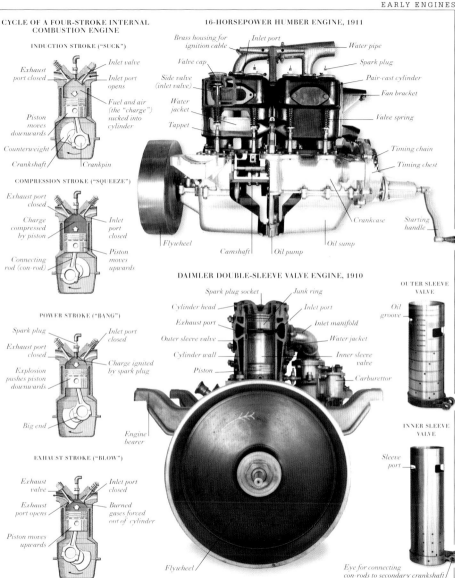

CYCLE OF A FOUR-STROKE INTERNAL COMBUSTION ENGINE

INDUCTION STROKE ("SUCK")

Exhaust port closed
Inlet valve
Inlet port opens
Fuel and air (the "charge") sucked into cylinder
Piston moves downwards
Counterweight
Crankshaft
Crankpin

COMPRESSION STROKE ("SQUEEZE")

Exhaust port closed
Charge compressed by piston
Inlet port closed
Piston moves upwards
Connecting rod (con-rod)

POWER STROKE ("BANG")

Spark plug
Inlet port closed
Exhaust port closed
Explosion pushes piston downwards
Charge ignited by spark plug
Big end

EXHAUST STROKE ("BLOW")

Exhaust valve
Inlet port closed
Exhaust port opens
Burned gases forced out of cylinder
Piston moves upwards

16-HORSEPOWER HUMBER ENGINE, 1911

Brass housing for ignition cable
Inlet port
Water pipe
Valve cap
Spark plug
Side valve (inlet valve)
Pair-cast cylinder
Water jacket
Fan bracket
Tappet
Valve spring
Timing chain
Timing chest
Crankcase
Starting handle
Flywheel
Camshaft
Oil pump
Oil sump

DAIMLER DOUBLE-SLEEVE VALVE ENGINE, 1910

Spark plug socket
Junk ring
Cylinder head
Inlet port
Exhaust port
Inlet manifold
Outer sleeve valve
Water jacket
Cylinder wall
Inner sleeve valve
Piston
Carburettor
Engine bearer
Flywheel

OUTER SLEEVE VALVE

Oil groove

INNER SLEEVE VALVE

Sleeve port
Eye for connecting con-rods to secondary crankshaft

Modern engines

TODAY'S PETROL ENGINE WORKS on the same basic principles as the first car engines of a century ago, although it has been greatly refined. Modern engines, often made from special metal alloys, are much lighter than earlier engines. Computerized ignition systems, fuel injectors, and multi-valve cylinder heads achieve a more efficient combustion of the fuel/air mixture (the charge) so that less fuel is wasted. As a result of this greater efficiency, the power and performance of a modern engine are increased, and the level of pollution in the exhaust gases is reduced. Exhaust pollution levels today are also lowered by the increasing use of special filters called catalytic converters, which absorb many exhaust pollutants. The need to produce ever more efficient engines means that it can take up to seven years to develop a new engine for a family car, at a cost of many millions of pounds.

FRONT VIEW OF A FORD COSWORTH V6 12-VALVE

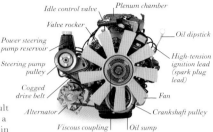

Idle control valve
Plenum chamber
Valve rocker
Oil dipstick
Power steering pump reservoir
High-tension ignition lead (spark plug lead)
Steering pump pulley
Cogged drive belt
Fan
Alternator
Crankshaft pulley
Viscous coupling
Oil sump

FRONT VIEW OF A FORD COSWORTH V6 24-VALVE

Idle control valve
Plenum chamber
Exhaust gas recirculation valve
Camshaft timing gear
Camshaft chain
Steering pump drive pulley
Belt tensioner
Air conditioning pump
Alternator cooling fan
Drive belt
Oil sump
Crankshaft pulley

SECTIONED VIEW OF A JAGUAR STRAIGHT 6

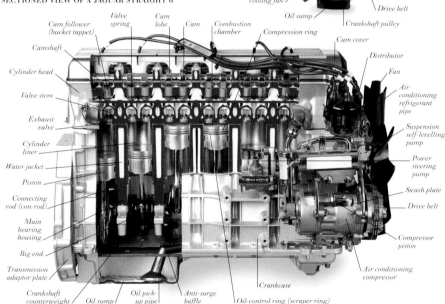

Cam follower (bucket tappet)
Valve spring
Cam lobe
Cam
Combustion chamber
Compression ring
Camshaft
Cam cover
Cylinder head
Distributor
Fan
Valve stem
Air conditioning refrigerant pipe
Exhaust valve
Cylinder liner
Suspension self-levelling pump
Water jacket
Power steering pump
Piston
Swash plate
Connecting rod (con-rod)
Drive belt
Main bearing housing
Big end
Compressor piston
Transmission adaptor plate
Air conditioning compressor
Crankshaft counterweight
Oil sump
Oil pick-up pipe
Anti-surge baffle
Crankcase
Oil-control ring (scraper ring)

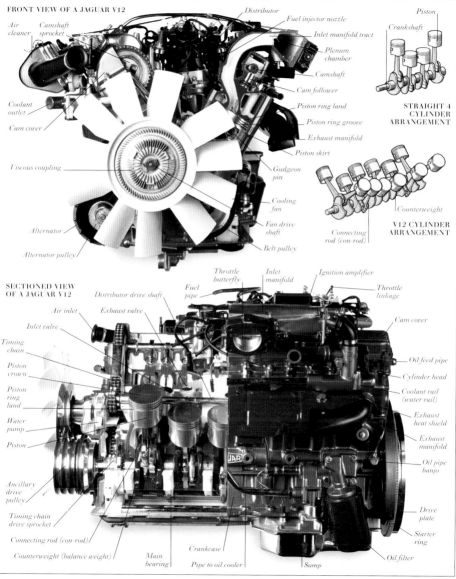

FRONT VIEW OF A JAGUAR V12

Air cleaner

Camshaft sprocket

Distributor

Fuel injector nozzle

Inlet manifold tract

Piston

Crankshaft

Plenum chamber

Camshaft

Cam follower

Coolant outlet

Piston ring land

Cam cover

Piston ring groove

Exhaust manifold

Piston skirt

STRAIGHT 4 CYLINDER ARRANGEMENT

Viscous coupling

Gudgeon pin

Cooling fan

Fan drive shaft

Alternator

Connecting rod (con-rod)

Counterweight

V12 CYLINDER ARRANGEMENT

Alternator pulley

Belt pulley

SECTIONED VIEW OF A JAGUAR V12

Throttle butterfly

Inlet manifold

Ignition amplifier

Fuel pipe

Throttle linkage

Distributor drive shaft

Air inlet

Exhaust valve

Cam cover

Inlet valve

Oil feed pipe

Timing chain

Cylinder head

Piston crown

Coolant rail (water rail)

Piston ring land

Exhaust heat shield

Water pump

Exhaust manifold

Piston

Oil pipe banjo

Ancillary drive pulley

Timing chain drive sprocket

Drive plate

Connecting rod (con-rod)

Starter ring

Counterweight (balance weight)

Main bearing

Crankcase

Pipe to oil cooler

Sump

Oil filter

Alternative engines

ROTARY-ENGINED MAZDA RX-7

THE MOST COMMON TYPE OF ALTERNATIVE ENGINE is the diesel engine, which, instead of igniting the compressed fuel/air mixture with a spark, uses compression alone, heating the mixture to the point where it explodes. A diesel engine's fuel consumption is low in comparison with similarly sized piston engines, despite its heavier, reinforced moving parts and cylinder block. Another type of engine is the rotary-combustion, first successfully developed by Felix Wankel in the 1950s. Its two trilobate (three-sided) rotors revolve in housings shaped in a fat figure-of-eight. The four sequences of the four-stroke cycle, which occur consecutively in a piston engine, occur simultaneously in a rotary engine, producing power in a continuous stream.

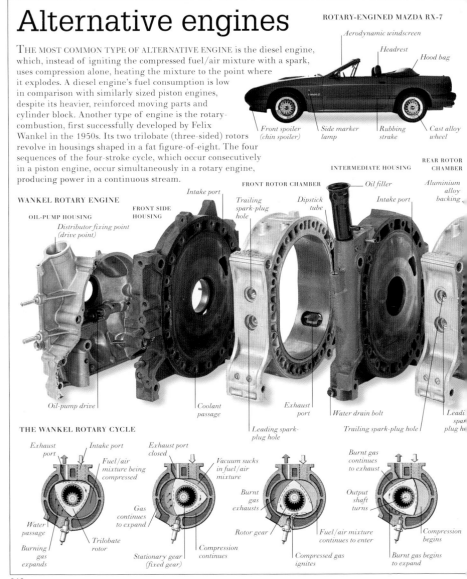

Aerodynamic windscreen

Headrest

Hood bag

Front spoiler (chin spoiler)

Side marker lamp

Rubbing strake

Cast alloy wheel

WANKEL ROTARY ENGINE

OIL-PUMP HOUSING

Distributor fixing point (drive point)

FRONT SIDE HOUSING

Intake port

FRONT ROTOR CHAMBER

Trailing spark-plug hole

Dipstick tube

INTERMEDIATE HOUSING

Oil filler

Intake port

REAR ROTOR CHAMBER

Aluminium alloy backing

Oil-pump drive

Coolant passage

Exhaust port

Leading spark-plug hole

Water drain bolt

Trailing spark-plug hole

Leading spark-plug hole

THE WANKEL ROTARY CYCLE

Exhaust port

Intake port

Fuel/air mixture being compressed

Water passage

Burning gas expands

Trilobate rotor

Gas continues to expand

Exhaust port closed

Vacuum sucks in fuel/air mixture

Stationary gear (fixed gear)

Compression continues

Burnt gas exhausts

Rotor gear

Compressed gas ignites

Burnt gas continues to exhaust

Output shaft turns

Fuel/air mixture continues to enter

Burnt gas begins to expand

Compression begins

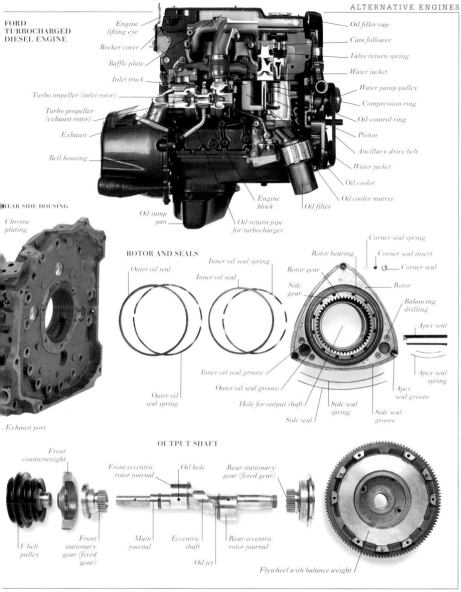

FORD TURBOCHARGED DIESEL ENGINE

Engine lifting eye

Oil filler cap

Cam follower

Rocker cover

Valve return spring

Baffle plate

Water jacket

Inlet track

Water pump pulley

Turbo impeller (inlet rotor)

Compression ring

Turbo propeller (exhaust rotor)

Oil-control ring

Piston

Exhaust

Ancillary drive belt

Bell housing

Water jacket

Oil cooler

Oil cooler matrix

Engine block

Oil filter

Oil sump pan

Oil return pipe for turbocharger

REAR SIDE HOUSING

Chrome plating

Exhaust port

ROTOR AND SEALS

Outer oil seal

Inner oil seal spring

Inner oil seal

Rotor bearing

Corner seal spring

Corner seal insert

Corner seal

Rotor gear

Side gear

Rotor

Balancing drilling

Apex seal

Inner oil seal groove

Outer oil seal groove

Apex seal spring

Outer oil seal spring

Hole for output shaft

Side seal spring

Side seal

Apex seal groove

Side seal groove

OUTPUT SHAFT

Front counterweight

Front eccentric rotor journal

Oil hole

Rear stationary gear (fixed gear)

V-belt pulley

Front stationary gear (fixed gear)

Main journal

Eccentric shaft

Rear eccentric rotor journal

Oil jet

Flywheel with balance weight

Bodywork

THE BODY OF A MODERN mass-produced car is built on the monocoque (single-shell) principle, in which the roof, side panels, and floor are welded into a single integral unit. This bodyshell protects and supports the car's internal parts.

RENAULT LOGO Steel and glass are used to construct the bodyshell, creating a unit that is both light and strong. Its lightness helps to conserve energy, while its strength protects the occupants. Modern bodywork is designed with the aid of computers, which are used to predict factors such as aerodynamic efficiency and impact-resistance. High-technology is also employed on the production line, where robots are used to assemble, weld, and paint the body.

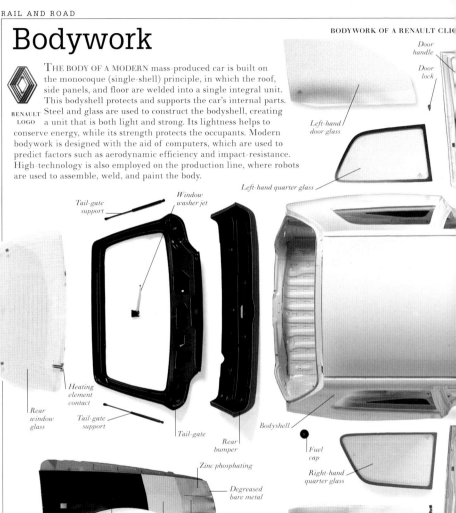

Door handle

Door lock

Left-hand door glass

Left-hand quarter glass

Tail-gate support

Window washer jet

Rear window glass

Heating element contact

Tail-gate support

Tail-gate

Rear bumper

Bodyshell

Fuel cap

Right-hand quarter glass

Zinc phosphating

Degreased bare metal

Right-hand door glass

Primer

Base coat colour

Cataphoresic coating

Chrome passivation

Varnish

Door key and lock

Door handle

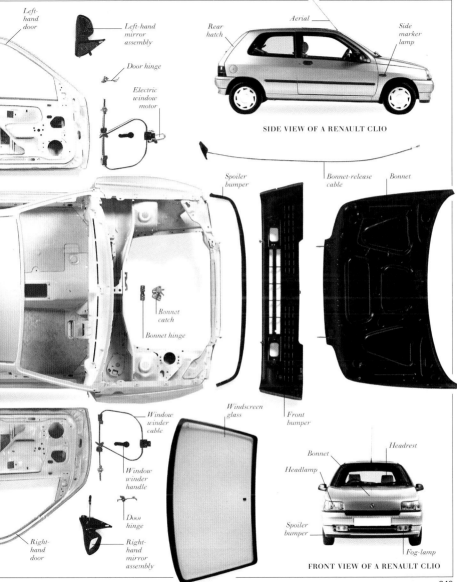

Left-hand door

Left-hand mirror assembly

Door hinge

Electric window motor

Aerial

Rear hatch

Side marker lamp

SIDE VIEW OF A RENAULT CLIO

Spoiler bumper

Bonnet-release cable

Bonnet

Bonnet catch

Bonnet hinge

Window winder cable

Window winder handle

Windscreen glass

Front bumper

Door hinge

Right-hand door

Right-hand mirror assembly

Headrest

Bonnet

Headlamp

Spoiler bumper

Fog-lamp

FRONT VIEW OF A RENAULT CLIO

Mechanical components

A TYPICAL MODERN CAR has several thousand individual mechanical components. These are assembled to form the car's various mechanical systems: engine and exhaust, transmission, steering, suspension, and brakes. To ensure that each system functions properly, components are manufactured to extremely fine tolerances – to within a five-hundredth of a millimetre (about one ten-thousandth of an inch) in some cases.

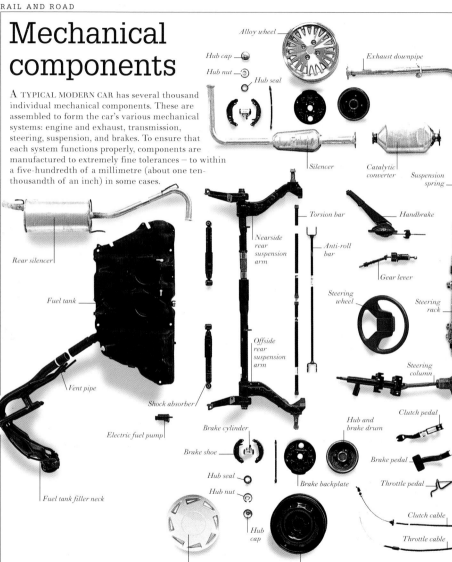

Alloy wheel

Hub cap

Hub nut

Hub seal

Exhaust downpipe

Silencer

Catalytic converter

Suspension spring

Rear silencer

Torsion bar

Handbrake

Nearside rear suspension arm

Anti-roll bar

Fuel tank

Gear lever

Steering wheel

Steering rack

Offside rear suspension arm

Steering column

Vent pipe

Shock absorber

Hub and brake drum

Clutch pedal

Electric fuel pump

Brake cylinder

Brake pedal

Brake shoe

Throttle pedal

Hub seal

Brake backplate

Hub nut

Clutch cable

Hub cap

Throttle cable

Fuel tank filler neck

Wheel trim

Steel wheel

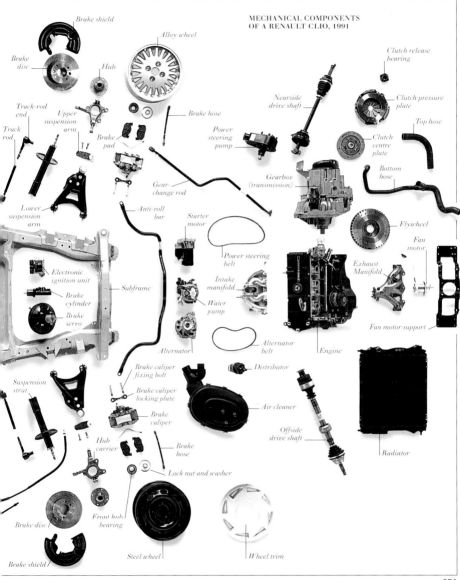

MECHANICAL COMPONENTS OF A RENAULT CLIO, 1991

Brake shield

Alloy wheel

Clutch release bearing

Brake disc

Hub

Nearside drive shaft

Clutch pressure plate

Track-rod end

Upper suspension arm

Brake hose

Top hose

Clutch centre plate

Track rod

Brake pad

Power steering pump

Bottom hose

Gear-change rod

Gearbox (transmission)

Lower suspension arm

Anti-roll bar

Starter motor

Flywheel

Fan motor

Electronic ignition unit

Power steering belt

Exhaust Manifold

Brake cylinder

Subframe

Intake manifold

Brake servo

Water pump

Fan motor support

Alternator

Alternator belt

Engine

Suspension strut

Brake caliper fixing bolt

Distributor

Brake caliper locking plate

Air cleaner

Brake caliper

Hub carrier

Offside drive shaft

Brake hose

Radiator

Lock nut and washer

Brake disc

Front hub bearing

Brake shield

Steel wheel

Wheel trim

Car trim

A MODERN CAR HAS TWO TYPES OF TRIM, according to the materials used: hard (chrome and plastics) and soft (upholstery materials). Safety and comfort are priorities in the trim's design: seats help the occupants to maintain a comfortable posture, rubber seals keep out dirt and moisture, and headlamps light the way. Older cars had interior or leather panelling cut and fitted by craftsmen; modern cars use precisely moulded plastics and seat fabrics cut by robot-controlled lasers to reduce costs and production time. Doors are now trimmed off the production line so that complex wiring can be built in.

TRIM OF A RENAULT CLIO, 1991

Rear quarter trim panel

Inner roof trim

Roof seal

Quarter trim panel

Quarter panel moulding

Rear seat belt

Centre seat belt

Rear seat belt stalk (catch)

Gear lever surround

Split, folding rear seat assembly

Rear tyre

Rear shelf

Rear shelf radio speaker

Rear shelf radio speaker

Rear wheel embellisher (wheel trim)

Untrimmed headrest

Rear seat belt

Quarter panel moulding

Tail-gate trim

Tail-gate seal

Rear wiper blade

Rear wiper arm

Number plate lamp

Rear indicator and stop lamp assembly

Rear tyre

HALOGEN HEADLAMP BULB

SPOTLAMP BULB

Filament

MARKER LAMP BULB

Filament

FESTOON BULB

Contact

Bayonet fixing

Contact

Contact

Contact

Contact

Rear quarter trim panel

Roof seal

Quarter trim panel

Inner roof trim

Roof moulding

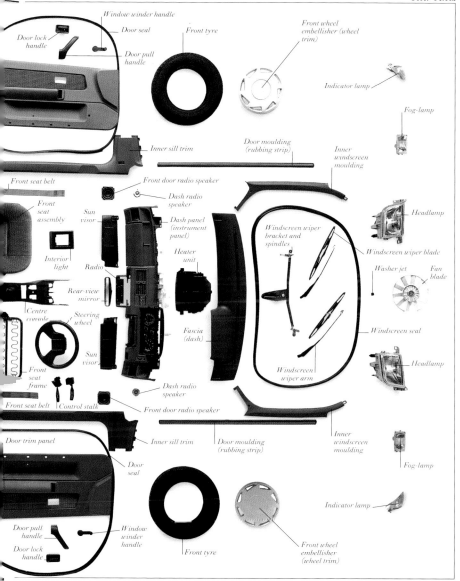

Window winder handle

Door lock handle

Door seal

Front tyre

Door pull handle

Front wheel embellisher (wheel trim)

Indicator lamp

Fog-lamp

Inner sill trim

Door moulding (rubbing strip)

Inner windscreen moulding

Front seat belt

Front door radio speaker

Dash radio speaker

Front seat assembly

Sun visor

Dash panel (instrument panel)

Windscreen wiper bracket and spindles

Headlamp

Windscreen wiper blade

Heater unit

Interior light

Radio

Washer jet

Fan blade

Rear-view mirror

Centre console

Steering wheel

Fascia (dash)

Windscreen seal

Sun visor

Front seat frame

Headlamp

Windscreen wiper arm

Dash radio speaker

Front seat belt

Control stalk

Front door radio speaker

Inner windscreen moulding

Door trim panel

Inner sill trim

Door moulding (rubbing strip)

Door seal

Fog-lamp

Door pull handle

Window winder handle

Door lock handle

Front tyre

Front wheel embellisher (wheel trim)

Indicator lamp

353

Hybrid car

THERE HAVE BEEN SEVERAL proposed alternatives to conventional petrol- or diesel-powered cars, including cars that use solar or battery power. The object is to lower harmful emissions and conserve natural resources. One of the alternatives already in production is the hybrid car. A hybrid vehicle uses two or more fuels. Examples include diesel-electric trains and mopeds. The latter combine the power of a petrol engine with pedal power. In a hybrid car, petrol consumption is reduced by the provision of additional power by an electric motor during acceleration. The motor is driven by power from on-board batteries that are recharged by an engine-driven generator when the car is decelerating or cruising. Some hybrid cars transfer energy from the wheels to a flywheel during braking. The flywheel drives the generator, which recharges the batteries.

HONDA INSIGHT

Aerial

Aerodynamic roof

Windscreen

Wing mirror

Plastic front wings

Front air dam

Plastic bumper

Aerodynamic underside components

Cooling intake

Aluminium bonnet

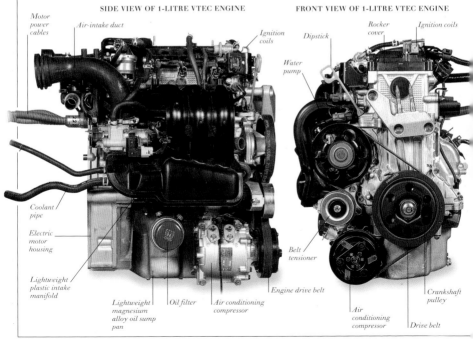

SIDE VIEW OF 1-LITRE VTEC ENGINE

Motor power cables

Air-intake duct

Ignition coils

Coolant pipe

Electric motor housing

Lightweight plastic intake manifold

Lightweight magnesium alloy oil sump pan

Oil filter

Air conditioning compressor

Engine drive belt

FRONT VIEW OF 1-LITRE VTEC ENGINE

Rocker cover

Ignition coils

Dipstick

Water pump

Belt tensioner

Air conditioning compressor

Crankshaft pulley

Drive belt

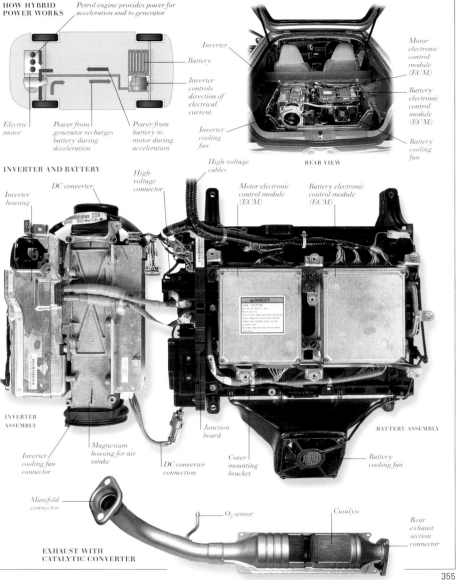

HOW HYBRID POWER WORKS

Petrol engine provides power for acceleration and to generator

Battery

Inverter controls direction of electrical current

Electric motor

Power from generator recharges battery during deceleration

Power from battery to motor during acceleration

Inverter

Inverter cooling fan

Motor electronic control module (ECM)

Battery electronic control module (ECM)

Battery cooling fan

REAR VIEW

INVERTER AND BATTERY

High-voltage cables

DC converter

High-voltage connector

Inverter housing

Motor electronic control module (ECM)

Battery electronic control module (ECM)

⚠ DANGER

INVERTER ASSEMBLY

Inverter cooling fan connector

Magnesium housing for air intake

DC converter connection

Junction board

Cover mounting bracket

BATTERY ASSEMBLY

Battery cooling fan

Manifold connector

O₂ sensor

Catalyst

Rear exhaust section connector

EXHAUST WITH CATALYTIC CONVERTER

Racing cars

SINCE MOTORING BEGAN, racing cars have been a major
focus of innovation in car design. Features that are now
commonplace, such as disc brakes, turbochargers, and even
safety belts, were used first on competition cars. Research into
racing cars has contributed to a new understanding of engine
performance, aerodynamics, and tyre adhesion, and has led
to the development of ultra-light materials such as carbon-
fibre for car bodies. A modern McLaren Formula One car has
a low, streamlined body and an open cockpit but, unlike its
forerunner, it also has front and rear wings that push the
wheels firmly on to the track, huge tyres for extra grip, and
electronic sensors that continually relay information to the
pits about the car's performance.

72° V10 ENGINE

Fuel injection trumpet guard

Cam cover

Gearbox fixing stud

Water and oil pump assembly

Mercedes-Benz

Harmonically-tuned exhaust system

Cylinder head

Stressed cylinder block

BACK VIEW OF MCLAREN MERCEDES MP4-13

Upper flap

Grooved racing tyre

Warning light

Half-shaft

West

BRIDGESTONE   *BRIDGESTONE*

Rear wing end-plate

One-piece side pod and engine cover

Side pod air outlet

Diffuser

Exhaust pipe

Differential

Engine air intake

On-board TV mini-camera

SIDE VIEW OF MCLAREN MERCEDES MP4-13

Engine cover

Winglet

Head rest

Hakkinen

BOSS
HUGO BOSS

Mobil 1   (E)

Mercedes-Benz

We

Rear wing end-plate

LOCTITE

CAMOZZI

WARSTEIN

BRIDGEST

BRIDGESTONE

ERKEL

POTENZA

Alloy wheel

Wheel nut

Side pod

We

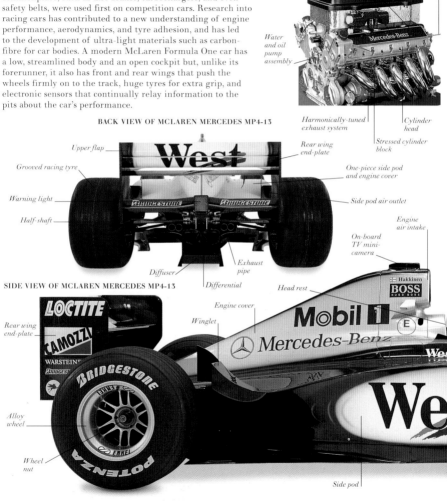

OVERHEAD VIEW OF MCLAREN MERCEDES MP4-13

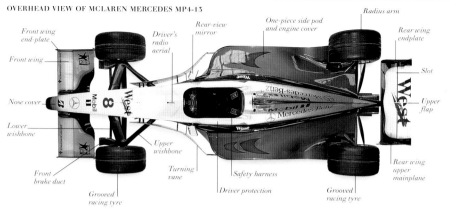

Front wing end-plate
Front wing
Nose cover
Lower wishbone
Front brake duct
Grooved racing tyre
Driver's radio aerial
Upper wishbone
Turning vane
Safety harness
Driver protection
Rear-view mirror
One-piece side pod and engine cover
Radius arm
Rear wing endplate
Slot
Upper flap
Rear wing upper mainplane
Grooved racing tyre

FRONT VIEW OF MCLAREN MERCEDES MP4-13

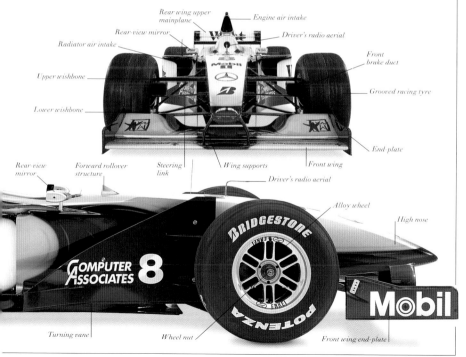

Rear wing upper mainplane
Rear-view mirror
Radiator air intake
Upper wishbone
Lower wishbone
Engine air intake
Driver's radio aerial
Front brake duct
Grooved racing tyre
End plate
Rear-view mirror
Forward rollover structure
Steering link
Wing supports
Front wing
Driver's radio aerial
Alloy wheel
High nose
Turning vane
Wheel nut
Front wing end-plate

BRIDGESTONE
POTENZA
COMPUTER ASSOCIATES 8
Mobil

Bicycle anatomy

THE BICYCLE IS A TWO-WHEELED, light-weight machine, which is propelled by human power. It is efficient, cheap, easily manufactured, and one of the world's most popular forms of transport. The first pedal-driven bicycle was built in Scotland in 1839. Since then the basic design – of a frame, wheels, brakes, handlebars, and saddle – has been gradually improved, with the addition of a chain, gear system, and pneumatic tyres (tyres inflated with air). The recent invention of the mountain bike (all-terrain bike) has been an important development. With its strong, rugged frame, wide tyres, and 21 gears, a mountain bike enables riders to reach rough and hilly areas that were previously inaccessible to cyclists.

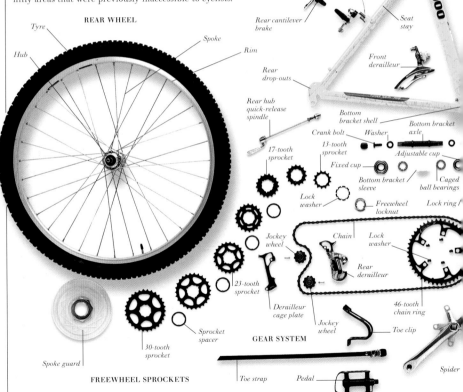

REAR WHEEL

Tyre

Spoke

Hub

Rim

Saddle

Seat post

Seat post quick-release bolt

Cable guide

Straddle wire

Seat tube

USA 6000

Rear cantilever brake

Seat stay

Front derailleur

Rear drop-outs

Rear hub quick-release spindle

Bottom bracket shell

Crank bolt

Washer

Bottom bracket axle

17-tooth sprocket

13-tooth sprocket

Adjustable cup

Fixed cup

Lock washer

Bottom bracket sleeve

Caged ball bearings

Freewheel locknut

Lock ring

Jockey wheel

Chain

Lock washer

23-tooth sprocket

Rear derailleur

Derailleur cage plate

Jockey wheel

46-tooth chain ring

Sprocket spacer

Toe clip

30-tooth sprocket

GEAR SYSTEM

Spoke guard

FREEWHEEL SPROCKETS

Toe strap

Pedal

Spider

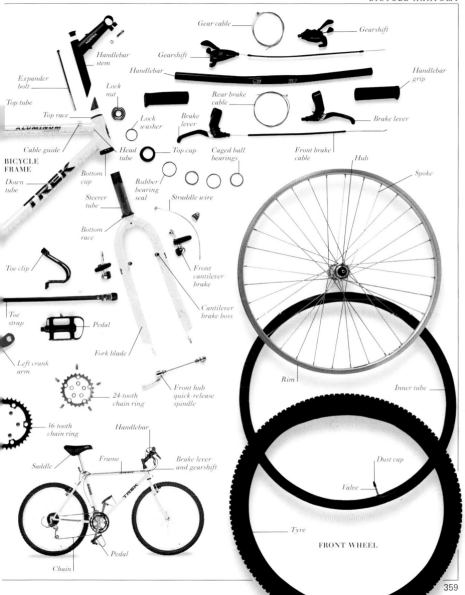

Gear cable

Gearshift

Handlebar
stem

Expander
bolt

Gearshift

Handlebar

Handlebar
grip

Top tube

Lock
nut

Rear brake
cable

Top race

Lock
washer

Brake
lever

Brake lever

ALUMINUM

Cable guide

Head
tube

Top cup

Caged ball
bearings

Front brake
cable

Hub

BICYCLE
FRAME

Bottom
cup

Spoke

Down
tube

Rubber
bearing
seal

TREK

Steerer
tube

Straddle wire

Bottom
race

Toe clip

Front
cantilever
brake

Toe
strap

Cantilever
brake boss

Pedal

Rim

Left crank
arm

Fork blade

24-tooth
chain ring

Front hub
quick-release
spindle

Inner tube

36-tooth
chain ring

Handlebar

Saddle

Frame

Brake lever
and gearshift

Dust cap

TREK

Valve

Pedal

Tyre

Chain

FRONT WHEEL

359

Bicycles

ALTHOUGH ALL BICYCLES are made up of the same basic components, they can vary greatly in design. A racing bike, such as the Eddy Merckx model, with its light frame and steep head- and seat-angles, is built for speed. Its design forces the rider to adopt the "aerotuck", a crouched, aerodynamic position. While a touring bike resembles the racing bike in many respects, it is designed for comfort and stability on long-distance journeys. Touring bikes are characterized by more relaxed frame angles, heavy chain stays that support the rear panniers, and a long wheelbase (the distance between the wheel axles) for reliable handling. All-round bicycles, known as "hybrids", combine the light weight and speed of sports bikes with the rugged durability of mountain bikes (see pp. 358-359). Bicycles that are not designed for conventional road use include time-trial bikes, which have a short head tube, sloping top tube, "aero" handlebars, and aerodynamic tubing. Most Human Powered Vehicles (HPVs) are recumbents – the rider has a recumbent position – which maximize power output and minimize drag (resistance). Essential to the safety of all riders are helmets, and both front and rear lights; locks protect against theft.

FRONT AND REAR LIGHTS

HELMET

White front light

Red rear light

Hard outer shell

Air vent

Polystyrene padding

Quick-release strap

EDDY MERCKX RACING BICYCLE

Saddle

Saddle clamp

Seat post

Seat-post bolt

Cable guide

Rear brake cable

Brake-block bolt

Top tube (crossbar)

Steel frame

Brake block

Seat stay

Seat tube

Down tube

Tyre

Tyre tread

Tyre wall

Wheel rim

Freewheel sprocket

Water-bottle cage

Front derailleur

STEEL LOCK

Key

Hardened steel

Pick-proof lock

Rear derailleur

Pulley bolt

Tension pulley

Chain

Chain stay

Chain ring

Crank bolt

Crank

Spider

Pedal

Toe clip

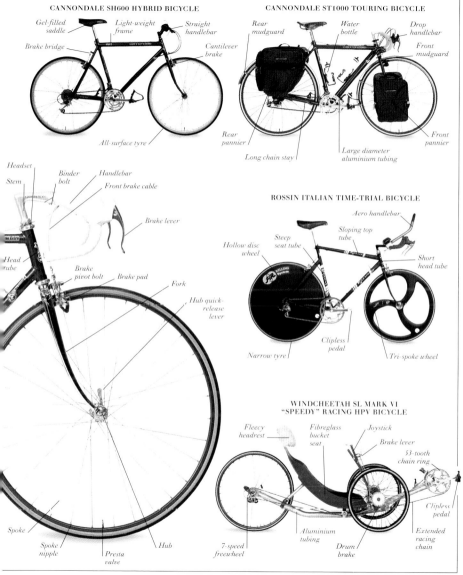

CANNONDALE SH600 HYBRID BICYCLE

Gel-filled saddle

Light-weight frame

Straight handlebar

Brake bridge

Cantilever brake

All-surface tyre

CANNONDALE ST1000 TOURING BICYCLE

Rear mudguard

Water bottle

Drop handlebar

Front mudguard

Rear pannier

Long chain stay

Large diameter aluminium tubing

Front pannier

Headset

Stem

Binder bolt

Handlebar

Front brake cable

Brake lever

Head tube

Brake pivot bolt

Brake pad

Fork

Hub quick-release lever

Spoke

Spoke nipple

Presta valve

Hub

ROSSIN ITALIAN TIME-TRIAL BICYCLE

Aero handlebar

Sloping top tube

Hollow disc wheel

Steep seat tube

Short head tube

Clipless pedal

Narrow tyre

Tri-spoke wheel

WINDCHEETAH SL MARK VI "SPEEDY" RACING HPV BICYCLE

Fleecy headrest

Fibreglass bucket seat

Joystick

Brake lever

53-tooth chain ring

Clipless pedal

Aluminium tubing

7-speed freewheel

Drum brake

Extended racing chain

The motorcycle

THE MOTORCYCLE HAS EVOLVED from a motorized cycle – a basic bicycle with an engine – into a sophisticated, high-performance machine. In 1901, the Werner brothers established the most viable location for the engine by positioning it low in the centre of the chassis (see pp. 364-365): the new Werner became the basis for the modern motorcycle. Motorcycles are used for many purposes – for commuting, delivering messages, touring, and racing – and different machines have been developed according to the demands of different types of riders. The Vespa scooter, for instance, which is small-wheeled, economical, and easy-to-ride, was designed to meet the needs of the commuter. Sidecars provided transport for the family until the arrival of cheap cars caused their popularity to decline. Enthusiast riders generally favour larger capacity machines that are capable of greater performance and offer more comfort. Four-cylinder machines have been common since the Honda CB750 appeared in 1969. Despite advances in motorcycle technology, many riders are attracted to the traditional looks of motorcycles like the twin-cylinder Harley-Davidson. The Harley-Davidson Glides exploit the style of the classic American V-twin engine, where the cylinders are placed in a V-formation.

1901 WERNER MOTORCYCLE

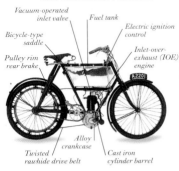

Vacuum-operated inlet valve
Fuel tank
Electric ignition control
Bicycle-type saddle
Inlet-over-exhaust (IOE) engine
Pulley rim rear brake
Alloy crankcase
Twisted rawhide drive belt
Cast iron cylinder barrel

1988 HARLEY-DAVIDSON FLHS ELECTRA GLIDE

1965 BMW R/60 WITH 1952 STEIB CHAIR

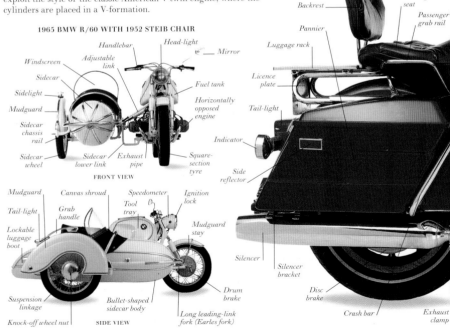

Handlebar
Head-light
Mirror
Windscreen
Adjustable link
Sidecar
Fuel tank
Sidelight
Horizontally opposed engine
Mudguard
Sidecar chassis rail
Sidecar wheel
Sidecar lower link
Exhaust pipe
Square-section tyre
Side reflector
Indicator

FRONT VIEW

Mudguard
Canvas shroud
Speedometer
Ignition lock
Tail-light
Grab handle
Tool tray
Mudguard stay
Lockable luggage boot
Silencer
Silencer bracket
Suspension linkage
Bullet-shaped sidecar body
Drum brake
Disc brake
Knock-off wheel nut
SIDE VIEW
Long leading-link fork (Earles fork)

Backrest
Passenger seat
Passenger grab rail
Pannier
Luggage rack
Licence plate
Tail-light
Crash bar
Exhaust clamp

1969 HONDA CB750

1963 VESPA GRAND SPORT 160 MARK 1

Tail-light

Seat

Mirror

Front brake lever

Shock absorber

Seat strap

Indicator

Oil tank

Telescopic fork

Mudguard stay

Disc brake

Clutch cover

Single overhead camshaft engine

Mirror

Heat shield

Passenger footrest

Exhaust pipe

Brake master cylinder

Handgrip

Front brake lever

Light switch

Twist grip gear change

Monocoque chassis

Seat strap

Throttle

Front brake lever

Clutch lever

Engine cover

Seat

Head-light

Cooling grille

Horn

Tail-light

Choke

Shock absorber

Petrol tap

Kick-starter

Centre stand

Foot brake

Drum brake

Silencer

Rubber foot mat

Single-sided trailing-link fork

Windscreen

Clutch cable

Throttle cable

Padded seat

Manufacturer's logo

Windscreen adjustor

Oil tank filler cap

Fuel tank

Head-light

Oil tank

Fog-lamp

Indicator

Telescopic fork

Side reflector

Mudguard

Passenger footrest

Gearbox

Air filter

45° V-twin engine

Exhaust pipe

Footrest

Brake pedal

Crash bar

Duplex tubular cradle frame

Brake calliper

Disc brake

Cast alloy wheel

The motorcycle chassis

THE MOTORCYCLE CHASSIS is the main "body" of the motorcycle, to which the engine is attached. Consisting of the frame, wheels, suspension, and brakes, the chassis performs various functions. The frame, which is built from steel or alloy, keeps the wheels in line to maintain the handling of the motorcycle, and serves as a structure for mounting other components. The engine and gearbox unit is bolted into place, while items such as the seat, the mudguards, and the fairing are more easily removable. Suspension cushions the rider from irregularities in the road surface. In most suspension systems, coil springs controlled by an oil damper separate the main mass of the motorcycle from the wheels. At the front, the spring and damper are usually incorporated in a telescopic fork; the rear employs a pivoted swingarm. The suspension also helps to retain maximum contact between the tyres and the road, necessary to effective braking and steering. Drum brakes were common until the 1970s, but modern motorcycles use disc brakes, which are more powerful.

1985 HONDA VF750 WITH BODYWORK

Racing number plate
Dual seat
Fuel tank
Frame-mounted fairing
Telescopic fork
Mudguard
V4 engine unit
Floating disc brake
Box-section tubular cradle frame
Box-section swingarm
Disc brake

1985 HONDA VF750 WITH BODYWORK REMOVED

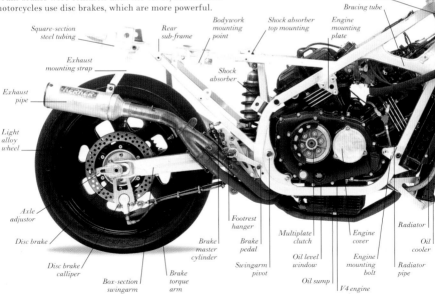

Brake master cylinder
Headstock
Bracing tube
Engine mounting plate
Shock absorber top mounting
Bodywork mounting point
Rear sub-frame
Square-section steel tubing
Exhaust mounting strap
Shock absorber
Exhaust pipe
Light alloy wheel
Axle adjustor
Disc brake
Disc brake calliper
Box-section swingarm
Brake torque arm
Brake master cylinder
Brake pedal
Footrest hanger
Swingarm pivot
Multiplate clutch
Oil level window
Oil sump
V4 engine unit
Engine cover
Engine mounting bolt
Radiator
Oil cooler
Radiator pipe

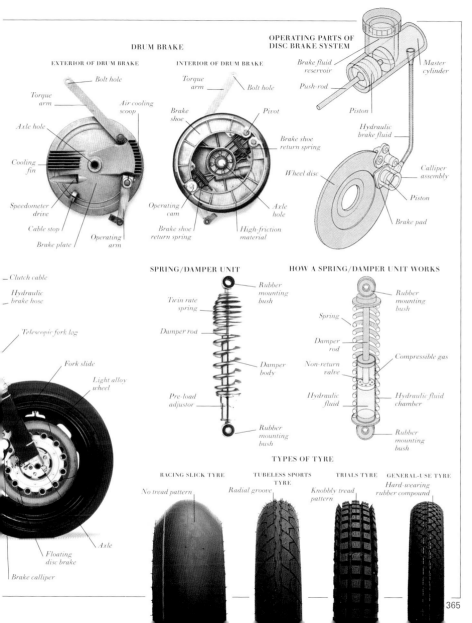

DRUM BRAKE

OPERATING PARTS OF DISC BRAKE SYSTEM

Brake fluid reservoir

Master cylinder

Push-rod

Piston

Hydraulic brake fluid

Wheel disc

Calliper assembly

Piston

Brake pad

EXTERIOR OF DRUM BRAKE

Bolt hole

Torque arm

Air cooling scoop

Axle hole

Cooling fin

Speedometer drive

Cable stop

Brake plate

Operating arm

INTERIOR OF DRUM BRAKE

Torque arm

Bolt hole

Brake shoe

Pivot

Brake shoe return spring

Operating cam

Axle hole

Brake shoe return spring

High-friction material

Clutch cable

Hydraulic brake hose

Telescopic fork leg

Fork slide

Light alloy wheel

Floating disc brake

Axle

Brake calliper

SPRING/DAMPER UNIT

Twin rate spring

Rubber mounting bush

Damper rod

Damper body

Pre-load adjustor

Rubber mounting bush

HOW A SPRING/DAMPER UNIT WORKS

Rubber mounting bush

Spring

Damper rod

Non-return valve

Hydraulic fluid

Compressible gas

Hydraulic fluid chamber

Rubber mounting bush

TYPES OF TYRE

RACING SLICK TYRE

No tread pattern

TUBELESS SPORTS TYRE

Radial groove

TRIALS TYRE

Knobbly tread pattern

GENERAL-USE TYRE

Hard-wearing rubber compound

Motorcycle engines

MOTORCYCLE ENGINES must be light-weight and compact, and have a good power output. They have between one and six cylinders, can be cooled by air or water, and the capacity of the combustion chamber varies from 49cc (cubic centimetres) to 1500cc. Two types of internal combustion engine are common: the four-stroke, which is used in cars (see pp. 342-343), and the two-stroke. A basic two-stroke engine has only three moving parts – the crankshaft, the connecting rod, and the piston – but the power output is high. The engine fires every two strokes (rather than every four), giving a "power stroke" every revolution (see p. 343). Power is conveyed from the engine to the rear wheel by the transmission system. This usually consists of a clutch, a gearbox, and a final drive system. Clutches are multiplate devices, which run in oil. Gearboxes have five or six speeds and are operated by foot pedal. Shaft and belt drive systems are used in some cases, but chain drive to the rear wheel is most common.

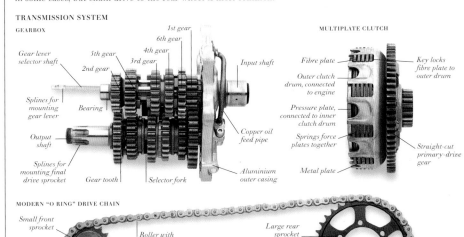

EXTERIOR OF STANDARD TWO-STROKE ENGINE

Spark plug cap

Fuel tap

Carburettor mounting

Kick-starter

Carburettor

Cylinder head

Cooling fin

Exhaust port

Case screw

Clutch activating arm

Engine cover

Gear lever

TRANSMISSION SYSTEM

GEARBOX

Gear lever selector shaft

1st gear

6th gear

4th gear

5th gear

3rd gear

2nd gear

Input shaft

Splines for mounting gear lever

Bearing

Output shaft

Copper oil feed pipe

Splines for mounting final drive sprocket

Gear tooth

Selector fork

Aluminium outer casing

MULTIPLATE CLUTCH

Fibre plate

Key locks fibre plate to outer drum

Outer clutch drum, connected to engine

Pressure plate, connected to inner clutch drum

Springs force plates together

Metal plate

Straight-cut primary-drive gear

MODERN "O RING" DRIVE CHAIN

Small front sprocket

Roller with sealed-in lubricant

Large rear sprocket

Mounting hole

Plate

Sprocket tooth

Hole for retaining bolt

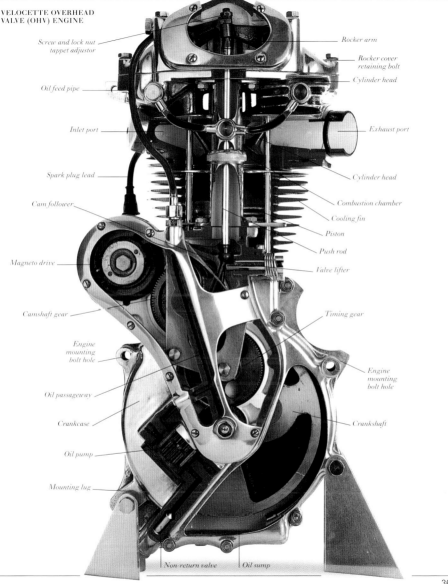

VELOCETTE OVERHEAD VALVE (OHV) ENGINE

Screw and lock nut tappet adjustor

Oil feed pipe

Inlet port

Spark plug lead

Cam follower

Magneto drive

Camshaft gear

Engine mounting bolt hole

Oil passageway

Crankcase

Oil pump

Mounting lug

Rocker arm

Rocker cover retaining bolt

Cylinder head

Exhaust port

Cylinder head

Combustion chamber

Cooling fin

Piston

Push rod

Valve lifter

Timing gear

Engine mounting bolt hole

Crankshaft

Non-return valve

Oil sump

Competition motorcycles

THERE ARE MANY TYPES of motorcycle sport and in each, a specialist machine has evolved to perform to specific requirements. Races take place on roads or tracks or "off-road", in fields, dirt tracks, and even the desert. "Grand Prix" world championships in road-racing are contested by three classes: 125cc, 250cc two-strokes; the top class of 500cc two-strokes; and 900cc four-stroke machines. The latest racing sidecars have more in common with racing cars than motorcycles. The rider and passenger operate within an all-enclosing, aerodynamic fairing. The Suzuki RGV500 shown here, like other Grand Prix machines, carries advertising, which helps to cover the cost of developing motorcycle technology. In Speedway, which originated in the US in 1902, motorcycles operate without brakes or a gearbox. Off-road competition motorcycles have less emphasis on high power output. In Motocross, for example, which is held on rough terrain, they must have high ground clearance, flexible long-travel suspension, and tyres with a chunky tread pattern.

1992 HUSQVARNA MOTOCROSS TC610

Throttle cable
Hand protector
Handlebar brace
Radiator air vent
Long seat
Racing number
Flexible plastic mudguard
Telescopic fork
Plastic guard
Axle
Light-weight exhaust system
Overhead camshaft engine
Gear lever
Disc brake
Knobbly tyre
Disc brake
Brake calliper
Shock absorber
Alloy swingarm
Shock absorber linkage

1992 SUZUKI RGV500
SIDE VIEW

Exhaust pipe
Racing number
Air vent
One-piece seat and tail unit
Shock absorber
Minimal seat padding
Arched alloy swingarm

Exhaust pipe
Vent
Handlebar
Footrest
Rear brake pedal
Drive chain
Wide, slick tyre

Exhaust pipe
Silencer
Shock absorber mounting
Three-spoke alloy wheel
Exhaust pipe
Axle adjustor
Disc brake
Rear brake calliper
Slick racing tyre
Drive chain
Footrest
Brake pedal
Disc brake master cylinder
Light-weight alloy frame

REAR VIEW

1981 WESLAKE SPEEDWAY

Throttle
Throttle cable
Carburettor cover
Fuel tank filler cap
Oil filler cap
Mudguard
Seat
Fuel tank
Mudguard
Wheel cover
Telescopic fork
Wheel cover
Narrow tyre
Wide tyre
Brakeless wheel hub
Silencer
Footrest
Oil pump
Overhead valve engine
Tubular open cradle frame

Fairing stay
Fuel tank breather
Throttle cable
Fuel tank
Throttle
Front brake lever
Telescopic fork
Mudguard

TEAM LUCKY STRIKE SUZUKI MOTUL

Sponsor's logo
Air vent
Braided steel hydraulic hose
Brake calliper
Carbon-fibre disc brake
Three-spoke alloy wheel
Slick tyre
Quickly detachable (QD) fairing

1968 KIRBY BSA RACING SIDECAR

FRONT VIEW

Rev counter
Windscreen
All-enclosing fairing
Fuel tank
Wheel guard
Battery
60
BSA
Square section tyre
Passenger windscreen
Passenger grab rail

SIDE VIEW

Throttle cable
Rev counter
Exhaust pipe
All-enclosing fairing
60
Sidecar chassis
Engine
Fuel cap
Fibreglass wheel guard

Windscreen
Racing number
Clutch lever
Fairing
LUCKY STRIKE TEAM LUCKY STRIKE SUZUKI MOTUL
34
Radiator
Front brake lever
Hydraulic brake hose
Mudguard
Axle
Slick tyre

FRONT VIEW

SEA AND AIR

Ancient Greek and Roman ships

ROMAN ANCHOR

Stock

Shank

Palm

Acutely angled arm

Ring

Crown

IN THE EXPANSIVE EMPIRES OF GREECE AND ROME, powerful fleets were needed for batt[le], trade, and communication. Greek galleys were powered by a sail and many oars. A new armament, the embolos (ram), was fitted on to the galley bow. As ramming duels required fast and manoeuvrable boats, extra rows of oarsmen were added, culminating in the trireme. During the fifth and fourth centuries B.C., the trireme dominated the Mediterranean. It was powered by 170 oarsmen, rowing with one oar each. The oarsmen were ranged on three levels, as the model opposite shows. The trireme also carried archers and soldiers for boarding.

Galleys were pulled out of the water when not in use, and were kept in dockyard ship-sheds. The merchant ships of the Greeks and Romans were mighty vessels too. The full-bodied Roman corbita, for example, could hold up to 400 tons and carried a cargo of spices, gems, silk, and animals. The construction of these boats was based on a stout hull with planking secured by mortice and tenon. Some of these ships embarked on long voyages, sailing even as far as India. To make them easier to steer, corbitas set a fore sail called an "artemon". It flew from a forward-leaning mast that was a forerunner of the long bowsprits carried by the great clipper ships of the 19th century.

ATTIC VASE SHOWING A GALLEY

Kalos (brailing rope)

Mast

Embolos (ram; beak)

Ophthalmos (eye)

Bronze mast truck

Keraia (yard)

Kubernetes (helmsman)

Sternpost

Pedalia (twin rudder)

Oar port sleeve

Kope (oar)

ROMAN CORBITA

Roband (rope band)

Ceruchi (lift)

Heraldic device

Ring

Ruden (brail line)

Double halyard

Bullseye

Fore mast

Buntline

Brace

Fore stay

Antenna (yard)

Artemon (fore sail)

Oculus (eye)

Tabling

Bolt rope

Prow

Windlass

Scala (ladder)

Catena (riding bitt)

Ancorale (anchor rope; anchor rode)

Anchor

Sheet

Hatch board

Deck beam

Zosteres (rubbing strake)

Cargo hold

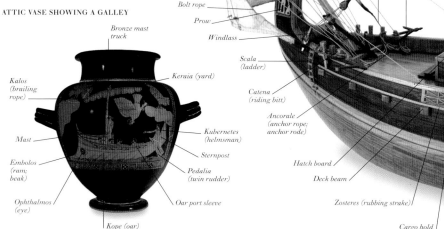

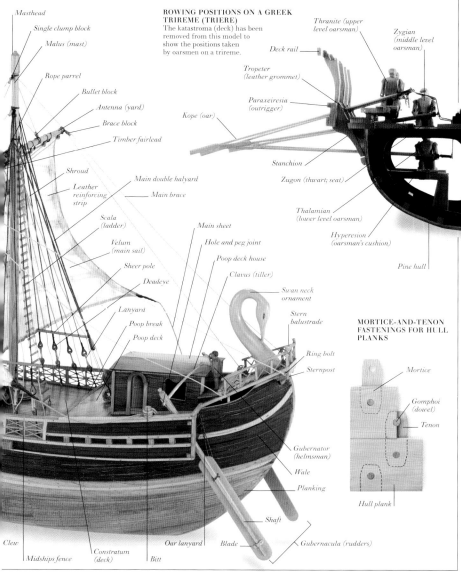

Masthead

Single clump block

Malus (mast)

Rope parrel

Bullet block

Antenna (yard)

Brace block

Timber fairlead

Shroud

Leather reinforcing strip

Scala (ladder)

Velum (main sail)

Sheer pole

Deadeye

Lanyard

Poop break

Poop deck

Clew

Midships fence

Constratum (deck)

Bitt

Oar lanyard

ROWING POSITIONS ON A GREEK TRIREME (TRIERE)
The katastroma (deck) has been removed from this model to show the positions taken by oarsmen on a trireme.

Thranite (upper level oarsman)

Zygian (middle level oarsman)

Deck rail

Tropeter (leather grommet)

Paraxeiresia (outrigger)

Kope (oar)

Stanchion

Zugon (thwart; seat)

Thalamian (lower level oarsman)

Hyperesion (oarsman's cushion)

Pine hull

Main double halyard

Main brace

Main sheet

Hole and peg joint

Poop deck house

Clavus (tiller)

Swan neck ornament

Stern balustrade

Ring bolt

Sternpost

Gubernator (helmsman)

Wale

Planking

Shaft

Blade

Gubernacula (rudders)

MORTICE-AND-TENON FASTENINGS FOR HULL PLANKS

Mortice

Gomphoi (dowel)

Tenon

Hull plank

Viking ships

IN THE DARK AGES and early medieval times, the longships of Scandinavia were one of the most feared sights for people of northern Europe. The Vikings launched raids from Scandinavia every summer in longships equipped with a single steering oar on the right, or "steerboard", side (hence "starboard"). A longship had one row of oars on each side and a single sail. The hull had clinker (overlapping) planks. Prowheads adorned fighting ships during campaigns of war. The sailing longship was also used for local coastal travel. The karv below was probably built as transport for an important family, while the smaller faering (top right) was a rowing boat only. The fleet of William of Normandy that invaded England in 1066 owed much to the Viking boatbuilding tradition, and has been depicted in the Bayeux Tapestry (above). Seals used by port towns and royal courts through the ages provide an excellent record of contemporary ship design. The seal opposite shows how ships changed from the Viking period to the end of the Middle Ages. The introduction of the fighting platform – the castle – and the addition of extra masts and sails changed the character of the medieval ship. Note also that the steering oar has been replaced by a centred rudder.

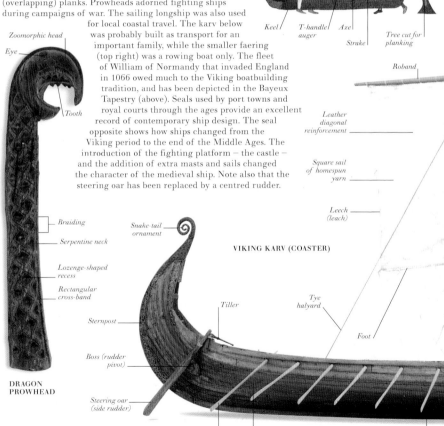

BOATBUILDERS' TOOLS

Shave

Broad axe

Breast auger

Sheer

Master shipwright

Stempost

Hood end

Keel

T-handle auger

Axe

Strake

Tree cut for planking

Roband

Leather diagonal reinforcement

Square sail of homespun yarn

Leech (leach)

Zoomorphic head

Eye

Tooth

Braiding

Serpentine neck

Lozenge-shaped recess

Rectangular cross-band

Sternpost

Boss (rudder pivot)

DRAGON PROWHEAD

Steering oar (side rudder)

Snake-tail ornament

VIKING KARV (COASTER)

Tiller

Tye halyard

Foot

Oar

Starboard (steerboard) side

Keel

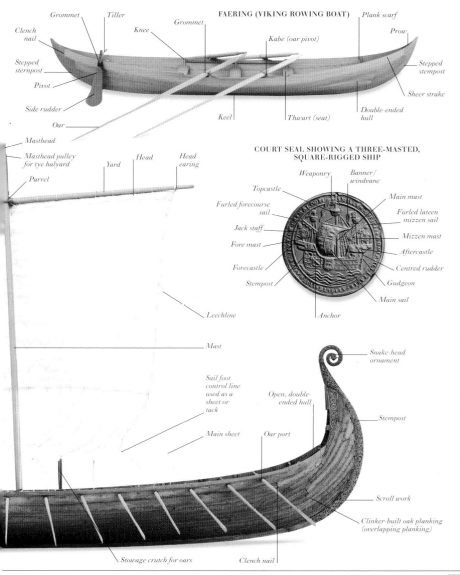

FAERING (VIKING ROWING BOAT)

Grommet

Tiller

Grommet

Plank scarf

Clench nail

Knee

Prow

Kabe (oar pivot)

Stepped sternpost

Stepped stempost

Pivot

Side rudder

Sheer strake

Oar

Keel

Thwart (seat)

Double-ended hull

COURT SEAL SHOWING A THREE-MASTED, SQUARE-RIGGED SHIP

Masthead

Masthead pulley for tye halyard

Yard

Head

Head earing

Weaponry

Banner/ windvane

Parrel

Topcastle

Main mast

Furled forecourse sail

Furled lateen mizzen sail

Jack staff

Mizzen mast

Fore mast

Aftercastle

Forecastle

Centred rudder

Stempost

Gudgeon

Leechline

Main sail

Anchor

Mast

Snake-head ornament

Sail foot control line used as a sheet or tack

Open, double-ended hull

Stempost

Main sheet

Oar port

Scroll work

Clinker-built oak planking (overlapping planking)

Stowage crutch for oars

Clench nail

Medieval warships and traders

FROM THE 16TH CENTURY, SHIPS WERE BUILT WITH A NEW FORM OF HULL, constructed from carvel (edge-to-edge) planking. Warships of the time, like King Henry VIII of England's Mary Rose, boasted awesome fire power. Th ship carried both long-range cannon in bronze, and short-range, anti-personnel guns in iron. Elsewhere, ships took on a multiformity of shapes. Dhows transported slaves from East Africa to Arabia, their fore-and-aft rigged lateen sails allowing them to sail close to the wind around the lands of the Indian Ocean. The Chinese sailed to East Africa and Arabia in junks, trading goods that were carried in watertight compartments. New astronomical tools helped medieval sailors to find their way. Cross-staves and astrolabes were used to measure the altitude of the sun or stars. One of a choice of four cross-pieces was slid up or down the staff of the cross-stave – which was graduated in degrees of altitude – until its top aligned with the celestial body and its base with the horizon. The sighting rule of the astrolabe was simply lined up with a known body, and its altitude read from marks on the metal disc. With sundials, the sailor could use the shadow of the sun to show the time of day.

DHOW

- Main yard
- Furled lateen main sail
- Mizzen yard
- Furled lateen mizzen sail
- Parrel
- Main mast
- Shroud
- Parrel tackle
- Mizzen mast
- Stem head
- Tiller
- Eye
- Rudder
- Raking stempost

JUNK

- Su-wei (fourth mast)
- Topsail
- Chung-ta-wei (main mast)
- Wei-wei (mizzen mast)
- Halyard
- Erh-wei (second mast)
- Sail batten
- T'on-wei (port fore-mast)
- Sprit yard
- Lug sail
- Rudder head
- Transom
- Rudder
- Quarterdeck house
- Cargo hatch
- Oar
- Grapnel-type anchor

SAILING WARSHIP

- Fore top yard
- Fore topmast
- Fore topcastle
- Lift
- Fore yard
- Fore mast
- Ratline
- Shroud
- Fore stay
- Woolding
- Forecastle
- Forecastle castle-deck gunport
- Beakhead
- Rigging rail
- Chain wale (channel)
- Hawse hole
- Anchor cable
- Stempost
- Fore topmast stay
- Bowsprit

Main topgallant mast

Main topgallant yard

Main topmast topcastle

Main top yard

Mizzen topmast

Mizzen top yard

Main topmast stay

Mizzen topcastle

Main topmast

Lift

Main topcastle

Bonaventure top yard

Lift

Bonaventure topmast

Main yard

Parrel

Tye

Bonaventure topcastle

Jeer

Brace

Bonaventure yard

Main stay

Bonaventure mast

Mizzen mast

Aftercastle

Mizzen yard

Main mast

Swifting tackle

Aftercastle castle-deck gunport

Upper deck gunport

Chain wale (channel)

Lid

Deadeye

Gangway

Gun carriage

Transom

Rudder

Sternpost

Keel

Blindage (removable archery screen)

Wale

Main deck gunport

Carvel planking

Port bower anchor

CROSS-STAVE (CROSS-STAFF)

90 degree cross-piece (transversary)

Clamp

Boxwood staff

60 degree cross-piece

Altitude scale in degrees and minutes

30 degree cross-piece

Ocular end

10 degree cross-piece (dutch shoe)

SUNDIAL

Style of the gnomon (edge)

Needle

Gnomon

Outrigger

Pivot

Hour line

Dial

Swivel suspension ring

ASTROLABE

Graduated ring

Scale of degrees

Pivot

Alidade (sighting rule)

Bottom ballast

Scribed arc decoration

377

The expansion of sail

BY THE 18TH CENTURY, SAILING SHIPS had become fast and effective floating fortresses. The navies of the north European powers competed with each other by building heavily-armed fighting ships called "men-of-war". The distinctive round stern of the ship below, with its open gallery, balcony, and elaborate wood carving is typical of the period. Hulls around this time were semicircular in cross section, although many boat designers were soon to return to the V-shaped hulls used by the Vikings. Ships of the period carried more sail than ever before. A labyrinth of rigging supported the masts and yards from which the profusion of square sails were set. Ships grew higher, as extra masts were fitted above the lower mast, and the bowsprit became longer to allow the ship to carry staysails, spritsails, and jibsails. Ships went into battle in single file, so that broadsides from the multiple decks of guns would have maximum effect. Ships were classified by rates, the rating of a vessel depending on how many guns it had. A first rate ship had more than 100 guns. The guns fired solid round shot, usually made of iron.

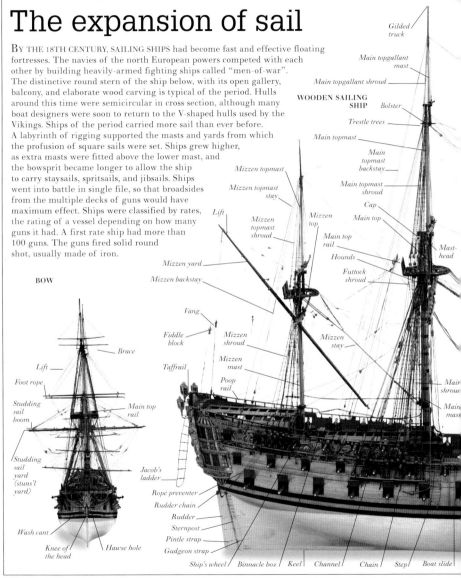

Gilded truck

Main topgallant mast

Main topgallant shroud

WOODEN SAILING SHIP

Bolster

Trestle trees

Main topmast

Main topmast backstay

Main topmast shroud

Cap

Main top

Masthead

Mizzen topmast

Mizzen topmast stay

Lift

Mizzen top

Mizzen topmast shroud

Main top

Main top rail

Hounds

Futtock shroud

Mizzen yard

Mizzen backstay

Mizzen stay

Vang

Fiddle block

Mizzen shroud

Mizzen mast

Taffrail

Poop rail

Main shroud

Main mast

BOW

Brace

Lift

Foot rope

Studding sail boom

Main top rail

Studding sail yard (stuns'l yard)

Jacob's ladder

Rope preventer

Rudder chain

Rudder

Sternpost

Pintle strap

Gudgeon strap

Wash cant

Knee of the head

Hawse hole

Ship's wheel

Binnacle box

Keel

Channel

Chain

Step

Boat slide

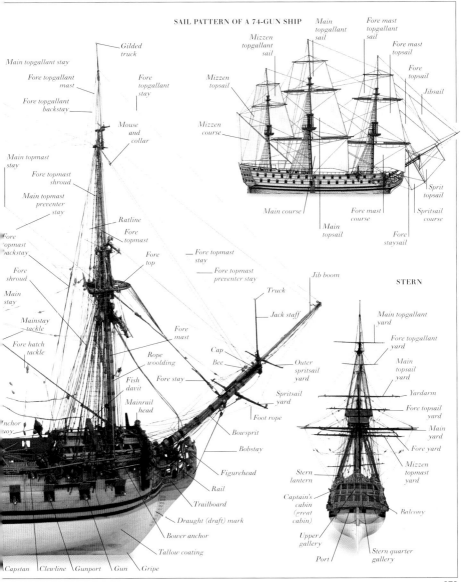

SAIL PATTERN OF A 74-GUN SHIP

Main topgallant stay

Fore topgallant mast

Fore topgallant backstay

Gilded truck

Fore topgallant stay

Mouse and collar

Main topmast stay

Fore topmast shroud

Main topmast preventer stay

Fore topmast backstay

Ratline

Fore topmast

Fore top

Fore shroud

Main stay

Mainstay tackle

Fore hatch tackle

Rope woolding

Fish davit

Mainrail head

Anchor buoy

Fore topmast stay

Fore topmast preventer stay

Fore mast

Cap

Bee

Fore stay

Truck

Jack staff

Jib boom

Outer spritsail yard

Spritsail yard

Foot rope

Bowsprit

Bobstay

Figurehead

Rail

Trailboard

Draught (draft) mark

Bower anchor

Tallow coating

Capstan   Clewline   Gunport   Gun   Gripe

Mizzen topgallant sail

Main topgallant sail

Fore mast topgallant sail

Fore mast topsail

Fore topsail

Mizzen topsail

Mizzen course

Main course

Fore mast course

Main topsail

Main topsail

Jibsail

Sprit topsail

Spritsail course

Fore staysail

Main topsail

STERN

Main topgallant yard

Fore topgallant yard

Main topsail yard

Yardarm

Fore topsail yard

Main yard

Fore yard

Mizzen topsail yard

Stern lantern

Captain's cabin (great cabin)

Upper gallery

Port

Stern quarter gallery

Balcony

A ship of the line

THE 74-GUN WOODEN SHIP WAS A MAINSTAY of British and French battlefleets in the late 18th and early 19th centuries. This "ship of the line" was heavy enough to fight with the most potent of rivals, yet nimble too. The length of such a ship was determined by the number of guns required for each deck, allowing enough room for crews to man them. The gun deck was about 52 m (170 ft) long. The decks had to be very strong to carry the weight of the guns. The deck planks have been removed on the vessel pictured below, to show just how close together the beams had to be to make the hull strong enough. Only timber with a perfect grain was used. The upper deck was open at the waist, but afore and abaft were officers' cabins. The forecastle and quarterdeck carried light guns and acted as platforms for working rigging and for reconnaissance. The ship's longboats (launches) were carried on booms between the gangways.

LONGBOAT

Truck
Mast
Jib halyard
Fore stay halyard
Shroud
Fore sail halyard
Parrel
Bowsprit
Traveller
Stempost
Waterline
Deadeye
Oar
Side bench
Flag halyard
Backstay
Topping lift
Peak halyard
Main sheet
Gaff
Boom

Thole pin
Planking
Rabbit line
Sheerplank
Windlass bar
Frame
Floor
Transom
Keel
Thwart (seat)
Tiller
Rudder

UPPER DECK OF A 74-GUN SHIP

Hoop
Stock
Cathead
Ring
Knighthead
Heads (privy)
Figurehead
Head beam
Head rail
Roundhouse
Boomkin
Anchor cable
Sheave for cat tackle
Fluke
Hoop
Arm
Stock
Deck beam
Foremast hole
Timber head
Fore bitt
Steam grating
Galley stove chimney
Belfry
Deadeye
Waterway
Gangway
Capstan
Breastwork
Carling (carline)
Forked beam
Bulwark
Main companion way
Pawl
Skid beam

Head
Forecastle (fo'c'sle)
Waist

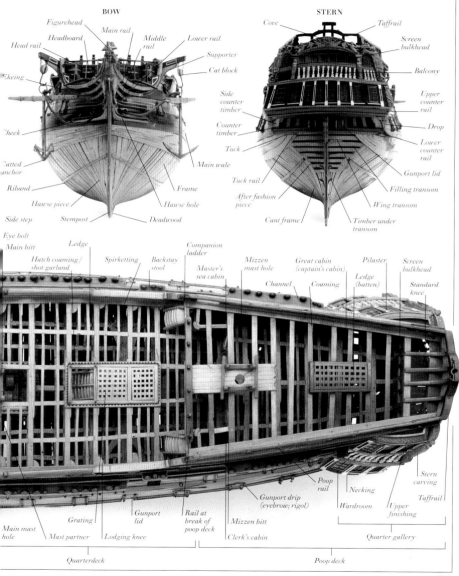

BOW

Figurehead

Main rail

Headboard

Middle rail

Head rail

Lower rail

Supporter

Cat block

Ekeing

Cheek

Catted anchor

Riband

Main wale

Frame

Hause piece

Hause hole

Side step

Stempost

Deadwood

Eye bolt

Main bitt

STERN

Cove

Taffrail

Screen bulkhead

Balcony

Upper counter rail

Side counter timber

Drop

Counter timber

Lower counter rail

Tuck

Gunport lid

Tuck rail

Filling transom

After fashion piece

Wing transom

Cant frame

Timber under transom

Ledge

Companion ladder

Hatch coaming / shot garland

Spirketting

Backstay stool

Master's sea cabin

Mizzen mast hole

Great cabin (captain's cabin)

Pilaster

Screen bulkhead

Channel

Coaming

Ledge (batten)

Standard knee

Poop rail

Stern carving

Gunport drip (eyebrow; rigol)

Necking

Taffrail

Main mast hole

Mast partner

Grating

Gunport lid

Lodging knee

Rail at break of poop deck

Mizzen bitt

Clerk's cabin

Wardroom

Upper finishing

Quarter gallery

Quarterdeck

Poop deck

Rigging

MOST SAILING SHIPS HAVE TWO TYPES OF RIGGING. Standing rigging – kept taut by rigging screws or old-fashioned lanyards and deadeyes – refers to the ropes, wires, and chains that support the masts and yards (horizontal spars). Running rigging, which includes types of block and tackle, halyards, and sheets, is used to hoist, lower, or trim sails.

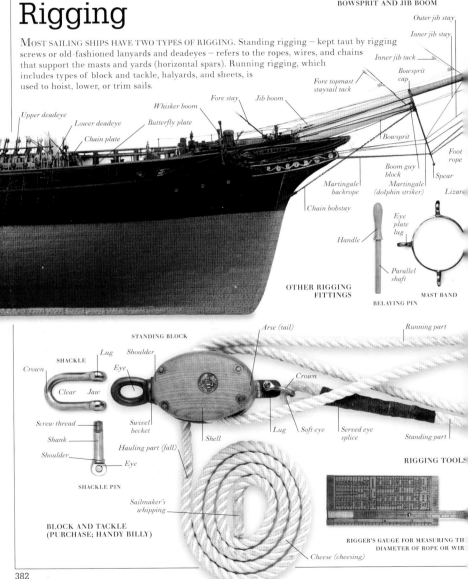

BOWSPRIT AND JIB BOOM

Outer jib stay

Inner jib stay

Inner jib tack

Bowsprit cap

Fore topmast staysail tack

Fore stay

Jib boom

Bowsprit

Whisker boom

Butterfly plate

Upper deadeye

Lower deadeye

Chain plate

Foot rope

Boom guy block

Martingale (dolphin striker)

Spear

Lizard

Martingale backrope

Chain bobstay

OTHER RIGGING FITTINGS

Handle

Eye plate lug

Parallel shaft

BELAYING PIN

MAST BAND

Running part

STANDING BLOCK

Arse (tail)

Lug

Shoulder

Crown

SHACKLE

Eye

Clear   Jaw

Crown

Screw thread

Shank

Shoulder

Swivel becket

Soft eye

Lug

Served eye splice

Standing part

Eye

Hauling part (fall)

Shell

SHACKLE PIN

RIGGING TOOLS

Sailmaker's whipping

BLOCK AND TACKLE (PURCHASE; HANDY BILLY)

RIGGER'S GAUGE FOR MEASURING THE DIAMETER OF ROPE OR WIRE

Cheese (cheesing)

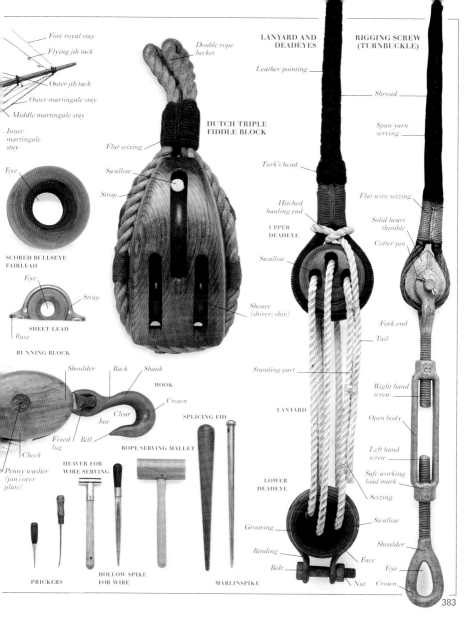

Fore royal stay

Flying jib tack

Outer jib tack

Outer martingale stay

Middle martingale stay

Inner martingale stay

Eye

SCORED BULLSEYE FAIRLEAD

Eye

Strap

SHEET LEAD

Base

RUNNING BLOCK

Double rope becket

Flat seizing

Swallow

Strop

DUTCH TRIPLE FIDDLE BLOCK

Sheave (shiver; shiv)

Shoulder   Back   Shank

HOOK

Crown

Clear

Jaw

Fixed lug   Bill

ROPE SERVING MALLET

Cheek

Penny washer (pin cover plate)

HEAVER FOR WIRE SERVING

SPLICING FID

PRICKERS

HOLLOW SPIKE FOR WIRE

MARLINSPIKE

LANYARD AND DEADEYES

RIGGING SCREW (TURNBUCKLE)

Leather pointing

Shroud

Spun yarn serving

Turk's head

Hitched hauling end

UPPER DEADEYE

Swallow

Flat wire seizing

Solid heart thimble

Cotter pin

Fork end

Tail

Standing part

Right hand screw

LANYARD

Open body

Left hand screw

Safe working load mark

LOWER DEADEYE

Seizing

Grooving

Swallow

Binding

Shoulder

Bolt

Face

Eye

Nut

Crown

Sails

THERE ARE TWO MAIN TYPES OF SAIL, often used in combination. Square sails are driving sails. They are usually attached by parrels to yards, square to the mast to catch the following wind. On fore-and-aft sails, such as lateen and lug sails, the luff (leading edge) usually abuts a mast or a stay. The head of the sail may abut a gaff, and the foot a boom. Around the world, a great range of rigs (sail patterns), such as the ketch, lugger, and schooner, have evolved to suit local needs. Sails are made from strips of cloth, cut to give the sail a belly and strong enough to resist the most violent of winds. Cotton and flax are the traditional sail materials, but synthetic fabrics are now commonly used.

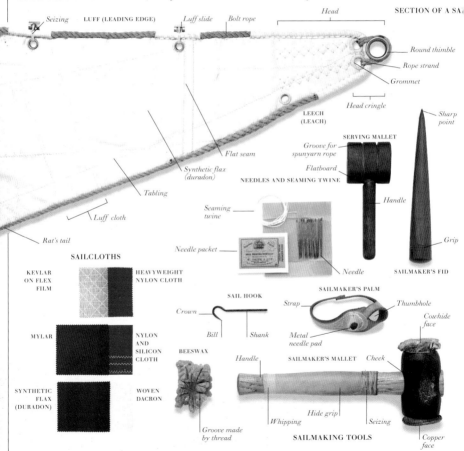

SECTION OF A SA...

Seizing — LUFF (LEADING EDGE) — Luff slide — Bolt rope — Head

Round thimble

Rope strand

Grommet

Head cringle

LEECH (LEACH)

Sharp point

Flat seam

Synthetic flax (duradon)

Tabling

Luff cloth

Rat's tail

SERVING MALLET

Groove for spunyarn rope

Flatboard

NEEDLES AND SEAMING TWINE

Seaming twine

Needle packet

Handle

Needle

Grip

SAILMAKER'S FID

SAILCLOTHS

KEVLAR ON FLEX FILM

HEAVYWEIGHT NYLON CLOTH

MYLAR

NYLON AND SILICON CLOTH

SYNTHETIC FLAX (DURADON)

WOVEN DACRON

SAIL HOOK

Crown

Bill — Shank

BEESWAX

Groove made by thread

Handle

SAILMAKER'S PALM

Strap

Thumbhole

Metal needle pad

Cowhide face

SAILMAKER'S MALLET

Cheek

Whipping

Hide grip

Seizing

Copper face

SAILMAKING TOOLS

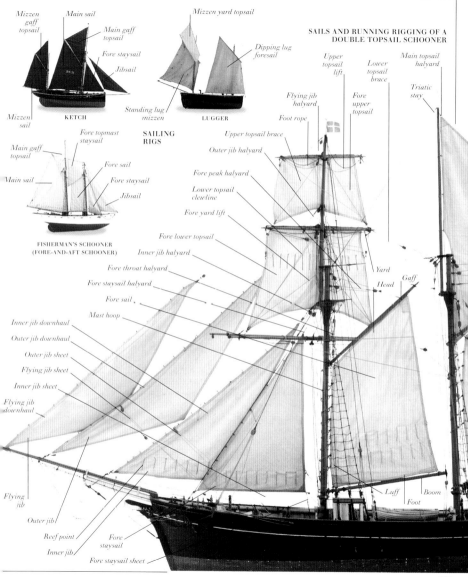

Mizzen gaff topsail

Main sail

Main gaff topsail

Fore staysail

Jibsail

Mizzen sail

KETCH

Mizzen yard topsail

Dipping lug foresail

Standing lug mizzen

LUGGER

SAILS AND RUNNING RIGGING OF A DOUBLE TOPSAIL SCHOONER

Main gaff topsail

Fore topmast staysail

SAILING RIGS

Main sail

Fore sail

Fore staysail

Jibsail

FISHERMAN'S SCHOONER (FORE-AND-AFT SCHOONER)

Upper topsail lift

Lower topsail brace

Main topsail halyard

Triatic stay

Flying jib halyard

Fore upper topsail

Foot rope

Upper topsail brace

Outer jib halyard

Fore peak halyard

Lower topsail clewline

Fore yard lift

Fore lower topsail

Inner jib halyard

Fore throat halyard

Fore staysail halyard

Fore sail

Mast hoop

Inner jib downhaul

Outer jib downhaul

Outer jib sheet

Flying jib sheet

Inner jib sheet

Flying jib downhaul

Yard

Head

Gaff

Flying jib

Outer jib

Reef point

Fore staysail

Inner jib

Fore staysail sheet

Luff

Boom

Foot

385

Mooring and anchoring

FOR LARGE VESSELS IN OPEN WATER, ANCHORAGE IS ESSENTIAL.. By holding a ship securely to the seabed, an anchor prevents the vessel from being at the mercy of wave, tide, and current. The earliest anchors were nothing more than stones. In later years, many anchors had a standard design, much like the Admiralty pattern anchor shown on this page. The Danforth anchor is somewhat different. It has particularly deep flukes to give it great holding power. On large sailing ships, anchors were worked by teams of sailors. They turned the drum of a capstan by pushing on bars slotted into the revolving cylinder. This, in turn, lifted or lowered the anchor chain. In calm harbours and estuaries, ships can moor (make fast) without using anchors. Berthing ropes can be attached to bollards both inboard and on the quayside. Berthing ropes are joined to each other by bends, like those opposite.

TYPES OF ANCHOR

STONE ANCHOR (KILLICK)

Rope hole

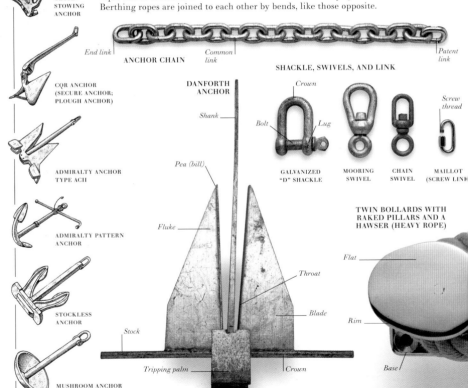

CLOSE-STOWING ANCHOR

CQR ANCHOR (SECURE ANCHOR; PLOUGH ANCHOR)

ADMIRALTY ANCHOR TYPE ACII

ADMIRALTY PATTERN ANCHOR

STOCKLESS ANCHOR

MUSHROOM ANCHOR (PERMANENT MOORING ANCHOR)

End link | Common link | Patent link
ANCHOR CHAIN

SHACKLE, SWIVELS, AND LINK

DANFORTH ANCHOR

Shank

Pea (bill)

Fluke

Stock

Tripping palm

Crown

Throat

Blade

Crown

Crown

Bolt

Lug

GALVANIZED "D" SHACKLE

Screw thread

MOORING SWIVEL

CHAIN SWIVEL

MAILLOT (SCREW LINK)

TWIN BOLLARDS WITH RAKED PILLARS AND A HAWSER (HEAVY ROPE)

Flat

Rim

Base

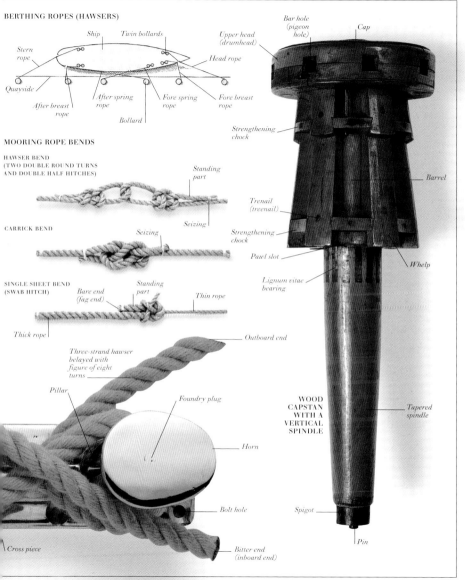

BERTHING ROPES (HAWSERS)

Ship
Twin bollards
Stern rope
Head rope
Quayside
After breast rope
After spring rope
Bollard
Fore spring rope
Fore breast rope

Bar hole (pigeon hole)
Cap

Upper head (drumhead)

Strengthening chock

Barrel

Trenail (treenail)

Strengthening chock

Pawl slot

Lignum vitae bearing

Whelp

MOORING ROPE BENDS

HAWSER BEND
(TWO DOUBLE ROUND TURNS
AND DOUBLE HALF HITCHES)

Standing part

Seizing

CARRICK BEND

Seizing

SINGLE SHEET BEND
(SWAB HITCH)

Bare end (fag end)
Standing part
Thin rope

Thick rope

Three-strand hawser belayed with figure of eight turns

Outboard end

Pillar

Foundry plug

Horn

Bolt hole

Cross piece

Bitter end (inboard end)

WOOD
CAPSTAN
WITH A
VERTICAL
SPINDLE

Tapered spindle

Spigot

Pin

Ropes and knots

ALL KINDS OF ROPES ARE USED AT SEA, from thin twines and yarns to thick hawsers. Synthetic fibres have been developed specifically for use at sea. Nylon ropes stretch, and so are ideal for anchoring; polypropylene has little stretch, so is ideal for halyards and sheets. Different types of knots are used for different purposes. Knots that join two ropes are called bends; hitches join a rope to another object; and bowlines produce an eye (loop) in the end of a rope. Ropes can be joined by splicing (unravelling the ends and weaving them together) or seizing (lashing the ropes together side by side).

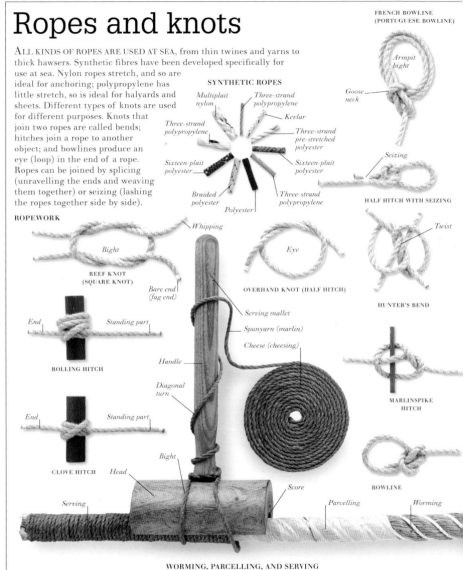

FRENCH BOWLINE (PORTUGUESE BOWLINE)

Armpit bight

Goose neck

Seizing

HALF HITCH WITH SEIZING

SYNTHETIC ROPES

Multiplait nylon

Three-strand polypropylene

Three-strand polypropylene

Kevlar

Three-strand pre-stretched polyester

Sixteen-plait polyester

Sixteen-plait polyester

Braided polyester

Three-strand polypropylene

Polyester

ROPEWORK

Whipping

Bight

REEF KNOT (SQUARE KNOT)

Bare end (fag end)

Eye

OVERHAND KNOT (HALF HITCH)

Twist

HUNTER'S BEND

Serving mallet

Spunyarn (marlin)

Cheese (cheesing)

End

Standing part

ROLLING HITCH

Handle

Diagonal turn

MARLINSPIKE HITCH

End

Standing part

CLOVE HITCH

Head

Bight

Score

BOWLINE

Serving

Parcelling

Worming

WORMING, PARCELLING, AND SERVING

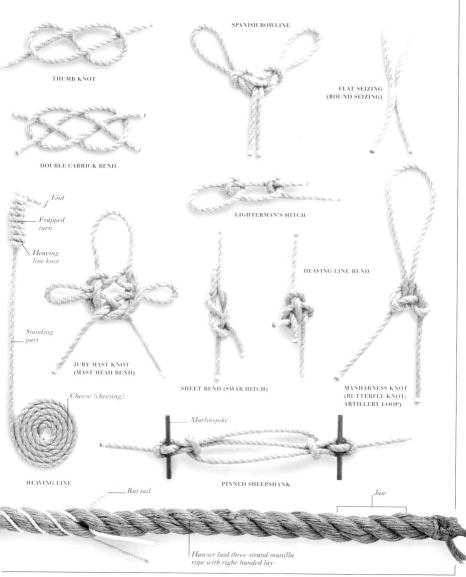

THUMB KNOT

SPANISH BOWLINE

FLAT SEIZING
(ROUND SEIZING)

DOUBLE CARRICK BEND

End

Frapped turn

Heaving line knot

LIGHTERMAN'S HITCH

HEAVING LINE BEND

Standing part

JURY MAST KNOT
(MAST HEAD BEND)

SHEET BEND (SWAB HITCH)

MANHARNESS KNOT
(BUTTERFLY KNOT;
ARTILLERY LOOP)

Cheese (cheesing)

Marlinspike

HEAVING LINE

Rat tail

PINNED SHEEPSHANK

Jaw

*Hawser laid three-strand manilla
rope with right-handed lay*

Paddle wheels and propellers

THE INVENTION OF THE STEAM ENGINE IN THE 18TH CENTURY made mechanically driven ships fitted with paddle wheels or propellers a viable alternative to sails. Paddle wheels have fixed or feathered floats, and the model shown below features both types. Feathered floats give more propulsive power than fixed floats because they are almost upright at all times in the water. Paddle wheels were superseded by the propeller on ocean-going vessels in the mid-19th century. Propellers are more efficient, work better in rough water, and are less vulnerable in collisions. The first propellers were two-bladed but later three- and four-bladed versions are more powerful; the shape and pitch of blades have also been refined over the years. At the beginning of the 18th century, tillers were superseded on many larger ships by the ship's wheel as a means of steering.

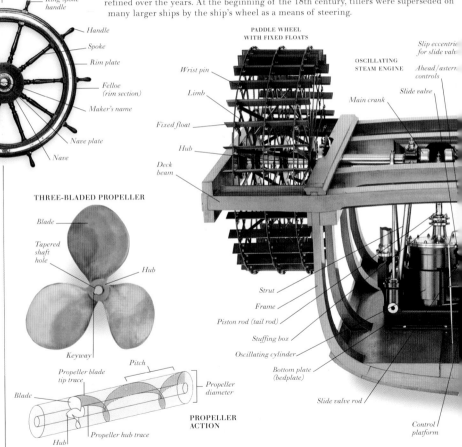

SHIP'S WHEEL

King spoke handle

Handle

Spoke

Rim plate

Felloe (rim section)

Maker's name

Nave plate

Nave

THREE-BLADED PROPELLER

Blade

Tapered shaft hole

Hub

Keyway

Blade

Hub

Pitch

Propeller blade tip trace

Propeller diameter

Propeller hub trace

PROPELLER ACTION

PADDLE WHEEL WITH FIXED FLOATS

Wrist pin

Limb

Fixed float

Hub

Deck beam

OSCILLATING STEAM ENGINE

Slip eccentric for slide valve

Ahead/astern controls

Slide valve

Main crank

Strut

Frame

Piston rod (tail rod)

Stuffing box

Oscillating cylinder

Bottom plate (bedplate)

Slide valve rod

Control platform

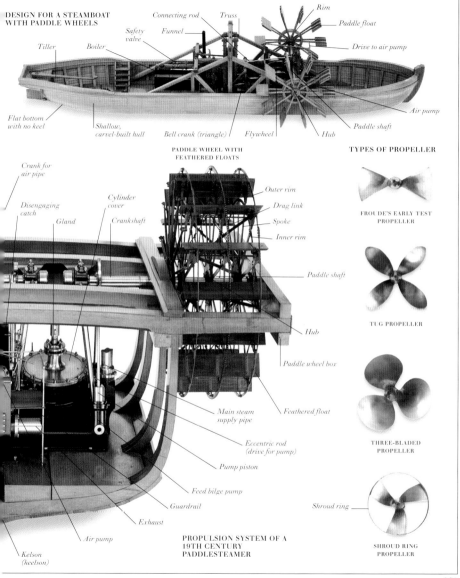

DESIGN FOR A STEAMBOAT WITH PADDLE WHEELS

Tiller

Safety valve

Boiler

Funnel

Connecting rod

Truss

Rim

Paddle float

Drive to air pump

Flat bottom with no keel

Shallow, carvel-built hull

Bell crank (triangle)

Flywheel

Hub

Paddle shaft

Air pump

PADDLE WHEEL WITH FEATHERED FLOATS

Crank for air pipe

Disengaging catch

Gland

Cylinder cover

Crankshaft

Outer rim

Drag link

Spoke

Inner rim

Paddle shaft

Hub

Paddle wheel box

Main steam supply pipe

Feathered float

Eccentric rod (drive for pump)

Pump piston

Feed bilge pump

Guardrail

Exhaust

Air pump

Kelson (keelson)

PROPULSION SYSTEM OF A 19TH CENTURY PADDLESTEAMER

TYPES OF PROPELLER

FROUDE'S EARLY TEST PROPELLER

TUG PROPELLER

THREE-BLADED PROPELLER

Shroud ring

SHROUD RING PROPELLER

Anatomy of an iron ship

IRON PARTS WERE USED IN THE HULLS OF WOODEN SHIPS AS EARLY AS 1675, often in the same form as the wooden parts that they replaced. Eventually, as on the tea clipper Cutty Sark (below), iron rigging was found to be stronger than the traditional rope. The first "ironclads" were warships whose wooden hulls were protected by iron armour plates. Later ironclads actually had iron hulls. The model opposite is based on the British warship HMS Warrior, launched in 1860, the first battleship built entirely of iron. The plan of the iron paddlesteamer (bottom), built somewhat later, shows that this vessel was a sailing ship; but it also boasted a steam propulsion plant amidships that turned two side paddlewheels. Early iron hulls were made from plates that were painstakingly rivetted together (as below), but by the 20th century vessels began to be welded together, whole sections at a time. The Second World War "liberty ship" was one of the first of these "production-line vessels".

TEA CLIPPER

Steel yard
Iron wire stay
Steel lower mast
Steel bowsprit
Wooden planking with copper sheathing
Forged iron anchor

RIVETTED PLATES

Pan head rivet
Plate
Button head rivet (snap head)
Seam

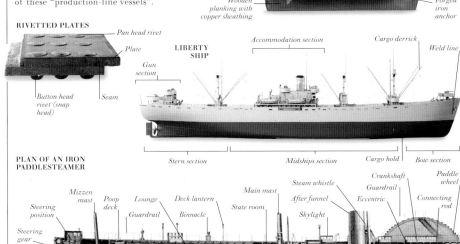

LIBERTY SHIP

Gun section
Accommodation section
Cargo derrick
Weld line
Stern section
Midships section
Cargo hold
Bow section

PLAN OF AN IRON PADDLESTEAMER

Steering position
Steering gear
Stern
Vertical frame ladder
Mast step
Rudder
Rudder post
Heel of rudder post
Mizzen mast
Poop deck
Guardrail
Lounge
Deck lantern
Binnacle
Main mast
State room
Steam whistle
After funnel
Skylight
Crankshaft
Guardrail
Eccentric
Paddle wheel
Connecting rod

Bar keel
Afterpeak
Cabin
Tank
Main mast step
Donkey boiler
Box boiler
Foundation
Reversing wheel
Bottom plate
Side lever
Cylinder

Stern framing

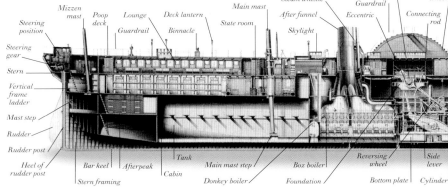

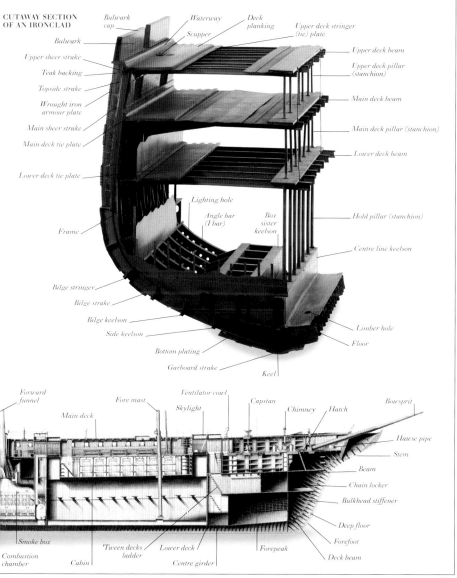

CUTAWAY SECTION OF AN IRONCLAD

Bulwark cap
Waterway
Deck planking
Upper deck stringer (tie) plate
Bulwark
Upper sheer strake
Teak backing
Topside strake
Wrought iron armour plate
Main sheer strake
Main deck tie plate
Lower deck tie plate
Frame
Bilge stringer
Bilge strake
Bilge keelson
Side keelson
Bottom plating
Garboard strake
Keel
Lighting hole
Angle bar (I bar)
Box sister keelson
Upper deck beam
Upper deck pillar (stanchion)
Main deck beam
Main deck pillar (stanchion)
Lower deck beam
Hold pillar (stanchion)
Centre line keelson
Limber hole
Floor

Forward funnel
Main deck
Fore mast
Skylight
Ventilator cowl
Capstan
Chimney
Hatch
Bowsprit
Hawse pipe
Stem
Beam
Chain locker
Bulkhead stiffener
Deep floor
Forefoot
Deck beam
Smoke box
Combustion chamber
Cabin
'Tween decks ladder
Lower deck
Centre girder
Forepeak

The battleship

IN THE EARLY YEARS OF THE 20TH CENTURY, sea warfare – attacking enemy vessels or defending a ship – was revolutionized by the introduction of Dreadnought-type battleships like the Brazilian vessel below. These new ships combined the latest advances in steam propulsion, gunnery, and armour plating. The gun turret was designed to fire shells over huge distances. It was protected by armour 30 cm (12 in) thick. The measurements given for the guns of this ship refer to the bore diameter. Where "weight" is quoted, this is the weight of the shell that the gun fires. Torpedoes – as portrayed on the upper cigarette card (right) – were self-propelled underwater missiles, often steered by gyro-control. Depth charges were designed in the First World War for use against submerged U-boats. They are canisters filled with explosives that are detonated by depth-sensitive pistols. The lower cigarette card shows depth charges being fired by a "thrower", fired from a torpedo tube, and rolled from the stern. Ship's shields were fitted to warships from the late 19th century onwards. The shield shown opposite depicts a traditional ship's cannon.

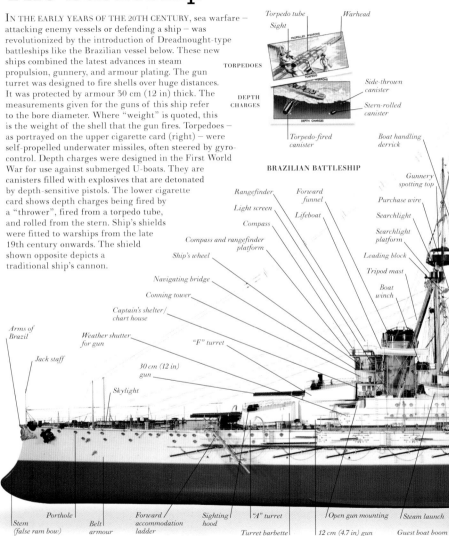

20TH CENTURY WEAPONRY

Torpedo tube
Sight
Warhead

TORPEDOES

Side-thrown canister

DEPTH CHARGES

Stern-rolled canister

Torpedo-fired canister

Boat handling derrick

BRAZILIAN BATTLESHIP

Rangefinder
Forward funnel
Gunnery spotting top
Light screen
Lifeboat
Purchase wire
Compass
Searchlight
Compass and rangefinder platform
Searchlight platform
Ship's wheel
Leading block
Tripod mast
Navigating bridge
Boat winch
Conning tower
Captain's shelter / chart house
Arms of Brazil
Weather shutter for gun
"F" turret
Jack staff
30 cm (12 in) gun
Skylight

Stem (false ram bow)
Porthole
Belt armour
Forward accommodation ladder
Sighting hood
"A" turret
Turret barbette
Open gun mounting
12 cm (4.7 in) gun
Steam launch
Guest boat boom

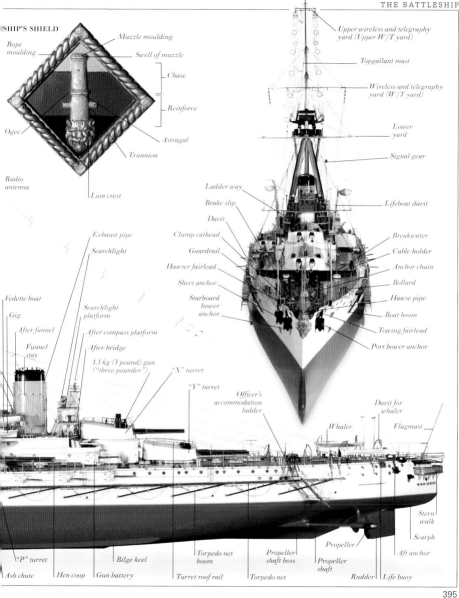

SHIP'S SHIELD

Rope moulding

Muzzle moulding

Swell of muzzle

Chase

Reinforce

Ogee

Astragal

Trunnion

Lion crest

Radio antenna

Upper wireless and telegraphy yard (Upper W/T yard)

Topgallant mast

Wireless and telegraphy yard (W/T yard)

Lower yard

Signal gear

Ladder way

Brake slip

Davit

Clump cathead

Guardrail

Hawser fairlead

Sheet anchor

Starboard bower anchor

Lifeboat davit

Breakwater

Cable holder

Anchor chain

Bollard

Hawse pipe

Boat boom

Towing fairlead

Port bower anchor

Exhaust pipe

Searchlight

Vedette boat

Gig

After funnel

Funnel stay

Searchlight platform

After compass platform

After bridge

1.3 kg (3 pound) gun ("three pounder")

"X" turret

"Y" turret

Officer's accommodation ladder

Whaler

Davit for whaler

Flagmast

"P" turret

Ash chute

Hen coop

Bilge keel

Gun battery

Torpedo net boom

Turret roof rail

Torpedo net

Propeller shaft boss

Propeller shaft

Propeller

Rudder

Aft anchor

Life buoy

Stern walk

Scarph

Frigates and submarines

From the mid-19th century, armoured ships provided a new challenge to enemy craft. In response, huge revolving gun turrets were developed. These could fire in any direction, could be loaded from the breech very rapidly, and, instead of cannonballs, they discharged exploding shells. Modern fighting ships, like the frigate, combine heavy ship-borne armament with light helicopter weaponry. Submarines function below the surface of the sea. Their speed and ability to fire missiles from under water are their major assets. The nuclear submarine can stay under water for several years without refuelling.

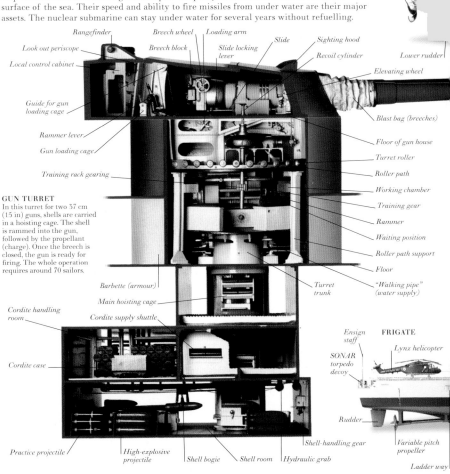

Stabilizer fin

Aft hydroplane

Propeller

Rangefinder
Loading arm
Breech wheel
Slide
Sighting hood
Look out periscope
Breech block
Slide locking lever
Recoil cylinder
Lower rudder
Local control cabinet
Elevating wheel

Guide for gun loading cage

Blast bag (breeches)

Rammer lever
Floor of gun house
Gun loading cage
Turret roller
Roller path
Training rack gearing
Working chamber

GUN TURRET
In this turret for two 37 cm (15 in) guns, shells are carried in a hoisting cage. The shell is rammed into the gun, followed by the propellant (charge). Once the breech is closed, the gun is ready for firing. The whole operation requires around 70 sailors.

Training gear
Rammer
Waiting position
Roller path support
Floor

Barbette (armour)
Turret trunk
"Walking pipe" (water supply)
Main hoisting cage
Cordite handling room
Cordite supply shuttle

Ensign staff

FRIGATE

Lynx helicopter

SONAR torpedo decoy

Cordite case

Rudder

Practice projectile
High-explosive projectile
Shell bogie
Shell room
Hydraulic grab
Shell-handling gear
Variable pitch propeller
Ladder way

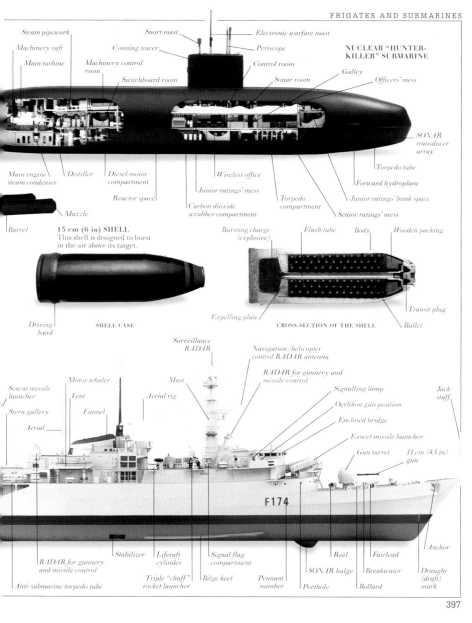

Steam pipework
Machinery raft
Main turbine
Machinery control room
Switchboard room
Conning tower
Snort mast
Periscope
Electronic warfare mast
Control room

NUCLEAR "HUNTER-KILLER" SUBMARINE

Sonar room
Galley
Officers' mess
SONAR transducer array
Torpedo tube
Forward hydroplane
Junior ratings' bunk space
Senior ratings' mess
Torpedo compartment
Carbon dioxide scrubber compartment
Junior ratings' mess
Wireless office
Reactor space
Diesel motor compartment
Distiller
Main engine steam condenser

Barrel
Muzzle

15 cm (6 in) SHELL
This shell is designed to burst in the air above its target.

Driving band
SHELL CASE

Bursting charge (explosive)
Expelling plate
Flash tube
Body
Wooden packing
Transit plug
Bullet
CROSS-SECTION OF THE SHELL

Surveillance RADAR
Navigation/helicopter control RADAR antenna
RADAR for gunnery and missile control
Mast
Signalling lamp
Oerlikon gun position
Enclosed bridge
Exocet missile launcher
Gun turret
11 cm (4.5 in) gun
Jack staff

Seacat missile launcher
Motor whaler
Vent
Aerial rig
Funnel
Stern gallery
Aerial

F174

RADAR for gunnery and missile control
Stabilizer
Liferaft cylinder
Triple "chaff" rocket launcher
Signal flag compartment
Bilge keel
Pennant number
Reel
SONAR bulge
Porthole
Fairlead
Breakwater
Bollard
Anchor
Draught (draft) mark
Anti-submarine torpedo tube

Pioneers of flight

FLIGHT HAS FASCINATED MANKIND for centuries, and countless unsuccessful flying machines have been designed. The first successful flight was made by the French Montgolfier brothers in 1783, when they flew a balloon over Paris. The next major advance was the development of gliders, notably by the Englishman Sir George Cayley, who in 1845 designed the first glider to make a sustained flight, and by the German Otto Lilienthal, who became known as the world's first pilot because he managed to achieve controlled flights. However, powered flight did not become a practical possibility until the invention of lightweight, petrol-driven internal combustion engines at the end of the 19th century. Then, in 1903, the American brothers Orville and Wilbur Wright made the first powered flight in their Wright Flyer biplane, which used a four-cylinder, petrol-driven engine. Aircraft design advanced rapidly, and in 1909 the Frenchman Louis Blériot made his pioneering flight across the English Channel (see pp. 400-401). The American Glenn Curtiss also achieved several "firsts" in his Model-D Pusher and its variants, most notably winning the world's first competition for airspeed at Reims in 1909.

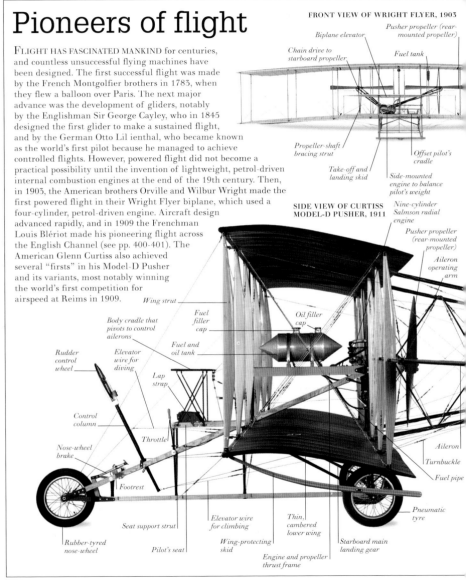

FRONT VIEW OF WRIGHT FLYER, 1903

Pusher propeller (rear-mounted propeller)

Biplane elevator

Chain drive to starboard propeller

Fuel tank

Propeller-shaft bracing strut

Offset pilot's cradle

Take-off and landing skid

Side-mounted engine to balance pilot's weight

SIDE VIEW OF CURTISS MODEL-D PUSHER, 1911

Nine-cylinder Salmson radial engine

Pusher propeller (rear-mounted propeller)

Aileron operating arm

Wing strut

Fuel filler cap

Oil filler cap

Body cradle that pivots to control ailerons

Fuel and oil tank

Rudder control wheel

Elevator wire for diving

Lap strap

Control column

Throttle

Nose-wheel brake

Aileron

Turnbuckle

Fuel pipe

Footrest

Pneumatic tyre

Rubber-tyred nose-wheel

Seat support strut

Pilot's seat

Elevator wire for climbing

Wing-protecting skid

Thin, cambered lower wing

Engine and propeller thrust frame

Starboard main landing gear

SIDE VIEW OF WRIGHT FLYER, 1903

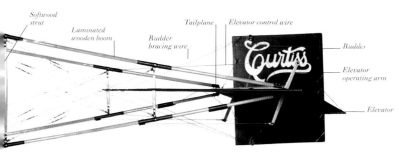

Plain cotton fabric

Interplane strut

Front diagonal strut

Water-filled radiator

Wing warping wire

Chain drive

Pusher propeller (rear-mounted propeller)

Rigid leading edge

Steel hub

Elevator drive wheel

Water pipe

Steel propeller shaft

Rudder

Front-mounted biplane elevator

Bracing wire

Landing skid

Elevator control cable

Pilot's cradle

Magneto

Rudder control cable

Braced rudder strut

Warping connection strut

Four-cylinder 12-HP engine

Propeller-shaft bracing strut

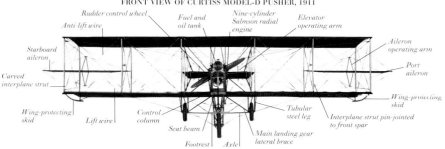

Softwood strut

Laminated wooden boom

Rudder bracing wire

Tailplane

Elevator control wire

Rudder

Elevator operating arm

Elevator

FRONT VIEW OF CURTISS MODEL-D PUSHER, 1911

Rudder control wheel

Fuel and oil tank

Nine-cylinder Salmson radial engine

Elevator operating arm

Anti-lift wire

Starboard aileron

Aileron operating arm

Port aileron

Carved interplane strut

Wing-protecting skid

Wing-protecting skid

Lift wire

Control column

Seat beam

Footrest

Axle

Main landing gear lateral brace

Tubular steel leg

Interplane strut pin-jointed to front spar

Early monoplanes

RUMPLER MONOPLANE, 1908

MONOPLANES HAVE ONE WING on each side of the fuselage. The principal disadvantage of this arrangement in early, wooden-framed aircraft was that single wings were weak and required strong wires to brace them to king-posts above and below the fuselage. However, single wings also had advantages: they experienced less drag than multiple wings, allowing greater speed; they also made aircraft more manoeuvrable because single wings were easier to warp (twist) than double wings, and warping the wings was how pilots controlled the roll of early aircraft. By 1912, the French pilot Louis Blériot had used a monoplane to make the first flight across the English Channel, and the Briton Robert Blackburn and the Frenchman Armand Deperdussin had proved the greater speed of monoplanes. However, a spate of crashes caused by broken wings discouraged monoplane production, except in Germany, where all-metal monoplanes were developed in 1917. The wings of all-metal monoplanes did not need strengthening by struts or bracing wires, but despite this, such planes were not widely adopted until the 1930s.

FRONT VIEW OF BLACKBURN MONOPLANE, 1912

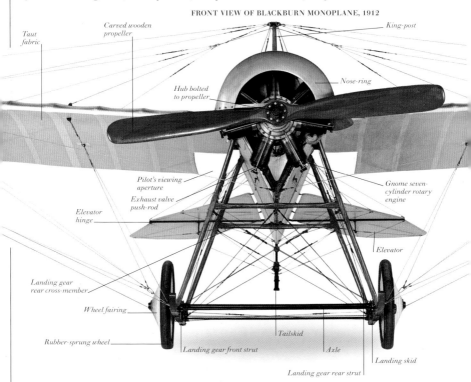

Taut fabric

Carved wooden propeller

King-post

Nose-ring

Hub bolted to propeller

Pilot's viewing aperture

Exhaust valve push-rod

Gnome seven-cylinder rotary engine

Elevator hinge

Elevator

Landing gear rear cross-member

Wheel fairing

Rubber-sprung wheel

Tailskid

Landing gear front strut

Axle

Landing skid

Landing gear rear strut

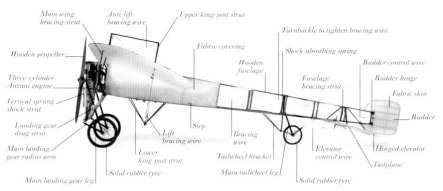

Main wing bracing-strut

Anti-lift bracing wire

Upper king-post strut

Fabric covering

Turnbuckle to tighten bracing wire

Wooden propeller

Wooden fuselage

Shock-absorbing spring

Rudder control wire

Three-cylinder Anzani engine

Fuselage bracing strut

Rudder hinge

Fabric skin

Vertical sprung shock-strut

Rudder

Landing gear drag strut

Step

Lift bracing wire

Main landing gear radius arm

Bracing wire

Elevator control wire

Hinged elevator

Lower king-post strut

Tailwheel bracket

Tailplane

Main landing gear leg

Solid rubber tyre

Main tailwheel leg

Solid rubber tyre

SIDE VIEW OF BLÉRIOT XI, 1909

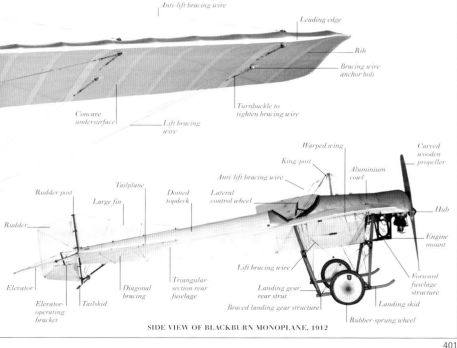

Anti-lift bracing wire

Leading edge

Rib

Bracing wire anchor bolt

Concave undersurface

Turnbuckle to tighten bracing wire

Lift bracing wire

Warped wing

Carved wooden propeller

King-post

Aluminium cowl

Anti-lift bracing wire

Lateral control wheel

Rudder post

Tailplane

Domed topdeck

Hub

Large fin

Engine mount

Rudder

Elevator

Diagonal bracing

Triangular-section rear fuselage

Lift bracing wire

Forward fuselage structure

Landing gear rear strut

Landing skid

Elevator-operating bracket

Tailskid

Braced landing gear structure

Rubber-sprung wheel

SIDE VIEW OF BLACKBURN MONOPLANE, 1912

Biplanes and triplanes

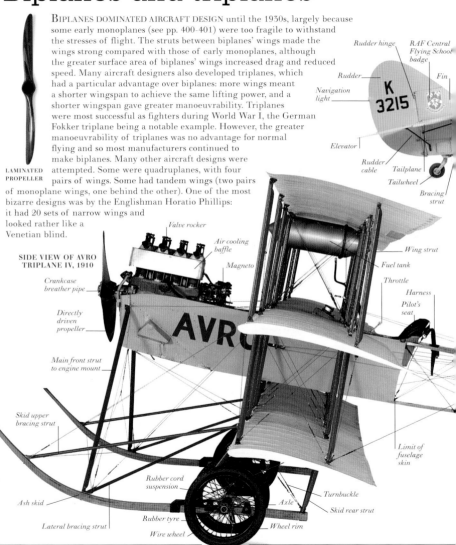

BIPLANES DOMINATED AIRCRAFT DESIGN until the 1930s, largely because some early monoplanes (see pp. 400-401) were too fragile to withstand the stresses of flight. The struts between biplanes' wings made the wings strong compared with those of early monoplanes, although the greater surface area of biplanes' wings increased drag and reduced speed. Many aircraft designers also developed triplanes, which had a particular advantage over biplanes: more wings meant a shorter wingspan to achieve the same lifting power, and a shorter wingspan gave greater manoeuvrability. Triplanes were most successful as fighters during World War I, the German Fokker triplane being a notable example. However, the greater manoeuvrability of triplanes was no advantage for normal flying and so most manufacturers continued to make biplanes. Many other aircraft designs were attempted. Some were quadruplanes, with four pairs of wings. Some had tandem wings (two pairs of monoplane wings, one behind the other). One of the most bizarre designs was by the Englishman Horatio Phillips: it had 20 sets of narrow wings and looked rather like a Venetian blind.

LAMINATED PROPELLER

Rudder hinge

RAF Central Flying School badge

Rudder

Fin

Navigation light

K 3215

Elevator

Rudder cable

Tailplane

Tailwheel

Bracing strut

SIDE VIEW OF AVRO TRIPLANE IV, 1910

Valve rocker

Air cooling baffle

Magneto

Wing strut

Fuel tank

Throttle

Harness

Pilot's seat

Crankcase breather pipe

Directly driven propeller

AVRO

Main front strut to engine mount

Skid upper bracing strut

Limit of fuselage skin

Ash skid

Rubber cord suspension

Turnbuckle

Axle

Skid rear strut

Lateral bracing strut

Rubber tyre

Wheel rim

Wire wheel

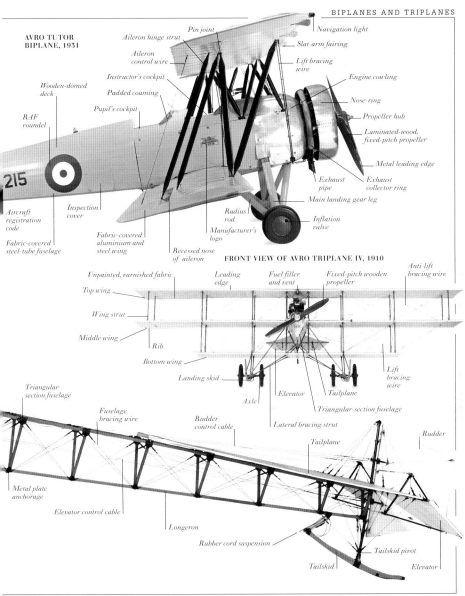

**AVRO TUTOR
BIPLANE, 1931**

Pin joint

Aileron hinge strut

Navigation light

Aileron control wire

Slat-arm fairing

Lift bracing wire

Instructor's cockpit

Engine cowling

Wooden-domed deck

Padded coaming

Nose-ring

Pupil's cockpit

Propeller hub

RAF roundel

Laminated-wood, fixed-pitch propeller

Metal leading edge

215

Exhaust pipe

Exhaust collector ring

Aircraft registration code

Inspection cover

Main landing gear leg

Fabric-covered steel-tube fuselage

Radius rod

Inflation valve

Fabric-covered aluminium and steel wing

Manufacturer's logo

Recessed nose of aileron

FRONT VIEW OF AVRO TRIPLANE IV, 1910

Unpainted, varnished fabric

Leading edge

Fuel filler and vent

Fixed-pitch wooden propeller

Anti-lift bracing wire

Top wing

Wing strut

Middle wing

Rib

Bottom wing

Landing skid

Axle

Elevator

Tailplane

Lift bracing wire

Triangular-section fuselage

Triangular-section fuselage

Fuselage bracing wire

Rudder control cable

Lateral bracing strut

Tailplane

Rudder

Metal plate anchorage

Elevator control cable

Longeron

Rubber cord suspension

Tailskid

Tailskid pivot

Elevator

World War I aircraft

FLYING HELMET

WHEN WORLD WAR I STARTED in 1914, the main purpose of military aircraft was reconnaissance. The British-built BE 2, of which the BE 2B was a variant, was well-suited to this duty; it was very stable in flight, allowing the occupants to study the terrain, take photographs, and make notes. The BE 2 was also one of the first aircraft to drop bombs. One of the biggest problems for aircraft designers during the war was mounting machine-guns. On aircraft that had front-mounted propellers, the field of fire was restricted by the propeller and other parts of the aircraft. The problem was solved in 1915 by the Dutchman Anthony Fokker, who designed an interrupter gear that prevented a machine-gun from firing when a propeller blade passed in front of the barrel. The German LVG CVI had a forward-firing gun to the right of the engine, as well as a rear-cockpit gun, and a bombing capability. It was one of the most versatile aircraft of the war.

PORT WINGS FROM A BE 2B

Interplane-strut attachment
Intermediate leading-edge rib
Airspeed-indicator tube
Leading edge
Wingtip
Airspeed-indicator tube
Main rib
Root
Interplane strut
Trailing edge
Airspeed pilot tube
Interplane-strut attachment
Upper side of lower wing
Attachment lug

BE 2B, 1914

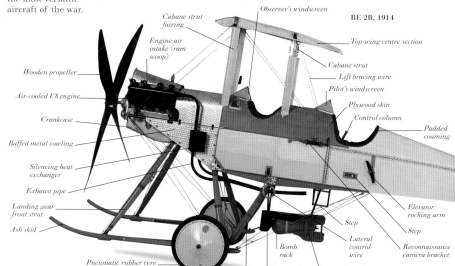

Observer's windscreen
Cabane strut fairing
Engine air intake (ram scoop)
Top-wing centre section
Cabane strut
Lift bracing wire
Pilot's windscreen
Wooden propeller
Air-cooled V8 engine
Plywood skin
Control column
Crankcase
Padded coaming
Buffed metal cowling
Silencing heat exchanger
Exhaust pipe
Elevator rocking arm
Landing gear front strut
Step
Ash skid
Step
Lateral control wire
Reconnaissance camera bracket
Pneumatic rubber tyre
Bomb rack
Wheel cover
V-strut
Lower-wing attachment
112 lb (51 kg) bomb

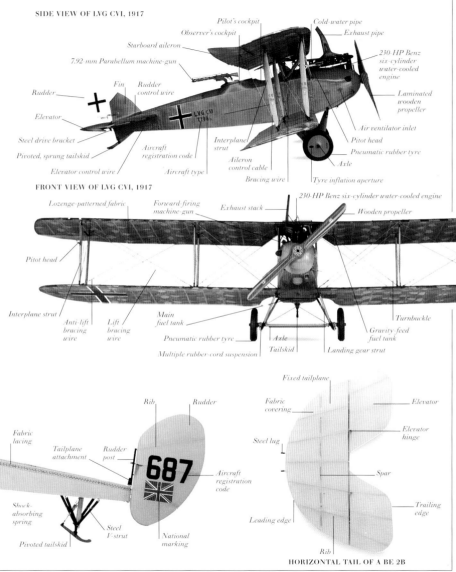

SIDE VIEW OF LVG CVI, 1917

Pilot's cockpit

Observer's cockpit

Cold-water pipe

Exhaust pipe

Starboard aileron

7.92-mm Parabellum machine-gun

230-HP Benz six-cylinder water-cooled engine

Fin

Rudder control wire

Rudder

Elevator

Laminated wooden propeller

Steel drive bracket

Air ventilator inlet

Pitot head

Pivoted, sprung tailskid

Pneumatic rubber tyre

Aircraft registration code

Interplane strut

Elevator control wire

Aileron control cable

Axle

Aircraft type

Bracing wire

Tyre inflation aperture

FRONT VIEW OF LVG CVI, 1917

Lozenge-patterned fabric

Forward-firing machine-gun

Exhaust stack

230-HP Benz six-cylinder water-cooled engine

Wooden propeller

Pitot head

Interplane strut

Anti-lift bracing wire

Lift bracing wire

Main fuel tank

Pneumatic rubber tyre

Axle

Multiple rubber-cord suspension

Tailskid

Landing gear strut

Turnbuckle

Gravity-feed fuel tank

Fixed tailplane

Fabric covering

Elevator

Rib

Rudder

Elevator hinge

Fabric lacing

Steel lug

Tailplane attachment

Rudder post

687

Aircraft registration code

Spar

Shock-absorbing spring

Steel V-strut

Trailing edge

Leading edge

Pivoted tailskid

National marking

Rib

HORIZONTAL TAIL OF A BE 2B

Early passenger aircraft

UNTIL THE 1930s, most passenger aircraft were biplanes, with two pairs of wings and a wooden or metal framework covered with fabric or, sometimes, plywood. Such aircraft were restricted to low speeds and low altitudes because of the drag on their wings. Many had an open cockpit, situated behind or in front of an enclosed – but unpressurized – cabin that carried a maximum of ten people. The passengers usually sat in wicker chairs that were not bolted to the floor, and the journey could be bumpy when flying through turbulence. Warm clothing, and ear plugs to reduce the effects of prolonged noise, were often required. During the 1930s, powerful, streamlined, all-metal monoplanes, such as the Lockheed Electra shown here, became widespread. By 1939, the advent of pressurized cabins allowed fast flights at high altitudes, where there is less turbulence.

Flying boats were still necessary on many routes until 1945 because of inadequate runways and the frequency of emergency sea-landings. World War II, however, resulted in enough good runways being built for land-planes to become standard on all major airline routes.

Green starboard navigation light

Flush-riveted metal-skinned wing

Leading edge

Fuel-jettison valve

Static discharge wick

Split flap in landing position

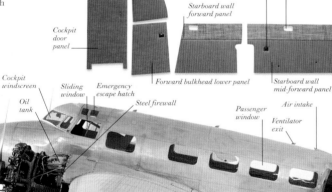

PASSENGER CABIN TRIM

Roof trim panel

Forward bulkhead upper panel

Passenger service-panel aperture

Ash-tray

Starboard wall forward panel

Cockpit door panel

Forward bulkhead lower panel

Starboard wall mid-forward panel

SIDE VIEW OF LOCKHEED ELECTRA, 1934

Cockpit windscreen

Sliding window

Emergency escape hatch

Steel firewall

Passenger window

Air intake

Oil tank

Ventilator exit

Nose

Propeller pitch-change cylinder

Blade counterweight

Spinner mounting disc

Variable-pitch propeller

Exhaust collector ring

Landing gear door

Electrically driven split flap

Pratt & Whitney nine-cylinder radial engine

Red port navigation light

Exhaust pipe

Passenger door

Main landing gear

Brake pipe

Static discharge wick

Aileron

Aluminium wheel

Mudguard

Metal-skinned wing

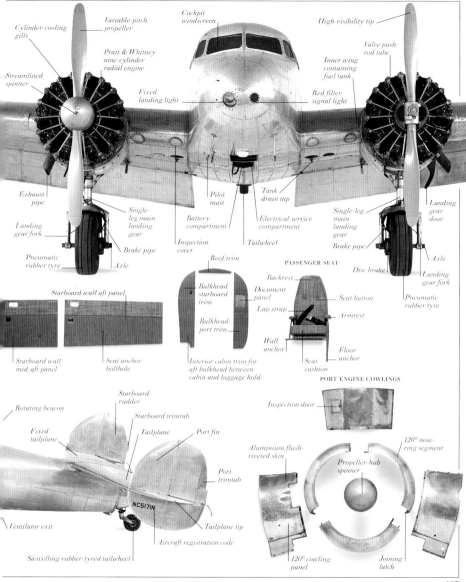

Cockpit windscreen

Variable-pitch propeller

High-visibility tip

Cylinder-cooling gills

Valve push-rod tube

Pratt & Whitney nine-cylinder radial engine

Inner wing containing fuel tank

Streamlined spinner

Fixed landing light

Red filter signal light

Exhaust pipe

Single-leg main landing gear

Pilot mast

Tank drain tap

Single-leg main landing gear

Landing gear door

Landing gear fork

Battery compartment

Electrical service compartment

Brake pipe

Axle

Pneumatic rubber tyre

Brake pipe

Axle

Inspection cover

Tailwheel

Disc brake

Landing gear fork

Pneumatic rubber tyre

PASSENGER SEAT

Roof trim

Backrest

Starboard wall aft panel

Bulkhead starboard trim

Document panel

Seat button

Lap strap

Armrest

Bulkhead port trim

Wall anchor

Floor anchor

Starboard wall mid-aft panel

Seat anchor bolthole

Interior cabin trim for aft bulkhead between cabin and luggage hold

Seat cushion

PORT ENGINE COWLINGS

Rotating beacon

Starboard rudder

Inspection door

Starboard trimtab

Fixed tailplane

Tailplane

Port fin

Aluminium flush-riveted skin

120° nose-ring segment

Propeller-hub spinner

Port trimtab

NC517IN

Ventilator exit

Tailplane tip

Aircraft registration code

Swivelling rubber-tyred tailwheel

120° cowling panel

Joining latch

World War II aircraft

WHEN WORLD WAR II began in 1939, air forces had already replaced most of their fabric-skinned biplanes with all-metal, stressed-skin monoplanes. Aircraft played a far greater role in military operations during World War II than ever before. The wide range of aircraft duties, and the introduction of radar tracking and guidance systems, put pressure on designers to improve aircraft performance. The main areas of improvement were speed, range, and engine power. Bombers became larger and more powerful – converting from two to four engines – in order to carry a heavier bomb load; the US B-17 Flying Fortress could carry up to 6.2 tonnes (6.1 tons) of bombs over a distance of about 3,200 km (2,000 miles). Some aircraft increased their range by using drop tanks (fuel tanks that were jettisoned when empty to reduce drag). Fighters needed speed and manoeuvrability: the Hawker Tempest shown here had a maximum speed of 700 kph (435 mph), and was one of the few Allied aircraft capable of catching the German jet-powered V1 "flying bomb". By 1944, Britain had introduced its first turbojet-powered aircraft, the Gloster Meteor fighter, and Germany had introduced the fastest fighter in the world, the turbojet-powered Me 262, which had a maximum speed of 868 kph (540 mph).

PROPELLER

High-visibility yellow tip

Light-alloy propeller spinner

Variable-pitch aluminium-alloy blade

COMPONENTS OF A HAWKER TEMPEST MARK V, c.1943

Radiator-access cowling

Lower side-cowling

Upper side-cowling

STARBOARD ENGINE COWLINGS

Cowling fastener

2,400-HP Napier Sabre 24-cylinder engine

Cartridge starter

Propeller governor

Radiator header tank

Propeller drive shaft

Distributor

Ejector exhaust

Magneto

Starter motor

Engine top cowling

Upper side-cowling

Lower side-cowling

Radiator-access cowling

Cowling fastener

PORT ENGINE COWLINGS

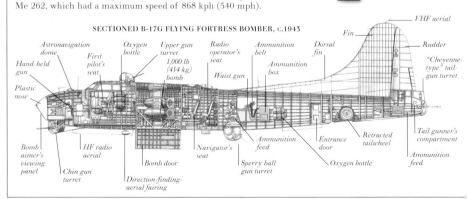

SECTIONED B-17G FLYING FORTRESS BOMBER, c.1943

VHF aerial

Fin

Rudder

"Cheyenne-type" tail-gun turret

Astronavigation dome

Oxygen bottle

Upper gun turret

Radio operator's seat

Ammunition belt

Dorsal fin

First pilot's seat

1,000 lb (454 kg) bomb

Ammunition box

Waist gun

Hand-held gun

Plastic nose

Tail gunner's compartment

Bomb aimer's viewing panel

HF radio aerial

Navigator's seat

Ammunition feed

Entrance door

Retracted tailwheel

Ammunition feed

Chin gun turret

Bomb door

Sperry ball gun turret

Oxygen bottle

Direction-finding aerial fairing

PORT WING UNDERSIDE

Flap

Cockpit starboard access panel

Starboard tailplane

Landing gear door

Elevator hinge

Wing front fillet panel

Wing rear fillet panel

Starboard elevator

Elevator control rod

Wing fillet panel

Leading edge

Canopy rail

Seat pan

Harness strap

FUSELAGE

Canopy rail

VHF radio whip aerial

Fin

Tail fairing

Trimtab operating rod

Dorsal fin

Tailplane root

Rudder

Flat, bulletproof windscreen

Armoured seat back

Cockpit front belly panel

Cockpit centre belly panel

Tail band

Tailplane front attachment bracket

Tailplane rear attachment bracket

Gyroscopic gunsight

Plastic cockpit canopy

RAF C1-type roundel

Port elevator trimtab

Rear spar trunnion

Cockpit rear belly panel

Trailing edge

Wing fillet panel

Camouflage

Port tailplane

TAIL

Wing front fillet panel

Wing rear fillet panel

Outboard ammunition-feed blister

Cockpit port access panel

Trailing edge

Wing upper surface

HAWKER TEMPEST MARK V FIGHTER, c.1943

Aileron

Hispano Mark V 20-mm cannon

Armour-plated seat back

Rudder

Dorsal fin

Headrest

Gyroscopic gunsight

Squadron code

Exhaust pipe

RAF C1-type roundel

Propeller spinner

RAF B-type roundel

Engine air intake

Radiator

Yellow-painted leading edge

PORT WING

Wingtip

Radiator outlet

Pitot head

Instant-identification "invasion" stripes

Retracted tailwheel

Rudder trimtab

Modern piston aero-engines

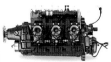

MID WEST TWO-STROKE, THREE-CYLINDER ENGINE

PISTON ENGINES today are used mainly to power the vast numbers of light aircraft and microlights, as well as crop-sprayers and crop-dusters, small helicopters, and fire-bombers (which dump water on large fires). Virtually all heavier aircraft are now powered by jet engines. Modern piston aero-engines work on the same basic principles as the engine used by the Wright brothers in the first powered flight in 1903. However, today's engines are more sophisticated than earlier engines. For example, modern aero-engines may use a two-stroke or a four-stroke combustion cycle; they may have from one to nine air- or water-cooled cylinders, which may be arranged horizontally, in-line, in V formation, or radially; and they may drive the aircraft's propeller either directly or through a reduction gearbox. One of the more unconventional types of modern aero-engine is the rotary engine shown here, which has a trilobate (three-sided) rotor spinning in a chamber shaped like a fat figure-of-eight.

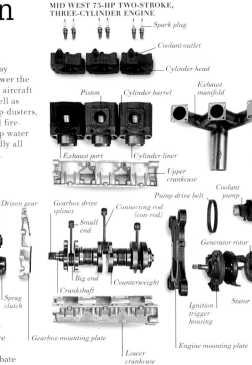

MID WEST 75-HP TWO-STROKE, THREE-CYLINDER ENGINE

Spark plug
Coolant outlet
Cylinder head
Exhaust manifold
Piston
Cylinder barrel
Exhaust port
Cylinder liner
Upper crankcase
Coolant pump
Pump drive belt
Reduction gearbox
Driven gear
Gearbox drive splines
Connecting rod (con-rod)
Small end
Generator rotor
Propeller drive flange
Big end
Counterweight
Crankshaft
Stator
Torsional vibration damper
Sprag clutch
Ignition trigger housing
Gearbox mounting plate
Engine mounting plate
Lower crankcase

ROTOR AND HOUSINGS OF A MID WEST SINGLE-ROTOR ENGINE

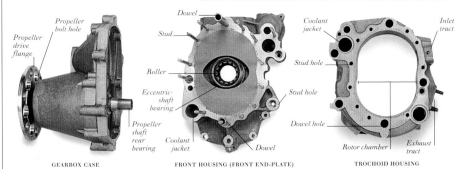

Propeller bolt hole
Propeller drive flange
Dowel
Stud
Roller
Eccentric-shaft bearing
Propeller shaft rear bearing
Coolant jacket
Dowel
Coolant jacket
Stud hole
Stud hole
Dowel hole
Inlet tract
Rotor chamber
Exhaust tract

GEARBOX CASE   **FRONT HOUSING (FRONT END-PLATE)**   **TROCHOID HOUSING**

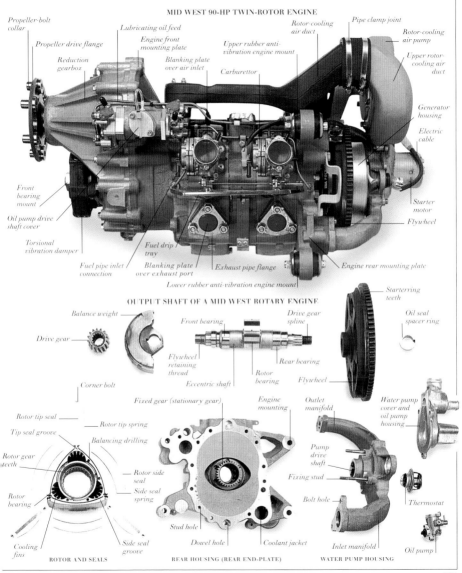

MID WEST 90-HP TWIN-ROTOR ENGINE

Propeller-bolt collar

Propeller drive flange

Reduction gearbox

Lubricating oil feed

Engine front mounting plate

Blanking plate over air inlet

Upper rubber anti-vibration engine mount

Carburettor

Rotor-cooling air duct

Pipe clamp joint

Rotor-cooling air pump

Upper rotor-cooling air duct

Generator housing

Electric cable

Starter motor

Flywheel

Engine rear mounting plate

Front bearing mount

Oil pump drive shaft cover

Torsional vibration damper

Fuel pipe inlet connection

Fuel drip tray

Blanking plate over exhaust port

Exhaust pipe flange

Lower rubber anti-vibration engine mount

OUTPUT SHAFT OF A MID WEST ROTARY ENGINE

Balance weight

Drive gear

Front bearing

Drive gear spline

Starter ring teeth

Oil seal spacer ring

Flywheel retaining thread

Rear bearing

Eccentric shaft

Rotor bearing

Flywheel

Corner bolt

Rotor tip seal

Tip seal groove

Rotor gear teeth

Rotor bearing

Cooling fins

Rotor tip spring

Balancing drilling

Rotor side seal

Side seal spring

Side seal groove

ROTOR AND SEALS

Fixed gear (stationary gear)

Engine mounting

Stud hole

Dowel hole

Coolant jacket

REAR HOUSING (REAR END-PLATE)

Outlet manifold

Pump drive shaft

Fixing stud

Bolt hole

Inlet manifold

Water pump cover and oil pump housing

Thermostat

Oil pump

WATER PUMP HOUSING

411

Modern jetliners 1

BAE-146 JETLINER

MODERN JETLINERS HAVE ENABLED ordinary people to travel to places where once only the wealthy could afford to go. Compared with the first jetliners (which were introduced in the 1940s), modern ones are much quieter, burn fuel more efficiently, and produce less air pollution. These advances are largely due to the replacement of turbojet engines with turbofan engines (see pp. 418-419). The greater power of turbofan engines at low speeds enables modern jetliners to carry more fuel and passengers than turbojet aircraft; a modern Boeing 747-400 (popularly known as a "jumbo jet") can fly 400 people for 13,700 km (8,500 miles) without needing to refuel. Jetliners fly at high altitudes, typically cruising at 8,000-11,000 m (26,000-36,000 ft), where they can use fuel efficiently and usually avoid bad weather. The pilot always controls the aircraft during take-off and landing, but at other times the aircraft is usually controlled by an autopilot. Autopilots are complex on-board mechanisms that detect deviations from an aircraft's route and make appropriate adjustments to the flight controls. Flight decks are also equipped with radars that warn pilots of approaching hazards, such as mountain ranges, bad weather, and other aircraft.

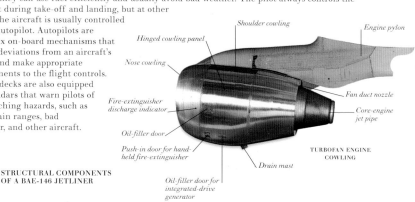

Shoulder cowling

Hinged cowling panel

Engine pylon

Nose cowling

Fan duct nozzle

Fire-extinguisher discharge indicator

Core-engine jet pipe

Oil-filler door

Push-in door for hand-held fire-extinguisher

Drain mast

TURBOFAN ENGINE COWLING

STRUCTURAL COMPONENTS OF A BAE-146 JETLINER

Oil-filler door for integrated-drive generator

FUSELAGE NOSE-SECTION

FUSELAGE MID-SECTION

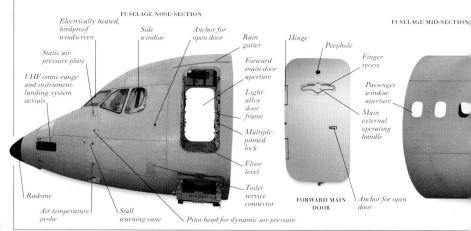

Electrically heated, birdproof windscreen

Side window

Anchor for open door

Rain gutter

Hinge

Peephole

Static air-pressure plate

Forward main door aperture

Finger recess

VHF omni-range and instrument-landing-system aerials

Light-alloy door frame

Passenger window aperture

Multiple-pinned lock

Main external operating handle

Floor level

Radome

Toilet service connector

Air temperature probe

Stall warning vane

Pitot head for dynamic air pressure

FORWARD MAIN DOOR

Anchor for open door

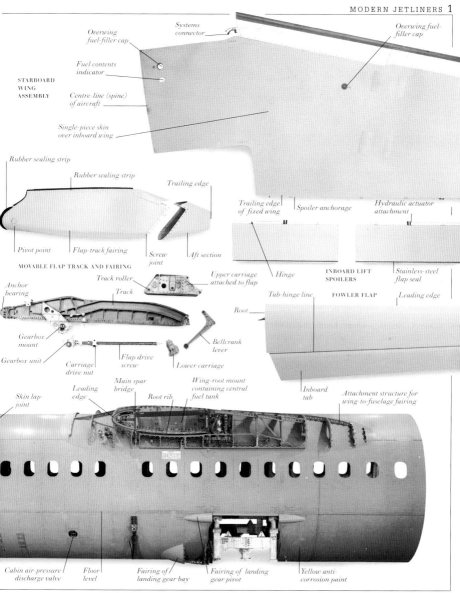

STARBOARD WING ASSEMBLY

Overwing fuel-filler cap

Systems connector

Overwing fuel-filler cap

Fuel contents indicator

Centre-line (spine) of aircraft

Single-piece skin over inboard wing

Rubber sealing strip

Rubber sealing strip

Trailing edge

Trailing edge of fixed wing

Spoiler anchorage

Hydraulic actuator attachment

Pivot point

Flap-track fairing

Screw joint

Aft section

Hinge

INBOARD LIFT SPOILERS

Stainless-steel flap seal

MOVABLE FLAP TRACK AND FAIRING

Upper carriage attached to flap

Track roller

Tab-hinge line

FOWLER FLAP

Leading edge

Anchor bearing

Track

Root

Gearbox mount

Gearbox unit

Carriage drive nut

Flap drive screw

Bellcrank lever

Lower carriage

Skin lap joint

Leading edge

Main spar bridge

Root rib

Wing-root mount containing central fuel tank

Inboard tab

Attachment structure for wing-to-fuselage fairing

Cabin air-pressure discharge valve

Floor level

Fairing of landing gear bay

Fairing of landing gear pivot

Yellow anti-corrosion paint

413

Modern jetliners 2

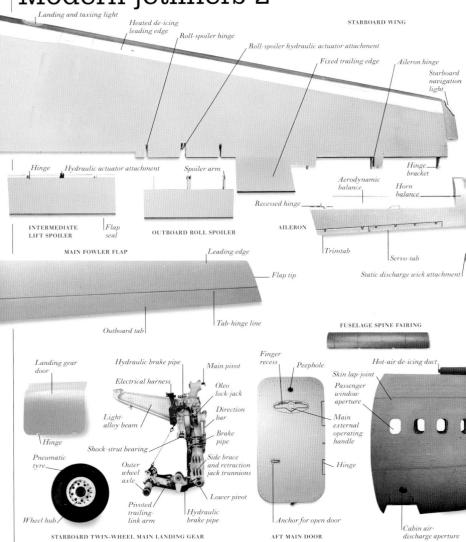

Landing and taxiing light

Heated de-icing leading edge

Roll-spoiler hinge

STARBOARD WING

Roll-spoiler hydraulic actuator attachment

Fixed trailing edge

Aileron hinge

Starboard navigation light

Hinge

Hydraulic actuator attachment

Spoiler arm

Hinge bracket

Aerodynamic balance

Horn balance

Recessed hinge

INTERMEDIATE LIFT SPOILER

Flap seal

OUTBOARD ROLL SPOILER

AILERON

MAIN FOWLER FLAP

Leading edge

Trimtab

Servo-tab

Flap tip

Static discharge wick attachment

FUSELAGE SPINE FAIRING

Outboard tab

Tab-hinge line

Landing gear door

Hydraulic brake pipe

Main pivot

Finger recess

Peephole

Hot-air de-icing duct

Electrical harness

Oleo lock-jack

Skin lap-joint

Passenger window aperture

Light-alloy beam

Direction bar

Brake pipe

Main external operating handle

Hinge

Shock-strut bearing

Pneumatic tyre

Outer wheel axle

Side brace and retraction jack trunnions

Hinge

Lower pivot

Wheel hub

Pivoted trailing-link arm

Hydraulic brake pipe

Anchor for open door

Cabin air-discharge aperture

STARBOARD TWIN-WHEEL MAIN LANDING GEAR

AFT MAIN DOOR

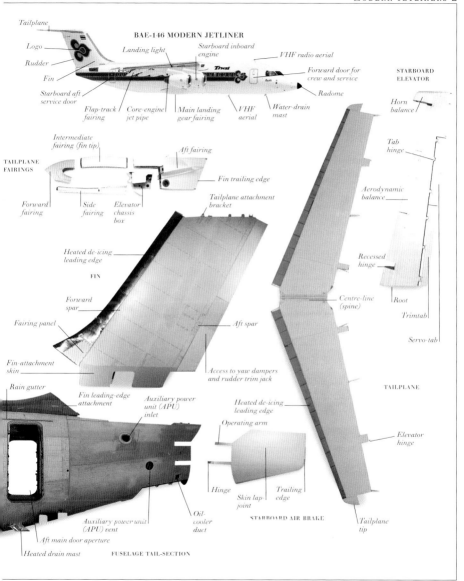

BAE-146 MODERN JETLINER

Tailplane

Logo

Rudder

Fin

Starboard aft service door

Landing light

Flap-track fairing

Core-engine jet pipe

Starboard inboard engine

Main landing gear fairing

VHF aerial

VHF radio aerial

Forward door for crew and service

Radome

Water-drain mast

STARBOARD ELEVATOR

Horn balance

Tab hinge

Aerodynamic balance

Recessed hinge

Root

Trimtab

Servo-tab

TAILPLANE FAIRINGS

Intermediate fairing (fin tip)

Aft fairing

Fin trailing edge

Forward fairing

Side fairing

Elevator chassis box

Tailplane attachment bracket

Heated de-icing leading edge

FIN

Forward spar

Fairing panel

Fin-attachment skin

Aft spar

Access to yaw dampers and rudder trim jack

Centre-line (spine)

TAILPLANE

Rain gutter

Fin leading-edge attachment

Auxiliary power unit (APU) inlet

Heated de-icing leading edge

Operating arm

Hinge

Skin lap-joint

Trailing edge

Auxiliary power unit (APU) vent

Oil-cooler duct

Aft main door aperture

Heated drain mast

FUSELAGE TAIL-SECTION

STARBOARD AIR BRAKE

Elevator hinge

Tailplane tip

Supersonic jetliners

COMPUTER-DESIGNED SST

SUPERSONIC AIRCRAFT FLY FASTER than the speed of sound (Mach 1). There are many supersonic military aircraft, but only two supersonic passenger-carrying aircraft (also called SSTs, or supersonic transports) have been produced: the Russian Tu-144, and Concorde, produced jointly by Britain and France. The Tu-144 was withdrawn in 1978, after only seven months in service. The concorde remained in service from 1976 until 2003, with a break for modifications from July 2000 until October 2001. Its features included a droop nose, which lowered during take-off and landing to aid visibility from the cockpit; the pumping of fuel between forward and aft trim tanks helped stabilize the aircraft. The concorde had a narrow fuselage and shortspan wings to reduce drag during supersonic flight. Its noisy turbojet engines with afterburners enabled it to carry 100 passengers at a cruising speed of Mach 2 at 15,000-18,000 m (50,000-60,000 ft). Once an aircraft is flying faster than Mach 1, it produces a continuous air-pressure wave, which is heard as a "sonic boom".

FRONT VIEW OF CONCORDE

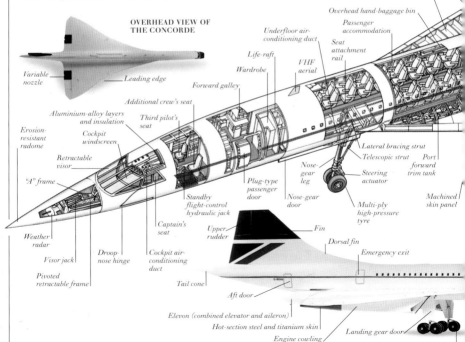

OVERHEAD VIEW OF
THE CONCORDE

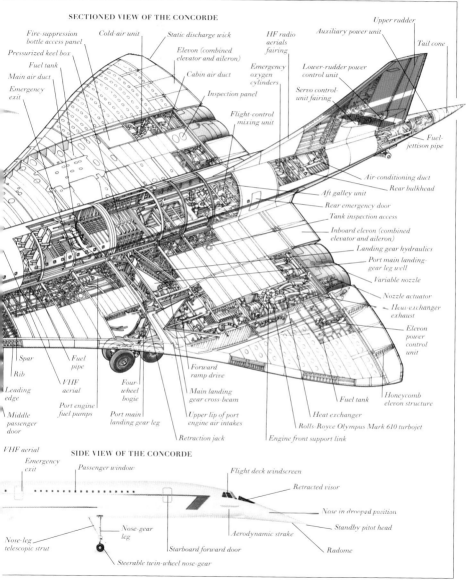

SECTIONED VIEW OF THE CONCORDE

Fire-suppression bottle access panel
Cold-air unit
Static discharge wick
Upper rudder
Auxiliary power unit
Tail cone
Pressurized keel box
Elevon (combined elevator and aileron)
HF radio aerials fairing
Fuel tank
Lower-rudder power control unit
Main air duct
Cabin air duct
Emergency oxygen cylinders
Servo control-unit fairing
Emergency exit
Inspection panel
Flight-control mixing unit
Fuel-jettison pipe
Air-conditioning duct
Rear bulkhead
Aft galley unit
Rear emergency door
Tank inspection access
Inboard elevon (combined elevator and aileron)
Landing gear hydraulics
Port main landing-gear leg well
Variable nozzle
Nozzle actuator
Heat-exchanger exhaust
Elevon power control unit
Spar
Fuel pipe
Forward ramp drive
Rib
VHF aerial
Four-wheel bogie
Main landing gear cross-beam
Leading edge
Fuel tank
Honeycomb elevon structure
Port engine fuel pumps
Port main landing gear leg
Upper lip of port engine air intakes
Heat exchanger
Rolls-Royce Olympus Mark 610 turbojet
Middle passenger door
Retraction jack
Engine front support link

SIDE VIEW OF THE CONCORDE

VHF aerial
Emergency exit
Passenger window
Flight deck windscreen
Retracted visor
Nose in drooped position
Standby pitot head
Nose-gear leg
Aerodynamic strake
Nose-leg telescopic strut
Radome
Starboard forward door
Steerable twin-wheel nose-gear

Jet engines

JET ENGINES ARE USED BY MOST MILITARY and heavy aircraft, and by many helicopters. The simplest type of jet engine, or gas turbine, is the turbojet. It works by continuously burning a mixture of fuel and air in a combustion chamber to produce a jet of hot exhaust gas that is expelled through a nozzle to produce thrust. The hot gas also spins turbine blades, which, in turn, spin the blades of an air compressor; the compressor forces air into the combustion chamber. Many of the fastest aircraft use turbojets, with additional booster units called afterburners, but their use is restricted by their high noise emission. Most jetliners use turbofan jet engines, which are quieter. An enormous fan, driven by a low-pressure turbine, feeds some air into the compressor but feeds most of it through bypass ducts to join the exhaust jetstream in the tail cone. The bypass stream produces most of the thrust. Many smaller, propeller-driven aircraft use turboprop jet engines, in which the engine powers a propeller.

NPT 301 MODERN TURBOJET

Fuel sprayer
Reverse-flow combustion chamber
Radial diffuser
Turbine rotor
Centrifugal compressor
Exhaust diffuser
Inducer
Tail cone
Air intake
Jet pipe
Exhaust nozzle
Nose cone
Igniter
Alternator
Nozzle guide vane
Air impingement starter
Combustion chamber casing

Plenum ring for hot anti-icing air
Gearbox bevel drive
Combustion chamber
High-pressure compressor
High-pressure turbine
Flow splitter
Integral oil tank
Fuel manifold
Fuel nozzle
Centrifugal compressor
Temperature and pressure sensor
Low-pressure fan
Inlet cone (rotating spinner)
Pressure line
Fan case with special structure to contain broken fan
Electronic engine control and airframe interface connector
Electronic engine control (EEC) unit
Fan duct
Compressor front bearing
Engine front mount
Electrical wiring harness
Fuel and oil heat exchanger
Oil filter
Compressor air-bleed connection

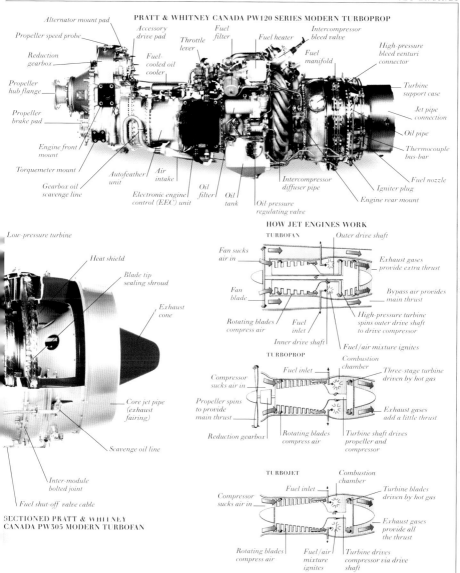

PRATT & WHITNEY CANADA PW120 SERIES MODERN TURBOPROP

Alternator mount pad
Propeller speed probe
Accessory drive pad
Throttle lever
Fuel filter
Fuel heater
Intercompressor bleed valve
High-pressure bleed venturi connector
Reduction gearbox
Fuel-cooled oil cooler
Fuel manifold
Propeller hub flange
Turbine support case
Jet pipe connection
Propeller brake pad
Oil pipe
Engine front mount
Thermocouple bus-bar
Torquemeter mount
Fuel nozzle
Gearbox oil scavenge line
Autofeather unit
Air intake
Oil filter
Oil tank
Intercompressor diffuser pipe
Igniter plug
Engine rear mount
Electronic engine control (EEC) unit
Oil-pressure regulating valve

HOW JET ENGINES WORK

TURBOFAN

Fan sucks air in
Outer drive shaft
Exhaust gases provide extra thrust
Fan blade
Bypass air provides main thrust
Rotating blades compress air
Fuel inlet
High-pressure turbine spins outer drive shaft to drive compressor
Inner drive shaft
Fuel/air mixture ignites

TURBOPROP

Compressor sucks air in
Fuel inlet
Combustion chamber
Three-stage turbine driven by hot gas
Propeller spins to provide main thrust
Exhaust gases add a little thrust
Reduction gearbox
Rotating blades compress air
Turbine shaft drives propeller and compressor

TURBOJET

Compressor sucks air in
Fuel inlet
Combustion chamber
Turbine blades driven by hot gas
Exhaust gases provide all the thrust
Rotating blades compress air
Fuel/air mixture ignites
Turbine drives compressor via drive shaft

Low-pressure turbine
Heat shield
Blade tip sealing shroud
Exhaust cone
Core jet pipe (exhaust fairing)
Scavenge oil line
Inter-module bolted joint
Fuel shut-off valve cable

SECTIONED PRATT & WHITNEY CANADA PW305 MODERN TURBOFAN

Modern military aircraft

MODERN MILITARY AIRCRAFT ARE AMONG THE MOST SOPHISTICATED and expensive products of the 21st century. Fighters need computer-operated controls for manoeuvrability, powerful engines, and effective air-to-air weapons. Most modern fighters also have guided missiles, radar, and passive, infra-red sensors. These developments enable today's fighters to engage in combat with adversaries that are outside visual range. Bombers carry a large weapon load and enough fuel for long-range flights. A few military aircraft, such as the Tornado and the F-14 Tomcat, have variable-sweep ("swing") wings. During take-off and landing their wings are fully extended, but for high-speed flight and low-level attacks the wings are pivoted fully back. A recent development is the "stealth" bomber, which is designed to absorb or deflect enemy radar in order to remain undetected. Earlier bombers, such as the Tornado, use terrain-following radars to fly so close to the ground that they avoid enemy radar detection.

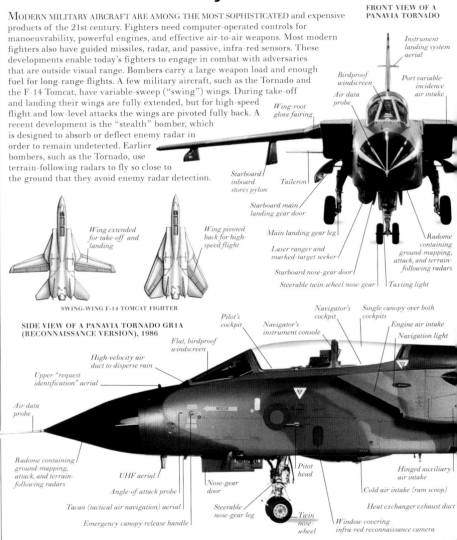

FRONT VIEW OF A PANAVIA TORNADO

Instrument landing system aerial

Birdproof windscreen

Port variable-incidence air intake

Air data probe

Wing-root glove fairing

Starboard inboard stores pylon

Taileron

Starboard main landing gear door

Main landing gear leg

Laser ranger and marked-target seeker

Starboard nose-gear door

Steerable twin-wheel nose-gear

Radome containing ground-mapping, attack, and terrain-following radars

Taxiing light

Wing extended for take-off and landing

Wing pivoted back for high-speed flight

SWING-WING F-14 TOMCAT FIGHTER

SIDE VIEW OF A PANAVIA TORNADO GR1A (RECONNAISSANCE VERSION), 1986

Pilot's cockpit

Navigator's cockpit

Navigator's instrument console

Single canopy over both cockpits

Engine air intake

Navigation light

Flat, birdproof windscreen

High-velocity air duct to disperse rain

Upper "request identification" aerial

Air data probe

Radome containing ground-mapping, attack, and terrain-following radars

UHF aerial

Angle-of-attack probe

Tacan (tactical air navigation) aerial

Emergency canopy release handle

Nose-gear door

Steerable nose-gear leg

Pitot head

Twin nose-wheel

Window covering infra-red reconnaissance camera

Hinged auxiliary air intake

Cold air intake (ram scoop)

Heat exchanger exhaust duct

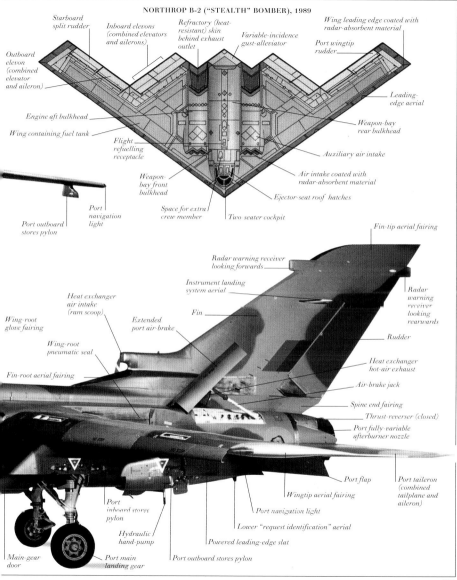

NORTHROP B-2 ("STEALTH" BOMBER), 1989

Starboard split rudder

Inboard elevons (combined elevators and ailerons)

Refractory (heat-resistant) skin behind exhaust outlet

Variable-incidence gust-alleviator

Wing leading edge coated with radar-absorbent material

Port wingtip rudder

Outboard elevon (combined elevator and aileron)

Leading-edge aerial

Engine aft bulkhead

Weapon-bay rear bulkhead

Wing containing fuel tank

Flight refuelling receptacle

Auxiliary air intake

Weapon-bay front bulkhead

Air intake coated with radar-absorbent material

Ejector-seat roof hatches

Space for extra crew member

Two-seater cockpit

Port outboard stores pylon

Port navigation light

Fin-tip aerial fairing

Radar warning receiver looking forwards

Instrument landing system aerial

Radar warning receiver looking rearwards

Heat exchanger air intake (ram scoop)

Fin

Extended port air-brake

Wing-root glove fairing

Rudder

Wing-root pneumatic seal

Heat exchanger hot-air exhaust

Fin-root aerial fairing

Air-brake jack

Spine end fairing

Thrust-reverser (closed)

Port fully-variable afterburner nozzle

Port flap

Port taileron (combined tailplane and aileron)

Wingtip aerial fairing

Port navigation light

Lower "request identification" aerial

Powered leading-edge slat

Port outboard stores pylon

Port inboard stores pylon

Hydraulic hand-pump

Main-gear door

Port main landing gear

Helicopters

HELICOPTERS USE ROTATING BLADES for lift, propulsion, and steering. The first machine to achieve sustained, controlled flight using rotating blades was the autogiro built in the 1920s by the Spaniard Juan de la Cierva. His machine had unpowered blades above the fuselage that relied on the flow of air to rotate them and provide lift as the autogiro was driven forwards by a conventional propeller. Then, in 1939, the Russian-born American Igor Sikorsky produced his VS-300, the forerunner of modern helicopters. Its engine-driven blades provided lift, propulsion, and steering. It could take off vertically, hover, and fly in any direction, and had a tail rotor to prevent the helicopter body from spinning. The introduction of gas turbine jet engines to helicopters in 1955 produced quieter, safer, and more powerful machines. Because of their versatility in flight, helicopters are today used for many purposes, including crop-spraying, traffic surveillance, and transporting crews to deep-sea oil rigs, as well as acting as gunships, air ambulances, and air taxis.

BELL 47G-3B1

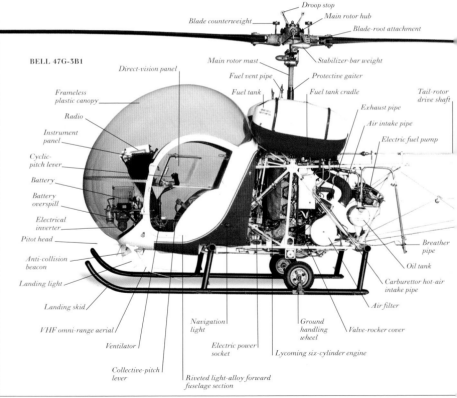

BELL 47G-3B1

Droop stop
Blade counterweight
Main rotor hub
Blade-root attachment
Main rotor mast
Stabilizer-bar weight
Direct-vision panel
Fuel vent pipe
Protective gaiter
Frameless plastic canopy
Fuel tank
Fuel tank cradle
Tail-rotor drive shaft
Radio
Exhaust pipe
Instrument panel
Air intake pipe
Cyclic-pitch lever
Electric fuel pump
Battery
Battery overspill
Electrical inverter
Pitot head
Breather pipe
Anti-collision beacon
Oil tank
Landing light
Carburettor hot-air intake pipe
Landing skid
Air filter
VHF omni-range aerial
Navigation light
Ground handling wheel
Valve-rocker cover
Ventilator
Electric power socket
Lycoming six-cylinder engine
Collective-pitch lever
Riveted light-alloy forward fuselage section

422

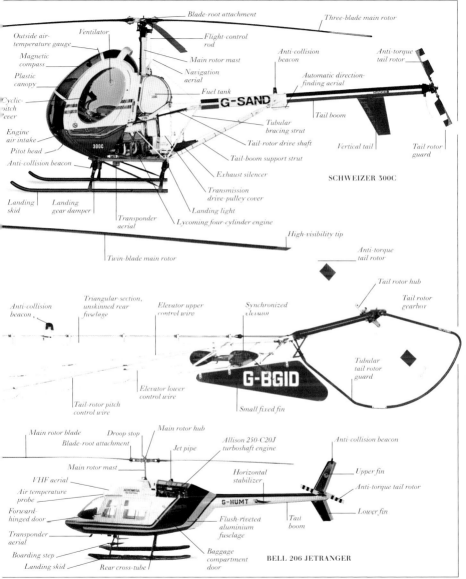

Blade-root attachment

Three-blade main rotor

Outside air-temperature gauge

Ventilator

Magnetic compass

Flight-control rod

Plastic canopy

Main rotor mast

Anti-collision beacon

Anti-torque tail rotor

Navigation aerial

Automatic direction-finding aerial

Cyclic-pitch lever

Fuel tank

Tail boom

G-SAND

Engine air intake

Tubular bracing strut

Tail rotor guard

Pitot head

Tail-rotor drive shaft

Vertical tail

Anti-collision beacon

Tail-boom support strut

300C

Exhaust silencer

SCHWEIZER 300C

Landing skid

Transmission drive-pulley cover

Landing gear damper

Landing light

Transponder aerial

Lycoming four-cylinder engine

High-visibility tip

Anti-torque tail rotor

Twin-blade main rotor

Tail rotor hub

Anti-collision beacon

Triangular-section, unskinned rear fuselage

Elevator upper control wire

Synchronized elevator

Tail rotor gearbox

Tubular tail rotor guard

Tail-rotor pitch control wire

Elevator lower control wire

G-BGID

Small fixed fin

Main rotor blade

Droop stop

Main rotor hub

Anti-collision beacon

Blade-root attachment

Jet pipe

Allison 250-C20J turboshaft engine

Main rotor mast

Upper fin

VHF aerial

Horizontal stabilizer

Air temperature probe

Anti-torque tail rotor

Forward-hinged door

G-HUMT

Lower fin

Transponder aerial

Flush-riveted aluminium fuselage

Tail boom

Boarding step

BELL 206 JETRANGER

Landing skid

Rear cross-tube

Baggage compartment door

423

Light aircraft

LIGHT AIRCRAFT, SUCH AS THE ARV SUPER 2 shown here, are small, lightweight, and of simple construction. More than a million have been built since World War I, mainly for recreational use by private owners. Virtually all light aircraft have piston engines, most of which are air-cooled, although some are liquid-cooled. Open cockpits, almost universal in the 1920s, have today been replaced by enclosed cabins. The cabins of high-wing aircraft have one or two doors, whereas those of low-wing aircraft usually have a sliding or hinged canopy. Most modern light aircraft are made of aluminium alloy, although some are made of wood or of fibre-reinforced materials. Light aircraft today also usually have navigational instruments, an electrical system, cabin heating, wheel brakes, and a two-way radio.

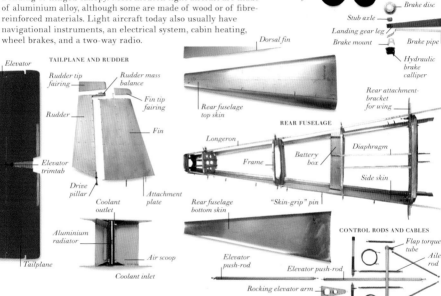

Port wingtip

Aileron mass balance

Aileron torque tube

Port aileron

PORT MAIN LANDING GEAR

Tyre
Inner tube
Hub
Brake disc
Stub axle
Landing gear leg
Brake mount
Brake pipe
Hydraulic brake calliper

TAILPLANE AND RUDDER

Elevator
Rudder tip fairing
Rudder mass balance
Fin tip fairing
Rudder
Fin
Elevator trimtab
Drive pillar
Attachment plate
Coolant outlet
Aluminium radiator
Air scoop
Coolant inlet
Tailplane

Dorsal fin
Rear fuselage top skin

REAR FUSELAGE

Longeron
Frame
Battery box
Diaphragm
Side skin
Rear attachment-bracket for wing
Rear fuselage bottom skin
"Skin-grip" pin

CONTROL RODS AND CABLES

Flap torque tube
Aileron rod
Elevator push-rod
Elevator push-rod
Rocking elevator arm
Aileron torque tube
Rudder cable
Flap drive-rod
Flap drive-rod

SIDE VIEW OF ARV SUPER 2

Spinner
Engine cowling
Canopy
Wing
Communications aerial
Navigational aerial
Fin
Dorsal fin
Rudder
Elevator
Tailplane
Tailskid
Radiator
Nose-gear
Venturi for instruments
Step
Wing strut
Main landing gear
Aircraft registration code

G-BNHB

STARBOARD MAIN LANDING GEAR

Brake calliper
Brake pipe
Landing gear leg
Brake disc
Inner tube
Stub axle
Hub
Tyre

PORT WING

Port top-wing fairing

Port underwing fairing

Wing strut

Port flap

Headrest

Backrest

Pitot head

Airspeed-indicator tube

SEAT ASSEMBLY

Seat cushion

Quick-release mechanism

Lap strap

Lap-strap length adjuster

Bolted anchor

CANOPY

Direct-vision panel

Pressurized strut

Hinge

Leading-edge fairing

Canopy latch

Moulded plastic

Outside air-temperature gauge

COCKPIT

Fibreglass canopy frame

Rudder pedal

Cockpit coaming

Fuel tank top skin

Forward attachment bracket for wing

Control-column aperture

Semi-bulkhead

Nose-leg upper mount

Fibreglass fuel tank

Bulkhead

Lap-strap attachment bracket

"Skin-grip" pin

Firewall

THREE-CYLINDER ENGINE

Port engine cowling

Air intake box

Carburettor

Water outlet

Backplate

Fuel hose

Cylinder head

Gearbox

Propeller drive flange

Exhaust manifold

Engine mount

PROPELLER

Spinner

Flanged plate

Starboard engine cowling

INSTRUMENT PANEL

Flight instruments

Engine instruments

Glove box

Radio plugs

NOSE-GEAR

Steering stop

Nose-leg down tube

Rubber bungee (elasticated cord) shock absorber

Damper unit

Pivoted fork

Hoop

Axle bolt

Nose-wheel

CONTROL COLUMN AND FLAP LEVER

Elevator arm

Torque tube assembly

Control column

Throttle lever

Brake lever

Elevator push-rod

Flap lever

Elevator trimtab lever

Flap lever detent box

Release button

Carburettor hot air lever

Bearing assembly

Pilot's handgrip

STARBOARD WING

Starboard underwing fairing

Wing strut

Starboard top-wing fairing

Gliders, hang-gliders, and microlights

MODERN GLIDERS ARE AMONG the most graceful and aerodynamically efficient of all aircraft. Unpowered but with a large wingspan (up to about 25 m, or 82 ft), gliders use currents of hot, rising air (thermals) to stay aloft, and a rudder, elevators, and ailerons for control. Modern gliders have achieved flights of more than 1,450 km (900 miles) and altitudes above 15,000 m (49,000 ft). Hang-gliders consist of a simple frame across which rigid or flexible material is stretched to form the wings. The pilot is suspended below the wings in a harness or body-bag and, gripping a triangular A-frame, steers by shifting weight from side to side. Like gliders, hang-gliders rely on thermals for lift. Microlights are basically powered hang-gliders. A small engine and an open fibreglass car (trike), which can hold a crew of two, are suspended beneath a stronger version of a hang-glider frame; the frame may have rigid or flexible wings. Microlight pilots, like hang-glider pilots, steer by shifting their weight against an A-frame. Microlights can reach speeds of up to 160 kph (100 mph).

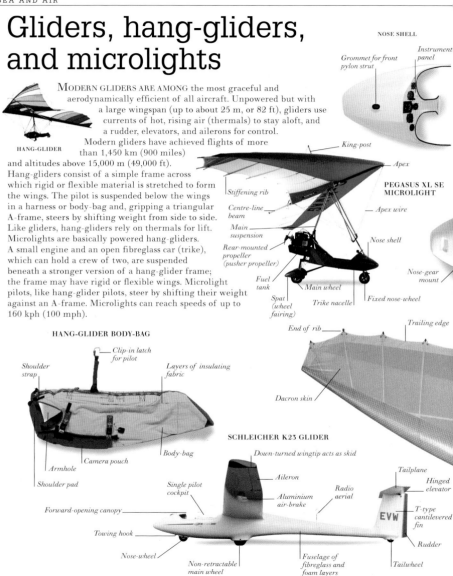

HANG-GLIDER

NOSE SHELL

Grommet for front pylon strut

Instrument panel

King-post

Apex

PEGASUS XL SE MICROLIGHT

Stiffening rib

Centre-line beam

Apex wire

Main suspension

Nose shell

Rear-mounted propeller (pusher propeller)

Fuel tank

Main wheel

Nose-gear mount

Spat (wheel fairing)

Trike nacelle

Fixed nose-wheel

Trailing edge

End of rib

HANG-GLIDER BODY-BAG

Clip-in latch for pilot

Shoulder strap

Layers of insulating fabric

Dacron skin

Camera pouch

Body-bag

Armhole

Shoulder pad

Single pilot cockpit

Forward-opening canopy

Towing hook

Nose-wheel

Non-retractable main wheel

SCHLEICHER K23 GLIDER

Down-turned wingtip acts as skid

Aileron

Aluminium air-brake

Radio aerial

Tailplane

Hinged elevator

EVW

T-type cantilevered fin

Rudder

Tailwheel

Fuselage of fibreglass and foam layers

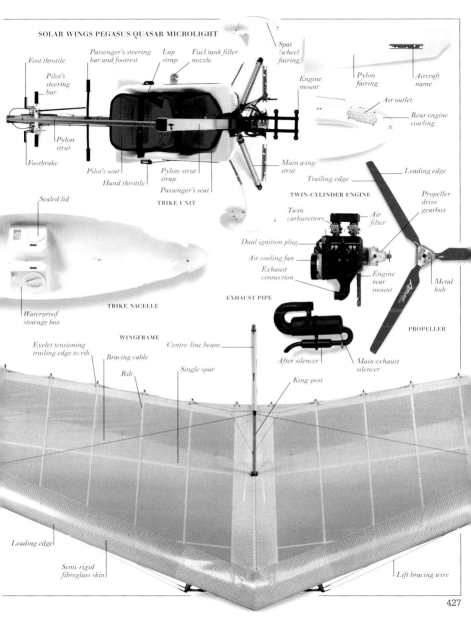

SOLAR WINGS PEGASUS QUASAR MICROLIGHT

Foot throttle

Passenger's steering bar and footrest

Lap strap

Fuel tank filler nozzle

Spat (wheel fairing)

Pilot's steering bar

Engine mount

Pylon fairing

Aircraft name

Air outlet

Rear engine cowling

Pylon strut

Footbrake

Pilot's seat

Hand throttle

Pylon-strut strap

Passenger's seat

Main wing-strut

Trailing edge

Leading edge

TRIKE UNIT

TWIN-CYLINDER ENGINE

Propeller drive gearbox

Sealed lid

Twin carburettors

Air filter

Dual ignition plug

Air cooling fan

Exhaust connection

Engine rear mount

Metal hub

Waterproof stowage box

TRIKE NACELLE

EXHAUST PIPE

PROPELLER

WINGFRAME

Centre-line beam

Eyelet tensioning trailing edge to rib

Bracing cable

Rib

Single spar

King-post

After silencer

Main exhaust silencer

Leading edge

Semi-rigid fibreglass skin

Lift bracing wire

427

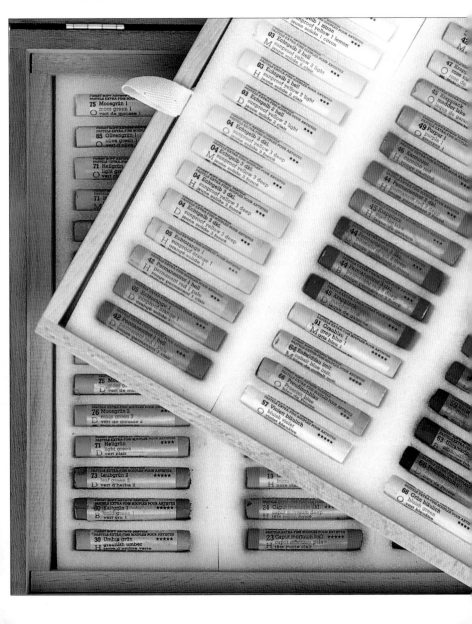

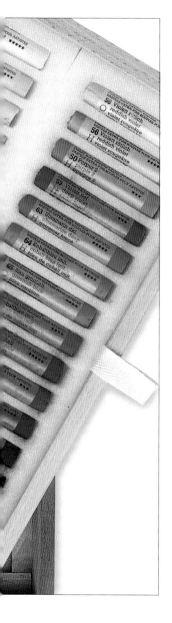

THE
VISUAL ARTS

Drawing

DRAWINGS CAN BE FINISHED WORKS OF ART, or preparatory studies for paintings and other visual arts. They can be made using a wide variety of drawing instruments such as pencils, graphite sticks, chalks, charcoal, pens and inks, and silver wires. The most common drawing instrument is the graphite pencil. A graphite pencil consists of a thin rod of graphite mixed with clay, encased in wood. Charcoal is one of the oldest drawing instruments. It is produced by firing twigs of willow, vine, or other woods at high temperatures in airtight containers. Erasers can be used to rub out marks made by drawing materials such as graphite pencils or charcoal, or to achieve a particular effect – such as smudging. Fixative is often applied – using a mouth diffuser or aerosol spray fixative – to prevent smudging once a drawing is finished. Silver lines can be produced by drawing silver wire across specially prepared paper – a technique known as silverpoint. The lines are permanent and cannot be erased. In time the silver lines oxidize and turn brown.

FIXATIVE AND MOUTH DIFFUSER

Hinge

Liquid fixative consisting of dissolved resin

Fixative is sucked into tube and sprayed on to drawing

CHALK, CRAYON, AND CHARCOAL

Calcite (calcium carbonate) mixed with pigment

BLUE CHALK

Iron oxide mixed with chalk

SANGUINE CRAYON

Carbonized wood

WILLOW CHARCOAL

ERASERS

Hard texture

Medium-soft, light line

PLASTIC ERASER

Soft texture

Very soft, dark line

PUTTY ERASER

DRAWING INSTRUMENTS

2B GRAPHITE PENCIL

8B GRAPHITE PENCIL

SILVER WIRE IN A METAL HOLDER

DRAWING BOARD

DRAWING MATERIALS

Graphite stick

Bulldog clip

Coloured pencil

Drawing board

Paper

Dip pen

Pencil sharpener

Sketch book

Ink bottle

Drawing clip

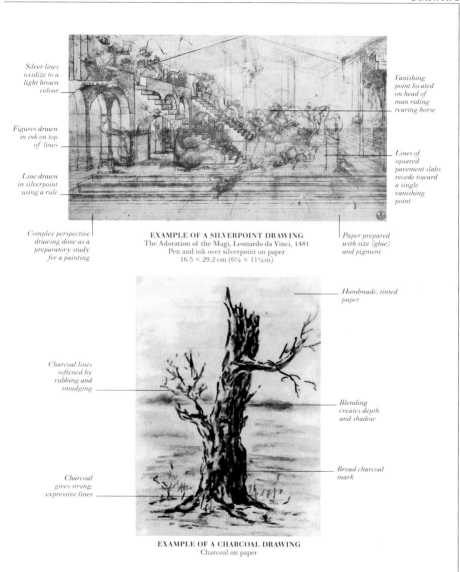

Silver lines oxidize to a light brown colour

Figures drawn in ink on top of lines

Line drawn in silverpoint using a rule

Complex perspective drawing done as a preparatory study for a painting

Vanishing point located on head of man riding rearing horse

Lines of squared pavement slabs recede toward a single vanishing point

Paper prepared with size (glue) and pigment

EXAMPLE OF A SILVERPOINT DRAWING
The Adoration of the Magi, Leonardo da Vinci, 1481
Pen and ink over silverpoint on paper
16.5 × 29.2 cm (6½ × 11½ in)

Handmade, tinted paper

Charcoal lines softened by rubbing and smudging

Blending creates depth and shadow

Broad charcoal mark

Charcoal gives strong, expressive lines

EXAMPLE OF A CHARCOAL DRAWING
Charcoal on paper

Tempera

THE TERM TEMPERA is applied to any paint in which pigment is tempered (mixed) with a water-based binding medium – usually egg yolk. Egg tempera is applied to a smooth surface such as vellum (for illuminated manuscripts) or more commonly to hardwood panels prepared with gesso – a mixture of chalk and size (glue). Hog hair brushes are used to apply the gesso. A layer of gesso grosso (coarse gesso) is followed by successive layers of gesso sotile (fine gesso) that are sanded between coats to provide a smooth, yet absorbent ground. The paint is applied with fine sable brushes in thin layers, using light brushstrokes. Tempera dries quickly to form a tough skin with a satin sheen. The luminous white surface of the gesso combined with the overlaid paint produces the brilliant crispness and rich colours particular to this medium. Egg tempera paintings are frequently gilded with gold. Leaves of finely beaten gold are applied to a bole (reddish-brown clay) base and polished by burnishing.

MATERIALS FOR GILDING

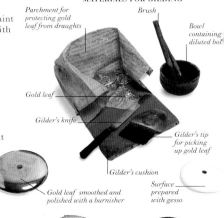

Parchment for protecting gold leaf from draughts

Brush

Bowl containing diluted bol

Gold leaf

Gilder's knife

Gilder's tip for picking up gold leaf

Gilder's cushion

Gold leaf smoothed and polished with a burnisher

Surface prepared with gesso

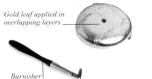

Gold leaf applied in overlapping layers

Bole brushed on to gesso

Burnisher

Agate tip

MATERIALS FOR TEMPERA PANEL PAINTING

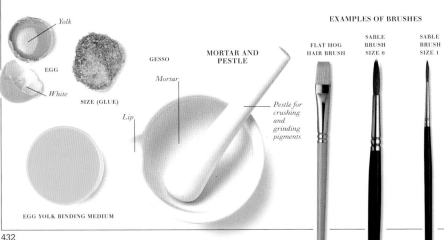

Yolk

EGG

White

SIZE (GLUE)

GESSO

MORTAR AND PESTLE

Mortar

Lip

Pestle for crushing and grinding pigments

EXAMPLES OF BRUSHES

FLAT HOG HAIR BRUSH

SABLE BRUSH SIZE 6

SABLE BRUSH SIZE 1

EGG YOLK BINDING MEDIUM

EXAMPLE OF A TEMPERA PAINTING
Presentation in the Temple, Ambrogio Lorenzetti, 1342
Tempera on wood, 257 × 168 cm (8 ft 5⅛ in × 5 ft 6 ⅛ in)

Altarpiece commissioned for Siena Cathedral, Italy

The red tinge of the bole is just visible beneath the gold

Textured gold ornament made by punching motifs into the gilded surface

Edge of a sheet of gold leaf

Crisp edge characteristic of tempera painting

Vine black used to create the dim cathedral interior

Highlights on the beard made by applying thin layers of white over dried paint

Red drapery painted in vermilion

Raised right hand and pointing finger is the gesture of prophecy

Receding floor tiles create the impression of depth

Patch of discoloured varnish, left from last cleaning

PIGMENTS FOR FLESH-COLOUR PAINTING

VERDACCIO

VERMILION AND LEAD WHITE

VERMILION

RED EARTH (IRON OXIDE)

EXAMPLES OF PIGMENTS

MALACHITE

ULTRAMARINE LAPIS LAZULI

VINE BLACK

LEAD TIN YELLOW

Warm flesh tones achieved by layering vermilion and white over an undercoat of verdaccio

Ultramarine lapis lazuli, as costly as gold, was reserved for significant figures such as the Virgin Mary

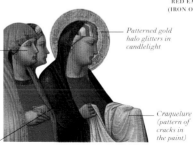

Patterned gold halo glitters in candlelight

Craquelure (pattern of cracks in the paint)

DETAIL FROM "PRESENTATION IN THE TEMPLE"

Fresco

FRESCO IS A METHOD OF WALL PAINTING. In buon fresco (true fresco), pigments are mixed with water and applied to an intonaco (layer of fresh, damp lime-plaster). The intonaco absorbs and binds the pigments as it dries making the picture a permanent part of the wall surface. The intonaco is applied in sections called giornate (daily sections). The size of each giornata depends on the artist's estimate of how much can be painted before the plaster sets. The junctions between giornate are sometimes visible on a finished fresco. The range of colours used in buon fresco are limited to lime-resistant pigments such as earth colours (below). Slaked lime (burnt lime mixed with water), bianco di San Giovanni (slaked lime that has been partly exposed to air), and chalk can be used to produce fresco whites. In fresco secco (dry fresco), pigments are mixed with a binding medium and applied to dry plaster. The pigments are not completely absorbed into the plaster and may flake off over time.

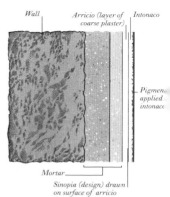

Wall

Arricio (layer of coarse plaster)

Intonaco

Pigmen[t] applied [to] intonac[o]

Mortar

Sinopia (design) drawn on surface of arricio

EXAMPLES OF EARTH COLOUR PIGMENTS

RAW UMBER

RED EARTH (IRON OXIDE)

GREEN EARTH

RAW SIENNA

EXAMPLES OF FRESCO BRUSHES

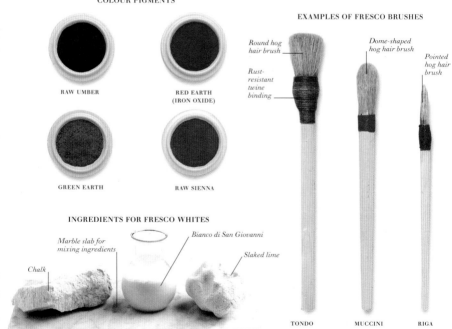

Round hog hair brush

Rust-resistant twine binding

Dome-shaped hog hair brush

Pointed hog hair brush

INGREDIENTS FOR FRESCO WHITES

Marble slab for mixing ingredients

Bianco di San Giovanni

Slaked lime

Chalk

TONDO

MUCCINI

RIGA

EXAMPLE OF A FRESCO
The Expulsion of the Merchants from the Temple, Giotto, c.1306
Fresco, 200 × 185 cm (78 × 72 in)

One of a series of frescoes in the Arena Chapel, Padua, Italy

Temple acts as a backdrop for the action

Patches of azurite blue have turned green due to reaction with carbon dioxide

Bianco di San Giovanni often used for fresco whites

Gold leaf applied to apostle's halo

Hairline junction between giornate is visible

Green earth pigment applied to robe

Child painted on top of apostle's robe

Red earth pigment applied in buon fresco has retained rich hue

Azurite blue applied in fresco secco has flaked off to reveal the plaster beneath

Dry, matt surface characteristic of buon fresco

Paint applied in buon fresco to child's face

White dove represents the Holy Ghost

Paint applied in fresco secco to child's body has flaked off

Sinopia (design) sketched in red earth

DETAIL FROM "THE EXPULSION"

Artist has to finish giornata before plaster dries

Junction between giornate

A fresco was generally worked in zones from the top down

Area with little detail can be painted quickly, allowing a larger giornata to be completed

Highly detailed area takes a longer time to paint, restricting the size of the giornata

GIORNATE (DAILY SECTIONS) IN "THE EXPULSION"

Oils

OIL PAINTS ARE MADE BY MIXING and grinding pigment with a drying vegetable oil such as linseed oil. The paint can be applied to many different surfaces and textures – the most common being canvas. Before painting, the canvas is stretched on a wooden frame and its surface is prepared with layers of size (glue) and primer. The two main types of brushes used in oil painting are stiff hog hair bristle brushes – generally used for covering large areas; and soft hair brushes made from sable or synthetic material – generally used for fine detail. Other tools, including painting knives, can also be used to achieve different effects. Oil paint can be applied thickly (a technique known as impasto), or can be thinned down using a solvent – such as turpentine or white spirit. Varnishes are sometimes applied to finished paintings to protect their surface and to give them a matt or gloss finish.

KIDNEY-SHAPED PALETTE

DAMMAR RESIN VARNISH

Crystals are dissolved and applied to painting to protect its surface

COMMERCIAL OIL PAINTS

CADMIUM RED

Lightfast opaque colour

ULTRAMARINE

Transparent colour

LINSEED OIL

Oil derived from seeds of flax plant

EXAMPLES OF PIGMENTS

CADMIUM RED

CERULEAN BLUE

DOUBLE DIPPER (PALETTE ATTACHMENT)

Screw-top lid

Container for storing solvent or drying oil

HOG HAIR BRISTLE BRUSHES

Flat hog hair brush

Filbert hog hair brush

Flat hog hair brush

Filbert hog hair brush

EQUIPMENT FOR MAKING OIL PAINT

Airtight jar for storing paint

Palette knife for mixing drying oil and pigment

Glass muller for grinding drying oil and pigment

Glass slab with abrasive surface

PAINTING KNIVES

TROWEL-SHAPED PAINTING KNIFE

Blade

DIAMOND-SHAPED PAINTING KNIFE

Blade

Cranked, steel shank

Cranked, steel shank

SYNTHETIC BRUSH

EXAMPLES OF BRUSHES

SABLE BRUSH

Round hog hair brush

Long, wooden handle

Protective, plastic case

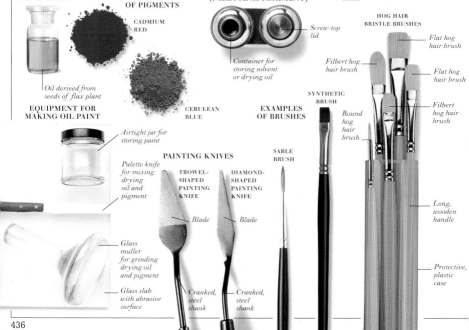

EXAMPLE OF AN OIL PAINTING
Fritillarias, Vincent van Gogh, 1886
Oil on canvas, 73.5 × 60.5 cm (29 × 24 in)

Artist's signature scratched in wet paint with the end of the brush

Background enlivened by dabs of white and green

Each leaf painted in a single, rapid stroke

Orange and blue (complementary colours) placed together to give maximum contrast and enhance one another to appear brighter

Impasto (deep ridges of paint applied in thick strokes)

Strong directional brushstrokes on table draw attention to the vase

Features of vase highlighted by generous touches of yellow

RADIAL STUDIO EASEL

Top sliding-block adjusts to canvas height

Canvas support

Height adjustment key

Angle adjustment key

CANVAS STRETCHED ON WOODEN FRAME (VIEWED FROM THE BACK)

Staple

Canvas prepared with glue (size) and primer

Wooden frame

Unprimed canvas

EXAMPLES OF CANVASES

COTTON DUCK

FINE LINEN

COARSE LINEN

Tripod

Watercolour

WATERCOLOUR PAINT IS MADE OF GROUND PIGMENT mixed with a water-soluble binding medium, usually gum arabic. It is usually applied to paper using soft hair brushes such as sable, goat hair, squirrel, and synthetic brushes. Watercolours are often diluted and applied as overlaying washes (thin, transparent layers) to build up depth of colour. Washes can be laid in a variety of ways to create a range of different effects. For example, a wet-in-wet wash can be achieved by laying a wash on top of another wet wash. The two washes blend together to give a fused effect. Sponges are used to modify washes by soaking up paint so that areas of pigment are lightened or removed from the paper. Watercolours can also be applied undiluted – a technique known as dry brush – to create a broken-colour effect. Watercolours are generally transparent and allow light to reflect from the surface of the paper through the layers of paint to give a luminous effect. They can be thickened and made opaque by adding body colour (Chinese white).

*Natural sap fro
acacia tree*

NATURAL SPONGE

ANATOMY OF A SABLE BRUSH

*Soft red
sable hair*

Toe (tip)

Wooden handle

SOFT HAIR BRUSHES

*Hair trimmed
and cemented
into ferrule*

ROUND SABLE BRUSH (SIZE 6)

*Round
ferrule*

*Hair tied with
clove hitch knot*

ROUND SABLE BRUSH (SIZE 1)

TUBES OF
WATERCOLOUR PAINT

WINSOR GREEN

SYNTHETIC WASH BRUSH

SQUIRREL MOP
WASH BRUSH

CADMIUM YELLOW

PORTABLE BOX OF
WATERCOLOUR PAINTS

Painted colour swatch

Chinese white

*Pan of
watercolour paint*

*Lid can be used for
mixing colours*

LARGE GOAT HAKE
WASH BRUSH

EXAMPLE OF A WATERCOLOUR
Burning of the Houses of Parliament, Turner, 1834
Watercolour on paper, 29.2 × 44.5 cm (11½ × 17½ in)

Transparent washes laid on top of each other to create tonal depth

Transparent washes allow light to reflect off the surface of the paper to give a luminous effect

Highlight scratched out with a scalpel

Paper shows through thin wash to give flames added highlight

Crowd painted with thin strokes laid over a pale wash

Undiluted paint applied, then partly washed out, to create the impression of water

EXAMPLES OF WATERCOLOUR PAPERS

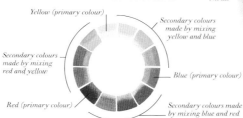

SMOOTH-TEXTURED PAPER

MEDIUM-TEXTURED PAPER

ROUGH-TEXTURED PAPER

EXAMPLES OF WASHES

WASH OVER DRY BRUSH
Wash laid over paint applied with dry brush gives two-tone effect

GRADED WASH
Strong wash applied to tilted paper gives graded effect

DRY BRUSH
Undiluted paint dragged across surface of paper gives broken effect

WET-IN-WET
Two diluted washes left to run together to give fused effect

COLOUR WHEEL OF WATERCOLOUR PAINTS

Yellow (primary colour)

Secondary colours made by mixing yellow and blue

Secondary colours made by mixing red and yellow

Blue (primary colour)

Red (primary colour)

Secondary colours made by mixing blue and red

Pastels

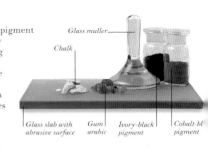

Glass muller

Chalk

Glass slab with abrasive surface

Gum arabic

Ivory-black pigment

Cobalt-bl pigment

PASTELS ARE STICKS OF PIGMENT made by mixing ground pigment with chalk and a binding medium, such as gum arabic. They vary in hardness depending on the proportion of the binding medium to the chalk. Soft pastel – the most common form of pastel – contains just enough binding medium to hold the pigment in stick form. Pastels can be applied directly to any support (surface) with sufficient tooth (texture). When a pastel is drawn over a textured surface, the pigment crumbles and lodges in the fibres of the support. Pastel marks have a particular soft, matt quality and are suitable for techniques such as blending, scumbling, and feathering. Blending is a technique of rubbing and fusing two or more colours on the support using fingers or various tools such as tortillons (paper stumps), soft hair brushes, putty erasers, and soft bread. Scumbling is a technique of building up layers of pastel colours. The side or blunted tip of a soft pastel is lightly drawn over an underpainted area so that patches of the colour beneath show through. Feathering is a technique of applying parallel strokes of colour with the point of a pastel, usually over an existing layer of pastel colour. A thin spray of fixative can be applied – using a mouth diffuser (see pp. 430-431) or aerosol spray fixative – to a finished pastel painting, or in between layers of colour, to prevent smudging.

EXAMPLES OF SOFT PASTELS

COBALT-BLUE
HALF PASTEL

VERMILION
HALF PASTEL

OLIVE-GREEN
FULL PASTEL

MAUVE
FULL PASTEL

BOXED PASTEL SET

Boxed set containing a mixture of portrait and landscape colours

Foam compartments protect the pastels

Soft pastel

Wooden tray

EQUIPMENT USED WITH PASTELS

PUTTY ERASER

BREAD

Soft bread suitable for erasing and blending

AEROSOL
SPRAY FIXATIVE

SOFT
HAIR BRUSH

TORTILLONS
(PAPER STUMPS)

Soft point used for blending

Tight roll of paper

EXAMPLE OF A PASTEL PAINTING
Woman Drying her Neck, Edgar Degas, c.1898
Pastel on cardboard, 62.5 x 65.5 cm (24½ x 25½in)

Pastels applied directly to support

Rich colour of fabric created by overlaying yellows and oranges

Broken colours, characteristic of scumbling technique

Colours are blended together using fingers or tools such as tortillons

Built up layers of pastel

Toned colour of paper visible beneath thinly applied pastels

Pure bright colours laid side by side produce strong contrasts

DETAIL FROM "WOMAN DRYING HER NECK"

Feathering technique used to produce skin tones

EXAMPLES OF TEXTURED PAPERS AND PASTEL BOARDS

WATERCOLOUR PAPER(ROUGH TEXTURE)

GLASS PAPER

WATERCOLOUR PAPER (MEDIUM TEXTURE)

INGRES PAPER

FLOCKED PASTEL BOARD

CANSON PAPER

EXAMPLES OF COLOURED AND TINTED PAPERS

Acrylics

ACRYLIC PAINT IS MADE BY MIXING PIGMENT with a synthetic
resin. It can be thinned with water but dries to become water
insoluble. Acrylics are applied to many surfaces, such as
paper and acrylic-primed board and canvas. A variety of
brushes, painting knives, rollers, air-brushes, plastic
scrapers, and other tools are used in acrylic painting.
The versatility of acrylics makes them suitable for a wide
range of techniques. They can be used opaquely or – by
adding water – in a transparent, watercolour style. Acrylic
mediums can be added to the paint to adjust its consistency
for special effects such as glazing and impasto (ridges of paint
applied in thick strokes) or to make it more matt or glossy.
Acrylics are quick-drying, which allows layers of paint to
be applied on top of each other almost immediately.

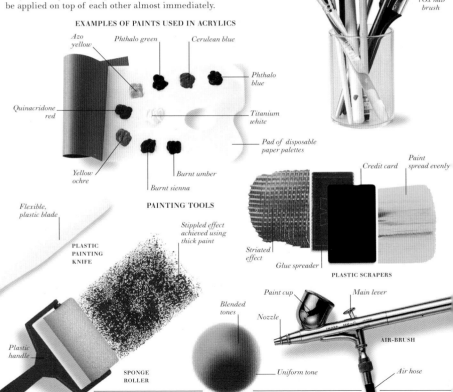

EXAMPLES OF BRUSHES

Sable
brush

Hog hair
sash
brush

Synthetic hog
hair brush

Synthetic
sable
brush

Hog
hair
brush

Goat hair
brush

Synthetic
wash
brush

Ox hair
brush

EXAMPLES OF PAINTS USED IN ACRYLICS

Azo
yellow

Phthalo green

Cerulean blue

Phthalo
blue

Quinacridone
red

Titanium
white

Yellow
ochre

Burnt umber

Burnt sienna

Pad of disposable
paper palettes

PAINTING TOOLS

Flexible,
plastic blade

PLASTIC
PAINTING
KNIFE

Stippled effect
achieved using
thick paint

Striated
effect

Glue spreader

Credit card

Paint
spread evenly

PLASTIC SCRAPERS

Plastic
handle

SPONGE
ROLLER

Paint cup

Main lever

Blended
tones

Nozzle

Uniform tone

AIR-BRUSH

Air hose

EXAMPLE OF AN ACRYLIC PAINTING
Acrylic on canvas, 20.5 x 26.6 cm (8 x 10½ in)

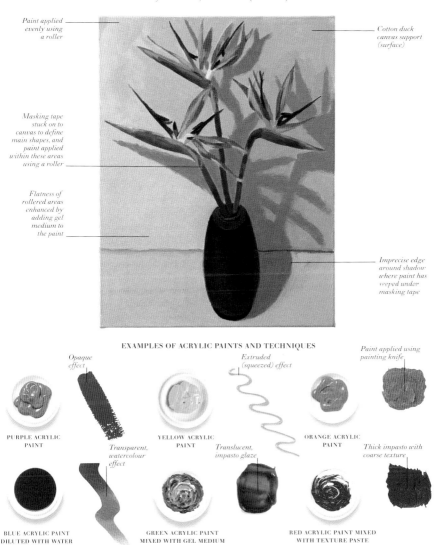

Paint applied evenly using a roller

Cotton duck canvas support (surface)

Masking tape stuck on to canvas to define main shapes, and paint applied within these areas using a roller

Flatness of rollered areas enhanced by adding gel medium to the paint

Imprecise edge around shadow where paint has weeped under masking tape

EXAMPLES OF ACRYLIC PAINTS AND TECHNIQUES

Opaque effect

Extruded (squeezed) effect

Paint applied using painting knife

Transparent, watercolour effect

Translucent, impasto glaze

Thick impasto with coarse texture

PURPLE ACRYLIC PAINT

YELLOW ACRYLIC PAINT

ORANGE ACRYLIC PAINT

BLUE ACRYLIC PAINT DILUTED WITH WATER

GREEN ACRYLIC PAINT MIXED WITH GEL MEDIUM

RED ACRYLIC PAINT MIXED WITH TEXTURE PASTE

Calligraphy

CALLIGRAPHY IS BEAUTIFULLY FORMED LETTERING. The term applies
to written text and illumination (the decoration of manuscripts using
gold leaf and colour). The essential materials needed to practise
calligraphy are a writing tool, ink, and a writing surface. Quills
are among the oldest writing tools. They are usually made from
goose or turkey feathers, and are noted for their flexibility and
ability to produce fine lines. A quill point, however, is not very
durable and constant recutting and trimming is required.
The most commonly used writing instrument in western
calligraphy is a detachable, metal nib held in a penholder.
The metal nib is very durable, and there are a wide range
of different types. Particular types of nibs – such as
copperplate, speedball, and roundhand nibs – are used
for specific styles of lettering. Some nibs have integral ink
reservoirs and others have reservoirs that are detachable.
Brushes are also used for writing, and for filling in outlined
letters and painting decoration. Other writing tools used in
calligraphy are fountain pens, felt-tip pens, rotring pens,
and reed pens. Calligraphy inks may come in liquid form,
or as a solid ink stick. Ink sticks are ground down in
distilled water to form a liquid ink. The most
common writing surfaces for calligraphy are good quality, smooth
-surfaced papers. To achieve the best writing position,
the calligrapher places the paper on a drawing
board set at an angle.

EQUIPMENT USED IN BRUSH LETTERING

Brush rest

Wolf hair brush

Goat hair brush

BRUSHES AND BRUSH REST

Liquid ink made by grinding down ink stick in distilled water

Solid carbon ink stick

Ink stone

INK STICK AND STONE

PENS, NIBS, AND BRUSHES USED IN CALLIGRAPHY

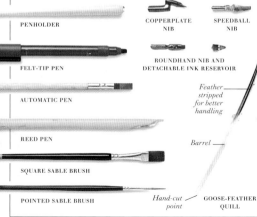

PENHOLDER

COPPERPLATE NIB

SPEEDBALL NIB

GOAT HAIR BRUSH

FELT-TIP PEN

ROUNDHAND NIB AND DETACHABLE INK RESERVOIR

WOLF HAIR BRUSH

AUTOMATIC PEN

Feather

Feather stripped for better handling

REED PEN

Barrel

SQUARE SABLE BRUSH

POINTED SABLE BRUSH

Hand-cut point

GOOSE-FEATHER QUILL

FOUNTAIN PEN AND INK

Bottle of permanent black ink

Barrel

Clip

Nib

Cuter cap

EXAMPLES OF LETTERING STYLES

ROMAN CAPITALS

Apex
Bowl
Curved stroke
Stem
Inner counter
Stem
Stem
Arm
Counter
Crossbar
Inner counter
Counter
Inner counter

A B C D E

ITALIC ROMAN

Cap line
X line
Base line
Descender line
Ascender
Curved stroke
Ear
Arch
Crossbar
Height of letter determined by number of nib widths
Serif
Neck
Descender

A b c g m p t

VERSAL

Slightly pinched (curved) vertical stroke
Letter filled in using brush
Inner counters
Tail
Spine
Pointed apex

O R S W

AN ILLUMINATED MANUSCRIPT

Style of lettering called Gothic book script
Large decorative letter used to mark the opening of a chapter
Words written carefully by hand
Gold leaf
Grid lines provide guide to position of words and pictures

CHINESE LETTERING

Rice paper
Broad brush stroke
Chinese character meaning long life
Artist's stamped signature

ARTIST'S STAMP

Stamp
Ink pad
Stamped signature of the artist

DRAWING BOARD

Adjustable set square
Blade with parallel motion

EXAMPLES OF CALLIGRAPHY PAPERS

Standard European paper
Indian handmade paper
Flecked, tinted paper
Imitation parchment paper

Printmaking 1

PRINTS ARE MADE BY FOUR BASIC printing processes – intaglio, lithographic, relief, and screen. In intaglio printing, lines are engraved or etched into the surface of a metal plate. Lines are engraved by hand using sharp metal tools. They are etched by corroding the metal plate with acid, using acid-resistant ground to protect the areas not to be etched. The plate is then inked and wiped, leaving the grooves filled with ink and the surface clean. Dampened paper is laid over the plate, and both paper and plate are passed through the rollers of an etching press. The pressure of the rollers forces the paper into the grooves, so that it takes up the ink, leaving an impression on the paper. Lithographic printing is based on the antipathy between grease and water. An image is drawn on a surface – usually a stone or metal plate – with a greasy medium, such as tusche (lihographic ink). The greasy drawing is fixed on to the plate by applying an acidic solution, such as gum arabic. The surface is then dampened and rolled with ink. The ink adheres only to the greasy areas and is repelled by the water. Paper is laid on the plate and pressure is applied by means of a press. In relief printing, the non-printing areas of a wood or linoleum block are cut away using gouges, knives, and other tools. The printing areas are left raised in relief and are rolled with ink. Paper is laid on the inked block and pressure is applied by means of a press or by burnishing (rubbing) the back of the paper. The most common forms of relief printing are woodcut, wood engraving, and linocut. In screen printing, the printing surface is a mesh stretched across a wooden frame. A stencil is applied to the mesh to seal the nonprinting areas and ink is scraped through the mesh to produce an image.

Paper
Printed image
Engraved or etched image
Metal plate
Inked area

INTAGLIO

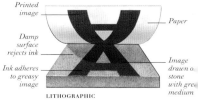

Printed image
Paper
Damp surface rejects ink
Ink adheres to greasy image
Image drawn on stone with greasy medium

LITHOGRAPHIC

Paper
Printed image
Raised figure
Inked surface
Wood block

RELIEF

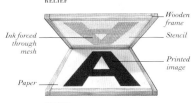

Wooden frame
Ink forced through mesh
Stencil
Printed image
Paper

SCREEN

LEATHER
INK DABBER

EQUIPMENT USED IN INTAGLIO PRINTING

ROCKER   SCRIBER   ROULETTE   SCRAPER   BURNISHER   CLAMP

ETCHING PRESS USED FOR INTAGLIO PRINTMAKING

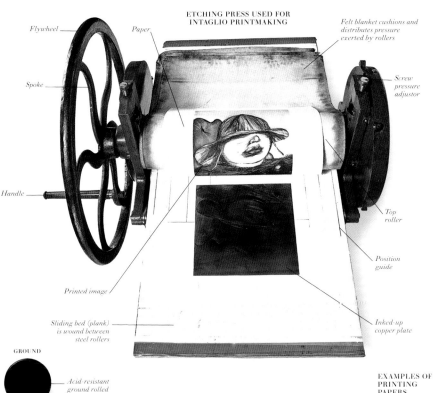

Flywheel

Spoke

Handle

Paper

Felt blanket cushions and distributes pressure exerted by rollers

Screw pressure adjustor

Top roller

Position guide

Printed image

Sliding bed (plank) is wound between steel rollers

Inked-up copper plate

GROUND

Acid-resistant ground rolled on to metal plate before etching

GROUND ROLLER

Gelatine roller

Wooden handle

EXAMPLES OF PRINTING PAPERS

EXAMPLE OF AN INTAGLIO PRINT
Annie with a Sun Hat, Jock McFadyen, 1995
Etched copper plate, 41 × 40 cm (16 × 15¾ in)

Printmaking 2

EXAMPLE OF A LITHOGRAPHIC STONE AND PRINT
Untitled, Frederic M. Pannebaker, 1972

IMAGE DRAWN ON STONE

LITHOGRAPIC PRINT

EXAMPLE OF A SCREEN PRINT
Patrons In An Art Deco Club, Unknown, 1931

SCREEN AND SQUEEGEE

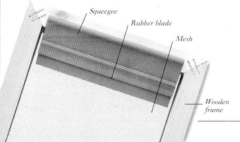

Squeegee

Rubber blade

Mesh

Wooden frame

EQUIPMENT USED IN LITHOGRAPHIC PRINTING

CRAYON AND HOLDER

LITHOGRAPHIC PENCIL

TUSCHE (LITHOGRAPHIC INK) PEN

ERASING STICK

EXPANDABLE SPONGE

TUSCHE (LITHOGRAPHIC INK) STICK

RUBBING INK

INK ROLLER

MILD ACIDIC SOLUTION

GUM ARABIC SOLUTION

WATER-BASED SCREEN PRINTING INKS

BLUE ACRYLIC INK

RED ACRYLIC INK

BROWN TEXTILE INK

EQUIPMENT USED IN RELIEF PRINTING

V-SHAPED GOUGE

INK ROLLER

Rubber roller

LINOLEUM AND WOODCUT BLOCK

Linoleum

U-SHAPED GOUGE

GRAVER

KNIFE

SCORPER

WOOD ENGRAVING

Side-grain wood block

END-GRAIN WOOD BLOCK

INKED-UP ENGRAVED BLOCK

WOOD ENGRAVING PRINT

RELIEF-PRINTING PRESS

Spiral spring

Crown

Piston

Staple (frame)

Tympan lowered on to printing block

Printed image

Bar (pressure handle)

Platen

Printing block

Bed is rolled under platen

Drum handle

Rail

Drum (rounce)

Leg

Counterweight

Pillar (post)

Foot

Mosaic

MOSAIC IS THE ART OF MAKING patterns and pictures from tesserae (small, coloured pieces of glass, marble, and other materials). Different materials are cut into tesserae using different tools. Smalti (glass enamel) and marble are cut into pieces using a hammer and a hardy (a pointed blade) embedded in a log. Vitreous glass is cut into pieces using a pair of nippers. Mosaics can be made using a direct or indirect method. In the direct method, the tesserae are laid directly into a bed of cement–based adhesive. In the indirect method, the design is drawn in reverse on paper or cloth. The tesserae are then stuck face-down on the paper or cloth using water-soluble glue. Adhesive is spread with a trowel on to a solid surface – such as a wall – and the back of the mosaic is laid into the adhesive. Finally, the paper or cloth is soaked off to reveal the mosaic. Gaps between tesserae can be filled with grout. Grout is forced into gaps by dragging a grouting squeegee across the face of the mosaic. Mosaics are usually used to decorate walls and floors, but they can also be applied to smaller objects.

EQUIPMENT FOR BREAKING MARBLE

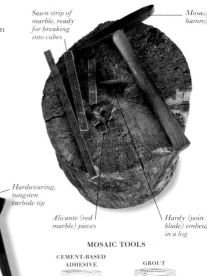

Sawn strip of marble, ready for breaking into cubes

Mosa hamm

Alicante (red marble) pieces

Hardy (poin blade) embe in a log

NIPPERS *Harduearing, tungsten carbide tip*

MOSAIC TOOLS

CEMENT-BASED ADHESIVE

GROUT

Handle with rubber grip

SMALTI (GLASS ENAMEL)

RED SMALTI

YELLOW SMALTI

BLUE SMALTI

EXAMPLE OF A MOSAIC (DIRECT METHOD)
Seascape, Tessa Hunkin, 1993
Smalti mosaic on board
80 cm (31½ in) diameter

Gold-leaf smalti

TROWEL

Notch

GROUTING SQUEEGEE

Wooden handle

Steel blade

Wooden handle

Ru bla

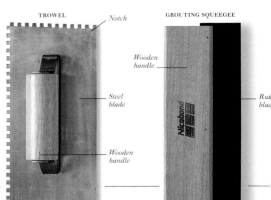

STAGES IN THE CREATION OF A MOSAIC (INDIRECT METHOD)

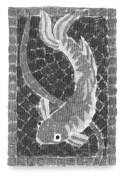

COLOUR SKETCH
A colour sketch is drawn in oil pastel to give a clear impression of how the finished mosaic will look.

REVERSE IMAGE
Tesserae are glued face-down on reverse image on paper. Mosaic is then attached to solid surface and paper is removed.

MOSAIC POT

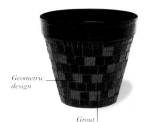

Geometric design

Grout

MOSAIC MOSQUE DESIGN

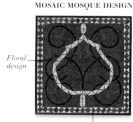

Floral design

Geometric border

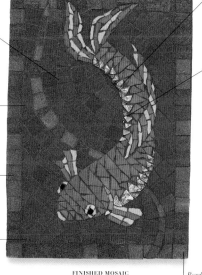

Andamenti (line along which tesserae are laid)

Grout fills the gaps between the tesserae

Mosaic mounted on board

Vitreous glass cut into triangular shape with nippers

Gold tessera with ripple finish

Gold tessera placed upside-down

FINISHED MOSAIC
Goldfish, Tessa Hunkin, 1993
Vitreous glass mosaic on board
35.5 × 25.5 cm (14 × 10 in)

Border of square vitreous glass

VITREOUS GLASS

GREEN VITREOUS GLASS WITH GOLD LEAF

Plain finish

Ripple finish

RED VITREOUS GLASS

BLUE VITREOUS GLASS

SHEETS OF VITREOUS GLASS

Sculpture 1

THE TWO TRADITIONAL METHODS OF MAKING SCULPTURE are carving and modelling. A carved sculpture is made by cutting away the surplus from a block of hard material such as stone, marble, or wood. The tools used for carving vary according to the material being carved. Heavy steel points, claws, and chisels that are struck with a lump hammer are generally used for stone and marble. Sharp gouges and chisels that are struck with a wooden mallet are used for wood. Sculptures formed from hard materials are generally finished by filing with rasps, rifflers, and other abrasive implements. Modelling is a process by which shapes are built up, using malleable materials such as clay, plaster, and wax. The material is cut with wire-ended tools and modelled with the fingers or a variety of hardwood and metal implements. For large or intricate modelled sculptures an armature (frame), made from metal or wood, is used to provide internal support. Sculptures formed in soft materials may harden naturally or can be made more durable by firing in a kiln. Modelled sculptures are often first designed in wax or another material to be cast later in a metal (see pp. 454-455) such as bronze. The development of many new materials in the 20th century has enabled sculptors to experiment with new techniques such as construction (joining preformed pieces of material such as machine components, mirrors, and furniture) and kinetic (mobile) sculpture.

EXAMPLES OF MARBLE CARVING TOOLS

1.1 kg (2½ lb) iron head

Ash handle

LUMP HAMMER

WIDE MARBLE CLAW

NARROW MARBLE CLAW

POINT

FLAT CHISEL

BULLNOSE CHISEL

EXAMPLES OF WOODCARVING TOOLS

CABINET RASP

STRAIGHT GOUGE

SALMON BEND GOUGE

CHISEL

Stone for sharpening woodcarving tools

Cedar box

ARKANSAS HONE-STONE

CARVING MALLET

CALLIPERS

Curved leg

Gap measures distance between two points on a sculpture

Wing nut

EXAMPLES OF RIFFLERS (FOR STONE, MARBLE, AND WOOD)

30 CM (12 IN) RIFFLER

15 CM (6 IN) RIFFLER

Surface for sharpening stonecarving tools

DIAMOND WHETSTONE

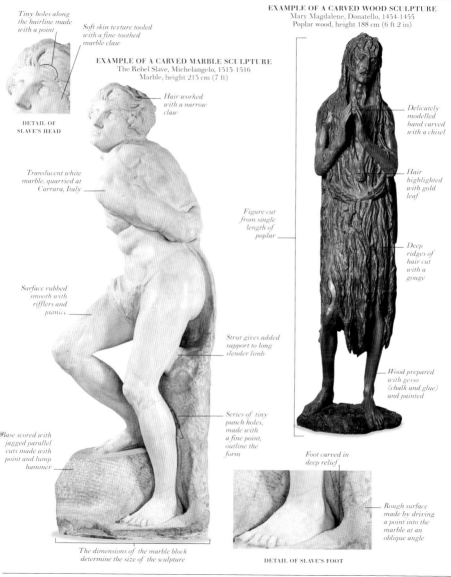

Tiny holes along the hairline made with a point

Soft skin texture tooled with a fine-toothed marble claw

DETAIL OF SLAVE'S HEAD

EXAMPLE OF A CARVED WOOD SCULPTURE
Mary Magdalene, Donatello, 1454-1455
Poplar wood, height 188 cm (6 ft 2 in)

EXAMPLE OF A CARVED MARBLE SCULPTURE
The Rebel Slave, Michelangelo, 1513-1516
Marble, height 213 cm (7 ft)

Hair worked with a narrow claw

Translucent white marble, quarried at Carrara, Italy

Surface rubbed smooth with rifflers and pumice

Base scored with jagged parallel cuts made with point and lump hammer

Figure cut from single length of poplar

Strut gives added support to long slender limb

Series of tiny punch holes, made with a fine point, outline the form

Delicately modelled hand carved with a chisel

Hair highlighted with gold leaf

Deep ridges of hair cut with a gouge

Wood prepared with gesso (chalk and glue) and painted

Foot carved in deep relief

Rough surface made by driving a point into the marble at an oblique angle

The dimensions of the marble block determine the size of the sculpture

DETAIL OF SLAVE'S FOOT

Sculpture 2

EXAMPLES OF MODELLING TOOLS

WIRE-ENDED CUTTING TOOL

CURVED MOULDING TOOL

SPATULA-ENDED WAX MODELLING TOOL

ROUNDED WAX MODELLING TOOL

EXAMPLES OF BRONZE FINISHING TOOLS

HOOKED RIFFLER

POINTED RIFFLER

SPIRIT LAMP (FOR HEATING WAX MODELLING TOOLS)

Wick

Brass holder

Glass bowl

Methylated spirit

STAGES IN THE LOST-WAX METHOD OF CASTING
Based on Mars, Giambologna, c.1546

Wax-covered wire armature

ORIGINAL MODEL
An original, solid wax model is made and preserved so that numerous replicas can be cast.

Wax riser (vertical, hollow rod)

Chaplet (iron nail)

Wax runner (horizontal, hollow rod)

HOLLOW WAX FIGURE IS CAST
A new, hollow wax model is cast from the original model. It is filled with a plaster core that is held in place with nails. Wax runners and risers are attached.

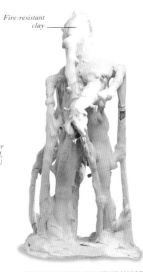

Fire-resistant clay

FIGURE IS BAKED IN CASTING MOULD
The model is encased in clay and baked. The wax melts away (through the channels made by the wax rods) and is replaced by molten bronze.

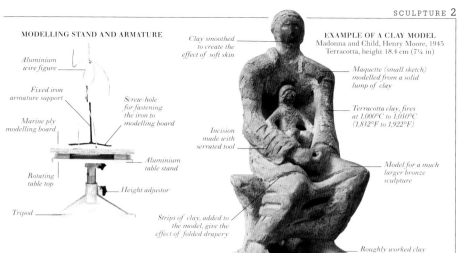

MODELLING STAND AND ARMATURE

Aluminium wire figure

Fixed iron armature support

Marine ply modelling board

Screw-hole for fastening the iron to modelling board

Rotating table top

Aluminium table stand

Tripod

Height adjustor

EXAMPLE OF A CLAY MODEL
Madonna and Child, Henry Moore, 1943
Terracotta, height 18.4 cm (7¼ in)

Clay smoothed to create the effect of soft skin

Maquette (small sketch) modelled from a solid lump of clay

Terracotta clay, fires at 1,000°C to 1,050°C (1,832°F to 1,922°F)

Incision made with serrated tool

Model for a much larger bronze sculpture

Strips of clay, added to the model, give the effect of folded drapery

Roughly worked clay

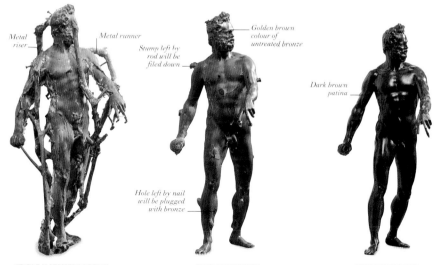

Metal riser

Metal runner

Golden brown colour of untreated bronze

Stump left by rod will be filed down

Dark brown patina

Hole left by nail will be plugged with bronze

STATUE IS STRIPPED OF CLAY
When the bronze has cooled, the clay mould is broken open to reveal the bronze statue with solid metal runners and risers.

STATUE IS FINISHED
The nails are pulled out and a large hole is made to remove the plaster core. When the metal rods have been sawn off, the sculpture is filed to refine the surface.

STATUE IS CLEANED
Finally the work is cleaned and polished. An artificial patina (colouring) is achieved by treating the surface with chemicals.

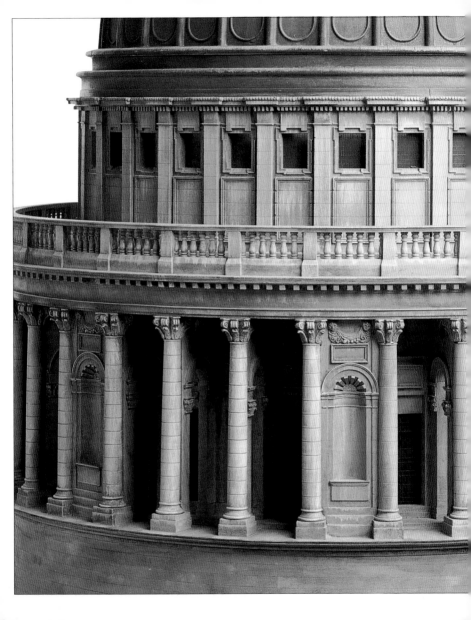

ARCHITECTURE

Ancient Egypt

THE CIVILIZATION OF THE ANCIENT EGYPTIANS (which lasted from about 3100 BC until it was finally absorbed into the Roman empire in 30 BC) is famous for its temples and tombs. Egyptian temples were often huge and geometric, like the Temple of Amon-Re (below and right). They were usually decorated with hieroglyphs (sacred characters used for picture-writing) and painted reliefs depicting gods, Pharaohs (kings), and queens. Tombs were particularly important to the Egyptians, who believed that the dead were resurrected in the after-life. The tombs were often decorated – as, for example, the surround of the false door opposite – in order to give comfort to the dead. The best-known ancient Egyptian tombs are the pyramids, which were designed to symbolize the rays of the sun. Many of the architectural forms used by the ancient Egyptians were later adopted by other civilizations; for example, columns and capitals were later used by the ancient Greeks (see pp. 460-461) and ancient Romans (see pp. 462-465).

SIDE VIEW OF HYPOSTYLE HALL, TEMPLE OF AMON-RE, KARNAK, EGYPT, c.1290 BC

Cornice decorated with cavetto moulding

Campaniform (open papyrus) capital

Architrave

Papyrus-bud capital

Socle

Side aisle

Central nave

Side aisle

Horus, the sun-god

Architrave

Stone slab forming flat roof of side ais

Kepresh crown with disc

Chons, the moon-god

Amon-Re, king of the gods

Hathor, the sky-goddess

Papyrus motif

Cartouche (oval border) containing the titles of the Pharaoh (king)

Socle

Aisle running north-south

LIMESTONE FALSE DOOR WITH HIEROGLYPHS, TOMB OF KING TJETJI, GIZA, EGYPT, c.2400 BC

Lintel

Hieroglyph representing a house

Disc representing sun or light

Eroded image of Tjetji

Limestone stela (slab)

Hoe-shaped hieroglyph representing "mr" sound

Head of false door

Image of Tjetji's wife

Image of Tjetji's daughter

PLANT CAPITAL OF THE PTOLEMAIC-ROMAN PERIOD, EGYPT, 332-30 BC

Palm leaf

Papyrus flower

Papyrus leaf

Papyrus stem

Lotus bud

Lotus stem

Cornice decorated with cavetto moulding

Bead moulding

Trellis window

Rectangular pier decorated with hieroglyphs

Elevated roof of central nave

Clerestory

Disc representing sun or light

Architrave

Square abacus

Papyrus-bud capital

Papyriform column

Shaft

Scene depicting a Pharaoh (king) paying homage to the god Amon-Re

Central nave

ANCIENT EGYPTIAN BUILDING DECORATION

DECORATED WINDOW, MEDINET HABU, EGYPT, C.1198BC

ROPE AND PATERAE DECORATION

CAPITAL WITH THE HEAD OF THE SKY-GODDESS HATHOR, TEMPLE OF ISIS, PHILAE, EGYPT, 283-47 BC

LOTUS AND PAPYRUS FRIEZE DECORATION

Ancient Greece

THE CLASSICAL TEMPLES OF ANCIENT GREECE were built according to the belief that certain forms and proportions were pleasing to the gods. There were three main ancient Greek architectural orders (styles), which can be distinguished by the decoration and proportions of their columns, capitals (column tops), and entablatures (structures resting on the capitals). The oldest is the Doric order, which dates from the seventh century BC and was used mainly on the Greek mainland and in the western colonies, such as Sicily and southern Italy. The Temple of Neptune, shown here, is a classic example of this order. It is hypaethral (roofless) and peripteral (surrounded by a single row of columns). About a century later, the more decorative Ionic order developed on the Aegean Islands. Features of this order include volutes (spiral scrolls) on capitals and acroteria (pediment ornaments). The Corinthian order was invented in Athens in the fifth century BC and is typically identified by an acanthus leaf on the capitals. This order was later widely used in ancient Roman architecture.

CAPITALS OF THE THREE ORDERS OF ANCIENT GREEK ARCHITECTURE

Abacus
Echinus
Annulet
Trachelion (neck)

DORIC CAPITAL, THE PROPYLAEUM (GATEWAY), THE ACROPOLIS, ATHENS, GREECE, 449 BC

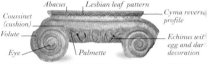

Abacus
Lesbian leaf pattern
Coussinet (cushion)
Cyma reverse profile
Volute
Echinus with egg and dart decoration
Eye
Palmette

IONIC CAPITAL, THE PROPYLAEUM (GATEWAY), TEMPLE OF ATHENA POLIAS, PRIENE, GREECE, c.334 BC

Mask
Abacus
Volute
Cauliculus
Bell-shaped core
Acanthus leaf

CORINTHIAN CAPITAL FROM A STOA (PORTICO), PROBABLY FROM ASIA MINOR

TEMPLE OF NEPTUNE, PAESTUM, ITALY, c.460 BC

Raking cornice
Pediment
Trachelion (neck)
Taenia
Triglyph
Metope
Glyph (channel)
Doric entablature
Pteron (external colonnade)
Euthynteria
Drum
Stylobate
Column of the Doric order

PLAN OF THE TEMPLE OF NEPTUNE, PAESTUM

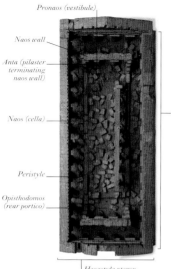

Pronaos (vestibule)

Naos wall

Anta (pilaster terminating naos wall)

Naos (cella)

Peristyle

Opisthodomos (rear portico)

Pteron (external colonnade)

Hexastyle pteron (colonnade of six columns)

ANCIENT GREEK BUILDING DECORATION

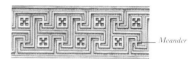

Volute

FACADE, TREASURY OF ATREUS, MYCENAE, GREECE, 1350-1250 BC

Meander

FRETWORK, PARTHENON, ATHENS, GREECE, 447-436 BC

ACROTERION, TEMPLE OF APHAIA, AEGINA, GREECE, 490 BC

Griffon (gryphon)

Raking cornice

ANTEFIXA, TEMPLE OF APHAIA, AEGINA, GREECE, 490 BC

Palmette

Volute

Regula (short fillet beneath taenia)

Eaves

Cornice

Frieze

Architrave

Capital

Shaft

Crepidoma (stepped base)

Entasis (slight curve of a column)

Intercolumniation

Fluting

Ancient Rome 1

IN THE EARLY PERIOD OF THE ROMAN EMPIRE extensive use was made of ancient Greek architectural ideas, particularly those of the Corinthian order (see pp. 460-461). As a result, many early Roman buildings – such as the Temple of Vesta (opposite) – closely resemble ancient Greek buildings. A distinctive Roman style began to evolve in the first century AD. This style developed the interiors of buildings (the Greeks had concentrated on the exterior) by using arches, vaults, and domes inside the buildings, and by ornamenting internal walls. Many of these features can be seen in the Pantheon. Exterior columns were often used for decorative, rather than structural, purposes, as in the Colosseum and the Porta Nigra (see pp. 464-465). Smaller buildings had timber frames with wattle-and-daub walls, as in the mill (see pp. 464-465). Roman architecture remained influential for many centuries, with some of its principles being used in the 11th century in Romanesque buildings (see pp. 468-469) and also in the 15th and 16th centuries in Renaissance buildings (see pp. 474-477).

ANCIENT ROMAN BUILDING DECORATION

FESTOON, TEMPLE OF VESTA, TIVOLI, ITALY, C.80 BC

RICHLY DECORATED ROMAN OVUM

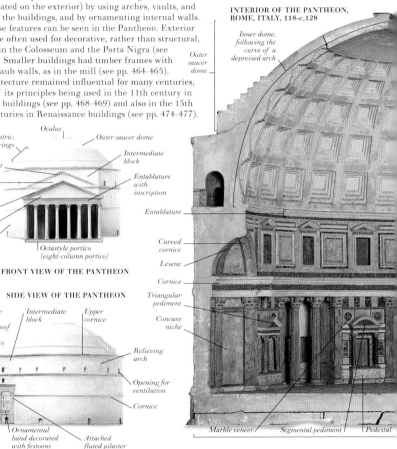

INTERIOR OF THE PANTHEON, ROME, ITALY, 118-c.128

- Inner dome, following the curve of a depressed arch
- Outer saucer dome
- Entablature
- Curved cornice
- Lesene
- Cornice
- Triangular pediment
- Concave niche
- Marble veneer
- Segmental pediment
- Pedestal

FRONT VIEW OF THE PANTHEON

- Oculus
- Series of concentric, step-like rings
- Outer saucer dome
- Intermediate block
- Dentil ornament
- Engaged pediment
- Entablature with inscription
- Raking cornice
- Entablature
- Pediment
- Rotunda
- Octastyle portico (eight-column portico)

SIDE VIEW OF THE PANTHEON

- Entablature
- Intermediate block
- Upper cornice
- Pitched roof
- Eaves
- Relieving arch
- Opening for ventilation
- Cornice
- Colonnade
- Ornamental band decorated with festoons
- Attached fluted pilaster

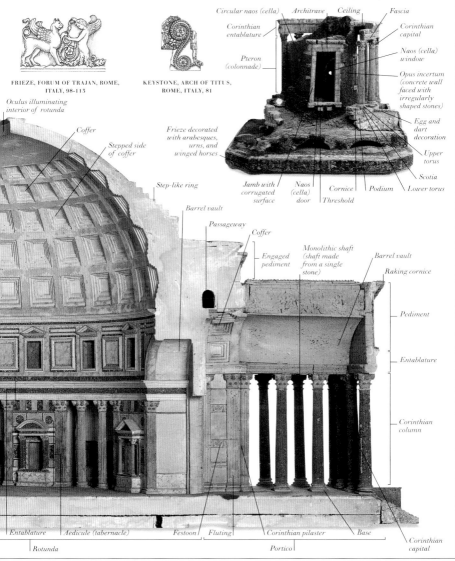

FRIEZE, FORUM OF TRAJAN, ROME, ITALY, 98-113

KEYSTONE, ARCH OF TITUS, ROME, ITALY, 81

TEMPLE OF VESTA, TIVOLI, ITALY, c.80 BC

Circular naos (cella)

Architrave

Ceiling

Fascia

Corinthian entablature

Corinthian capital

Pteron (colonnade)

Naos (cella) window

Opus incertum (concrete wall faced with irregularly shaped stones)

Egg and dart decoration

Upper torus

Scotia

Lower torus

Oculus illuminating interior of rotunda

Coffer

Stepped side of coffer

Frieze decorated with arabesques, urns, and winged horses

Step-like ring

Barrel vault

Passageway

Coffer

Engaged pediment

Monolithic shaft (shaft made from a single stone)

Barrel vault

Raking cornice

Pediment

Entablature

Corinthian column

Jamb with corrugated surface

Naos (cella) door

Cornice

Threshold

Podium

Entablature

Aedicule (tabernacle)

Festoon

Fluting

Corinthian pilaster

Base

Corinthian capital

Rotunda

Portico

463

Ancient Rome 2

SIDE VIEW OF A ROMAN MILL

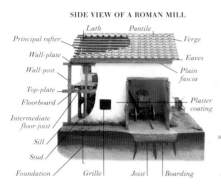

Principal rafter
Wall-plate
Wall-post
Top-plate
Floorboard
Intermediate floor-joist
Sill
Stud
Foundation

Lath
Pantile
Grille
Joist
Boarding

Verge
Eaves
Plain fascia
Plaster coating

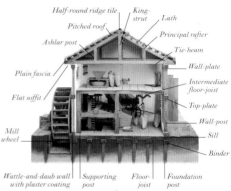

Half-round ridge tile
Pitched roof
Ashlar post
Plain fascia
Flat soffit
Mill wheel
Wattle-and-daub wall with plaster coating
Supporting post
Floor-joist
Foundation post

King-strut
Lath
Principal rafter
Tie-beam
Wall-plate
Intermediate floor-joist
Top-plate
Wall-post
Sill
Binder

THE COLOSSEUM (FLAVIAN AMPHITHEATRE), ROME, ITALY, 70-82

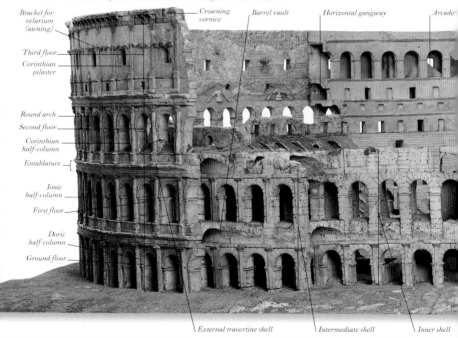

Bracket for velarium (awning)
Third floor
Corinthian pilaster
Round arch
Second floor
Corinthian half-column
Entablature
Ionic half-column
First floor
Doric half-column
Ground floor

Crowning cornice
Barrel vault
Horizontal gangway
Arcade

External travertine shell
Intermediate shell
Inner shell

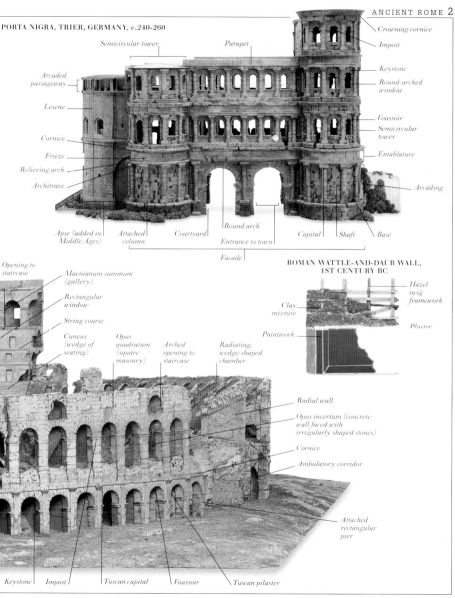

PORTA NIGRA, TRIER, GERMANY, c.240-260

Crowning cornice

Impost

Keystone

Round-arched window

Voussoir

Semicircular tower

Entablature

Arcading

Capital

Shaft

Base

Semicircular tower

Parapet

Arcaded passageway

Lesene

Cornice

Frieze

Relieving arch

Architrave

Apse (added in Middle Ages)

Attached column

Courtyard

Round arch

Entrance to town

Facade

Opening to staircase

Maenianum summum (gallery)

Rectangular window

String course

Cuneus (wedge of seating)

Opus quadratum (square masonry)

Arched opening to staircase

Radiating, wedge-shaped chamber

Radial wall

Opus incertum (concrete wall faced with irregularly shaped stones)

Cornice

Ambulatory corridor

Attached rectangular pier

Keystone

Impost

Tuscan capital

Voussoir

Tuscan pilaster

ROMAN WATTLE-AND-DAUB WALL, 1ST CENTURY BC

Hazel twig framework

Clay mixture

Plaster

Paintwork

Medieval castles and houses

WARFARE WAS COMMON IN EUROPE in the Middle Ages, and many monarchs and nobles built castles as a form of defence. Typical medieval castles have outer walls surrounding a moat. Inside the moat is a bailey (courtyard), protected by a chemise (jacket-wall). The innermost and strongest part of a medieval castle is the keep. There are two main types of keep: towers called donjons, such as the Tour de César and Coucy-le-Château, and rectangular keeps ("hall-keeps"), such as the Tower of London. Castles were often guarded by salients (projecting fortifications), like those of the Bastille. Medieval houses typically had timber cruck (tent-like) frames, wattle-and-daub walls, and pitched roofs, like those on medieval London Bridge (opposite).

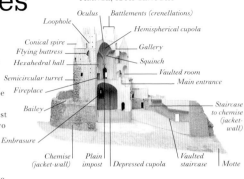

DONJON, TOUR DE CESAR, PROVINS, FRANCE, 12TH CENTURY

Loophole — Oculus — Battlements (crenellations) — Hemispherical cupola — Conical spire — Gallery — Flying buttress — Squinch — Hexahedral hall — Vaulted room — Semicircular turret — Main entrance — Fireplace — Bailey — Staircase to chemise (jacket-wall) — Embrasure — Chemise (jacket-wall) — Plain impost — Depressed cupola — Vaulted staircase — Motte

Loophole

SALIENT, CAERNARVON CASTLE, BRITAIN, 1283-1323

Timber cruck frame

CRUCK-FRAMED HOUSE, BRITAIN, c.1200

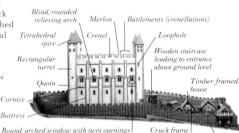

Blind, rounded relieving arch — Merlon — Battlements (crenellations) — Tetrahedral spire — Crenel — Loophole — Rectangular turret — Wooden staircase leading to entrance above ground level — Quoin — Timber-framed house — Cornice — Buttress — Round-arched window with twin openings — Cruck frame — Paling

TOWER OF LONDON, BRITAIN, FROM 1070

Curtain wall — Pointed relieving arch — Semicircular relieving arch — Plain string course — Bracket decorated with scroll moulding

Rectangular window — Sunken rectangular panel — Round-arched window — Semicircular salient — Loophole — Lateral circular salient

THE BASTILLE, PARIS, FRANCE, 14TH CENTURY

MEDIEVAL LONDON BRIDGE, BRITAIN, 1176 (WITH 14TH-CENTURY BATTLEMENTED BUILDING, NONESUCH HOUSE, AND TWO-TOWERED GATE)

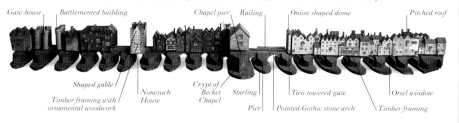

Gate-house
Battlemented building
Chapel pier
Railing
Onion-shaped dome
Pitched roof

Shaped gable
Nonesuch House
Crypt of Becket Chapel
Starling
Two-towered gate
Oriel window

Timber framing with ornamental woodwork
Pier
Pointed Gothic stone arch
Timber framing

DONJON, COUCY-LE-CHATEAU, AISNE, FRANCE, 1225-1245

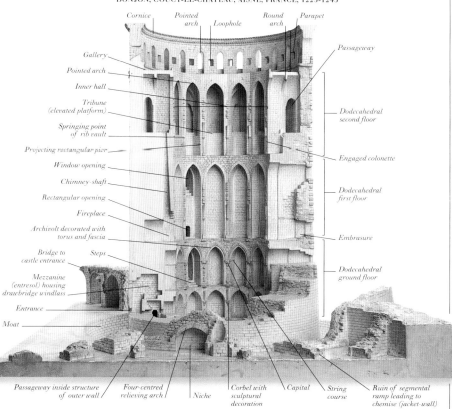

Cornice
Pointed arch
Loophole
Round arch
Parapet

Passageway

Gallery

Pointed arch

Inner hall

Tribune (elevated platform)

Springing point of rib vault

Projecting rectangular pier

Window opening

Chimney-shaft

Rectangular opening

Fireplace

Archivolt decorated with torus and fascia

Bridge to castle entrance
Steps

Mezzanine (entresol) housing drawbridge windlass

Entrance

Moat

Dodecahedral second floor

Engaged colonette

Dodecahedral first floor

Embrasure

Dodecahedral ground floor

Passageway inside structure of outer wall
Four-centred relieving arch
Niche
Corbel with sculptural decoration
Capital
String course
Ruin of segmental ramp leading to chemise (jacket-wall)

Medieval churches

ABBEY OF ST. FOI, CONQUES, FRANCE, c.1050-c.1130

DURING THE MIDDLE AGES, large numbers of churches were built in Europe. European churches of this period typically have high vaults supported by massive piers and columns. In the 10th century, the Romanesque style developed. Romanesque architects adopted many Roman or early Christian architectural ideas, such as cross-shaped ground-plans – like that of Angoulême Cathedral (opposite) – and the basilican system of a nave with a central vessel and side aisles. In the mid-12th century, flying buttresses and pointed vaults appeared. These features later became widely used in Gothic architecture (see pp. 470-471). Bagneux Church (opposite) has both styles: a Romanesque tower, and a Gothic nave and choir.

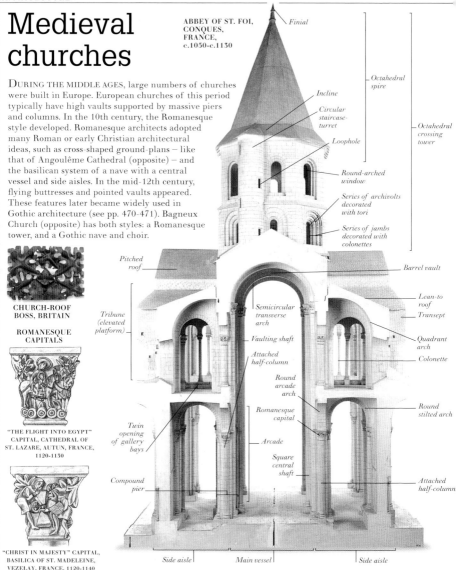

Finial

Octahedral spire

Incline

Circular staircase-turret

Loophole

Octahedral crossing tower

Round-arched window

Series of archivolts decorated with tori

Series of jambs decorated with colonettes

CHURCH-ROOF BOSS, BRITAIN

ROMANESQUE CAPITALS

Pitched roof

Barrel vault

Lean-to roof

Transept

Tribune (elevated platform)

Semicircular transverse arch

Quadrant arch

Vaulting shaft

Colonette

Attached half-column

Round arcade arch

"THE FLIGHT INTO EGYPT" CAPITAL, CATHEDRAL OF ST. LAZARE, AUTUN, FRANCE, 1120-1130

Twin opening of gallery bays

Romanesque capital

Round stilted arch

Arcade

Compound pier

Square central shaft

Attached half-column

"CHRIST IN MAJESTY" CAPITAL, BASILICA OF ST. MADELEINE, VEZELAY, FRANCE, 1120-1140

Side aisle

Main vessel

Side aisle

GROUND-PLAN OF ANGOULEME CATHEDRAL, FRANCE, FROM c.1105

CHOIR, CHURCH OF ST. SERGE, ANGERS, FRANCE, c.1215-1220

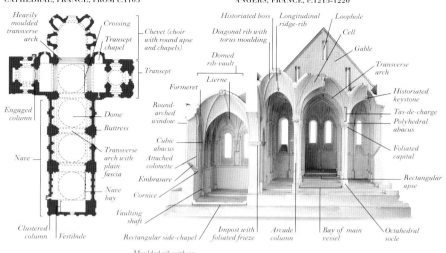

Heavily moulded transverse arch
Crossing
Transept chapel
Chevet (choir with round apse and chapels)
Transept
Engaged column
Dome
Buttress
Transverse arch with plain fascia
Nave
Nave bay
Clustered column
Vestibule

Historiated boss
Longitudinal ridge-rib
Loophole
Cell
Historiated keystone with torus moulding
Domed rib-vault
Gable
Transverse arch
Lierne
Formeret
Round-arched window
Historiated keystone
Tas-de-charge
Polyhedral abacus
Cubic abacus
Attached colonette
Embrasure
Cornice
Foliated capital
Rectangular apse
Vaulting shaft
Rectangular side-chapel
Impost with foliated frieze
Arcade column
Bay of main vessel
Octahedral socle

BAGNEUX CHURCH, FRANCE, 1170-1190

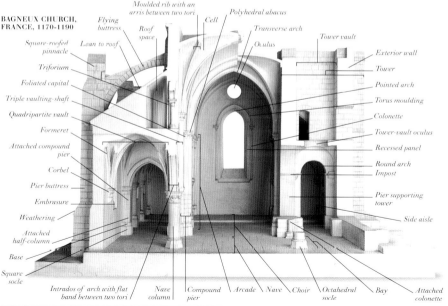

Moulded rib with an arris between two tori
Flying buttress
Cell
Polyhedral abacus
Roof space
Transverse arch
Square-roofed pinnacle
Lean to roof
Oculus
Tower vault
Exterior wall
Triforium
Tower
Foliated capital
Pointed arch
Triple vaulting-shaft
Torus moulding
Quadripartite vault
Colonette
Formeret
Tower-vault oculus
Attached compound pier
Recessed panel
Corbel
Round arch
Pier buttress
Impost
Embrasure
Pier supporting tower
Weathering
Side aisle
Attached half-column
Base
Square socle
Intrados of arch with flat band between two tori
Nave column
Compound pier
Arcade
Nave
Choir
Octahedral socle
Bay
Attached colonette

Gothic 1

GOTHIC STAINED GLASS WITH FOLIATED SCROLL MOTIF, ON WOODEN FORM

GOTHIC BUILDINGS are characterized by rib vaults, pointed or lancet arches, flying buttresses, decorative tracery and gables, and stained-glass windows. Typical Gothic buildings include the Cathedrals of Salisbury and old St. Paul's in England, and Notre Dame de Paris in France (see pp. 472-473). The Gothic style developed out of Romanesque architecture in France (see pp. 468-469) in the mid-12th century, and then spread throughout Europe. The decorative elements of Gothic architecture became highly developed in buildings of the English Decorated style (late 13th-14th century) and the French Flamboyant style (15th-16th century). These styles are exemplified by the tower of Salisbury Cathedral and the staircase in the Church of St. Maclou (see pp. 472-473), respectively. In both of these styles, embellishments such as ballflowers and curvilinear (flowing) tracery were used liberally. The English Perpendicular style (late 14th-15th century), which followed the Decorated style, emphasized the vertical and horizontal elements of a building. A notable feature of this style is the hammer-beam roof.

GROUND-PLAN OF SALISBURY CATHEDRAL

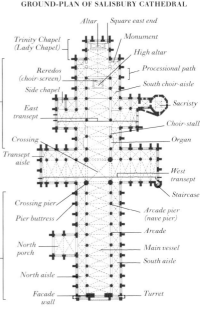

Altar
Square east end
Trinity Chapel (Lady Chapel)
Monument
High altar
Reredos (choir-screen)
Processional path
Side chapel
South choir-aisle
Choir
East transept
Sacristy
Choir-stall
Crossing
Organ
Transept aisle
West transept
Staircase
Crossing pier
Arcade pier (nave pier)
Pier buttress
Arcade
North porch
Main vessel
South aisle
Nave
North aisle
Facade wall
Turret

GOTHIC TORUS WITH BALLFLOWERS

Limestone block
Block members carved into rolls
Block members cut polygonally
Pencil guideline
Early stage of ballflower carving

BLOCK AFTER INITIAL CUTTING

BLOCK WITH MEMBERS CUT INTO ROLLS

Torus
Ballflower
Fillet
Mason's mark

FINISHED BLOCK

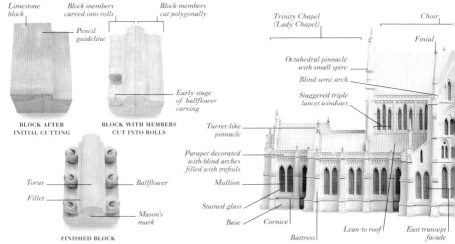

Trinity Chapel (Lady Chapel)
Choir
Finial
Octahedral pinnacle with small spire
Blind semi-arch
Staggered triple lancet windows
Turret-like pinnacle
Parapet decorated with blind arches filled with trefoils
Mullion
Stained glass
Base
Cornice
Buttress
Lean-to roof
East transept facade

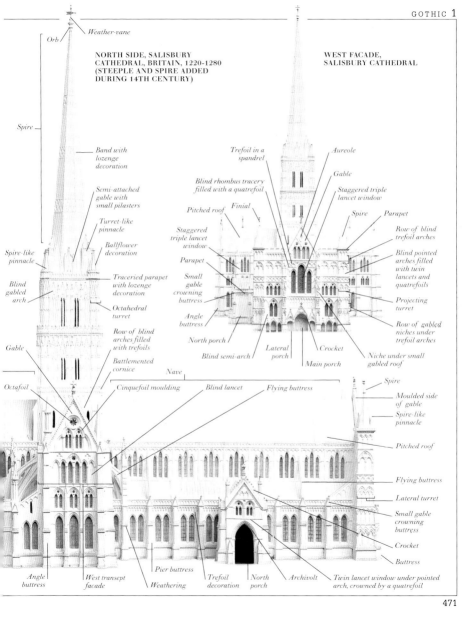

NORTH SIDE, SALISBURY CATHEDRAL, BRITAIN, 1220-1280 (STEEPLE AND SPIRE ADDED DURING 14TH CENTURY)

WEST FACADE, SALISBURY CATHEDRAL

Orb

Weather-vane

Spire

Band with lozenge decoration

Semi-attached gable with small pilasters

Turret-like pinnacle

Ballflower decoration

Spire-like pinnacle

Blind gabled arch

Traceried parapet with lozenge decoration

Octahedral turret

Row of blind arches filled with trefoils

Gable

Battlemented cornice

Octafoil

Cinquefoil moulding

Blind lancet

Flying buttress

Nave

Trefoil in a spandrel

Aureole

Gable

Blind rhombus tracery filled with a quatrefoil

Staggered triple lancet window

Pitched roof

Finial

Spire

Parapet

Staggered triple lancet window

Row of blind trefoil arches

Parapet

Blind pointed arches filled with twin lancets and quatrefoils

Small gable crowning buttress

Projecting turret

Angle buttress

Row of gabled niches under trefoil arches

North porch

Lateral porch

Crocket

Blind semi-arch

Niche under small gabled roof

Main porch

Spire

Moulded side of gable

Spire-like pinnacle

Pitched roof

Flying buttress

Lateral turret

Small gable crowning buttress

Crocket

Buttress

Angle buttress

West transept facade

Weathering

Pier buttress

Trefoil decoration

North porch

Archivolt

Twin lancet window under pointed arch, crowned by a quatrefoil

471

Gothic 2

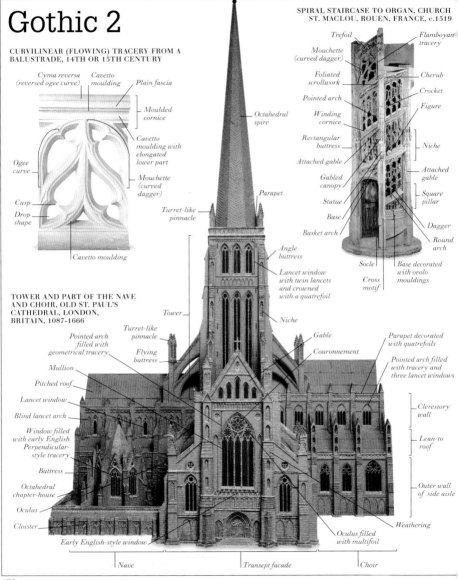

CURVILINEAR (FLOWING) TRACERY FROM A BALUSTRADE, 14TH OR 15TH CENTURY

- *Cyma reversa (reversed ogee curve)*
- *Cavetto moulding*
- *Plain fascia*
- *Moulded cornice*
- *Cavetto moulding with elongated lower part*
- *Ogee curve*
- *Mouchette (curved dagger)*
- *Cusp*
- *Drop shape*
- *Cavetto moulding*

SPIRAL STAIRCASE TO ORGAN, CHURCH ST. MACLOU, ROUEN, FRANCE, c.1519

- *Trefoil*
- *Flamboyant tracery*
- *Mouchette (curved dagger)*
- *Foliated scrollwork*
- *Cherub*
- *Pointed arch*
- *Crocket*
- *Winding cornice*
- *Figure*
- *Rectangular buttress*
- *Niche*
- *Attached gable*
- *Attached gable*
- *Gabled canopy*
- *Square pillar*
- *Statue*
- *Base*
- *Dagger*
- *Basket arch*
- *Round arch*
- *Socle*
- *Base decorated with ovolo mouldings*
- *Cross motif*

TOWER AND PART OF THE NAVE AND CHOIR, OLD ST. PAUL'S CATHEDRAL, LONDON, BRITAIN, 1087-1666

- *Octahedral spire*
- *Parapet*
- *Turret-like pinnacle*
- *Angle buttress*
- *Lancet window with twin lancets and crowned with a quatrefoil*
- *Tower*
- *Niche*
- *Turret-like pinnacle*
- *Pointed arch filled with geometrical tracery*
- *Flying buttress*
- *Mullion*
- *Pitched roof*
- *Lancet window*
- *Blind lancet arch*
- *Window filled with early English Perpendicular-style tracery*
- *Buttress*
- *Octahedral chapter-house*
- *Oculus*
- *Cloister*
- *Gable*
- *Couronnement*
- *Parapet decorated with quatrefoils*
- *Pointed arch filled with tracery and three lancet windows*
- *Clerestory wall*
- *Lean-to roof*
- *Outer wall of side aisle*
- *Weathering*
- *Early English-style window*
- *Oculus filled with multifoil*
- *Nave*
- *Transept facade*
- *Choir*

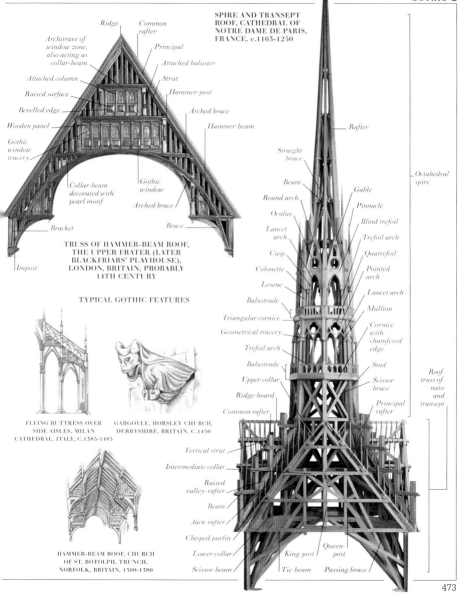

SPIRE AND TRANSEPT ROOF, CATHEDRAL OF NOTRE DAME DE PARIS, FRANCE, c.1163-1250

Ridge
Common rafter
Architrave of window zone, also acting as collar-beam
Principal
Attached baluster
Attached column
Strut
Raised surface
Hammer-post
Bevelled edge
Arched brace
Wooden panel
Hammer-beam
Gothic window tracery
Rafter
Collar-beam decorated with pearl motif
Gothic window
Arched brace
Bracket
Brace
Impost

TRUSS OF HAMMER-BEAM ROOF, THE UPPER FRATER (LATER BLACKFRIARS' PLAYHOUSE), LONDON, BRITAIN, PROBABLY 14TH CENTURY

TYPICAL GOTHIC FEATURES

FLYING BUTTRESS OVER SIDE AISLES, MILAN CATHEDRAL, ITALY, C.1385-1485

GARGOYLE, HORSLEY CHURCH, DERBYSHIRE, BRITAIN, C.1450

HAMMER-BEAM ROOF, CHURCH OF ST. BOTOLPH, TRUNCH, NORFOLK, BRITAIN, 1360-1380

Straight brace
Beam
Round arch
Oculus
Lancet arch
Cusp
Colonette
Lesene
Balustrade
Triangular cornice
Geometrical tracery
Trefoil arch
Balustrade
Upper collar
Ridge-board
Common rafter
Vertical strut
Intermediate collar
Raised valley-rafter
Beam
Jack-rafter
Clasped purlin
Lower collar
Scissor-beam

Gable
Pinnacle
Blind trefoil
Trefoil arch
Quatrefoil
Pointed arch
Lancet arch
Mullion
Cornice with chamfered edge
Stud
Scissor brace
Principal rafter
King-post
Queen-post
Tie-beam
Passing brace

Octahedral spire

Roof truss of nave and transept

473

Renaissance 1

THE RENAISSANCE was a European movement – lasting roughly from the 14th century to the mid-17th century – in which the arts and sciences underwent great changes. In architecture, these changes were marked by a return to the classical forms and proportions of ancient Roman buildings. The Renaissance originated in Italy, and the buildings most characteristic of its style can be found there, such as the Palazzo Strozzi shown here. Mannerism is a branch of the Renaissance style that distorts the classical forms; an example is the Laurentian Library staircase. As the Renaissance style spread to other European countries, many of its features were incorporated into the local architecture; for example, the Château de Montal in France (see pp. 476-477) incorporates aedicules (tabernacles).

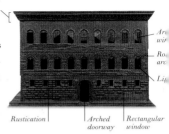

Crowning cornice

Ar... wir...

Ro... arc...

Li...

Rustication *Arched doorway* *Rectangular window*

SIDE VIEW OF PALAZZO STROZZI, FLORENCE, ITALY, 1489 (BY G. DA SANGALLO, B. DA MAIANO, AND CRONACA)

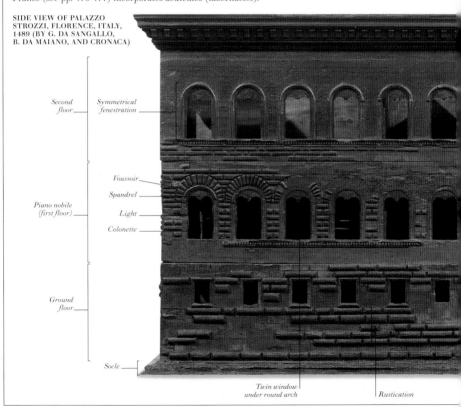

Second floor

Symmetrical fenestration

Voussoir

Spandrel

Piano nobile (first floor)

Light

Colonette

Ground floor

Socle

Twin window under round arch

Rustication

DETAILS FROM ITALIAN RENAISSANCE BUILDINGS

**PANEL FROM DRUM OF DOME,
FLORENCE CATHEDRAL, 1420-1436**

**COFFERING IN DOME,
PAZZI CHAPEL,
FLORENCE, 1429-1461**

**STAIRCASE,
LAURENTIAN LIBRARY,
FLORENCE, 1559**

**PORTICO, VILLA ROTUNDA,
VICENZA, 1567-1569**

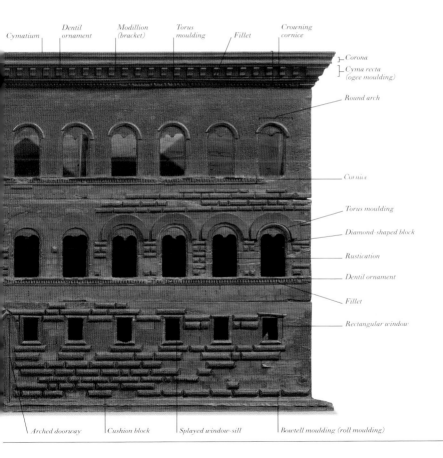

Cymatium

Dentil ornament

Modillion (bracket)

Torus moulding

Fillet

Crowning cornice

Corona

Cyma recta (ogee moulding)

Round arch

Cornice

Torus moulding

Diamond-shaped block

Rustication

Dentil ornament

Fillet

Rectangular window

Arched doorway

Cushion block

Splayed window-sill

Bowtell moulding (roll moulding)

Renaissance 2

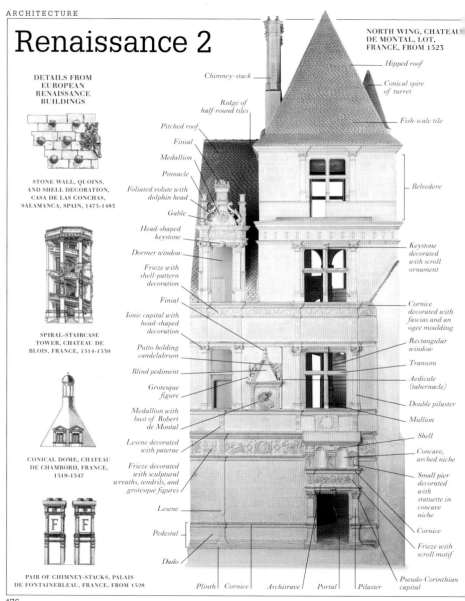

**DETAILS FROM
EUROPEAN
RENAISSANCE
BUILDINGS**

STONE WALL, QUOINS,
AND SHELL DECORATION,
CASA DE LAS CONCHAS,
SALAMANCA, SPAIN, 1475-1483

SPIRAL-STAIRCASE
TOWER, CHATEAU DE
BLOIS, FRANCE, 1514-1530

CONICAL DOME, CHATEAU
DE CHAMBORD, FRANCE,
1519-1547

PAIR OF CHIMNEY-STACKS, PALAIS
DE FONTAINEBLEAU, FRANCE, FROM 1528

Hipped roof

Conical spire
of turret

Fish-scale tile

Chimney-stack

Ridge of
half-round tiles

Pitched roof

Finial

Medallion

Pinnacle

Foliated volute with
dolphin head

Gable

Head-shaped
keystone

Dormer window

Frieze with
shell-pattern
decoration

Finial

Ionic capital with
head-shaped
decoration

Putto holding
candelabrum

Blind pediment

Grotesque
figure

Medallion with
bust of Robert
de Montal

Lesene decorated
with paterae

Frieze decorated
with sculptural
wreaths, tendrils, and
grotesque figures

Lesene

Pedestal

Dado

Belvedere

Keystone
decorated
with scroll
ornament

Cornice
decorated with
fascias and an
ogee moulding

Rectangular
window

Transom

Aedicule
(tabernacle)

Double pilaster

Mullion

Shell

Concave,
arched niche

Small pier
decorated
with
statuette in
concave
niche

Cornice

Frieze with
scroll motif

Pseudo-Corinthian
capital

Plinth   Cornice   Architrave   Portal   Pilaster

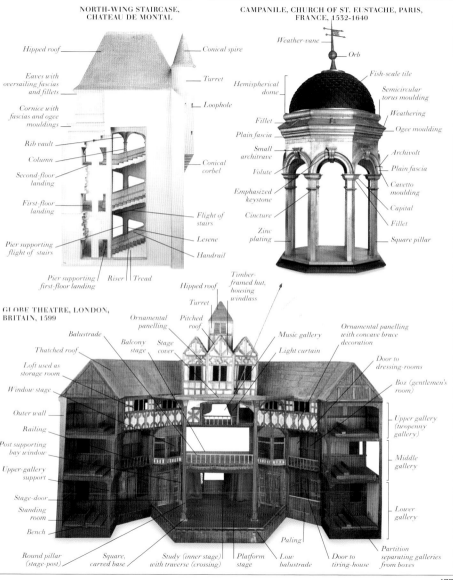

NORTH-WING STAIRCASE, CHATEAU DE MONTAL

- Hipped roof
- Conical spire
- Eaves with oversailing fascias and fillets
- Turret
- Cornice with fascias and ogee mouldings
- Loophole
- Rib vault
- Column
- Second-floor landing
- First-floor landing
- Conical corbel
- Flight of stairs
- Pier supporting flight of stairs
- Lesene
- Handrail
- Pier supporting first-floor landing
- Riser
- Tread

CAMPANILE, CHURCH OF ST. EUSTACHE, PARIS, FRANCE, 1532-1640

- Weather-vane
- Orb
- Hemispherical dome
- Fish-scale tile
- Semicircular torus moulding
- Weathering
- Fillet
- Plain fascia
- Ogee moulding
- Small architrave
- Archivolt
- Volute
- Plain fascia
- Emphasized keystone
- Cavetto moulding
- Cincture
- Capital
- Zinc plating
- Fillet
- Square pillar

GLOBE THEATRE, LONDON, BRITAIN, 1599

- Timber-framed hut, housing windlass
- Hipped roof
- Turret
- Ornamental panelling
- Pitched roof
- Music gallery
- Ornamental panelling with concave brace decoration
- Balustrade
- Balcony stage
- Stage cover
- Light curtain
- Door to dressing-rooms
- Thatched roof
- Box (gentlemen's room)
- Loft used as storage room
- Window stage
- Outer wall
- Upper gallery (twopenny gallery)
- Railing
- Post supporting bay window
- Middle gallery
- Upper-gallery support
- Stage-door
- Standing room
- Lower gallery
- Bench
- Paling
- Partition separating galleries from boxes
- Round pillar (stage-post)
- Square, carved base
- Study (inner stage) with traverse (crossing)
- Platform stage
- Low balustrade
- Door to tiring-house

Baroque and neoclassical 1

THE BAROQUE STYLE EVOLVED IN THE EARLY 17TH CENTURY in Rome. It is characterized by curved outlines and ostentatious decoration, as can be seen in the Italian church details (right). The baroque style was particularly widely favoured in Italy, Spain, and Germany. It was also adopted in Britain and France, but with adaptations. The British architects Sir Christopher Wren and Nicholas Hawksmoor, for example, used baroque features – such as the concave walls of St. Paul's Cathedral and the curved buttresses of the Church of St. George in the East (see pp. 480-481) – but they did so with restraint. Similarly, the curved buttresses and volutes of the Parisian Church of St. Paul-St. Louis are relatively plain. In the second half of the 17th century, a distinct classical style (known as neoclassicism) developed in northern Europe as a reaction to the excesses of baroque. Typical of this new style were churches such as the Madeleine (a proposed facade is shown below), as well as secular buildings such as the Cirque Napoleon (opposite) and the buildings of the British architect Sir John Soane (see pp. 482-483). In early 18th-century France, an extremely lavish form of baroque developed, known as rococo. The balcony from Nantes (see pp. 482-483) with its twisted ironwork and head-shaped corbels is typical of this style.

SCROLLED BUTTRESS, CHURCH OF ST. MARIA DELLA SALUTE, VENICE, 1631-1682

STATUE OF THE ECSTASY OF ST. THERESA, CHURCH OF ST. MARIA DELLA VITTORIA, ROME, 1645-1652

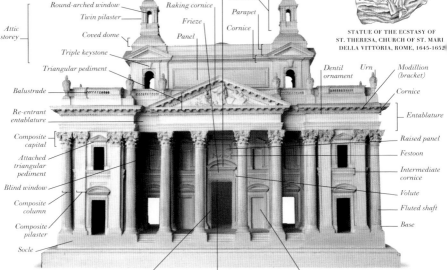

PROPOSED FACADE, THE MADELEINE (NEOCLASSICAL), PARIS, FRANCE, 1764 (BY P. CONTANT D'IVRY)

CIRQUE NAPOLEON (NEOCLASSICAL), PARIS, FRANCE, 1852 (BY J.I. HITTORFF)

EXTERIOR

Rectangular panel

Small polyhedral roof

Attached colonette

Projecting entablature

Polyhedral iron roof

Palmette

Sculpted frieze

Cornice

Pedestal

Smooth, vertical rustication

Statue of Amazon on horseback

Hanging wreath

Dado (die)

Plinth

Projecting pedestal

Eagle carrying festoons

INTERIOR

King-post

Statue of Minerva

Tie-beam

Orb

Painted inner roof

Brace

Polyhedral lantern

Roll moulding

Strut

Straight brace

Projecting entablature

Crest

Projecting socle

Outer wall

Attached Corinthian column

Frieze painted with scenes from classical mythology

Circle (auditorium)

Finial with cavetto moulding

Foliated panel

Transverse arch

Crowning cornice

Window hood-mould

Volute

Fascia

Barrel vault

Dentil

Clerestory level

Rectangular door leading to roofed space

Groin vault

Raised window jamb

Curved buttress

Gallery level

Semi-parabolic curve

Short pilaster

Pier-shaped pinnacle

Modillion (bracket)

Cornice

Architrave decorated with oversailing fascias

Semicircular arched window

Corinthian capital

Cornice

Foliated frieze

Gallery

Depressed arch

Small cupola

Oeil-de-boeuf ("ox-eye") window

Balustrade

Pendentive

Keystone decorated with scroll ornament

Archivolt

Archivolt decorated with plain fascias

Formeret (wall rib)

Cornice

Arcade

Round arch

Window jamb

Arcade level

Buttress

Window-sill

Outer wall

Round arch

Re-entrant corner

Base

Socle

Doorway connecting chapels

Side chapels

Main vessel

Side chapels

NAVE, CHURCH OF ST. PAUL-ST. LOUIS (FRENCH BAROQUE), PARIS, FRANCE, FROM 1627 (BY E. MARTELLANGE)

Baroque and neoclassical 2

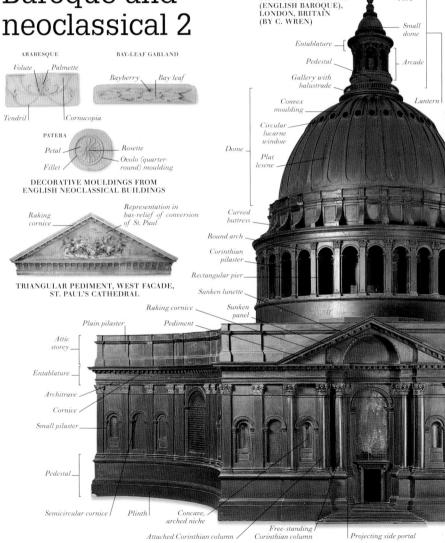

ARABESQUE

Volute · Palmette
Tendril · Cornucopia

BAY-LEAF GARLAND

Bayberry · Bay leaf

PATERA

Petal · Rosette
Fillet · Ovolo (quarter-round) moulding

DECORATIVE MOULDINGS FROM ENGLISH NEOCLASSICAL BUILDINGS

Raking cornice
Representation in bas-relief of conversion of St. Paul

TRIANGULAR PEDIMENT, WEST FACADE, ST. PAUL'S CATHEDRAL

MODEL BUILT IN 1674 OF PROPOSED EXTERIOR OF ST. PAUL'S CATHEDRAL (ENGLISH BAROQUE), LONDON, BRITAIN (BY C. WREN)

Cross
Orb
Small dome
Entablature
Pedestal — Arcade
Gallery with balustrade
Lantern
Convex moulding
Circular lucarne window
Dome
Plat lesene
Curved buttress
Round arch
Corinthian pilaster
Rectangular pier
Sunken lunette
Sunken panel
Raking cornice
Pediment
Plain pilaster
Attic storey
Entablature
Architrave
Cornice
Small pilaster
Pedestal
Semicircular cornice · Plinth
Concave, arched niche
Attached Corinthian column
Free-standing Corinthian column
Projecting side portal

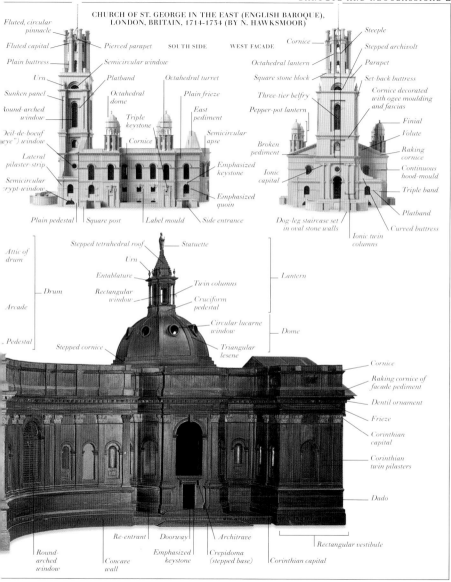

**CHURCH OF ST. GEORGE IN THE EAST (ENGLISH BAROQUE),
LONDON, BRITAIN, 1714-1734 (BY N. HAWKSMOOR)**

SOUTH SIDE   WEST FACADE

Fluted, circular pinnacle

Fluted capital

Plain buttress

Urn

Sunken panel

Round-arched window

Œil-de-boeuf ("eye") window

Lateral pilaster-strip

Semicircular crypt-window

Plain pedestal

Square post

Pierced parapet

Semicircular window

Plathband

Octahedral dome

Triple keystone

Cornice

Octahedral turret

Plain frieze

East pediment

Semicircular apse

Emphasized keystone

Emphasized quoin

Label mould

Side entrance

Steeple

Cornice

Octahedral lantern

Square stone block

Three-tier belfry

Pepper-pot lantern

Broken pediment

Ionic capital

Stepped archivolt

Parapet

Set-back buttress

Cornice decorated with ogee moulding and fascias

Finial

Volute

Raking cornice

Continuous hood-mould

Triple band

Plathband

Curved buttress

Dog-leg staircase set in oval stone walls

Ionic twin columns

Attic of drum

Drum

Arcade

Pedestal

Stepped tetrahedral roof

Urn

Entablature

Rectangular window

Statuette

Twin columns

Cruciform pedestal

Circular lucarne window

Triangular lesene

Stepped cornice

Lantern

Dome

Cornice

Raking cornice of facade pediment

Dentil ornament

Frieze

Corinthian capital

Corinthian twin pilasters

Dado

Round-arched window

Concave wall

Re-entrant

Emphasized keystone

Doorway

Crepidoma (stepped base)

Architrave

Corinthian capital

Rectangular vestibule

Baroque and neoclassical 3

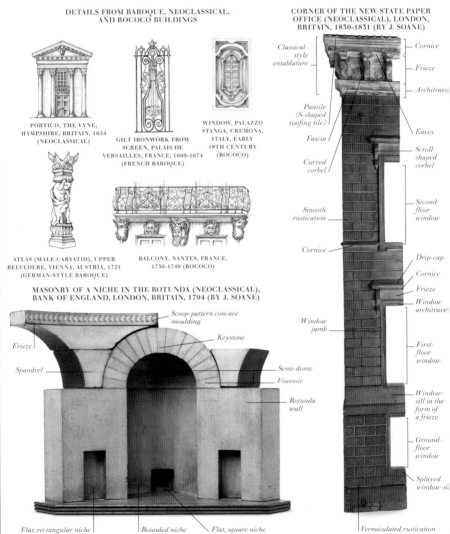

DETAILS FROM BAROQUE, NEOCLASSICAL, AND ROCOCO BUILDINGS

PORTICO, THE VYNE, HAMPSHIRE, BRITAIN, 1654 (NEOCLASSICAL)

GILT IRONWORK FROM SCREEN, PALAIS DE VERSAILLES, FRANCE, 1669-1674 (FRENCH BAROQUE)

WINDOW, PALAZZO STANGA, CREMONA, ITALY, EARLY 18TH CENTURY (ROCOCO)

ATLAS (MALE CARYATID), UPPER BELVEDERE, VIENNA, AUSTRIA, 1721 (GERMAN-STYLE BAROQUE)

BALCONY, NANTES, FRANCE, 1730-1740 (ROCOCO)

MASONRY OF A NICHE IN THE ROTUNDA (NEOCLASSICAL), BANK OF ENGLAND, LONDON, BRITAIN, 1794 (BY J. SOANE)

Scoop-pattern concave moulding

Keystone

Frieze

Spandrel

Semi-dome

Voussoir

Rotunda wall

Flat, rectangular niche

Rounded niche

Flat, square niche

CORNER OF THE NEW STATE PAPER OFFICE (NEOCLASSICAL), LONDON, BRITAIN, 1830-1831 (BY J. SOANE)

Classical-style entablature

Cornice

Frieze

Architrave

Pantile (S-shaped roofing tile)

Eaves

Fascia

Scroll-shaped corbel

Curved corbel

Second-floor window

Smooth rustication

Cornice

Drip-cap

Cornice

Frieze

Window architrave

Window jamb

First-floor window

Window-sill in the form of a frieze

Ground-floor window

Splayed window-sill

Vermiculated rustication

TYRINGHAM HOUSE (NEOCLASSICAL), BUCKINGHAMSHIRE, BRITAIN, 1793-1797 (BY J. SOANE)

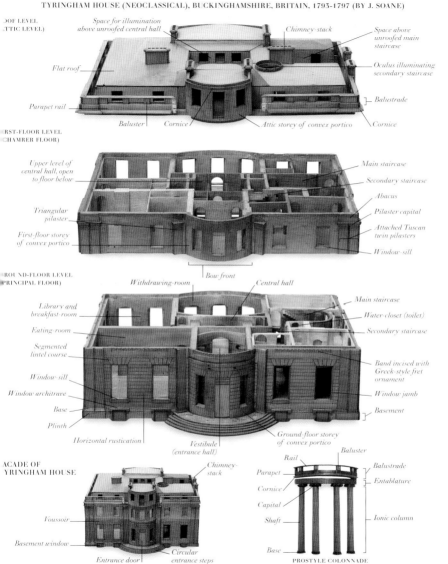

ROOF LEVEL (ATTIC LEVEL)

Space for illumination above unroofed central hall
Chimney-stack
Space above unroofed main staircase
Flat roof
Oculus illuminating secondary staircase
Parapet rail
Balustrade
Baluster
Cornice
Attic storey of convex portico
Cornice

FIRST-FLOOR LEVEL (CHAMBER FLOOR)

Upper level of central hall, open to floor below
Main staircase
Secondary staircase
Abacus
Triangular pilaster
Pilaster capital
Attached Tuscan twin pilasters
First-floor storey of convex portico
Window-sill

GROUND-FLOOR LEVEL (PRINCIPAL FLOOR)

Withdrawing-room
Central hall
Library and breakfast-room
Main staircase
Water-closet (toilet)
Eating-room
Secondary staircase
Segmented lintel course
Band incised with Greek-style fret ornament
Window-sill
Window architrave
Window jamb
Base
Basement
Plinth
Horizontal rustication
Vestibule (entrance hall)
Ground-floor storey of convex portico

FACADE OF TYRINGHAM HOUSE

Chimney-stack
Voussoir
Basement window
Entrance door
Circular entrance steps

Rail
Baluster
Parapet
Balustrade
Cornice
Entablature
Capital
Shaft
Ionic column
Base
PROSTYLE COLONNADE

Arches and vaults

ARCHES ARE CURVED STRUCTURES used to bridge spans and to support the weight of upper parts of buildings, such as domes, as in St. Paul's Cathedral (below) and the antique temple (opposite). The voussoirs (wedge-shaped blocks) that form an arch (right) support each other and convert the downward force of the weight of the building into an outward force. This outward force is in turn transferred to buttresses, piers, or abutments. A vault is an arched roof or ceiling. There are four main types of vault (opposite). A barrel vault is a single vault, semicircular in cross-section; a groin vault consists of two barrel vaults intersecting at right-angles; a rib vault is a groin vault reinforced by ribs; and a fan vault is a rib vault in which the ribs radiate from the springing point (where the arch begins) like a fan.

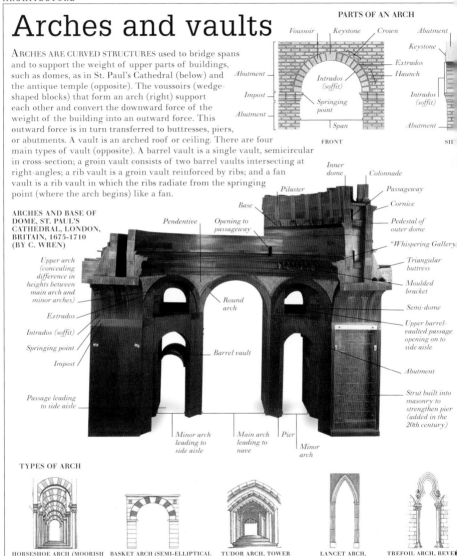

ARCHES AND BASE OF DOME, ST. PAUL'S CATHEDRAL, LONDON, BRITAIN, 1675-1710 (BY C. WREN)

TYPES OF ARCH

HORSESHOE ARCH (MOORISH ARCH), GREAT MOSQUE, CORDORA, SPAIN, 785

BASKET ARCH (SEMI-ELLIPTICAL ARCH), PALATINE CHAPEL, AIX-LA-CHAPELLE, FRANCE, 790-798

TUDOR ARCH, TOWER OF LONDON, BRITAIN, C.1086-1097

LANCET ARCH, WESTMINSTER ABBEY, LONDON, BRITAIN, 1503-1519

TREFOIL ARCH, BEVERLEY MINSTER, YORKSHIRE, BRITAIN, C.1300

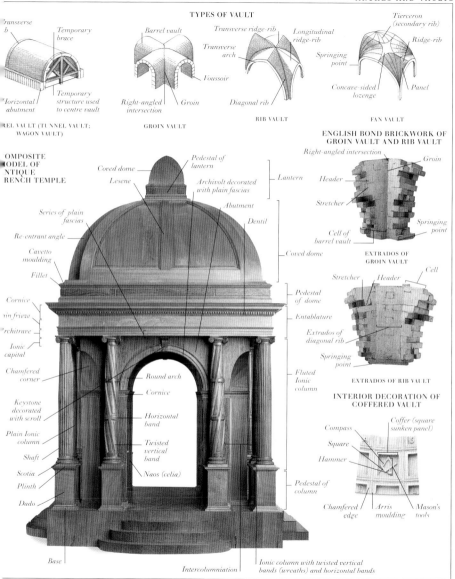

TYPES OF VAULT

Transverse rib

Temporary brace

Horizontal abutment

Temporary structure used to centre vault

BARREL VAULT (TUNNEL VAULT; WAGON VAULT)

Barrel vault

Voussoir

Right-angled intersection

Groin

GROIN VAULT

Transverse ridge-rib

Transverse arch

Diagonal rib

RIB VAULT

Tierceron (secondary rib)

Ridge-rib

Springing point

Concave-sided lozenge

Panel

FAN VAULT

COMPOSITE MODEL OF ANTIQUE FRENCH TEMPLE

Coved dome

Lesene

Series of plain fascias

Re-entrant angle

Cavetto moulding

Fillet

Cornice

Plain frieze

Architrave

Ionic capital

Chamfered corner

Keystone decorated with scroll

Plain Ionic column

Shaft

Scotia

Plinth

Dado

Base

Pedestal of lantern

Archivolt decorated with plain fascias

Abutment

Dentil

Round arch

Cornice

Horizontal band

Twisted vertical band

Naos (celia)

Intercolumniation

Lantern

Coved dome

Pedestal of dome

Entablature

Fluted Ionic column

Pedestal of column

Ionic column with twisted vertical bands (wreaths) and horizontal bands

ENGLISH BOND BRICKWORK OF GROIN VAULT AND RIB VAULT

Right-angled intersection

Header

Stretcher

Cell of barrel vault

Groin

Springing point

EXTRADOS OF GROIN VAULT

Stretcher

Header

Cell

Extrados of diagonal rib

Springing point

EXTRADOS OF RIB VAULT

INTERIOR DECORATION OF COFFERED VAULT

Compass

Square

Hammer

Coffer (square sunken panel)

Chamfered edge

Arris moulding

Mason's tools

485

Domes

A DOME IS A CONVEX ROOF. Domes are categorized according to the shapes of both the base and the section through the centre of the dome. The base may be circular, square, or polygonal (many-sided), depending on the plan of the drum (the walls on which the dome rests). The section of a dome may be the same shape as any arch (see pp. 484-485). Various types of dome are illustrated here: a hemispherical dome, which has a circular base and a semicircular section; a saucer dome, which has a circular base and a segmental (less than a semicircle) section; a polyhedral dome, which is a dome on a polygonal base whose sides meet at the top of the dome; and an onion dome, which has a circular or polygonal base and an ogee-shaped section. Many domes have a lantern (a turret with windows) to provide light inside.

LANTERN AND UPPER DOME TIMBERING, ST. PAUL'S CATHEDRAL

DOME TIMBERING, CHURCH OF THE SORBONNE PARIS, FRANCE, 1635-1642 (BY J. LEMERCIER)

Ogee-curved dome
Straight brace
Deeply projecting pier buttress
Window zone
Cornice
Depressedhood-mould
Pedestal
Circular lucarne window
Floorboard
Floor-joist
Ashlar piece
Hood-mould
Pin
Waisted-oval lucarne window
Short strut
Mortise-and-tenon joint
Ogee-curved window-frame
Principal rafter
Straight brace
Vertical post
Tie-beam
Circular baseplate
Common rafter
Shaft connecting lantern and church interior

ROOF WITH LANTERN AND ONION DOME

Weathercock
Ellipsoid orb
Keeled lesene
Onion dome
Fish-scaletile
Octahedral base
Oversailing fascia
Sloping roof
Round arch
Tetrahedral capital
Attached pillar
Return
Vertical band
Window
Oversailing fascia
Torus
Octahedral base of lantern
Fillet
Lantern
Tetrahedral roof

REPRESENTATION OF DOME METALLING, CHURCH OF THE SORBONNE

Cross
Orb
Square rib
Inverted ovolo (quarter-round)
Astragal
Fillet
Volute
Plain fascia
Roll moulding
Lantern
Round-arched window
Buttress
Ovolo (quarter-round)
Volute
Cornice
Fillet
Projecting pier buttress
Dome on a circular base
Fish-scale tile
Inverted demi-heart torus moulding
Hood-mould
Waisted-oval lucarne window
Small volute
Gutter
Parapet
Semicircular torus moulding
Small roll
Fillet
Plain fascia
Triple lesene

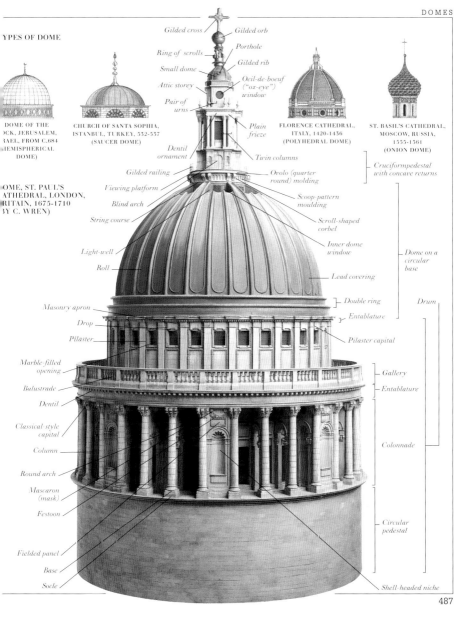

TYPES OF DOME

DOME OF THE
ROCK, JERUSALEM,
ISRAEL, FROM C.684
(HEMISPHERICAL
DOME)

CHURCH OF SANTA SOPHIA,
ISTANBUL, TURKEY, 532-537
(SAUCER DOME)

FLORENCE CATHEDRAL,
ITALY, 1420-1436
(POLYHEDRAL DOME)

ST. BASIL'S CATHEDRAL,
MOSCOW, RUSSIA,
1555-1561
(ONION DOME)

DOME, ST. PAUL'S
CATHEDRAL, LONDON,
BRITAIN, 1675-1710
(BY C. WREN)

Gilded cross
Gilded orb
Porthole
Ring of scrolls
Small dome
Gilded rib
Attic storey
Oeil-de-boeuf
("ox-eye")
window
Pair of
urns
Plain
frieze
Dentil
ornament
Twin columns
Gilded railing
Ovolo (quarter
round) molding
Viewing platform
Blind arch
Scoop-pattern
moulding
String course
Scroll-shaped
corbel
Light-well
Inner dome
window
Roll
Lead covering

Cruciform pedestal
with concave returns

Dome on a
circular
base

Masonry apron
Double ring
Drum
Drop
Entablature
Pilaster
Pilaster capital

Marble-filled
opening
Gallery
Balustrade
Entablature
Dentil
Classical-style
capital
Column
Colonnade
Round arch
Mascaron
(mask)
Festoon
Circular
pedestal
Fielded panel
Base
Socle
Shell-headed niche

Islamic buildings

OPUS SECTILE MOSAIC DESIGN

THE ISLAMIC RELIGION was founded by the prophet Muhammad, who was born in Mecca (in present-day Saudi Arabia) about 570 AD. In the following three centuries, Islam spread from Arabia to North Africa and Spain, as well as to India and much of the rest of Asia. The worldwide influence of Islam remains strong today. Common characteristics of Islamic buildings include ogee arches and roofs, onion domes, and walls decorated with carved stone, paintings, inlays, or mosaics. The most important type of Islamic building is the mosque – the place of worship – which generally has a minaret (tower) from which the muezzin (official crier) calls Muslims to prayer. Most mosques have a mihrab (decorative niche) that indicates the direction of Mecca. As figurative art is not allowed in Islam, buildings are ornamented with geometric and arabesque motifs, and inscriptions (frequently Koranic verses).

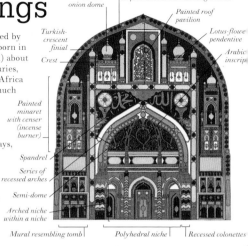

Bud-like onion dome
Depressed arch surrounding mihrab
Painted roof pavilion
Turkish-crescent finial
Lotus-flower pendentive
Crest
Arabic inscription
Painted minaret with censer (incense burner)
Spandrel
Series of recessed arches
Semi-dome
Arched niche within a niche
Mural resembling tomb
Polyhedral niche
Recessed colonettes

MIHRAB, JAMI MASJID (PRINCIPAL OR CONGREGATIONAL MOSQUE), BIJAPUR, INDIA, c.1636

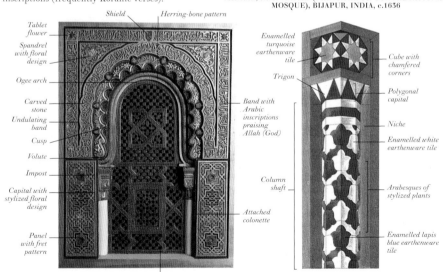

Shield
Herring-bone pattern
Tablet flower
Spandrel with floral design
Ogee arch
Carved stone
Undulating band
Cusp
Volute
Impost
Capital with stylized floral design
Panel with fret pattern
Band with Arabic inscriptions praising Allah (God)
Attached colonette
Jali (latticed screen) with geometrical patterns

ARCH, THE ALHAMBRA, GRANADA, SPAIN, 1333-1354

Enamelled turquoise earthenware tile
Trigon
Cube with chamfered corners
Polygonal capital
Niche
Enamelled white earthenware tile
Column shaft
Arabesques of stylized plants
Enamelled lapis blue earthenware tile

MIHRAB WITH COLUMN, EL-AINYI MOSQUE, CAIRO, EGYPT, 15TH CENTURY

EXAMPLES OF ISLAMIC MOSAICS, EGYPT AND SYRIA

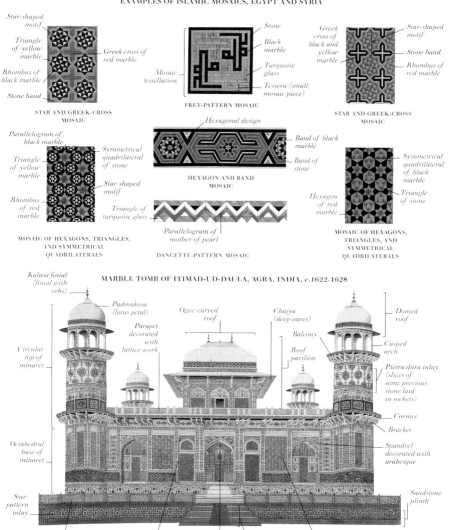

Star-shaped motif

Triangle of yellow marble

Greek cross of red marble

Rhombus of black marble

Stone band

STAR AND GREEK-CROSS MOSAIC

Stone

Black marble

Turquoise glass

Mosaic tessellation

Tessera (small mosaic piece)

FRET-PATTERN MOSAIC

Greek cross of black and yellow marble

Star-shaped motif

Stone band

Rhombus of red marble

STAR AND GREEK-CROSS MOSAIC

Parallelogram of black marble

Triangle of yellow marble

Symmetrical quadrilateral of stone

Rhombus of red marble

Star-shaped motif

MOSAIC OF HEXAGONS, TRIANGLES, AND SYMMETRICAL QUADRILATERALS

Hexagonal design

Band of black marble

Band of stone

HEXAGON AND BAND MOSAIC

Triangle of turquoise glass

Parallelogram of mother-of-pearl

DANCETTE-PATTERN MOSAIC

Symmetrical quadrilateral of black marble

Triangle of stone

Hexagon of red marble

MOSAIC OF HEXAGONS, TRIANGLES, AND SYMMETRICAL QUADRILATERALS

MARBLE TOMB OF ITIMAD-UD-DAULA, AGRA, INDIA, c.1622-1628

Kalasa finial (finial with orbs)

Padmakosa (lotus petal)

Ogee-curved roof

Chajya (deep eaves)

Domed roof

Parapet decorated with lattice-work

Balcony

Roof pavilion

Cusped arch

Circular top of minaret

Pietra dura inlay (slices of semi-precious stone laid in sockets)

Cornice

Bracket

Octahedral base of minaret

Spandrel decorated with arabesque

Star-pattern inlay

Sandstone plinth

Sandstone parapet decorated with lattice-work

Jali (latticed screen) with geometrical patterns

Depressed entrance arch

Sandstone stairway

Opus sectile mosaic (geometric mosaic) of stone, tile, glass, and enamel

South and east Asia

SEVEN-STOREYED
PAGODA IN
BURMESE STYLE,
c.9TH-10TH
CENTURY

THE TRADITIONAL ARCHITECTURE of south and east Asia has been profoundly influenced by the spread from India of Buddhism and Hinduism. This influence is shown both by the abundance and by the architectural styles of temples and shrines in the region. Many early Hindu temples consist of rooms carved from solid rock-faces. However, free-standing structures began to be built in southern India from about the eighth century AD. Many were built in the Dravidian style, like the Temple of Virupaksha (opposite) with its characteristic antarala (terraced tower), perforated windows, and numerous arches, pilasters, and carvings. The earliest Buddhist religious monuments were Indian stupas, which consisted of a single hemispherical dome surmounted by a chattravali (shaft) and surrounded by railings with ornate gates. Later Indian stupas and those built elsewhere were sometimes modified; for example, in Sri Lanka, the dome became bell-shaped, and was called a dagoba. Buddhist pagodas, such as the Burmese example (right), are multistoreyed temples, each storey having a projecting roof. The form of these buildings probably derived from the yasti (pointed spire) of the stupa. Another feature of many traditional Asian buildings is their imaginative roof-forms, such as gambrel (mansard) roofs, and roofs with angle-rafters (below).

DETAILS FROM EAST ASIAN BUILDINGS

KASUGA-STYLE ROOF WITH
SUMIGI (ANGLE-RAFTERS),
KASUGADO SHRINE OF
ENJOJI, NARA, JAPAN,
12TH-14TH CENTURY

TERRACES, TEMPLE OF
HEAVEN, BEIJING, CHINA,
15TH CENTURY

GAMBREL (MANSARD) ROOF
WITH UPSWEPT EAVES AND
UNDULATING GABLES,
HIMEJI CASTLE, HIMEJI,
JAPAN, 1608-1609

CORNER CAPITAL WITH
ROOF BEAMS, POPCHU-SA
TEMPLE, POPCHU-SA, SOUTH
KOREA, 17TH CENTURY

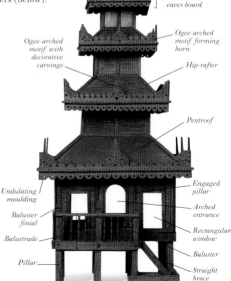

Gilded
band

Gilded iron
hti (crown)

Dubika (mast)

Arrow
motif

Torus moulding
with spiral
carving

Decorative
eaves board

Ogee-arched
motif with
decorative
carvings

Ogee-arched
motif forming
horn

Hip-rafter

Pentroof

Undulating
moulding

Baluster
finial

Balustrade

Pillar

Engaged
pillar

Arched
entrance

Rectangular
window

Baluster

Straight
brace

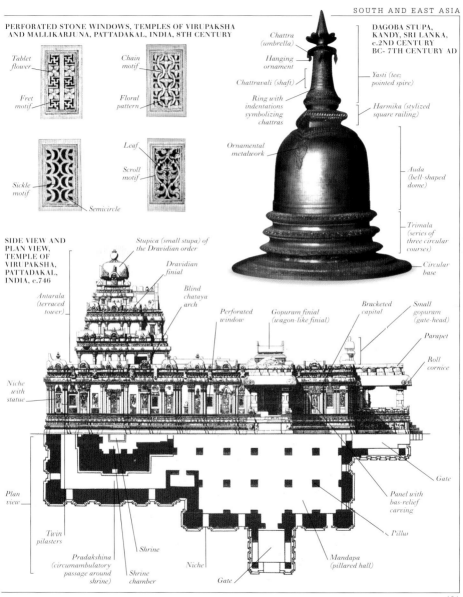

PERFORATED STONE WINDOWS, TEMPLES OF VIRUPAKSHA AND MALLIKARJUNA, PATTADAKAL, INDIA, 8TH CENTURY

Tablet flower

Fret motif

Chain motif

Floral pattern

Leaf

Scroll motif

Sickle motif

Semicircle

DAGOBA STUPA, KANDY, SRI LANKA, c.2ND CENTURY BC– 7TH CENTURY AD

Chattra (umbrella)

Hanging ornament

Chattravali (shaft)

Ring with indentations symbolizing chattras

Ornamental metalwork

Yasti (tee; pointed spire)

Harmika (stylized square railing)

Auda (bell-shaped dome)

Trimala (series of three circular courses)

Circular base

SIDE VIEW AND PLAN VIEW, TEMPLE OF VIRUPAKSHA, PATTADAKAL, INDIA, c.746

Stupica (small stupa) of the Dravidian order

Dravidian finial

Blind chataya arch

Antarala (terraced tower)

Perforated window

Gopuram finial (wagon-like finial)

Bracketed capital

Small gopuram (gate-head)

Parapet

Roll cornice

Niche with statue

Gate

Panel with bas-relief carving

Plan view

Pillar

Twin pilasters

Pradakshina (circumambulatory passage around shrine)

Shrine

Shrine chamber

Niche

Gate

Mandapa (pillared hall)

The 19th century

BUILDINGS OF THE 19TH CENTURY are characterized by the use of new materials and by a great diversity of architectural styles. From the end of the 18th century, iron and steel became widely used as alternatives to wood for the framework of buildings, as in the flax-spinning mill shown here. Built in Britain in 1796, this mill exemplifies an architectural style that became common throughout the industrialized world for more than a century. The Industrial Revolution also brought mass-production of building parts – a development that enabled the British architect Sir Joseph Paxton to erect London's Crystal Palace (a building made entirely of iron and glass) in only nine months, ready for the Great Exhibition of 1851. The 19th century saw a widespread revival of older architectural styles. For example, in the USA and Germany, Neo-Greek architecture was fashionable; in Britain and France, Neo-Baroque, Neo-Byzantine, and Neo-Gothic styles (as seen in the Palace of Westminster and Tower Bridge) were dominant.

**FLAX-SPINNING MILL,
SHREWSBURY, BRITAIN,
1796 (BY C. BAGE)**

Section through a flax-spinning mill. Labels: Cast-iron wall-plate; Pitched roof; Ridge; Verge; Gutter; Machinery space; Cast-iron mortise-and-tenon joint; Inverted T-section cast-iron beam; Segmentally arched brick vault; Anchor-joint; Drain-pipe; End flange; Concrete floor; Tapering part of column; Paved ground floor; Strengthened central column.

Flax-spinning mill. Labels: Multi-gabled roof (ridge and furrow roof); Ridge; Furrow; Verge; Timber rafter; Cast-iron wall-plate; Gutter; Gable; Drain-pipe; Tapering part of column; Three courses of stretchers; Segmentally arched brick vault; Course of headers; Cast-iron mortise-and-tenon joint; Course of decorative headers; Tie-rod; Cast-iron cruciform column; Cast-iron lattice window; Inverted T-section cast-iron beam; Cast-iron tenon; Anchor-joint; Strengthened central column; Bonded brick wall; Stone foundation; Quoin; Jamb; Gauged arch (segmental arch of tapered bricks).

492

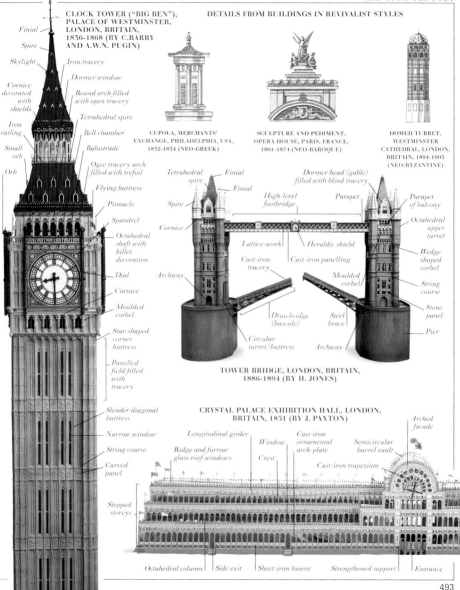

CLOCK TOWER ("BIG BEN"), PALACE OF WESTMINSTER, LONDON, BRITAIN, 1836–1868 (BY C. BARRY AND A.W.N. PUGIN)

Finial
Spire
Skylight
Cornice decorated with shields
Iron railing
Small orb
Orb
Iron tracery
Dormer window
Round arch filled with open tracery
Tetrahedral spire
Bell chamber
Balustrade
Ogee tracery arch filled with trefoil
Flying buttress
Pinnacle
Spandrel
Octahedral shaft with billet decoration
Dial
Cornice
Moulded corbel
Star-shaped corner buttress
Panelled field filled with tracery
Slender diagonal buttress
Narrow window
String course
Carved panel
Stepped storeys

DETAILS FROM BUILDINGS IN REVIVALIST STYLES

CUPOLA, MERCHANTS' EXCHANGE, PHILADELPHIA, USA, 1832–1834 (NEO-GREEK)

SCULPTURE AND PEDIMENT, OPERA HOUSE, PARIS, FRANCE, 1861–1874 (NEO-BAROQUE)

DOMED TURRET, WESTMINSTER CATHEDRAL, LONDON, BRITAIN, 1894–1903 (NEO-BYZANTINE)

TOWER BRIDGE, LONDON, BRITAIN, 1886–1894 (BY H. JONES)

Tetrahedral spire
Finial
Finial
Spire
Cornice
High-level footbridge
Dormer head (gable) filled with blind tracery
Parapet
Parapet of balcony
Octahedral upper turret
Lattice-work
Heraldic shield
Cast-iron panelling
Wedge-shaped corbel
String course
Cast-iron tracery
Archway
Moulded corbel
Stone panel
Drawbridge (bascule)
Steel brace
Pier
Circular turret/buttress
Archway

CRYSTAL PALACE EXHIBITION HALL, LONDON, BRITAIN, 1851 (BY J. PAXTON)

Longitudinal girder
Ridge and furrow glass roof-windows
Window
Crest
Cast-iron ornamental arch-plate
Semicircular barrel vault
Cast-iron trapezium
Arched facade
Octahedral column
Side exit
Sheet-iron louvre
Strengthened support
Entrance

The early 20th century

ARCHITECTURE OF THE EARLY 20TH CENTURY is notable for radical new types of steel-and-glass buildings – particularly skyscrapers – and the widespread use of steel-reinforced concrete. The steel-framed skyscraper was pioneered in Chicago in the 1880s, but did not become widespread until the first decades of the 20th century. As construction techniques were refined, skyscrapers became higher and higher; for example, the Empire State Building (right) of 1929-1931 has 102 storeys. Many buildings of this period were constructed from lightweight concrete slabs, which could be supported by cantilever beams or by pilotis (stilts). The early 20th century also produced a great variety of architectural styles, some of which are illustrated opposite. Despite their diversity, the styles of this period generally had one thing in common: they were completely new, with few links to past architectural styles. This originality is in marked contrast to 19th century architecture (see pp. 492-493), much of which was revivalist.

EMPIRE STATE
BUILDING, NEW
YORK, USA, 1929-19[
(BY R. H. SHREVE,
T. LAMB, AND
A. L. HARMON)

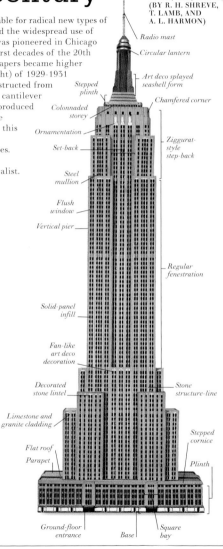

Radio mast

Circular lantern

Art deco splayed
seashell form

Stepped
plinth

Chamfered corner

Colonnaded
storey

Ornamentation

Ziggurat-
style
step-back

Set-back

Steel
mullion

Flush
window

Vertical pier

Regular
fenestration

Solid-panel
infill

Fan-like
art deco
decoration

Decorated
stone lintel

Stone
structure-line

Limestone and
granite cladding

Stepped
cornice

Flat roof

Parapet

Plinth

Ground-floor
entrance

Base

Square
bay

The Empire State Building's top 30 floors were first illuminated in colour in 1976 to honour the United States Bicentennial. This marked the beginning of the Lighting Partners Program that today sees the building lit up in specific colours for many occasions. Above, the blue, white, and red lights celebrate Independence Day.

MIDWAY GARDENS, CHICAGO, USA, 1914 (BY F. L. WRIGHT)

Flagpole

Plain coping-stone

Main floor

Orchestra shell

Tiled, shallow pitched roof

Terrace

Steps

Stage

Decorated cement frieze

Ridge

Projecting balustrade

Hip

Ornamental light

Main pavilion

Arcade

Terrace

Ornamental sculpture

Octagonal window

Stone plinth

Flat roof

EAST SIDE

Tiled frieze

Cantilevered, latticed shade

NORTH SIDE

Deep-set window

Planting bed

Brick pier

Slit window

Stepped flat-roofs

Terrace

Ornamented coping-stone

EARLY 20TH-CENTURY ARCHITECTURAL STYLES

DORMER WINDOW, STUDIO ELVIRA, MUNICH, GERMANY, 1902 (ART NOUVEAU)

AEG TURBINE HALL, BERLIN, GERMANY, 1909 (DEUTSCHER WERKBUND)

ROBIE HOUSE, CHICAGO, USA, 1909-1910 (PRAIRIE STYLE)

GRUNDTVIG CHURCH, COPENHAGEN, DENMARK, 1920 (EXPRESSIONIST)

VERTEX, CHRYSLER BUILDING, NEW YORK, USA, 1928-1930 (ART DECO)

TOWER, TOWN HALL, HILVERSUM, NETHERLANDS, 1930 (DUTCH CUBIST)

CASA DEL FASCIO, COMO, ITALY, 1932-1936 (GRUPPO SEVEN CUBIST)

MOTIF ABOVE DOORWAY, HOOVER FACTORY, LONDON, BRITAIN, 1933 (ART DECO)

495

Modern buildings 1

ARCHITECTURE SINCE ABOUT THE 1950s is generally known as modern architecture. One of its main influences has been functionalism – a belief that a building's function should be apparent in its design. Both the Centre Georges Pompidou (below and opposite) and the Hong Kong and Shanghai Bank (see pp. 498-499) are functionalist buildings: on each, elements of engineering and the building's services are clearly visible on the outside. In the 1980s, some architects rejected functionalism in favour of post-modernism, in which historical styles – particularly neoclassicism – were revived, using modern building materials and techniques. In many modern buildings, walls are made of glass or concrete hung from a frame, as in the Kawana House (right); this type of wall construction is known as curtain walling. Other modern construction techniques include the intricate interlocking of concrete vaults – as in the Sydney Opera House (see pp. 498-499) – and the use of high-tension beams to create complex roof shapes, such as the paraboloid roof of the Church of St. Pierre de Libreville (see pp. 498-499).

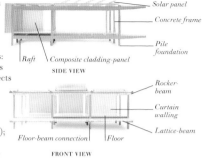

Solar panel
Concrete frame
Pile foundation
Raft | Composite cladding-panel

SIDE VIEW

Rocker-beam
Curtain walling
Lattice-beam
Floor-beam connection | Floor

FRONT VIEW

SERVICES FACADE, CENTRE GEORGES POMPIDOU, PARIS, FRANCE, 1977 (BY R. PIANO AND R. ROGERS)

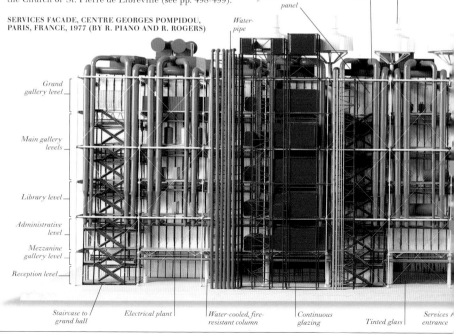

Metal-faced, fire-resistant panel
Air-conditioning duct
Cooling tower
Water-pipe

Grand gallery level
Main gallery levels
Library level
Administrative level
Mezzanine gallery level
Reception level

Staircase to grand hall | Electrical plant | Water-cooled, fire-resistant column | Continuous glazing | Tinted glass | Services / entrance

PRINCIPAL FACADE, CENTRE GEORGES POMPIDOU

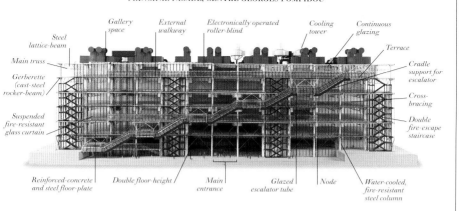

Gallery space

External walkway

Electronically operated roller-blind

Cooling tower

Continuous glazing

Steel lattice-beam

Terrace

Main truss

Cradle support for escalator

Gerberette (cast-steel rocker-beam)

Cross-bracing

Suspended fire-resistant glass curtain

Double fire-escape staircase

Reinforced-concrete and steel floor-plate

Double floor-height

Main entrance

Glazed escalator tube

Node

Water-cooled, fire-resistant steel column

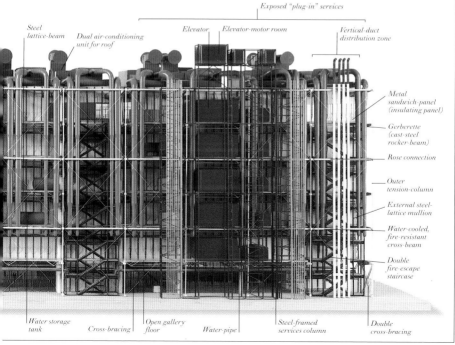

Exposed "plug-in" services

Steel lattice-beam

Dual air-conditioning unit for roof

Elevator

Elevator-motor room

Vertical-duct distribution zone

Metal sandwich-panel (insulating panel)

Gerberette (cast-steel rocker-beam)

Rose connection

Outer tension-column

External steel-lattice mullion

Water-cooled, fire-resistant cross-beam

Double fire-escape staircase

Double cross-bracing

Water storage tank

Cross-bracing

Open gallery floor

Water-pipe

Steel-framed services column

497

Modern buildings 2

HONG KONG AND SHANGHAI BANK, HONG KONG, 1981-1985 (BY N. FOSTER)

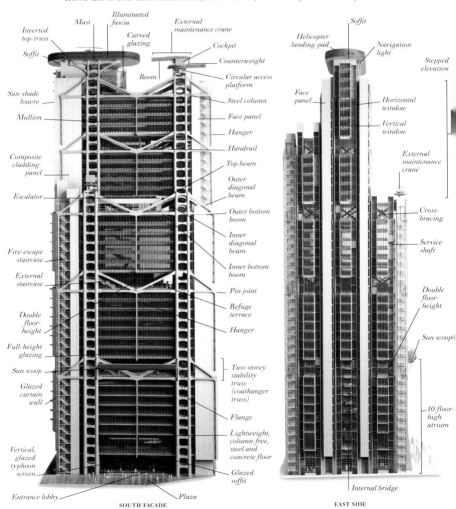

Inverted top-truss

Mast

Illuminated fascia

Curved glazing

External maintenance crane

Soffit

Helicopter landing-pad

Soffit

Navigation light

Stepped elevation

Sun-shade louvre

Mullion

Cockpit

Counterweight

Boom

Circular access platform

Steel column

Face panel

Face panel

Horizontal window

Vertical window

Hanger

Handrail

Composite cladding-panel

Top beam

External maintenance crane

Escalator

Outer diagonal beam

Outer bottom boom

Inner diagonal beam

Cross-bracing

Service shaft

Fire-escape staircase

Inner bottom boom

External staircase

Pin joint

Double floor-height

Double floor-height

Refuge terrace

Full-height glazing

Hanger

Sun scoop

Sun scoop

Glazed curtain wall

Two-storey stability truss (coathanger truss)

Flange

10-floor high atrium

Vertical, glazed typhoon screen

Entrance lobby

Lightweight, column-free, steel and concrete floor

Glazed soffit

Plaza

Internal bridge

SOUTH FACADE

EAST SIDE

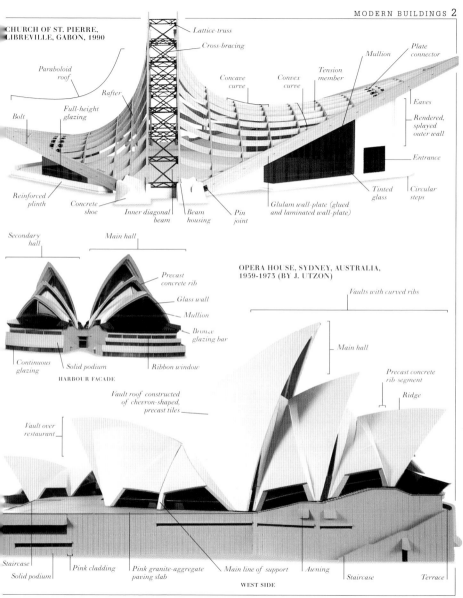

CHURCH OF ST. PIERRE, LIBREVILLE, GABON, 1990

Lattice-truss

Cross-bracing

Mullion

Plate connector

Paraboloid roof

Rafter

Concave curve

Convex curve

Tension member

Eaves

Rendered, splayed outer wall

Full-height glazing

Bolt

Entrance

Reinforced plinth

Concrete shoe

Inner diagonal beam

Beam housing

Pin joint

Glulam wall-plate (glued and laminated wall-plate)

Tinted glass

Circular steps

Secondary hall

Main hall

OPERA HOUSE, SYDNEY, AUSTRALIA, 1959-1973 (BY J. UTZON)

Vaults with curved ribs

Precast concrete rib

Glass wall

Mullion

Bronze glazing bar

Main hall

Precast concrete rib segment

Ridge

Continuous glazing

Solid podium

Ribbon window

HARBOUR FACADE

Vault roof constructed of chevron-shaped, precast tiles

Vault over restaurant

Staircase

Solid podium

Pink cladding

Pink granite-aggregate paving slab

Main line of support

Awning

Staircase

Terrace

WEST SIDE

499

MUSIC

Musical notation

MUSICAL NOTATION IS ANY METHOD by which sounds are written down so that they can be read and performed by others. The present-day conventional system of notation uses a five-line stave (staff) – divided by vertical lines into sections known as bars – on which notes, rests, clefs, key signatures, time signatures, accidentals, and other symbols are written. A note indicates the duration of a sound and, according to its position on the stave, its pitch. Notes can be arranged on the stave in order of pitch to form a scale. A silence in the music is indicated by a rest. The clef, which is placed at the begininng of a stave, fixes the pitch. The key signature, which is placed after the clef, indicates the key. The time signature, placed after the key signature, shows the number of beats in a bar. Accidentals are used to indicate the raising or lowering of the pitch of a note.

ELEMENTS OF MUSICAL NOTATION

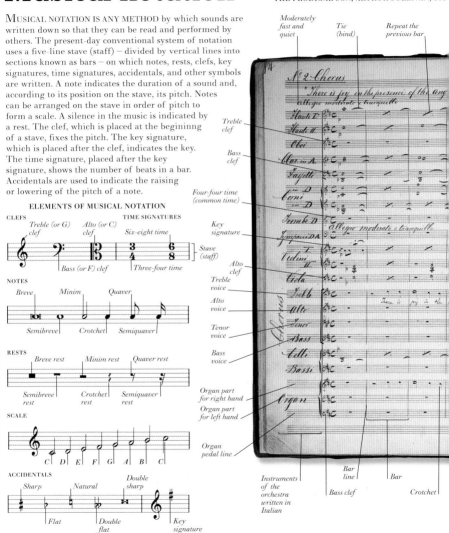

CLEFS

Treble (or G) clef

Alto (or C) clef

Bass (or F) clef

TIME SIGNATURES

Six-eight time

Three-four time

NOTES

Breve   Minim   Quaver

Semibreve   Crotchet   Semiquaver

RESTS

Breve rest   Minim rest   Quaver rest

Semibreve rest   Crotchet rest   Semiquaver rest

SCALE

C D E F G A B C

ACCIDENTALS

Sharp   Natural   Double sharp

Flat   Double flat   Key signature

Moderately fast and quiet

Tie (bind)

Repeat the previous bar

Treble clef

Bass clef

Four-four time (common time)

Key signature

Stave (staff)

Alto clef

Treble voice

Alto voice

Tenor voice

Bass voice

Organ part for right hand

Organ part for left hand

Organ pedal line

Instruments of the orchestra written in Italian

Bar line

Bar

Bass clef

Crotchet

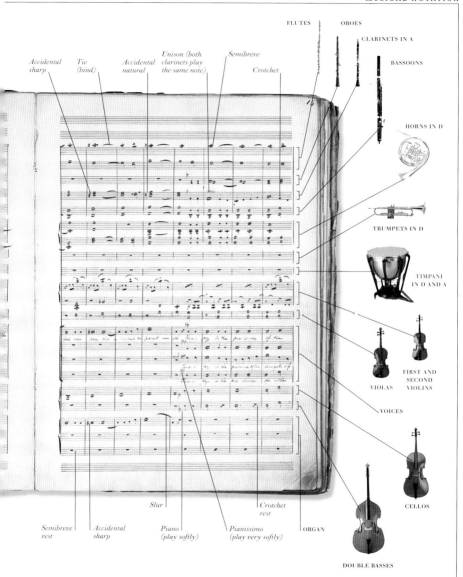

Accidental sharp

Tie (bind)

Accidental natural

Unison (both clarinets play the same note)

Semibreve

Crotchet

FLUTES

OBOES

CLARINETS IN A

BASSOONS

HORNS IN D

TRUMPETS IN D

TIMPANI IN D AND A

FIRST AND SECOND VIOLINS

VIOLAS

VOICES

CELLOS

Slur

Crotchet rest

ORGAN

Semibreve rest

Accidental sharp

Piano (play softly)

Pianissimo (play very softly)

DOUBLE BASSES

Orchestras

AN ORCHESTRA IS A GROUP of musicians that plays music written for a specific combination of instruments. The number and type of instruments included in the orchestra depends on the style of music being played. The modern orchestra (also known as a symphony orchestra) is made up of four sections of instruments – stringed, woodwind, brass, and percussion. The stringed section consists of violins, violas, cellos (violoncellos), double basses, and sometimes a harp (see pp. 510-511). The main instruments of the woodwind section are flutes, oboes, clarinets, and bassoons – the piccolo, cor anglais, bass clarinet, saxophone, and double bassoon (contrabassoon) can also be included if the music requires them (see pp. 508-509). The brass section usually consists of horns, trumpets, trombones, and the tuba (see pp. 506-507). The main instruments of the percussion section are the timpani (see pp. 518-519). The side drum, bass drum, cymbals, tambourine, triangle, tubular bells, xylophone, vibraphone, tam-tam (gong), castanets, and maracas can also be included in the percussion section (see pp. 516-517). The musicians are usually arranged in a semi-circle – strings spread along the front, woodwind and brass in the centre, and percussion at the back. A conductor stands in front of the musicians and controls the tempo (speed) of the music and the overall balance of the sound, ensuring that no instruments are too loud or too soft in relation to the others.

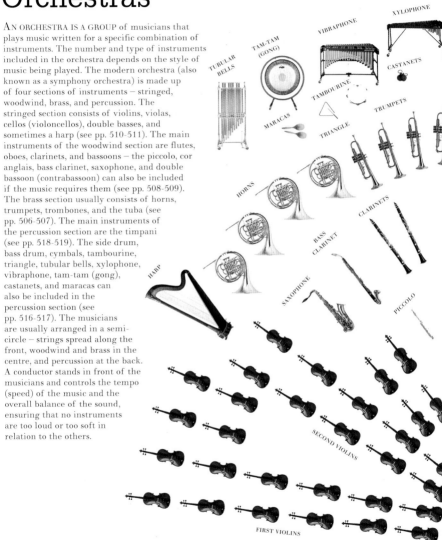

XYLOPHONE

VIBRAPHONE

TAM-TAM (GONG)

TUBULAR BELLS

CASTANETS

TAMBOURINE

TRUMPETS

MARACAS

TRIANGLE

HORNS

CLARINETS

BASS CLARINET

HARP

SAXOPHONE

PICCOLO

SECOND VIOLINS

FIRST VIOLINS

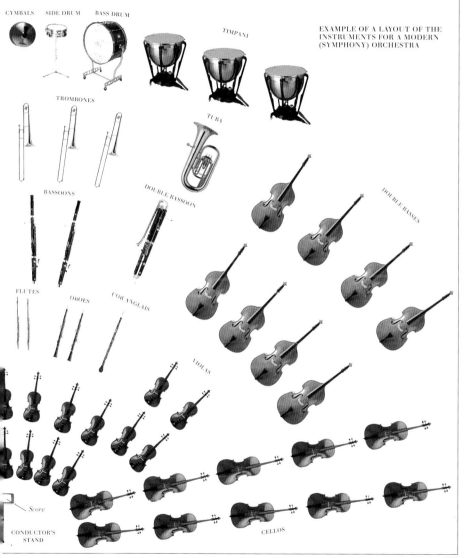

CYMBALS SIDE DRUM BASS DRUM

TIMPANI

EXAMPLE OF A LAYOUT OF THE
INSTRUMENTS FOR A MODERN
(SYMPHONY) ORCHESTRA

TROMBONES

TUBA

BASSOONS

DOUBLE BASSOON

DOUBLE BASSES

FLUTES

OBOES

COR ANGLAIS

VIOLAS

Score

CONDUCTOR'S
STAND

CELLOS

505

Brass instruments

BUGLE

BRASS INSTRUMENTS ARE WIND INSTRUMENTS that are made of metal, usually brass. Although they appear in many different shapes and sizes, all brass instruments have a mouthpiece, a length of hollow tube, and a flared bell. The mouthpiece of a brass instrument may be cup-shaped, as in the cornet, or cone-shaped, as in the horn. The tube may be wide or narrow, mainly conical, as in the horn and tuba, or mainly cylindrical, as in the trumpet and trombone. The sound of a brass instrument is made by the player's lips vibrating against the mouthpiece, so that the air vibrates in the tube. By changing lip tension, the player can vary the vibrations and produce notes of different pitches. The range of notes produced by a brass instrument can be extended by means of a valve system. Most brass instruments, such as the trumpet, have piston valves that divert the air in the instrument along an extra piece of tubing (known as a valve slide) when pressed down. The total length of the tube is increased and the pitch of the note produced is lowered. Instead of valves, the trombone has a movable slide that can be pushed away from or drawn toward the player. The sound of a brass instrument can also be changed by inserting a mute into the bell of the instrument.

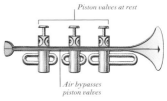

Brace

Tuning slide

Counterbalancing weight

SIMPLIFIED DIAGRAM SHOWING HOW A PISTON VALVE SYSTEM WORKS

Piston valves at rest

Air bypasses piston valves

PISTON VALVES AT REST

First piston valve pressed down

Second and third piston valves at rest

Air diverted through first valve slide

PISTON VALVE PRESSED DOWN

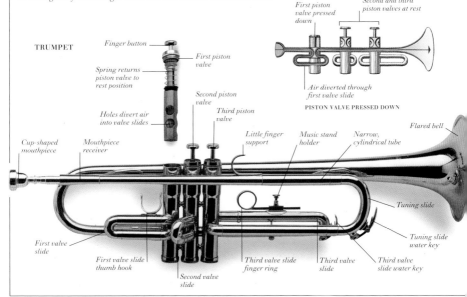

TRUMPET

Finger button

First piston valve

Spring returns piston valve to rest position

Second piston valve

Third piston valve

Holes divert air into valve slides

Little finger support

Music stand holder

Narrow, cylindrical tube

Flared bell

Cup-shaped mouthpiece

Mouthpiece receiver

Tuning slide

Tuning slide water key

First valve slide

First valve slide thumb hook

Second valve slide

Third valve slide finger ring

Third valve slide

Third valve slide water key

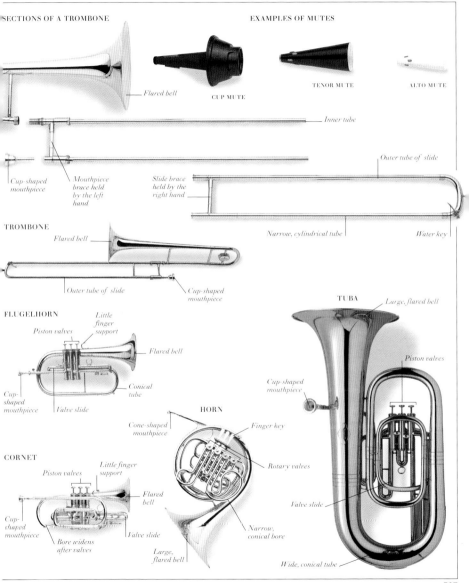

SECTIONS OF A TROMBONE

EXAMPLES OF MUTES

Flared bell

CUP MUTE

TENOR MUTE

ALTO MUTE

Inner tube

Outer tube of slide

Cup-shaped
mouthpiece

Mouthpiece
brace held
by the left
hand

Slide brace
held by the
right hand

Narrow, cylindrical tube

Water key

TROMBONE

Flared bell

Outer tube of slide

Cup-shaped
mouthpiece

FLUGELHORN

Little
finger
support

Piston valves

Flared bell

Cup-
shaped
mouthpiece

Conical
tube

Valve slide

TUBA

Large, flared bell

Piston valves

Cup-shaped
mouthpiece

HORN

Cone-shaped
mouthpiece

Finger key

Rotary valves

CORNET

Piston valves

Little finger
support

Flared
bell

Cup-
shaped
mouthpiece

Valve slide

Bore widens
after valves

Narrow,
conical bore

Large,
flared bell

Valve slide

Wide, conical tube

507

Woodwind instruments

WOODWIND INSTRUMENTS ARE wind instruments that are generally made of wood, although some are made of metal or plastic. The sound of a woodwind instrument is produced by the vibration of air in a hollow tube. The air is made to vibrate by blowing across a blow hole – as in the flute and piccolo – or by blowing through a single reed – as in the clarinet and saxophone – or a double reed – as in the bassoon, cor anglais, and oboe. The pitch of a woodwind instrument can be changed by opening or closing holes cut into the tube of the instrument.

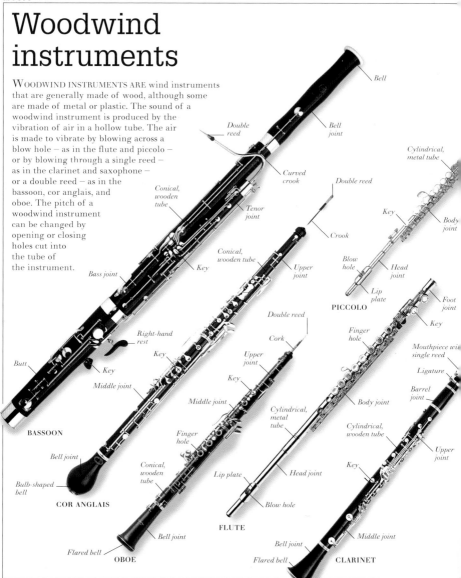

Bell

Double reed

Bell joint

Cylindrical, metal tube

Curved crook

Double reed

Conical, wooden tube

Tenor joint

Key

Body joint

Crook

Blow hole

Head joint

Conical, wooden tube

Upper joint

Key

Lip plate

Bass joint

PICCOLO

Key

Double reed

Foot joint

Cork

Finger hole

Key

Butt

Right-hand rest

Key

Upper joint

Mouthpiece with single reed

Key

Key

Middle joint

Ligature

Barrel joint

Body joint

BASSOON

Middle joint

Cylindrical, metal tube

Cylindrical, wooden tube

Finger hole

Bell joint

Conical, wooden tube

Lip plate

Head joint

Key

Upper joint

Bulb-shaped bell

COR ANGLAIS

Blow hole

FLUTE

Bell joint

Flared bell

OBOE

Bell joint

Middle joint

Flared bell

CLARINET

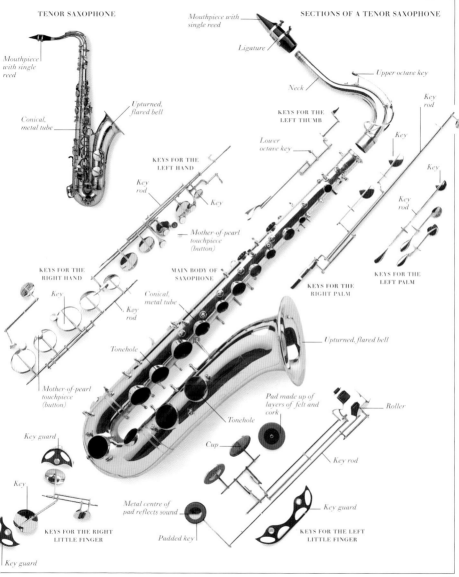

TENOR SAXOPHONE

SECTIONS OF A TENOR SAXOPHONE

Mouthpiece with single reed

Mouthpiece with single reed

Ligature

Upper octave key

Neck

Key rod

Conical, metal tube

Upturned, flared bell

KEYS FOR THE LEFT THUMB

Lower octave key

Key

Key

KEYS FOR THE LEFT HAND

Key rod

Key rod

Key

Key

Mother-of-pearl touchpiece (button)

KEYS FOR THE RIGHT HAND

MAIN BODY OF SAXOPHONE

KEYS FOR THE LEFT PALM

Key

KEYS FOR THE RIGHT PALM

Conical, metal tube

Key rod

Tonehole

Upturned, flared bell

Mother-of-pearl touchpiece (button)

Tonehole

Pad made up of layers of felt and cork

Roller

Key guard

Cup

Key rod

Key

Metal centre of pad reflects sound

Key guard

KEYS FOR THE RIGHT LITTLE FINGER

Padded key

KEYS FOR THE LEFT LITTLE FINGER

Key guard

509

Stringed instruments

STRINGED INSTRUMENTS PRODUCE SOUND by the vibration of stretched strings. This may be done by drawing a bow across the strings, as in the violin; or by plucking the strings, as in the harp and guitar (see pp. 512-513). The four modern members of the bowed string family are the violin, viola, cello (violoncello), and double bass. Each consists of a hollow, wooden body, a long neck, and four strings. The bow is a wooden stick with horsehair stretched across its length. The vibrations made by drawing the bow across the strings are transmitted to the hollow body, and this itself vibrates, amplifying and enriching the sound produced. The harp consists of a set of strings of different lengths stretched across a wooden frame. The strings are plucked by the player's thumbs and fingers – except the little finger of each hand – which produces vibrations that are amplified by the harp's soundboard. The pitch of the note produced by any stringed instrument depends on the length, weight, and tension of the string. A shorter, lighter, or tighter string gives a higher note.

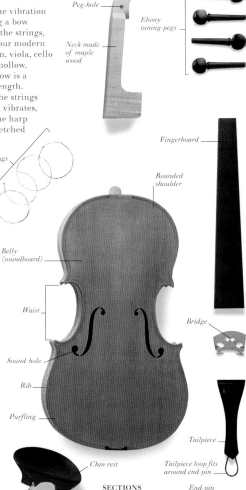

Scroll eye

Scroll

Peg-hole

Ebony tuning-pegs

Neck made of maple wood

Strings

Fingerboard

Rounded shoulder

Belly (soundboard)

Waist

Bridge

Sound hole

Tailpiece

Rib

Purfling

Tailpiece loop fits around end-pin

Chin rest

End-pin (tail-pin)

SECTIONS OF A VIOLIN

Head

Point

Stick

Scroll

Horsehair

Scroll eye

Peg-box

Tuning-peg

Nut

String

Fingerboard

Rounded shoulder

Belly (soundboard)

Purfling

Waist

Sound-hole

Bridge

Tuning adjustor

Frog

Tailpiece

Screw

Chin rest

VIOLIN BOW

VIOLIN

HARP

Crown
Tuning-peg
Neck (string arm)
Shoulder
String
Soundboard
Pillar
Pedestal
Foot
Pedal

Scroll
Scroll eye
Peg-box
Tuning-peg
Nut
Fingerboard
String
Belly (soundboard)
Rounded shoulder
Waist
Sound-hole
Bridge
Tailpiece
Spike
Tuning adjustor

CELLO (VIOLONCELLO)

Head
Point
Inward-curving stick
Horsehair
Frog
Screw

DOUBLE BASS BOW

Scroll
Scroll eye
Tuning-pegs at back of peg-box
Nut
Fingerboard
String
Sloping shoulder
Belly (soundboard)
Purfling
Waist
Bridge
Rib
Sound-hole
Sound-hole
Tailpiece
Spike

DOUBLE BASS

Scroll
Tuning-peg
Scroll eye
Peg-box
Nut
Fingerboard
String
Belly (soundboard)
Rounded shoulder
Purfling
Waist
Bridge
Sound-hole
Tuning adjustor
Chin rest
Tailpiece

VIOLA

Guitars

THE GUITAR IS A PLUCKED stringed instrument
(see pp. 510-511). There are two types of guitar –
acoustic and electric. Acoustic guitars have hollow
bodies and six or twelve strings. Plucking the strings
produces vibrations that are amplified by their hollow
bodies. Electric guitars usually have solid bodies and
six strings. Pick-ups placed under the strings convert
their vibrations into electronic signals that are magnified
by an amplifier, and sent to a loudspeaker where they are
converted into sounds (see pp. 520-521). Electric bass
guitars are very similar in structure to electric guitars,
and produce sound in the same way, but have four
strings and play bass notes.

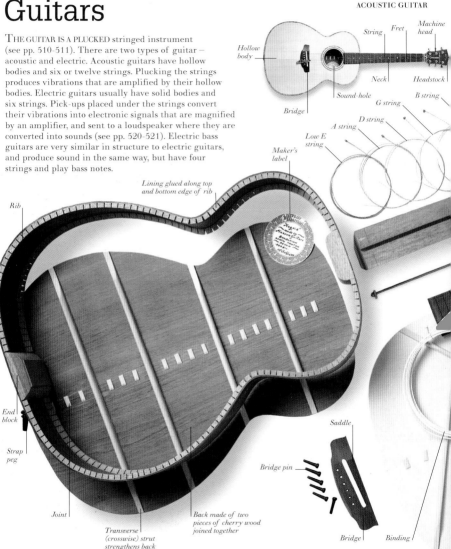

String

Fret

Machine head

Hollow body

Neck

Headstock

Sound-hole

B string

Bridge

G string

D string

A string

Low E string

Maker's label

Lining glued along top and bottom edge of rib

Rib

End block

Strap peg

Joint

Transverse (crosswise) strut strengthens back

Back made of two pieces of cherry wood joined together

Saddle

Bridge pin

Bridge

Binding

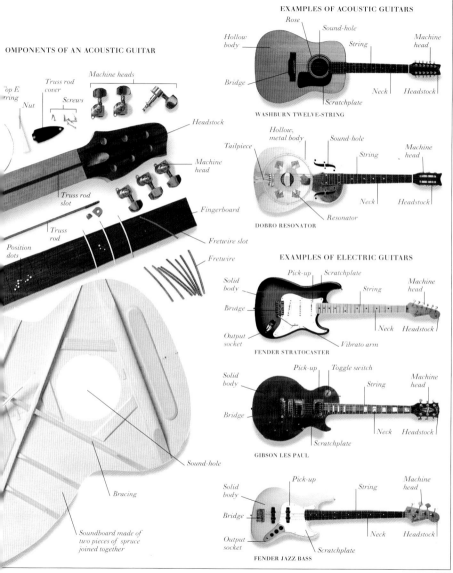

EXAMPLES OF ACOUSTIC GUITARS

Rose
Sound-hole
Hollow body
String
Machine head
Bridge
Neck
Headstock
Scratchplate

WASHBURN TWELVE-STRING

COMPONENTS OF AN ACOUSTIC GUITAR

Top E string
Truss rod cover
Machine heads
Nut
Screws
Headstock
Machine head
Truss rod slot
Fingerboard
Truss rod
Fretwire slot
Position dots
Fretwire

Hollow, metal body
Sound-hole
Tailpiece
String
Machine head
Neck
Headstock
Resonator

DOBRO RESONATOR

EXAMPLES OF ELECTRIC GUITARS

Pick-up
Scratchplate
Solid body
String
Machine head
Bridge
Neck
Headstock
Output socket
Vibrato arm

FENDER STRATOCASTER

Pick-up
Toggle switch
Solid body
String
Machine head
Bridge
Neck
Headstock
Scratchplate

GIBSON LES PAUL

Sound-hole

Bracing

Soundboard made of two pieces of spruce joined together

Pick-up
Solid body
String
Machine head
Bridge
Neck
Headstock
Output socket
Scratchplate

FENDER JAZZ BASS

Keyboard instruments

KEYBOARD INSTRUMENTS are instruments that are sounded by means of a keyboard. The organ and piano are two of the principal members of the keyboard family. The organ consists of pipes which are operated by one or more manuals (keyboards) and a pedal board. The pipes are lined up in rows (known as ranks or registers) on top of a wind chest. The sound of the organ is made when air is admitted into a pipe by pressing a key or pedal. The piano consists of wire strings stretched over a metal frame, and a keyboard and pedals that operate hammers and dampers. The piano frame is either vertical – as in the upright piano – or horizontal – as in the grand piano. When a key is at rest, a damper lies against the string to stop it vibrating. When a key is pressed down, the damper moves away from the string as the hammer strikes it, causing the string to vibrate and sound a note.

ORGAN PIPE

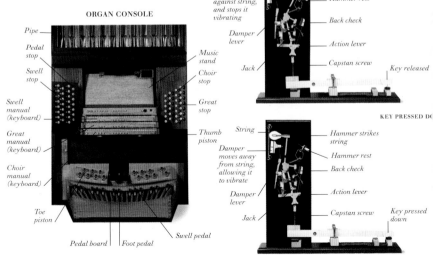

UPRIGHT PIANO

Muffler felt
Pressure bar
Tuning pin
Pin block
Hammer
88–note keyboard
Keybed
Soundboard
String
Treble bridge
Una corda (soft) pedal
Sostenuto pedal
Damper (sustaining) pedal

ORGAN CONSOLE

Pipe
Pedal stop
Swell stop
Swell manual (keyboard)
Great manual (keyboard)
Choir manual (keyboard)
Music stand
Choir stop
Great stop
Thumb piston
Toe piston
Pedal board
Foot pedal
Swell pedal

UPRIGHT PIANO ACTION

KEY AT REST

String
Damper lies against string, and stops it vibrating
Damper lever
Jack
Hammer
Hammer rest
Back check
Action lever
Capstan screw
Key released

KEY PRESSED DOWN

String
Damper moves away from string, allowing it to vibrate
Damper lever
Jack
Hammer strikes string
Hammer rest
Back check
Action lever
Capstan screw
Key pressed down

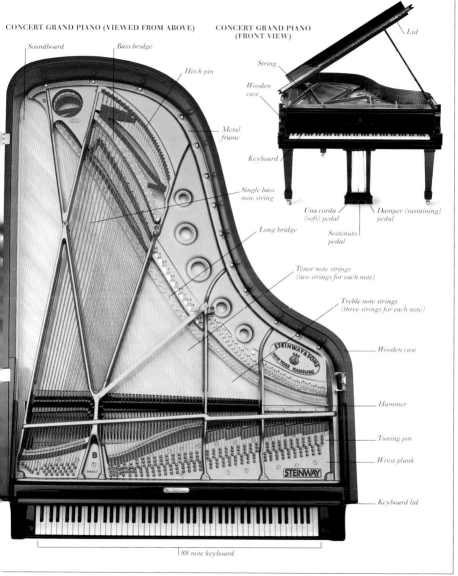

CONCERT GRAND PIANO (VIEWED FROM ABOVE)

CONCERT GRAND PIANO
(FRONT VIEW)

Lid

Soundboard

Bass bridge

Hitch pin

String

Wooden
case

Metal
frame

Keyboard

Single bass
note string

Una corda
(soft) pedal

Damper (sustaining)
pedal

Sostenuto
pedal

Long bridge

Tenor note strings
(two strings for each note)

Treble note strings
(three strings for each note)

Wooden case

STEINWAY & SONS
NEW YORK HAMBURG

Hammer

Tuning pin

Wrest plank

STEINWAY

B

Keyboard lid

88-note keyboard

515

Percussion instruments

TEMPLE BLOCKS

PERCUSSION INSTRUMENTS are a large group of instruments that produce sound by being struck, shaken, scraped, or clashed together. Most percussion instruments – such as the tam-tam (gong), cymbals, and maracas – do not have a definite pitch and are used for rhythm and impact, and the distinctive timbre (colour) of their sound. Other percussion instruments – such as the xylophone, vibraphone, and tubular bells – are tuned to a definite pitch and can play melody, harmony, and rhythms. The xylophone and vibraphone each have two rows of bars that are arranged in a similar way to the black and white keys of a piano. Metal tubes are suspended below the bars to amplify the sound. The vibraphone has electrically operated fans that rotate in the tubes and produce a vibrato (wavering pitch) effect.

EXAMPLES OF BEATERS

SOFT-HEADED BEATER

Fell-covered head

Rosewood head

HARD-HEADED BEATER

Leather-covered head

MALLET

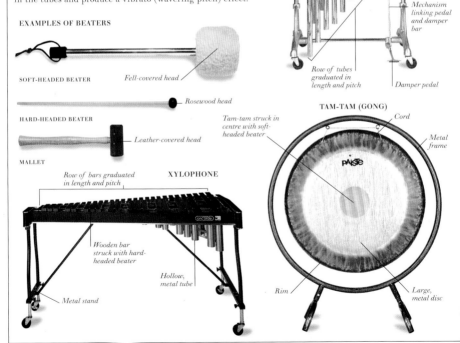

TUBULAR BELLS

Tube struck with mallet

Hollow, metal tube

Damper bar

Metal frame

Mechanism linking pedal and damper bar

Row of tubes graduated in length and pitch

Damper pedal

XYLOPHONE

Row of bars graduated in length and pitch

Wooden bar struck with hard-headed beater

Hollow, metal tube

Metal stand

Tam-tam struck in centre with soft-headed beater

TAM-TAM (GONG)

Cord

Metal frame

PAISTE

Rim

Large, metal disc

CYMBALS

Leather strap fits around player's hand

Pad protects hands from vibrations

Thin, convex disc of copper and tin alloy

SECTIONS OF A MARACA

Wooden handle

Lead shot

Hollow, wooden head

TRIANGLE

Steel rod bent into triangular shape

Steel beater

CLAVES

Hardwood sticks clashed together to give a sharp crack

CASTANETS

Cord

Hollowed wood

VIBRAPHONE

Row of bars graduated in length and pitch

Metal bar struck with soft-headed beater

Metal frame

Damper pedal

Metal tube containing electrically operated fan that produces vibrato (wavering pitch) effect

Electric cable

Drums

TAMBOURINE

A DRUM IS A percussion instrument that consists of a drumhead, made of skin or plastic, stretched over one or both ends of a hollow vessel (the body-shell). Drums are played in most parts of the world and are made in a number of different shapes and sizes. They can be divided into three groups according to the shape of the body-shell: frame drums (e.g., tambourines), bowl-shaped drums (e.g., timpani), and tubular drums (e.g., congas). Drums are usually sounded by striking the drumhead with the hands or with beaters, such as a hard-headed stick. The drumhead vibrates, and its vibrations are amplified by the hollow body-shell. The snare drum has wires – known as snares – stretched across the lower drumhead; the snares vibrate against the lower drumhead when the drum is played. Most drums, such as congas, do not have a definite pitch and can play only rhythms (see pp. 516-517). Other drums, such as timpani, have a definite pitch and can play melody, harmony, and rhythms. They can be tuned by adjusting the tension of the drumhead. Different types of drum can be combined together with other percussion instruments to form a drum kit. The basic components of the drum kit are bass drum, tom-toms, floor tom (tenor drum), snare drum, and cymbals.

DRUM KIT

Crash cymbal

Tension key

Tension rod

Tom-tom

Lug

Hi-hat cymbal

Snare drum

Tripod stand

SNARE DRUM (VIEWED FROM BELOW)

Snare mounting

Adjustable damper

Lug

Transparent lower drumhead

Chain

Tension screw

Felt-covered beater

Pedal

Upper drumhead

Snare

Stick

Snare release lever

Pedal

EXAMPLES OF BEATERS

HARD-HEADED STICK

Acorn

Taper

SOFT-HEADED STICK

Felt-covered head

WIRE BRUSH

Wire bristles

Ride cymbal

Tension key

m-tom

Tension rod

Lug

Height adjustment key

Floor tom (tenor drum)

Tension rod

Lug

Wooden body-shell

Height adjustment key

Bass drum

Leg

Rubber foot

CONGAS

Metal hoop

Drumhead

Tension rod

Wooden body-shell

Leg

Tripod stand

TIMPANUM (KETTLE DRUM)

Drumhead

Tension rod

Metal hoop

Tuning gauge

Copper body-shell

Strut

Crown

Tension rod

Tuning pedal

Castor

Electronic instruments

ELECTRONIC DRUMS

ELECTRONIC INSTRUMENTS generate electronic signals
that are magnified by an amplifier, and sent to a loudspeaker
where they are converted into sounds. Synthesizers, and other
electronic instruments, simulate the characteristic sounds of
conventional instruments, and also create entirely new sounds.
Most electronic instruments are keyboard instruments, but electronic
wind and percussion instruments are also popular. A digital sampler
records and stores sounds from musical instruments or other sources.
When the sound is played back, the pitch of the original sound can be
altered. A keyboard can be connected to the sampler so that a tune can
be played using the sampled sounds. With a MIDI (Musical Instrument
Digital Interface) system, a computer can be linked with other electronic
instruments, such as keyboards and electronic drums, to make sounds
together or in sequence. It is also possible, using music software, to
compose and play music on a home computer.

Drum pad

Height
adjustment key

HOME KEYBOARD

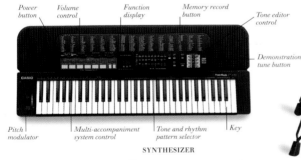

Power
button

Volume
control

Function
display

Memory record
button

Tone editor
control

Demonstration
tune button

Pitch
modulator

Multi-accompaniment
system control

Tone and rhythm
pattern selector

Key

Tripod

SYNTHESIZER

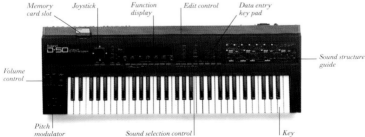

Memory
card slot

Joystick

Function
display

Edit control

Data entry
key pad

Sound structure
guide

Volume
control

Pitch
modulator

Sound selection control

Key

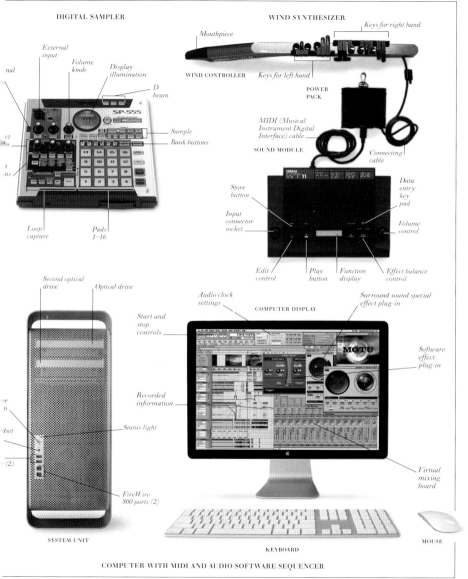

DIGITAL SAMPLER

- *nal*
- *External input*
- *Volume knob*
- *Display illumination*
- *D beam*
- *ct* / *3s*
- *Sample*
- *Bank buttons*
- *t* / *ns*
- *Loop capture*
- *Pads 1–16*

SP-555

WIND SYNTHESIZER

- *Mouthpiece*
- *Keys for right hand*
- WIND CONTROLLER
- *Keys for left hand*
- POWER PACK
- *MIDI (Musical Instrument Digital Interface) cable*
- *Connecting cable*
- SOUND MODULE
- YAMAHA WT11
- *Store button*
- *Data entry key pad*
- *Input connector socket*
- *Volume control*
- *Edit control*
- *Play button*
- *Function display*
- *Effect balance control*

- *Second optical drive*
- *Optical drive*
- *r* / *n*
- *dset*
- *(2)*
- *Status light*
- FireWire 800 ports (2)
- SYSTEM UNIT

- *Audio clock settings*
- COMPUTER DISPLAY
- *Start and stop controls*
- *Surround sound special effect plug-in*
- MOTU
- *Software effect plug-in*
- *Recorded information*
- *Virtual mixing board*

KEYBOARD

MOUSE

COMPUTER WITH MIDI AND AUDIO SOFTWARE SEQUENCER

Sports

Soccer

GAMES INVOLVING KICKING A BALL have a long history and were recorded in China as early as 300 BC; in medieval Europe, street football was banned as a menace to the public; only in 1863 were the rules established, specifically banning carrying the ball for all players except the goalkeeper, and separating rugby from soccer. Soccer, officially termed association football, is a team sport in which players attempt to score goals by passing and dribbling the ball down the field past opposing defenders, and kicking or heading the ball into the goal net, outwitting the defending goalkeeper. Each team consists of ten outfield players (defenders, midfielders, and strikers) and a goalkeeper. Players from the opposing team may challenge the player in possession of the ball, but an illegal or foul tackle results in a penalty if a foul occurs inside the penalty area or a free kick if outside the penalty area. The round ball used in soccer is more easily controlled than the oval balls used in American, Canadian, and Australian rules football and in rugby. The result is a more "open" or flowing game which is played and watched by millions of people worldwide.

ASSISTANT REFEREE'S FLAG

Lightweight, brightly coloured fabric

Handle with rubber grip

REFEREE'S EQUIPMENT

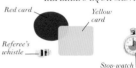

Red card

Yellow card

Referee's whistle

Stop-watch

SOCCER PITCH

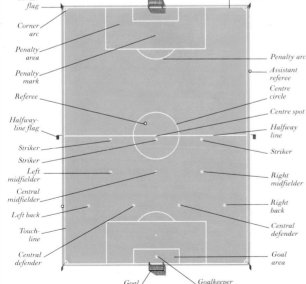

Corner flag

Corner arc

Penalty area

Penalty mark

Referee

Halfway-line flag

Striker

Striker

Left midfielder

Central midfielder

Left back

Touch-line

Central defender

46–91 m (150–300 ft)

Goal-line

Penalty arc

Assistant referee

Centre circle

Centre spot

Halfway line

Striker

Right midfielder

Right back

Central defender

Goal area

Goal

Goalkeeper

PITCH MARKINGS

Halfway line

1.5 m (5 ft)

HALFWAY-LINE FLAG

Corner arc

CORNER FLAG

7.3 m (24 ft)

Goal-line

GOAL

GOALKEEPER

Goalkeeper's shirt

Shorts

Glove

Shin guard

Sock

Soccer boot

SOCCER STRIP

Open-neck collar

Lightweight, man-made fabric team shirt

Team logo

Manufacturer's logo

Ribbed welt

Sponsor's logo

MAKING A SOCCER BALL

Hole punched in panel for stitching

Ball size number

Manufacturer's name

Edge cut to fit perfectly

Mitre

Mitre

MULTIPLEX

22–23 cm (8½–9 in)

Waxed thread

Needle

Bladder valve

Bladder made from latex rubber

Long cotton sock

Club crest

Laminated panel

Panels sewn together with ball inside out

Synthetic bootlace

Team shorts

Interchangeable nylon stud

SOCCER BOOT

American football

IN AMERICAN AND CANADIAN FOOTBALL, the object of the game is to get the ball across the opponent's goal line, either by passing or carrying it across (a touch-down), or by kicking it between their goalposts (a field goal). An American football team has 11 players on the field at a time, although up to 40 players can appear for each side in a single game. The agile "offence" tries to score points, and the heavy hitting "defence" holds back the opposition. When in possession of the ball, a team has four chances ("downs"), to move it at least ten yards (nine metres) up the field to make a "first down". The opposition gains possession if they fail, or by tackling and intercepting the ball. Canadian football is played on a larger field, with 12 men on each side. A team has only three chances to achieve a first down. Otherwise, the game is very similar to American football. Helmets, face masks, and layers of body padding are worn by the players for protection.

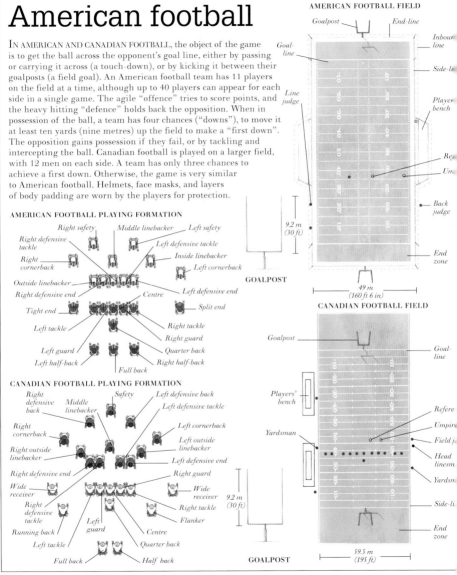

AMERICAN FOOTBALL FIELD

Goalpost
End-line
Goal-line
Inbound line
Side-line
Line judge
Player bench
Re
Un
Back judge
9.2 m (30 ft)
End zone
GOALPOST
49 m (160 ft 6 in)

CANADIAN FOOTBALL FIELD

Goalpost
Goal-line
Players' bench
Referee
Umpire
Yardsman
Field ju
Head linesm
Yardsm
Side-li
End zone
9.2 m (30 ft)
GOALPOST
59.5 m (195 ft)

AMERICAN FOOTBALL PLAYING FORMATION

Right safety
Middle linebacker
Left safety
Right defensive tackle
Left defensive tackle
Right cornerback
Inside linebacker
Left cornerback
Outside linebacker
Right defensive end
Centre
Left defensive end
Tight end
Split end
Left tackle
Right tackle
Right guard
Left guard
Quarter back
Left half-back
Right half-back
Full back

CANADIAN FOOTBALL PLAYING FORMATION

Right defensive back
Middle linebacker
Safety
Left defensive back
Left defensive tackle
Right cornerback
Left cornerback
Left outside linebacker
Right outside linebacker
Left defensive end
Right defensive end
Right guard
Wide receiver
Wide receiver
Right defensive tackle
Right tackle
Flanker
Left guard
Centre
Running back
Quarter back
Left tackle
Half back
Full back

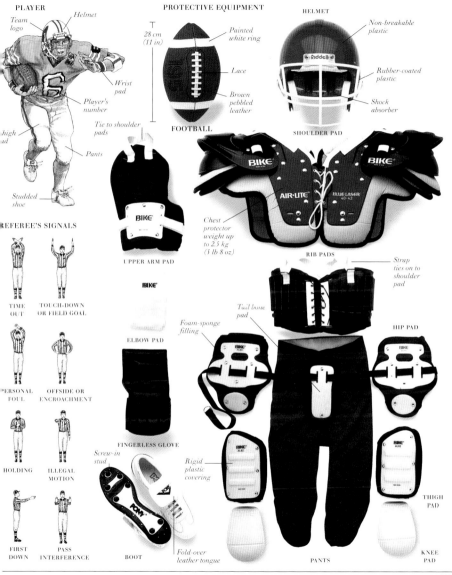

PLAYER

Team logo

Helmet

Wrist pad

Player's number

Thigh pad

Pants

Studded shoe

PROTECTIVE EQUIPMENT

28 cm (11 in)

Painted white ring

Lace

Brown pebbled leather

Tie to shoulder pads

FOOTBALL

HELMET

Non-breakable plastic

Rubber-coated plastic

Shock absorber

SHOULDER PAD

BIKE

BIKE

AIR·LITE

BLUE·LASER 40-42

Chest protector weight up to 2.5 kg (5 lb 8 oz)

UPPER ARM PAD

BIKE

RIB PADS

Strap ties on to shoulder pad

Tail bone pad

Foam-sponge filling

HIP PAD

BIKE

BIKE

ELBOW PAD

FINGERLESS GLOVE

Screw-in stud

Rigid plastic covering

BIKE

BIKE

THIGH PAD

BOOT

Fold-over leather tongue

PANTS

KNEE PAD

REFEREE'S SIGNALS

TIME OUT

TOUCH-DOWN OR FIELD GOAL

PERSONAL FOUL

OFFSIDE OR ENCROACHMENT

HOLDING

ILLEGAL MOTION

FIRST DOWN

PASS INTERFERENCE

527

Australian rules and Gaelic football

VARIETIES OF FOOTBALL have developed all over the world and Australian rules football is considered to be one of the roughest versions, allowing full body tackles although participants wear no protective padding. The game is played on a large, oval pitch by two sides, each of 18 players. Players can kick or punch the ball, which is shaped like a rugby ball, but cannot throw it. Running with the ball is permitted, as long as the ball touches the ground at least once every ten metres. The full backs defend two sets of posts. Teams try to score "goals" (six points) between the inner posts or "behinds" (one point) inside the outer posts. Each game has four quarters of 25 minutes, and the team with the most points at the end of the allotted time is the winner. In Gaelic football, an Irish version of soccer (see pp. 524–525), a size 5 soccer ball is used. Each team can have 15 players on the field at a time. Players are allowed to catch, fist, and kick the ball, or dribble it using their hands or feet, but cannot throw it. Teams are awarded three points for getting the ball into the net, and one point for getting it through the posts above the crossbar. Gaelic football is rarely played outside of Ireland.

Field umpire

Centre circle

SCORING

GOAL
(6 POINTS)

BEHIND
(1 POINT)

AUSTRALIAN RULES FOOTBALL FIELD

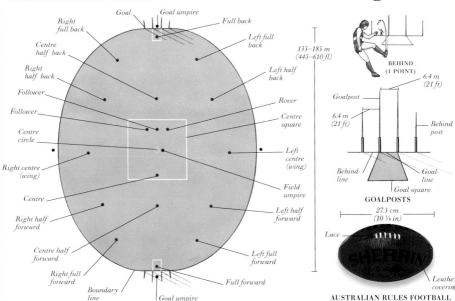

Right full back
Goal
Goal umpire
Full back
Left full back
Centre half back
Right half back
Left half back
Follower
Follower
Rover
Centre circle
Centre square
Right centre (wing)
Left centre (wing)
Centre
Field umpire
Right half forward
Left half forward
Centre half forward
Right full forward
Left full forward
Boundary line
Goal umpire
Full forward

135–185 m (445–610 ft)

Goalpost

6.4 m (21 ft)

6.4 m (21 ft)

Behind post

Behind-line

Goal-line

Goal square

GOALPOSTS

27.5 cm (10 7/8 in)

Lace

Leather covering

AUSTRALIAN RULES FOOTBALL

528

AUSTRALIAN RULES FOOTBALL SKILLS

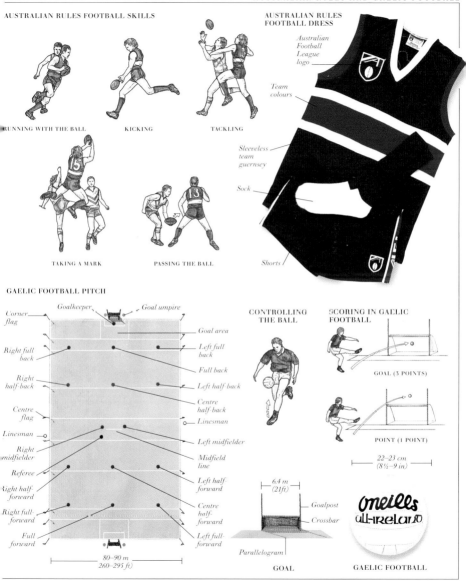

RUNNING WITH THE BALL

KICKING

TACKLING

TAKING A MARK

PASSING THE BALL

AUSTRALIAN RULES FOOTBALL DRESS

Australian Football League logo

Team colours

Sleeveless team guernsey

Sock

Shorts

GAELIC FOOTBALL PITCH

Corner flag

Goalkeeper

Goal umpire

Goal area

Right full back

Left full back

Full back

Right half-back

Left half-back

Centre half-back

Centre flag

Linesman

Linesman

Right midfielder

Left midfielder

Referee

Midfield line

Right half-forward

Left half-forward

Right full-forward

Centre half-forward

Full forward

Left full-forward

80–90 m (260–295 ft)

CONTROLLING THE BALL

SCORING IN GAELIC FOOTBALL

GOAL (3 POINTS)

POINT (1 POINT)

22–23 cm (8½–9 in)

6.4 m (21ft)

Goalpost

Crossbar

Parallelogram

GOAL

oneills
all-ireland

GAELIC FOOTBALL

529

Rugby

RUGBY IS PLAYED WITH AN OVAL BALL, which may be carried, thrown, or kicked. There are two codes of rugby, both played at amateur and professional levels. Rugby Union is played by two teams of 15 players. They can score points in two ways: by placing the ball by hand over the opponents' goal-line (a try, scoring four points) or by kicking it over the crossbar of the opponent's goal (a conversion of a try, scoring two points; a penalty kick, scoring three points; or a drop-kick, scoring three points). Rugby League developed from the Union game but is played by 13 players. In League games, a try scores four points; a conversion scores two points; a drop goal scores one point, and a penalty kick scores two points. Scrummages occur in both codes when play stops following an infringement.

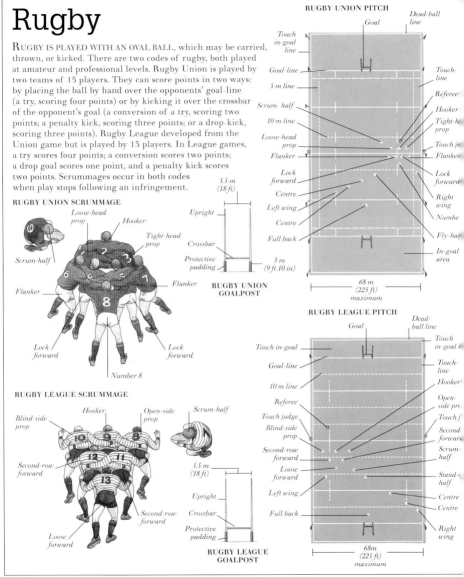

RUGBY UNION PITCH

Goal
Dead-ball line
Touch in-goal line
Goal-line
5 m line
Scrum-half
10 m line
Loose-head prop
Flanker
Lock forward
Centre
Left wing
Centre
Full back
Touch-line
Referee
Hooker
Tight-head prop
Touch judge
Flanker
Lock forward
Right wing
Number
Fly-half
In-goal area
68 m (225 ft) maximum

RUGBY UNION SCRUMMAGE

Loose-head prop
Hooker
Tight-head prop
Scrum-half
Flanker
Flanker
Lock forward
Lock forward
Number 8

RUGBY UNION GOALPOST

5.5 m (18 ft)
Upright
Crossbar
Protective padding
3 m (9 ft 10 in)

RUGBY LEAGUE SCRUMMAGE

Blind-side prop
Hooker
Open-side prop
Scrum-half
Second-row forward
Second-row forward
Loose forward

RUGBY LEAGUE GOALPOST

5.5 m (18 ft)
Upright
Crossbar
Protective padding

RUGBY LEAGUE PITCH

Goal
Dead-ball line
Touch in-goal
Goal-line
10 m line
Referee
Touch judge
Blind-side prop
Second-row forward
Loose forward
Left wing
Full back
Touch in-goal
Touch-line
Hooker
Open-side prop
Touch judge
Second-row forward
Scrum-half
Stand-off half
Centre
Centre
Right wing
68m (225 ft) maximum

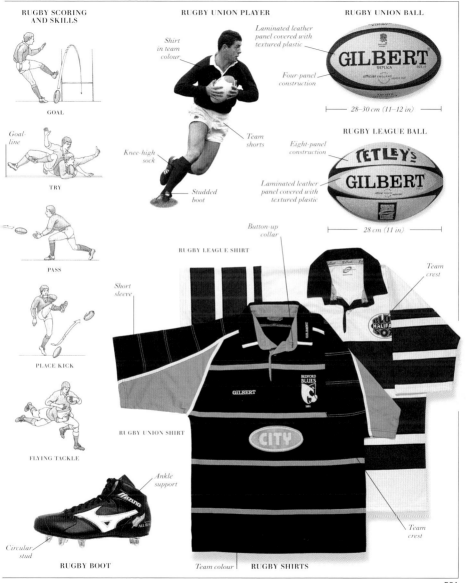

RUGBY SCORING AND SKILLS

GOAL

Goal-line

TRY

PASS

PLACE KICK

FLYING TACKLE

Ankle support

Circular stud

RUGBY BOOT

RUGBY UNION PLAYER

Shirt in team colour

Team shorts

Knee-high sock

Studded boot

RUGBY UNION BALL

Laminated leather panel covered with textured plastic

Four-panel construction

28–30 cm (11–12 in)

RUGBY LEAGUE BALL

Eight-panel construction

Laminated leather panel covered with textured plastic

28 cm (11 in)

Button-up collar

RUGBY LEAGUE SHIRT

Short sleeve

Team crest

BEDFORD BLUES

GILBERT

CITY

RUGBY UNION SHIRT

Team crest

Team colour   **RUGBY SHIRTS**

531

Basketball

BASKETBALL IS A BALL GAME for two teams of five players, originally devised
in 1890 by James Naismath for the Y.M.C.A. in Springfield, Massachusetts, U.S.A.
The object of the game is to take possession of the ball and score points by throwing
the ball into the opposing team's basket. A player moves the ball up and down the
court by bouncing it along the ground or "dribbling"; the ball may be passed
between players by throwing, bouncing, or rolling. Players may not run with or kick
the ball, although pivoting on one foot is allowed. The game begins with the referee
throwing the ball into the air and a player from each team jumping up to try and
"tip" the ball to a team-mate. The length of the game and the number of periods
played varies at different levels. There are amateur, professional, and international
rules. No game ends in a draw. An extra period of five minutes is played, plus as
many extra periods as are necessary to break the tie. In addition to the five players
on court, each team has up to seven substitutes, but players may only leave the
court with the permission of the referee. Basketball is a non-contact sport and fouls
on other players are penalized by a throw-in awarded against the offending team; a
free throw at the basket is awarded when a player is fouled in the act of shooting.
Basketball is a fast-moving game, requiring both physical and mental coordination.
Skilful tactical play matters more than simple physical strength and the agility of
the players makes the game an excellent spectator sport.

CHEST PASS

DRIBBLE

OVERHEAD PASS

INTERNATIONAL BASKETBALL COUBT

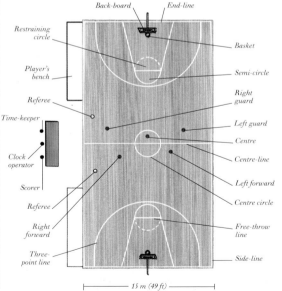

Back-board *End-line*

Restraining circle

Player's bench

Referee

Time-keeper

Clock operator

Scorer

Referee

Right forward

Three-point line

Basket

Semi-circle

Right guard

Left guard

Centre

Centre-line

Left forward

Centre circle

Free-throw line

Side-line

— *15 m (49 ft)* —

BASKET AND BACK-BOARD

Back-board

Metal rim

Cord net

1.8 m (6 ft)

BASKET AND BACK-BOARD STRUCTURE

3.05 m (10 ft)

LAY-UP SHOT

JUMP SHOT

LONG PASS

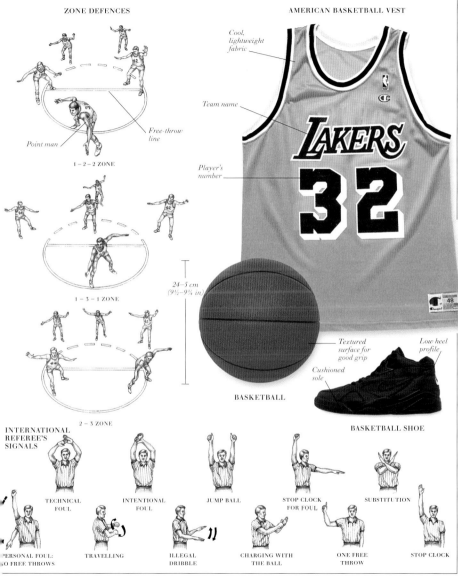

ZONE DEFENCES

Free-throw line

Point man

1 – 2 – 2 ZONE

1 – 3 – 1 ZONE

24–5 cm
(9½–9¾ in)

2 – 3 ZONE

AMERICAN BASKETBALL VEST

Cool, lightweight fabric

Team name

LAKERS

Player's number

32

48

BASKETBALL

Textured surface for good grip

Cushioned sole

Low heel profile

BASKETBALL SHOE

INTERNATIONAL REFEREE'S SIGNALS

TECHNICAL FOUL

INTENTIONAL FOUL

JUMP BALL

STOP CLOCK FOR FOUL

SUBSTITUTION

PERSONAL FOUL: 0 FREE THROWS

TRAVELLING

ILLEGAL DRIBBLE

CHARGING WITH THE BALL

ONE FREE THROW

STOP CLOCK

533

Volleyball, netball, and handball

VOLLEYBALL, NETBALL, AND HANDBALL are fast-moving team sports played with balls on courts with a hard surface. In volleyball, the object of the game is to hit the ball over a net strung across the centre of the court so that it touches the ground on the opponent's side. The team of six players can take three hits to direct the ball over the net, although the same player cannot hit the ball twice in a row. Players can hit the ball with their arms, hands or any other part of their upper body. Teams score points only while serving. The first team to score 15 points, with a two-point margin over its opponent, wins the game. Netball is one of the few sports played exclusively by women. Similar to basketball (see pp.532–533), it is played on a slightly larger court with seven players instead of five. A team moves the ball towards the goal by throwing, passing, and catching it with the aim of throwing the ball through the opponents' goal net. Players are confined by their playing position to specific areas of the court. Team handball is one of the world's fastest games. Each side has seven players. A team moves the ball by dribbling, passing, or bouncing it as they run. Players may stop, catch, throw, bounce, or strike the ball with any part of the body above the knees. Each team tries to score goals by directing the ball past the opposition's goalkeeper into the net, which is similar to a soccer net.

VOLLEYBALL SHOTS

OVERHAND SERVE   SPIKE (SMASH)

UNDERHAND SERVE   FOREARM PASS (DIG)

VOLLEYBALL COURT

Linesman

Side-line

Players' bench

Referee

Scorer

Net

Left forward

Back zone

Left back

Linesman

End-line

Linesman

Clear space

Attack zone

Attack line

Umpire

Centre forward

Right forward

Centre back

Linesman

Service area

Server

9 m (29 ft 6 in)

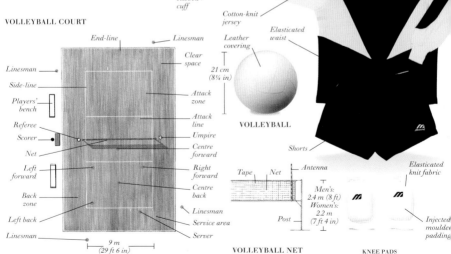

VOLLEYBALL KIT

Team colours

Ribbed cuff

Cotton-knit jersey

Leather covering

Elasticated waist

21 cm (8¼ in)

VOLLEYBALL

Shorts

Elasticated knit fabric

Tape   Net   Antenna

Men's: 2.4 m (8 ft)
Women's: 2.2 m (7 ft 4 in)

Post

VOLLEYBALL NET

Injected moulded padding

KNEE PADS

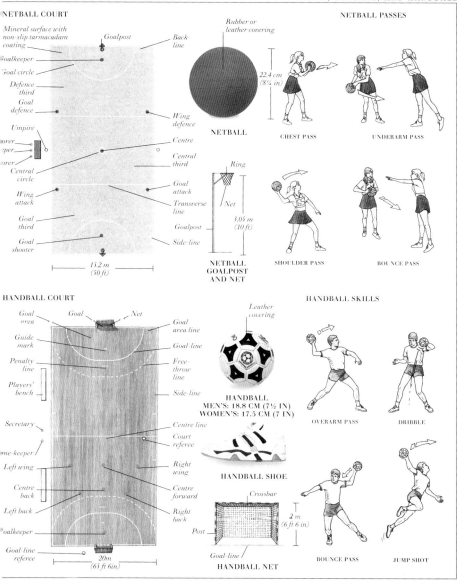

NETBALL COURT

Mineral surface with non-slip tarmacadam coating

Goalpost

Back-line

Goalkeeper

Goal circle

Defence third

Goal defence

Umpire

Wing defence

Scorer

Timekeeper

Scorer

Centre

Central third

Central circle

Goal attack

Transverse line

Wing attack

Goal third

Goalpost

Side-line

Goal shooter

15.2 m (50 ft)

NETBALL PASSES

Rubber or leather covering

22.4 cm (8¾ in)

NETBALL

CHEST PASS

UNDERARM PASS

Ring

Net

3.05 m (10 ft)

Goalpost

NETBALL GOALPOST AND NET

SHOULDER PASS

BOUNCE PASS

HANDBALL COURT

Goal area

Goal

Net

Goal area line

Guide mark

Goal-line

Penalty line

Free-throw line

Players' bench

Side-line

Secretary

Centre line

Court referee

Line-keeper

Left wing

Right wing

Centre back

Centre forward

Left back

Right back

Goalkeeper

Goal-line referee

20m (65 ft 6in)

HANDBALL SKILLS

Leather covering

**HANDBALL
MEN'S: 18.8 CM (7½ IN)
WOMEN'S: 17.5 CM (7 IN)**

HANDBALL SHOE

Crossbar

2 m (6 ft 6 in)

Post

Goal-line

HANDBALL NET

OVERARM PASS

DRIBBLE

BOUNCE PASS

JUMP SHOT

Baseball

BASEBALL IS A BALL GAME for two teams of nine players. The batter hits the ball thrown by the opposing team's pitcher, into the area between the foul lines. He then runs round all four fixed bases in order to score a run, touching or "tagging" each base in turn. The pitcher must throw the ball at a height between the batter's armpits and knees, a height which is called the "strike zone". A ball pitched in this area that crosses over the "home plate" is called a "strike" and the batter has three strikes in which to try and hit the ball (otherwise he is "struck out"). The fielding team tries to get the batting team out by catching the ball before it bounces, tagging a player of the batting team with the ball who is running between bases, or by tagging a base before the player has reached it. Members of the batting team may stop safely at a base as long as it is not occupied by another member of their team. When the batter runs to first base, his team-mate at first base must run on to second – this is called "force play". A game consists of nine innings and each team will bat once during an inning. When three members of the batting team are out, the teams swap roles. The team with the greatest number of runs wins the game.

BATTER'S HELMET

Plastic shell

Peak

Foam padding

CATCHER'S MASK

Wire coated in strong nylon

Plastic-coated foam padding

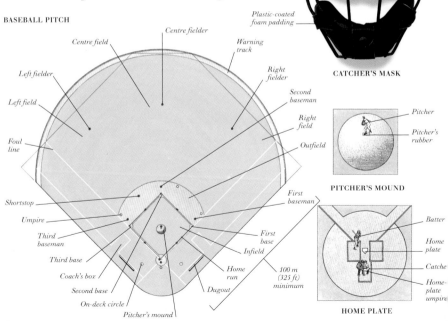

BASEBALL PITCH

Centre field

Centre fielder

Warning track

Right fielder

Left fielder

Left field

Second baseman

Right field

Foul line

Outfield

Shortstop

First baseman

Umpire

First base

Third baseman

Infield

Third base

Home run

Coach's box

Second base

Dugout

On-deck circle

Pitcher's mound

Home plate

100 m (325 ft) minimum

PITCHER'S MOUND

Pitcher

Pitcher's rubber

HOME PLATE

Batter

Home plate

Catche

Home-plate umpire

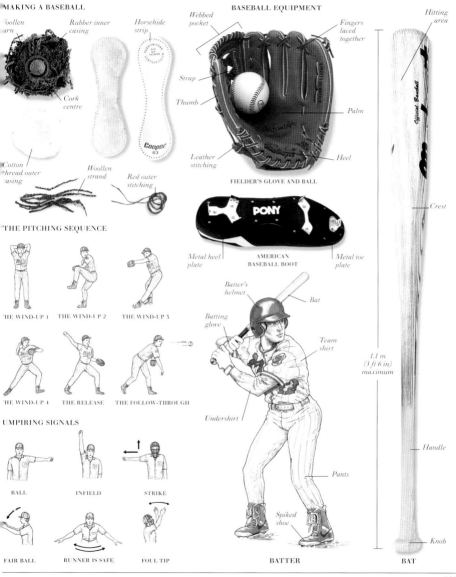

MAKING A BASEBALL

Woollen yarn

Rubber inner casing

Horsehide strip

Cork centre

Cotton thread outer casing

Woollen strand

Red outer stitching

THE PITCHING SEQUENCE

THE WIND-UP 1

THE WIND-UP 2

THE WIND-UP 3

THE WIND-UP 4

THE RELEASE

THE FOLLOW-THROUGH

UMPIRING SIGNALS

BALL

INFIELD

STRIKE

FAIR BALL

RUNNER IS SAFE

FOUL TIP

BASEBALL EQUIPMENT

Webbed pocket

Fingers laced together

Strap

Thumb

Palm

Leather stitching

Heel

FIELDER'S GLOVE AND BALL

Metal heel plate

AMERICAN BASEBALL BOOT

Metal toe plate

Batter's helmet

Bat

Batting glove

Team shirt

Undershirt

Pants

Spiked shoe

BATTER

Hitting area

Crest

1.1 m (3 ft 6 in) maximum

Handle

Knob

BAT

Cricket

CRICKET IS A BALL GAME PLAYED by two teams of eleven players on a pitch with two sets of three stumps (wickets). The bowler bowls the ball down the pitch to the batsman of the opposing team, who must defend the wicket in front of which he stands. The object of the game is to score as many runs as possible. Runs can be scored individually by running the length of the playing strip, or by hitting a ball which lands outside the boundary ("six"), or which lands inside the boundary but bounces or rolls outside ("four"); the opposing team will bowl and field, attempting to dismiss the batsmen. A batsman can be dismissed in one of several ways: by the bowler hitting the wicket with the ball ("bowled"); by a fielder catching the ball hit by the batsman before it touches the ground ("caught"); by the wicket-keeper or another fielder breaking the wicket while the batsman is attempting a run and is therefore out of his ground ("stumped" or "run out"); by the batsman breaking the wicket with his own bat or body ("hit wicket"); by a part of the batsman's body being hit by a ball that would otherwise have hit the wicket ("leg before wicket" ["lbw"]). A match consists of one or two innings and each innings ends when the tenth batsman of the batting team is out, when a certain number of overs (a series of six balls bowled) have been played, or when the captain of the batting team "declares" ending the innings voluntarily.

FORWARD DEFENSIVE STROKE

BACKWARD DEFENSIVE STROKE

ON-DRIVE

OFF-DRIVE

PULL

HOOK

SQUARE CUT

LEG GLANCE

POSSIBLE FIELD POSITIONS FOR AN AWAY SWING BOWLER TO A RIGHT-HANDED BATSMAN (IN RED) AND OTHER FIELD POSITIONS

Long on
Long off
Umpire
Boundary line
Deep mid-wicket
Bowler
Non-striking batsman
Mid-on
Silly mid-on
Extra cover
Forward short leg
Mid-off
Square leg
Silly mid-off
Deep square leg
Cover
Square-leg umpire
Point
Batsman
Gulley
Long leg
Third man
Leg slip
Second slip
Wicket-keeper
Return crease
Fine leg
First slip
Sight screen

CRICKET PITCH

Wicket-keeper
Batsman
Wicket
Bowling crease
20 m (66 ft)
Bowler
Umpire
Non-striking batsman

CRICKET BALL AND WICKET

Leather skin
Seam
BALL
Bail
WICKET
Stump

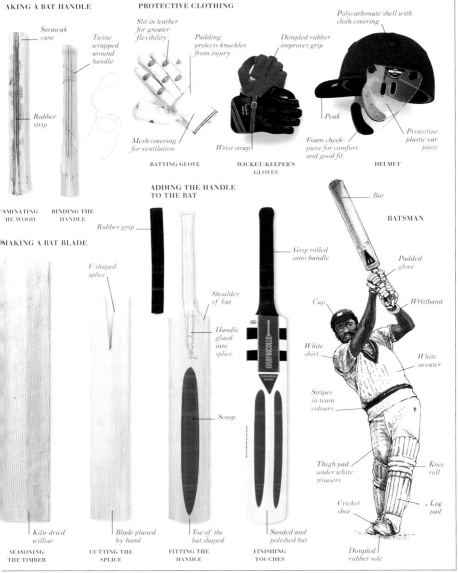

\AKING A BAT HANDLE

Sarawak cane

Twine wrapped around handle

Rubber strip

\AMINATING THE WOOD

BINDING THE HANDLE

\MAKING A BAT BLADE

V-shaped splice

Kiln-dried willow

SEASONING THE TIMBER

PROTECTIVE CLOTHING

Slit in leather for greater flexibility

Padding protects knuckles from injury

Dimpled rubber improves grip

Mesh covering for ventilation

Wrist strap

BATTING GLOVE

WICKET-KEEPER'S GLOVES

Polycarbonate shell with cloth covering

Peak

Foam cheek-piece for comfort and good fit

Protective plastic ear piece

HELMET

ADDING THE HANDLE TO THE BAT

Rubber grip

Grip rolled onto handle

Shoulder of bat

Handle glued into splice

Scoop

Blade planed by hand

Toe of the bat shaped

Sanded and polished bat

CUTTING THE SPLICE

FITTING THE HANDLE

FINISHING TOUCHES

Bat

BATSMAN

Padded glove

Wristband

Cap

White shirt

White sweater

Stripes in team colours

Thigh pad under white trousers

Knee roll

Cricket shoe

Leg pad

Dimpled rubber sole

Hockey, lacrosse, and hurling

ALL OVER THE WORLD, TEAM GAMES have evolved which require that a ball be struck or carried, and tossed at the end of a stick. Early forms of these games include hurling, shinty, bandy, and pelota. Hockey is played by men and women: two teams of eleven players try to gain and keep possession of the ball and score goals by using the hockey stick to propel the ball into their opponents' goal net. Skills such as passing, pushing, or hitting the ball by slapping or lifting it in a flicking movement, and shooting at goal are crucial. Hockey is played indoors and outdoors on grass or synthetic pitches. Lacrosse is played internationally as a 12-a-side game for women and as 10-a-side game for men. The women's pitch has no absolute boundaries but the men's pitch has clearly defined side-lines and end-lines. The ball is kept in play by being carried, thrown or batted with the crosse, and rolled or kicked in any direction. In men's and women's lacrosse, play can continue behind the marked goal areas. Similar skills are required in hurling – a Gaelic field game played on the same pitch as Gaelic football (see pp. 528–529), using the same goalposts and net. In hurling, the ball may be struck with or carried on the hurley and, when off the ground, may be struck with the hand or kicked. Goals (three points) are scored when the ball passes between the posts and under the crossbar; one point is scored when it passes between the posts and over the crossbar.

GOALKEEPER'S EQUIPMEN

Air vent

Hard shell

Face mask

HELMET

Str

HELMET

Rigid palm

Padded wrist

GAUNTLET

Steam-bent ash head

HOCKEY STICK AND BALL

STICK

Handle

Tape

Slazenger FLEX

Blade

91 cm (3 ft)

Stitched seam

7–7.5 cm (2¼–3 in)

BALL

HOCKEY FIELD

Corner flag

Side-line

Centre forward

Inside right

Right wing

Right half

Right back

Shooting circle

Goal

Penalty spot

Five yard mark

Goal-line

Inside left

Left wing

Umpire

Centre half

Left half

Left back

Goalkeeper

55 m (180 ft)

Protective overshoe

Padding protec toes against th hard ba

Strap

GOALKEEPER'S KICKER

2.1 m (7 ft)

HOCKEY GOAL

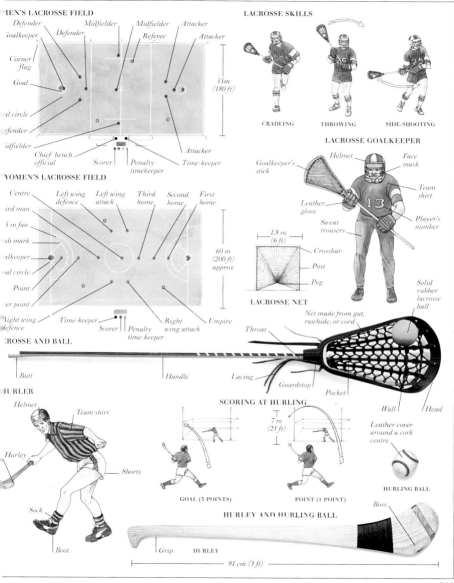

MEN'S LACROSSE FIELD

Defender
Goalkeeper
Midfielder
Defender
Midfielder
Referee
Attacker
Attacker
Corner flag
Goal
55m (180 ft)
Goal circle
Defender
Midfielder
Chief bench official
Scorer
Penalty timekeeper
Attacker
Time-keeper

LACROSSE SKILLS

CRADLING

THROWING

SIDE-SHOOTING

LACROSSE GOALKEEPER

Goalkeeper's stick
Helmet
Face mask
Team shirt
Leather glove
Player's number
Sweat trousers
Solid rubber lacrosse ball

WOMEN'S LACROSSE FIELD

Centre
Left wing defence
Left wing attack
Third home
Second home
First home
Third man
5 m fan
Goal crosse mark
Goalkeeper
Goal circle
Point
Cover point
Right wing defence
Time-keeper
Scorer
Penalty time-keeper
Right wing attack
Umpire

60 m (200 ft) approx

LACROSSE NET

1.8 m (6 ft)
Crossbar
Post
Peg

LACROSSE AND BALL

Butt
Handle
Lacing
Guardstop
Pocket

Net made from gut, rawhide, or cord
Throat
Wall
Head

HURLER

Helmet
Team shirt
Hurley
Shorts
Sock
Boot

SCORING AT HURLING

7 m (23 ft)

GOAL (3 POINTS)

POINT (1 POINT)

HURLEY AND HURLING BALL

Grip
HURLEY
91 cm (3 ft)

Leather cover around a cork centre

HURLING BALL

Boss

Athletics

THE SPORTS that make up athletics are divided into two main groups: track events – which include sprinting, middle, and long distance running, relay running, hurdling, and walking – and field events which require jumping and throwing skills. Contests designed to test the speed, strength, agility, and stamina of athletes were held by the ancient Greeks over 4,000 years ago. However, the abolition of the Olympic Games in 393 AD meant that athletics were neglected until the revival of large-scale competitions in the mid-nineteenth century. Modern stadia offer areas reserved for the long jump, triple jump, and pole vault usually situated outside the running track. The javelin, shot, hammer, and discus are thrown within the track area. Most athletes specialize in one or two events but, in the heptathlon, women compete in seven events, held over two days: 200 m and 800 m races, 100 m hurdles, javelin, shot put, high jump, and long jump. In the decathlon, men compete in ten events over two days: 100 m, 400 m, and 1,500 m races, 110 m hurdles, javelin, discus, shot put, pole vault, high jump, and long jump.

Steel wire
Head
Body
Swivel
Metal r
Cent weig
Hammer handle

DISCUS
MEN: 2 KG (4 LB 7 OZ)
WOMEN: 1 KG (2 LB 3 OZ)

HAMMER
7 KG (16 LB)

Rubber coating
Shot-pellet filling

12.7 cm (5 in)
10 cm (4 in)

MEN'S SHOT
7 KG (16 LB)

WOMEN'S SHOT
4 KG (8 LB 12 OZ)

JAVELIN   Cord grip   Shaft   Tip

Men: 2.6 m (8 ft 6 in)
Women: 2.3 m (7 ft 6 in)

ATHLETICS
TRACK AND FIELD

Finishing post
Pole-vault mat
Pole-vault runway
100 m starting line

Finishing line
Javelin fan
Steeplechase water jump

Hammer circle
Discus circle
Jave runu

Lane
Shot-put fan
Shot-put circle
Discus fan

One is 400

High-jump fe
High-jump mat
Hammer fan

Triple-jump take-off board
Triple-jump take-off line
Indicator board
Triple-jump runway
Long-jump take-off board
Landing area

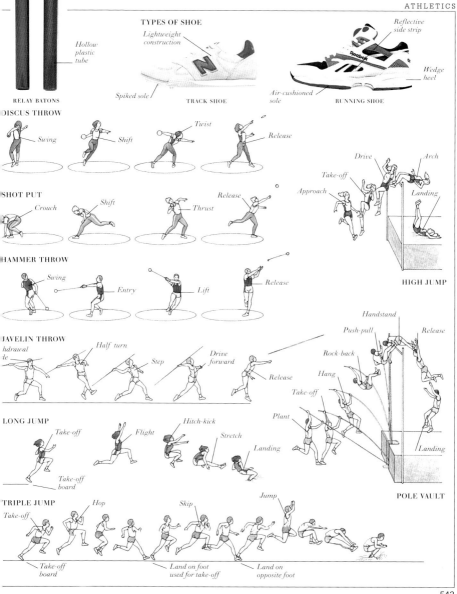

RELAY BATONS

Hollow plastic tube

TYPES OF SHOE

Lightweight construction

Spiked sole

TRACK SHOE

Reflective side strip

Wedge heel

Air-cushioned sole

RUNNING SHOE

DISCUS THROW

Swing

Shift

Twist

Release

SHOT PUT

Crouch

Shift

Thrust

Release

HAMMER THROW

Swing

Entry

Lift

Release

JAVELIN THROW

Withdrawal te

Half turn

Step

Drive forward

Release

LONG JUMP

Take-off

Flight

Hitch-kick

Stretch

Landing

Take-off board

TRIPLE JUMP

Take-off

Hop

Skip

Jump

Take-off board

Land on foot used for take-off

Land on opposite foot

HIGH JUMP

Drive

Arch

Take-off

Approach

Landing

POLE VAULT

Handstand

Push-pull

Release

Rock-back

Hang

Take-off

Plant

Landing

543

Racket sports

PROTECTIVE EYEWEAR

THE OBJECT OF ALL RACKET SPORTS is to make shots the opponent cannot return. Games are played by two players (singles) or four players (doubles). Racket shape and size is tailored to each sport, but all rackets are constructed of wood, plastic, aluminium, or high-performance materials such as fibreglass and carbon graphite. Racket strings are usually synthetic, although natural gut is still used. Tennis is played on a court divided by a low net. Opposing players serve alternate games. At least six games must be won to gain a set, and two or sometimes three sets are needed to win a match. Tennis courts may be concrete, grass, clay, or synthetic, each surface requiring a different style of play. Badminton is an indoor sport that is played with light, flexible rackets and a feather shuttlecock on a court with a high net. Players can score points only on their serve. The first to reach 15 points (11 points for women's singles) wins the game. Two games are needed to win a match. Squash and racketball are both played in enclosed courts. One player hits the ball against the front wall, and the other tries to return it before it bounces on the floor more than once. Squash rackets have smaller, rounder heads and stiffer frames than badminton rackets. In America, the game is played on a narrower court than an international court using a much harder ball. Squash games are played to nine points (international) or 15 points (American). In racketball, players use a ball that is larger and bouncier than a squash ball. The racket is thick and sturdy, with a large head, short handle, and a thong that loops around the wrist. Points can be won only when serving, and the first player to reach 21 points wins.

TENNIS RACKET

Synthetic string

Frame

Head

Logo

Throat

Grip

Butt

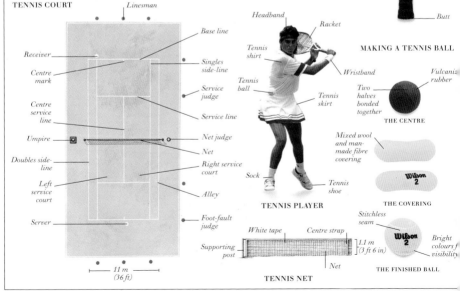

TENNIS COURT

Linesman

Base line

Receiver

Singles side-line

Centre mark

Service judge

Centre service line

Service line

Umpire

Net judge

Net

Doubles side-line

Right service court

Left service court

Alley

Server

Foot-fault judge

11 m (36 ft)

TENNIS PLAYER

Headband

Racket

Tennis shirt

Wristband

Tennis ball

Tennis skirt

Sock

Tennis shoe

MAKING A TENNIS BALL

Vulcanized rubber

Two halves bonded together

THE CENTRE

Mixed wool and man-made fibre covering

Wilson 2

THE COVERING

Stitchless seam

Wilson 2

Bright colours for visibility

THE FINISHED BALL

TENNIS NET

White tape

Centre strap

1.1 m (3 ft 6 in)

Supporting post

Net

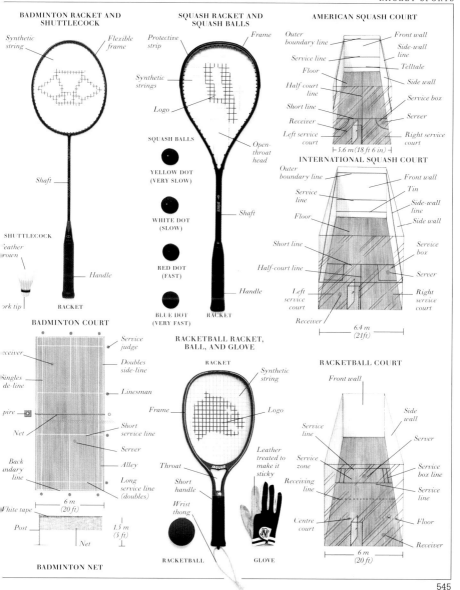

BADMINTON RACKET AND SHUTTLECOCK

Synthetic string

Flexible frame

Shaft

SHUTTLECOCK

Feather crown

Cork tip

Handle

RACKET

SQUASH RACKET AND SQUASH BALLS

Protective strip

Frame

Synthetic strings

Logo

Open-throat head

Shaft

Handle

RACKET

SQUASH BALLS

YELLOW DOT (VERY SLOW)

WHITE DOT (SLOW)

RED DOT (FAST)

BLUE DOT (VERY FAST)

AMERICAN SQUASH COURT

Outer boundary line

Front wall

Side-wall line

Service line

Telltale

Floor

Half court line

Side wall

Short line

Service box

Receiver

Server

Left service court

Right service court

⊢ 5.6 m (18 ft 6 in) ⊣

INTERNATIONAL SQUASH COURT

Outer boundary line

Front wall

Service line

Tin

Floor

Side-wall line

Side wall

Short line

Service box

Half-court line

Server

Left service court

Right service court

Receiver

6.4 m (21ft)

BADMINTON COURT

Receiver

Service judge

Doubles side-line

Singles side-line

Linesman

Umpire

Net

Short service line

Server

Back boundary line

Alley

Long service line (doubles)

6 m (20 ft)

White tape

Post

Net

1.5 m (5 ft)

BADMINTON NET

RACKETBALL RACKET, BALL, AND GLOVE

RACKET

Synthetic string

Frame

Logo

Leather treated to make it sticky

Throat

Short handle

JAGUAR

Wrist thong

RACKETBALL

GLOVE

RACKETBALL COURT

Front wall

Side wall

Service line

Server

Service zone

Service box line

Receiving line

Service line

Centre court

Floor

Receiver

6 m (20 ft)

545

Golf

GOLF BALL AND TEE

THE GAME OF GOLF was first played in Scotland some 400 years ago. Players are required to hit a ball, using a wooden or iron club, from a smooth level point or "teeing ground", down the "fairway", and on to a putting green where the target hole is located. The fairway is a strip of clear land along which there are natural hazards – such as ponds and streams, man-made hazards – such as bunkers (sand-pits), and rough (areas of uncut grass). Championship golf courses have 18 holes. The object of the game is to hit the ball into each hole in turn, and to complete the "round" using as few strokes as possible. Players compete individually or in teams, playing the course together in groups of two, three, or four. The two basic forms of competition are match play and stroke play. In match play, the side winning the majority of holes over a certain number of rounds wins the match. In stroke play, the winner is the player who finishes a certain number of rounds having made the fewest strokes.

GOLF BALL WITH BALATA SURFACE

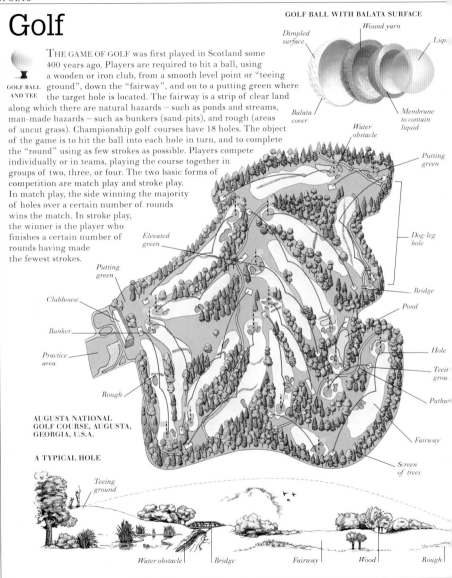

Dimpled surface

Wound yarn

Liqu

Balata cover

Membrane to contain liquid

Water obstacle

Putting green

Dog-leg hole

Elevated green

Bridge

Putting green

Pond

Clubhouse

Hole

Bunker

Teein grou

Practice area

Pathw

Rough

Fairway

AUGUSTA NATIONAL
GOLF COURSE, AUGUSTA,
GEORGIA, U.S.A.

Screen of trees

A TYPICAL HOLE

Teeing ground

Water obstacle | Bridge | Fairway | Wood | Rough

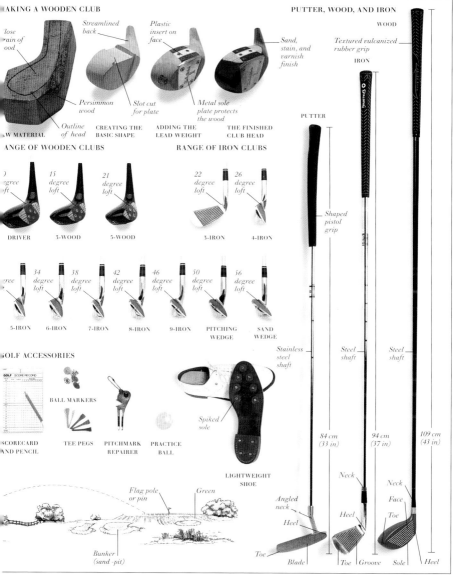

MAKING A WOODEN CLUB

PUTTER, WOOD, AND IRON

WOOD

Close grain of wood

Streamlined back

Plastic insert on face

Sand, stain, and varnish finish

Persimmon wood

Slot cut for plate

Metal sole plate protects the wood

Outline of head

RAW MATERIAL

CREATING THE BASIC SHAPE

ADDING THE LEAD WEIGHT

THE FINISHED CLUB HEAD

Textured vulcanized rubber grip

IRON

RANGE OF WOODEN CLUBS

degree loft

15 degree loft

21 degree loft

DRIVER

3-WOOD

5-WOOD

RANGE OF IRON CLUBS

22 degree loft

26 degree loft

3-IRON

4-IRON

PUTTER

Shaped pistol grip

34 degree loft

38 degree loft

42 degree loft

46 degree loft

50 degree loft

56 degree loft

5-IRON

6-IRON

7-IRON

8-IRON

9-IRON

PITCHING WEDGE

SAND WEDGE

Stainless steel shaft

Steel shaft

Steel shaft

GOLF ACCESSORIES

GOLF SCORE RECORD

BALL MARKERS

Spiked sole

SCORECARD AND PENCIL

TEE PEGS

PITCHMARK REPAIRER

PRACTICE BALL

84 cm (33 in)

94 cm (37 in)

109 cm (43 in)

LIGHTWEIGHT SHOE

Flag pole or pin

Green

Angled neck

Neck

Neck

Face

Heel

Heel

Toe

Bunker (sand-pit)

Toe

Blade

Toe

Groove

Sole

Heel

Archery and shooting

TARGET SHOOTING AND ARCHERY EVOLVED as practice for hunting and battle skills. Modern bows, although designed according to the principles of early hunting bows, use laminates, fibreglass, dacron, and carbon, and are equipped with sights and stabilizers. Competitors in target archery shoot over distances of 30 m (100 ft), 50 m (165 ft), 70 m (230 ft), and 90 m (300 ft) for men, and 30 m (100 ft), 50 m (165 ft), 60 m (200 ft), and 70 m (230 ft) for women. The closer the shot is to the centre of the target, the higher the score. The individual scores are added up, and the archer with the highest total wins the competition. Crossbows are used in match competitions over 10 m (33 ft), and 30. m (100 ft). Rifle shooting is divided into three categories: smallbore, bigbore, and air rifle. Contests take place over a variety of distances and further subdivisions are based on the type of shooting position used: prone, kneeling, or standing. The Olympic biathlon combines cross-country skiing and rifle shooting over a course of approximately 20 km (12½ miles). Additional magazines of ammunition are carried in the butt of the rifles. Bigbore rifles fitted with a telescopic sight can be used for hunting and running game target shooting. Pistol shooting events, using rapid-fire pistols, target pistols, and air pistols, take place over 10 m (33 ft), 25 m (82 ft), and 50 m (165 ft) distances. In rapid-fire pistol shooting, a total of 60 shots are fired from a distance of 25 m (83 ft).

CROSSBOW AND BOL

Laminated fibreglass bow

Bolt

Bolt rest

45 mm (1¼ in)

CROSSBOW TARGET

Sight

Stirr held betwe feet t draw bow

Hardwood laminate limb

Dacron string

Si

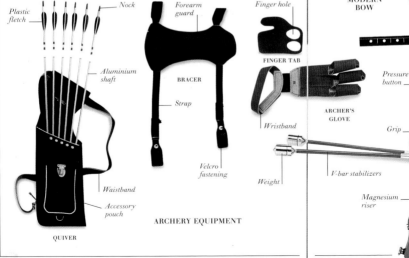

Plastic fletch

Nock

Forearm guard

Finger hole

MODERN BOW

Aluminium shaft

BRACER

Strap

FINGER TAB

Wristband

ARCHER'S GLOVE

Pressure button

Grip

Velcro fastening

Weight

V-bar stabilizers

Waistband

Accessory pouch

ARCHERY EQUIPMENT

Magnesium riser

QUIVER

SMALLBORE BIATHLON RIFLE

Rifle sight without magnifying lens

Fore sight

Barrel

Trigger

5.6 mm (0.22 in) calibre bullet

Trigger guard

Magazine

Extra magazine stored in rifle butt

155 mm (6 in)

SMALLBORE FREE RIFLE TARGET FOR 50 M (165 FT) RANGE

BIGBORE HUNTING RIFLE

Telescopic sight

Bolt handle

Bolt

Open sight

Open sight

Sling fixing point

7.62 mm (0.3 in) calibre bullet

1 m (39 in)

BIGBORE RIFLE TARGET FOR 300 M (100° FT) RANGE

155 mm (6 in)

TARGET PISTOL

Back sight

Fore sight

Hammer

Sight pin

Firing pin

197 mm (7¾ in)

PISTOL TARGET FOR 18 M (60 FT) RANGE

AIR PISTOL

Wooden grip shaped to fit the hand

Piston

Cocking lever and barrel

ht ring achment

Magazine

9 mm (0.35 in) calibre bullet

Trigger

Air-pistol pellet

AIR-PISTOL TARGET FOR 10 M (33 FT) RANGE

Nock

FIELD ARROW

Metal tip

Feathering

Wooden shaft

Straw butt

White inner 2 points

Aluminium longrod stabilizer

Blue outer 5 points

Yellow inner 10 points (bull's-eye)

ARCHERY TARGET

Ice hockey

ICE HOCKEY IS PLAYED by two teams of six players on
an ice rink, with a goal net at each end. The object of this
fast, and often dangerous, game is to hit a frozen rubber
puck into the opposing team's net with a ice hockey stick.
The game begins when the referee drops the puck between
the sticks of two players from opposing teams, who "face
off". The rink is divided into three areas: defending, neutral,
and attacking zones. Players may move with the puck and
pass the puck to one another along the ice, but may not
pass it more than two zones across the rink markings.
A goal is scored when the puck entirely crosses the goal-line
between the posts and under the crossbar of the goal.
A team may field up to 20 players although only six
players are allowed on the ice at one time; substitutions
occur frequently. Each game consists of three periods of
20 minutes, divided by breaks of 15 minutes.

GOALKEEPER

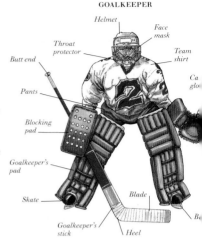

ICE HOCKEY RINK

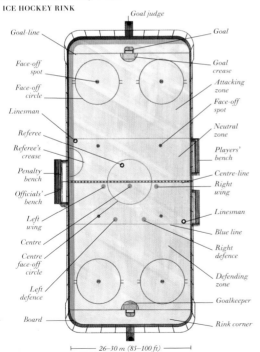

THE FACE-OFF

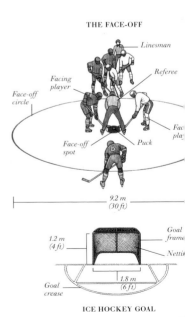

ICE HOCKEY GOAL

GOALKEEPER'S HELMET

Customized paintwork

Face guard

Chin protection

PLAYER'S BODY ARMOUR

Air vents

Rigid plastic shell

Manufacturer's logo

Foam padding

Chin strap

PLAYER'S HELMET

ICE HOCKEY STICKS

GOALKEEPER'S STICK

OUTFIELD PLAYER'S STICK

MADE IN FINLAND

147 cm (4 ft 9 in)

SHOULDER AND CHEST PADDING

Shoulder padding

ELBOW PADS

Strap

Chest padding

Wrist protection

Heavy padding

LEG PROTECTOR

Knee protection

Wide lower shaft

Thin shaft

Rigid plastic casing

Flexible gusset

Rigid finger cap

GLOVE

Thick foam backing

Vulcanized rubber

7.6 cm (3 in)

FROZEN PUCK

Ankle support

Leg pad

39 cm (15 in)

Blade

SKATE

Safety heel tip

Puck stopper

32 cm (12½ in)

Thick blade

Heel

Alpine skiing

DOWNHILL SKIER

COMPETITIVE ALPINE SKIING is divided into four disciplines: downhill, slalom, giant slalom, and super-giant slalom (Super-G). Each one tests different skills. In downhill skiing, competitors race down a slope marked out by control flags, known as "gates", and are timed on a single run only. Competitors wear crash helmets, one-piece Lycra suits, and long skis with flattened tips to minimize air resistance. Slalom and giant slalom skiers negotiate a twisting course requiring balance, agility, and quick reactions. Courses are defined by pairs of gates. Racers must pass through each pair of gates to complete the course successfully. Competitors are timed on two runs over different courses, and the skier who completes the courses in the shortest time wins. The equipment and protective guards used by slalom skiiers are shown opposite. In Super-G races, competitors ski a single run that combines the technical challenge of slalom with the speed of downhill. The course requires skiers to complete medium-to-long radius turns at high speed, and contain up to two jumps. Clothing is the same as for downhill, but slightly shorter skis are used.

Ski goggles
Helmet
One-piece lycra ski suit
Wrist strap
Ski pole
Basket
Ski boot
Safety binding
Tail

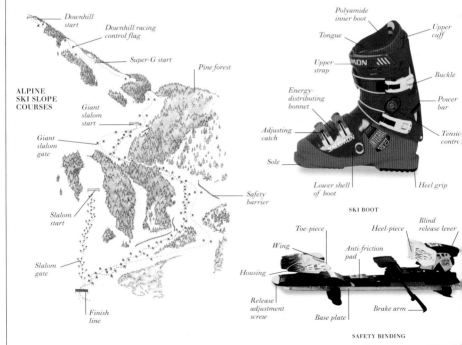

ALPINE SKI SLOPE COURSES

Downhill start
Downhill racing control flag
Super-G start
Pine forest
Giant slalom start
Giant slalom gate
Slalom start
Slalom gate
Finish line
Safety barrier

Polyamide inner boot
Tongue
Upper cuff
Upper strap
Buckle
Energy-distributing bonnet
Power bar
Adjusting catch
Tensi contr
Sole
Lower shell of boot
Heel grip

SKI BOOT

Toe-piece
Heel-piece
Blind release lever
Wing
Anti-friction pad
Housing
Release adjustment screw
Base plate
Brake arm

SAFETY BINDING

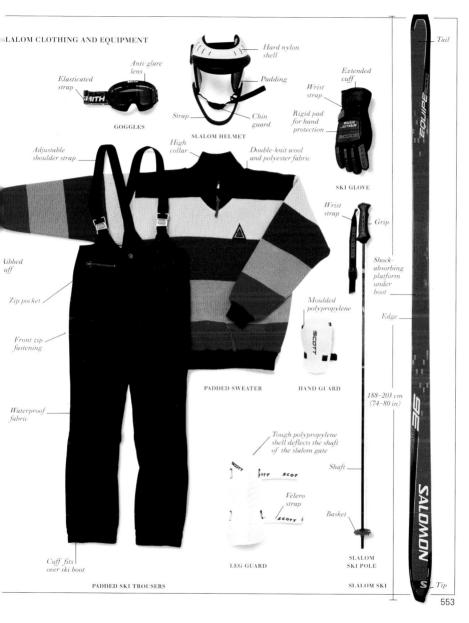

SLALOM CLOTHING AND EQUIPMENT

GOGGLES

Elasticated strap

Anti-glare lens

SLALOM HELMET

Hard nylon shell

Padding

Strap

Chin guard

High collar

SKI GLOVE

Extended cuff

Wrist strap

Rigid pad for hand protection

Double-knit wool and polyester fabric

Adjustable shoulder strap

Ribbed cuff

Zip pocket

Front zip fastening

Waterproof fabric

PADDED SWEATER

Moulded polypropylene

HAND GUARD

SLALOM SKI POLE

Wrist strap

Grip

Shock-absorbing platform under boot

Edge

188–203 cm (74–80 in)

Tough polypropylene shell deflects the shaft of the slalom gate

Shaft

Velcro strap

Basket

LEG GUARD

Cuff fits over ski boot

PADDED SKI TROUSERS

SLALOM SKI

Tail

Tip

553

Equestrian sports

EQUESTRIAN SPORTS HAVE TAKEN place throughout the world for centuries: events involving mounted horses were recorded in the Olympic Games of 642 BC. Showjumping, however, is a much more recent innovation, and the first competitions were held at the beginning of the 1900s. In this sport, horse and rider must negotiate a course of variable, unfixed obstacles, making as few mistakes as possible. Showjumping fences consist of wooden stands, known as standards or wings, that support planks or poles. Parts of the fence are designed to collapse on impact, preventing injury to the horse and rider. Judges penalise competitors for errors, such as knocking down obstacles, refusing jumps, or deviating from the course. Depending on the type of competition, the rider with the fewest faults, most points, or fastest time wins. There are two basic forms of horse racing – flat races and races with jumps, such as steeplechase or hurdle-races. Thoroughbred horses are used in this sport, as they have great strength and stamina and can achieve speeds of up to 65 kph (40 mph). Jockeys wear "silks" – caps and jackets designed in distinctive colours and patterns which help identify the horses. In harness racing, the horse is driven from a light, twowheeled carriage called a sulky. Horses are trained to trot and to pace, and different races are held for each of these types of gait. In pacing races, the horses wear hobbles to prevent them from breaking into a trot or gallop. Breeds such as the Standardbred and the French Trotter have been developed especially for this sport.

SHOWJUMPING SADDLE

High cantle

Deep seat

Pommel

Forward-cut flap

Knee roll

SHOWJUMPING FENCES

Standard

Foo

Plank

UPRIGHT PLANKS

Standard

Foo

Pole

UPRIGHT POLES

Back pole

Standard

Foot

Pole

TRIPLE BAR (STAIRCASE)

Standard

Pole

Foot

HOG'S-BACK

Pillar

Wo block pa to rese a

WALL

Hard hat

Riding jacket

Browband

Throat-latch

Rein

Jodhpurs

Cheek-piece

Showjumping saddle

Hindquarters

Dock

Running martingale

Noseband

Brushing boot

Sheepskin numnah

Girth

Stirrup iron

Riding boot

Hoof

Hock joint

Gaskin

Fetlock joint

Pastern

Coronet

**SHOWJUMPING
HORSE WITH RIDER**

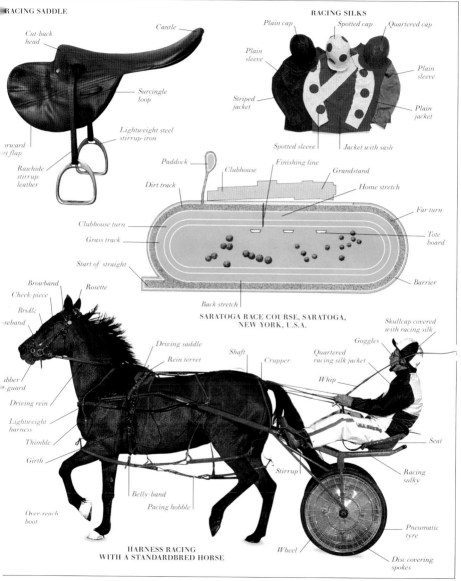

RACING SADDLE

Cantle

Cut-back head

Surcingle loop

Lightweight steel stirrup-iron

Forward cut flap

Rawhide stirrup-leather

RACING SILKS

Plain cap

Spotted cap

Quartered cap

Plain sleeve

Plain sleeve

Striped jacket

Plain jacket

Spotted sleeve

Jacket with sash

Paddock

Clubhouse

Finishing line

Grandstand

Dirt track

Home stretch

Far turn

Clubhouse turn

Grass track

Tote board

Start of straight

Back stretch

Barrier

SARATOGA RACE COURSE, SARATOGA, NEW YORK, U.S.A.

Browband

Rosette

Check-piece

Bridle

Noseband

Driving saddle

Rein terret

Shaft

Crupper

Skullcap covered with racing silk

Goggles

Quartered racing silk jacket

Whip

Rubber bit-guard

Driving rein

Lightweight harness

Thimble

Girth

Seat

Racing sulky

Stirrup

Belly-band

Pacing hobble

Over-reach boot

Pneumatic tyre

Wheel

Disc covering spokes

HARNESS RACING WITH A STANDARDBRED HORSE

Judo and fencing

COMBAT SPORTS ARE BASED ON THE SKILLS used in fighting. In these sports, the competitors may be unarmed – as in judo and boxing – or armed – as in fencing and kendo. Judo is a system of unarmed combat developed in the East. Translated from the Japanese the name means "the gentle way". Students learn how to turn an opponent's force to their own advantage. The usual costume is loose white trousers and a jacket, fastened with a cloth belt. The colour of belt indicates the student's level of expertise, from white-belted novices to the expert "black belts". Competitions take place on a mat or "shiaijo", 9 or 10 m (30 or 33 ft) square in size, bounded by "danger" and "safety" areas to prevent injury. Competitors try to throw, pin, or master their opponent by applying pressure to the arm joints or neck. Judo bouts are strictly monitored, and competitors receive points for superior technique, not for injuring their opponent. Fencing is a combat sport using swords, which takes place on a narrow "piste" 14 m (46 ft) long. Competitors try to touch specific target areas on their opponent with their sword or "foil" while avoiding being touched themselves. The winner is the one who scores the greatest number of hits. Fencers wear clothing made from strong white material, which affords maximum protection while allowing freedom of movement, steel mesh masks with padded bibs to protect the fencer's neck, and a long white glove on their sword hand. Fencing foils do not have sharpened blades, and their tips end in a blunt button to prevent injuries. Three types of swords are used – foils, épées, and sabres. Official foil and épée competitions always use an electric scoring system. The sword tips are connected to lights by a long wire that passes underneath each fencer's jacket. A bulb flashes when a hit is made.

JUDO HOLDS AND THROWS

SIDE FOUR QUARTER HOLD

SINGLE WING

BODY DROP

ONE ARM SHOULDER THROW

SHOULDER WHEEL

SWEEPING LOW THROW

STOMACH THROW

KNEE WHEEL

JUDO KIT

JUDO MAT

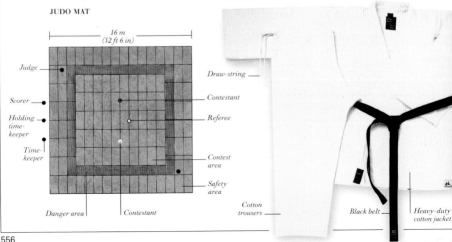

16 m
(52 ft 6 in)

Judge

Scorer

Holding time-keeper

Time-keeper

Draw-string

Contestant

Referee

Contest area

Safety area

Danger area

Contestant

Cotton trousers

Black belt

Heavy-duty cotton jacket

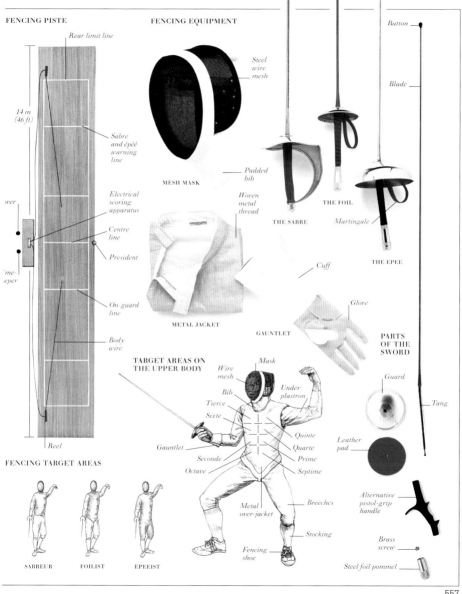

FENCING PISTE

Rear limit line

14 m
(46 ft)

Sabre
and épéé
warning
line

Electrical
scoring
apparatus

Centre
line

President

On-guard
line

Body
wire

Reel

rer

*me-
eper*

FENCING EQUIPMENT

Steel
wire
mesh

Padded
bib

MESH MASK

Woven
metal
thread

Cuff

METAL JACKET

Glove

GAUNTLET

Button

Blade

THE SABRE

THE FOIL

Martingale

THE EPEE

PARTS OF THE SWORD

Guard

Tang

Leather
pad

Alternative
pistol-grip
handle

Brass
screw

Steel foil pommel

FENCING TARGET AREAS

SABREUR **FOILIST** **EPEEIST**

TARGET AREAS ON THE UPPER BODY

Mask

Wire
mesh

Bib

Tierce

Sixte

Gauntlet

Seconde

Octave

Under
plastron

Quinte

Quarte

Prime

Septime

Metal
over-jacket

Breeches

Stocking

Fencing
shoe

557

Swimming and diving

SWIMMING GOGGLES

Swimming was included in the first modern Olympic Games in 1896 and diving events were added in 1904. Swimming is both an individual and a team sport and races take place over a predetermined distance in one of the four major categories of stroke – freestyle (usually front crawl), butterfly, breaststroke, and backstroke. Competition pools are clearly marked for racing and anti-turbulence lane lines are used to separate the swimmers and help keep the water calm. The first team or individual to finish the race is the winner. Competitive diving is divided into men's and women's springboard and platform (highboard) events. There are six official groups of dives: forward dives, backward dives, armstand dives, twist dives, reverse dives, and inward dives. Competitors perform a set number of dives and after each one a panel of judges awards marks according to the quality of execution and the degree of difficulty.

STYLES OF DIVES

Starting position

Hands above head

Legs fully stretched

Flight

Arched back

Toes pointed

Feet together

Entry

Hands close together

FORWARD DIVE

BACKWARD DIVE

SWIMMING POOL

Swimmer

Chief time-keeper

Lane number

Starting block

Lane time-keeper

End wall

Placing judge

Starter

Recorder

Side wall

Backstroke marker 15 m (49 ft) from end of pool

Anti-turbulence lane line

Referee

Stroke judge

Backstroke turn indicator 5 m (16 ft) from end of pool

Bottom line

Turning judge

Turning wall

Lane

23 m (75 ft 6 in)

SWIMWEAR

Latex rubber moulds to shape of head

High neckline

CAPS

Rubber-covered wire

NOSE CLIP

Moulded rubber

EARPLUG

Man-made stretch fabric

Drawstring

High-cut leg

Strong seam

SWIMSUIT

TRUNKS

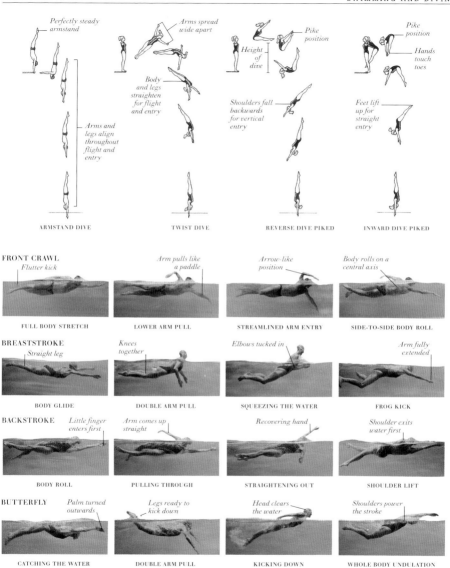

Perfectly steady armstand

Arms and legs align throughout flight and entry

ARMSTAND DIVE

Arms spread wide apart

Body and legs straighten for flight and entry

TWIST DIVE

Pike position

Height of dive

Shoulders fall backwards for vertical entry

REVERSE DIVE PIKED

Pike position

Hands touch toes

Feet lift up for straight entry

INWARD DIVE PIKED

FRONT CRAWL
Flutter kick

FULL BODY STRETCH

Arm pulls like a paddle

LOWER ARM PULL

Arrow-like position

STREAMLINED ARM ENTRY

Body rolls on a central axis

SIDE-TO-SIDE BODY ROLL

BREASTSTROKE
Straight leg

BODY GLIDE

Knees together

DOUBLE ARM PULL

Elbows tucked in

SQUEEZING THE WATER

Arm fully extended

FROG KICK

BACKSTROKE
Little finger enters first

BODY ROLL

Arm comes up straight

PULLING THROUGH

Recovering hand

STRAIGHTENING OUT

Shoulder exits water first

SHOULDER LIFT

BUTTERFLY
Palm turned outwards

CATCHING THE WATER

Legs ready to kick down

DOUBLE ARM PULL

Head clears the water

KICKING DOWN

Shoulders power the stroke

WHOLE BODY UNDULATION

Canoeing, rowing, and sailing

WATERBORNE SPORTS are as varied as the crafts used. There are two disciplines in rowing; sweep rowing, in which each rower has one oar and sculling, in which rowers use two oars. There are a number of different Olympic and competitive rowing events for both men and women. The number of rowers and weight classes vary. Some rowing events use a coxswain; a steersman who does not row but directs the crew. Kayaks and canoes are used in straight sprint and slalom races. Slalom races take place over a course consisting of 20 to 25 gates, including at least six upstream gates. In yacht racing, competitors must complete prescribed courses, organized by the race committees, in the shortest possible time, using sail power only. Olympic events include classes for keel boats, dinghies, and catamarans.

SAILING GEAR

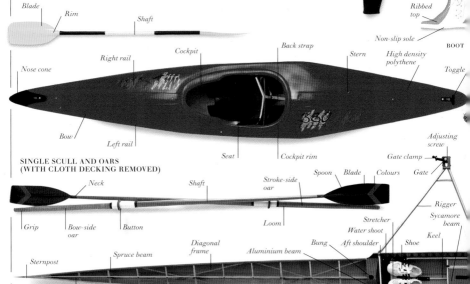

Sleeveless long johns

Buo... aid

Long-sleeved jacket

Neoprene material

Bel...

GLOVE

BOOT

Ribbed top

Non-slip sole

ONE-PERSON KAYAK AND PADDLE

Blade

Rim

Shaft

Back strap

Stern

High density polythene

Cockpit

Right rail

Nose cone

Toggle

Bow

Left rail

Seat

Cockpit rim

Adjusting screw

Gate clamp

SINGLE SCULL AND OARS (WITH CLOTH DECKING REMOVED)

Neck

Shaft

Stroke-side oar

Spoon

Blade

Colours

Gate

Grip

Bow-side oar

Button

Loom

Rigger

Stretcher

Water shoot

Sycamore beam

Diagonal frame

Bung

Aft shoulder

Shoe

Keel

Sternpost

Spruce beam

Aluminium beam

Kelson (keelson)

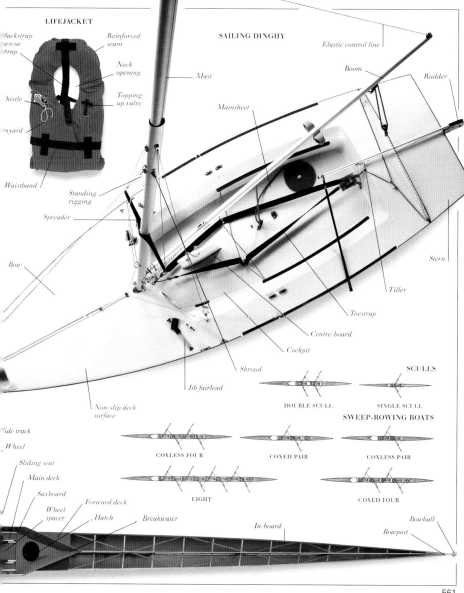

Backstrap
Rescue
strap

Reinforced
seam

Neck
opening

Elastic control line

Boom

Rudder

Mast

Whistle

Topping-
up valve

Mainsheet

Lanyard

Waistband

Standing
rigging

Spreader

Bow

Stern

Tiller

Toestrap

Centre-board

Cockpit

Shroud

SCULLS

Jib fairlead

Non-slip deck
surface

DOUBLE SCULL

SINGLE SCULL

SWEEP-ROWING BOATS

Side track

Wheel

COXLESS FOUR

COXED PAIR

COXLESS PAIR

Sliding seat

Main deck

Saxboard

Forward deck

EIGHT

COXED FOUR

Wheel
spacer

Hatch

Breakwater

In-board

Bowball

Bowpost

Angling

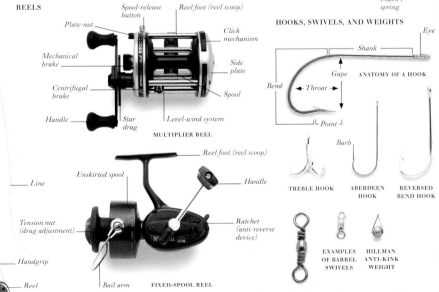

ANGLING MEANS FISHING WITH A ROD, reel, line, and lure. There are several different types of angling: freshwater coarse angling, for members of the carp family and pike; freshwater game angling, for salmon and trout; and sea angling, for sea fish such as flatfish, bass, and mackerel. Anglers use a variety of methods of catching fish. These include bait fishing, in which bait (food to allure the fish) is placed on a hook and cast into the water; fly fishing, in which a natural or artificial fly is used to lure the fish; and spinning, in which a lure that looks like a small fish revolves as it is pulled through the water. The angler uses the rod, reel, and line to cast the lure over the water. The reel controls the line as it spills off the spool and as it is wound back. Weights may be fixed to the line so that it will sink. Swivels are attached to prevent the line from twisting. When a fish bites, the hook must become embedded in its mouth and remain there while the catch is reeled in.

BUTT SECTION

Keeper ring

Drag spindle

Handgrip

Disk drag

Drag washer

Disk spring

Gear retainer

Dual click gear

Retaining screw

Check pawl cover

Check pawl

Check slide

Check spring

REELS

Plate-nut

Spool-release button

Reel foot (reel scoop)

Click mechanism

Mechanical brake

Side plate

Centrifugal brake

Spool

Handle

Star drag

Level-wind system

MULTIPLIER REEL

Reel foot (reel scoop)

Unskirted spool

Handle

Line

Tension nut (drag adjustment)

Ratchet (anti-reverse device)

Handgrip

Reel

Bail arm

FIXED-SPOOL REEL

HOOKS, SWIVELS, AND WEIGHTS

Eye

Shank

Gape

ANATOMY OF A HOOK

Bend

Throat

Point

Barb

TREBLE HOOK

ABERDEEN HOOK

REVERSED BEND HOOK

EXAMPLES OF BARREL SWIVELS

HILLMAN ANTI-KINK WEIGHT

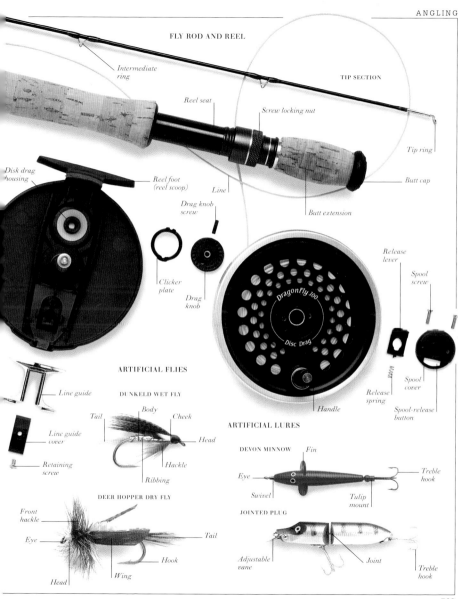

FLY ROD AND REEL

Intermediate ring

TIP SECTION

Reel seat

Screw locking nut

Tip ring

Disk drag housing

Reel foot (reel scoop)

Line

Butt cap

Drag knob screw

Butt extension

Release lever

Spool screw

Clicker plate

Drag knob

DragonFly 100

Disc Drag

Release spring

Spool cover

Spool-release button

Line guide

ARTIFICIAL FLIES

DUNKELD WET FLY

Tail *Body* *Cheek*

Head

Hackle

Ribbing

Handle

ARTIFICIAL LURES

Line guide cover

Retaining screw

DEER HOPPER DRY FLY

Front hackle

Eye

Tail

Hook

Head *Wing*

DEVON MINNOW

Fin

Eye

Treble hook

Swivel

Tulip mount

JOINTED PLUG

Adjustable vane

Joint

Treble hook

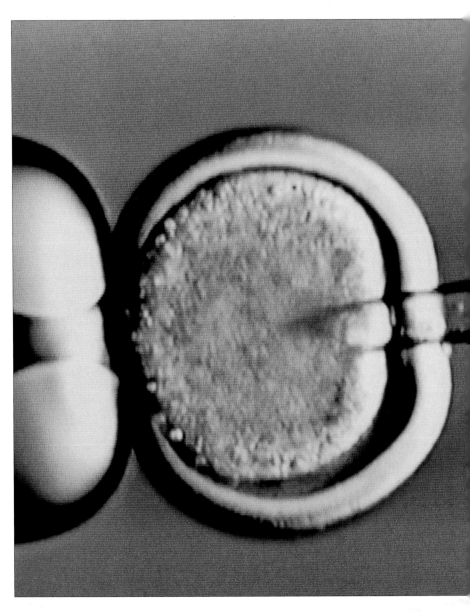

THE MODERN WORLD

Personal computer

PERSONAL COMPUTERS (PCs) fall into two main types: IBM-compatible PCs, known simply as PCs, and Apple Macintosh PCs, known as "Macs". They differ in the way files and programs, and the user's access to them, are organized, and programs must be tailored for each type. However, in most other respects PCs and Macs have much in common. Both contain microchips, or integrated circuits, that store and process data. The "brain" of any PC is a chip known as the central processing unit (CPU), which performs mathematical operations in order to run program instructions and receive, store, and output data. The most powerful personal computer CPUs today can perform more than a billion calculations a second. Data can be input via CDs, USB memory sticks, and other storage media. Highly portable laptop and network PCs are also in widespread use. Most PCs are able to communicate with many other devices, including digital cameras (see pp. 580-81) and smartphones (see pp. 588-89).

LE back glos wid scre

Keyboard

Mo

iMAC

Webcam

USB ports (4)

Audio in jack

Headphone jack

Firewire 800 port

Ethernet port

Mini display port

Powercord connector

REAR OF iMAC

LCD display

Keyboard

Touchpad

Fingerprint reader

Left touchpad button

Right touchpad button

Headphone jacks (2)

HP PAVILION DV4 LAPTOP

Audio in jack

Optical drive

Power connector

USB ports (2)

Expansion port

Remote control

Display

Digital media slot

Security cable slot

RG-45 (network) port

HDMI port

eSATA/ USB port

External monitor port

SIDE VIEW OF HP PAVILION DV4 LAPTOP

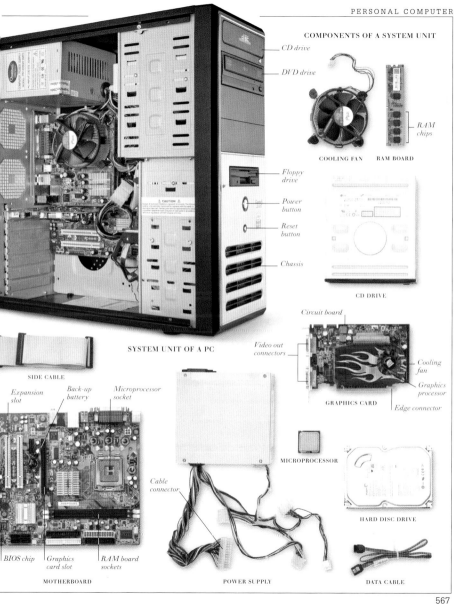

COMPONENTS OF A SYSTEM UNIT

CD drive

DVD drive

RAM chips

COOLING FAN   RAM BOARD

Floppy drive

Power button

Reset button

Chassis

CD DRIVE

Circuit board

Video out connectors

Cooling fan

Graphics processor

SYSTEM UNIT OF A PC

GRAPHICS CARD

Edge connector

SIDE CABLE

Expansion slot

Back-up battery

Microprocessor socket

MICROPROCESSOR

Cable connector

HARD DISC DRIVE

BIOS chip   Graphics card slot   RAM board sockets

MOTHERBOARD   POWER SUPPLY   DATA CABLE

Tablet computer

By THE EARLY 1990s electronic circuitry had been miniaturized to such an extent that it was possible to make small handheld computing devices. The first of these was the Personal Digital Assistant (PDA), which offered features including an address book, calendar, and notepad. In recent years, PDAs have been overtaken by smartphones with Internet and email access (see pp. 588–589). A related product is the e-book reader, which stores books in digital form and uses "electronic paper" to mimic the appearance of ink on real paper. An e-book reader no bigger than a thin paperback can store several thousand digital books in its memory. The most recent handheld computing device is the tablet computer. This looks like a thin flat display, but it is actually a complete computer. Tablet computers are typically controlled by a touch-sensitive screen and have a wireless link to other computers and the Internet. They run software applications, or apps, downloaded from the Internet. The most popular tablet computer currently is the Apple iPad. It has a multi-touch interface that enables its screen to detect the movements of fingertips. As well as selecting options and apps by touching the screen, images can be enlarged or shrunk by moving fingertips apart or together on the screen.

Sleep/wake button

APPLE IPAD

Home button

App icon

Touch data is sent as a list of finger positions to the controller where the information is used to zoom in and out of a web page

LCD with buttons displayed

Fingers alter the electric field around nearby sections of the grid

User touches clear protective screen

Touchscreen electronics interpret the outputs from the grid to work out exactly where the fingers are

Controller

MULTI-TOUCH INTERFACE

15-cm (6-in) screen

Next page button

Previous page button

Joyst *contr*

ACER LUMIREAD E-READER

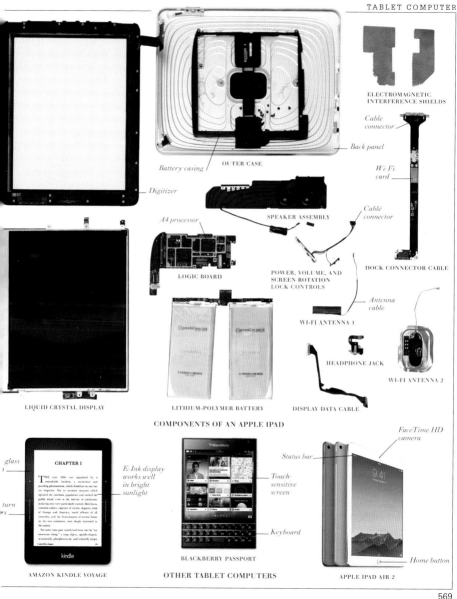

ELECTROMAGNETIC
INTERFERENCE SHIELDS

Cable connector

Back panel

Wi-Fi card

OUTER CASE

Battery casing

Digitizer

A4 processor

SPEAKER ASSEMBLY

Cable connector

DOCK CONNECTOR CABLE

LOGIC BOARD

POWER, VOLUME, AND
SCREEN ROTATION
LOCK CONTROLS

Antenna cable

WI-FI ANTENNA 1

HEADPHONE JACK

WI-FI ANTENNA 2

LIQUID CRYSTAL DISPLAY

LITHIUM-POLYMER BATTERY

DISPLAY DATA CABLE

COMPONENTS OF AN APPLE IPAD

glass

E-Ink display works well in bright sunlight

turn

CHAPTER I

FaceTime HD camera

Status bar

Touch-sensitive screen

Keyboard

Home button

kindle

AMAZON KINDLE VOYAGE

BLACKBERRY PASSPORT

OTHER TABLET COMPUTERS

APPLE IPAD AIR 2

Flatbed scanner

SCANNERS CONVERT physical images into electronic form, allowing them to be sent over the Internet, displayed on a website, stored on a computer, and manipulated using specialized software. Scanners work by detecting and analysing light reflected from an opaque image, such as a photographic print. Some can also scan photographic transparencies by analysing light that has passed through the image. Flatbed scanners contain a unit, called the scan head, that contains a lamp, mirrors, a lens, and an array of CCDs (Charge-Coupled Devices). The carriage passes beneath the image; the lamp shines light on to or through the original; the mirrors reflect the light on to the lens, which focuses it on to the CCD array. Each CCD detects the brightness of light from a particular pixel (picture element) along a· horizontal strip and converts this data into an electric signal. For colour images, the light is usually passed through red, green, and blue filters and then directed to the CCD array so that it can be broken down into its component colours. This information is then converted to digital form. The quality of the image depends on its resolution, measured in dpi (Dots Per Inch).

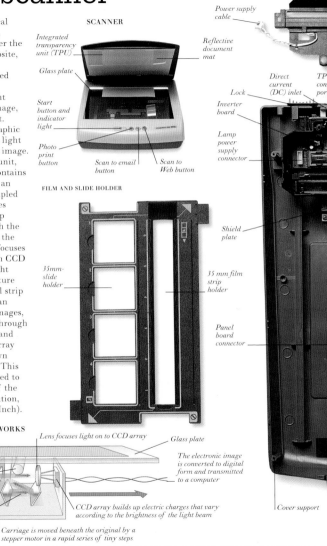

SCANNER

Integrated transparency unit (TPU)

Glass plate

Start button and indicator light

Photo print button

Scan to email button

Scan to Web button

Power supply cable

Reflective document mat

Direct current (DC) inlet

Lock

Inverter board

Lamp power supply connector

TP conn port

Shield plate

FILM AND SLIDE HOLDER

35mm-slide holder

35 mm film strip holder

Panel board connector

HOW A FLATBED SCANNER WORKS

Original image (photograph or artwork)

Lamp

Lens focuses light on to CCD array

Glass plate

The electronic image is converted to digital form and transmitted to a computer

CCD array builds up electric charges that vary according to the brightness of the light beam

Light beam is reflected from the original to a series of mirrors

Carriage is moved beneath the original by a stepper motor in a rapid series of tiny steps

Cover support

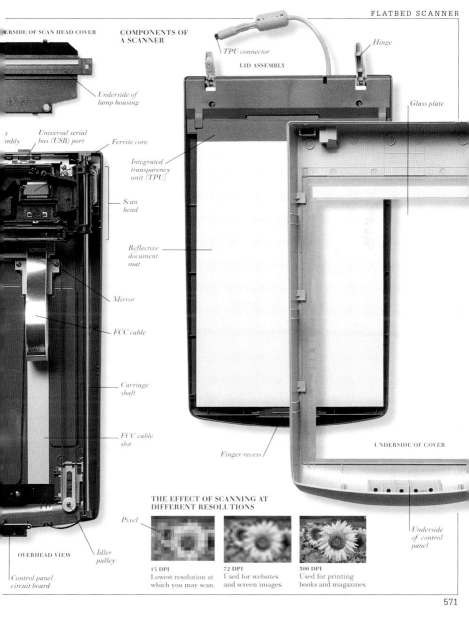

UNDERSIDE OF SCAN HEAD COVER

COMPONENTS OF A SCANNER

TPU connector

Hinge

LID ASSEMBLY

Underside of lamp housing

Glass plate

s mbly

Universal serial bus (USB) port

Ferrite core

Integrated transparency unit (TPU)

Scan head

Reflective document mat

Mirror

FCC cable

Carriage shaft

FCC cable slot

Finger recess

UNDERSIDE OF COVER

THE EFFECT OF SCANNING AT DIFFERENT RESOLUTIONS

Pixel

OVERHEAD VIEW

Idler pulley

Control panel circuit board

Underside of control panel

15 DPI
Lowest resolution at which you may scan.

72 DPI
Used for websites and screen images.

300 DPI
Used for printing books and magazines.

Airbus 380

CROSS-SECTION OF FUSELAGE

THE AIRBUS A380 WAS CONCEIVED in the early 1990s to compete with, and if possible replace, the Boeing 747. Work began in earnest on what was then called the A3XX in 1994. Its maiden flight was in April 2005. The A380's shape is subtly moulded to minimize drag from its ovoid fuselage. The structure makes extensive use of composite materials, such as thermoplastics and GLARE (aluminium and glass fibre). Its engines are very powerful, but also very efficient. It is claimed that when carrying 550 passengers, the A380 uses only 2.9 litres (¾ gallon) of fuel per passenger per 100km (60 miles).

INTERIOR VIEW OF BUSINESS CLASS CABIN

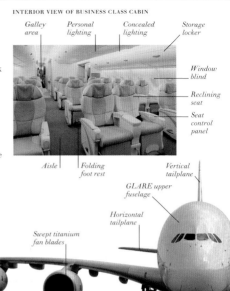

Galley area

Personal lighting

Concealed lighting

Storage locker

Window blind

Reclining seat

Seat control panel

Aisle

Folding foot rest

Vertical tailplane

GLARE upper fuselage

Horizontal tailplane

Obstruction light

Swept titanium fan blades

Wing landing gear

FRONT VIEW

Company logo

Split rudder

Jupp-Reese winglet

Upper deck windows

Overwing emergency exit

A380

F-WWOW

Auxiliary Power Unit (APU) exhaust

Horizontal tailplane

Tailcone fairing

Aft door

SIDE VIEW

Belly fairing

Flap track fairings

Body landing gear

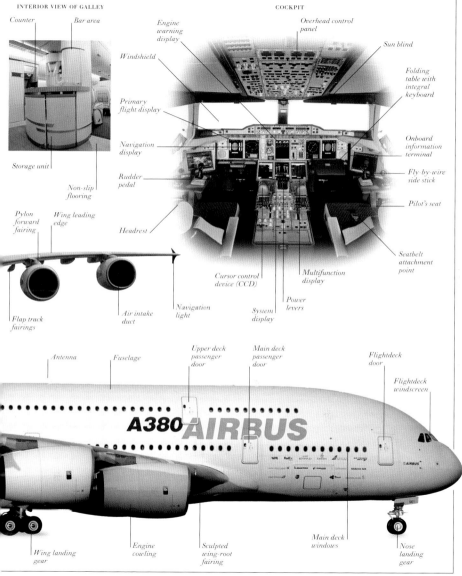

INTERIOR VIEW OF GALLEY

Counter

Bar area

Storage unit

Non-slip flooring

COCKPIT

Engine warning display

Windshield

Primary flight display

Navigation display

Rudder pedal

Headrest

Overhead control panel

Sun blind

Folding table with integral keyboard

Onboard information terminal

Fly-by-wire side stick

Pilot's seat

Seatbelt attachment point

Pylon forward fairing

Wing leading edge

Flap track fairings

Air intake duct

Navigation light

Cursor control device (CCD)

System display

Power levers

Multifunction display

Antenna

Fuselage

Upper deck passenger door

Main deck passenger door

Flightdeck door

Flightdeck windscreen

A380 AIRBUS

Main deck windows

Wing landing gear

Engine cowling

Sculpted wing-root fairing

Nose landing gear

573

Inkjet printer

INKJET PRINTERS EXPEL ink droplets from hundreds of tiny jets, or nozzles, on to a medium, such as paper, to print an image. Each droplet corresponds to a single pixel (picture element). Black-and-white printers use only black ink, while colour printers overprint combinations of the printing colours (cyan, yellow, magenta, and black) to create a full colour range. The printhead containing the nozzles moves sideways across the paper, creating a line of pixels, before the paper moves slightly forward so the next line can be printed. Two basic methods are used to eject ink: thermal, in which ink is heated to form an expanding bubble that expels a droplet from the nozzle, and piezoelectric, in which an electric current expands a crystal causing it to push out the ink droplet. The printer shown here can print digital photographs directly from a memory card.

EPSON STYLUS PHOTO 895 COLOUR INKJET PRINTER

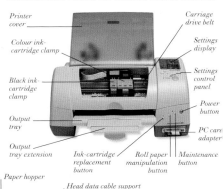

Printer cover

Colour ink-cartridge clamp

Black ink-cartridge clamp

Output tray

Output tray extension

Carriage drive belt

Settings display

Settings control panel

Power button

PC card adapter

Ink-cartridge replacement button

Roll paper manipulation button

Maintenance button

OVERHEAD VIEW WITH OUTER CASING REMOVED

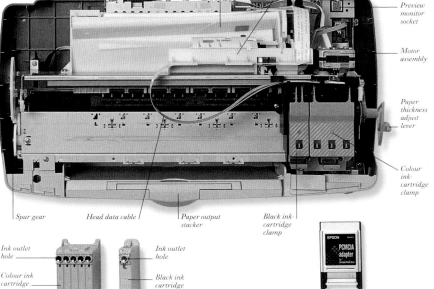

Paper hopper

Head data cable support

Preview monitor socket

Motor assembly

Paper thickness adjust lever

Colour ink-cartridge clamp

Spur gear

Head data cable

Paper output stacker

Black ink-cartridge clamp

Ink outlet hole

Colour ink cartridge

Ink outlet hole

Black ink cartridge

INK CARTRIDGES

PC CARD ADAPTER

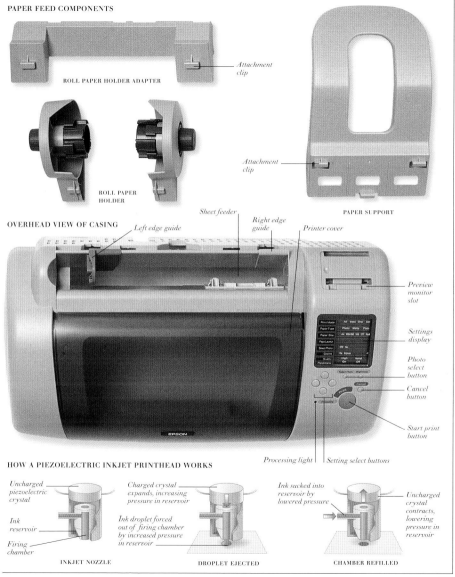

PAPER FEED COMPONENTS

Attachment clip

ROLL PAPER HOLDER ADAPTER

ROLL PAPER HOLDER

Attachment clip

PAPER SUPPORT

OVERHEAD VIEW OF CASING

Sheet feeder

Left edge guide

Right edge guide

Printer cover

Preview monitor slot

Settings display

Photo select button

Cancel button

Start print button

Processing light

Setting select buttons

EPSON

HOW A PIEZOELECTRIC INKJET PRINTHEAD WORKS

Uncharged piezoelectric crystal

Ink reservoir

Firing chamber

INKJET NOZZLE

Charged crystal expands, increasing pressure in reservoir

Ink droplet forced out of firing chamber by increased pressure in reservoir

DROPLET EJECTED

Ink sucked into reservoir by lowered pressure

Uncharged crystal contracts, lowering pressure in reservoir

CHAMBER REFILLED

575

The Internet

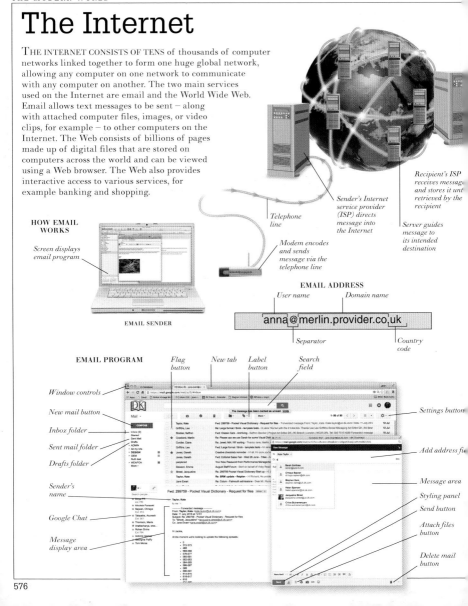

THE INTERNET CONSISTS OF TENS of thousands of computer networks linked together to form one huge global network, allowing any computer on one network to communicate with any computer on another. The two main services used on the Internet are email and the World Wide Web. Email allows text messages to be sent – along with attached computer files, images, or video clips, for example – to other computers on the Internet. The Web consists of billions of pages made up of digital files that are stored on computers across the world and can be viewed using a Web browser. The Web also provides interactive access to various services, for example banking and shopping.

Recipient's ISP receives message and stores it until retrieved by the recipient

Sender's Internet service provider (ISP) directs message into the Internet

Server guides message to its intended destination

Telephone line

Modem encodes and sends message via the telephone line

HOW EMAIL WORKS

Screen displays email program

EMAIL SENDER

EMAIL ADDRESS

User name

Domain name

anna@merlin.provider.co.uk

Separator

Country code

EMAIL PROGRAM

Flag button

New tab

Label button

Search field

Window controls

New mail button

Inbox folder

Sent mail folder

Drafts folder

Sender's name

Google Chat

Message display area

Settings button

Add address field

Message area

Styling panel

Send button

Attach files button

Delete mail button

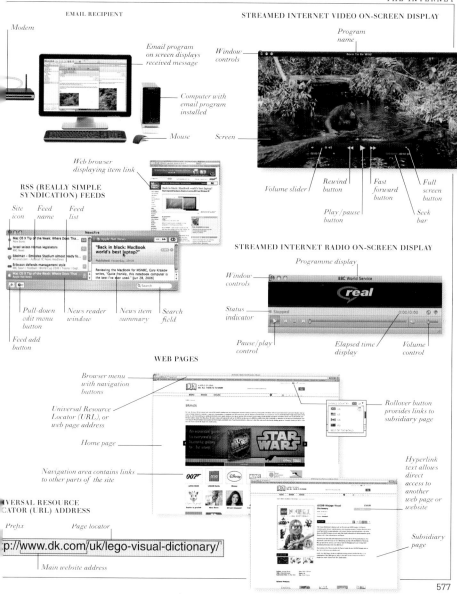

EMAIL RECIPIENT

STREAMED INTERNET VIDEO ON-SCREEN DISPLAY

Modem

Email program on screen displays received message

Window controls

Program name

Computer with email program installed

Mouse

Screen

Volume slider

Rewind button

Play/pause button

Fast forward button

Seek bar

Full screen button

Web browser displaying item link

RSS (REALLY SIMPLE SYNDICATION) FEEDS

Site icon

Feed name

Feed list

Pull-down edit menu button

News reader window

News item summary

Search field

Feed add button

STREAMED INTERNET RADIO ON-SCREEN DISPLAY

Programme display

Window controls

Status indicator

Pause/play control

Elapsed time display

Volume control

WEB PAGES

Browser menu with navigation buttons

Universal Resource Locator (URL), or web page address

Rollover button provides links to subsidiary page

Home page

Navigation area contains links to other parts of the site

Hyperlink text allows direct access to another web page or website

VERSAL RESOURCE CATOR (URL) ADDRESS

Prefix

Page locator

p://www.dk.com/uk/lego-visual-dictionary/

Main website address

Subsidiary page

Electronic games

MARIO SPORTS MIX WII

VIDEO GAMES HAVE BEEN around since the early 1970s. They are played on PCs, arcade machines, on a TV using a home console, and on portable hand-held consoles. Players use devices such as joysticks and control pads with buttons to control movement and action on screen. The latest generation of consoles uses motion sensor technology to allow players to manipulate objects on screen by simply moving the controller. The most advanced game systems respond to gestures and commands spoken by a player, without any need to use a hand controller. The game itself is stored in the form of digital information on CD, DVD, or microchip – which may be integral or stored in a removable cartridge – or on an internal hard disk. A central processing unit (CPU) (see pp. 566–567) is needed to process commands from the players, while specialized graphics chips are used to process the complex mapping and texturing functions that make modern games appear so realistic.

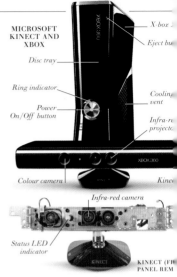

MICROSOFT
KINECT AND
XBOX

X-box
Eject bu
Disc tray
Ring indicator
Cooling
vent
Power
On/Off button
Infra-re
projecto
Colour camera
Kine
Infra-red camera
Status LED
indicator
KINECT (FI
PANEL REM

NINTENDO 3DS

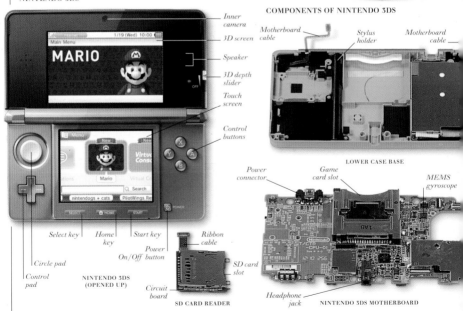

Inner camera
3D screen
Speaker
3D depth slider
Touch screen
Control buttons

Select key
Home key
Start key
Power On/Off button
Circle pad
Control pad

NINTENDO 3DS
(OPENED UP)

COMPONENTS OF NINTENDO 3DS

Motherboard cable
Stylus holder
Motherboard cable

LOWER CASE BASE

Power connector
Game card slot
MEMS gyroscope

Ribbon cable
SD card slot
Circuit board

SD CARD READER

Headphone jack
NINTENDO 3DS MOTHERBOARD

NINTENDO Wii FIT PLUS

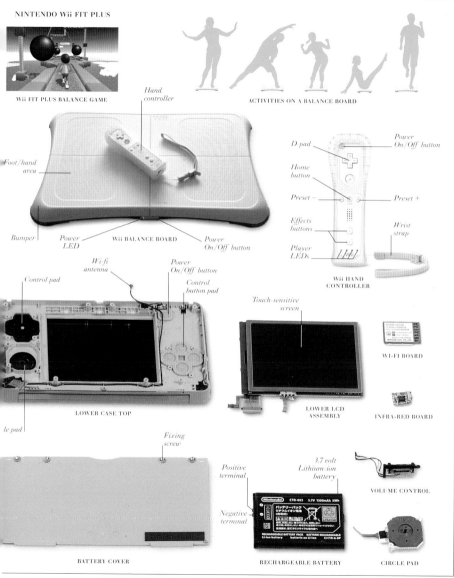

Wii FIT PLUS BALANCE GAME

Hand controller

ACTIVITIES ON A BALANCE BOARD

D pad

Power On/Off button

Home button

Preset −

Preset +

Effects buttons

Wrist strap

Player LEDs

Wii HAND CONTROLLER

Foot/hand area

Bumper

Power LED

Wii BALANCE BOARD

Power On/Off button

Wi-fi antenna

Power On/Off button

Control button pad

Control pad

Touch-sensitive screen

WI-FI BOARD

LOWER CASE TOP

LOWER LCD ASSEMBLY

INFRA-RED BOARD

le pad

Fixing screw

Positive terminal

Negative terminal

3.7 volt Lithium-ion battery

VOLUME CONTROL

BATTERY COVER

RECHARGEABLE BATTERY

CIRCLE PAD

Digital camera

FOR MORE THAN 200 YEARS, CAMERAS recorded
pictures as chemical changes in silver-containing
substances, on a strip of flexible, celluloid film.
The digital camera records pictures in electronic
form. At its heart is a specialized integrated
circuit known as a charge-coupled device (CCD).
This has millions of micro-units known as pixels.
It works in the opposite way to a miniature
computer or TV screen. Instead of electric signals
making pixels shine, when light hits a pixel it
generates a tiny electrical signal, according to
the light's colour and brightness. The signals
from the CCD's millions of pixels are analogue:
they vary continuously in a wave-like fashion.
They are converted by a microchip to digital
codes of numbers, represented as on-off electronic
pulses. The digital signals are processed and fed
to the camera's internal memory or a removable
memory device such as a data card or memory
stick. Photographs can be downloaded from a
digital camera to a computer via a cable or in
some cases a wireless link. Some digital cameras
automatically reduce blurring caused by camera
shake or fast movement, some can record video
clips as well as still pictures.

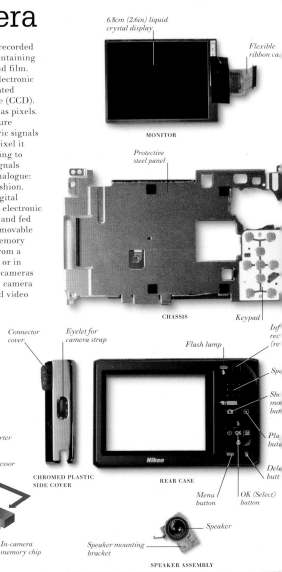

6.8cm (2.6in) liquid
crystal display

Flexible
ribbon ca

MONITOR

Protective
steel panel

CHASSIS

Keypad

Inf
rec
(re

Flash lamp

Sp

Sho
mo
but

Pla
but

Del
butt

REAR CASE

Menu
button

OK (Select)
button

HOW A DIGITAL CAMERA WORKS

CCD
turns
light into
electronic
signals

Lens focuses
light

Light
from
scene

Analogue
signals

Analogue to
digital converter
microchip

Microprocessor

Digital
signals

LCD
screen

Memory
stick

In-camera
memory chip

Connector
cover

Eyelet for
camera strap

**CHROMED PLASTIC
SIDE COVER**

Speaker

Speaker mounting
bracket

SPEAKER ASSEMBLY

COMPONENTS OF NIKON COOLPIX S1000PJ

Shutter release button

Focusing lens

Filters

Projector assembly cover

TOP PANEL

Projector button

Projector LED

Ribbon cable

PROJECTOR ASSEMBLY

CODEC with speaker driver and video buffet

Display controller chip

SIDE-B

LOGIC BOARD

TYPES OF DIGITAL CAMERA

Mode selector

Shutter button

Nikon

Lens release button

DIGITAL SLR

18–55mm zoom lens

On/off button

Shutter button

Lens release button

16mm interchangeable lens

DIGITAL CAMERA WITH INTERCHANGEABLE LENS

Projector window

Flash window

Lens

Self-timer lamp

Infra-red receiver (front)

Camera module connector

Nikon

COOLPIX

NIKKOR 5X WIDE OPTICAL ZOOM VR 5.0-25.0mm 1:3.9-5.8

FRONT CASE

CCD image sensor

CAMERA MODULE

Water-resistant case

Shutter button

Electronic flash

Strap mount

Canon

Lamp

Microphone

Lens

UNDERWATER DIGITAL CAMERA

Nikon

LITHIUM ION BATTERY PACK EN-EL12

JFBC

NIKON CORPORATION JAPAN

EN-EL12 RECHARGEABLE BATTERY

Lithium-ion battery

Lens cover motor

LENS COVER

Shutter button

Microphone

Left lens

Right lens

Flash

Lens cover

3D HD

FUJIFILM

3D DIGITAL CAMERA

Digital camcorder

A CAMCORDER records a scene as a sequence of 25 or 30 still images per second, along with sound. It comprises a video camera to capture light from the scene, a viewfinder through which the scene may be viewed, a screen on which the recorded scene may be viewed, a charge-coupled device (CCD) to convert the visual data into an electric signal, and a means of storing the signal. Digital video cameras convert the signal into digital form – a series of separate measurements of the initial analogue (continuously varying) signal. They record the digital signal, usually on a chip or hard disk. Camcorders often have a slot where a memory card can be inserted to expand the memory and store longer recordings or more still pictures.

COMPONENTS OF A JVC EVERIO CAMCORDER

JVC Everio

MONITOR SHELL

MONITOR MOUNT

MONITOR FRAME

Screen connector

6.8-cm (2.7-in) LCD screen

MONITOR SCREEN

Speaker

Play button

Auto/Manual recording b

Info button

Menu butto

AV termina

LEFT SIDE

OK button

Grip belt

Battery

Power/ Charge lamp

Access lamp

Zoom select lever

Power/charge lamp

Access lamp

LEFT OUTER SHELL

Lens cover

Microphone

LCD monitor

TOP VIEW

LENS COVER ASSEMBLY

Speaker

SPEAKER CIRCUIT BOARD

MOTHERBOARD

Monitor frame

USB terminal

DC terminal

Start/Stop button

LCD monitor

Battery

REAR VIEW

Grip belt

CHASSIS

Lens cover switch

RIGHT OUTER SHELL

Grip belt release lever

SanDisk SDHC Card 32GB

SDHC CARD

Lens

CCD mounting peg

CCD chip

SENSOR BOARD

LENS UNIT

Start/Stop button

3.6-volt lithium-ion battery

LENS UNIT MOUNT

GRIP BELT FASTENER

Zoom select lever

OK button

GRIP BELT

REAR PANEL

CONTROL UNIT

RECHARGEABLE BATTERY

583

Home cinema

HOME CINEMA REPLICATES a real "movie theatre" using pictures displayed on a high-quality widescreen television set, such as an LED TV, and surround sound from strategically sited loudspeakers. The source for sound and vision is a DVD (Digital Versatile Disc). Its player uses standard CD (Compact Disc) digital technology, but with a higher density of laser-read microscopic pits – more than 20 billion such pits in multi-level spiral tracks that, stretched out, would extend nearly 40km (25 miles). Blu-ray is a high-quality DVD system that fits much more data on its disc than standard DVDs, allowing High Definition video files to be stored. It is hard for the human ear to discern the direction of low-pitched sounds, so these emanate from a central bass speaker, often built into or below the screen unit. High-pitched sounds, the direction of which is easier to detect, emanate from mid- and high-frequency speakers positioned around the viewer. Light Emitting Diode (LED) TVs shine LEDs through a Liquid Crystal Display (LCD) panel. LCD screens are made up of millions of three-cell pixels, each containing a red, green, and blue sub-pixel. These pixels are controlled by the liquid crystals in the display panel, which regulate the light emitted by the LEDs. This allows all the different combinations of the three colours to be produced, creating the image on-screen. Organic Light Emitting Diode (OLED) TVs have an organic carbon-based layer that produces coloured light. While traditional LED screens use several layers to make light and colour, OLED screens have just one, and can therefore be thinner and use less energy.

BLU-RAY PLAYER

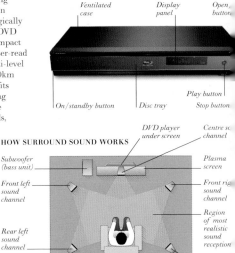

Ventilated case

Display panel

Open button

On/standby button

Disc tray

Play button

Stop button

HOW SURROUND SOUND WORKS

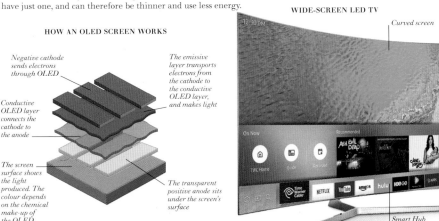

DVD player under screen

Centre sound channel

Subwoofer (bass unit)

Plasma screen

Front left sound channel

Front right sound channel

Rear left sound channel

Region of most realistic sound reception

Rear right sound channel

HOW AN OLED SCREEN WORKS

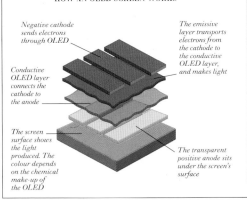

Negative cathode sends electrons through OLED

The emissive layer transports electrons from the cathode to the conductive OLED layer, and makes light

Conductive OLED layer connects the cathode to the anode

The screen surface shows the light produced. The colour depends on the chemical make-up of the OLED

The transparent positive anode sits under the screen's surface

WIDE-SCREEN LED TV

Curved screen

Smart Hub

On Now

Recommended

TWC Home   Guide   Recorded

Time Warner Cable   NETFLIX   YouTube   amazon   hulu   HBO GO

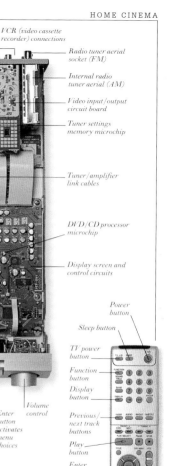

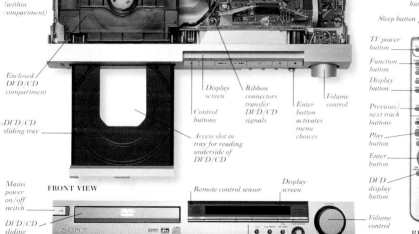

Mains electricity supply lead

INTERNAL VIEW OF SONY DAV-S300

Tweeter speaker connectors

Woofer speaker connector

VCR (video cassette recorder) connections

Radio tuner aerial socket (FM)

Internal fuse overload protection

Internal radio tuner aerial (AM)

Video input/output circuit board

Voltage reduction and regulation circuits

Tuner settings memory microchip

Power transistors

Tuner/amplifier link cables

Power transistor heat sink (dissipator)

DVD/CD processor microchip

DVD/CD drive turntable

Display screen and control circuits

DVD/CD laser-reader (within compartment)

Power button

Sleep button

TV power button

Function button

Display button

Enclosed DVD/CD compartment

Display screen

Ribbon connectors transfer DVD/CD signals

Enter button activates menu choices

Volume control

Previous/ next track buttons

Play button

Control buttons

Access slot in tray for reading underside of DVD/CD

Enter button

DVD/CD sliding tray

DVD display button

Mains power on/off switch

FRONT VIEW

Remote control sensor

Display screen

SONY

AV SYSTEM

DVD/CD sliding tray

Volume control

REMOTE CONTROL

Vibration-reducing damper foot

Radio tuner FM/AM selector

Muting button

DVD/CD control buttons

Headphones socket

Personal music

THE FIRST BATTERY-DRIVEN PORTABLE source of sound and music was the transistor radio of the 1950s. In the 1970s, the magnetic audio cassette tape allowed recordings to be played on portable tape players. Also, new metal alloys permitted the tiny but high-power magnets needed for lightweight earphones. In the 1980s, compact discs brought music into the digital era. Sony's MD, or minidisc, introduced re-recordable CDs that used magnetic and optical technology. From the mid 1990s, music could be stored in all-electronic digital form in a microchip, usually in the MP3 file format. These files can be transferred between devices and via the Internet. Today, a variety of portable media gadgets can record, play, and store video, photographs, and music in electronic form.

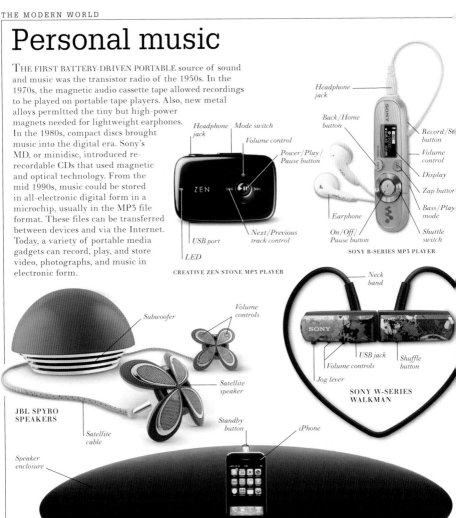

Headphone jack
Mode switch
Volume control
Power/Play/Pause button
USB port
Next/Previous track control
LED
ZEN

CREATIVE ZEN STONE MP3 PLAYER

Headphone jack
Back/Home button
Record/St button
Volume control
Display
Zap button
Bass/Play mode
Earphone
On/Off/Pause button
Shuttle switch

SONY B-SERIES MP3 PLAYER

Subwoofer
Volume controls
Satellite speaker
Satellite cable

JBL SPYRO SPEAKERS

Neck band
USB jack
Shuffle button
Volume controls
Jog lever

SONY W-SERIES WALKMAN

Speaker enclosure
Standby button
iPhone

ZEPPELIN IPOD SPEAKER DOCK

Remote control

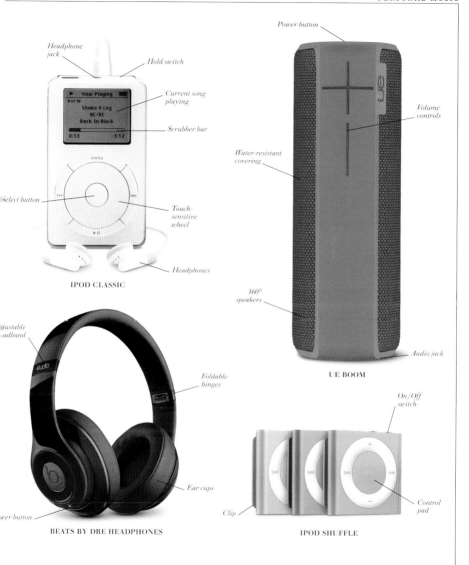

Headphone jack

Hold switch

Current song playing

Scrubber bar

Select button

Touch-sensitive wheel

Headphones

IPOD CLASSIC

Power button

Volume controls

Water-resistant covering

360° speakers

Audio jack

UE BOOM

Adjustable headband

Foldable hinges

Ear cups

Power button

BEATS BY DRE HEADPHONES

On/Off switch

Control pad

Clip

IPOD SHUFFLE

Mobile phones

IN THE EARLY 1990s, THE MOBILE PHONE (or cellphone) was a rare luxury, but in recent years it has outsold almost every other electrical gadget – as a professional tool, domestic convenience, and even a fashion accessory. Mobile phones have also generally shrunk in size, due to improvements in rechargeable batteries, which now store more electricity for longer in a smaller package, and to smaller, more efficient electronics that use less electricity. A "mobile" is basically a low-power radio receiver-transmitter, plus a tiny microphone to convert sounds into electrical signals, and a small speaker that does the reverse. When the mobile phone is activated, it sends out a radio signal that is answered by nearby mast transmitter-receivers. The phone locks onto the clearest signal and uses this while within range (the range of each transmitter is known as a cell). The phone continuously monitors signal strength and switches to an alternative transmitter when necessary. The phone's liquid crystal display (LCD) shows numbers, letters, symbols, and colour pictures. Newer models have a larger screen for more complex colour images, and commonly incorporate a camera, radio, and MP3 functionality. Smartphones, which are increasingly widespread, contain additional software and more may be downloaded. Smartphones typically offer Internet and email access, PDA-like functions (see pp. 568–569), and may even contain GPS navigation software.

Camera
Rear microphone
Top microphone
App i...
Lightning connector
Headphone jack
Home key
Spe...

I-PHONE 6

HOW A MOBILE PHONE WORKS

Phone locks onto signals from local mast within home cell

Caller sends call signal to nearest cell tower

Recipient's land-line phone (fixed at wall socket or cordless with base-set) emits ring tone

Cells are smal... in areas where many calls occ... simultaneously (cities, suburbs...

Phone out of signal range – no reception

Activated phone auto-switches to signals from next cell as it moves across cell boundary

Landlines (or tower-to-tower links) carry phone signals to local exchange

Local mobile phone network exchange

Main telephone network exchange

Signals forwarded to non-mobile phone

Recipient's mobil... phone emits ring

Signals forwarde... to relevant cell fo... transmission

COMPONENTS OF BLACKBERRY CURVE 8520

LCD screen

Ribbon connector

Front housing

DISPLAY

Locating tabs

...el

Keypad keys

FASCIA

KEYPAD

...zen
...nector

Camera

Trackpad

Keypad circuit board

LOGIC BOARD (FRONT)

Trackpad module

SIM card slot

LOGIC BOARD (REAR)

BlackBerry

SCREEN LENS

BATTERY COVER

BLACKBERRY CURVE 8520

Headphone jack

Volume control keys

Screen lens

Micro USB port

Left convenience key

Right convenience key

Trackpad

Send/call key

End/power key

Menu key

Escape/back key

Delete key

Speakerphone key

Left shift key

Right shift key

🔆 BlackBerry

EDGE

12:21
Thursday, May 21

(3) Messages

Headphone jack

Volume control keys

Lithium-ion battery

Negative terminal

Positive terminal

REAR HOUSING

RECHARGEABLE BATTERY

589

Wearable technology

WEARABLE TECHNOLOGY DEVICES are clothing or accessories, such as jewellery or glasses, that have connected computer devices incorporated in their design. Such devices contain many smart sensors and are connected wirelessly – either via the Internet or Bluetooth – to another device, such as a smartphone, that tracks the data the wearable device collects. Wearable technology has been around since the late 1970s, with devices such as the calculator watch and digital hearing aid. However, progress in wearable technology advanced rapidly in the early twenty-first century when sensors and chip sets became much cheaper and more readily available. Wearable technology can have many different functions. Some devices are used to track medical data, such as measuring heart rate, breathing patterns, and temperature. Others are used to monitor fitness, with many using GPS (below) to track how many steps a user has walked, or how many miles they have run, for example. Some wearable technology is designed to merge the digital world with the physical world – for example Google Glass, which projects digital information, such as maps and text notifications, onto the glasses' screen without obstructing the view of the real world.

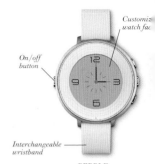

*Customiz\
watch fac*

*On/off\
button*

*Interchangeable\
wristband*

PEBBLE

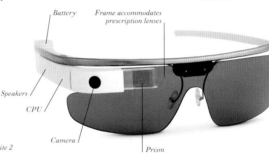

Battery

*Frame accommodates\
prescription lenses*

Speakers

CPU

Camera

Prism

GOOGLE GLASS

HOW GPS WORKS

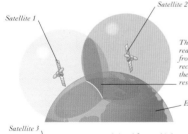

Satellite 1

Satellite 2

*The receiver takes a\
reading of its distance\
from two satellites. The\
receiver is located along\
the plane where the two\
resultant spheres meet*

Earth

Satellite 3

*A signal from a third\
satellite defines two\
positions on that plane.\
The position on the\
earth's surface is read\
as the correct location*

*Optical\
touchpad*

HD camera

RECON JET

*Polarized\
lens*

Batt

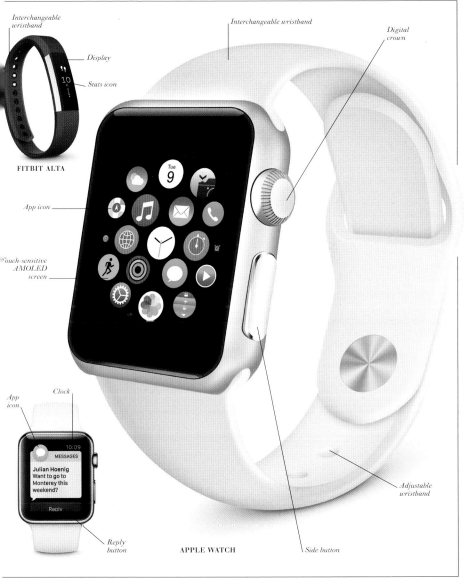

Interchangeable wristband

Display

Stats icon

FITBIT ALTA

Interchangeable wristband

Digital crown

App icon

Touch-sensitive AMOLED screen

App icon

Clock

10:09
MESSAGES

Julian Hoenig
Want to go to
Monterey this
weekend?

Reply

Reply button

APPLE WATCH

Side button

Adjustable wristband

591

Vacuum cleaner

IN A CONVENTIONAL VACUUM CLEANER, an electric motor spins a fan that sucks in air carrying dust and debris. The air is forced through tiny pores in a dust bag, trapping most particles. In the 1990s, James Dyson's dual cyclone "bag-less" design did away with the dust bag – and the reduced airflow caused by clogging of its pores. An electrically driven fan creates a partial vacuum within the machine. This sucks air into the machine past a rotating brush that loosens dirt. The air flows into a cylinder-shaped bin. As the air whirls around the bin like a miniature storm, or cyclone, larger particle are flung outwards and fall to the bottom of the bin. The air then passes through perforations into a cone-shaped inner bin and then into a series of smaller cones, spinning faster all the time and flinging smaller and smaller particle out. The nearly clean air exits the machine through micro-filters that trap the tiniest particles. Some Dyson vacuum cleaners run on a large ball instead of wheels. The ball makes it easier to steer the cleaner.

WAND HANDLE AND BRUSHBAR CONTROLS
Wand handle and brushbar controls

Upper wand

Lower wand

Motorized brushbar floor tool

CYCLONE ASSEMBLY

Air intake from hose

Air exit to bin/cyclone cover

DYSON DC05 MOTORHEAD

Hose electricity connector

Inner cyclone cone

Hose slider

WASHABLE PRE-MOTOR FILTER

Microporous filter

Bin upper seal seating

Perforated shroud

Bin handle clip

Hose slider seating

Central retaining screw

Hose electricity supply

Post-motor micropore filter

Filter rim casing

DUST COLLECTION BIN

Inner bin fin

Bin upper seal

Bin base

Bin handle

Bin lower seal

Inner bin dust collection area

Polycarbonate plastic bin body

Bin cover retaining clip

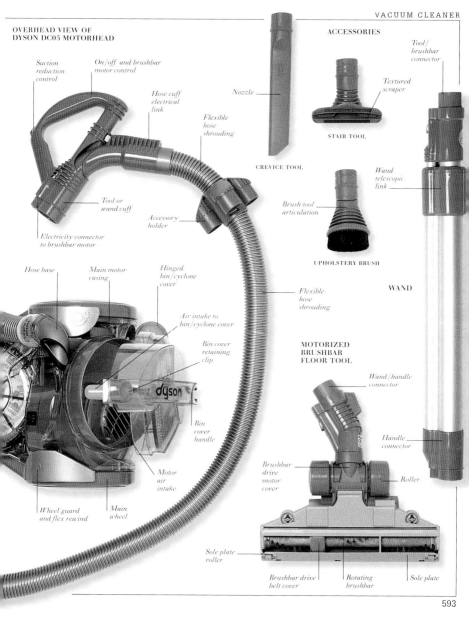

OVERHEAD VIEW OF DYSON DC05 MOTORHEAD

Suction reduction control

On/off and brushbar motor control

Hose cuff electrical link

Flexible hose shrouding

Tool or wand cuff

Accessory holder

Electricity connector to brushbar motor

ACCESSORIES

Nozzle

CREVICE TOOL

Textured scraper

STAIR TOOL

Tool/ brushbar connector

Brush tool articulation

UPHOLSTERY BRUSH

Wand telescopic link

WAND

Hose base

Main motor casing

Hinged bin/cyclone cover

Air intake to bin/cyclone cover

Bin cover retaining clip

Flexible hose shrouding

MOTORIZED BRUSHBAR FLOOR TOOL

dyson

Bin cover handle

Motor air intake

Wheel guard and flex rewind

Main wheel

Wand/handle connector

Handle connector

Brushbar drive motor cover

Roller

Brushbar drive belt cover

Rotating brushbar

Sole plate

Sole plate roller

Iron and washer-dryer

IN THE DAYS BEFORE WASHING MACHINES, laundry was done by hand – washed in a barrel, squeezed in a roller-mangle, hung on a line, and smoothed with an iron heated on the hob or stove. In the 1880s electrically heated irons were one of the first home electrical appliances. Today's iron still applies heat, sometimes moistened with steam, to dampen and flatten garment fibres. Machines with electric heaters and motors took the strain out of washing from the 1910s. Up to the 1960s, three machines were needed to wash, spin, and dry. Now clothes are swirled in a rotating ribbed tub of hot water, then spun fast to throw off most of the water, before slowly tumbling in electrically heated air to dry – all in one appliance.

FRONT VIEW OF A MIELE WASHER-DRYER

- Detergent tray
- Control panels
- Door
- Filter access flap

COMPONENTS OF A STEAM IRON

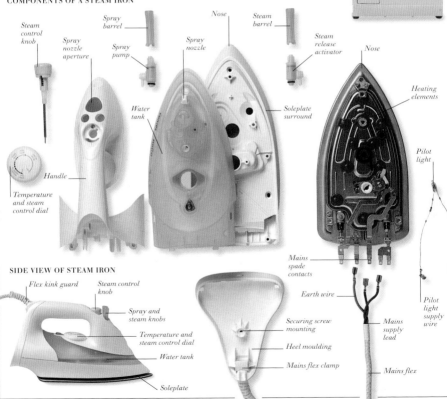

- Steam control knob
- Spray barrel
- Spray nozzle aperture
- Spray pump
- Spray nozzle
- Nose
- Steam barrel
- Steam release activator
- Nose
- Water tank
- Soleplate surround
- Heating elements
- Handle
- Temperature and steam control dial
- Pilot light
- Mains spade contacts
- Earth wire
- Pilot light supply wire

SIDE VIEW OF STEAM IRON

- Flex kink guard
- Steam control knob
- Spray and steam knobs
- Temperature and steam control dial
- Water tank
- Soleplate
- Securing screw mounting
- Heel moulding
- Mains flex clamp
- Mains supply lead
- Mains flex

COMPONENTS OF A MIELE WASHER-DRYER

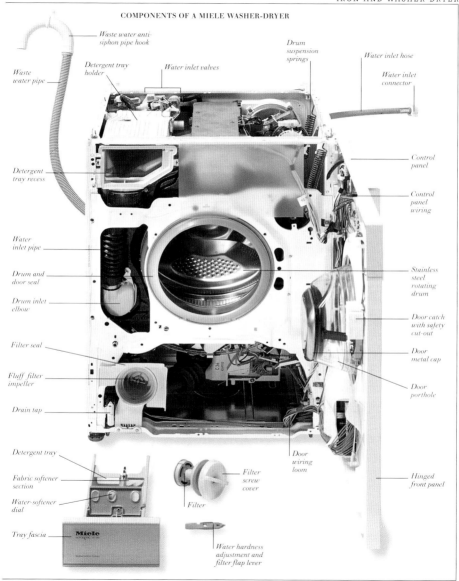

Waste water anti-siphon pipe hook

Waste water pipe

Detergent tray holder

Water inlet valves

Drum suspension springs

Water inlet hose

Water inlet connector

Detergent tray recess

Control panel

Control panel wiring

Water inlet pipe

Drum and door seal

Drum inlet elbow

Stainless steel rotating drum

Door catch with safety cut-out

Door metal cap

Door porthole

Filter seal

Fluff filter impeller

Drain tap

Detergent tray

Fabric softener section

Water-softener dial

Filter screw cover

Filter

Tray fascia

Miele

Door wiring loom

Hinged front panel

Water hardness adjustment and filter flap lever

Microwave combination oven

CONVENTIONAL OVENS use electrically warmed elements or a flame to heat food. In a microwave oven heat energy is created by electromagnetic waves produced by a magnetron and led by waveguides into the oven compartment. These microwaves cannot pass through the compartment's metal casing, being reflected within and spread evenly by a fan. But they do pass through most types of plastic, ceramics, and glass. Therefore platters or containers made from these materials are suitable for use in microwave ovens. A combination oven also has conventional heating elements, to grill and "brown" in the traditional fashion, either alone or in conjunction with microwaves.

MICROWAVE COMBINATION OVEN

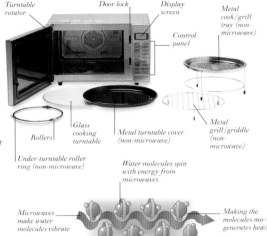

Turntable rotator
Door lock
Display screen
Metal cook/grill tray (non-microwave)
Control panel
Glass cooking turntable
Rollers
Metal turntable cover (non-microwave)
Metal grill/griddle (non-microwave)
Under-turntable roller ring (non-microwave)

HOW MICROWAVES HEAT FOOD

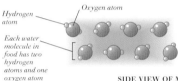

Hydrogen atom
Oxygen atom
Each water molecule in food has two hydrogen atoms and one oxygen atom

Water molecules spin with energy from microwaves
Microwaves make water molecules vibrate
Making the molecules mo generates hea

SIDE VIEW OF MICROWAVE COMBINATION OVEN

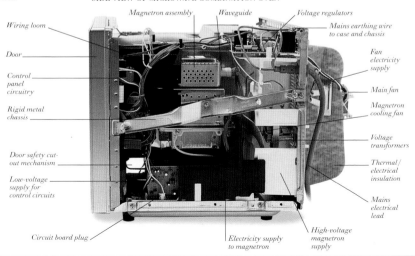

Magnetron assembly
Waveguide
Voltage regulators
Wiring loom
Mains earthing wire to case and chassis
Door
Fan electricity supply
Control panel circuitry
Main fan
Rigid metal chassis
Magnetron cooling fan
Voltage transformers
Door safety cut-out mechanism
Thermal/electrical insulation
Low-voltage supply for control circuits
Mains electrical lead
Circuit board plug
Electricity supply to magnetron
High-voltage magnetron supply

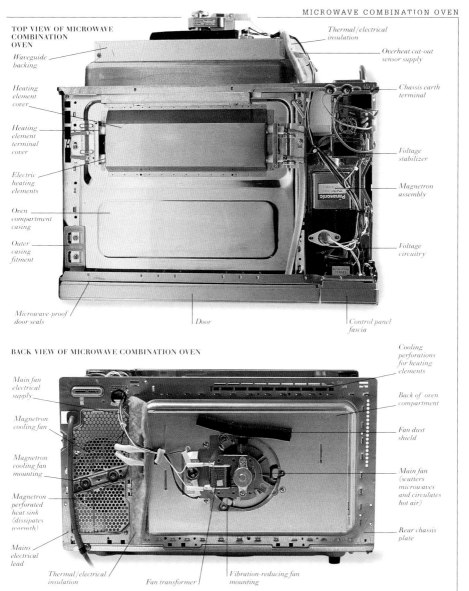

TOP VIEW OF MICROWAVE COMBINATION OVEN

Waveguide backing

Heating element cover

Heating element terminal cover

Electric heating elements

Oven compartment casing

Outer casing fitment

Microwave-proof door seals

Door

Control panel fascia

Thermal/electrical insulation

Overheat cut-out sensor supply

Chassis earth terminal

Voltage stabilizer

Magnetron assembly

Voltage circuitry

BACK VIEW OF MICROWAVE COMBINATION OVEN

Main fan electrical supply

Magnetron cooling fan

Magnetron cooling fan mounting

Magnetron perforated heat sink (dissipates warmth)

Mains electrical lead

Thermal/electrical insulation

Fan transformer

Vibration-reducing fan mounting

Cooling perforations for heating elements

Back of oven compartment

Fan dust shield

Main fan (scatters microwaves and circulates hot air)

Rear chassis plate

597

Toaster

MOST ELECTRIC TOASTERS not only grill slices of bread, they also pop them up when ready. While the slices rest on a spring-loaded rack, electric heating elements toast the bread. At the same time, a bimetallic strip heats and expands. One of the two metals in this strip expands more quickly than the other, causing the strip to curve. As it bends, it completes an electrical circuit and activates an electromagnet. The magnet attracts a catch, releasing the spring that holds the rack down in the toaster. The elements switch off, and the toasted slices pop up.

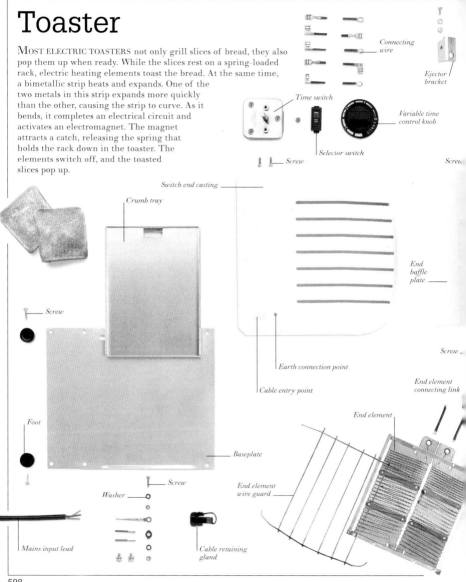

Connecting wire

Ejector bracket

Time switch

Variable time control knob

Selector switch

Screw

Screw

Switch end casting

Crumb tray

End baffle plate

Screw

Screw

Earth connection point

Cable entry point

End element connecting link

End element

Foot

Baseplate

Washer

Screw

End element wire guard

Mains input lead

Cable retaining gland

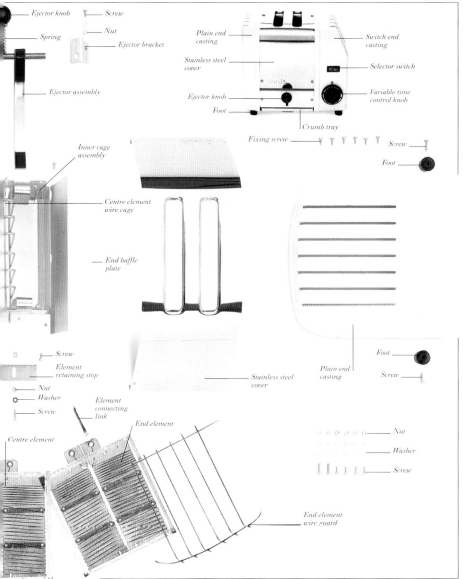

Ejector knob

Screw

Spring

Nut

Ejector bracket

Ejector assembly

Plain end casting

Switch end casting

Stainless steel cover

Selector switch

Ejector knob

Variable time control knob

Foot

Crumb tray

Fixing screw

Screw

Foot

Inner cage assembly

Centre element wire cage

End baffle plate

Foot

Plain end casting

Screw

Screw

Element retaining stop

Nut

Washer

Screw

Stainless steel cover

Nut

Washer

Screw

Element connecting link

End element

Centre element

End element wire guard

599

Drills

THE ELECTRICALLY POWERED MOTOR OF A POWER DRILL, cooled by a fan, turns a shaft at high speed. The shaft connects, in turn, to a system of gears that rotates a chuck even faster. Clamped by the chuck, a sharp bit cuts out the hole, and at the same time the bit's screw-shaped grooves channel the waste out of the hole. For drilling hard materials, many power drills have a hammer mechanism: when this is operated a ratchet in the gearcase causes the chuck and bit to pound in and out as they drill. A hand drill, although slower and less forceful than a power drill, is easier to control. For cutting wide holes, carpenters often prefer a brace-and-bit. This acts like a lever: the bowed handle of the brace moves a larger distance than the bit, turning the bit with extra force.

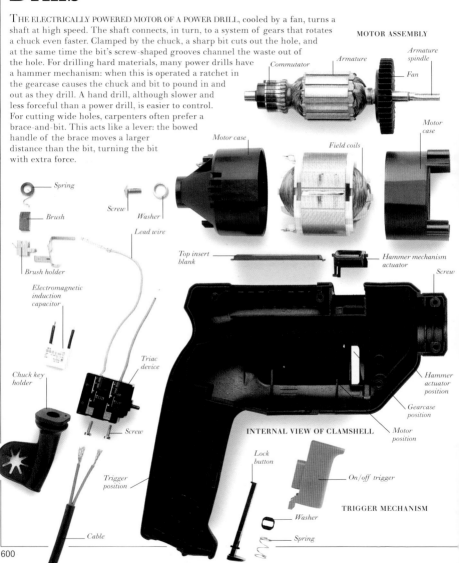

MOTOR ASSEMBLY

Commutator

Armature

Armature spindle

Fan

Motor case

Motor case

Field coils

Spring

Brush

Screw

Washer

Lead wire

Brush holder

Electromagnetic induction capacitor

Top insert blank

Hammer mechanism actuator

Screw

Chuck key holder

Triac device

Screw

Hammer actuator position

Gearcase position

INTERNAL VIEW OF CLAMSHELL

Motor position

Trigger position

Cable

Lock button

On/off trigger

TRIGGER MECHANISM

Washer

Spring

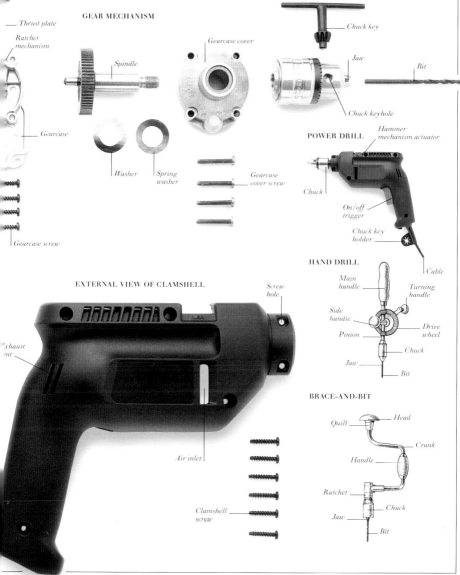

GEAR MECHANISM

Thrust plate

Ratchet mechanism

Spindle

Gearcase cover

Chuck key

Jaw

Bit

Chuck keyhole

Gearcase

Washer

Spring washer

Gearcase cover screw

Gearcase screw

POWER DRILL

Hammer mechanism actuator

Chuck

On/off trigger

Chuck key holder

Cable

HAND DRILL

Main handle

Turning handle

Side handle

Drive wheel

Pinion

Chuck

Jaw

Bit

EXTERNAL VIEW OF CLAMSHELL

Screw hole

Exhaust vent

Air inlet

Clamshell screw

BRACE-AND-BIT

Quill

Head

Crank

Handle

Ratchet

Chuck

Jaw

Bit

601

House of the future

HOUSES IN THE FUTURE are likely to be more environmentally friendly and energy-efficient than older dwellings, by making better use of materials and intelligent control systems. The Integer house was designed by Cole Thompson Associates, Bree Day Partnership, and Paul Hodgkins Associates, and built in conjunction with the Building Research Establishment in the UK. One of its key features is a large conservatory that warms one side of the house. Extensive use is made of recycled, natural, and renewable materials and energy. The walls are made from timber and insulated with fibre from recycled newspaper; waste water from the bathrooms is saved and used to flush the toilets; and a wind turbine and solar panels contribute some of the electricity requirements. Many elements were prefabricated off site for ease of construction. The Integer house uses only half the energy and a third less water than a traditionally built house.

WALL CONSTRUCTION

Cellulose fibre insulation

Vertical batten

Plasterboard

Vertical batten

Red cedar boarding

Noggin

Skirting board

Breather paper

Floating floor

Cables and ducting

Wooden boarding

SIDE AND REAR VIEW OF THE INTEGER HOUSE

Single-glazed conservatory

Gutter collects rain water for use in the garden

Composter for recycling kitchen waste

FRONT VIEW OF THE INTEGER HOUSE

Turfed roof helps to regulate temperature

Passive stack vents from bathroom and toilet

Automatic louvres cool conservatory

Small windows reduce heat loss

Red cedar walls that do not require painting or staining

Intelligent electronic door-lock

Hatch for home deliveries

ROOF CONSTRUCTION

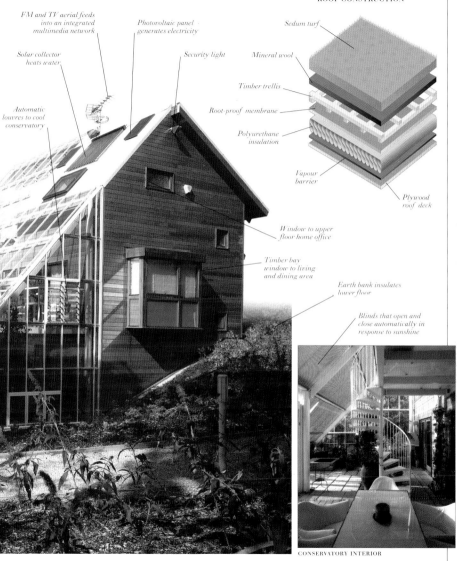

FM and TV aerial feeds into an integrated multimedia network

Photovoltaic panel generates electricity

Solar collector heats water

Security light

Automatic louvres to cool conservatory

Sedum turf

Mineral wool

Timber trellis

Root-proof membrane

Polyurethane insulation

Vapour barrier

Plywood roof deck

Window to upper floor home office

Timber bay window to living and dining area

Earth bank insulates lower floor

Blinds that open and close automatically in response to sunshine

CONSERVATORY INTERIOR

Renewable energy

RENEWABLE ENERGY COMES from sources that do not become depleted as we use the energy. When a fossil fuel such as coal is burned, it is gone forever, but a renewable source remains available no matter how much is used. The tides, waves, flowing water, sunlight, and the wind are all renewable sources of energy. Wind and water energy are captured by a device called a turbine. The turbine spins and drives an electricity generator. Energy from sunlight, or solar energy, is changed into electricity in two main ways. One uses mirrors to concentrate solar energy and magnify its heating effect which is used to change water into steam to drive turbines. Photovoltaic cells change sunlight directly into electricity. A cell is made from two layers of silicon. One gives out electrons (negative particles) and the other receives them. Sunlight knocks electrons out of atoms where the two layers meet, separating them from the positive particles. The electrons are attracted to one layer of the cell, the positive particles to the other layer. Electrons are naturally attracted to the positive particles, but to come together again, the electrons must flow out of the cell, through an external electric circuit, or load, and back to the other side of the cell, creating a charge. The cell supplies electric current for as long as light keeps falling on it.

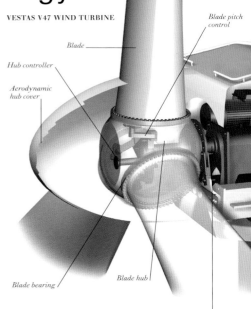

VESTAS V47 WIND TURBINE

Blade pitch control

Blade

Hub controller

Aerodynamic hub cover

Blade bearing

Blade hub

Rotor lock

TIDAL POWER

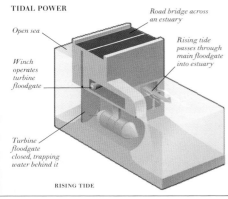

Open sea

Road bridge across an estuary

Rising tide passes through main floodgate into estuary

Winch operates turbine floodgate

Turbine floodgate closed, trapping water behind it

RISING TIDE

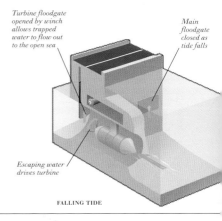

Turbine floodgate opened by winch allows trapped water to flow out to the open sea

Main floodgate closed as tide falls

Escaping water drives turbine

FALLING TIDE

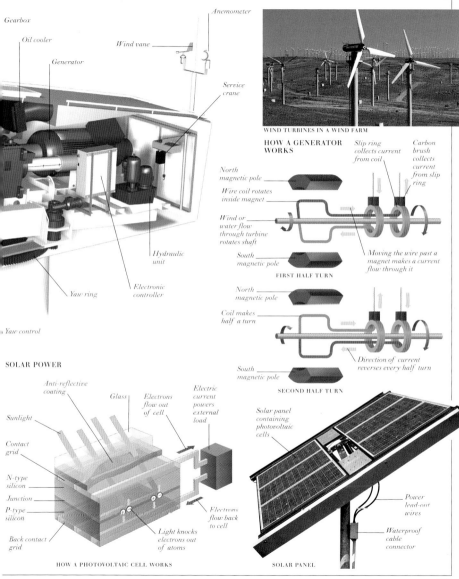

Gearbox

Oil cooler

Generator

Anemometer

Wind vane

Service crane

Hydraulic unit

Yaw ring

Electronic controller

Yaw control

WIND TURBINES IN A WIND FARM

HOW A GENERATOR WORKS

Slip ring collects current from coil

Carbon brush collects current from slip ring

North magnetic pole

Wire coil rotates inside magnet

Wind or water flow through turbine rotates shaft

South magnetic pole

Moving the wire past a magnet makes a current flow through it

FIRST HALF TURN

North magnetic pole

Coil makes half a turn

South magnetic pole

Direction of current reverses every half turn

SECOND HALF TURN

SOLAR POWER

Anti-reflective coating

Glass

Electrons flow out of cell

Electric current powers external load

Sunlight

Contact grid

N-type silicon

Junction

P-type silicon

Back contact grid

Light knocks electrons out of atoms

Electrons flow back to cell

HOW A PHOTOVOLTAIC CELL WORKS

Solar panel containing photovoltaic cells

Power lead-out wires

Waterproof cable connector

SOLAR PANEL

Cloning technology

IN A LIVING CELL THE GENETIC MATERIAL DNA (deoxyribonucleic acid) contains thousands of units called genes that carry instructions for development, growth, and repair of the living creature. During normal reproduction, half the mother's genetic material contained in an egg cell joins with half the genetic material from the father carried in a sperm cell, to form a unique new genome (set of genes) for a new life. During the early stages of embryo development, the fertilized egg divides into stem cells, which have the potential to become specialized into the hundreds of cell types in a body. Through therapeutic cloning, stem cells can be produced in a laboratory. It is hoped that in the future this technology can be used to grow new tissue that can be transplanted back into the donor to treat illness, without fear of rejection — when the body recognizes a transplanted part as "foreign" because it has different genes, and tries to destroy it. In another form of cloning, performed experimentally using animals, genetic material from a donor animal has been inserted into an egg from another animal that has been emptied of its own genetic material, to produce an animal genetically identical to the donor.

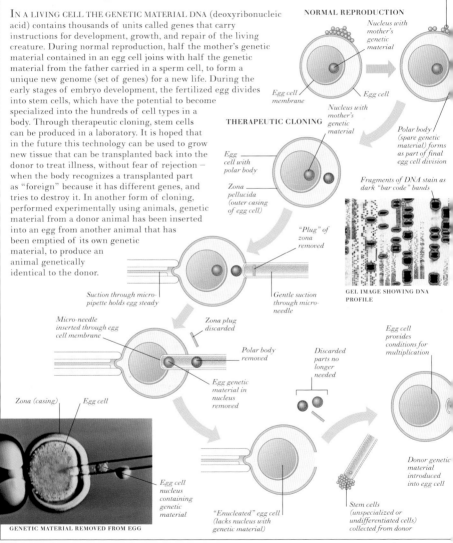

NORMAL REPRODUCTION

Spare cells from egg development

Nucleus with mother's genetic material

Egg cell

Egg cell membrane

Nucleus with mother's genetic material

Polar body (spare genetic material) forms as part of final egg cell division

THERAPEUTIC CLONING

Egg cell with polar body

Zona pellucida (outer casing of egg cell)

Fragments of DNA stain as dark "bar code" bands

"Plug" of zona removed

GEL IMAGE SHOWING DNA PROFILE

Suction through micro-pipette holds egg steady

Gentle suction through micro-needle

Micro-needle inserted through egg cell membrane

Zona plug discarded

Polar body removed

Discarded parts no longer needed

Egg cell provides conditions for multiplication

Egg genetic material in nucleus removed

Zona (casing)

Egg cell

Egg cell nucleus containing genetic material

"Enucleated" egg cell (lacks nucleus with genetic material)

Donor genetic material introduced into egg cell

Stem cells (unspecialized or undifferentiated cells) collected from donor

GENETIC MATERIAL REMOVED FROM EGG

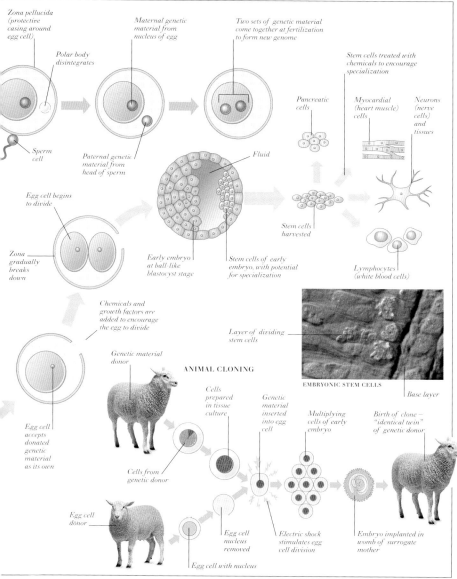

Zona pellucida (protective casing around egg cell)

Polar body disintegrates

Maternal genetic material from nucleus of egg

Two sets of genetic material come together at fertilization to form new genome

Stem cells treated with chemicals to encourage specialization

Pancreatic cells

Myocardial (heart muscle) cells

Neurons (nerve cells) and tissues

Sperm cell

Paternal genetic material from head of sperm

Fluid

Egg cell begins to divide

Zona gradually breaks down

Early embryo at ball-like blastocyst stage

Stem cells of early embryo, with potential for specialization

Stem cells harvested

Lymphocytes (white blood cells)

Chemicals and growth factors are added to encourage the egg to divide

Layer of dividing stem cells

Genetic material donor

ANIMAL CLONING

EMBRYONIC STEM CELLS

Base layer

Cells prepared in tissue culture

Genetic material inserted into egg cell

Multiplying cells of early embryo

Birth of clone — "identical twin" of genetic donor

Egg cell accepts donated genetic material as its own

Cells from genetic donor

Egg cell donor

Egg cell nucleus removed

Electric shock stimulates egg cell division

Embryo implanted in womb of surrogate mother

Egg cell with nucleus

607

Robots

ROBOTS ARE
MACHINES THAT CAN
carry out a variety of
tasks on their own,
with little or no human
control. Most robots are
mechanical arms used to build
things in factories. The end of the
robot's arm can be fitted with
different tools for gripping, drilling,
cutting, welding, and painting. Robot
toys have become popular, too. They
incorporate sensors that respond to
sounds and sometimes touch. Some of them
can even understand spoken words. Scientists are
also trying to create more advanced, human-like
robots that can see, hear, learn, and make their own
decisions. ASIMO, a robot developed by the Japanese
car manufacturer Honda, is one of these advanced
humanoid robots. ASIMO stands for Advanced Step
in Innovative MObility. It looks like a small astronaut
wearing a backpack. ASIMO can walk, talk, carry things,
recognize familiar faces, and respond to its name. It was
the first robot that could walk independently and climb
stairs. There are robot toys too, in the shape of animals
with simple artificial intelligence.

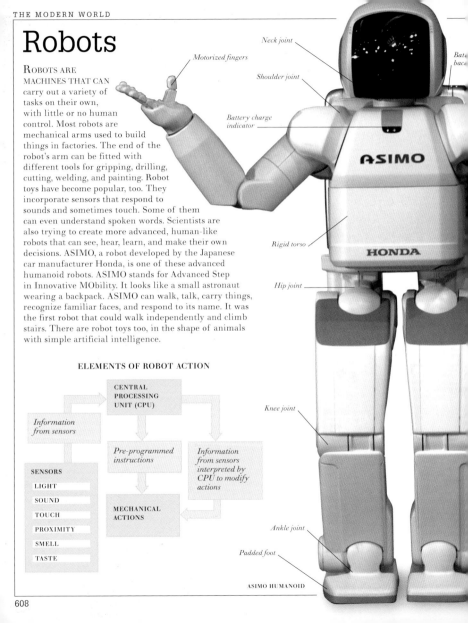

Motorized fingers

Neck joint

Shoulder joint

Battery charge indicator

Bat... back...

ASIMO

HONDA

Rigid torso

Hip joint

Knee joint

Ankle joint

Padded foot

ASIMO HUMANOID

ELEMENTS OF ROBOT ACTION

Information from sensors

CENTRAL PROCESSING UNIT (CPU)

Pre-programmed instructions

Information from sensors interpreted by CPU to modify actions

SENSORS

LIGHT

SOUND

TOUCH

PROXIMITY

SMELL

TASTE

MECHANICAL ACTIONS

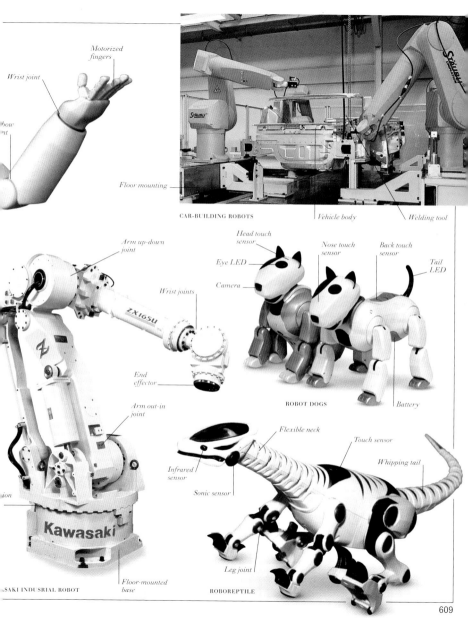

Wrist joint

Motorized fingers

bow nt

Floor mounting

CAR-BUILDING ROBOTS

Vehicle body

Welding tool

Arm up-down joint

Wrist joints

End effector

Arm out-in joint

ion

Kawasaki

ZX165U

ₛASAKI INDUSRIAL ROBOT

Floor-mounted base

Head touch sensor

Eye LED

Camera

Nose touch sensor

Back touch sensor

Tail LED

ROBOT DOGS

Battery

Flexible neck

Touch sensor

Infrared sensor

Sonic sensor

Whipping tail

Leg joint

ROBOREPTILE

609

High-performance microscopes

OPTICAL MICROSCOPES FORM A MAGNIFIED image by using lenses to bend light. Some special-purpose optical microscopes used in industry and research are designed for observing particular materials, such as living cells. They produce magnifications of up to about 2,000. Electron microscopes produce magnifications of as much as 50 million, although 2 million is more typical. Their images are formed by means of electrons focused by magnetic lenses. There are two main types: scanning electron microscopes (SEMs) scan electrons back and forth across the surface of a specimen; transmission electron microscopes (TEMs) transmit electrons through a thin slice of the specimen.

FEI TECNAI G² TRANSMISSION ELECTRON MICROSCOPE

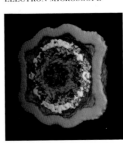

TEM IMAGE OF A VIRUS

OPTICAL MICROSCOPE IMAGE OF DYING NERVE CELLS

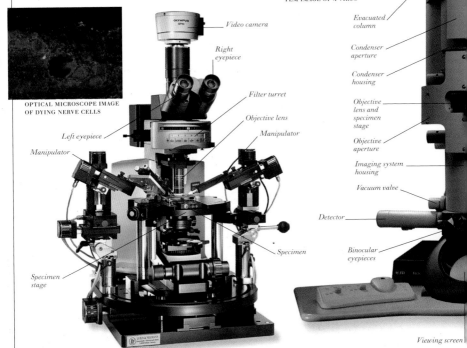

Electron gun housing

Video camera

Right eyepiece

Evacuated column

Condenser aperture

Condenser housing

Filter turret

Objective lens

Objective lens and specimen stage

Left eyepiece

Manipulator

Manipulator

Objective aperture

Imaging system housing

Vacuum valve

Detector

Specimen

Binocular eyepieces

Specimen stage

Viewing screen

OLYMPUS BX51W1 OPTICAL MICROSCOPE

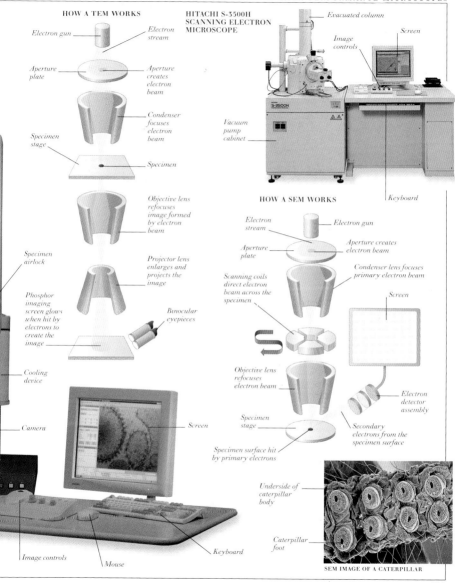

HOW A TEM WORKS

Electron gun

Electron stream

Aperture plate

Aperture creates electron beam

Condenser focuses electron beam

Specimen stage

Specimen

Objective lens refocuses image formed by electron beam

Projector lens enlarges and projects the image

Specimen airlock

Phosphor imaging screen glows when hit by electrons to create the image

Binocular eyepieces

Cooling device

Camera

Screen

Image controls

Mouse

Keyboard

HITACHI S-3500H SCANNING ELECTRON MICROSCOPE

Evacuated column

Image controls

Screen

Vacuum pump cabinet

S-3500H

Keyboard

HOW A SEM WORKS

Electron stream

Electron gun

Aperture plate

Aperture creates electron beam

Scanning coils direct electron beam across the specimen

Condenser lens focuses primary electron beam

Screen

Objective lens refocuses electron beam

Specimen stage

Specimen surface hit by primary electrons

Electron detector assembly

Secondary electrons from the specimen surface

Underside of caterpillar body

Caterpillar foot

SEM IMAGE OF A CATERPILLAR

Space telescope

SPACE TELESCOPES ORBIT THE EARTH hundreds of kilometres above the ground, their instruments collecting light from stars and galaxies. Telescopes in space have a clearer view than those on Earth, because they are unaffected by the Earth's atmosphere, which absorbs or distorts much of this radiation. There are a variety of types of space telescopes designed to observe different types of light. The Hubble Space Telescope observes infra-red, ultraviolet, and visible light. It can detect objects that are 100 times fainter than those any telescopes on Earth can see. When this 11,000-kilogram (12-ton), 13-metre (43-foot) long telescope was launched by the Space Shuttle in 1990, it was found that its primary mirror was faulty and its images were blurred. Astronauts fitted extra optics to correct the problem in 1993.

IMAGES TAKEN BY HUBBLE

Pillar of gas

CONE NEBULA

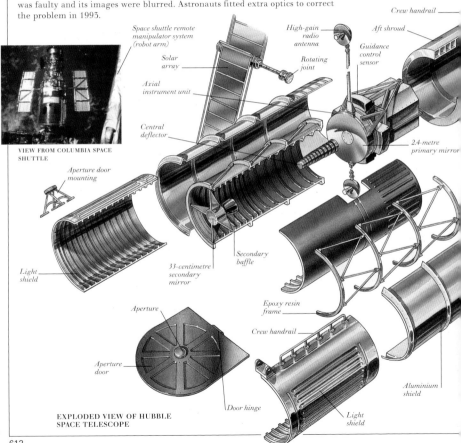

VIEW FROM COLUMBIA SPACE SHUTTLE

Space shuttle remote manipulator system (robot arm)

Solar array

Axial instrument unit

Central deflector

Aperture door mounting

Light shield

33-centimetre secondary mirror

Secondary baffle

High-gain radio antenna

Rotating joint

Guidance control sensor

Crew handrail

Aft shroud

2.4-metre primary mirror

Aperture

Aperture door

Door hinge

Epoxy resin frame

Crew handrail

Light shield

Aluminium shield

EXPLODED VIEW OF HUBBLE SPACE TELESCOPE

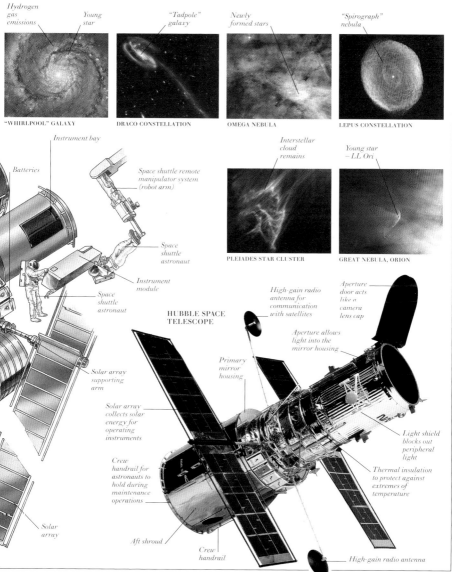

Hydrogen gas emissions

Young star

"Tadpole" galaxy

Newly formed stars

"Spirograph" nebula

"WHIRLPOOL" GALAXY

DRACO CONSTELLATION

OMEGA NEBULA

LEPUS CONSTELLATION

Interstellar cloud remains

Young star – LL Ori

PLEIADES STAR CLUSTER

GREAT NEBULA, ORION

Instrument bay

Batteries

Space shuttle remote manipulator system (robot arm)

Space shuttle astronaut

Instrument module

Space shuttle astronaut

Solar array supporting arm

Solar array collects solar energy for operating instruments

Crew handrail for astronauts to hold during maintenance operations

Solar array

Aft shroud

Crew handrail

HUBBLE SPACE TELESCOPE

High-gain radio antenna for communication with satellites

Primary mirror housing

Aperture door acts like a camera lens cap

Aperture allows light into the mirror housing

Light shield blocks out peripheral light

Thermal insulation to protect against extremes of temperature

High-gain radio antenna

Probing the Solar System

S<small>PACE PROBES HAVE VISITED</small> every planet in the Solar System. They take photographs and gather data that cannot be collected using Earth-based equipment. Some probes fly past or orbit around planets or moons, while others land. Two Voyager space probes flew past the outer planets in the 1970s and 1980s. Two Viking spacecraft landed on Mars in 1976. The Magellan spacecraft orbited Venus from 1989 and mapped its surface. The Pathfinder spacecraft landed on Mars in 1997 and released a rover vehicle to explore the surface. The Mars Exploration Rover (MER) Mission landed two rovers in 2003. The Cassini space probe reached Saturn in 2004, and in 2005 its mini-probe, Huygens, landed on one of its moons, Titan, and became the first probe to land on a moon of another planet.

A MAP OF JUPITER'S VAST MAGNETIC FIELD PRODUCED BY CASSINI'S INSTRUMENTS

DIONE, ONE OF SATURN'S MOONS, ORBITING ABOVE THE "A" RING

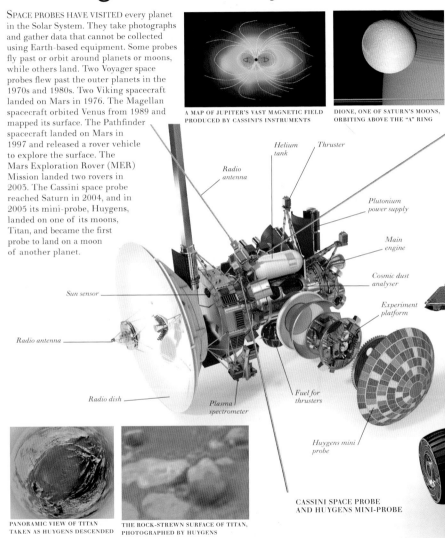

Helium tank

Thruster

Radio antenna

Plutonium power supply

Main engine

Cosmic dust analyser

Sun sensor

Experiment platform

Radio antenna

Radio dish

Plasma spectrometer

Fuel for thrusters

Huygens mini probe

CASSINI SPACE PROBE AND HUYGENS MINI-PROBE

PANORAMIC VIEW OF TITAN TAKEN AS HUYGENS DESCENDED

THE ROCK-STREWN SURFACE OF TITAN, PHOTOGRAPHED BY HUYGENS

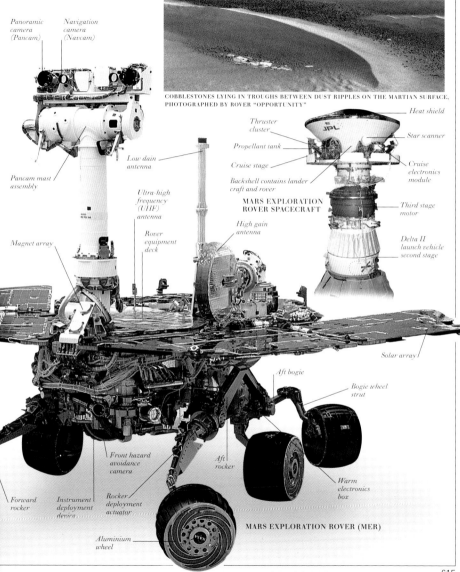

Panoramic camera (Pancam)

Navigation camera (Navcam)

COBBLESTONES LYING IN TROUGHS BETWEEN DUST RIPPLES ON THE MARTIAN SURFACE, PHOTOGRAPHED BY ROVER "OPPORTUNITY"

Heat shield

Thruster cluster

Star scanner

Propellant tank

Low gain antenna

Cruise stage

Cruise electronics module

Pancam mast assembly

Backshell contains lander craft and rover

MARS EXPLORATION ROVER SPACECRAFT

Ultra-high frequency (UHF) antenna

Third stage motor

Magnet array

Rover equipment deck

High gain antenna

Delta II launch vehicle second stage

Solar array

Aft bogie

Bogie wheel strut

Forward rocker

Front hazard avoidance camera

Aft rocker

Warm electronics box

Instrument deployment device

Rocker deployment actuator

MARS EXPLORATION ROVER (MER)

Aluminium wheel

Physical map of the world

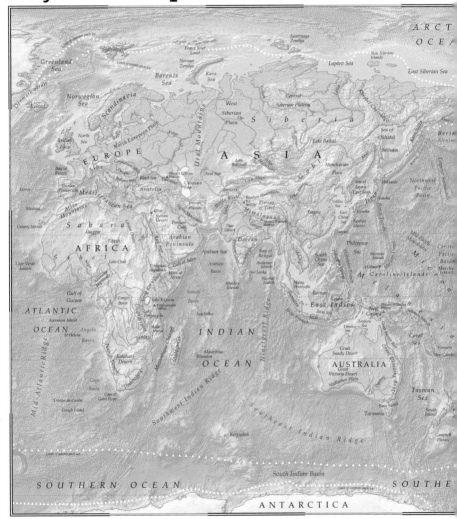

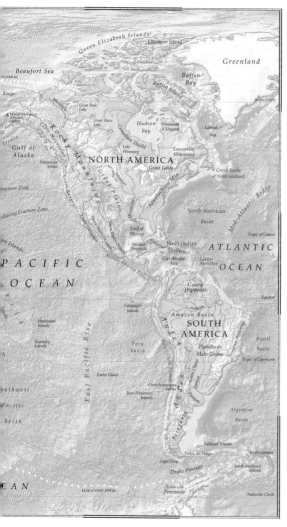

THIS MAP DEPICTS the surface of the Earth today, showing its physical features both above and below sea level. The outer layer of the Earth is called the crust, and it is broken into several pieces called tectonic plates. These plates move slowly on the upper mantle of the Earth. Although tectonic plates move only a few centimetres every year, over the course of Earth's history the plates have moved thousands of kilometres to create new oceans, mountain chains, and continents. Continental drift determines the distribution of the continents, which are propelled by currents rising from the intense heat at the Earth's centre. There are seven continents on Earth; these are (from largest to smallest) Asia, Africa, North America, South America, Antarctica, Europe, and Australasia. The physical features of the land are remarkably varied. Among the most notable are mountain ranges, rivers, and deserts. The largest mountain ranges – the Himalayas in Asia and the Andes in South America – extend for thousands of kilometres. The Himalayas include the world's highest mountain, Mount Everest (8,848 metres). The longest rivers are the River Nile in Africa (6,695 kilometres) and the Amazon River in South America (6,457 kilometres). Deserts cover about 20 per cent of the total land area. The largest is the Sahara, which covers nearly a third of Africa. Most of Earth is not made up of land, however, but of water – it accounts for about 70 per cent of the Earth's surface. The largest single body of water, the Pacific Ocean, alone covers about 30 per cent of Earth. The physical features of Earth are not permanent – tectonic forces, weathering and erosion, means that the Earth's surface is constantly changing.

Elevation

-6000m	-4000m	-2000m	-1000m	-500m	-250m	Below sea level 0		250m	500m	1000m	2000m	3000m	4000m	6000m
-19,658ft	-13,124ft	-6562ft	-3281ft	-1640ft	-820ft	-328ft/-100m	0	820ft	1640ft	3281ft	6562ft	9843ft	13,124ft	19,685ft

Time zones

The world is divided into 24 time zones, measured in relation to 12 noon Coordinated Universal Time (UTC), on the Greenwich Meridian (0°). Time advances by one hour for every 15° longitude east of Greenwich (and goes back one hour for every 15° west), but the system is adjusted in line with administrative boundaries. Numbers on the map indicate the number of hours that must be added to, or subtracted from UTC to calculate the time in each zone. Thus, eastern USA (−5) is 5 hours behind UTC.

TYPES OF CALENDAR

GREGORIAN

The 365-day Gregorian calendar was introduced by Pope Gregory XIII in 1582 and is now in use throughout most of the Western world. Every four years (leap year) an extra day is added. Below are the names of the months (and number of days).

January (31)	July (31)
February (28, 29 in leap years)	August (31)
	September (30)
March (31)	October (31)
April (30)	November (30)
May (31)	December (31)
June (30)	

JEWISH

The Jewish calendar is a lunar calendar adapted to the solar year. It normally has 12 months but in leap years, which occur seven times in every cycle of 19 years, there are 13 months. The years are reckoned from the Creation (which is placed at 3761 BC); the months are Nisan, Iyyar, Sivan, Thammuz, Ab, Elul, Tishri, Hesvan, Kislev, Tebet, Sebat, and Adar, with an intercalary month (First Adar) being added in leap years.

ISLAMIC

The Islamic calendar is based on a year of 12 months, each month beginning roughly at the time of the New Moon. The months are Muharram, Safar, Rabi'I, Rabi'II, Jumada I, Jumada II, Rajab, Sha'ban, Ramadan, Shawwal, Dhu l-Qa'dah, and Dhu l-Hijja.

CHINESE

The Chinese calendar is a lunar calendar, with a year consisting of 12 months. Intercalary months are added to keep the calendar in step with the solar year of 365 days. Months are referred to by a number within a year, but also by animal names that, from ancient times, have been attached to years and hours of the day.

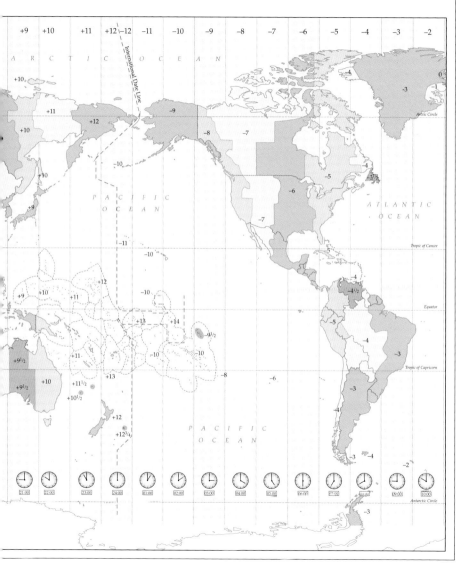

Useful data

UNITS OF MEASUREMENT

METRIC UNIT	EQUIVALENT
Length	
1 centimetre (cm)	10 millimetres (mm)
1 metre (m)	100 centimetres
1 kilometre (km)	1,000 metres
Mass	
1 kilogram (kg)	1,000 grams (g)
1 tonne (t)	1,000 kilograms
Area	
1 square centimetre (cm²)	100 square millimetres (mm²)
1 square metre (m²)	10,000 square centimetres
1 hectare	10,000 square metres
1 square kilometre (km²)	1,000,000 square metres
Volume	
1 cubic centimetre (cc)	1 millilitre (ml)
1 litre (l)	1,000 millilitres
1 cubic metre (m³)	1,000 litres
Capacity (liquid and dry measures)	
1 centilitre (cl)	10 millilitres (ml)
1 decilitre (dl)	10 centilitres
1 litre (l)	10 decilitres
1 decalitre (dal)	10 litres
1 hectolitre (hl)	10 decalitres
1 kilolitre (kl)	10 hectolitres

IMPERIAL UNIT	EQUIVALENT
Length	
1 foot (ft)	12 inches (in)
1 yard (yd)	3 feet
1 rod (rd)	5.5 yards
1 mile (mi)	1,760 yards
Mass	
1 dram (dr)	27.344 grains (gr)
1 ounce (oz)	16 drams
1 pound (lb)	16 ounces
1 hundredweight (cwt) (long)	112 pounds
1 hundredweight (cwt) (short)	100 pounds
1 ton (long)	2,240 pounds
1 ton (short)	2,000 pounds
Area	
1 square foot (ft²) (in²)	144 square inches
9 square feet	1 square yard (yd²)
1 acre	4,840 square yards
1 square mile	640 acres
Volume	
1 cubic foot	1,728 cubic inches
1 cubic yard	27 cubic feet
Capacity (liquid and dry measures)	
1 fluidram (fl dr)	60 minims (min)
1 fluid ounce (fl oz)	8 fluidrams
1 gill (gi)	5 fluid ounces
1 pint (pt)	4 gills
1 quart (qt)	2 pints
1 gallon (gal)	4 quarts
1 peck (pk)	2 gallons
1 bushel (bu)	4 pecks

ROMAN	ARABIC
I	1
II	2
III	3
IV	4
V	5
VI	6
VII	7
VIII	8
IX	9
X	10
XI	11
XII	12
XIII	13
XIV	14
XV	15
XX	20
XXI	21
XXX	30
XL	40
L	50
LX	60
LXX	70
LXXX	80
XC	90
C	100
CI	101
CC	200
CCC	300
CD	400
D	500
DC	600
DCC	700
DCCC	800
CM	900
M	1,000
MM	2,000

METRIC - IMPERIAL CONVERSIONS

TO CONVERT	INTO	MULTIPLY BY
Length		
Centimetres	inches	0.3937
Metres	feet	3.2810
Kilometres	miles	0.6214
Metres	yards	1.0940
Mass		
Grams	ounces	0.0352
Kilograms	pounds	2.2050
Tonnes	long tons	0.9843
Tonnes	short tons	1.1025
Area		
Square centimetres	square inches	0.1550
Square metres	square feet	10.7600
Hectares	acres	2.4710
Square kilometres	square miles	0.3861
Square metres	square yards	1.1960
Volume		
Cubic centimetres	cubic inches	0.0610
Cubic metres	cubic feet	35.3100
Capacity		
Litres	pints	1.7600
Litres	gallons	0.2200

IMPERIAL - METRIC CONVERSIONS

TO CONVERT	INTO	MULTIPLY BY
Length		
Inches	centimetres	2.5400
Feet	metres	0.3048
Miles	kilometres	1.6090
Yards	metres	0.9144
Mass		
Ounces	grams	28.3500
Pounds	kilograms	0.4536
Long tons	tonnes	1.0160
Short tons	tonnes	0.9070
Area		
Square inches	square centimetres	6.4520
Square feet	square metres	0.0929
Acres	hectares	0.4047
Square miles	square kilometres	2.5900
Square yards	square metres	0.8361
Volume		
Cubic inches	cubic centimetres	16.3900
Cubic feet	cubic metres	0.0283
Capacity		
Pints	litres	0.5683
Gallons	litres	4.5460

RULES OF ALGEBRA

EXPRESSION	COMMENTS	EXPRESSION BECOMES
$a + a$	Simple addition	$2a$
$a + b = c + d$	Subtract b from either side	$a = c + d - b$
$ab = cd$	Divide both sides by b	$a = cd \div b$
$(a + b)(c + d)$	Multiplication of bracketed terms	$ac + ad + be + bd$
$a^2 + ab$	Use parentheses	$a(a + b)$
$(a + b)^2$	Expand brackets	$a^2 + 2ab + b^2$
$a^2 - b^2$	Difference of two squares	$(a + b)(a-b)$
$1/a + 1/b$	Find common denominator	$(a + b)/ab$
$a/b \div c/d$	Dividing by a fraction is the same as multiplying by its reciprocal	$a/b \times d/c$

POWERS OF TEN USED WITH SCIENTIFIC UNITS

FACTOR	NAME	PREFIX	SYMBOL
10^{18}	quintillion	exa-	E
10^{15}	quadrillion	peta-	P
10^{12}	trillion	tera-	T
10^9	billion	giga-	G
10^6	million	mega-	M
10^5	thousand	kilo-	k
10^2	hundred	hecto-	h
10^1	ten	deca-	da
10^{-1}	one tenth	deci-	d
10^{-2}	one hundredth	centi-	c
10^{-3}	one thousandth	milli-	m
10^{-6}	one millionth	micro-	u
10^{-9}	one billionth	nano-	n
10^{-12}	one trillionth	pico-	p
10^{-15}	one quadrillionth	femto-	f
10^{-18}	one quintillionth	atto-	a

Note: The American system of numeration for denominations above one million is used in this book. In this system, each of the denominations above one billion (1,000 millions) is 1,000 times the preceding one.

BIOLOGY SYMBOLS

SYMBOL	MEANING
O	female individual (used in inheritance charts)
□	male individual (used in inheritance charts)
♀	female
♂	male
×	crossed with; hybrid
+	wild type
F_1	offspring of the first generation
F_2	offspring of the second generation

TEMPERATURE SCALES

To convert from Celsius (C) to Fahrenheit (F): $F = (C \times 9 \div 5) + 32$
To convert from Fahrenheit to Celsius: $C = (F - 32) \times 5 \div 9$
To convert from Celsius to Kelvin (K): $K = C + 273$
To convert from Kelvin to Celsius: $C = K - 273$

Celsius	-20	-10	0	10	20	30	40	50	60	70	80	90	100
Fahrenheit	-4	14	32	50	68	86	104	122	140	158	176	194	212
Kelvin	253	263	273	283	293	303	313	323	333	343	353	363	373

MATHEMATICAL SYMBOLS

SYMBOL	EXPLANATION
+	addition
-	subtraction
×	multiplication
÷	division
=	equals
≠	does not equal
>	greater than
<	less than
≥	greater than or equal to
≤	less than or equal to
∞	infinity
%	per cent
π	pi (5.1416)
°	degree
≈	is approximately equal to
∠	angle
∏	parallel to
∑	summation
u, u	vectors
f(x)	function
!	factorial
√	square root
ξ	universal set
A ∩ B	intersection
A ∪ B	unison
A ⊂ B	subset
Ø	null set

CHEMISTRY SYMBOLS

SYMBOL	MEANING
+	plus; together with
−	single bond
•	single bond; single unpaired electron; two separate parts or compounds regarded as loosely joined
=	double bond
≡	triple bond
R	group
X	halogen atom
Z	atomic number

PHYSICS SYMBOLS

SYMBOL	MEANING
α	alpha particle
β	beta ray
γ	gamma ray; photon
ε	electromotive force
η	efficiency; viscosity
λ	wavelength
μ	micro-; permeability
ν	frequency; neutrino
ρ	density; resistivity
σ	conductivity
c	velocity of light
e	electronic charge

SCIENTIFIC NOTATION

NUMBER	NUMBER BETWEEN 1 AND 10	POWER OF TEN	SCIENTIFIC NOTATION
10	1	10^1	1.5×10^1
150	1.5	$10^2 (= 100)$	1.5×10^2
274,000,000	2.74	$10^8 (= 100,000,000)$	2.74×10^8
0.0023	2.3	$10^{-3} (= 0.001)$	2.3×10^{-3}

TRIGONOMETRY

Angle A (degrees)	sin A	cos A	tan A
0	0	1	0
30	$1/2$	$\sqrt{3}/2$	$1/\sqrt{3}$
45	$1/\sqrt{2}$	$1/\sqrt{2}$	1
60	$\sqrt{3}/2$	$1/2$	$\sqrt{3}$
90	1	0	∞

Shapes: Plane

Two-dimensional shapes are termed plane (or flat) shapes. Plane shapes constructed with straight sides, as illustrated here, are called polygons. They are categorized according to the number of sides they have − for example, three-sided polygons are known as triangles. A polygon that has sides of equal length and internal angles of equal size, such as a square, is said to be regular.

SCALENE TRIANGLE
A triangle (three-sided polygon) with no equal sides or angles.

ISOSCELES TRIANGLE
A triangle with only two sides and two angles equal.

RIGHT-ANGLED TRIANGLE
A triangle with one angle as a right angle (90°).

EQUILATERAL TRIANGLE
A regular triangle. All angles are 60°.

SQUARE
A regular quadrilateral. All angles are 90°.

RHOMBUS
A quadrilateral with all sides equal and two pairs of equal angles.

RECTANGLE
A quadrilateral with four right angles and opposite sides of equal length.

PARALLELOGRAM
A quadrilateral with two pairs of parallel sides.

TRAPEZIUM
A quadrilateral with one pair of parallel sides.

PENTAGON
A five-sided polygon. A regular pentagon is shown above.

HEXAGON
A six-sided polygon. A regular hexagon is shown above.

OCTAGON
An eight-sided polygon. A regular octagon is shown above.

AREAS AND PERIMETERS

The formulae for calculating the areas and perimeters of simple plane shapes were devised by Classical Greek mathematicians.

CIRCLE
r = radius
d = diameter = 2 × r

Circumference = 2 × π × r
Area = π × r²
(π = 3.1416)

TRIANGLE
Height = h
Sides = a, b, c

Perimeter = a + b + c
Area = ½ × b × h

RECTANGLE
Sides = a, b

Perimeter = 2 × (a + b)
Area = a × b

Shapes: Solid

Three-dimensional shapes are known as solid shapes, and include spheres, cubes, and pyramids. A solid shape with a polygon at each face is called a polyhedron.

SURFACE AREAS AND VOLUMES

Volume refers to the amount of space that a solid object occupies. Its surface area is the sum of the area of each of its faces.

TETRAHEDRON
A four-sided polyhedron. A regular tetrahedron is shown.

CUBE
A regular hexahedron. All sides are equal and all angles are 90°.

OCTAHEDRON
A polyhedron with eight sides.

CYLINDER
Surface area = $2 \times \pi \times r \times h + 2\pi r^2$
Volume = $\pi \times r^2 \times h$

Height = h
Radius = r

PRISM
A polyhedron of constant cross-sections in planes perpendicular to its longitudinal axis.

PYRAMID
A polygonal base and triangular sides that meet at a point.

TORUS
A doughnut-like, ring shape.

CONE
Surface area = $\pi \times r \times l + \pi r^2$
Volume = $\frac{1}{3} \times \pi \times r^2 \times l$

Height = h
Radius = r
Side = l

SPHERE
A round shape, as in a ball or an orange.

HEMISPHERE
Formed when a sphere is cut exactly in half.

SPHEROID
An egg-shaped solid object whose cross-section is a circle or an ellipse.

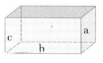

RECTANGULAR BLOCK
Surface area = $2 (a \times b + b \times c + a \times c)$
Volume = $a \times b \times c$

Sides = a, b, c

CONE
An elliptical or circular base with sides tapering to a single point.

RIGHT CYLINDER
A tube-shaped, solid figure. A right cylinder has parallel faces.

HELIX
A twisted curve. The distance moved in one revolution is its pitch.

Index

624

627

637

648

654

656

666

Acknowledgments

Dorling Kindersley would like to thank
(in order of sections):

The Universe
(consultant editors – Sue Becklake,
Gevorkyan Tatyana Alekseyevna):

John Becklake; the Memorial Museum of
Cosmonautics, Moscow; The Cosmos Pavilion,
Moscow; The United States Space and Rocket Centre,
Alabama; Broadhurst, Clarkson and Fuller Ltd;
Susannah Massey

Prehistoric Earth
(consultant editors – William Lindsay, Martyn
Bramwell, Dr Ralph E. Molnar, David
Lambert):

Dr Monty Reid, Andrew Neuman, and the staff of the
Royal Tyrrell Museum of Palaeontology, Drumheller,
Alberta; Dr Angela Milner and the staff of the
Department of Palaeontology, the Natural History
Museum, London; Professor W. Ziegler and the
staff, in particular Michael Loderstaedt, of the
Naturmuseum Senckenburg, Frankfurt; Dr Alexander
Liebau, Axel Hungrebüller, Reiner Schoch, and the
staff of the Institut und Museum für Geologie und
Paläontologie der Universität, Tübingen; Rupert Wild
of the Institut für Paläontologie, Staatliches Museum
für Naturkunde, Stuttgart; Dr Scheiber of the
Stadtmuseum, Nördlingen; Professor Dr Dietrich
Herm of Staatssammlung für Paläontologie und
Historische Geologie, München; Dr Michael Keith-
Lucas of the Department of Botany, University of
Reading; Richard Walker; American Museum of
Natural History, New York

Plants
(consultant editor – Richard Walker):

Diana Miller; Lawrie Springate; Karen Sidwell; Chris
Thody; Michelle End; Susan Barnes and Chris Jones
of the EMU Unit of the Natural History Museum,
London; Jenny Evans of Kew Gardens, London; Kate
Biggs of the Royal Horticultural Society Gardens,
Wisley, Surrey; Spike Walker of Microworld Services;
Neil Fletcher; John Bryant of Bedgebury Pinetum,
Kent; Dean Franklin

Animals
(consultant editor – Richard Walker):

David Manning's Animal Ark; Intellectual Animals;
Howletts Zoo, Canterbury; John Dunlop; Alexander
O'Donnell; Sue Evans of the Royal Veterinary
College, London; Dr Geoff Potts and Fred Frettsome
of the Marine Biological Association of the United
Kingdom, Plymouth; Jeremy Adams of the Booth
Museum of Natural History, Brighton; Derek Telling
of the Department of Anatomy, University of Bristol;
the Natural History Museum, London; Andy Highfield
of the Tortoise Trust; Brian Harris of the Aquarium,
London Zoo; the Invertebrate Department, London
Zoo; Dr Harold McClure of the Yerkes Regional
Primate Research Center, Emory University, Atlanta,
Georgia; Nielson Lausen of the Harvard Medical
School, New England Regional Primates Research

Centre, Southborough, Massachusetts; Dr Paul
Hopwood of the Department of Veterinary Anatomy,
University of Sydney; Dean Franklin

The Human Body
(consultant editors – Dr Frances Williams,
Dr Fiona Payne, Richard Cummins FRCS):

Derek Edwards and Dr Martin Collins, British School
of Osteopathy; Dr M.C.E. Hutchinson of the
Department of Anatomy, United Medical and Dental
Schools of Guy's and St Thomas' Hospitals, London.
Models – Barry O'Rorke (Bodyline Agency) and
Pauline Swaine (MOT Model Agency)

Geology, Geography, and Meteorology
(consultant editor – Martyn Bramwell):

Dr John Nudds of the Manchester Museum,
Manchester; Dr Alan Wooley and Dr Andrew Clark
of the Natural History Museum, London; Graham
Bartlett of the National Meteorological Library and
Archive, Bracknell; Tony Drake of BP Exploration,
Uxbridge; Jane Davies of the Royal Society of
Chemistry, Cambridge; Dr Tony Waltham of
Nottingham Trent University, Nottingham; staff of
the Smithsonian Institute, Washington; staff of the
United States Geological Survey, Washington; staff
of the National Geographic Society, Washington;
staff of Edward Lawrence Associates (Export Ltd);
Midhurst; John Farndon; David Lambert

Rail and Road
Rail (consultant editor – John Coiley)
Michael Ashworth of the London Transport Museum

Road (consultant editors – David Burgess-Wise,
Hugo Wilson)
The National Motor Museum, Beaulieu; Alf Newell of
Renault UK Ltd; David Suter of Cheltenham Cutaway
Exhibits Ltd; Francesca Riccini of the Science
Museum, London. Signore Amadelli of the Museo
dell' Automobile Carlo Biscaretti di Ruffia; Paul
Bolton of the Mazda MCL Group; Duncan Bradford
of Reg Mills Wire Wheels; John and Leslie Brewster
of Autocavan; David Burgess-Wise; Trevor Cass of
Garrett Turbo Service; John Corbett of The Patrick
Collection; Gary Crumpler of Williams Grand Prix
Engineering Ltd; Mollie Easterbrooke and Duncan
Gough of Overland Ltd; Arthur Fairley of the
Vauxhall Motor Company; Paul Foulkes-Halbard of
Filching Manor Motor Museum; Frank Gilbert of
I. Wilkinson and Son Ltd; Paolo Gratton of Gratton
Museum; Colvin Gunn of Gunn and Son; Judy Hogg
of Ecurie Bertelli; Milton Holman of Dream Cars;
Ian Matthews of IMAT Electronics; Eric Neal of
Jaguar Cars Ltd; Paul Niblett, Keith Davidson, Mark
Reumel, and David Woolf of Michelin Tyre plc; Doug
Nye; Kevin O'Keefe of O'Keefe Cars; Seat UK; Ian
Whitley; Raj Johal and Andy Faiers of the Honda
Institute; Roger Smith; Jim Stirling of Ironbridge
Gorge Museum, Staffordshire; Jon Taylor; Doug
Thompson; Martyn Watkins of Ford Motor Company
Ltd; John Cattermole, Customer Services Manager at
London Northern Buses; F. W. Evans Cycles Ltd;
Trek UK Ltd (Bicycle); Sam Grimmer; Colin Uttley

Physics and Chemistry
(consultant editor – Jack Challoner)

Sea and Air
Sea (consultant editors – Geoff Hales and
Harvey B. Loomis):
David Spence, Gillian Hutchinson, David Topliss,
Simon Stephens, Robert Baldwin, Jonathan Betts, all
of the National Maritime Museum, London; Ian Friel;
Simon Turnage of Captain O.M. Watts of London Ltd;
Davey and Company Ltd, Great Dunmow; Avon
Inflatables Ltd, Llanelli; Musto Ltd, Benfleet; Peter
Martin of Spencer Rigging Ltd, Southampton; Peter
Rowson of Ratseys Sailmakers, Southampton;
Swiftech Ltd, Wallingford; Colin Scattergood of the
Barrow Boat Company Ltd, Colchester; Professor J.S.
Morrison of the Trireme Trust, Cambridge; The Cutty
Sark Maritime Trust; Adrian Daniels of Kelvin
Hughes Marine Instruments, London; Arthur
Credland of Hull City Council Museums and Art
Galleries; The Hull Maritime Society; Gerald Clark;
Peter Fitzgerald of the Science Museum, London;
Alec Michael of HMB Subwork Ltd, Great Yarmouth,
and Ray Ward of the OSEL Group, Great Yarmouth;
Richard Bird of UWI, Weybridge; Walker Marine
Instruments, Birmingham; The International Sailing
Craft Association; The Exeter Maritime Museum;
Jane Wilson of the Trinity Lighthouse Company,
London; The Imperial War Museum Collections;
Thorn Security Ltd; Michael Bach

Air (consultant editor – Bill Gunston):
Aeromega Helicopters, Stapleford; Aero Shopping,
London; Avionics Mobile Services Ltd, Watford;
Roy Barber and John Chapman of the RAF Museum,
Hendon; Mitch Barnes Aviation, London; Mike Beach;
British Caledonian Flight Training Ltd; Fred Coates
of Helitech (Luton) Ltd; Michael Cuttell and CSE
Aviation Ltd, Oxford; Dowty Aerospace Landing Gear,
Gloucester; Guy Harteup of the Airship Association;
Anthony Hooley, Chris Walsh, and David Cord of
British Aerospace Regional Aircraft Ltd; Ken Huntley
of Mid-West Aero Engines Ltd; Imperial War
Museum, Duxford; The London Gliding Club,
Dunstable; Musée des Ballons, Calvados; Noel Penny
Turbines Ltd; Andy Pavey of Aviation Scotland Ltd;
Tony Pavey of Thermal Aircraft Developments,
London; the Commanding Officer and personnel
of RAF St Athan; the Commanding Officer and
personnel of RAF Wittering; The Science Museum,
London; Ross Sharp of the Science Museum,
Wroughton; The Shuttleworth Collection; Skysport
Engineering; Mike Smith; Solar Wings Ltd,
Marlborough; Julian Temple of Brooklands Museum
Trust Ltd; Kelvin Wilson of Flying Start

Architecture
(consultant editor – Alexandra Kennedy):
Stephen Cutler for advice and text; Gavin Morgan of
the Museum of London, London; Chris Zeuner of the
Weald and Downland Museum, Singleton, Sussex;
Alan Hills and James Putnam of the British Museum,
London; Dr Simon Penn and Michael Thomas of the
Avoncroft Museum of Buildings, Bromsgrove,

Worcestershire; Christina Scull of Sir John Soane's Museum, London; Paul Kennedy and John Williamson of the London Door Company, London; Lou Davis of The Original Box Sash Window Company, Windsor; Goddard and Gibbs Studios Ltd, London, for access to stained glass windows; The Royal Courts of Justice, Strand, London; Charles Brooking and Peter Dalton for access to the doors and windows in the Charles Brooking Collection, University of Greenwich, Dartford, Kent; Clare O'Brien of the Shakespeare Globe Trust, Shakespeare's Globe Museum, Bear Gardens, Southwark, London; Ken Teague of the Horniman Museum, London; Canon Haliburton, Mike Payton, Ken Stones, and Anthony Webb of St Paul's Cathedral, London; Roy Spring of Salisbury Cathedral; Reverend Gillean Craig of the Church of St George in the East, London; the Science Museum, London; Dr Neil Bingham; Lin Kennedy of Historic Royal Palaces; Katy Harris of Sir Norman Foster and Partners; Production Design, Thames Television plc, London; Dominique Reymer of Le Centre Georges Pompidou, Paris; Denis Roche of Le Musée National des Monuments Français, Paris; Franck Gioria and students of Les Compagnons du Devoir, Paris, for access to construction models; Frank Folliot of Le Musée Carnavalet, Paris; Dr Martina Harms of Hessische Landesmuseums, Darmstadt; Jefferson Chapman of the University of Tennessee, Knoxville, for access to the model of the Hypostyle Hall, Temple of Amon-Re; staff of the Palazzo Strozzi, Florence; staff of the Sydney Opera House, Sydney; staff of the Empire State Building, New York; Nick Jackson; Ann Terrell

The Visual Arts
(consultant editor – Pip Seymour):
Rosemary Simmons; Michael Taylor of Paupers Press, London; Tessa Hunkin and Emma Biggs of Mosaic Workshop, London; John Tiranti, Jonathan Lyons of Alec Tiranti Ltd, London; Chris Hough; Dr Ashok Roy; Satwinder Sehmi of Alphabet Soup, London; Phillip Poole of Cornelissens, London; George Weil and Sons Ltd, London; The National Gallery, London; Chris Webster of the Tate Gallery, London; China Art Cultural Centre, London; London Graphic Centre, London; A.P. Fitzpatrick, London; Flowers Graphics, London; Intaglio Printmaker, London; Falkiner Papers, London; Edgar Udny and Co, London; John Green

Music
(consultant editor – Susan Sturrock):
Boosey and Hawkes Music Publishers Ltd, London, for permission to reproduce extract from The Prodigal Son by Arthur Sullivan; The Bass and Drum Cellar, London; Empire Drums and Percussion, London; Argents (part of World of Music), London; Bill Lewington Ltd, London; Frobenius organ at Kingston Parish Church, Surrey; Yamaha-Kemble Music (UK) Ltd, Tilbrook, Milton Keynes; Yamaha Atelier, London; Akai (UK) Ltd, Hounslow, Middlesex; Casio Electronics Co. Ltd, London; Roland (UK) Ltd, Fleet, Hampshire; Richard Schulman; Andy Brown of Musictrack

Sports
The Sports Council Information Centre, London; The British Olympic Games Committee; Brian Crennell of Black's Leisure Group (First Sport); Lillywhites of Piccadilly, London; Mitre Sports International Ltd, Huddersfield; David Bloomfield of the Football Association; Denver Athletics Ltd, Norfolk; Greg Everest and Keith Birley of the British League of Australian Rules Football; Peter McNally of the Gaelic Athletic Association; Jeremy Garman of James Gilbert Ltd.; Rex King of the Rugby Football Union, Twickenham; Neil Tunnicliffe and John Huxley of the Rugby Football League, Leeds; Wayne Patterson of the Basketball Hall of Fame, Springfield, Connecticut; Brian Coleman of the English Basketball Association; All American Imports, Northampton; George Bulman of the English Volleyball Association; Julie Longdon of Mizuno Mallory (UK) Ltd; Juliet Stanford of the All-England Netball Association; Jeff Rowland of the British Handball Association; Cally Melin of Adidas UK Ltd; Patrick Donnely of the Baseball Hall of Fame, Cooperstown, New York; Ian Lepage and Stephen Barlow of the Hockey Association, Milton Keynes; Alison Taylor and Anita Mason of the All England Women's Lacrosse Association, Birmingham; David Shuttleworth of the English Lacrosse Union; Les Barnett and Jock Bentley of the British Athletic Federation Ltd, Birmingham; Mike Gilks of the Badminton Association of England; Gurinder Purewall for advice on archery; Chris McCartney of the US Archery Association; Geoff Doe of the National Smallbore Rifle Association, Bisley, Surrey, for information and reference material on shooting; Fagan Sports Goods Distributors, Surrey; Konrad Bartelski for advice on skiing; The British Ski Federation, Edinburgh; Mike Barnett of Snow and Rock of London; Sally Spurway of Mast Co. Ltd, Reading; Sarah Morgan for advice on equestrian sports; Steve Brown and the New York Racing Association Inc, New York; Danrho of London; Alan Skipp and James Chambers of the Amateur Fencing Association, London; Carla Richards of the US Fencing Association; Hamilton Bland and John Dryer of the Amateur Swimming Association, Loughborough; Cotswold Camping Ltd, London; Tim Spalton of Glyn Locke (Racing Shells) Ltd, Chalgrove; Terry Friel of the US Rowing Association; House of Hardy; Leeda Fishing Tackle

The Modern World
John Lewis, Brent Cross, for the loan of products for photography; Apple Computers UK; Palm Inc.; Epson UK; Navnesh Mistry of Brother UK; Nintendo; Sony UK; Nokia Mobile Phones Ltd; Sony Ericsson; Tony Broad of Garmin Europe; Dualit Ltd; Black and Decker Ltd; James Honour of the Buildings Research Establishment; Craig Anders of Cole Thompson Associates; Vestas Wind Systems; Bryan Adams of MIT; Dr Julian Heath of Microscopy and Analysis; Fei UK Ltd; Steve Parker; Ian Graham

PHOTOGRAPHY:
M. Alexander; Peter Anderson; Colin Bowling; Charles Brooks; Jane Burton; Peter Chadwick; Simon Clay; Gordon Clayton; John Coiley; Andy Crawford; Geoff Dann; Philip Dowell; John Downs; Mike Dunning; Torla Evans; David Exton; Paul Forrester; Robert and Anthony Fretwell of Fretwell Photography Ltd.; Philip Gatward; Steve Gorton; Anna Hodgson; Gary Kevin; J. Heseltine; Cyril Laubscher; John Lepine; Lynton Gardiner (American Museum of Natural History, New York); Steve Gorton; Michelangelo Gratton; Judith Harrington; Peter Hayman; Anna Hodgson; Colin Keates; Gary Kevin; Dave King; Bob Langrish; Brian D.Morgan; Nick Nicholls; Nick Parfitt; Tim Parmenter and Colin Keates (Natural History Museum, London); Tim Ridley; Dave Rudkin; Philippe Sebert; James Stevenson; Clive Streeter; Harry Taylor; Matthew Ward; Jerry Young

PHOTOGRAPHIC ASSISTANCE:
Kevin Zak; Gary Ombler; Govind Mittal

ILLUSTRATORS:
Julian Baum; Rick Blakeley; Kuo Rang Chen; Karen Cochrane; Simone End; Ian Fleming; Roy Flooks; Mark Franklin; David Gardner; Will Giles; Mick Gillah; David Hopkins; Selwyn Hutchinson; Mei Lim; Linden Artists; Nick Loates; Chris Lyon; Kathleen McDougall; Coral Mula; Sandra Pond; Dave Pugh; Colin Rose; Graham Rosewarne; John Temperton; Halli Verrinder; John Woodcock; Chris Woolmer

MODEL MAKERS:
Roby Braun; David Donkin; Morrison Frederick; Gordon Models; John Holmes; Graham High and Jeremy Hunt of Centaur Studios; Richard Kemp; Kelvin Thatcher; Paul Wilkinson

ADDITIONAL DESIGN ASSISTANCE:
Stefan Morris; Ulysses Santos; Suchada Smith; Niyati Gosain; Jomin Johny; Ridhi Khanna; Amit Malhotra; Payal Rosalind Malik; Anamica Roy; Ira Sharma; Balwant Singh

ADDITIONAL EDITORIAL ASSISTANCE:
Helen Castle; Colette Connolly; Camela Decaire; Nick Harris; Andrea Horth; Stewart McEwen; Damien Moore; Melanie Tham; Pragati Nagpal; Suparna Sengupta; Anita Kakar; Divya Chandhok

INDEX: Kay Wright; Lynn Bresler

Picture credits:

The publisher would like to thank the following for their kind permission to reproduce their photographs:

2011 Research In Motion Limited 589tr; Action Plus 550tc; Alamy images David Kilpatrick 581tr, 581cra; Nikreates 586ca; NordicImages 591tr; © PG Pictures/Apple Inc. 591r; Oleksiy Maksymenko Photography 568cra; © Stanca Sanda/Apple Inc. 588tr; Arthur Turner 579cla; © Chris Wilson/Apple Inc. 587tl; © Amazon. com, Inc. 569bl; Anglo Australian Telescope Board 11cl, 11cra, 11cbl, 12tr, 12bc, 13tl, 13bl, 14tl, 16b, 17tc, 17bl, 22tl/D.Malin 16tl, 26tr, 27tl; © Apple Inc. 569br, 587br, 591bl; Austin Brown and the Aviation Picture Library 426tl; Baptistery, Florence/Alison Harris 453r; © Beats Electronics 587bl; © Blackberry 569bc; Biophoto Associates 217ca, 217cra, 228cbc, 228cbc 250tr; BRE Imaging 602bl, 602r, 603tr, 605br; Paul Brierley 311bra; Bowers & Wilkins: B&W Group Ltd 586b; British Aerospace/Anthony Hooley 412tl, 415tl; British Aerospace (Commercial Aircraft) Ltd 416tl; By permission of the British Library 432tl, 445bl; British Museum 459tl, 459tr, 460tr, 460tc, 460tb, 489b; BP Exploration 299; Duncan Brown 25tl; Frank Lloyd Wright, American, 1867-1959, Model of Midway Gardens, 1914, executed by Richard Tickner, mixed media, 1987, 41.9 x 81.3 x 76.2, 1989.48. view 1. Photography courtesy of the Art Institute of Chicago 495t; J.A. Coiley 331cr; Bruce Coleman Ltd/Andy Price 272tl; Canon Europe 581crb; Corbis Joseph Sohm/Visions of America 494l; Paul Sounders/Terra 328b; Jon Stokes/ Science Photo Library 576cl; Wu Ching-teng/ Xinhua Press 568br; Haruyoshi Yamaguchi/ Sygma 608r; Courtesy of the Board of Trustees of the Victoria and Albert Museum, London 454-455b; Creative Labs. Inc. 586tc; Dorling Kindersley Owen Peyton Jones 566cr, 582-583, 589; Dreamstime.com Vasimila 431b; Dyson 592tr; European Passenger Services 329tl; ESA / PLV 11bl; European Southern Observatory (ESO) 55tl; Fei Co. 610tc, 610r; © Fitbit 591tl; French Railways 329c; FUJIFILM UK 581br; Geoscience Features 311cla; Robert Harding Picture Library 62tl; Getty Images Tony Cordoza 584tr; GraphicaArtis 448clb; Bill Johnson/The Denver Post 448tl; © MacFormat Magazine/James Looker 590cr; Photodisc/Ryan McVay 577tl; Harman International Industries, Incorporated JBL 586cl; Hitachi High-Technologies Co. Ltd 61 1tr; Michael Holford/British Museum 372bl, Michael Holford 374tr; Honda 354tr, 555b; Hutchison Picture Library 60cl; iFixit Miroslav Djuric 580-581 (Nikon Coolpix S1000PJ); Brett Hartt 578cra; The Image Bank/ Edward Bower 506tr; Jet Propulsion Laboratory 11cbr; 30bc; 31bc; 31bcr; 38tl; 42crb; 44cb; 44cbr; 44bc; 46tl; 46cr; 46cb; 46bc; 46br; 50tl; 50cra; 50cl; 50c; 50cr; 50br; Kawasaki (UK) 609bl; KeyMed Ltd 248bl, 249bl, 249bcl; Department of Prints and Drawings, Uffizi, Florence/Philip Gatward 451tc/Uffizi, Florence/ Philip Gatward 433tl; Robin Kerrod/Spacecharts 615br; Dr D.N. Landon (Institute of Neurology) 228bl,br; Life Science Images/Ron Boardman 244bl, 244br; The Lund Observatory 15bc; Brian Morrison 329tl, 329tr; © The Henry Moore Foundation 455tr; Used with permission from Microsoft 578tr; Musée d'Orsay, Paris/Philippe Sebert 457tc, 441tc; Musée du Louvre, Paris/ Philippe Sebert 453tl, 453l, 453br; Musictrack/ MOTU Digital performer 521bcl; NASA/AUI 15tr; NASA and The Hubble Heritage Team (AURA/STScI) 44tl; NASA Dr. R. Albrecht, ESA/ESO Space Telescope European Coordinating Facility 31fbr; CXC/ASU/J. Hester et al 28cra; JPL/DLR 44br; JPL JHUAPL 42br; JPL-Caltech/University of Arizona 42fbr; NASA/JPL 11 cbr, 11br, 30tl, 30bl, 30br, 30bc, 31bc, 31bcr, 31bl, 34ct, 38tl, 40tl, 40cr, 42cr, 44cb, 44cbr, 44bc, 44cr, 46crb, 46tl, 46cr, 46cb, 46bc, 46br, 48tl, 48cra, 48bca, 48bc, 48br, 50tl, 50bc, 50bc, 50cbr, 50br, 50cr, 52cr, 612cr, 612tr, 613tl, 613tcl, 613tcr, 613tr, 613c, 613cr, 615tr, 615cr, 615c; National Maritime Museum 373br, 392-395b; National Medical Slide Bank 217cr; Nature Photographers/Paul Sterry 286tl; Newage International 517bl; Nintendo 578tl, 578clb, 579tl, 579tr, 579cra; Olympus 610cl, 61 0bi; Oxford Scientific Films/Breck P. Kent 166tl; © Pebble 590tr; Planet Earth 274tr; Press Association Images AP 609cr; Quadrant 326tr; Margaret Robinson 332tl; Giotto The Expulsion of the Merchants from the Temple Scala 435tc, 435bl, 435br; RapidRepair.com Ben Levy 569ca (iPad Components); © Recon Instruments Inc 590br; Rex Features Jonathan Hordle 609bl; Roland UK 521tl; © Samsung 584br; © SanDisk/Western Digital Corporation (WDC) 583crb; Science Photo Library 10bl, 13tr, 214bcr, 214bl, 256tr/Michael Abbey 225tc/Agema Infrared Systems 518tl/AGFA 220tl/Alex Barte 605tr/David Becker 607cr/ Biophoto Associates: 217crb/Dr Jeremy Burgess/ Science Photo Library 132tr; Dr Jeremy Burgess 255bl/CNRI 214tl, 214cl, 214c, 214cr, 214bl, 214clb, 214crb, 214blc, 214br, 217cb, 235bcr, 238tl, 249bcr, 253tr, 253cra, 256tl; Science Photo library /Earth Satellite Corporation 288cl, 293br/Dr Brian Eyden 228cbr/Professor C. Ferlaud 245bl/ Vaughan Fleming 311tl/Simon Fraser/U.S. Dept. of Energy 214bcl, 266tl/Eric Grave 217br/Hale Observatories 32br/Max Planck Institute for Radio Astronomy 15tl/Jan Hinsch 225tc/Jodrell Bank 11tr, 13c /Manfred Kage 217c, 255br, 257br/Dr William C. Keel 15br/Keith Kent 564c/ James King-Holmes 316tl, 606bl/Russ Lappa 310bra/John Mead 605br/Astrid & Hans-Freider Michler 217tr/ Dennis Milon 52bl/NASA 11cla, 12tl, 15tr, 50c, 32tl, 35tl, 36tl, 36cl, 36cr, 36bc, 42tr, 52tl, 291tr, 300tl/National Optical Astro Observatory 52tr/NIBSC 253crb/Omikron 244bc/David Parker 63bl, 304-305, 308br/Alfred Pasieka 606cr/Philippe Plailly 308tl/Quest 611br/Roussel-UCLAF/CNRI 217tc/Rev Ronald Royer 32cr/Royal Observatory, Edinburgh/D Malin 11tl, 11cr,12c, 16cl, 16cr, 17br/David Scharf 253bl/Dr Kaus Schiller 248bcl, 248bcr, 248br/Secchi-Lecaque/Koussel-UCLAF/CNRI 255br/H. Sochurek 214cb/Stammers/Thompson 250tl/Sheila Terry 234tl/US Department of Energy 310bc/US Geological Survey/Science Photo Library 8-9, 30bcr, 42tl, 42bl/Tom Van Sant/Geosphere Project, Santa Monica/Science Photo Library 275tr, 281tr, 296tr, 297tl/Dr Christopher B. Williams (Saint Marks Hospital) 249br; Oxford Scientific Films/Animals/ Breck P. Kent 167tl; Pratt & Whitney Canada 418-419b, 419t; Science Museum 506bl, 506bcl; 306 bcr, 524t, 526-527b), 530tr, 351ct, 531 ct; © Sony Corporation 586tr, 586cr; Sporting Pictures 524tl, 544cr; TechRepublic Bill Detwiler 578-579b; Tony Stone Worldwide 280tl; J.M.W. Turner The Burning of the Houses of Parliament Tate Gallery 439tc; © Ultimate Ears/UE Boom 2 587tr; Vision 26tr, 27c; Jerry Young 306tl; Dr Robert Youngson 241cr; courtesy of Vestas Wind Systems 604t; Zefa 217bc/Janicek 276tl/H. Sochurek 210tl, 250tl, 254tl/G. Steenmans 292tl

(a=above, b=below/bottom, c=centre, f=far, l-left, r=right, t=top)

All other images © Dorling Kindersley
For further information see: www.dkimages.com

Every effort has been made to trace the copyright holders. Dorling Kindersley apologizes for any unintentional omissions and would be pleased, in any such cases, to add an acknowledgment in future editions.

Some pages in this book previously appeared in the Visual Dictionary series published by Dorling Kindersley. Contributors to these series include:

Project Art Editors: Duncan Brown, Ross George, Nicola Liddiard, Andrew Nash, Clare Shedden, Bryn Walls

Designers: Lesley Betts, Paul Calver, Simone End, Ellen Woodward

Additional design assistance: Sandra Archer, Christina Betts, Alexandra Brown, Nick Jackson, Susan Knight

Project Editors: Fiona Courtney-Thompson, Paul Docherty, Tim Fraser, Stephanie Jackson, Mary Lindsay

Editorial Assistant: Emily Hill

Additional editorial assistance: Susan Bosanko, Edward Bunting, Candace Burch, Deirdre Clark, Jeanette Cossar, Danièle Guitton, Jacqui Hand, David Harding, Nicholas Jackson, Edwina Johnson, David Lambert, Gail Lawther, David Learmount, Paul Jackson, Christine Murdock, Bob Ogden, Cathy Rubinstein, Louise Tucker, Dr Robert Youngson

Picture Researchers: Vere Dodds, Danièle Guitton, Anna Lord, Catherine O'Rourke, Christine Rista, Sandra Schneider, Vanessa Smith, Clive Webster

Series Editor: Martyn Page

Series Art Editor: Paul Wilkinson

Managing Art Editors: Philip Gilderdale, Steve Knowlden

Art Director: Chez Picthall

Managing Editor: Ruth Midgley

Production: Jayne Simpson